THE PAPERS

of

JOHN C. CALHOUN

FORT HILL

*The main house of Fort Hill plantation, home of
John C. Calhoun from 1826 to 1850, as it stands
now in the midst of the Clemson University Campus.*

THE PAPERS

of

JOHN C. CALHOUN

⑪

Volume XX, 1844

Edited by

Clyde N. Wilson

Shirley Bright Cook, *Associate Editor*

Alexander Moore, *Assistant Editor*

University of South Carolina Press, 1991

*Publication of this book was made possible
by a grant from the National Historical Publications
and Records Commission.*

International Standard Book Number: 0—87249—769—0
Library of Congress Catalog Card Number: 59—10351

Manufactured in the United States of America

CONTENTS

◫

v

PREFACE

This volume continues the documentation of Calhoun's service as Secretary of State. The worth of its materials, reflecting as they do not only the career of one of the great triumvirs of the middle period of American history but also the dynamic and multifarious activities of the American people, is limited only by the imagination of the historian who makes use of them.

While the publication space devoted to Calhoun's relatively brief tenure in the State Department must seem ample, it should be remembered that almost two-thirds of the extant documents have been omitted. The policies of selection and omission which have governed our publication of official documents are explained in detail in the Introduction to *The Papers of John C. Calhoun,* Volume XVIII, pages xii–xxiv. The volume of the edition which will swiftly follow the one now in hand will conclude the State Department period and include as well a period following that, before Calhoun returned to the Senate for the last time. The summary of omitted documents, which in the Preface to Volume XVIII was promised to be given in Volume XX, will instead be given in Volume XXI.

The enterprise in which we are engaged, to provide a comprehensive and enduring record of an American statesman of perennial significance, is now more than three decades old. It proceeds apace and its end is in sight. Such progress has only been possible because of the dedication and skill of the staff. No editor has ever had more skillful, dedicated, and cheerful associates than Shirley B. Cook and Alexander Moore. Thanks are also in order for the continuing support of the Program for Editions of the National Endowment for the Humanities, the National Historical Publications and Records Commission, the University of South Carolina, and the University South Caroliniana Society.

The frontispiece has been supplied by the courtesy of Mrs. Carroll C. Brannon and the United Daughters of the Confederacy. The University of South Carolina Institute of Southern Studies gave some timely logistical assistance. Mark G. Malvasi participated ably in the publication of this volume while he was N.H.P.R.C. National Documentary Editing Fellow with the Calhoun project.

CLYDE N. WILSON

Columbia, June 1989

INTRODUCTION

〚〛

During the third quarter of Calhoun's service as Secretary of State a great many significant matters were under way, but few of them came to a clear resolution. The only really decisive event of the last months of 1844 was the Presidential election in November, which provided a narrow victory for James K. Polk and the Democratic Party—that vast, tumultuous organization to which Calhoun had been giving his support since 1838.

Though the electoral results provided a mandate of sorts for Calhoun's main objective, the annexation of Texas, the consummation of that objective would be deferred to early the next year. And the new President and the new Congress would not take office until the following March.

The continuing and unresolved events which are reflected in this volume can be characterized under three somewhat superficial but useful headings: personal, diplomatic, and political.

As to the personal, after a month's fall holiday at Fort Hill during the harvest, Calhoun returned to Washington in early November, 1844. For the first time in many years he was accompanied by his wife. Their second daughter, Martha Cornelia, who was twenty in 1844, came to Washington also. It was doubtless hoped that a stay in the federal city would be useful to her medically and socially, for Cornelia had been partly crippled and somewhat deaf from childhood. She was to survive her father only by seven years and die in her early thirties.

From the point of view of the historian working from documents, the most significant personal event is that Calhoun's son-in-law and daughter took up station in Brussels, where Thomas Clemson was to serve as the U.S. Chargé d'Affaires until 1851. Distance somewhat altered the content and quality of Calhoun's correspondence with the Clemsons. The many letters of Anna Maria Calhoun Clemson, an intelligent and articulate Southern woman in Europe, to her father and other kin constitute a group of papers interesting in their own right, quite apart from the public significance of Calhoun. And in writing to loved ones across the sea, Calhoun broadened to a degree

ix

his customary focus and scope in commenting on public and private affairs.

Except for one return to the United States, the Clemsons remained in Europe until Calhoun's death, so that for most of the rest of his life he was deprived of the company of the beloved daughter who in intellectual gifts and temperament resembled him more than any of his five sons.

As to diplomacy, most of the matters discussed in the Introduction to Volume XIX of this series were still in course. Calhoun's administration of the State Department is interesting in itself, at least to his editors, but perhaps even more interesting is the light shed by his papers on the far-flung activities of the American people. As in the case of the frontier, the dynamism of the American people abroad—as traders, whalers, adventurers, students, missionaries, tourists—drew the government in its wake.

We had expected the editing of Calhoun's official papers in the State Department to be a matter of presenting in context the most authentic versions of the familiar major documents and of coping with a vast amount of dead and routine matters. An unexpected bonus has been the vivid portrayal in the papers of American society at its expansive edge, thrusting out into the larger world. While this material has been long available for research, most of it has not been gathered and published in readily usable form, and we may hope that the eyes of a few historians at least may be opened to riches that are yet to be mined for almost any imaginable aspect of American life in the diplomatic and consular records of the National Archives.

The major continuing issue of late 1844 was the annexation of Texas, a domestic political conflict with bitter sectional ramifications. It was also a major diplomatic issue in terms of what it portended for U.S. relations with the large and militant Latin-American neighbor to the South—especially when coupled, as it inevitably was, with American covetousness toward the sparsely settled, vast northern regions of the Mexican Republic known as New Mexico and California.

During the period of this volume Andrew Jackson Donelson carried out his duties as American Chargé d'Affaires in the Texan Republic. Donelson enjoyed the inestimable advantage of being not only an experienced soldier and lawyer but also a nephew of Andrew Jackson. He thus had a basis for rapport with the dominant public figure of Texas, General Sam Houston. Houston was a giant leader of men, but also a guileful politician and a magnificent hater. He had hated Calhoun since the time when Calhoun was Secretary of War and Houston was an Indian Agent and some difficulty had arisen about Houston's accounts. Fortunately, in regard to Texas annexation, Calhoun and the aged and feeble Andrew Jackson were at one.

Donelson's reports indicate that public opinion in Texas was overwhelming for joining the Union of the States. But it was also obvious that not insignificant negative factors had to be countered and that annexation had to be pursued with some urgency. British machinations, the ambitions of some leaders, and discouragement and irritation among the Texans themselves over vehement opposition to annexation among the politicians and press of the Northern United States were all potentially troublesome.

Also extensively documented herein are the reports of the Kentucky-born former Governor of Ohio, Wilson Shannon, whom John Tyler and Calhoun had sent to manage American relations with Mexico City. It was hoped, undoubtedly, that Shannon would be able to secure official Mexican acquiescence in the annexation of Texas, probably in return for cash and a guarantee of future boundaries. The facts that Americans hoped to arrange for California and New Mexico as well as Texas to fall on their side of the future boundaries, and that anti-Americanism was the chief principle of political life and national cohesion in Mexico, made the hope of peaceful settlement a forlorn one from the beginning.

Calhoun's friends continued to believe that he might have managed it had he kept the controls that soon would pass to James K. Polk and James Buchanan.[1] At any rate, the papers herein document important stages of that continuing tension that was to erupt into war in 1846.

Of some interest though no lasting importance in regard to the Texas question was Calhoun's sending his old ally and kinsman Duff Green to Texas and Mexico. Green went with appointments as U.S. Consul at Galveston and as despatch bearer to Shannon in Mexico City. Probably he carried oral advice to supplement the official instructions Calhoun had sent to Shannon under date of June 20, September 10, and September 11, 1844.[2]

---

[1] This was a commonplace to Calhoun's supporters and was being put forward as late as 1889 by Ben E. Green, who had been Acting U.S. Chargé d'Affaires in Mexico City. See Green's extended argument in his letter to Lyon G. Tyler (son of President John Tyler), August 8, 1889. ALS (copy) in Duff Green Papers, University of North Carolina, Southern Historical Collection (published microfilm, roll 17, frames 803–812).

[2] In the letter cited in footnote 1, Ben E. Green wrote: "I am very confident that there were no *written* instructions, in reference to the proposed treaty for the acquisition of New Mexico and California beyond the general proposal in Mr. Calhoun's letter to Gov. [Wilson] Shannon, to settle all questions of boundary with

As usual, wherever Green passed he left behind him a chain of controversies that continued to explode for some time afterward. Duff Green aspired to be, and to a considerable extent succeeded in being the Calhoun of the Southern economy. In Texas and Mexico he was inspired with the visions of transcontinental railroads and other vast schemes of development that he was to pursue in coming years.[3]

A less tangible objective than the annexation of Texas, but to Calhoun an important and related one, was a concert of international opinion to be developed as a weight against the imperial economic motives he saw behind the humanitarian facade of British emancipationism. One of the difficulties in implementing this subtle policy was the American Minister in London, Edward Everett. A Massachusetts Whig and an Anglophile, Everett was an unlikely vehicle for the administration's antiabolition policy, and he exercised as much diplomatic skill in evading the President and Secretary of State as in dealing with the British.

Everett, former Governor of Massachusetts and future Secretary of State and President of Harvard University, was thought to be one of the great learned men of the time. Of all American representatives abroad he was in the most important, active, and varied post, and could communicate with Washington most readily and frequently. He was energetic and businesslike and interpreted the duties of his post broadly.

From the point of view of a documentary editor forced to be selective, Everett's despatches are ideal because each deals with one single issue in a businesslike manner (with the result that there are often many despatches in one week or even in one day). Only a small part of Everett's correspondence with Calhoun could be published in this edition. He was a man with something to say on every subject. (It was Everett who, nineteen years later, was to speak for several hours on the same occasion at Gettysburg during which Abraham Lincoln delivered a notable but considerably briefer address.)

The American Minister to France, William R. King, a former Representative from North Carolina and Senator from Alabama (and later to be elected Vice-President of the United States), was in full

Mexico on liberal terms. The verbal instructions were sent by my father [Duff Green]."

[3] The lack of any biography of this Southern entrepreneur, whose activities lasted from the War of 1812 to the Greenback era and encompassed a huge territory and a great variety of enterprises, is a major gap in nineteenth century American historiography.

and intelligent sympathy with Calhoun's strategy. France, which still had plantation interests in the New World and which could naturally be expected to be dubious of British motives and influence, was the key link in Calhoun's plan of bringing weight against the British. It was a somewhat intangible goal with somewhat intangible results. Texas was a fairly small question when weighed in the balance against Louis Philippe's interest in Anglo-French concord.

Diplomacy and politics, of course, could not be entirely separated. Calhoun, as always, was hopeful that the results of one of the most clear-cut election campaigns in recent history would be to clarify principles and allow the government of the Union to work along the lines of restraint, honesty, and consensus which he envisioned as the ideal. As always, the amorphousness and evasiveness of American politicians were to defeat him.

One aspect of the politics of the period has to do with South Carolina, the unique base with which Calhoun enjoyed a relationship perhaps unlike that of any other major leader in American public life at any time. The meeting of the South Carolina General Assembly in the late fall of 1844 gave occasion for ferment beneath the surface of unity.

Part of this ferment came from the restless dissatisfaction of Southern nationalists to whom Calhoun represented an irksome force of moderation. Of a generation later than Calhoun, such men rejected any program which put preservation of the Union on a par with the defense of the South. They saw in compromise with the temporizing politics of the North and moderate Southerners only a path to disaster.

Another and perhaps larger, though less clear-cut and philosophical, source of dissent was personal ambition. The aristocratic society of South Carolina produced an extraordinary number of prima donnas, who imagined that their own wisdom and foresight were superior to Calhoun's. For such men Calhoun was a hateful obstacle to their own glory.

One such man was the outgoing Governor, James H. Hammond, who confided continually to his diary his imaginings of Calhoun's mistakes and his relentless machinations to slight and manipulate him.[4] It would have been out of character and totally unnecessary for Calhoun to devote thought and energy to such petty affairs. With

[4] Carol Bleser, ed., *Secret and Sacred: The Diaries of James Henry Hammond, a Southern Slaveholder* (New York and Oxford: Oxford University Press, 1988). See especially pp. 141, 145, 162, 163, 198.

very considerable talents Hammond combined the most extreme pride of a self-made Southern grandee and the most extreme self-righteousness inherited from his New England forebears.

Another such man was Francis W. Pickens, a young kinsman of Calhoun, who grew increasingly alienated for reasons that seemed sufficient to no one but himself. Though wealthy and of distinguished lineage (the son of a governor and the grandson of a Revolutionary general), Pickens owed most of his prominence to his relationship with Calhoun. From the election of 1844 onward Pickens apparently concluded that his own political judgment was superior to Calhoun's.[5] His was a fairly familiar case of a man of privileged background but limited ability overestimating his own importance.

While such problems were to characterize South Carolina political life for the rest of Calhoun's career, it is notable that they were muted and that the preponderance of opinion remained solidly behind Calhoun—the opinion of the public and of most of the remarkable number of able men that the State produced.

Calhoun felt, and many of his correspondents agreed, that the election of 1844 had finished off Henry Clay and the Whig party—and thereby also the "American System." The first part of the prediction was true, although the Whigs would take a little longer than expected to die. But to expect that the "American System," the linking of national politics with economic development and profit, which Calhoun saw as the fundamental obstacle to his own conception of American destiny, would disappear was as forlorn a hope as peace with Mexico. The premises of the "American System" coincided too deeply with the economic interests and the conception of social good of too many Americans.

If defeat was to kill the Whig party, success boded most ambiguously for its rival, more and more frequently known as the Democratic party, though Calhoun and others always referred to it as "the Republicans." This party had once been described by an ally of Calhoun's as "An immense mass of *ignorance* moved by the necessary momentum of *knavery*."[6] Or put another way, in the Calhounian view, the party rested upon a huge grass roots of decent republican instincts and patriotism in all parts of the Union—a naive mass un-

---

[5] A recent and detailed biography, which finds Pickens always wrong except when he disagrees with Calhoun, is John B. Edmunds, *Francis W. Pickens and the Politics of Destruction* (Chapel Hill and London: University of North Carolina Press, 1986).

[6] From James Hamilton, Jr., November 21, 1843, in *The Papers of John C. Calhoun*, 17:556.

fortunately helpless before the manipulations of the spoilsmen who had ridden to power on the coattails of Andrew Jackson.

As Calhoun's correspondence reveals, tensions were evident in the party from the moment of victory if not before. The victory in which they had expected to share left Calhoun's followers, especially in the absence of any clear signal from the President-elect, at sea.[7] As Calhoun and most of his friends saw it, the primary problems were two—the swarms of Van Burenite patronage seekers and party operatives whose goal was pay and power rather than principle, and the opportunistic ambitions of Thomas H. Benton.[8] Either of these forces could deprive the Democratic victory of meaning for those who pursued, as did Calhoun, a politics of principle and policy.

The primary hope was that the President-elect, Polk, would be able to surmount these obstacles and take what Calhoun always called the "high ground." As matters were to turn out, Polk certainly would not meet Calhoun's hopes. But it was also true that the elements represented by Van Buren and Benton would cause as much difficulty for Polk as they always had for Calhoun.

[7] Evident from many letters herein. See also James A. Seddon to Robert M.T. Hunter, November 16, 1844, in Charles Henry Ambler, ed., *Correspondence of Robert M.T. Hunter, 1826–1876*, in the *American Historical Association Annual Report* for 1916 (2 vols. Washington: U.S. Government Printing Office, 1918), 2:73–74.

[8] For Benton's maneuvering on the Texas annexation question see *Congressional Globe*, 28th Cong., 2nd Sess., pp. 19, 43.

THE PAPERS

of

JOHN C. CALHOUN

Ⅲ

Volume XX

OCTOBER 1–15
1844

▨

The Oregon negotiations had been carried as far as they could be for the time. A number of initiatives had been set in motion. The sixty-two-year-old Secretary of State had just finished six months of intensive labor on diplomatic and administrative matters large and small. It was time for a holiday, which to Calhoun usually meant joining in the productive outdoor labor of his plantation.

By October 1 he was at Charleston and by the fourth at home—to remain for a month, leaving the Department of State in the capable hands of Richard K. Crallé, Chief Clerk and Acting Secretary. (Crallé knew his chief's mind as well as any man.) The local paper reported of Calhoun, on arrival home, that he was "in excellent health and spirits." (Pendleton, S.C., Messenger, October 11, 1844.)

Harvest was under way, and, despite serious drought, Calhoun found the crops good, so he wrote, shortly after his arrival, to his son-in-law across the sea in Brussels. Similar news was had from the second plantation in Alabama. Farmer Calhoun could not have been anything but pleased by a report issued on October 10 by a visiting committee of the local agricultural society, which found Fort Hill to be exemplary in nearly every respect.

Official business continued in the far corners of the world. Calhoun's and the President's choice for Minister to Texas, during this troubled period while the fate of annexation tottered in the balance, accepted on October 2 and made plans to hasten to that Republic. There could not have been a better choice than Andrew Jackson Donelson, not only an experienced soldier and lawyer but a nephew of Andrew Jackson who could establish the proper relations with that difficult giant, President Sam Houston. Another giant, Duff Green, was already in Texas and found public opinion there sound. He continued his fact-finding mission for the Secretary of State on to Mexico and reached Vera Cruz on October 6.

There was, of course, a campaign going on for the White House and the Congress, and Calhoun received the usual supply of political correspondence. An Ohioan had written that Whig stump dema-

3

gogues in that State, in response to the Southern zeal for Texas annexation, were raising the old cries of South Carolina "disunionism." "It is a great mistake . . . both North and West," Calhoun replied, "that South Carolina is hostile to the Union. There is not a member of our Union more devoted to it than she is; I mean the Federal Union, as it came from the hands of its framers."

As to the larger currents of events, Calhoun was guardedly optimistic. The Democratic Party had at last overthrown Van Burenism, and the election itself portended the overthrow of Clay. It was Clay who was "the author of that system of plunder, which has oppressed the South & corrupted the North," and Van Buren who "has perpetuated it & fixed it on the country."

On October 4, the Washington Spectator, *which had struggled along since mid-1842 as an organ of Calhoun's supporters, published its last issue. To take its place, friends were already organizing the* Constitution, *which would begin publishing within two weeks under the editorship of William A. Harris, until recently a Representative from Virginia.*

⫿

R[ichard] K. Crallé to Brig. Gen. Don J[uan] N. Almonte

Department of State
Washington, 1st October, 1844

The Undersigned, Acting Secretary of State of the United States, has the honor to inform General Almonte, Envoy Extraordinary and Minister Plenipotentiary of the Mexican Republic, that information has been received by the Undersigned that the officers in command of the Mexican war steamers which came into the Port of New York for the purpose of undergoing repairs and which are designed to be employed in military operations against Texas, a country with which the United States are at peace, have, most probably through ignorance of the laws of the United States, since their arrival in our waters, enlisted seamen other than Mexican citizens transiently within the same, for service on board the ships, and have also increased the number of their guns and added equipments solely applicable to war. For the information of General Almonte, the Undersigned begs leave to refer

4

him to the 2nd and 5th Sections of an Act of Congress, passed on the 20th of April, 1818, to preserve the neutrality of the United States. By the 2nd section of said Act, it will be perceived that all persons are forbidden within the jurisdiction or territory of the United States (except the citizens or subjects of the foreign power making the enlistment transiently within the United States) from enlisting or entering themselves, or from hiring or enlisting other persons in the service of any foreign Prince, State, District or People, as a soldier or as a marine or seaman on board of any vessel of war, Letter of Marque or Privateer; and the Section declares every person offending against this provision to be guilty of a misdemeanor and to be punishable by a fine not exceeding a thousand dollars, and imprisonment not exceeding one year.

The 5th Section prohibits the increase or augmentation of the force of any ship of war, cruiser or other armed vessel, which, at the time of her arrival within the United States, was a ship of war or cruiser in the service of any foreign power, the same being at war with any other foreign power with whom the United States are at peace, by adding to the number of guns of such vessel or by changing those on board of her for guns of a larger calibre, or by the addition thereto of any equipment solely applicable to war; and denounces against the violators of this provision forfeiture and punishment of the same extent with that contained in the 2nd Section.

While the President [John Tyler], reflecting in his own feelings those of the entire people and government of the United States, would be the last person who would desire to present any obstacle in the way of Mexican ships or vessels, either public or private, from enjoying all the advantages of the ports of the United States, and would most earnestly desire to see all the rights of hospitality extended to all ships or vessels of the Republic of Mexico visiting our waters, it is nevertheless made his imperative duty to see that no violation of the provisions of the Acts of Congress, passed to secure the neutrality of the United States, takes place. He feels a deep conviction that the Mexican Government would not knowingly countenance any proceeding involving that neutrality, on the part of any one in her service; and he has, therefore, instructed the Undersigned to bring this matter to your consideration and to request that you will institute inquiries into this subject and that an order may be given to prevent the sailing of the Guadalupe and Montezuma, until a full investigation be made in the premises. Nor does he permit himself to doubt that an order will be given that all additional guns and munitions of war received on board said ships or vessels, be immediately relanded, and all persons enlisted, other than Mexican citizens transiently in in [*sic*] the United States, be forthwith discharged.

In evidence of the well-grounded apprehension of the Undersigned that the laws of the United States have been violated, the Undersigned submits to General Almonte the accompanying copies of affidavits and extracts from a letter received from Mr. Ogden Hoffman, the United States District Attorney for the Southern District of New York, and Mr. Richard S. Coxe, who have been unitedly instructed to make inquiries into the matter.

The Undersigned avails himself of this occasion to offer General Almonte the assurance of his very distinguished consideration. R.K. Crallé.

FC in DNA, RG 59 (State Department), Notes to Foreign Legations, Mexico, 6: 183–185 (M-99:69).

From Clement C. Biddle, Philadelphia, 10/1. He encloses a petition of 9/28 signed by 24 merchants and recommending Joshua Clibborn as U.S. Consul at Liverpool. Clibborn is a gentleman, an experienced businessman and merchant, and a former U.S. Consul at Antwerp. He "would cherish and promote the mercantile interests" of the U.S. ALS with En in DNA, RG 59 (State Department), Applications and Recommendations, 1837–1845, Clibborn (M-687:5, frames 507–509).

From ROBERT B. CAMPBELL

Consulate of the United States of America, Havana
October 1st 1844

Sir, I have the honor to acknowledge having received on yesterday by the ship C. Colon your official communication of the 31st August last, in which I am instructed to demand of the Government of this Island, in the name of the Government of the United States That the cases of the American citizens imprisoned, be immediately brought before the proper tribunal, and that no delay may be made in the disposition of them, further than a fair and impartial trial may render necessary.

I am further instructed to request a prompt answer to the demand it conveys, in a manner not to cause offence. This duty was discharged, immediately, on the receipt of your communication in an official note a copy of which is herewith transmitted.

Previous to the receipt of your official letter of the 31st August, I had written you under date of the 14th Sept. stating that Messrs. [William] Bisby, [Samuel] Moffat and [Thomas] Savage were liberated and [John] Thompson was the only American remaining in Prison at Matanzas. By a letter received this morning dated 30th Sept. (a copy of which accompanies this communication) I have received information of Thompson[']s discharge, his discharge consequently preceding the receipt of my letter of yesterday by the Capt[ai]n General.

Dr. [Elias] Wolf of Villa Clara who has been detained (but so far as I can learn not imprisoned) has been ordered to be discharged under date of the 19th Sept. Of which I have already informed you. It thus appears that no American Citizen is now incarcerated upon charges of participation in the insurrection or for other cause. That these Americans have been arrested[,] some of them cruelly and inhumanly treated, long and rigidly confined upon charges frivolous or unsustained, is beyond controversy. That resident foreigners are amenable to the laws for their viola[tion?] for conspiring against the institutions of the country and the lives of the inhabitants is admitted I presume by all foreign governments, and none could rightfully complain of their punishment upon conviction. In this instance however so far as I can learn and beleive, there is no evidence entitled to credence of overt act or design on the part of any American to violate law, or disturb the public peace. Those arrested are represented to me as correct, inoffensive, and incapable of thought or deed tending to subvert the relations of Master and slave. Admitting this representation to be true Are they entitled to compensation for their sufferings and losses? If entitled (as I beleive they are) how is it to be obtained? Am I authorised to demand it here? If authorised how is the am[oun]t to be fixed? If I am not authorised to apply to this government, shall I advise the discharged Americans to make out accounts, & forward them to the State Department to be sent to the American Minister at Madrid? Your instructions on this subject I am desirous of having at the earliest possible period of time. Mr. Savage having already applied for information and the others may do the same.

In the different communications received from the Department no mention is made of any being received from this Consulate. Will you favor me with the information whether they have been received, as in the event of miscarriage copies will be forwarded. I have the honor to be Y[ou]r Mo[st] Ob[edien]t Serv[an]t, Robert B. Campbell.

7

ALS with Ens in DNA, RG 59 (State Department), Consular Despatches, Havana, vol. 19 (T-20:19), received 10/25.

From C[ALEB] CUSHING

United States Brig Perry
October 1st 1844

Sir: I cannot forbear to express a strong conviction of the expediency of making some new and permanent provision for the future official intercourse between the United States and China, in consideration both of the magnitude of our existing interests in that Empire, and still more of those which may be expected to grow up under the provisions of the Treaty of Wang-Hiya.

The ordinary commercial & other concerns of the United States in China call for the appointment of a public functionary there of a higher class than a mere unpaid consul, himself engaged in mercantile concerns, and for that reason not possessing the independence of position, which is desirable in relation to his own countrymen, as well as to the Chinese, among whom commercial pursuits are not held in distinguished estimation.

The force of these considerations is augmented by the fact of the privilege of ex[tra]territoriality being conferred on Citizens of the United States in China, and great additional power & responsibility being thus deferred to & imposed on our public officers there, as explained in my despatch of the 29th of September, numbered (97) ninety-seven.

What opinion the British Government entertains of this matter may be inferred from their practise. In addition to their military establishment, they have a Plenipotentiary permanently residing in Hong-kong; and they have besides paid consuls in each of the Five Ports, one of whom is of the rank of Consul General. The French have, also, both a Plenipotentiary & a Consul General.

And I do not well see how our own interests in China can be guarded, or our national character honorably maintained, without the appoint[ment] of a resident Minister or Commissioner from the United States. I am With great respect Your ob[edien]t S[er]v[an]t, C. Cushing.

ALS (No. 98) in DNA, RG 59 (State Department), Diplomatic Despatches, China, vol. 2 (M-92:3), received 1/21[?]/1845; PC in Senate Document No. 58, 28th Cong., 2nd Sess., p. 14; PC in House Document No. 69, 28th Cong., 2nd Sess., pp. 14–15.

R[ichard] K. Crallé to OGDEN HOFFMAN and RICHARD S. COXE, New York [City]

Department of State
Washington, 1st Oct. 1844
Gentlemen, Your several and joint letters relative to the duties with which you have been specially charged with respect to the Mexican War-Steamers at New York, have been received and laid before the President [John Tyler]. He has duly considered the subject and has requested the opinion of [John Nelson] the Attorney General upon the points of law which you have stated. A copy of the opinion is herewith transmitted for your information and guidance and, also; a copy of a note which has been addressed by this Department to General [Juan N.] Almonte the Mexican Minister to this Government. I am Gentlemen, Your Ob[edien]t Serv[an]t, R.K. Crallé, Act[in]g Secretary.

FC in DNA, RG 59 (State Department), Domestic Letters, 34:397 (M-40:32).

From GEO[RGE] W. HOUK

Dayton O[hio,] Oct. 1st 1844
D[ea]r Sir, The character which the coming political contest is assuming is my apology for addressing one, so well known to all his fellow-citizens, though personally unknown to the under signed. Your public course however, has far from remained by me, unnoticed, unstudied. I have looked upon it with more interest than upon that of any other public man, who has partaken in the councils of the nation in your time. As the great political conflict approaches nearer & nearer, it waxes warmer & warmer, & the more direct and severe do our opponents point their charges. You are not unaware perhaps of the feeling which pervades the North regarding the question of the annexation of Texas and your course upon that subject. That measure has met with the most unrelenting opposition from the whigs, chiefly based upon the ground of the extension of slavery, a far different ground I apprehend from that assumed by the same party upon the same question in the South. It is also denounced here as a pretext upon which the South seeks to dissolve the Union. South Carolina is accused of taking the lead in the move with you at her head. Such are the base, baseless, tho' high sounding charges here made daily

9

when this great question of reannexation is brot' up for discussion. I need scarcely ask your opinion, your sentiments regarding the preservation of the honourable Union of the States which form our noble Republic; Union as it is, & always under the Constitution. I am well satisfied regarding your sentiments upon this subject for I have studied your course in the memorable session of '32. Nor need I make inquiry concerning your opinions upon the Texas Question for they are fully shown in your Texas Correspondence. But I wish to know the general sentiment in South Carolina respecting both and whether it is averse to a continuation in the Union if Texas is not admitted. I do not write this with the intention of receiving an answer for publication.

If you will favor me with an answer at your convenience communicating your views upon the above, I will be under the greatest obligations to you. Any other observations you may be pleased to make, concerning the policies of the respective parties[?] on the questions involved will be highly acceptable & I trust appreciated.

I am not unaware of the probable extent of your correspondence and of the favor I am asking at your hands, but I have found my justification in the high regard in which I have always held your character and public course & the admiration I have felt, the approbation I have expressed for your disinterested Statesmanlike public career. Be pleased Sir to accept the earnest assurances of my highest esteem. Truly y[ou]rs, Geo. W. Houk.

ALS in ScCleA; PEx in Boucher and Brooks, eds., *Correspondence*, p. 252.

From STEWART NEWELL

Consulate of the United States
Galveston, Oct. 1st 1844

Sir, In my No. 6 from this Consulate I had the honor to communicate to the Department the arrival here of Duff Green Esq[ui]r[e] who *verbally* informed me of his being on his way to Mexico bearing despatches to the Minister from the United States to Mexico [Wilson Shannon]. He however did not exhibit any document to me from the Department by which I might know the fact officially, but many of the Citizens of this place who make it a point to beset every stranger and particularly one with communications from the Government to extract from them all the information possible after which circulate it to the community ["as appears to be the case in this instance" *inter-lined*]. I did not consider it my duty to ask of Gen[era]l Green any thing, excepting if he had any communications from the Department to me to which he replied no he had none, yet I can hear at every corner the nature of the despatches of which he is the bearer and upon his arrival in this place in the Evening in public proclaimed himself the Consul when asked by Cap[tai]n [Winslow] Foster of the "Wood-berry" if he had seen me, supposing such had been the case. On the next morning after his arrival he address[e]d a note to me requesting an interview which in defference to his *Age* was promptly and cheer-fully granted, I expecting to receive some authentic information rela-tive to his Appointment and a proper demand of the Books, Papers &C of this Consulate. This not having been done I could only infer the intention on his part that I should continue to Act until his return, but to my surprise I was told by Mr. Green this morning that he should transmit his Commission to this Government for an Exequator and had appointed Elisha A. Rhodes former Consul at this Port to Act as Vice-Consul being the same to whom the late Consul A[rchibald] M. Green Esq[ui]r[e] refers the Department in his Letters No. 9 ["& 8" *interlined*] and to which a reply from the Hon. Daniel Webster, Secretary of State is now in this Office under date of April 20th 1843. I felt it my duty to make reference to said Letters in reply to Mr. Green and deeming his whole course while here to be irregular from first to last and wanting in that courtesy towards me as an Officer and gentleman I have felt it my duty to communicate the facts to the Department and await instructions if the Appointment of E.A. Rhodes as Vice-Consul will be recognized by the Department and to deliver to him the Books papers &C of the Consulate and Archives of the Legation now secure from any danger until a Chargé shall be ap-pointed. If so it shall be done immediately, but a sense of duty and Courtesy to ["myself" *interlined*] & total disregard as I deem it to-wards me in this case induces me to say that further instructions from the department will be requisite to induce a deviation on my part from a strict observance of that line of duty which under present circum-stances now unhap[p]ily exist and should I not do so would feel as if a duty to my Government had been by me neglected and I can only attribute the Hostile feelings in this whole matter towards me as ema-nating from the promptings of a base and malicious faction existing ["here" *canceled*] against any man who cannot or will not indulge in the low petty intrigues and disapation of the parties here to whom one of the late Chargés, and I fear Gen[era]l Green has lent too willing an Ear for personal interest or the good of our Country.

11

I have used no improper means to lay my claims to the Appointment to this Consulate relying solely upon a knowledge of them to the Department and now do not desire to be so understood, but I must be permitted to protest against such a course as has been pursued towards me without having merited it and if my services have been of any advantage to the American interests in this Country they cannot long be so with such conduct towards me suffer[e]d by the Department and of which I trust no more will be permitted by the Department. Open enemies, I fear not, but the Assassin like darts in secret hurled at me cannot always be guarded against, and I challenge any man to the proof ["of any Act" *canceled*] of my whole life Official or private for any single act of wrong done by me, and which I could wish was the case with many here, and those, who are most energetic in reccommending for thier own interests, improper persons to the consideration of the Govt. I have the honor to be Most Respectfully Your Ob[edien]t Servant, Stewart Newell.

ALS (No. 7) in DNA, RG 59 (State Department), Consular Despatches, Galveston, vol. 2 (T-151:2), received 10/16. NOTE: An AEI by R[obert] S. C[hew], Clerk in the Consular Bureau, reads "What answer shall I give Mr. Newell to this letter[?]" In the same file is a document indicating that Newell claimed payment of $106 from the State Department for "Transcribing, Binding, Pageing, Indexing and affixing Marginal Notes" for records of the Galveston Consulate. An ES by Calhoun in response to the claim reads "The expense having been incurred under instructions from Mr. [Daniel] Webster, in his letter referred to above, the account is, Approved, to be paid out of the appropriation for the Contingent expenses of Foreign intercourse. Dept. of State, 18 Nov. 1844."

From A[lphonse] Pageot, [French Minister to the U.S.], Washington, 10/1. John Baptiste Demerlier, born at Ghent, Belgium, in 1788 and naturalized in Philadelphia in 1818, has applied to the French government for letters of naturalization. Pageot seeks to learn Demerlier's official status with respect to American authority and whether the granting to him of French naturalization will absolve him of allegiance to the U.S. LS (in French) and State Dept. translation in DNA, RG 59 (State Department), Notes from Foreign Legations, France, vol. 12 (M-53:8, frames 716–719).

From Charles P. Traub, [Acting Consul], Matanzas, [Cuba], 10/1. He informs Calhoun that John Thompson, "the last remaining prisoner of those taken up as concerned in the late conspiracy," was released on bail on 9/29 under the same terms as W[illia]m Bisby. ALS (No. 24) in DNA, RG 59 (State Department), Consular Despatches, Matanzas, vol. 4 (T-339:4), received 11/15.

From T[homas] Wynns

New York [City,] October 1st 1844

Sir, Having been on a visit to Marianna in West Florida in March and April last I was induced to make a visit to St. Andrews Bay, about 50 miles distant; and I was surprised at finding that so ample a Harbor had never been brought into requisition by the General Government, as it occurs to me that its locality, its capabalities, and resources, together with the acknowledged salubrity of the Climate, render it one of the most valuable and desirable places for a Naval and Commercial Depot, that can be found perhaps upon the American Coast; and should the United States happen to be involved in a War, or should the Island of Cuba happen to fall into other hands than its present possessors, the value of St. Andrews Bay would be incalculable, affording as it does all the requisite facilities for a great Commercial Emporium, as well as a Naval Station, having a safe and Capacious Harbor, and abounding with Live Oak and other Timber requisite in the construction of Vessels of War and being so easy of access from the Gulph.

Under the foregoing impressions, I had several conversations with Gentlemen in the neighborhood who appeared to be conversant with the subject, and I subsequently addressed a communication to my friend Doctor Simmons Ba[ker?] who is an extensive planter in that vicinity, and I beg leave to subjoin an abstract of his reply, dated Raleigh N.C. 31st May.

"Believing St. Andrews Bay is susceptible of very important improvement, by which it could be made a place of great commercial importance, far superior to any in the Gulf of Mexico excepting New Orleans I am particularly gratified at the interest you take in it—there is some discrepancy in regard to the depth of water at the pass. I have a Map made from a Survey of Gen. [Simon] Bernard, which represents it at 18 feet—a later Survey by U.S. Engineers represent it 16 ft. Col[one]l [John W.] Campbell to the best of my recollection says 24 feet, and I think Felix Long, who was Surveyor of the Port for several years, ["I think" *canceled*] confirms that statement—the depth inside is ample, and I understand that at[?] Robertson's House, a large vessel may lay along side the Bank; there is a considerable quantity of live Oak about the Bay, and Mr. Watson had a Contract with the Government for a large supply of that article—the Canals are most important to the improvement of the place; one of four miles in length communicating with the Choctawhatchie Bay, and from there to Santa Rosa Sound, and Pensacola, an inland pas[sage?] of great importance in time of War. I have never heard of any estimate of the cost of this; the other Canal would be from the Apalachicola River to a Navigable Creek, name not recollected entering the East arm of the Bay—this has been twice surveyed by U.S. Engineers, the distance 10¼ miles, with a fall from the River to the Creek of 10 feet, firm land and no deep cutting, for more than half a mile, and on the side next the Creek no cutting, but embankments to retain the water, of which an unlimited supply Can be procured from the River. This Canal would turn all the Cotton from above, to St. Andrews Bay, say at this time 130 thousand Bales—Estimated cost by one Engineer 300,000$— by another, 400,000$—at a time when labor was more than double the present price in that Country.

Apalachicola is too sickly for any one to live at, being surrounded by fresh water marsh; no vessel drawing more than six feet water can get nearer than three miles, and ships, nine miles, below the Town in an exposed situation, now the outlet of a considerable portion of Georgia, Alabama, and Florida; all the produce of which would at once go to that delightful and healthy place, St. Andrews, if the Canal was cut. Choctawhatchie is navigable to Steam Boats for 100 to 150 miles, into the heart of Alabama." From the foregoing, Your Excellency will perhaps concur with me in believing, that the Harbour of St. Andrews Bay, might be easily brought into notice, by the action of the General Government, and at a Comparatively trifling expenditure of money, which it is presumed might very soon be refunded by a moderate Toll, to say nothing of the vast and incalculable importance of the place in a Commercial and Naval point of view, and the immense quantity of Land now lying dormant, which would by such a measure, be immediately brought into the market, and which consideration alone may perhaps be quite an equivalent for the necessary expenditure. During my visit to St. Augustine in May last I availed myself of the opportunity to mention the Subject to that Patriotic and indefatigable Officer, Gen[era]l [William J.] Worth, who very kindly promised me, that he would take an early opportunity of bringing the matter under the notice of Government, and obtaining a new Survey of the Harbor, in[?] a view to its accomplishment. And I have now only to beg [the] favor of submitting it to Your Excellency's favorable consideration with a hope that this feeble attempt towards the welfare and aggrandisement of our common Country, may in some wise prove available, and I shall be amply compensated by such a result. I have the honor to remain Very Respectfully, Your Excellency's Most Ob[edien]t Serv[an]t, T. Wynns.

ALS in DNA, RG 59 (State Department), Miscellaneous Letters (M-179:107, frames 268–270). NOTE: This letter was not sent to Calhoun at the time of its writing, but was enclosed in a later letter from Wynns of 1/15/1845. Thomas Wynns was a native of N.C. and had been U.S. Consul at Turks Island during 1817–1835.

From D[AVID] LEVY [YULEE, Delegate from Fla. Territory]

Washington, Oct[obe]r 1, 1844
Dear Sir, The failure of my printer to furnish my circular in season prevented my being able to accompany you on y[ou]r route South, for your kind invitation to do which I was very grateful.

I now enclose you [*not found*] a copy of my circular, by a glance over the leaves of which you will see the view I present to my constituents. The leading point I seek to impress, is that the South needs our ["aid" *interlined*] in maintaining as far as possible a defensive power in the Federal councils, and that such aid is more essential now, than it can be at any future day.

Our people place their reliance in you as the true representative of the South & her policy, and you w[oul]d do me great favor, if you can spare a leisure moment, to give me your opinion as to the course proper for us to pursue, & best for our own & the Southern interests. Sh[oul]d you have time to do so, please address me at St. Augustine, where I shall be in about ten days. Your letter is not desired for publication, but to show to those of our citizens to whom it may be properly and usefully exhibited.

Nothing of much interest has transpired since your departure. Mr. [Henry] Clay[']s private letter to Cassius M. C[lay] is the subject of chief[?] curiosity & commentary. I cannot admire the morals which brought it into publicity, any more than the morals which dictated it. Yet it is clear its publication will have a serious effect upon Mr. Clay[']s present prospects, and upon ["his" *interlined*] standing and charachter as a public man.

A gentleman recently from Ohio tells me the Abolitionists will preserve their separate organization there—if so, we may have some hope even of that State. With high regard & respect I am Y[ou]r ob[edien]t S[ervan]t, D. Levy.

ALS in ScCleA. NOTE: David Levy, a native of the West Indies and subsequently Senator from Fla. and a member of the Confederate Congress, became David Levy Yulee in 1846.

From RUFUS CHOATE, [Senator from Mass.]

Boston, 2 Oct. 1844

Sir, I have the honour to introduce Mr. [Charles] Tyng of Newburyport in Massachusetts. He is engaged in his profession of merchant in Cuba, although his residence & that of his family is here; & is a gentleman of character, & bears the name of one of our oldest & most respectable families. He desires to engage the attention of the department to some business of interest in Europe. I have the honor to be Your obedient Servant, Rufus Choate.

ALS in DNA, RG 59 (State Department), Miscellaneous Letters (M-179:105, frame 503); CC in DNA, RG 84 (Foreign Posts), Great Britain, Instructions, 8: 466. NOTE: Tyng had a claim against the British for the seizure of a Bremen ship on the coast of Africa in 1840 with a cargo of his goods. This was the subject of later correspondence of the State Department with Tyng and with the U.S. Minister in London, Edward Everett, which is not included herein.

From A[NDREW] J. DONELSON

Near the Hermitage, Oct. 2d 1844

D[ea]r Sir, I reached home last night and found there awaiting my arrival your letter of the 16[t]h ult[im]o enclosing the appointment which the President [John Tyler] was pleased to forward to me, and also the instructions which had been given to Gen[era]l [Tilghman A.] Howard whose untimely death has been so much regretted.

Although at a great sacrifice of my private interests, which require all my attention to relieve them from embarrassment, I have accepted the appointment, and will proceed to the seat of Government of Texas in the course of a few days or the time necessary to provide for the comfort of my family during my absence.

I regard as you do the question of annexing Texas as most important to the future peace of our own country, and if not settled soon, favorably to the United States, as likely to produce difficulties which will affect this whole continent. As a good citizen, therefore, I could not withhold my aid in endeavoring to avert such difficulties; and it will be gratifying to me indeed if I can requite your confidence and that of President Tyler by a faithful and useful vindication and support of the true interests of my country at so critical a juncture.

I shall of course use the draft brought to me by Mr. [James] Broome: and will keep you advised of my progress to Texas and of all that concerns the objects of the mission. I must, however, ask of you permission to visit the United States in the course of the winter to complete the arrangement of my private affairs, after the course of events in Texas shall have settled the fate of the annexation question, and when the interests of our Government will not suffer from my temporary absence.

Gen[era]l [Andrew] Jackson is in feeble health, but is still in a condition to attend to business and to examine questions of public interest. He highly approves of the course adopted by the Government in relation to Texas and has no doubt of its success.

Thanking you for your kindness, and tendering you my sincere wishes for your health & prosperity I remain Y[ou]rs truly, A.J. Donelson.

ALS in ScCleA.

From BEN E. GREEN

Legation of the U.S. of A.
Mexico [City], Oct. 2d 1844

Dear Sir, Accompanying Mr. [Wilson] Shannon's last despatch were some papers relating to the case of a boy [Thomas Farrington] taken by the Governor of San Luis Potosi from an American citizen, named Bensley. This case originated, while I was in charge of the legation. Immediately on being informed of the circumstances by a letter from Bensley then at San Luis, I went personally to the palace to see the Minister of Foreign Relations on the subject. Mr. [José M. Ortiz] Monasterio, then Minister, told me that he had received an account of the transaction from the Governor, & promised that the boy should be restored. On the strength of this promise, I assured Mr. Bensley that his apprentice should be restored to him without delay.

When the boy was taken, Bensley was doing a good business; but by the loss of the boy, who was the chief attraction of his [circus] company, he has been completely broken up, & his company dispersed. He has now waited here three months patiently confiding in the assurance which I gave him, & is of course much disappointed at the result. His company being dispersed, he has now determined to await here the determination of the case. I feel interested in it, both because of the assurance, which, on the strength of Mr. Monasterio's promise, I gave him, and because neither the property nor the lives of our citizens will be safe in Mexico, should our Government easily pass over so flagrant an outrage as this. I deem it therefore proper to call your attention particularly to this case to request your immediate action thereon, and to explain the reason, why there has been so much difficulty in obtaining justice from the Mexican Govt. in a case like this.

The Governor of San Luis Potosi, who committed this outrage, is Rincon Gallardo, ex-marquis of Guadalupe, a man of immense wealth and extensive family connexions, and who, having been some time Governor of San Luis Potosi, exercises no inconsiderable influence over a large portion of the Army, stationed at that place. He is connected by marriage with [José M.] Tornel, the latter enemy of every thing American, and as you may judge from this transaction (vide [Andrew] Harris' affidavit) shares in all the bitterness of his spleen. At the time the outrage was committed (the 8th July) it was generally thought in the interior that there would be a rupture between Mexico and the U.S. about Texas, & Gov. Gallardo probably supposed that any outrage committed on an American would be looked upon as good service, for which he would not be called to account.

The Mexican Govt., through its minister of Foreign Relations, promised that the boy should be restored. This promise, however, was not complied with, because the Government is at war with the Congress, whose refractory spirit must soon be curbed by force of arms. I know, positively, that several Cabinet meetings have been held, the subject of which was to put down the Congress by force. To this it must come, & that very soon, and in the contest that must ensue, the army at San Luis Potosi will make a considerable part of the Govt. force. Over this army Gov. Gallardo exercises much control, and to Santa Anna, whose only support is the army, & who is generally detested, his opposition would be formidable. Already Gallardo must be somewhat displeased at Tornel's disgrace, and should he be baulked in (I do not say punished for) his highhanded conduct, which from its wantonness has attracted general attention, his pride would be most deeply wounded, & his disaffection might be turned into open opposition.

This is the secret of the difficulty. The Govt., detested and with reason, by the popular body, is unable or afraid to repress or chastise the misconduct of its officers. In fact the Minister of Foreign Relations intimated as much, in an interview, which I had with him on the case, for he declared his anxiety to do justice, but at the same time cited the difficulties of the Govt., the opposition of the Congress and the recent accusations of the Ministry as excuses for not ordering the boy to be restored.

The Mexican Govt. is either unwilling or unable to restrain the excesses of one of its own officers, or to do justice in this flagrant case. To me its inability appears as inexcusable as its *unwillingness*, and I trust our Govt. will view the matter in the same light, & act promptly in this matter.

I do not believe however that the present Mexican Govt. is more *willing* than *able* to protect & do justice to our citizens. I believe its good *will* is less than its ability, and I differ *toto ca[e]lo* from Gen[era]l [Waddy] Thompson [Jr.] in his opinion of its present head, Santa Anna. The Gen[era]l has been very lavish of praise of Santa Anna in the U. States. Yet in one of his despatches (30 July 1842 no. 4) he says: "The rights of American citizens of every grade & character are subject to constant outrage." From whom? From the officers of the Mexican Govt. itself; from Santa Anna's friends and partisans, holding office under him. But can it be supposed that *they* would dare to commit these "constant outrages on the rights of American citizens," unless they know that it is not unacceptable to their master? I regret that Gen[era]l Thompson's praises are calculated to create an erroneous impression of Santa Anna's character, in the U. States. Better that his true character should be known, and it is to be hoped that the Govt. at least will not be led astray as to his true character, and as to his *feelings towards the U. States.* Your ob[edien]t Serv[an]t & friend, Ben E. Green.

ALS in DNA, RG 59 (State Department), Diplomatic Despatches, Mexico, vol. 12 (M-97:13), received 11/13; draft in NcU, Duff Green Papers (published microfilm, roll 5, frames 830–835). NOTE: An undated memorandum [of *ca.* 11/-1844], found among Calhoun's papers and in the hand of William Hunter, Jr., a State Department Clerk, indicates that Farrington was an 11-year-old circus rider, a "regularly" indentured apprentice to Bensley, whose abduction by Gallardo was completely unjustified. The report concludes, "The United States would seem to be justified in compelling him either directly or through the Mexican government, to release the boy and to make amends for his detention." (ADU in ScCleA.)

From MEMUCAN HUNT, "Private"

Galveston, Texas, October 2nd 1844

My Dear Sir, The present momentous position of this country induces me to take the liberty of addressing you this note with view of stating our situation and making some suggestions in relation to what should be our present policy and actions & of asking yours in reply.

It is doubtful from the course he has heretofore pursued & from what I can learn whether Mr. Anson Jones, the Pres[iden]t elect of Texas is favorable to our union with the U.S. The recent appointments of Mr. [George W.] Terrell as minister to Great Britain & Mr. [James] Reily to the U.S. both of whom are avowed opponents of annexation when added to the recent zealous support of the British party in Texas of Mr. Jones for Pres[iden]t with the declaration, in some instances on their part, that they voted for Mr. Jones because he was opposed to annexation is calculated to increase these doubts. I hope however they are unfounded. When I saw him last, which was in February, we held frequent conversations on the subject & I can assure you that he was, at that time an unreserved advocate of the measure, yet he may have changed since the defeat of the treaty for that object, by the U.S. Senate. Whether he has, or has not, I am satisfied that if your congress will pass a law providing for the union within the next twelve months, that at least two thirds of both houses of the congress of Texas will ratify the same.

There is no guaranty however that this would be the case at a later date. The very policy, I, as one of the citizens of the country, shall recommend to my friends in congress to adopt—whilst I believe it is calculated to hasten your action in favor of the measure will at the same time tend to create a powerful party in this country opposed to it. The recommendation I shall offer is a simple reduction by law of our import duties to 10 per cent, or even 8, or 6, ad valorem on all products and manufactories of any country which will admit the products and manufactories of Texas on the same conditions, & to such countries as refuse an acquiescence a requisition of discriminating duties of from 25 to 200 per cent. This proposition would, doubtless, be exceeded [*sic*] to by Great Britain, France & Belgium—Texas being being [*sic*] exclusively an agricultural country. The result of this if it is adopted will be great, very great, injury to both the manufactures & revinues of the U.S., for, as I stated officially to your Govt. in 1837 it will be impossible to prevent smuggleing from one country to the other when their tariffs of duties materially differ. The passage of such a law, as the one I have refer[r]ed to, in the event of its being

20

met with reciprocal regulations in Great Britain & the other powers of Europe with which we have treaties, of which there is little doubt, would at once engage capital enough at this place to supply the valley of the Mississippi with all the goods they need the duties of which exceed 20 per cent. The prop[r]ietors of the great manufacturing interests in the U.S. foreseeing this result, will, it appears to me, become advocates of immediate annexation, for, without it, the state of trade above depicted will destroy or greatly impair their prosperity and they are surely wise enough to foresee that if Texas once adopts this, almost free trade system & its citizens derive the benefits that will certainly accrue to them from it they will become opposed in a very short time to annexation. The expences of our government is a mere nothing & 8 or 10 per cent duties will pay them. Agriculture would be greatly promoted by such a system of trade and the wealth of the mercantile interest in such a state of things would soon greatly control all classes of our citizens and I can not say but that in twelve months after its adoption a majority of the people of Texas would be opposed to annexation, and backed as they would be, doubtless, by Great Britain and France it would be impossible for the U.S. to force a connexion at an after time.

As an individual & one who consulted alone his individual happiness & prosperity for life I should be opposed to annexation myself and were it [not] coupled with the paramount security of Republican institutions in the U.S. and the prosperity and happiness of so many millions of the human family I should now oppose it.

If you think I am wrong in my views as regards the best policy to be adopted by Texas to procure speedy annexation be pleased to communicate to me any other policy you may think is better. There is no public measure, whatever, the result of which causes me half the solicitude. I believe that the success of mankinkind [*sic*] in sustaining republican institutions depend upon it.

I have the pleasure to forward a slip from a news paper along with this announcing the arrival of Gen[era]l Duff Green as U.S. Consul at this place. No officer of any Government, or of any grade has ever been welcomed among us with as much cordiality & respect as the Gen[era]l was on his arrival. It is a matter of surprise here to every person, with whom I have conversed upon the subject that Gen[era]l Green had not been appointed minister to Texas. I assure you the appointment could not be confer[r]ed on a gentleman who would be more welcome to the Texian nation in that capacity.

I have written in great haste—The Steam packet that bears this has wrang its last bell—I have not time to read over what I have written and make the necessary corrections. You will be pleased therefore to excuse errors & omissions. I have the honor to be with great regard your friend & s[er]v[an]t, Memucan Hunt.

ALS in ScCleA; PC in Jameson, ed., *Correspondence*, pp. 973–975.

From J[oseph] C. Luther, U.S. Commercial Agent, Port-au-Prince, 10/2. "I have the honor to inform the Department that, by a decree of the President and Counsel of this Republic, under date of the 30th of September, ultimo; the duty, on all foreign refined sugar imported into any of the Haytien ports, shall be four cents per pound, instead of ten cents as formerly charged." ALS (No. 10) in DNA, RG 59 (State Department), Consular Despatches, Port-au-Prince, vol. 2 (T-346:2), received 11/5.

From FRANKLIN DEXTER

District Attorney's Office
Boston, Oct. 3d 1844

Sir, In further answer to your letter of the 25 ult[im]o I have now the honor to report the following facts.

The House of Greely & Guild of this City were applied to by Ramon de Zaldo a naturalized Spanish merchant living in New York to procure for him 1000 tents to be shipped in his Brig Ramon de Zaldo from Boston to such port as he should afterwards direct. Mess[rs]. Greely & Guild employed Prince & Baker Sailmakers to make the tents and they were shipped by Greely & Guild the Consignees of the Ramon de Zaldo for Havana in that Vessel without waiting the further order of de Zaldo—to which course I presume they were induced by apprehension of detention from the publication of the Statement referred to in your letter. The House of Philo S. Shelton & Co. I cannot learn had any concern in the matter. Nor can I learn that it was done in any manner through British Agency. Mr. Draper from whom, (as it will appear from Mr. [George] Roberts letter herewith enclosed) the information was given to the Editor of the Times newspaper, stated to me that he had no information to that effect it being only his own conjecture.

Since the sailing of the Vessel I have had an interview with Mess[rs]. Greely & Guild (to whom I was satisfied it would be in vain to apply before) and they have stated to me all the facts, frankly, as

I believe. They deny all participation of any other agency in the business except that of Don Ramon de Zaldo, and any knowledge or intimation that the Government of Mexico had any concern in the contract, although they suppose the fact to be that the tents are finally intended for the Mexican Government. It is notorious here that very large shipments of shells and other munitions of war are made directly to Vera Cruz for the use of the Mexican Government.

I was informed on the day that the Ramon de Zaldo sailed that these tents were on board under the denomination of "100 bales of manufactured Sail Cloth" and I should have caused her to be detained, if it had appeared to me that in any aspect of the transaction the case could come within the provisions of the Neutrality Act of 1818 or of any other law of Congress; but I do not perceive that even if the contract had been made directly with the Mexican Government, & the Vessel had sailed directly for a Mexican port with these munitions of war, either the tents, or the parties, could be held responsible here for it; the Ramon de Zaldo being an American Merchant Vessel.

It has not been as easy to ascertain the facts in this case as it appeared at first, which must be my apology for delay. The sailmakers declined stating for whom they had made the tents, saying only that the person was unknown to them; and it is only since the Vessel sailed & all apprehension of detention was over, that I could learn with certainty the true character of the transaction. I am very Respectfully Your Ob[edien]t Ser[van]t, Franklin Dexter, U.S. District Attorney.

ALS with En in DNA, RG 59 (State Department), Miscellaneous Letters (M-179:105, frames 466–469). NOTE: Dexter enclosed a letter of 10/2 from George Roberts to himself. Roberts was editor of the Boston, Mass., *Times*.

From EDWARD EVERETT

London, 3 October 1844
Dear Sir, I returned to town on the morning of the 1st from my little excursion to the North. My despatches by this steamer will acquaint you with those matters of public business to which I have already been able to give my attention. I hope to have it in my power before long, to address you officially on various questions of public moment, which have formed the subject of some of your recent communications.

I notice in the late papers that formal possession has been taken by this Government, of the very extensive territory usually known as the "Mosquito shore," between Central America and New Granada.

This appears to have been done in virtue of a nominal act of cession on the part of the native King. This personage, as I have understood from the New Granada Chargé d'Affaires, has for some time been employed by the Agents of the British Government as an instrument for extending its influence in that region.

You will find some allusion to this subject in my despatch No. 90 of the 27th of February. I have never received the communication from Mr. [M.M.] Mosquera, to which reference is there made, but I dare say the representative of New Granada at Washington would be able to give you, if indeed he has not already done so, full information on the subject, which I am inclined to think is one of equal delicacy and importance.

I forward by this steamer for the department a copy of a work just published by Mr. [Cayetano] Moro on the long agitated subject of a Canal to connect the isthmus between the two oceans; in reference to which, as you perceive from my despatch just referred to, the Government of New Granada is very anxious to engage the co-operation of the United States. I am inclined to think that this anxiety springs not more from a view to the Commercial importance of the object itself, than from a desire to create barriers to what it regards as the encroachments of Great Britain, in that direction. I am, dear Sir, with great respect, faithfully Yours, Edward Everett.

LS (Private) in DNA, RG 59 (State Department), Diplomatic Despatches, Great Britain, vol. 53 (M-30:49), received 10/22; FC in MHi, Edward Everett Papers, 50:96–99 (published microfilm, reel 23, frames 317–318). NOTE: Moro's work on the canal was *Survey of the Isthmus of Tehuantepec, Executed in 1842 and 1843* (London: 1844).

From THEO[DORE] S. FAY

Berlin, 3 Oct., 1844

Dear Sir, In my Despatch, No. 21, under date of the 18 September, I had the honor to communicate the intention of the Prussian Government, acting on behalf of the other States of the Zollverein, to refuse to prolong the time for the exchange of the Ratifications of the Convention of the 25 March. It subsequently struck me that, if the convention were ratified by us, the mere fact of the expiration of the very short period named for that purpose, need not in reality operate against the conclusion of a mutually advantageous arrangement equally desired by both parties.

After several attempts to see Baron [Heinrich von] Bülow, frustrated by his engagements with the King or at conferences, I this morning, in order to save the next steamer, drove to his chateau at Tegel, about two hours from the city, where he resides during the summer. After some preliminary conversation, I asked him whether, if a messenger had arrived to day with the ratification of our Convention, the expiration of the time *appointed* for the exchange, would operate as an obstacle. Upon a moment's reflection he answered "no." I then asked whether the obstacle would be insurmountable, if the ratification were to Come at a later period during the winter. He replied that he had just, the day before, taken the resolution to address a communication, either to me or to the Prussian Minister at Washington, declaring that all the States of the Association of Customs & Commerce felt themselves slighted & that they would not prolong the time. I then represented to him my views, prefacing them with the observation that I was not authorized to promise any certainty as to the future action of the Senate & wished the conversation to be more frank than would be perhaps consistent with strict official responsibility. He asked me many questions & did me the honor to say I presented the subject to him in a new light. I proposed to write you what passed between us & asked his advice whether it should be in the form of a Despatch or of a private letter. He said he would not authorize me to communicate officially the results of our interview, but I might address to you a private Letter & advise you according to my own judgment as to your future course. I stated that, if he did not forbid it, I should advise the ratification of the Convention by our Government, in the hope that an arrangement of such importance would not be laid aside from a consideration of mere form. He acquiesced fully, & altho, without a further consultation with Mr. Eichmann & Mr. [Otto] Michaelis, he was not in a position to say that the negative answer of the States of the Customs' Association should be withheld or delayed, yet he would consult with them, & did not doubt the ratification would be accepted if it arrived during the winter. He pointed out to me that he also was not acting alone for Prussia, but that Saxony, Bavaria, &c., if he delayed communicating their negative to our application for longer time, might say to him, "You are deciding, yourself, a question which you profess to have left to us." & that there was even a great deal of embarrassment in the least delay on his part to make such a communication; but nevertheless he knew there were ninety nine chances out of the hundred of his being able to carry it through were the ratification really here—& that in case of its subsequent arrival, although he could not decide without his colleagues, yet he could explain to, & reason with them.

You may judge how far he was serious by his begging me to call your attention to the fact that he had signed the Convention without being aware that any other nation was entitled, by existing Treaties, to the *gratuitous* enjoyment of the Equivalents granted in it to the States of the Zollverein.

Whether or not an official reply will now be returned to Mr. [Henry] Wheaton's late application for time, I have no authority to say, but Baron Bülow went so far as to state ["that" *interlined*] a long delay was to him a delicate matter, & to intimate that a speedy action on the part of our Government would relieve him from a certain perplexity.

In all I stated I scrupulously avoided committing either the President or yourself, more than you were already committed by the mere application for ["a" *interlined*] longer time, & I wish, on the other hand, with equal care, to keep before you the unofficial character of my Conversation with Baron Bülow, although it has convinced me that no real obstacle exists, here, to the successful termination of the negotiation. The suggestion that I should advise you according to my own judgment I follow with diffidence, but without doubt.

I need scarcely add, what is already so well known to you, that Baron Bülow is distinguished, not more for his profound knowledge & great talents as a statesman, than for his sterling integrity as a man.

I have just seen the Ratifications of a Treaty quietly Exchanged sometime after the date appointed for the exchange.

There is a report that our consul at Hamburg, Mr. [John] Cuthbert, is dead.

I have thrown together these lines in the greatest haste with scarcely time for the English Courier. I have the honor to be, Dear Sir, with the greatest consideration, Y[ou]r Ob[e]d[ien]t Serv[an]t, Theo. S. Fay [Secretary of Legation].

ALS (Private & confidential) in DNA, RG 59 (State Department), Diplomatic Despatches, Germany, vol. 3 (M-44:4), received 11/14; variant FC in DNA, RG 84 (Foreign Posts), Germany, Despatches, 4:154–157; CC in DNA, RG 46 (U.S. Senate), 28B-B11; two CC's in ScCleA.

From THEO[DORE] S. FAY

Legation U. States
Berlin, Oct. 3, 1844

Dear Sir, In my Letter, by the courier of the English Legation of to day, I find I have left unintelligible the paragraph commencing: "You may judge how serious he was," &c. To its close should be added the words: "and he several times repeated the wish that this point, which had been already too much discussed in the newspapers, might be urged upon your particular consideration."

I understood this to mean that, if possible, in the event of your sending the ratification of the Convention, some guarantee might be given as to the extent to which this liberty would be permitted to other nations by our present Treaties. With great Consideration, I have the honor to be Dear Sir, Y[ou]r Ob[e]d[ien]t Serv[an]t, Theo. S. Fay.

ALS (Private & confidential) in DNA, RG 59 (State Department), Diplomatic Despatches, Germany, vol. 3 (M-44:4), received 11/14.

R[ichard] K. Crallé to OGDEN HOFFMAN and R[ICHARD] S. COXE, New York [City]

Department of State
Washington, 3d Oct. 1844

Gentlemen, The President [John Tyler] awaits with anxiety any further information which it may have been in your power to obtain in regard to the increase of the ["amount"(?) *altered to* "armament"] or the enlistment of the Crews of the Mexican War Steamers at N. York in violation of the laws of the United States. He trusts that you will continue to pursue your inquiries with diligence and discretion and will not delay a communication of their results to this Department, in order that such ulterior proceedings may be adopted as may be called for. I am Gentlemen Your Ob[edien]t Serv[an]t, R.K. Crallé, Act[in]g Secretary of State.

FC in DNA, RG 59 (State Department), Domestic Letters, 34:398 (M-40:32).

O [GDEN] HOFFMAN to "J. K." [*sic*; Richard K.] Crallé, Sec[retar]y of State Ad interim

U.S. Attorney[']s Office

New York [City], 3rd Oct[obe]r 1844

Sir, I have the honor to inclose four additional copies of Affidavits, in relation to the Mexican Steamers "Montezuma" and "Guadeloupe." In the present state of the nogotiation [*sic*] in relation to these vessels, the facts stated in the affidavits, may be useful and necessary for the further action of the Department.

Mr. [Richard S.] Coxe will hand you these papers, and as he will be able, personally to communicate to you, the present position of affairs, a formal communication from me, in relation to them, is deemed unnecessary. I have the honor to be Very Respectfully Your Obed[ien]t Serv[an]t, O. Hoffman, U.S. Attorney.

LS with Ens in DNA, RG 59 (State Department), Miscellaneous Letters (M-179: 105, frames 469–473). NOTE: Among the enclosed affidavits, those of Frederick Booth and Benjamin Miller, dated 9/27, reported the shipping aboard the Mexican vessels of American citizens as seamen. The affidavit of Solomon Morling, of 9/28, stated that nine men, "not being subjects of Mexico," had joined the crew of the *Montezuma*. The final, undated, deposition of Peter V. Garrett, a machinist, described the nature of the repair and refitting of the *Montezuma*.

Tubman Jones, Washington, to R.T. Queen, "2nd Auditor's Office, War Department," 10/3. Jones encloses his account "against the Dept., which I would ask the favor of you to lay before Mr. Cralley" [*sic*; Richard K. Crallé]. He wishes to be advanced some of the money due him "until the Secretary returns" because he is without the means of paying his board or getting away. ALS in ScCleA.

J [UAN] N. ALMONTE to "R. R." [*sic*; Richard K.] Crallé

Mexican Legation

New York [City], October 4, 1844

The Undersigned, Envoy Extraordinary and Minister Plenipotentiary of the Mexican Republic, had the honour to receive the note, which Mr. R.R. Crallé Acting Secretary of State of the United States, addressed to him under date of the 1st instant; stating that his Government, had received information, that the Commanders of the

Mexican Steamers of war, lying in this port, were recruiting seamen, increasing the number of their guns &c.

The Undersigned believes that an attempt has been made by ["giving" *interlined*] such information, to take ["improper" *interlined*] advantage of the good faith of the ["American" *canceled*] Government of the United States; and he does not hesitate now to assure, the Acting Secretary of State, that it is entirely false, that the Mexican ships in question, have ["neither" *changed to* "either"; "increased their" *canceled*] taken on board any artillery in this port, ["nor" *changed to* "or"] increased their marine force, ["nor" *changed to* "or"] much less, have they made any provision of munitions of war. Nevertheless, in order to proceed with more accuracy, the Undersigned will make an investigation into the matter, and will in due time, have the honour to communicate ["the result" *interlined*] to the Acting Secretary of State ["the result" *canceled*].

The Undersigned avails himself of this occasion to offer to the Acting Secretary of State the assurances of his distinguished consideration. J.N. Almonte.

State Department translation of LS (in Spanish) in DNA, RG 59 (State Department), Notes from Foreign Legations, Mexico, vol. 4 (M-54:2).

From J[AMES] HAMILTON, [JR.]

Oswichee Bend [Ala.,] Oct. 4[t]h 1844
My Dear Sir, Your most kind & friendly favor of the 20[t]h Sept. was forwarded to me at this place where I have been detained by indisposition having taken a severe cold in the late change in the weather.

I need scarcely reiterate my sincere satisfaction at the appointment of Major Doneldson [*sic*; Andrew J. Donelson]. Nothing could have been more judicious. It is possible that some domestic circumstance may make it inconvenient for Major Doneldson to accept the mission. As I know no man except Gen[era]l [Andrew] Jackson ["who" *interlined*] can exercise more influence on the Question of Annexation than myself—in that Country, if backed by that official authority which a U.S. appointment would give me, ["I say without mock modesty" *interlined*]—If therefore Doneldson ["resigns" *canceled and* "declines" *interlined*] & you want me, I will guarantee that I ["will" *interlined*] go down to Texas & by the first of January next bring to Washington with me a better Treaty than your last—one more likely to pass the Senate.

In reference to the Mission to St. James allow me to remark, that with all Everitt[']s [*sic*; Edward Everett's; *one or two words canceled and* "learning & accomplishments" *interlined*] for he undoubtedly is one of the most highly educated men in our Country, he is as you say "an unfit representative of this Country to Great Britain." I am satisfied that his tone is at best nothing more than apologetic on the Slave Question whilst all his secret *sympathies* are against us.

If you were President it would indeed be the height of my ambition to represent the ["Court" *canceled and* "Country" *interlined*] at St. James—and to endeavour by a Treaty of Reciprocity to modify ["a Compact" *canceled*] the tariff by a compact which would carry the whole West & So. West, with the South, in the overthrow of that base system of plunder. I should glory in doing something so catholic in behalf of our principles. Whilst I feel prouud [*sic*] that you should deem me fit for such a *post*, I hope that in your esteem I shall not be regarded as indulging in an inordinate self [love] when I say that for ["such a" *canceled and* "the" *interlined*] Mission, I should not not [*sic*] consider that I brought small advantages from the ["past" *interlined*] intimate associations which I formed with the public men of England during ["my" *canceled and* "a" *interlined*] residence off & on of nearly four years in that Country. For my associations with the Ministry of Sir Rob[ert] Peel were quite as ["when(?)" *canceled*] as [*sic*] close as with that of Lord Melb[o]urne. Should [James K.] Polk be elected and you remain Sec[retar]y of State, I will go out to England if he thinks proper to appoint me Minister on the 1st of April—and conclude, under your instructions & directions a ["new" *interlined*] Commercial Treaty. As [*sic*] the moment I have effected such a Treaty[,] which I believe I can do before the meeting of Congress, I will return, as it would not suit me to be a *resident Minister*. Of course I would decline receiving the outfit ["sh" *canceled*] and only take the salary for the time in which I might be actually employed in the public service. From my intimacy with Lord Aberdeen, with whom I have corresponded privately since my Texian Mission & who is a *strenuously hard working man*, I think in six months I could conclude a treaty which would do something for us both. If in accordance with ["your" *canceled and* "the" *interlined*] voluntary expression of your opinion of my fitness & your strong wish to see me ["in the Mission" *interlined*] the time should arrive when you would as Sec[retar]y of State or Pres[i]d[en]t have an influential voice in this matter, I will be prepared ["t" *canceled*] to give my whole soul to the objects of such an ["Mission" *canceled and* "Embassy" *interlined*].

Now, a word on the position you ought to take in Polk[']s administration if he is elected. My opinion is that you ought to remain *where you are*. You can be eminently serviceable to the South, & indeed to the whole Union. [*Marginal interpolation*: "Would we have had the reply to Packenhams (*sic*; Richard Pakenham's) Slave Letter, if you had not been in the Department? which silenced the British Battery on this subject. No[,] from some sleek headed Temporiser like Everitt we should have had a canting apology for Slavery."]

I shall write to Alfred Huger to induce Judge [Daniel E.] Huger to hold over until after the 4[t]h of March. If [Henry] Clay is elected your position will be in the Senate from So. Carolina leading the opposition to what I fear will be the pernicious measures of his administration. In the mean time *So. C. ought* to adopt no course calculated to alienate from her the sympathies of the other Southern States. And only in the last alternative resort to separate action. I believe with a little patience & better temper this resort will be altogether unnecessary altho I am prepared for it if it comes. I shall write ["Gov." *interlined*; James H.] Hammond today enforcing[?] these views & confer freely with our friends in Charleston. There is as much wisdom in doing a *right* thing in the *right* time as in the *thing itself*.

I leave for Charleston on Monday the 7[t]h & will remain there until the 23d *inst*. and deeply regret that I shall not have the gratification of seeing you before your return to Washington. Let me know when that will be & if possible I will at an *appointed day* go on in the night Steamer from Savannah to meet you. Have you read [Daniel] Webster[']s speech on the 19[t]h Sept. on Boston Common? It combines with an outpouring & spouting malice to the South ["& p" *canceled and "a" interlined*] remarkable & hollow perfidy to Clay Occult & insidious but still the Treachery is *there*. What a Swiss—God has made him all head but no principle. Ever My Dear Sir with sincere esteem faithfully yours, J. Hamilton.

P.S. I have written most urgently to Alfred Huger to induce his cousin to hold on during the next Session. If Clay is elected you must return & lead in the Senate the opposition & we must from all the Southern States fortify you with the strongest friends & most able men as your allies. If Polk [is elected] then you must retain your present post & of course give the impulse to his Cabinet.

[P.P.S.] In reference to the Texian Mission if Doneldson does not accept & I were appointed—I could not reach there before [Samuel] Houston was out of office. But if he had been in with six months to run he would ["have" *canceled and "given" changed to "give"*] me no trouble. I would have ["had" *canceled*] him in my interest in a week.

ALS in ScCleA; PEx in Boucher and Brooks, eds., *Correspondence*, pp. 252–253.

From Thomas Jefferson Sutherland, New York [City], 10/4. He asks that Calhoun transmit to him a list of the U.S. citizens imprisoned at Van Diemen's Land [from the Canadian rebellion] and who have been pardoned by the British government. Having learned that about 40 prisoners are still confined, Sutherland wishes to write to the British government requesting that these men be released. He encloses a copy of resolutions adopted at a public meeting in Rensselaer County, N.Y. ALS with Ens in DNA, RG 59 (State Department), Miscellaneous Letters (M-179:105, frames 474–479).

From B[ENJAMIN] G. WRIGHT

Belmont [Ohio] Oct[obe]r 4th 1844

My Dear Sir, After my respects let me say to you that, in the event of Col. [James K.] Polk[']s election & his wish to retain your services as Secratary of State, it is the anxious desire of your friends here, (as we believe it will be of those every where,) that you should continue in the department of State, at least till the Texas question is satisfactorily adjusted.

The success of Col. Polk, I grant, is somewhat problamatical but we feel assured here that, if the South is true to the best interests of the whole Union, & especially to herself, he cannot be defeated should Mr. [Henry] Clay carry Ohio, New York, & even Indiana. But the question, here suggests itself, will Col. Polk if elected tender to you a continuance in the Cabinet?

If Col. Polk tenders you a continuance in the Cabinet you know our views, & I assure you that we have full confidince [*sic*] that your decission will be made with an eye single to the best interests of the Confederacy. But if Col. Polk should not tender you a continuance in the Cabinet it will be conclusive evidence to your friends, & those of the President, every where, that the coming Dynasty will be only a new edition of *"Hunkerism"*—that the old corrupt party organization will be re-established—that every State Rights Democrat will be ostracised, & the country be again cursed by a party whose only principles of cohesion are the *"Spoils of Victory."*

Should this state of things take place you will agree with your friends here that the election of Mr. Clay would be less injurious to the best interests of the country than the election of Col. Polk. 1st. Because, even, on the question of annexation there could be no confidence in an Administration that would promote such reckless politicians as [Thomas H.] Benton[,] [William] Allen[,] [Benjamin] Tappan &c. &c.

2nd. Because a second defeat of the Democratic party would ["rid" *interlined*] it of false friends & prove unequivocally that to regain power the party must retrace its wayward course, return to its "*first love*", & plant itself immovably on the old Republican State Rights platform of '98 & rally under the ample folds of the good "Old Republican Flag" on which is inscribed, in the words of [Thomas] Jefferson, "*Nullification is the rightful remedy*." This re-organization of the party under its Old Flag would necessarily plant the Republican States on their reserved rights of sovereignty, &, aided by the powerful minorities in the Federal[ist] States, they would check the reckless course of the administration, or if failing in this, they would compell the F[ederal] Government (as S.C. did in 1833) to back out from its unconstitution[al] & oppressive measures. Thus re-organised the party would rally on its old & time honored principles under the lead of [a] firm, fearless & intellectual Standard Bearer, who would conduct it to victory in '48—to a vic[t]ory worth acheiving [*sic*]—a victory which ["could" *altered to* "would"] secure peace, happiness & prosperity to the people, & stability to our complex yet admirable system of government for the next fifty years.

This much on politics. A word now on business of interest to me because of deep interest to a worthy & much esteemed brother, whom I introduce to your kind attention as James J. Wright, Esq. ["late" *canceled*] of St. Jago de Cuba, & formerly, for some years, American ["Consulate" *altered to* "Consul"] at that city. Mr. Wright is a partner in the extensive & well known mercantile firm of "Wright[,] Brooks & Co." in St. Jago de Cuba. He was formerly a citizen of the [United] States, but by a residence of near 30 years in Cuba he has consequently forfeited his right of citizenship here. Mr. Wright is now on a visit to his friends in Ohio ["& though he" *interlined*] will return to Cuba ["though" *canceled*] he intends ["to" *interlined*] make the States his permanent place ["of residence" *interlined*] at some future time. The South from his habits, (having been an extensive slave holder,) will most likely be the place ["in" *interlined*] which ["he" *interlined*] may ["determine" *interlined*] to settle.

A vacancy being likely to occur in the American Consulate at

St. Jago de Cuba, my object in addressing you is to learn (should that vacancy occur) whether Mr. Wright would, under all the circumstances of the case, have say 3 or 4 chances in 5 of procuring the appointment from the President should he make ["the" *canceled*] application backed by the recommendation of the principle [*sic*] merchants of Boston, N[ew] York, Philadelphia & Baltimore.

The facts which would recommend Mr. Wright to favourable consideration of President Tyler would be these:

1st. He stands at the head of the anti-British & anti-abolition party in St. Jago de Cuba.

2nd. He is a Texas annexationist in interest, in feeling, & in every thing else.

3rd. In any attempt of the Brittish Government to acquire a footing in Cuba, or to interfere with the institutions of that island, or with those of the southern States he would be its firm[,] fearless & uncompromising enemy. In fact the South could not select from [its] own *true* sons a truer[,] firmer & more energetic representative of her rights.

4th. His recommendations, should he make application will be from the most influential merchants of the above named cities.

5th. He is, from his long business habits both as a merchant & as an extensive coffee Planter, as well as from his former experience fully competent to ["the duties" *canceled*] perform the duties of Consul with credit to himself & advantage to the interests of ["the" *interlined*] country whose representative he would be.

In conclusion I ask of you the favour to lay the subject before the President as soon as convenient & inform me by letter of the prospect of success should the application be made.

Since writing the above Mr. Wright has advice from his partner Mr. Brooks of the death of the late Consul, & also intelligence that the official despatch for this governme[n]t ["is now in" *canceled and* "has been forwarded to" *interlined*] the States—It, most likely, will reach the President ere this reaches you.

With the best wishes for your personal & political prosperity I subscribe myself Your obedient servant, B.G. Wright.

ALS in ScCleA.

R[ichard] K. Crallé to Thomas Davis, Minerva, Mason County, Ky., 10/5. "I have received the letter [*not found*] which you addressed to this Department on the 30th Ult[im]o relative to a female slave, belonging to you, who recently committed a robbery in Kentucky and afterwards fled to Canada. I have to state in reply that if the charge can be properly substantiated, the case would appear to be one coming within the terms of the 10th Article of our recent treaty with Great Britain. I therefore transmit to you for your information two printed papers, which may prove useful to you in pursuing this matter." FC in DNA, RG 59 (State Department), Domestic Letters, 34:406 (M-40:32).

O [GDEN] HOFFMAN to R[ichard] K. Crallé

U.S. Attorney's Office
New York [City,] Oct. 5, 1844
Sir, I have the honor to acknowledge the receipt of your letter of the 3d inst. in relation to the Mexican war-steamers now lying in this port.

The President [John Tyler] may be assured that I shall continue to pursue my enquiries with diligence, and that their results shall be immediately communicated to your Department. I am Sir With great respect Your ob[edien]t Serv[an]t, O. Hoffman, U.S. Att[orne]y.

LS in DNA, RG 59 (State Department), Miscellaneous Letters (M-179:105, frame 484).

R[ichard] K. Crallé to A[lbert] Schumacher, Consul General of Hamburg for the U[nited] States, Baltimore, 10/5. Crallé acknowledges Schumacher's letter of 9/21. In compliance he sends Schumacher an exequatur and returns his consular commission. FC in DNA, RG 59 (State Department), Notes to Foreign Legations, German States, 6:99 (M-99:27).

From ALBERT SMITH

Boundary Line [Maine,] Oct. 5th 1844
Sir—I am informed by Lt. W[illiam] H. Emory, U.S. Top[ographical] Eng[inee]r now engaged upon the survey of the N[orth] E[ast] boundary line, that no provision has been made by the War Department for the return transportation of the military detachment under his immediate command.

Without any request from, or consultation with me, a detachment from the U.S. Artillery was detailed for this service in 1843. I had nothing to do with the transportation of that detachment, & I had good reason to suppose that, if any aid from the Army were to be rendered to this service the present season, a similar course would be pursued.

Having preferred no request for any military force the present season—& having received no notice or information that there would be a detail for this service—I made no estimate for their expenses, & *have no funds for their transportation.*

I am at a loss to understand why the Department of War, has adopted a different rule in regard to the expenses of this detachment, from that of the last year.

It certainly was important, that I should have been apprized of the fact.

As the duties of these men upon this line will expire in two or three weeks, it is necessary, to prevent their being discharged here, without money or even clothing, that some measures should be *immediately* adopted for their relief. I have the honor to be With great regard and high Consideration Your ob[edien]t Serv[an]t, Albert Smith, U.S. Com[missione]r N[orth] E[astern] B[oundary] Survey.

ALS in DNA, RG 76 (Records of Boundary and Claims Commissions and Arbitrations), Letters Received by the Department of State Concerning the Northeast Boundary Line.

From STEPHEN SMITH

Baltimore, October 5th 1844

Sir, For many years I have been engaged in the South American trade. I have frequently visited Ecuador, and the other Republics in the Pacific. The object of the present is to call your attention to the propriety of having our Government represented at Quito. Our trade with Ecuador is considerable and in my opinion the appointment of a Representative of the United States to Quito would not only promote the interests of our commerce but that of many American Citizens having claims and interests with that Republic. Hoping that you may find it for the interest of the United States to send a Representative to Ecuador for the purpose of protecting the American Citizens I have the honor to be Sir Very Respectfully Your Ob[edien]t S[er]v[an]t, Stephen Smith.

ALS in DNA, RG 59 (State Department), Miscellaneous Letters (M-179:105, frames 485–486).

From WILLIAM R. KING

Legation of the United States
Paris, 6 October 1844

Sir, I have the honor to acknowledge the receipt of your despatches No. 4, 5 and 6. It affords me great satisfaction to learn that the President approves of my course in the interviews which I had with the King [Louis Philippe] and Mr. [François P.G.] Guizot; and that the assurances which I received upon those occasions are deemed acceptable. I am also happy to find the opinions which I expressed, corroborated by the views so amply and ably developed in your despatch of the 12th August, which I shall not fail to present and enforce upon all suitable occasions.

Since I last wrote I have nothing of particular interest to communicate. The Texas question has ceased to be a topic of interest or even of allusion here, though it is not improbable, now that the harmonious relations of France and England have been at least temporarily restored, the designs of Mexico against the young Republic may once more direct the attention of the French cabinet to that remote quarter. Prudent, however, as is the King of the French, and ever solicitous to maintain peace and good will, both for his own sake and that of France whose strength and resources are rapidly developing with this temperate policy, I entertain very little apprehension that he will connect himself actively, if at all, with the hostile manoeuvres of England in relation to the annexation of Texas to the United States, from a mistaken view of the true interests of this country in the question, and at the hazard of forfeiting the friendship and regard of the American government and people. I delayed writing with the hope that the steamers from New York and Boston would bring me something from Washington, but I was disappointed although despatches were received by Messrs. [Henry] Wheaton and [Washington] Irving, who are in Paris, at this time. The former gentleman was kind enough to show me the copy of your despatch of the 10th September to Mr. [Wilson] Shannon, on the subject of the threatened invasion of Texas by Mexico, a transcript of which, I make no doubt was also directed to me, as its early receipt at this legation, was of no slight urgency and importance. The failure or delay of this important communication

37

makes a word opportune with regard to the transmission of my correspondence from the Department of State. It happens, strangely enough, that nearly all the communications which I receive are forwarded, or rather delayed, by the ordinary packets, instead of being transmitted by the more prompt conveyance of the steamers. A few days ago, for example, when others had intelligence from America up to the 16th September, the legation received letters and papers by a Havre packet, which were not later than the 27th August. Thus my intelligence, official and private is always of an old date, and the legation is the last informed of what it should be the first to know. I need not dwell upon the public injury and private inconvenience produced by this delay. I would, therefore, request that instructions be given to the Despatch agents, to transmit ["m" *canceled*] communications for this legation, when not too bulky, by the steamers which will convey them with more promptitude and regularity.

I have delivered to Mr. [Robert] Walsh his Commission [as U.S. Consul at Paris] together with his exequatur. I am Sir very respectfully your obedient servant, William R. King.

LS (No. 4) in DNA, RG 59 (State Department), Diplomatic Despatches, France, vol. 30 (M-34:33), received 10/29.

From R[OBERT] WICKLIFFE, JR.

Legation of The United States
Turin, Oct. 6, 1844

Sir, By the same steamer with this you will receive my quarterly account. You will observe that the Contingent expenses are much less than the sum allowed for this Legation. If you have the power to dispose of the residue, I would suggest that the best application of it, would be to the purchase of the Reports of the Supreme Court of the United States. Not having brought my own copy of [*one word altered to* "those"] reports with me and not of course being able to procure one in Europe, I feel the want of it nearly every day. If I had been aware that this Legation was destitute of those indispensable books, I should certainly have brought them with me. You are aware that often on knotty questions of International law, the Text Books are unsatisfactory, and that it is in the Reports alone that their solution can be found. The English Admiralty Decisions, I have procured on my own account, but many points have been adjudicated differently in America and England. I think the Library quite bare, and that a copy of the American Reports would be infinitely more valuable than all the Congressional Documents sent out by the Department.

In November & December of each year the Court goes to Genoa and the Diplomatic Corps is expected to attend. This arrangement nearly or quite doubles my personal expenses during those months, and in addition I have to employ a Secretary to sign passports and attend to the ordinary routine of my office. It occurs to me that an additional Contingency ought to be allowed for that purpose.

You have doubtless observed that [Ferdinand] the Emperor of Austria and Prince Metternich ["having" *altered to* "have"] during the last month visited Trieste and that several Princes and Ministers of Italy, repaired to that City for the purpose of consulting upon the affairs of this country. With their political arrangements we of course have no concern. But it is said by well-informed persons, that Prince Metternich desires to establish among the Italian States a Zollverein or Customs Union. It is also credibly stated that [Leopold II] the Grand Duke of Tuscany, who is connected with the House of Austria has acceded to the idea. The Lombardo-Venetian Kingdom, you know is governed by a Vice-Roy of Austria. Some of the smaller states, such as Parma, Modena & Lucca are also more or less related to and under the influence of the Court of Vienna. The difficulty, I presume, lies with Naples and Sardinia. I have taken great pains to inform myself as far as possible of the views of the ministry and [Charles Albert,] sovereign of this Kingdom. Government and all its affairs are studiously wrapped in the profoundest mystery and secrecy at Turin and nothing is ever published on the subject. Those, who I think are the best informed assure me that the Government of Sardinia will not listen to the proposition of a Zollverein. They are very jealous of their independence, and although they could not perhaps uphold their government long, without the friendship of Austria and the *prestige* of her power, yet they fear very much the impairment of their sovereignty and the *direct* subjection to Austrian influence, which they fancy an Italian Customs Union would produce. I am inclined to think that a Zollverein would operate favorably to our Commerce. The Tobacco monopoly certainly restricts the extension of the sale of that article but its oppression falls upon the people here and not upon us. Indeed their manufactures of Silk, which would be the greatest source of wealth, if free trade existed with the United States, daily decay. The monopoly however secures us one advantage, which I believe is not generally known in the United States. There are many parts of Italy well suited to the cultivation of Tobacco, but the proprietors are prohibited the culture, because it would diminish the value of this monopoly. If the monopoly were destroyed, the motive for this prohibition would cease and we should have a Competitor. I am not able to make a accurate calculation, but I believe that this Monopoly in *Italy* is not so *wholly* injurious to our interests as is generally thought. It falls however with deadly weight upon the poor subjects of the Country, who already so impoverished by absolutism and restrictions, appear to be getting poorer & poorer every day. I can do nothing now nor do I see any prospect of doing anything that would lead to the destruction of this monopoly. Together with that of salt it forms a main branch of their Revenue and the remotest hint at the subject, still a [*sic*] less a formal discussion of the question is in the highest degree offensive to this Government. I avail myself of this occasion to renew to you the assurances of my most distinguished Consideration, R. Wickliffe, Jr.

LS (No. 14) in DNA, RG 59 (State Department), Diplomatic Despatches, Sardinia, vol. 4 (M-90:5), received 11/6; FC in DNA, RG 84 (Foreign Posts), Italy, Diplomatic and Other Correspondence of the U.S. Legation to Sardinia, 2: [253–255].

From ROBERT B. CAMPBELL

Consulate of the United States of America
Havana, Oct. 7th 1844

Sir, In my communication of the 1st Oct. asking information of the course to be pursued by American Consuls in behalf of American Citizens, who expect and will endeavour to obtain remuneration from this Government for their arrests, ill usage and long incarceration I had assumed that the Department knew under what obligations, renunciations and other circumstances, Americans and other foreigners became residents of Cuba. An assumption perhaps not justified. The attention of the Department may not have been drawn to the subject, and Consuls may not have communicated the information. Should neither the one or the other have happened, you cannot correctly judge of the embarrassing situation of your Consuls under the recent occurrences, nor of the extent and justice of demands for compensation. Cuba like other Colonies of Spain was governed under the laws of the Indies. Under these laws this Colony was not open to foreign commerce, and no foreigner could reside in it, for transaction of business. These laws were subsequently modified by Royal edicts opening the Ports to foreign commerce, and permitting foreigners to become matriculated for all the purposes of agricultural, commercial, professional & mechanical pursuits &c. To enable them to embark in any one, or all of these pursuits, or to remain on the Island for more than three consecutive months, it is required by law and usage to take out what are here called letters of domiciliation. To obtain these letters a memorial is addressed to the Capt. General by the individual (or his authorized agent) expressive of his wish. To this memorial is attached a certificate from the Consul of his Country stating the memorialist to be a citizen or subject of the country to which he professes to belong, that he is of good habits and of the Catholic religion. The applicant in person or his agent in his name then appears before a notary of the Government who records him as having sworn fidelity to the Catholic religion, to her Majesty & her laws, as renouncing every privilege, right & protection pertaining to him as a foreigner, all dependence upon, and all civil relation with the Country of his birth, except those of parentage and domestic family relations and economy of interest and property he may have.

The Government of the United States making in numberless instances citizens of the Citizens and subjects of other Powers and upon principles of justice and reciprocity allowing Americans to become citizens or subjects of other Governments. It may be questioned whether an individual prompted by interest or other causes to reside here, who acquires that residence, voluntarily relinquishes the protection of his Government renouncing all rights as a foreigner, and ending all civil relations with the land of his birth or adoption, can with propriety be allowed to claim the protection of the Government renounced, against that of his new allegiance for wrongs sustained under the forms of law.

I said in a previous communication that I beleived them entitled to redress to be obtained through the intervention of our Government. That opinion was rather dictated by sympathies in the behalf of the sufferers, than the deliberate convictions of my judgement, and if the Christian rule of doing to others as we would that others should do unto us, is admitted as a rule of action as binding and obligatory upon Governments as upon individuals the right would at least be doubtful.

For I presume the United States neither could or would permit foreign Governments to interfere in the arrests, mode of trial, punishment or acquittal, or redress for wrongs of naturalized foreigners. Not that I design to be understood that persons taking out letters of domiciliation acquire here all the rights pertaining to naturalized citizens in the United States; for five years residence and the observance of other forms are necessary to entitle them to the privileges of Spanish subjects.

With the English Government whose subjects arrested have been more numerous, and sufferings equal to that of the Americans the case is perhaps different That Government never recognizing the right of the subject to denationalize himself and transfer his ["allegiance &" *interlined*] Altho' policy would prompt them under circumstances similar to those occurring here, to slumber over rights they claim where the offending party was strong enough to be dreaded, they rarely decline to assert them to the utmost extent with powers so weak as Spain.

These suggestions & information are submitted to your consideration to be determined by your better & less fallible judgement. I have the honor to be with great respect & esteem y[ou]r mo[st] ob[edien]t Ser[van]t, Robert B. Campbell.

LS in DNA, RG 59 (State Department), Consular Despatches, Havana, vol. 19 (T-20:19), received 11/15.

To T[HOMAS] G. CLEMSON, [Brussels]

Fort Hill, 7th Oct[obe]r 1844
My dear Sir, After a long delay, I left Washington on the 28th last month, and arrived here on the 4th Inst.; and had the pleasure of finding all well. There had been much sickness, but no deaths on the place. I am forced to conclude, that the place is sickly in the fall, in very dry seasons, attributable, I think, to the low state of the [Seneca] River & the exposure of its bed to the action of the sun. We have never had fevers, but in very dry seasons. This has been the most so of any we have ever had.

My crop is good, considering how severe the drought has been. The corn crop is fully equal to last year. The ears are not so large, but the stand better. The pea crop is almost a failure. The pumpkin entirely so. The cotton is about equal to last year. I have in 65 acres; and have harvested 43,000 pounds & will probably make 10,000 more, making in the whole say 53,000.

I enclose a letter from Col. [Francis W.] Pickens, which will give you the fullest account I have of your place [in Edgefield District] and crop. The result certainly speaks well for the place, as well as the management. On my return to Washington, which, if not called back sooner, will not be untill the 1st week in Nov[embe]r[,] I will take your place in my route and spend a day or two there & give you a full account of every thing.

I had a letter from Andrew [Pickens Calhoun], the day I left Washington. Our crop of corn & cotton [in Ala.] is good. We shall make about 12,000 bushels of corn & 450 or 500 bales of cotton. The place still enjoys perfect health. There was not a case of sickness on the place, & this is the third year without a physician's bill. Our only draw back is the low price of produce.

The friends of [James K.] Polk now regard his election as almost certain. I think the prospect good; but the whigs are making great efforts, which may tell deeper than their opponents calculate. A few weeks, however, will now decide, which side shall prevail.

There has been a good deal of excitement in our State in consequence of the movement of Mr. [Robert Barnwell] Rhett in favour of seperate action of the State. The publick sentiment has settled down ag[ai]nst his course, & all is now quiet; but the feeling of the State is deep both on the subject of the Tariff & Abolition. If [Henry] Clay should be elected or Polk not fulfil ["the" *canceled*] expectation, in the event of his election, the feeling will burst forth into action.

Mrs. [Floride Colhoun] Calhoun will write Anna [Maria Calhoun Clemson] by the conveyance that takes this, & give all the local news. We have not heard from Patrick [Calhoun] & John [C. Calhoun, Jr.] since they left Ioway; now about 2 months, & do not expect to hear from them untill their return to St. Louis.

I am waiting to hear of your arrival by the next steamer with not a little anxiety. I conclude, that you had a long voyage, as the voyages this way have been short; I hope, however, that it was safe & not unpleasant, and that you have been comp[en]sated for its tardiness by the enjoyment & pleas[ure] since your arrival.

All join their love to you & Anna. Kiss the children [John Calhoun Clemson and Floride Elizabeth Clemson] for their Grandfather. Your affectionate father, J.C. Calhoun.

[P.S.] I notice in Mathew[e]s & Bonneau's ac[coun]t a payment to you of $64 on the 27th March last. I forget whether it was on my own individual account, or on the joint transaction of Andrew & myself. I will thank you to state in your next. J.C.C.

ALS in ScCleA; PEx in Jameson, ed., *Correspondence,* p. 624.

W[illia]m S. Derrick, "Acting Ch[ief] Cl[er]k," State Department, to John L. Graham, Postmaster, New York [City], 10/7. "It being desirable that the accompanying package for General [Juan N.] Almonte should reach him with certainty, I will thank you to hand it to him in person and to inform this Department thereof." FC in DNA, RG 59 (State Department), Domestic Letters, 35:8 (M-40:33).

From DUFF GREEN

Vera Cruz, 7th Oc[tobe]r 1844
My dear Sir, I reached here yesterday and leave tonight for Mexico [City]. Santa Anna is at Mango de Clava twelve miles from here, and has just married a young wife *by proxy*, who was to leave the city of Mexico yesterday. He will spend some time on his estate, Gen[era]l [Valentín] Canalizo, being charged, *ad interim* with the Government. The Texan prisoners were liberated on the 16th of June, with the exception of Mr. [José Antonio] Navarro of the Santa Fee [*sic*] Expedition, and most of them are here on their way home. They have been taken by the hand by Mr. [Lewis S.] Hargous, who in the absence of proper government influence is the protection of the citizens of Texas as well as of the oppressed citizens of the United States, and in the absence of Mr. Diamond [*sic*; Francis M. Dimond] is the acting Consul of the United States. He has chartered a Vessel, and [will] send them to New Orleans. I avail myself of this occasion to say that he is a native of Philadelphia, that his house have extensive relations in this country, that every person whom I have heard speak of him, do so in the most favorable terms, and that you who have not been abroad cannot appreciate the service which such a man can render to the citizens of the United States under circumstances constantly occurring. Is it not the duty of the Government to do all they can to sustain the influence and means of such men in such important positions abroad? & should you not instantly [act] to reinstate him in the office of Consul? To him the fees of office are nothing. The confidence of his government and the opportunity of serving his countrymen is his chief inducement to act at all. I write this without his asking it for your consideration.

The Congress have granted the 4 millions to Santa Anna, but it is not yet realised nor is it probable that it soon will be. There is no confidence here that there will be any efficient invasion of Texas. It is supposed that there may be a predatory war intended chiefly to haras[s] the country and prevent the introduction of merchandise from that quarter, but no one supposes that he (Santa Anna) supposes that he can reconquer Texas. I learn from Col. [George] Fisher who has just been released from Perote, that he has heard from a person to be relied on, that [Antonio] Canales is now in the neighbourhood of Zacatecas at the head of 4000 men—that they are sustained by popular opinion & side so far with Texas as to demand free trade, and opposition to forced loans and high duties. I learn that a powerful influence in favor of a free trade is springing up into a perfect organisation against Santa Anna's Govt. throughout the northern provinces and that this alone will be sufficient to prevent a formidable invasion of Texas.

I find that the best informed people of Texas are [of] opinion that there will be no difficulty in achieving annexation. The election of [Anson] Jones [as President of Texas] was a triumph of the peace party over the party for an invasion of Mexico—[*one word or partial word canceled*] & not the triumph of an English party. This whole matter however must be treated with great delicacy. I think I understand it. I will write to you fully from Mexico. Your sincere friend, Duff Green.

P.S. The President [John Tyler] must not send my name before the Senate [as Consul at Galveston].

ALS in DNA, RG 59 (State Department), Diplomatic Despatches, Special Agents, vol. 13 (M-37:13, frames 17–19), received 11/14.

From Lt. M[atthew] F. M[aury], U.S. N[aval] Observatory, [Washington], 10/7. "I enclose for such action as you may think proper . . . a letter this day received by me" from a reliable source. [The En is a letter of 9/17 from R.B. Bate, London, to Maury, warning of the recent discovery of a high-quality counterfeit English gold sovereign which it is believed is to be circulated in America and Europe.] (A Clerk's EU indicates that the information was to be published in the Washington, D.C., *Madisonian*.) ALI with En in DNA, RG 59 (State Department), Miscellaneous Letters (M-179:105, frames 486–489).

From Geo[rge] W. Paschal

Van Buren Ark., 7th October 1844
Sir: I notice with regret the death of the Hon[orab]le Tilghman A. Howard, Minister to Texas from the United States.

Should the vacancy, thus created, not have been already filled, I would most respectfully ask the appointment for myself. I trust that my intimate knowledge of the affairs of Texas; and my earnest desire to aid the views of the administration in regard to that Republic, added to your knowledge of my general deportment and moral character will be a sufficient guaranty to you that I would discharge the duties of the office faithfully.

The State of Arkansas has never had conferred upon any one of her citizens any considerable appointment—and I have no doubt but my appointment would meet the universal approbation of the State which has already honored me beyond my merits.

I may add as personal to myself that an accident on a steam boat, on my homeward trip from Washington caused me an injury, which renders a short residence farther south necessary.

Should you approve my application you will please forward this letter to the President, with such remarks as you may feel authorized to make. Very Respectfully Your ob[edien]t Serv[an]t, Geo. W. Paschal.

ALS in DNA, RG 59 (State Department), Applications and Recommendations, 1837–1845, Ponhal [*sic*] (M-687:26, frames 343–345). Note: Paschal (1812–1878) had been acquainted with Calhoun in Lumpkin County, Ga., where he had taken part in the gold rush. He was married to a daughter of the Cherokee chief John Ridge, and had been a few years previous to this letter a justice of the Ark. Supreme Court.

From JOHN CAMPBELL,
[Representative from S.C.]

Montgomery C[oun]ty, No. Ca., Oct. [*ca.* 8, 18]44
Dear Sir, I have the honor herewith to enclose you a letter from John S. Rich of Williamsburg District So. Ca. who is desirous of obtaining a consulship in Greece or Egypt. My personal acquaintance with Mr. Rich is limited, but I know him to be of respectable family, and suppose him well qualified to discharge the duties of the situation for which he applies. With much respect & Esteem Y[ou]r Ob[edien]t Serv[an]t, John Campbell.

N.B. A letter directed to my usual Post Office in So. Ca. will reach me.

ALS with En in DNA, RG 59 (State Department), Applications and Recommendations, 1837–1845, Rich (M-687:28, frames 2–5). Note: Campbell enclosed a letter to himself from John S. Rich, dated 9/14, from Kingstree, S.C.

From Joseph W. Hale and Ch[arle]s H. Todd, New York [City], 10/8. They state that in 6/1843 they chartered a vessel to carry goods to several ports in Mexico, having first ascertained through Henry W. Holmes, the captain of the vessel, from both the State Department and the Mexican Chargé d'Affaires in the U.S., that the goods shipped were admissible into Mexican ports. Despite assurances that their goods were admissible, certain of them were declared on arrival to be illegal imports by virtue of a newly-passed law . The Mexican government not only refused to let these goods be landed but also dictated terms of sale for the remainder of their cargo. Hale and Todd claim to have lost $2,793.82. They ask that compensation be sought for this loss. LS in DNA, RG 76 (Records of Boundary and Claims Commissions and Arbitrations), Records of United States and Mexican Claims Commissions.

Rich[ar]d K. Crallé to ALPHONSE PAGEOT

Department of State
Washington, 8th Oct. 1844

Sir: I have the honor to acknowledge the receipt of your note of the 1st instant, addressed to the Secretary of State, in which you inform this Department that M. John Baptiste Demerlier, a naturalized citizen of the United States, has applied for letters of naturalization in France; and that the Government of His Majesty the King of the French desires to know what relation this individual bears to the American authority; and whether, should his application be allowed, he would be absolved from all allegiance to the United States.

In reply, I have the honor to inform you that questions growing out of the acts of Congress on the subject of naturalization, are not considered as coming properly under the cognizance of the Executive Department of the Government, and that the President [John Tyler] does not feel himself warranted in venturing any decision of, or expressing any opinion in regard to them. I have the honor to be, with high consideration, Sir, Your obedient servant, Richd. K. Crallé, Acting Secretary of State.

LS in DNA, RG 59 (State Department), Notes from Foreign Legations, France, vol. 12 (M-53:8, frames 720–721). NOTE: A Clerk's EU reads "Returned by Mr. Pageot 2d December, 1844."

From David Levy [Yulee], Washington, 10/8. Levy [Yulee] encloses two letters vindicating the conduct of Charles S. Sibley, U.S. District Attorney for Middle Fla., from charges made against him. [One letter, from George Walker, former U.S. District Attorney, to Sibley, dated 9/14, verified the local practice of assessing court costs in cases resolved by *nolle prosequi* rulings. The other, from E.E. Blackburn to Levy [Yulee], dated 9/21, described the dismissal of criminal charges against Blackburn and Sibley's role in the proceedings.] ALS with Ens in DNA, RG 59 (State Department), Applications and Recommendations, 1837–1845, Sibley (M-687:30, frames 292–298).

From JUNIUS BOYLE

Washington D.C., October 9th 1844

Sir: In case the present incumbent [James Rich] of the Consulate at Port Mahon [Minorca] should resign his commission, I should like to receive the appointment. The fees are of no importance, amounting, during the last year to less than fifty dollars; but I deem it of importance to the public service, that I should ["obtain" *interlined*] it.

I have been appointed Naval Storekeeper, and the two situations have always heretofore, been held by the same person; and, by holding it, my interest with the [Spanish] authorities will be much increased.

There is no law against my holding both appointments; and, I would ["refer" *interlined*] to my character and standing for twenty-one years in the navy to Judge [John Y.] Mason.

Should I receive the appointment, I trust it will be sent to me with as little delay as possible. I am very respectfully Your Ob[edien]t Serv[an]t, Junius Boyle, U.S. Navy.

ALS in DNA, RG 59 (State Department), Applications and Recommendations, 1845–1853, Boyle (M-873:9, frames 252–254). NOTE: A Clerk's EU reads "Mr. Calhoun said he would make the appointment requested should Mr. Rich resign—and the Sec[retar]y of the Navy give his consent."

From E[DWARD] G. W. BUTLER

Dunboyne Plantation
near Bayou Goula P.O. [La.]
Oct. 9, 1844

My dear Sir: Many of our sugar canes having greatly degenerated (owing, probably, to long culture in the same climate and soil,) it is the determination of many planters to try the effect of importations from the various Islands and countries in which the different canes grow, and it has occurred to me that you may have it in your power to aid us in our efforts, thro' the Agents of your Department in Foreign Countries; especially in the East Indies, with which we have but little direct commercial intercourse.

Any shipments to the care of my Agents, (A. Ledoux & Co.) in New Orleans, will be promptly attended to, and I feel that to one so deeply interested in agricu[l]tural pursuits, no apology will be required for thus trespassing upon your time and attention. With great respect, Your ob[edien]t Serv[an]t, E.G.W. Butler.

ALS in DNA, RG 59 (State Department), Miscellaneous Letters (M-179:105, frames 495–496); FC in DNA, RG 59 (State Department), Consular Instructions, 12:104–105; PC in DNA, RG 59 (State Department), Circulars of the Department of State, 1:96.

R[ichard] K. Crallé to R[OBERT] B. CAMPBELL, U.S. Consul, "Havanna"

Department of State
Washington, Oct. 9, 1844

Sir; Your letters of the 14th & 19th of September have been submitted to the President.

The President is highly gratified to learn from these despatches that our citizens who have been so long imprisoned at Matanzas, have at last been released; and he directs me to say that the exertions you have used in their behalf are fully appreciated.

With regard to the suggestion that a demand should be made on the Government of Cuba for redress for the incarceration of these individuals, I am instructed to state that it is not considered proper that the interposition of this Government should be extended so far, inasmuch as it appears that a fair trial, according to the laws of the

Island (with which we have no right to interfere) has been accorded to each of the persons imprisoned.

Perhaps redress for false imprisonment &c might be obtained by an appeal to the proper tribunal by the individuals themselves; and if upon a full view of the circumstances, you should feel justified in recommending that course to them, the President would be much pleased at your using all honorable means to aid them in their suit.

We have just heard, unofficially of the arrival in the U.S. of Capt. [P.C.] Dumas, of the Brig Cyrus. Before taking any measures in regard to the outrage committed upon his vessel, which formed the subject of one of your despatches of the 14th Ult., we await his evidence in the case. I am &c, R.K. Crallé, Acting Sec[retar]y.

FC in DNA, RG 59 (State Department), Consular Instructions, 10:270.

From DUFF GREEN

Jalapa, Mexico, Oc[tobe]r 9th 1844

My dear Sir, The stage lies over here a day—and I have improved the occasion to see a Mr. [James L.?] Kennedy[,] a very intelligent American merchant, a man of reputed property who proposes soon to remove to the United States. He tells me that a man of war lately arrived [at] Vera Cruz and that the Consul there has[?] sent a special messenger to go in advance of the mail with despatches for the British Minister [Charles Bankhead] and that he understood from the Mexican Governor of Vera Cruz and from another reliable source that the despatches had relation to a loan of ten millions of dollars which it is said Santa Anna is negociating with the British Government. It was his confident belief that the loan was about to be concluded. I do not think so—but I think it more than probable that England is negociating for California under a belief that war between Mexico & the United States is probable, and that having possession of California she may use that possession as a means of strengthening herself in the possession of Oregon.

Santa Anna is expected here tomorrow to meet his new wife & a striking fact is that he employed [Juan de Dios] Canedo, the author of the essay in favor of the recognition of the Independence of Texas as the negociator in arranging the marriage[,] which was by proxy.

The rumor has just reached us that the Army at Tampico have declared in favor of Santa Anna as Dictator & the Troops here about 6000 strong are expected to pronounce in his favor in a few days.

I write this hoping that it may reach Vera Cruz in time to go by the Curtis, which takes home the Texan Prisoners. Yours truly, Duff Green.

ALS in DNA, RG 59 (State Department), Diplomatic Despatches, Special Agents, vol. 13 (M-37:13, frames 20–22), received 11/14.

From JOHN HASTINGS, [former Representative from Ohio]

New Garden, Col[umbian]a C[ount]y, Ohio
Oct. 9, 1844

Dear Sir, Perhaps you may think proper to have the enclosed remarks [*not found*] which I have had occasion to make on the tariff, published in your State, coming as they do, from a democrat who lives in an abolition region, and speaking truths which will, to my mind, be appreciated by all whose assumed interests and aspirations are not obnoxious to them. They are brief: and the south and west will entertain them in the true light; but some sections in the east are incorrigible on tariffing, and it is worse than useless to mince the matter with them. The Union in its plenitude demands the truth, and as far as my voice goes it shall not be wanting[.]

Democracy must give up trimming and tampering with the impositions practiced on the people through banking and tariffing, and with that reckless factionism of British sympathies, called abolition, (an associative power that, in relation to the Union and the States, involves the conduct both of the parricide and the fratricide) before she can tap the pinnacle of confidence with the people that her principles would enable her to do. The amount is: she, or rather many among the professionists she trusts, unfortunately resort too much to the wretched and weak expedients of trimming and tampering and temporizing with the violative action of the constitution, and the desecration of the great principles which conserve the integrity of the Union; and until the people experience our persevering adherence to pure democratic principle and truth without prevarication, we will not be able to establish ourselves in their confidence as trustfully as we otherwise should do—a trustfulness that would enable democracy to defy anti-democracy under all the protean forms she assumes[.]

We had our general election yesterday, and from the returns so far, hopes of carrying the State are not flattering. A portion of the abolitionists illustrated by their vote the applicable no-people definition in my tariff remarks[.]

I had hopes of seeing you at Washington ere this, having some conceptions to submit to you that involve the weal and ["pow"(?) *canceled*] integrity and strength of the Union, (and do not deem me egotistical, when I indulge in saying that, my whole being is devoted to the conservation of ["these" *canceled and then interlined*] two last essentials—compassing as they do, the first—for keeping us a free people) but circumstances have not, so far, permitted it. However, if I do not get there, I will trouble ["you" *interlined*] with them on paper; and in this reference, will you, my dear Sir, just write me one line, saying when you may be in Washington? *As ever*, yours most earnestly, John Hastings.

P.S. If you should deem it any way useful to have the tariff remarks published, please send me a paper.

ALS in ScCleA. NOTE: Hastings was a native of Ireland and had been Representative from Ohio during 1839–1843.

From S[tephen] Rapalje

United States' Naval Lyceum
Navy Yard, New York [City,] October 9, 1844
Sir, I have the honor to transmit to you a "diploma," in testimony of your election as an honorary member of the U.S. Naval Lyceum.

This mark of consideration on the part of an institution, whose main object will be to promote the essential interests of the Navy, by encouraging in its members the active and strenuous pursuit of professional and general knowledge, is tendered to you, in respect for the prominent position you occupy among the distinguished men of our country.

It will be a source of pleasure to the Lyceum to learn that it meets with your acceptance. I am Sir, very respectfully Your obed[ien]t Serv[an]t, S. Rapalje, Corresponding Secr[etar]y.

LS with En in ScCleA. NOTE: In the enclosed certificate, dated 9/8/1844, S[ilas] H. Stringham, President, and other officers, attest Calhoun's election.

From W[illia]m Pinkney Starke

Paris France, October 9th 1844

Mr. Calhoun[']s request that I would write to him from Europe was too great a compliment to be forgotten and if I have not till this time availed myself of such a privilege, it was from a desire to see something of foreign countries before venturing to express an opinion about them.

I employed the first months after my arrival in traveling over Great Britain. That country was interesting to me as the source of our institutions; from the intimate relations, commercial and political, subsisting between it and my own country and lastly; from its having carried to the highest developement the arts most contributing to National Wealth and aggrandizement. I there saw how far Wealth, Science, and Legislative patronage have contributed towards the solution of the problem, to make of an island not large nor fertile a great Agricultural country. Although we produce much more in the aggr[eg]ate yet how much greater is the difference in extent ["of territory" *interlined*] cultivated than the difference in amount of produce between us! The upper house of Parliament being composed of landed proprietors, the attention of the Government has become very much directed to ["the" *interlined*] Agricultural Interest, which is in fact a Monopoly. In this respect their legislation is the reverse of ours. But though the English boast much of the beauty of their country, which is indeed a garden, yet it cannot be pleasant to reflect that the point of greatest possible produce having been very nearly attained, their great endeavour henceforth must be to remain *stationary.*

It is to Commerce however and Manufacturing that England is principally indebted for her present, and prospects for ["her" *interlined*] future, wealth. How magnificent are her docks and Warehouses? how vast, how admirable her Commercial arrangements? Formerly merchants on the ["unexpected" *interlined*] arrival of vessels from a distance with heavy cargoes, were called upon frequently for the sudden payment of such immense amount[?] in way of duties, that many were crushed. The consequence of course was that commercial enterprise was cramped. Now however the cargo is, on being landed, immediately deposited in ["the" *interlined*] Public Warehouses, from which the merchant withdraws his goods in amounts and at times to suit the course and demands of trade; paying duty only when and on what he withdraws. There are at any one time goods to the amount of fifty millions Sterling in the Warehouses of

Great Britain and the amazing increase of London ["within forty years" *interlined*] in wealth and population, has been very much owing to the adoption of the *Warehousing System.*

Marriages between the sons of the Nobility and the daughters of the formerly despised London traders are not uncommon, for many of the London merchants have incomes of two & three hundred thousand pounds. While the tendency of commerce has thus been to equalize ranks, to favour the progress of liberty, And to render a people naturally surly and quarrelsome, peaceable and in a measure polite, ["yet there has been" *canceled*] it has had its counterbalancing ill effect on the public character. No man can obtain a seat in Parliament without wealth. No man can rise at the bar without (strange as it may seem) having wealth to commence with. Erskine, Eldon, Ellenborough &c—with many others might be mentioned as instances in the last century of men who rose solely by talents. Nay there may be a few now, but they ["are" *interlined*] only accidents. The English Government has become, and more particularly I think within the last forty years, *an Oligarchy of wealth.* A man without money is a cypher. Their public exhibitions, statuary, painting, museums, libraries are opened to those who can pay for them and their Parliament is a place where a number of ["men" *canceled and* "wealthy" *interlined*] men meet together for the purpose of discussing business matters in a colloquial way. In point of eloquence they fall immeasurably below us. I here take occasion to mention the pride it gave an American and more particularly a Southerner to hear Mr. Calhoun quoted in the House of Lords in terms of the highest eulogium ["as one" *interlined*] "whose views on this point *singularly* lucid in themselves, must be considered ["as" *canceled*] entitled to greater attention as coming from the head of ["the" *interlined*] Free Trade Party in the United States."

I remained in England until the commencement of the fishing season when I visited Scotland, the Orkney & Zetland [*sic*; Shetland] Islands. These fisheries are important to England, not from any direct revenue they afford but from the great numbers of hardy seamen they train up to man her navy. The single harbour of Wick on the extreme N.E. point of Scotland sheltered when I visited it over 900 boats. Now to each boat there must be at least five men often more, besides very nearly as many engaged in curing the fish caught. By running up the calculation and considering that this is but a single harbour, though the most important, we are able to form an idea of the value of the fisheries.

I spent the latter part of July in the Orkney & Zetland Islands.

The latter are immense rocks ["rocks" *canceled*] rising suddenly out of the water sometimes to the height of a thousand feet, with only a vegetation of heath & moss. Not a tree is to be found and the main employment of the inhabitants in the few months during which they can labour without, is to lay in a supply of peat fuel against the winter season, with salt fish. For though the land denies produce to the hand of labour the sea by a Beneficent Providence pours forth its plenty. The sheep is small, but the wool which is pulled off by hand is fine and the flesh very delicate like that of all which feed on the heath flower. The horse never exceeds 44 inches in height the ["average" *interlined*] being 38. In the month preceeding and that succeeding the ["winter" *canceled and* "summer" *interlined*] solstice there is no night properly speaking. I could read at midnight without moonlight. The people subsist almost entirely on fish. In some vallies, I saw the oat & rye growing but the former could not have exceeded the height of eight inches. But notwithstanding the cold and bad living I had to put up with, I was more than repaid for my trip by the appearance of a country so utterly different from my own and by the kind and hospitable treatment of the inhabitants.

Scotland seems to be an entire stone quarry. Aberdeen is built of ["much" *canceled*] granite, the other cities entirely of stone. The scenery in many parts is beautiful, but I think has been exaggerated in the writings of Walter Scott. His "Ben An high" is 1800 feet, and the neighboring mountains are quite bare, add to this that it ["it" *altered to* "is"] impossible at almost any time to see any distance from the continual mists and you will agree with me that with the advantage of sky in our favour—the difference is with us.

As I returned through England I descended into the celebrated coal mines of New Castle. There were at the time 30,000 miners who had struck for ["higher" *interlined*] wages. The life below ["in" *interlined*] these mines is very singular.

I have been in Paris two months and can speak the language with a moderate degree of fluency. The French and English character is radically different. The hatred between the people of the two countries is intense. The French are emphatically a Military people. Napoleon has ruined them in my opinion—for the immense sacrifices France was forced to submit to under the Empire, ought, one would suppose, to have inclined them to forget War, it has in fact produced the reverse. Napoleon's is the only name known in France—they have ["erected" *interlined*] magnificent monuments ["erected" *canceled*] to him every where in public and in private there is scarcely a house in which there is not a bust or a print of him. They talk of him, they write of him, and they are continually hurling his name over Europe. The consequence is that now as under the Empire there are in Europe ["France" *canceled and* "two" *interlined*] parties, France and Europe. The Emperour ["of Russia" *interlined*] whom I saw in England has begun openly to speak of his intention ["of his intention" *canceled*] to seize Turkey. The merchants are to suffer him quietly to seize it for the privilege of taking a part of Egypt so as to gain a free passage to India and on condition of commanding the Russian army in case of a French war. To retaliate the French papers have lately revived the claim to Belgium. There are in Paris at present about 80,000 men—the standing force ["in France" *interlined*] about 450,000 and the war force, a million of trained men. Consider that the French live almost entirely out of doors, in conversation and sight-seeing that they are a people whose ruling passions are Pleasure and Glory, that they are a brave people, that they have large resources, that after conquering Europe they have not been suffered to possess even the Rhine as a limit and you will ["perceive" *canceled and* "agree" *interlined*] that I am not far wrong in saying that the Millenium has not yet come.

In hopes that you are enjoying fine health and may be long spared to the country; I remain with very great respect Your Fellow Citizen, Wm. Pinkney Starke.

P.S. I start in three days for Italy.

[P.P.S.] From Rome or Athens I shall again take the liberty of writing to Mr. Calhoun.

ALS in ScCleA.

From D[avid] Levy [Yulee], [Delegate from Fla. Territory], 10/- 9. He requests that Charles S. Sibley be sent copies of any charges against him that have been made by [Richard K.] Call since "the first one." ALS in DNA, RG 59 (State Department), Applications and Recommendations, 1837–1845, Sibley (M-687:30, frames 299–300).

From EDWARD EVERETT

London, 10 October 1844

Sir, In my correspondence with the department last winter, I had frequent occasion to advert to the duty on Tobacco and to the appointment of a Committee of the House of Commons on the subject of Smuggling.

I forward by the "Great Western" which sails on the 12th a copy of the report of this Committee, which will be found to embody a great deal of information on the subject.

The Committee in question was granted on the motion of Mr. [Joseph] Hume, who is decide[d]ly of opinion that the only effectual remedy against smuggling would be a reduction of the duty to one shilling per pound. This opinion appears also to have been held by several other members of the Committee, and is emphatically expressed by many of the witnesses, including those most extensively engaged in the Tobacco trade, whose evidence is contained in the printed report. A majority of the Committee with the Chancellor of the Exchequer at their head entertained a different opinion.

A detailed Report was submitted by Mr. Hume recapitulating those portions of the evidence which illustrated the extent of smuggling and adulteration, and concluding in favor of a reduction of the duty. A counter Report was offered by Mr. [George] Darby; and the Committee finally determined, instead of adopting either, to lay the evidence before the House, with the following brief report:

"That, considering the period, to which the enquiries of your Committee have necessarily been protracted, and the various important matters which are involved in a decision upon the several points to which the evidence has been directed, it appears to your Committee impracticable to present to the House a full report upon the subject referred to them and therefore confine themselves to reporting the Minutes of Evidence and their proceedings to the House."

Although the reduction of the duty appears to have been strenuously resisted by the Chancellor of the Exchequer, as a member of Mr. Hume's Committee, I remain of the opinion, which I have already taken occasion to intimate to the Department, that should it be decided next spring to continue the property tax, a material reduction of other taxes will take place, among which the duty on tobacco is very likely to be included. If, on the contrary, the Property tax is repealed, there is not the least probability that it will be deemed expedient to make the experiment of a reduction of the duty on tobacco; that duty being one of the most considerable sources of revenue. I am, Sir, with great respect, Your obedient Servant, Edward Everett.

LS (No. 188) in DNA, RG 59 (State Department), Diplomatic Despatches, Great Britain, vol. 53 (M-30:49), received 10/30; FC in DNA, RG 84 (Foreign Posts), Great Britain, Despatches, 8:409–412; FC in MHi, Edward Everett Papers, 50: 120–121 (published microfilm, reel 23, frames 329–330).

From ALLEN A. HALL

Legation of the United States
Caracas, October 10th, 1844

Sir, Mr. P.J. Caduc, bearer of despatches, has handed me your despatches numbered 21 and 22. I have pleasure in informing you that the Morris claim has been paid. The Executive could not direct it to be done in the absence of an appropriation by Congress. But the National Bank, after consultation with him, agreed to anticipate the action of Congress, and to advance the money to Mr. Caduc, the authorized agent of Mr. [Henry H.] Williams. To such an arrangement I could see no objection, more particularly as Mr. Caduc came out with full powers from Mr. Williams to arrange the matter in any way he might deem expedient. It is virtually a payment by the Government, and while it relieves the Executive will be of great advantage to the owner of the claim.

Being perfectly satisfied that Mr. Williams is "in fact the principal claimant, and that in the prosecution of the claim he has represented the other claimants," I have in conformity with the instructions contained in your despatch of the 25th of April, disposed of the amount as directed by him, first, however, taking from ["him" *interlined*] such acknowledgments as will secure your Department from any further accountability in the matter.

There is a misconception in your despatch of the 15th of August which, as it presupposes extreme ignorance on my part in relation to a very important provision in the Constitution of the United States, I beg permission to correct. You say "the remedy which you (I) advise would no doubt prove effective, but it cannot be adopted without the sanction of Congress." Now, it so happens that I have "advised" no "remedy" at all—much less one which, under the circumstances, the President could not have adopted without a violation of one of the most important provisions in our Constitution. If you will have the goodness to turn to my despatch of the 15th of August, in which I acquainted you with the failure of the Venezuelan Congress to make the appropriation in the case of the Brig Morris, you will find in it the following paragraph:

"Before this reaches you, the Congress of the United States will probably have adjourned. By the time they meet again in December, I shall have brought under the consideration of this Government all the residue of the claims of our citizens against the late Republic of Colombia, and then, with a knowledge of the disposition manifested in the interim by the States which formerly composed that Republic to afford a fair and satisfactory indemnification, the President may perhaps have no difficulty in deciding whether the United States will not consult their dignity by either promptly enforcing the payment of the claims or as promptly abandoning their further prosecution."

It was precisely because I knew that Congress would have adjourned before my despatch could reach Washington, and that without the sanction of that body the President had no power under the constitution to resort to coercive measures, that I forbore to "advise" any "remedy" whatever. Instead of "advising" a blockade or the issuing of letters of marque and reprisal without the sanction of Congress, as you suppose, I expressly assumed that nothing could be done until that body assembled again in December, "*when*, the President &c. &c.*"

The mortification I have felt at the bare supposition on your part of such discreditable ignorance on mine must plead my apology for the foregoing correction. I have the honor to be Sir, with great respect Your obedient servant, Allen A. Hall.

ALS (No. 41) in DNA, RG 59 (State Department), Diplomatic Despatches, Venezuela, vol. 2 (M-79:3), received 12/2; CCEx in DNA, RG 233 (U.S. House of Representatives), 28A-E1; PEx in House Document No. 6, 28th Cong., 2nd Sess.

From C H [R I S T O P H E R] H U G H E S, "Private"

The Hague; 10th Oct[obe]r 1844
My dear Sir, I am sorry that the hope I entertained—and that I communicated to you—in my last despatch concerning the Exequatur to [William H. Freeman] our Consul at Curaçoa—has been completely disappointed.

The fact is I had received (though quite in an informal & unofficial way) encouragement *to hope it*—from one of the most Considered & confidential of the *Employés* in the Foreign office! and I am sure—*He believed* it when he gave me reason to hope—that the exception in favour of our Consul at Curaçoa would be Continued. However, it has turned out otherwise; and it seems that the Netherlands Government has come to a firm & fixed resolution to return to the old System of Exclusion of *all Consuls* in their Colonies.

Such agents will be tolerated & allowed quietly to exercise their functions; but the Government *will not officially recognize them.*

In this state of things the question presents itself—is it not better

59

to leave the matter quiet; and to take all we can get—than to make the case worse—by insisting on what I feel pretty sure this Government will not grant?

If I were to write volumes—I could say no more—than what is conveyed by the above paragraph.

Mr. Freeman will not meet with any interruption in his Consular functions; I know the Governor of Curaçoa well; and I am sure that Baron Raders will be always ready to—not merely tolerate the U.S. Consul—but sanction—support & protect him in the fair & full exercise of all the duties & functions of a *Consul*! but Consuls in Colonies are apt to play *"the Swell"*; & it is to keep the Governor free from *Rivals*—that this Exclusive system is adopted; & *will be rigidly enforced*—as far as formal recognition goes: this self-protection is—in a great measure—the motive of the refusal—*not* to *Exequo* Consuls.

I shall be happy to receive your Instructions & to obey them—on the subject; but we shall gain nothing by pressing the matter—at least for the present—on the Netherlands Government. They visit the same principle of Exclusion upon all Nations without exception.

This is my view of the case—as it now is!

You may remember, my dear Sir—that I did not avail myself of the very kind permission, so promptly granted me, by the ["Present" *canceled and* "President" *interlined*]; to return home this autumn—to see into my private affairs at Baltimore; my presence *seemed* indispensable—and my mind was made up to go home; a great family affliction had fallen upon me. The President knew of the death of my sister Mrs. Moore & he shared I am sure in the sorrows of his old Friend—Col. [Samuel] Moore my Brother in Law. Colonel Moore—soon after his loss—came on to Europe & is now with his Family at Londonderry! It is highly important—nay, necessary—that I should see him. His Gout & *Weight* (The President *knows* him!) make it very inconvenient for him to move. I intend running over to Ireland for a few days; I shall ["not" *canceled*] be absent from the Hague but [a] few days—& no sort of ["public" *canceled*] inconvenience whatever will—or can—occur to the service by my short absence. Still—I think it proper to mention the fact to you & to the President; for now a days—the Newspapers meddle—& announce—& invent & add—whenever and wherever a public man moves! it is impossible to escape this nuisance! & I should rather you & the President should know of my movements *from myself*—than from any other source of Intelligence.

I feel quite sure that the President will not merely sanction my going to see my poor Brother—Col. Moore—but he will be pleased to know that we *have seen each other* after so heavy an affliction;

though our meeting must be a sad one; there is consolation even in sadness at times. I shall *"stop"* (as the English say) at Londonderry—but 3 or 4 days. I pray you, my dear Sir, to present my respects to the President and to believe me to be—very respectfully & Sincerely Yours, Ch. Hughes.

P.S. I received *the Answer* from my Friend—Mr. [Joseph R.] Ingersoll—& I have to thank you for y[ou]r kindness. C.H.

ALS in DNA, RG 59 (State Department), Diplomatic Despatches, Netherlands, vol. 12 (M-42:16, frames 205–207), received 11/11.

From W ILLIAM R. K ING, "(Private)"

[Paris, *ca.* October 10, 1844?]

My Dear Sir, Mr. [Seth T.] Otis our Consul at Basle, has recently been in Paris, to confer with me relative to the affair of [Gerard H.] Koster. I found him to be an intel[l]igent gentleman, and judging from his conduct and efforts to procure Koster[']s arrest, I should say he is a zealous and active agent of the government. The compensation his Consulate affords is insufficient for his support. Mr. Otis could, without any inconvenience to persons engaged in commerce with Switzerland, discharge all the duties of Consul for the whole Confederation; this would afford to him the means of living as an American Consul should. The Consul at Zurich is a Swiss permanently settled there, and extensively engaged in commerce; and the Merchants are generally opposed to submitting their Invoices to a Consul whose commercial opperations conflict with their own. The objection seems to be reasonable; and whenever our government can command the services of native citizens who are not engaged in commerce, it would certainly be desirable to do so. Would it not also be advantageous to reduce the number of our Consular agents and extend the sphere of the duties of those employed? I make this suggestion from a conviction that the character of our Country not unfrequently suffers, by the improper conduct of its Consuls at points where the fees of office are insufficient to afford them a support. Their official station gives to them a credit, which unfortunately they but too often abuse. Would it not be well to present to the next Congress a plan for the revision of our entire Consular system[?]

The subject of emancipation in the French Colonies, engages much attention here, and will probably be brought before the Chambers this winter. The abolitionists of England, commanding imence [*sic*] pecuniary resources, are opperating I fear but too successfully, through the medium of the French press; which is altogether venal. It is well understood that many of the prominent Journals in Paris are in the pay of the society of Exeter Hall; and ["they" *interlined*] abound in publications containing the most false and exag[g]erated statements on the subject of slavery. If France influenced by the efforts now making, should abolish slavery in her Colonies; Spain, and Brazill, will be compelled to yield to the pressure which will be brought to bear upon them; and the United States will be left to stand alone, with the whole civilized world against her. Tis here then, that this great question, so vitally affecting our interests, should be met. The selfish objects of the British government should be clearly, and fully presented to the people of France. They should be made to understand that under the pretext of humanity towards the slave, the real object is to engross to herself the entire production of Shugar; and in a great degree, that of Cotton & Rice, through the medium of her East India possessions. To effect this the Press must be employed, which can only be effected with money. The Delegates of the French Colonies, are doing all they can, to enlighten the public mind, & to counteract the efforts of England; but, as I know, their means are limited, I have thought that a small portion of the secret ["service" *canceled and* "or contingent" *interlined*] fund at your disposal, could not be more usefully employed, than by procuring the insertion in the Paris papers (now closed against us) of well written articles, calculated to disabuse the public mind here, as to the actual condition of the Slaves of our Country. Indeed I have long thought that our Representatives abroad, could greatly subserve the public interest, could they be allowed access to the press in the countries to which they are accredited; as it is, they see our Institutions stigmatized, and our people calumniated, without the means of counteracting the false impressions thus made to our prejudice. Should you think my suggestions worthy of your attention, and that you can with propriety apply a part of the fund to the object designated; I would recommend Mr. [Robert] Walsh, our present Consul [at Paris], as admirably qualified to prepare the proper articles for publication, ["while" *canceled*] as his long residence in France has enabled him to form correct opinions, not only of its government, and people; but as to the best mode of opperating either on their Judgement or feelings. He would engage in it with the utmost zeal; for his heart is truly American.

I had the pleasure of seeing Mr. [Thomas G. Clemson] & Mrs. [Anna Maria Calhoun] Clemson often during their short stay in Paris; and of presenting Mr. Clemson to the King [Louis Philippe] & Royal

Family; by whom he was most cordially received. I have no doubt they will be pleased with Brussels, which I consider a much more agreeable residence than Paris. The climate here is execrable; cold, and damp. I have suffered much from rheumatism, and my hand is so disabled, that it is with difficulty I can hold my pen. I fear the winter will knock me up entirely. The accounts I receive of the Presidential contest, are cheering. [James K.] Polk & [George M.] Dallas have united our distracted Party, and with the aid of the Texas question, are carrying all before them. God grant them success, for I should view the election of [Henry] Clay, as a death blow to our national prosperity; if not to the government itself. Two children have been born to the Royal Family, since my arrival here, and the King informed me, that he had, with his own hand, written two letters to the President informing him of the interesting events—no answer to them has as quet [sic] been received by me. In matters of that kind, there should be as little delay as possible, as much importance is attached to them here. Neither have I received your letter [of 9/10/-1844] to Governor [Wilson] Shannon although those addressed to Mr. [Washington] Irving & Mr. [Henry] Wheaton arrived safely and were delivered to them. If there is any place where it is of importance that the American Minister should be constantly advised of all that relates to to [sic] the movements connected with the Texas question, it certainly is here. At present all looks well, and I have no reason to apprehend any action on the part of this government to which we could reasonably object. Still it is of the utmost importance that I should be kept advised of all that takes place on our side of the water. The King of the French has returned from his visit to Queen Victoria. He is much elated with the reception he met with, which was no doubt flattering. But all this billing & cooing of the Sovereigns, cannot change the character of their people; nor eradicate the deep rooted hostility which the[y] entertain towards each other. Louis Phillippe [sic] manifests, I fear too anxious a desire to maintain peace with his haughty Neighbour. Tis certainly his true policy, but may be pressed too far. The French are a proud and sensitive people; and any manifestation on his part, of truckling to England, would arouse a spirit in the nation, which would probably prove fatal to his dynasty. I regret that he is not as popular as he deserves to be, for France was never more prosperous than under his wise and pacific policy, and I sincerely wish that his reign may be long. He is emphatically a man suited to the times; for having been taught in the school of adversity, he has a just appreciation of men, & things, which peculiarly fits him for the high destiny to which he has been called. I converse with him

63

often, and freely, and my intercourse with him has been all that I could desire. Mr. [F.P.G.] Guizot is able and adroit. He has a strong leaning towards England, whose government is his beau ideal. He is also represented by those who profess to know him well, to be deceptive & false. Had this character of the prime Minister been furnished me on my arrival, I should have reduced his conversation relative to Texas to writing, and submitted to him for correction, so as to bind him to his declarations, beyond the possibility of cavil or denyal. His enemies say he will not hesitate to lie, whenever he thinks he can gain by so doing. He is probably at this very time one of the most unpopular men in France. Yet sustained by the King, he will command a decided majority of the Chambers, and for the present, is secure in his position. Present me respectfully to the President [John Tyler] & Lady [Julia Gardiner Tyler], also to my Friends [William] Wilkins, [John Y.] Mason, [George M.] Bibb, & [John] Nelson & Krawley [*sic*; Richard K. Crallé]. With the highest respect I am faithfully your Ob[edien]t Ser[van]t, William R. King.

ALS in ScCleA; variant PC in Jameson, ed., *Correspondence*, pp. 986–990. NOTE: An AEU by Calhoun reads: "About a treaty with the Switz [*sic*] Confederacy, Abolition, The King's letters to the Pres[iden]t & my letter to Gov[erno]r Shannon."

R[ichard] K. Crallé to STEWART NEWELL, U.S. Consul at Sabine

Department of State
Washington, Oct. 10, 1844

Sir, Your letters Nos. 25 & 26 with their enclosures & No. 3 dated at U.S. Consulate Galveston, have been received.

The zeal which you have evinced in taking steps to inform the Department of the State of the public Archives and other matters connected with the interests of our Country, is highly appreciated. A Chargé d'Affaires [Andrew J. Donelson] has been appointed to succeed the late Gen[era]l [Tilghman A.] Howard, and I have to request that you will retain in your possession the letter alluded to in your No. 25 and all others you may receive, under the frank of the Department, addressed to Gen[era]l Howard, until the arrival of his successor, by whom they will be opened. It is also desired that the Archives and public papers which are at Washington [Texas] and at Austin, the late Capitol, be suffered to remain at those places 'till Gen[era]l

Howard's successor arrives & takes the proper measures to get possession of them.

Your Draft for $100, in compensation to a Bearer of Despatches, on the Collector of the Customs at New Orleans has been paid. Should you have occasion hereafter, to incur a similar expense, your draft should be upon this Department and not upon a Collector of the Customs, as such officer has no authority to meet it.

In regard to the conduct of J[ames] J. Wright, your vigilance entitles you to the approbation of the Department, and it is hoped that you will keep a strict eye upon his movements, and report them when important to do so. I am, Sir &c, R.K. Crallé, Act[in]g Sec[re]t[ar]y.

FC in DNA, RG 59 (State Department), Consular Instructions, 11:284–285; CC in DNA, RG 59 (State Department), Applications and Recommendations, 1845–1853, Newell (M-873:63, frames 23–24).

Rich[ar]d K. Crallé to R[ICHARD] PAKENHAM

Department of State
Washington, 10th Oct. 1844

The Undersigned, Acting Secretary of State of the United States, has the honor to acknowledge the receipt of the note addressed to this Department on the 22d of August last, by the Right Honorable Mr. Pakenham, Her Britannic Majesty's Envoy Extraordinary and Minister Plenipotentiary, referring to a previous correspondence between the Secretary of State and Her Majesty's Legation at Washington, relative to the injury alleged to have been suffered by British merchants trading with this country, in consequence of a particular clause in the tariff law of August, 1842, whereby it was provided that goods imported in vessels bound to any part of the United States which had left their ports of lading eastward of the Cape of Good Hope, or beyond Cape Horn, prior to the 1st of September, 1842, should be subjected only to the lower rate of duties specified in the tariff regulations existing before the 30th of June, 1842, while, on the contrary, like goods imported into the United States from British ports, although shipped prior to the aforesaid date of 1st September, 1842, were subjected to the heavy duties imposed by the tariff of 29th August of that same year; and renewing the application on behalf of the claimants, for the restitution of the excess of duties which should have been thus levied on goods shipped from British ports, on the ground that the operation of the act complained of, amounts to a violation of the convention between the two countries.

The Undersigned has the honor to acquaint Mr. Pakenham that his note above referred to has been duly communicated to the Treasury Department, and that the Secretary of the Treasury, after a mature consideration of the subject, is of opinion that the claim for reimbursement on the part of the British merchants, is inadmissible, as will be seen from his letter to the Secretary of State, dated the 18th of September, a copy of which is herewith transmitted.

The Undersigned avails himself of this occasion to offer to Mr. Pakenham the assurance of his high consideration. Richd. K. Crallé.

FC in DNA, RG 59 (State Department), Notes to Foreign Legations, Great Britain, 7:57–58 (M-99:36).

Report of a committee of the Pendleton Agricultural Society, 10/-10. This published report describes in detail the conditions and practices on seven farms in the Pendleton vicinity. In regard to Calhoun's "farm," the committee reported that "although it may be truly stated that nature has done much for it, yet to its proprietor clearly belongs the merit of very superior management." The committee was particularly impressed with an extensive but simple system of drains designed to prevent the washing away of topsoil on upland fields. This system was so successful that the committee "have deemed it a duty incumbent on them, to bring to the notice of our planters, not only the principles upon which this measure has been conducted, but also the results which have followed." Calhoun's stock, "consisting of horses, hogs and cattle, were of good blood and in fine condition." The farm dwellings were described as "sufficiently numerous, and both comfortable and convenient. And this was more especially the case with the negro house, which consisted of a building of stone of superior masonry, two hundred and ten feet in length, divided into apartments, with separate fire-places, sufficiently large for all the purposes of comfort and healthful ventilation." In conclusion the committee found "the management upon this farm highly superior. The useful and the ornamental have been most happily blended . . . ." The committee was composed of O[zey] R. Broyles, R[obert] A. Maxwell, Tho[ma]s M. Sloan, Andrew F. Lewis, and R[ichard] F. Simpson. PC in the Pendleton, S.C., *Messenger*, October 18, 1844, p. 4, and October 25, 1844, p. 4; PC in the *Carolina Planter*, vol. I, no. 10 (April, 1845), pp. 219–221; PC in the Richmond, Va., *Enquirer*, May 26, 1845, p. 4; PC in the *Southern Cultivator*, vol. III, no. 7 (July, 1845), pp. 97–98; PC in *The American Farmer,* new series, vol. I, no. 1 (July, 1845), pp. 4–5.

From Joseph A. Wright, [Representative from Ind.]

Rockville Ind., Oct. 10th 1844

Sir, The death of my personal and political friend T[ilghman] A. Howard in Texas, induces me to call your attention to some Subjects that his family have an interest in.

The Gen[era]l left a will and letters testamentary will be taken out in this county. What steps is necessary to be taken in order to procure whatever is due to his Estate from the Government[?]

Is there such a thing as an *In*fit, or some equivalent for an outfit, in cases of ministers or Char[gés] De affair[e]s dying abroad[?]

Is there any precedent established on the Subject of bringing the remains of ministers dying abroad, home[?] If there is any rule or practice on this subject, I should be glad to know the nature of the same. The Gen[era]l has left a large family and I feel a deep anxiety to see his Family receive from the Government whatever is proper & right, and what is in accordance with the practice of the Government. I shall leave for Washington about the 15th of Nov., and will bring with me, whatever vouchers or ["authority" *altered to* "authorities"] may be needed, in order to settle the claims of the Deceased.

I am requested by a relation of Gen[era]l Howard to enclose you the within letter to Gen[era]l [Sam] Houston of Texas, and to request that you would see that the letter is forwarded by some conveyance, to Texas.

There is one universal feeling overspreading this community, expressive of the attachment of the people to Gen[era]l Howard, his place in this community cannot be filled.

Your attention to this, will bring the undersigned under many obligations, and his large family join with me in assurances of respect & Esteem for the kindness you have manifested for the deceased. Yours very Respectfully, Joseph A. Wright.

ALS in ScCleA.

From JOHN R. BRADY

N[ew] Y[ork City,] Oct. 11, 1844

D[ea]r Sir, I take great pleasure in presenting for your consideration John H. Albers who desires to be appointed Consul for Elberfeld and Russian [*sic*; Prussian] Provinces of the Rhine and Westphalia, and Egidius Franz Goettner who also desires to be appointed Consul for the Kingdom of Bavaria to reside in the City of Munich.

Both of these gentlemen from the interest manifested for them are no doubt well qualified in every point of view for the appointments which they respectively solicit. I shall therefore esteem any aid rendered them by you as entitled to my gratitude. I am y[ou]rs very resp[ectfull]y, Jno. R. Brady.

ALS in DNA, RG 59 (State Department), Applications and Recommendations, 1845–1853, Albers (M-873:1, frames 414–417).

From LOUIS MARK, "Private"

Bamberg (Bavaria), 11h October 1844

Sir, As from my Infancy I have allways been taught to look up to you as one of the most distinguished of our Citizens for Character and talents, and as I feel assured you would be the last Person in the United States, who would knowingly suffer any injustice to be done to an American Citizen, I take the liberty of troubling you with a few lines on the subject of my late connection with our Government.

I was born of German Parents and resided in the City of New York from the time I was two years old. I was brought up in the Protestant Religion and married a Sister of General [Alexander] Macomb and early in life made several Voyages to Germany, and thus became acquainted with its Commerce and Manufactures, which induced Mr. [Henry] Wheaton to avail himself of my Experience and knowledge of the language and the Country. I wrote a great deal in the German News Papers and Reviews against England and in favor of the United States, and as you know was sent by Mr. Wheaton last October to Washington where I gave all the information in my Power, which so pleased the late Mr. [Abel P.] Upshur and the President [John Tyler], that I was sent back to Mr. Wheaton with a Dispatch now on file in your Department, saying that I had in every way made myself worthy of the Confidence he placed in me and on my return to Berlin I was again employed in most difficult and delicate negotiations which completely succeeded, and the Part I took in them so pleased Mr. Wheaton that he requested me to go with the Treaty to Washington to give any explanations which might be required.

I again left my Family and crossed the Atlantic, and in place of being received as one who had assisted in defeating England and laying the corner Stone to a prosperous Commerce between Germany and the United States, you may imagine my Chagrin and disappointment to find your Mind prejudiced by all kind of Calumnies with which the Enemies of this Treaty and my personal Enemies mostly caused by jealousy as to the part I took in it, had in vain attempted to prevent my getting the Exequatur from the Prussian and Bavarian Governments who after examining all the Facts acknowledged me in the most flattering terms. As to the circumstance of my first Bond, there was considerable carelessness and so soon as I returned to New York I got a sufficient one executed and sent to you and could not without injuring a young unexperienced Man who acted without thought, but no bad intention, prove what I might have done, but who promised personally to explain to you the Facts, and there being thus no farther necessity to remain in the United States I returned to my Family but without pretending to carry Dispatches which was a mere squib of the [New York] Herald without my knowledge. I did not see Mr. [Edward] Everett and immediately wrote on my arrival in England ["wrote" *interlined*] to Mr. Wheaton that I had no communication from you. Since my return to Europe I have not meddled with the Consulship of the Prussian Provinces which is in the hands of Mr. Charles Hecker, President of the Board of Trade in Elberfeld who acted as my Consular Agent as notified by me to the Department—that Consulate issues yearly about 200 Certificates which at $2 each is worth about 400 Dollars per annum—the Bavarian Consulate issues about 100 Certificates and is worth about 200 Dollars per Annum—of course it would be unpleasant for me to see the latter given to any other Person whilst I remain in this Country. Since my return I have only as a private Individual explained to the King of Bavaria the causes of the Treaty not being ratified at once, and the part England took against it, and under all Circumstances I shall continue as I ["have" *canceled*] hitherto have done, in or out of office, to promote the Interests of our Country wherever I may be.

As I do not trouble the President with a Letter, but highly value his good opinion, may I beg the favor of you to mention to him the

Contents of this Letter. I remain with the greatest Respect Your Obedient Servant, Louis Mark.

ALS in DNA, RG 59 (State Department), Consular Despatches, Munich, vol. 1 (T-261:1).

From H[ARVEY] M. WATTERSON

Special Agency of the U.S.
Buenos Ayres, Oct. 11th 1844

Sir, The accompanying documents will acquaint you with all the facts in regard to the recent capture of the Buenos [Ayrean] blockading Squadron off Monte Video, by the United States Frigate Congress, whose Commander [Philip F. Voorhees], to say the least of it, acted with great precipitancy. This Government was much incensed at his conduct, and you will perceive ["that" *altered to* "from"] my reply to the letter of Señor Don Felipe Arana, Minister of Foreign ["Relations" *altered to* "Affairs"], that I have not defended it, further than the capture of the Schooner and crew, which committed the outrage on the American Barque Rosalba, was concerned. Commodore [Daniel] Turner is daily expected in the River Plate from Rio [de] Janeiro, and I trust he will act with that prudence, which the circumstances demand. I have reason to know the ardent desire of Governor [Juan M.] Rosas, to draw still closer the bonds of friendship between his Government and that of the United States—indeed he is more anxious to cultivate our good opinion and our well wishes than those of any other nation, and now when diplomatic relations are about to be completely re-established, this rash proceeding of Capt. Voorhies [*sic*] is much to be regretted.

Mr. [William] Brent [Jr.] has not yet arrived. Until he does so, I shall continue to use all the means in my power, consistent with self respect, and the honor of my country[,] to allay the excitement which this unfortunate affair has produced, and to preserve the amicable relations of the two Republics. Very Respectfully Your Ob[edien]t S[er]v[an]t, H.M. Watterson.

ALS with Ens (in Spanish, with State Department translations) in DNA, RG 59 (State Department), Diplomatic Despatches, Argentina, vol. 5 (M-69:6), received 12/11; FC (dated 10/12) with En (in English) in DNA, RG 84 (Foreign Posts), Argentina. NOTE: Watterson enclosed a formal protest, dated 10/6, from Don Felipe Arana, Argentine Foreign Minister, against the actions of Capt. Philip F. Voorhees, commander of the U.S.S. *Congress*. On 9/29 Voorhees captured the

Argentine warship *Sancala,* removed and imprisoned its crew, and struck its flag. He then commandeered the vessel with an American crew, flying the U.S. flag, and captured two vessels of the Argentine Blockading Squadron, the *9th of July* and the *Republicano.* Watterson also transmitted documents enclosed with Arana's protest that described these actions.

From HENRY A. WISE

Legation of the United States
Rio de Janeiro, October 11th 1844

Sir, The accompanying papers will show you what I have been doing in the business of this mission. The paper marked No. 1 is a copy of the letter [of 9/24/1844] which I deemed it my duty to address to the Govt. of Brazil on the subject of the Texas treaty. I trust that, neither transcending nor coming short of your instructions, it will meet with your approbation. The subject was difficult for me to manage after its change of aspect since my departure from the U. States. To some my letter may appear to partake of the tone of the partizan against Great Britain. In the sense of a partizan of American interests and influence, in opposition to those of England or any other European power, I am willing that it should so appear. There is no doubt but what sympathy enough with that feeling is to be found in the Government and among the people of Brazil. Their partiality to the U. States is apparent, and no less manifest is their distrust of Great Britain. Mr. [Ernesto Ferreira] França, Secretary of State, in my personal interview with him did not with[h]old the expression of his approval of the measure of the treaty with Texas by the Govt. of the U. States.

No. 2 is a copy of my letter to Mr. França on the subject of the claims of citizens of the U. States upon this Govt. To it I have as yet received no reply.

No. 3 is a copy of my letter to H.B.M. Minister, Mr. [Hamilton] Hamilton, touching the capture of the American brig Cyrus by a British cruiser on the coast of Africa. Whilst the Capt[ai]n of this brig, Capt[ai]n [P.C.] Dumas, was making his protest and taking the depositions of witnesses before the U. States Consul, the British Consul intimated to him in my presence that there were rumors of facts which would perhaps invalidate the statements of himself and his witnesses, and which would tend to convict him of the offences of the slave-trade. This at once suggested to me the view of the case that if Capt[ai]n Dumas was guilty, he ought to be convicted, and none

71

would be more ready or likely to succeed in furnishing whatever evidence there was to be found here against him than the British authorities; and, if he was an innocent & lawful trader who had been searched and captured as he described, he was entitled to have his case strengthened by giving due notice to the British authorities here, so that they might have the opportunity to take other testimony, or cross-examine his witnesses who were all in this port, and so that the British Govt. should not hereafter have it in its power to plead that they could or might have proved the contrary of Capt[ai]n Dumas' statement by witnesses in this port at the time. I myself am fully convinced that the case was one of great outrage upon the flag and commerce of the U. States, in any and every aspect in which it can be viewed. If I understand the position taken by our Govt. it is that the flag of the U. States shall be a positive protection to their own vessels, and that if any power attempts to exercise the authority to search a vessel sailing under that flag, it must be at its peril. That is to say, if the vessel belongs to the U. States and is under their flag, it is, under any circumstances, even where there are slaves themselves found on board, a case for reparation. If the vessel belongs not to the U. States, or be under false colors, it is a case of which the U. States will not take cognizance. The Earl of Aberdeen, as I understand, yields the point that where the vessel is found on visit (which means practically the act of search) to belong to the U. States, even though she have slaves on board, the British Govt. or cruisers will not pretend to the right of interfering with her. The U. States insist that they shall not search to find out whether the vessel be a vessel of the U. States or not; and, if they do, and the vessel does belong to their flag, whether slaves be found on board or not, they shall be held answerable. The suspicions then respecting Capt[ai]n Dumas, whether groundless or not, would not affect the case of a violation of our flag; for it is not pretended that the Cyrus was not a vessel belonging to the U. States & sailing under their flag. As between Great Britain and the U. States, a wrong at all events has been perpetrated by the armed force of the former upon the flag of the latter. As between Capt[ai]n Dumas and the U. States, he may or may not be a culprit under *their* laws, but Great Britain had no right to exercise any authority whatever over him or his vessel. As soon, therefore, as Mr. Gordon could copy and inclose to me the papers, I addressed my letter to Mr. Hamilton, inclosing to him copies of the papers now sent to the Department. He has since expressed to me his thanks for so doing, and said he would forward my communication to his Govt. I have not heard since of any attempt to justify the capture of the Cyrus. I trust that a case so flagrant will not be overlooked by the U. States.

No. 4 is a correspondence with our Consul, Mr. [George William] Gordon, and with the British Minister, Mr. Hamilton, touching the case of the brig "Sooy." In the early part of September last, whilst on board the Congress frigate in this port, my attention was called to a brig evidently of American construction and reported to be a vessel of the U. States, then lately captured and brought in here under a British prize flag. In pulling from the frigate to the shore, I caused the boat to be hauled under the stern of the brig which I found to have plainly lettered upon it the names "Sooy, Newport." Having ["occasion" *canceled*] on Monday, the 16th of Sept[embe]r, to call upon Mr. França at the Foreign Office, I took occasion to mention the fact to him, and that it was also rumored that this vessel was captured in the waters of Brazil. The U. States were interested to know whether this vessel belonged to their flag; if so, what were the pretexts of her capture; and whether such captures were permitted by this Govt. to Great Britain or any other powers. He replied that mine was the first information he had on the subject, and he would immediately inquire and act according to the circumstances of the case. On the 19th of September, Mr. Gordon, our Consul, addressed to me a letter, and on the 21st of September I addressed to Mr. Hamilton a letter, of which the inclosed marked "A" & "B" are copies. Mr. Hamilton called immediately upon me in person. He at first intimated that he could not communicate with me *officially*. It would not be "diplomatic." I did not remind him that he had reversed that position when he addressed my predecessor, Mr. [George H.] Proffit, directly on a similar subject lately; but replied that my letter to him stated its bona fide objects, and that the information called for was all I asked, and it mattered not in what character he gave it so it came from him. He then very promptly showed me a number of papers found on board the "Sooy," most in Portuguese and a few in English, which in no view whatever implicated any citizen of the U. States, but which pretty clearly showed the vessel was a slaver, that she was then owned by Brazilians, belonged to the port of Bahia, and was captured within the maritime jursidiction of Brazil. He further showed me a letter from Mr. França making reclamation of the vessel, and admitted that under his instructions from the British Govt. he would be obliged to give her up. Since then Mr. Gordon has addressed to me two letters, of which the inclosed "C" & "D" are copies. Mr. Hamilton promised to obtain all the further information he could and to communicate it as soon as it was received by him. During my interview with him, I took occasion, in a becoming way, to endeavor to impress upon him the conviction that the attempt on the part of Great Britain to subject our vessels to her acts of visit or search, was among other causes an obstacle to the successful suppression of the African slave trade.   The U. States never could so [*one word canceled and* "cordially" *interlined*] and efficiently cooperate in the benevolent work of arresting that odious traffic, so long as there was a pretence even of the right to search their vessels.   The jealousy with which they would guard their rights of free navigation and commerce would naturally and inevitably, to some extent, cover and protect illicit trade.   That if the British Govt. would waive all claim to this right of search of U. States vessels; and would no longer pay bounties of so many pounds sterling per capita for every recaptured African to the officers of her cruisers and thereby remove from them the temptation to encourage actually the shipping of the slaves on the coast of Africa in order that they may win the reward of their capture on the high seas, which they are accused of doing; and if the British Govt. would cease itself to partake in some sense of the slave trade by carrying every captured slave into her colonies—at Demerara and other places—to bind them out for a limited period of servitude, instead of restoring them to some African colony, there to be taught the arts of civilized life in manual labor or other schools, and thence to be dispersed throughout Africa for its improvement; the attempts to suppress the slave trade would prove much more successful, and the roots of the evil would soon be reached in Africa herself where they take their growth.   I urged that moral means were much preferable to physical force, and referred him to the confirmation of these views in the lately expressed opinions of the Earl of Clarendon in the British Parliament.   His only reply was that his Govt. had changed its place of operation by withdrawing nearly all its force from the South American coast and transferring it to the Eastern and Western shores of Africa, as explained lately by the Earl of Aberdeen in the House of Lords.   This terminated our conversation, and I avoided adding what I am sure of, that this transfer of force means nothing more and will result in nothing less than the destruction of all, except British, trade with Africa, and in a necessity for increased vigilance on the part of the U. States for the protection of their vessels and crews in all the East.   I submit, whether under our treaty with England, some inquiry should not be made which will elicit information as to her mode of enslaving captured Africans in her colonies.   Is it not in fact a part of the slave-trade to take them away from their own country without their consent, to bind them out under a system of apprenticeship? Are proper steps taken to guard their *identity* and to prevent them from being enslaved for life? If they may be lawfully held in bondage for a term of 5 or 10 years, why not 50 or 100 years or any period beyond the duration of human life? It is openly avowed here, from various quarters, that many of these apprentices, after being bound out, are reported to be *dead* by their masters, their names are changed and flesh marks taken out, and they are transformed into slaves for life. Has England, under her treaties with and pledges to the world, a right to carry on a system like this, which leads to the direct encouragement of the trade she professes to suppress, and which, by fraud and cruelty, increases its horrors, inhumanities & crimes? But this is for me merely to suggest.

In all that I have said and done respecting any and all of these subjects, I have looked alone to the honor and interests of my country, and ask for nothing more than the approval of my own conscience and of the authorities appointed over me. With the highest consideration and respect, I am, Sir, Your obedient Servant, Henry A. Wise.

ALS with Ens in DNA, RG 59 (State Department), Diplomatic Despatches, Brazil, vol. 13 (M-121:15), received 12/9; FC (No. 5) in DNA, RG 84 (Foreign Posts), Brazil, Despatches, 11:87–92; autograph draft in Henry A. Wise Papers, Eastern Shore of Virginia Historical Society, Onancock, Va. (microfilm in NcU and ViHi); CCEx's with En in DNA, RG 84 (Foreign Posts), Great Britain, Instructions, 8:565–569; CCEx in DNA, RG 233 (U.S. House of Representatives), 28A-E1; PEx with Ens in House Document No. 148, 28th Cong., 2nd Sess., pp. 3–39; PEx with En in Senate Document No. 300, 29th Cong., 1st Sess., pp. 39–41.

From HENRY A. WISE

Legation of the United States
Rio de Janeiro, October 11th, 1844
Sir, Accompanying this despatch is a receipt, marked No. 1, for the records, papers, and effects belonging to this Legation, made after a careful examination and after having them cleaned and put in order. Mr. [Robert M.] Walsh will describe as well as he can hereafter the deficiencies of the records; and I trust that they will, if possible, be supplied by the Department, and I beg that the missing volumes of books and those wanting from the last dates may be sent on. Nothing can be of more importance to a minister, either for information, or for facilitating the business of his office than to have full and complete

records to which he may turn and see what has been done or proposed before his own time. The archives are still more valuable for the great purposes of history. A mission addresses itself to and is addressed by at least two Governments, and it treats of facts and principles of the highest concern which in part guide and govern their conduct and destiny and which illustrate their relations. Nothing can be more unworthy of a great nation than to be careless of its records, and I repeat that nothing of the kind could be more disgraceful than the condition of those of this Legation when they came into my hands. They were wholly neglected, were never completed, were partially destroyed and all more or less injured. This climate, it is true, is very damp and moulds every thing very soon, and generates the white ant which in a single night, I am told, destroys hundreds of dollars worth of property. Great care must therefore be taken to air and dust the books and papers, and I shall not hesitate to pay out of the contingent fund the necessary hire of servants to have this done.

Soon after my arrival here Mr. [Alexander] Thomson, the U.S. Consul at Maranham, addressed to me a correspondence with the Vice President of the Province touching the remission of a Provincial tax on cigars and tobacco imported from the U. States since 1837. I saw the Secretary of State in person on this subject and have since addressed to him an argument in full, in reply to the Vice President's views, but have not as yet received a reply.

No. 2 is a copy of a letter from me to Mr. [Lemuel] Wells, our Consul at St. Catherine's. I send it for your inspection because it assumes, as I considered it my duty, to disapprove of certain complaints which he has been pressing upon the Vice President of that Province, and upon the Imperial Govt. here through Mr. [George H.] Proffit, and which he seeks to urge still further through me. It seems that for some mere private business claim—the right or wrong of which the tribunals of justice ought to decide—an Englishman named Wilson, publickly insulted him. He complained to the Vice President, and insisted that Wilson should be ordered to quit the Province. The Vice President referred him for redress to the Municipal Authorities, and required of them to protect Mr. Wells. They reported that they had offered to do all in their power, to exact surety to keep the peace from Wilson, and to hear any complaints of actual injury done to Mr. Wells. He refused to appear before them, and wrote to our Minister here complaining that no redress was afforded him for this insult, and that a small Provincial tax was levied upon him as a retail dealer, against the letter and spirit of our treaty with Brazil, and intimating that the U. States did not protect their officers or citizens. I refused to present the complaint respecting the personal insult. The matter of the tax I presented to Mr. [Ernesto Ferreira] França, who seemed willing to do all in his power to have it remitted. The difficulty is that Mr. Wells suffered a judgment by default to be entered against him in a court of Law, under the impression that he as Consul was not compellable to plead before that tribunal, without distinguishing his character as Consul from his private character of merchant and trader. The case is submitted to legal advice by the Minister of State.

Just as Mr. Proffit was about leaving for home, he procured from the Emperor the revocation of the appointment of a Brazilian citizen named Souto as Vice Consul of the U.S. at Victoria for the Province of Espirito Santo, but no publication was made of the decree. This man, it seems, is a very prince of slave-dealers, and has actually, since the date of the revocation of his commission on the 3d August, been using his pretended office under the U. States for the purpose of aiding and abetting the Slave-trade. He was appointed many years ago by our former Chargé here, Mr. [John M.] Baker. I addressed the Secretary of State two communications and have obtained the publication of the orders revoking his appointment, with a decree notifying the Vice President of the Province and all others that he is no longer to be accredited as an officer or agent of the U. States in any character whatever.

I send an abstract of my account with the Govt. up to the 16th of the present month. Hereafter I shall draw on the Messrs. Baring Brothers & Co. or bills payable in the U. States, for the balances as stated. I have heretofore explained that the draft for $3000 was sold here before the power to draw on London came to hand.

Inclosed is the "Jornal do Commercio" of the 21st Sept[embe]r containing the first publication here of the audiences of Mr. Proffit and myself on the 8th of August.

Several weeks ago, it was communicated to me that a few days previously to the 15th of Sept[embe]r when Capt[ai]n [Philip F.] Voorhe[e]s sailed for the La Plata, the English Commodore [John B.] Purvis requested him (Capt[ai]n V.) to take sundry stores to the English squadron at Monte-Video, assigning as a reason for not sending them by the English ship America, Capt[ai]n Gordon, which had lately sailed from this port, that it was desirable she should not stop or be delayed on her passage around the Cape Horn, as that ship was to join the English squadron in the Pacific as soon as possible, in the expectation that a treaty would be concluded immediately between England & Mexico whereby the latter was to cede to the former the Country of California. Certain it is that Capt[ai]n Voorhe[e]s took the stores, and Mr. [Hamilton] Hamilton expressed his acknowledgments of the kindness to my Secretary, Mr. Walsh. But hearing that Capt[ai]n Voorhe[e]s had himself written home what was said to him by Commodore Purvis, and not trusting to the truth or probability of what thus carelessly fell from that high functionary, I have omitted until now the mention of the circumstance of this rumor. I should not, however, be surprised if, notwithstanding England's horror of the cession by Texas, she should make it the pretext of a cession by Mexico.

Every thing here is at a pause awaiting the result of the pending elections. The last assembly was suddenly dissolved by the Emperor [Pedro II], and a new Ministry, that now in, was singularly enough appointed, as it is said, favorable to a spirit of revolt even which had manifested itself in various quarters against the policy of their predecessors. The present Ministry will retire or not as the elections turn favorably or unfavorably to them. This shows some advance in the power of popular representation. The Provinces near the seat of the Imperial Govt. will probably go decidedly for Ministers; those more remote are doubtful and it will be some time before they are heard from.

There are no developments as yet of a disposition on the part of Brazil to open new negotiations with any of the Powers. No intimations have been given me, except that it will be impossible for England ever to obtain another treaty so favorable as the last, and all nations will probably be placed upon an equal footing. The U. States, at all events, have no reason whatever to apprehend any injustice from Brazil. With the highest regard and esteem, I have the honor to be, Your obedient Servant, Henry A. Wise.

ALS with Ens in DNA, RG 59 (State Department), Diplomatic Despatches, Brazil, vol. 13 (M-121:15), received 12/9; FC (No. 6) with En in DNA, RG 84 (Foreign Posts), Brazil, Despatches, 11:93–104.

From ROBERT B. CAMPBELL

Consulate of the United States of America, Havana
Oct. 12, 1844

Sir, I have the honor to enclose you copies of a communications [*sic*] addressed me by Mr. Thomas Savage, whose arrest & long imprisonment have been mentioned in former communications to the Department. I have the honor to be with great respect & esteem y[ou]r most ob[edien]t Ser[van]t, Robert B. Campbell.

LS with Ens in DNA, RG 59 (State Department), Consular Despatches, Havana, vol. 19 (T-20:19), received 11/15. NOTE: Campbell enclosed copies of a letter dated 9/16 and of an appended statement by Savage describing his arrest on 5/23 for alleged complicity in the slave insurrection at Cardenas. Savage was an engineer on the plantation called "Casualidad" and had been named as a conspirator by a slave Ambrosio Garcia while the latter was under torture. In the statement Savage described his arrest, imprisonment, and interrogation by Cuban authorities at Matanzas.

R[ichard] K. Crallé to J[ames] C. Pickett, [Lima], 10/12. "Mr. J[ohn] A. Bryan having been appointed Chargé d'Affaires of the United States to the Republic of Peru, you will transfer to him the books and papers of the Legation. Herewith are enclosed a sealed letter [dated 8/24] to the Minister for Foreign Affairs announcing your intended departure from Peru and an open copy of the same." FC (No. 23) in DNA, RG 59 (State Department), Diplomatic Instructions, Peru, 15:37 (M-77:130).

From [NATHANIEL] B[EVERLEY] TUCKER

Williamsburg Va., Oct. 12, 1844

I can hardly flatter myself that Mr. Calhoun will pardon the liberty I take in addressing him. But, if I have not been misinformed, the subject of this letter will be accepted as an apology for my intrusion.

I have been assured that Mr. Calhoun has been pleased to take a considerable interest in my unfortunate friend & neighbour Dr. Thomas Griffin Peachy. If this be so, that feeling will be much increased by this communication. Dr. P[eachy]'s misfortunes have been brought on him in part by causes he could not control, and in part by a magnanimous resolve to abandon himself to the best interests of his Children. He has five Sons; and when he saw the alternative of preserving his own independence at the expense of their education, or cultivating their minds to the utmost, tho' by doing this he should not only send them pennyless into the world; but perhaps reduce himself to want, he nobly chose the latter. I believe Mr. Calhoun knows his second Son who resides in Georgetown. If so, he has seen that good seed has been sown in good ground. I trust it will produce bountifully. But as yet it produces nothing but the means of bare subsistence, and affords nothing from which aid to the father can be given. The oldest Son is prosperous—not rich, but making money & quite able to assist in the education of the younger. I believe he had the disposition to do this; but he has married a wicked woman who has, with great art, and yet greater audacity, effected such a breach as to make it impossible that any aid can come from that quarter. It would be impertinent to give particulars: and I beg Mr. C[alhoun] to believe my assurance, founded on the most intimate knowledge, that Dr. P[eachy] and his family are not only blameless in the affair, but up to the last moment lavished on this woman every manifestation of kindness, until she, deliberately and of premeditated purpose, left their house, which was her home, under circumstances of outrage, such as would make it impossible for a man of proud spirit to accept bread from her hand, if he was starving. It is but just to the young man to say that in this he has been the reluctant instrument of an imperious and artful woman. But she has moulded him to her purpose, and he can now only lament what his acquiescence in her dictation has made irreparable.

The Doctor's situation is now one of destitution. He has no property. The house he lives in has been conveyed to his creditors and may be sold tomorrow. He is too old to push his fortune on a new theatre; and the profits of the profession in this place, divided among four, are not more than enough to afford a handsome practice to one. Ill health in his youth prevented him from contending successfully for a fair share of it, and he is now too old to hope to succeed. He has still with him three Sons. The oldest a well educated youth of 21 would fill with fidelity and ability any of those stations in which young men are commonly placed. I have known him from his childhood, and vouch for him as an amiable honourable upright man of the steadiest habits and of good education. His name is John Blair Peachy. Any post which would afford him a bare subsistence, and the means of supplying something to his mother would be accepted with gratitude. He has had Mr. [John] Tyler's *volunteer* promise. But all Mr. T[yler]'s promises are alike.

The other two boys are at [William and Mary] College here. One of them is a lad of the highest promise, and if the rest of the family can be in any way provided for, I will charge myself with his education. The other might accompany his father abroad, if any of the hopes held out to him are to be realized. I should then hope that the mother, with her two lovely little daughters (nine and three years old) might live in an humble way with her dutiful son in Georgetown, until his merit begins to reap its full reward.

I have been told that Mr. Calhoun was good enough to interest himself on behalf of Dr. P[eachy] for the consulship at Liverpool. It is understood that the two parasites to whom this has been offered have had wit enough to decline it. They were right. The Senate ought not to have confirmed them. Dr. P[eachy]'s is a different case. His character is too high to be assailed. As a politician he is a S[tate] R[ights] man, ardent and earnest but no partizan. If he were nominated, I have little doubt that he would be confirmed, and retained, whether by Clay or Polk. I hope, if it be true, as [has] been said, that Mr. Calhoun interests himself on behalf of Dr. P[eachy] he will do so the more earnestly because of this new and unexpected calamity. How Mr. Tyler might be affected by the knowledge of the same facts I am unable to guess. The constitution of his mind is one which I am happy to think I shall never be able to comprehend. It can certainly do no good to Dr. P[eachy] to name me to Mr. T[yler] in connexion with him. A magnanimous man may forgive an injury; but a vain man can never forgive the undissembled contempt with which I have treated Mr. T[yler] ever since he ["sacraf" *canceled*] sacrificed the opportunity of nobly serving his principles and his country, to the ridiculous hope of being made President of the U.S. by the people's choice.

Mr. Calhoun will see, in what I have just said, evidence that, however I may heretofore have differed from him on political questions, I can never regard him but with the highest respect. In this sentiment I remain, B. Tucker.

ALS in ScCleA.

J[uan] N. Almonte, [Mexican Minister to the U.S.], New York [City], to Richard K. Crallé, 10/14. Almonte acknowledges Crallé's letter of 10/7 [*sic*] with its enclosures concerning charges that two Mexican war steamers in New York harbor, the *Guadalupe* and the *Montezuma*, were acquiring munitions and cannon and enlisting seamen other than Mexicans. Almonte has found that the allegations were made by deserters from the two vessels and are not to be relied on. Enclosed is a letter of 9/8 from Pedro A. Diaz y Miron, Commander of the vessels, to Almonte, denying the charges. LS (in Spanish) with partial State Department translation, and En (in Spanish) with translation, in DNA, RG 59 (State Department), Notes from Foreign Legations, Mexico, vol. 4 (M-54:2).

From ROBERT B. CAMPBELL

Consulate of the United States of America
Havana, Oct. 14, 1844

Sir, By the public Journals forwarded by this Consulate, you will have seen that all duties for six months have been taken off the articles of rice, corn, corn-meal, lumber, potatoes &c. In this condition of things, I would respectfully suggest that the discriminating tonnage duties between Spanish & American Vessels in the Ports of the United States, where the former are loading with free articles for this Island be removed for the space of time in which they are admitted free from duty. Such a modification would not injuriously affect our navigating interest, nor benefit that of Spain, for it is doubted if any Spanish Vessel would enter into the trade. The effect however might be beneficial as evidencing on the part of the United States a disposition of reciprocity in the removal of commercial restrictions. Not that the authorities here in the present instance have been prompted in their action by aught, but the necessities of the Island. They are however disposed to lessen duties generally on American products so far as, the Intendente and his Council feel authorised.

In the article of flour in which our Western States are so vitally interested, I have endeavoured in conversation to impress upon them the importance to the Island of more moderate duties and have discovered a favorable disposition. My suggestion in relation to the tonnage duty is made with a view to this great interest, the extent & importance of which needs no comment from me. I cannot however promise that the adoption of my recommendation will ensure a modification of the present onerous duty upon flour, but am satisfied the effect would be to strengthen the parties interesting themselves to bring about a reduction.

In the various accounts you will see of loss & destruction by the late gale, you must receive them as all other reports from this Island, magnified at *least* tenfold. The loss will be in Coffee & plantains in all else comparatively trifling so far as the Island is concerned. I have the honor to be with great respect & esteem y[ou]r mo[st] ob[edien]t Ser[van]t, Robert B. Campbell.

LS in DNA, RG 59 (State Department), Consular Despatches, Havana, vol. 19 (T-20:19), received 11/12.

To George W. Houk, [Dayton, Ohio], "Private"

Fort Hill, 14th Oct[obe]r 1844

Dear Sir: Your letter of the 1st ins[tan]t followed me from Washington to my residence here, where I am on a short visit.

It is a great mistake, either way, both North and West, that South Carolina is hostile to the Union. There is not a member of our Union more devoted to it than she is; I mean the Federal Union, as it came from the hands of its framers. But she believes that the Union may be destroyed as well by consolidation as by despotism [*sic*; dissolution?]; and that of the two, there is much more danger of the former than the latter. And, hence it is, that while other States look with indifference for the most part at the tendency of the system to consolidation, she regards it with the veriest jealousy as the exposed point, and one that ought to be guarded with the greatest care. According to her creed consolidation must necessarily lead in succession to injustice, oppression, fraud, corruption, violence, anarchy and despotism; and her efforts, accordingly, have been directed to averting these and not to dissolving the Union. And hence her devotion to State rights, which she regards as the only effectual means of averting them, and saving both liberty and Union. She considers those who advocate doctrines and measures tending to consolidation as the most dangerous enemies to both.

If she has taken high ground on the question of admitting Texas into the Union it is not because she has any pecuniary interest whatever in her annexation. On the contrary, she clearly sees that it must act as a powerful drain both on her population and capital; but sees, also, that it is necessary for the safety of the West and South, while it is calculated to advance the interest and prosperity of the North and East. Thus regarding it, she cannot but see that the ground on which annexation is opposed by leading Whigs in the latter sections implies not only a total indifference, but deep hostility to the South and its domestic institutions, a hostility unless resisted and put down destructive of the great object for which the Union was formed—the mutual safety and protection of the members composing it. It is this view of the subject which has given utterance to the strong expressions of some of our people, which has been construed as evidence of the hostility of the State to the Union by those whose acts and declarations clearly prove them to be wholly indifferent to it, except as an instrument of plunder and oppression. What I have written is intended exclusively for yourself.

PC in Jameson, ed., *Correspondence*, pp. 624–625; variant PEx in G.P. Thruston, "Autograph Collections and Historic Manuscripts," *Sewanee Review*, vol. X, no. 1 (January, 1902), p. 33.

To J[OHN] R. MATHEW[E]S, Clark[e]sville, Ga.

Fort Hill, 14th Oct[obe]r 1844

My dear Sir, My stay will be so short, & I have so much to attend to before I leave home to return to Washington, that it will not be in my power to visit Lumpkin [County, Ga.]. I expect to return early in Nov., & hope I may have an opportunity of seeing you on my way in Charleston. I have much that I would be glad to say to you.

I am happy to infer from what you write & what I hear, that Georgia is lost to the whigs. It is a most important point; and forebodes the certain downfall of [Henry] Clay. His defeat, and the overthrow of Mr. [Martin] V[an] B[uren] & his wing of the party by the Baltimore Convention, I regard as a great political revolution. They give us much to hope. No two men have done more to bring & keep the party & the country in their present condition, than Clay & Mr. V[an] Buren. If the former is the author of that system of plunder, which has oppressed the South & corrupted the North, the latter has perpetuated it & fixed it on the country. Had it not been for him & his immediate friends, it would have been prostrated in 1828 & 1842. Yours truly & sincerely, J.C. Calhoun.

ALS in DLC, John C. Calhoun Papers.

From John Bartlett Saunders, New Orleans, 10/14. Saunders requests a passport to visit Havana and Mexico in his search for a treatment for leprosy. A graduate of the Medical College of S.C., he gives his physical description and encloses a label from a bottle of Saunders' No. 1 Compound Syrup of Stillingia. (Clerks' EU's read "Rec[eive]d Oct. 24" and "Sent to Coll[ecto]r N. Orleans.") ALS with En in DNA, RG 59 (State Department), Passport Applications, 1795–1905, vol. 33, no. 2591 (M-1372:15).

R[ichard] K. Crallé to Th[omas] Jefferson Sutherland, New York [City], 10/14. Crallé encloses, in answer to Sutherland's letter of 10/4 and its enclosure, a list of American prisoners in the British penal colony at Van Diemen's Land, imprisoned for participating in "political disturbances in Canada in 1838, of whose pardon notice has reached this Department." For information on obtaining the release of those Americans still imprisoned there, Crallé refers Sutherland to the Washington *Madisonian* of 2/28/1844. FC in DNA, RG 59 (State Department), Domestic Letters, 34:412 (M-40:32).

From ROBERT WALSH

Paris, 14th October 1844

Sir, Within even the short period of my experience as Consul of the United States for this capital, I have become much more strongly impressed with the necessity of a full collection of the laws of the Union & the several States, and of American commercial regulations of every description, towards ["and" *altered to* "an"] adequate and creditable performance of the duties of the office. No such library has ever been formed here; the materials are few, imperfect and scattered. Questions, proper in themselves, are constantly propounded by Frenchmen and strangers having business professional or casual, which cannot be answered with precision and confidence and which we cannot set aside without loss of repute. The ability to satisfy reasonable consultation is essential to the Consulate, and common to all the other Consular bureaux. I am making efforts to obtain similar sources of information, British & continental, for the service of my countrymen, whose affairs require frequent and intelligent reference to them. The Departments of Commerce and the Navy offer whatever volumes and documents they may issue; the same liberality may be expected from the other branches of the administration, & from the two Chambers whose Reports & bills possess, in general, instructive value.

An appeal is ventured to your patriotic and enlightened spirit for assistance in the object mentioned above. A card or request from the office in this capital, might be addressed in your official journal, to the authorities of the States and Territories, with a view to the transmission to your Department, of Laws and Digests which some one of your functionaries could cause to be sent to the Legation in Paris, for the Consulate. The destitution in which we are, of these means, and the urgency of possessing them, embolden me to trouble you with such suggestions, and have prompted me to apply, for like aid, to some of my acquaintanc[es] in the cities of Boston, New York and Philadelphia, whose stations or pursuits qualify them to assist me by selection or indication.

I would take the liberty of adding that it might be well to assign a column or division in the official paper for such commercial & statistical information as I could regularly supply, & to direct the journal to be furnished to this bureau, where it may be often useful to meet enquiries about acts of the American government. All American Custom-house regulations and formulas are particularly desirable. I have the honor to be, Sir, Your very respectful & ob[edien]t Servant, Robert Walsh.

ALS (No. 2) in DNA, RG 59 (State Department), Consular Despatches, Paris, vol. 9 (T-1:9).

W[illia]m Wilkins, [Secretary of War], to R[ichard] K. Crallé, 10/14. In answer to a letter of 10/5 from Albert Smith, referred by Crallé to the War Department, in which transportation is requested for those engaged in the Northeastern boundary survey, Wilkins encloses a copy of an earlier order that granted transportation to the site but stipulated that no other transportation would be furnished. LS with En in DNA, RG 59 (State Department), Miscellaneous Letters (M-179:105, frames 516–517).

From J[OSEPH] BALESTIER

Consulate of the United States
Singapore, 15 Oct. 1844

Sir, I have the honor to wait on you with dupl[icate] of my letter of the 1 November 1843 calling your attention to the injury done to our commerce by the Revenue act of August 1842 laying heavy duties on Tea & Coffee imported into the United States from other than the place of growth.

Since the date of my former communication many American vessels have touched here, but although they found abundance of teas of suitable descriptions for our home trade, & at two thirds the Canton prices, and also plenty of Coffee from the adjacent native states, still these ships left the Port, with their original home cargoes which might have been bartered[?] to advantage, leaving the trade in the hands of other nations. I have the honor to be Sir, Your most Ob[edient] S[ervant], J. Balestier, U.S. Consul.

ALS (No. 64) with En in DNA, RG 59 (State Department), Consular Despatches, Singapore, vol. 1 (M-464:1, frame 350), received 2/28/[1845].

From EDWARD EVERETT

London, 15 October 1844

Sir, In the box of books forwarded to the Department by the "Great Western" on the 12th instant, will have been found a copy of the correspondence of this Government with Foreign Powers and its own Representatives abroad, for the year 1843 on the subject of the suppression of the Slave Trade. The correspondence of the former years has been annually sent to me but I have retained it in the office for reference in the course of my official intercourse with this Government. Thinking however that it might be convenient for the department to have access to these papers, I transmitted the portion last received by the "Great Western," proposing to send the preceding volumes by an early opportunity.

On casually examining the list of papers for the year 1843 under the head of "the United States," I was surprised to see the term "mis-statement" applied to the President's Message to Congress of December 1842 in a manner which I deemed gratuitous and offensive. Supposing the "list of papers" or index, in which the use of the term occurs, to be the work of some subordinate person employed in the Foreign Office, I should not have deemed it a proper subject of notice on my part, had it not appeared in a parliamentary document officially communicated to me by Lord Aberdeen, in the note which accompanies this despatch.

Such however being the case, I have felt that it ought not to pass without remark; and I have accordingly addressed a note to Lord Aberdeen on the subject, a copy of which is herewith transmitted. I am, Sir, with great respect, Your obedient Servant, Edward Everett.

Transmitted with despatch Nro. 192.

1. The Earl of Aberdeen to Mr. Everett 27th August 1844.
2. Mr. Everett to the Earl of Aberdeen, 15 October 1844.

LS (No. 192) with Ens in DNA, RG 59 (State Department), Diplomatic Despatches, Great Britain, vol. 53 (M-30:49), received 11/6; FC in DNA, RG 84 (Foreign Posts), Great Britain, Despatches, 9:5–7; FC in MHi, Edward Everett Papers, 50:141–142 (published microfilm, reel 23, frames 339–340).

Rich[ar]d K. Crallé to ALLEN A. HALL, [Caracas]

Department of State
Washington, 15th October, 1844

Sir: Mr. Vespasian Ellis having been appointed Chargé d'Affaires of the United States to the Republic of Venezuela, you will deliver to him the books and papers of the Legation of the United States at Caracas. A sealed letter [dated 10/15] to the Minister for Foreign Affairs of that Republic [Juan Manuel Manrique] announcing your intended departure, and an open copy of the same, are herewith transmitted. I am, Sir, your obedient servant, Richd. K. Crallé, Acting Secretary.

LS (No. 22) with En in DNA, RG 84 (Foreign Posts), Venezuela; FC in DNA, RG 59 (State Department), Diplomatic Instructions, Venezuela, 1:49–50 (M-77: 171).

O[GDEN] HOFFMAN to R[ichard] K. Crallé

U.S. Attorney[']s Office
New York [City], October [*ca.* 15,] 1844

Sir, My attention has been directed, to the affidavits, which I have had the honor to transmit to the Department, in relation to the Mexican Steamers.

The Deponents Martin Tosney, Frederick Booth, and Henry Cook, were furnished and brought to my office, by Mr. [Alanson] Nash, a Lawyer of this City, to whom I referred in my communication of the 23d of September last. The Deponents Solomon Muling [*sic*] and Benjamin Miller, were brought to my office, by Mr. Smith, a Deputy Marshal, whom I had employed, for the purpose of watching those vessels, and obtaining evidence of their movements. It appears from the depositions, that most of the Deponents, had been at one time, serving on board the Steamers, but whether they are Deserters, from said vessels, or whether their allegations, that the time for which they shipped, had expired, is [*sic*] true, I have no evidence of, beyond what their own depositions afford. The deposition[s] of Benjamin Miller and Solomon Muling are, if true, conclusive as to the fact, that illegal shipments have been made, but there certainly is, "a strange discrepancy" between their depositions, and the statements of the Mexican Officers. On the 11th inst. I addressed a letter to Capt. [Silas

H.] Stringham, a copy of which, together with his reply, I have the honor to inclose. You will perceive, that I have made every exertion, to ascertain from competent testimony, the truth of the case, but so far, my exertions, have been attended with no success, beyond what may be found in the depositions, already transmitted to you. If the law has been violated by these Steamers, it has been done, with so much secrecy, as to defy conclusive proof, or it may be, that the statements of the Mexican Officers are true, and that the adverse allegations, are the offspring of private grief, on the part of their accusers. I shall however continue my endeavours to establish the truth. I have the honor to be, Very Respectfully, Your obed[ien]t Serv[an]t, O. Hoffman, U.S. Attorney.

LS with Ens in DNA, RG 59 (State Department), Miscellaneous Letters (M-179:105, frames 455–459). Note: In his letter of 10/11 Hoffman requested Stringham's assistance to ascertain whether any laws were violated in the refitting of the Mexican steamers. Stringham, Commander of the New York Navy Yard, replied on 10/12 that he knew of no increase of the steamers' armaments and that, from his knowledge, all Americans who had worked on the vessels had been discharged.

R[ichard] K. Crallé, Acting Secretary [of State], to [Juan Manuel Manrique], Venezuelan Minister for Foreign Affairs, 10/15. Crallé informs Manrique of the impending return of Allen A. Hall, former U.S. Chargé d'Affaires to Venezuela, to the United States. Hall has been directed to take leave of the Venezuelan government with an expression of the U.S. desire to maintain and promote the present good relations between the two countries. CC in DNA, RG 84 (Foreign Posts), Venezuela.

From W[illia]m Wilkins, Secretary of War, 10/15. He transmits a copy of an order issued today [to Maj. James D. Graham] "for the relief of the detachment of the Army serving with the commission on the North Eastern boundary." LS with En in DNA, RG 59 (State Department), Miscellaneous Letters (M-179:105, frames 514–515); FC in DNA, RG 107 (Secretary of War), Letters Sent Relating to Military Affairs, 1800–1861, 25:398 (M-6:25).

OCTOBER 16–31, 1844

◫

Calhoun was at Fort Hill and at work on the plantation. He thus had to delay until his return to Washington next month dealing with such matters of official business as the arrival of a Russian Minister and the first reports reaching the United States of troublesome incidents off the coast of South America in late September. Capt. Philip F. Voorhees, United States Navy, had made a summary response to the difficulties created for American neutral commerce by the Argentinian blockade of Montevideo. Provoked by Argentinian firing on an American ship, he had captured the entire Argentine blockading squadron.

The Calhouns' only son-in-law, Thomas G. Clemson, was digging into his new official duties as U.S. Chargé d'Affaires in Belgium. But doubtless it was the unofficial letters written by Clemson that interested Calhoun most. These brought him into as close contact as he was ever to experience with the fascinations of Europe. Thomas Clemson told Calhoun, among much else, of his grandson, John Calhoun Clemson: "The little fellow speaks of you often." And Anna Maria Calhoun Clemson wrote of the care she had exercised and the difficulty she had experienced in finding a suitable present to send her father from the Continent: "For Mother & Sister there were a thousand things one might send but you are a man so utterly without fancies that it is hard to know what would suit you."

As to politics, with an election drawing near its climax, Calhoun wrote to a Northern friend: "I agree with you, that Democracy must give up its trim[m]ing & place itself on principles to save itself from distraction." The Democrats' departure from their original and true principles had raised the Whigs to power. Nothing else could save the Democracy but a "return to its original policy & purity."

The new American Minister to Mexico, Wilson Shannon, wrote on October 28 his first extended report of the tangled affairs of that country and its relationship with the United States. There was little room for optimism about any aspect of the relationship. But the key sentence of Shannon's report was this: "There is no room to doubt that Mexico some time since determined to renew the war against

Texas and immediately commenced extensive preparations for that purpose." Of course, between the purpose and its implementation, there yet remained some space.

Ⅲ

Vespasian Ellis, Baltimore, to President [John] Tyler, 10/16. Ellis seeks the appointment of his son, Joseph C.C. Ellis, as U.S. Consul at Maracaibo. The younger Ellis stands high in the legal profession in Missouri and "is an *original Tyler man*, but can't go for Polk." ALS in ScCleA.

From WASHINGTON IRVING, [U.S. Minister to Spain]

Paris, October 16th 1844

Sir, I have duly received your despatches enclosing ["the" *canceled*] copies of ["the" *interlined*] letters from the department of State to our Ministers at Paris and Mexico [William R. King and Wilson Shannon] on the subject of Texas. I have read those two important documents with deep attention and with no common interest, and shall bear them in mind in any communications I may have to make or any conversations I may have to hold, in regard to the topics and views contained in them, in my diplomatic capacity.

In recent conversations with Mr. [Ashbel] Smith the Texian Chargé d'Affaires at the Court of France he assured me that he considered all likelihood of annexation at an end, and that the hope of it was generally given up in Texas. That they felt they would have to act for themselves, and rely upon themselves as an independent power, and that, under this conviction, instructions had been given him by his Government to ascertain whether there was a probability of opening diplomatic relations with the Spanish government, and establishing a direct and unembarrassed trade between Texas and the Island of Cuba. He wanted to know my opinion in the matter. I did not hold out any very encouraging prospects to him, in the present agitated state of Spain and the precarious situation of its government: indeed, I considered his whole conversation on the subject as intended

91

merely to draw out my own views and feelings on the question of annexation. I cannot persuade myself that the Texians consider the case hopeless, seeing the encreasing popularity of the question in the United States.

I have had conversations also with Mr. [Adolphe] Jollivet, member of the Chamber of Deputies and delegate for the Island of Martinique; who is earnestly prosecuting the scheme of organizing a coalition between the French and Spanish colonies, Brazil and the Southern parts of the United States to protect themselves from the Abolition intrigues and machinations of England. He finds much difficulty to contend with in France, several of the leading papers such as the Journal des Debats, the Presse, the Constitutionnel &c being, as he says, in the pay of Anti slavery societies in England or under the influence of British Diplomacy. He is endeavoring to interest the Spanish government in the subject, and to that effect has just written a letter to Mr. [Francisco] Martinez de la Rosa, who, while Ambassador at Paris, professed himself favorable to the measure. I have promised to take a copy of his letter and have it, safely delivered into the hands of Martinez de la Rosa.

I believe the actual government of Spain is very distrustful of the policy of England with respect to their West India possessions, and would gladly concur in any measure to counteract it; but should the progresista party come into power and the Esparterists once more have sway, the English influence would revive and might be detrimental to the colonial interests. England is endeavoring to regain the footing she has lost in Spain; and the good offices, such as they were, rendered by her Minister Mr. [William Henry L.E.] Bulwer in aiding to settle the difficulties between Spain and Marocco, are constantly placed in the strongest light to catch the public eye.

I have not numbered this letter as I do not intend it as a regular despatch. I regret that I have to date it from Paris having expected, before this time to have been at my post at Madrid. In availing myself of the two months leave of absence kindly granted me by the President, I extended my tour of health to England to pass some little time with a sister, now advanced in years, from whom I have long been separated, and who, of late has suffered from a dangerous illness. After a visit of about three weeks I set out on my return, but had an attack of bile in Paris which brought on a temporary return of my herpetic malady; ["which" *canceled*] and obliged me to have recourse to mineral baths. I am now nearly recovered and trust in the course of a few days to be able to resume my journey to Madrid.

I have felt it proper to make this explanation of my delay in returning to my post; lest the President should think I was heedlessly exceeding ["the term of" *canceled*] my leave of absence, or was availing myself of his indulgence for purposes of personal gratification. I am Sir, very respectfully your ob[edien]t Serv[an]t, Washington Irving.

ALS in DNA, RG 59 (State Department), Diplomatic Despatches, Spain, vol. 34 (M-31:34), received 11/6; PC in Aderman et al., eds., *Complete Works of Washington Irving, Letters*, 3:822–824.

From Anson Jones, Department of State, Washington, [Republic of Texas], 10/16. James Reily has been appointed Minister "from this Government to the Government of the United States" and should receive credence as such. [These credentials were never delivered to Calhoun.] LS in Tx, Records of the Texas Republic Department of State, U.S. Diplomatic Correspondence.

Charles A. Leas, Baltimore, to John Tyler, 10/16. Leas resigns his appointment as U.S. Consul at Maracaibo because he feels that he can be more useful in the U.S. ALS in DNA, RG 59 (State Department), Consular Despatches, Maracaibo, vol. 2 (T-62:2).

From J[ohn] Y. Mason, Navy Department, 10/16. Mason replies to Calhoun's letter of 8/2 enclosing a letter from C. F[rederick] Hagedorn, Bavarian Consul at Philadelphia. Hagedorn seeks information relating to canal steam navigation, particularly [William W.] Hunter's propellers. Because of limited contingent funds, Mason cannot comply with Hagedorn's request to make "drafts or drawings." LS in DNA, RG 59 (State Department), Miscellaneous Letters (M-179:105, frame 521); FC in DNA, RG 45 (Naval Records), Letters Sent by the Secretary of the Navy to the President and Executive Agencies, 5:41 (M-472:3, frame 62).

Richard K. Crallé to Stewart Newell, U.S. Consul, Sabine, 10/16. Newell's letters nos. 6 and 7 have been received. Gen. Duff Green has it fully within his power to appoint a temporary agent to transact the business of the Consulate at Galveston while he is away from his post. Therefore, Newell is instructed to turn over to E[lisha] A. Rhodes the records of the consular office at Galveston. FC in DNA, RG 59 (State Department), Consular Instructions, 11:286.

From T[HOMAS] W. ROBESON

Consulate of the United States
Santa Martha New Granada
16 October 1844

Sir, I regret to inform You that I have been put in the Hospital Prision of this City, by the Collector of the Customs, for my Bonds unpaid to the Amount of Three Thousand Seven hundred dollars. In order to prevent so harsh a measure being taken I tendered the Collector Debts, and Obligations, to the Amount of Thirteen thousand dollars, as Security. This he refused to receive, except to hold as my property taken in execution. These were handed him but without relieving me from Imprisonment.

I immediately wrote Mr. [William M.] Blackford on the subject and he was pleas'd to to [*sic*] see Mr. [Joaquin] Acosta Secretary of State who informed him that he would write the Governor of St. Martha to interfere in matter and have me released. The Governor on receipt of the Secretary[']s letter informed me that he had no power to interfere in my case unless they would send him positive instructions from Bogota. As the Post takes Forty days to perform the Journey there is not Yet sufficient time to have heard of the effect the Governor[']s Communication will have on the Executive. I solicited to be confined to my House until the affair could be arranged and Mr. Blackford has informed me that he would use his utmost exertions in my behalf. It was certainly a Very harsh Measure of the Collector and entirely uncall'd for.

I will advise you by the first opportunity of the result of Mr. Blackford['s] efforts. I have the honor to be Sir Your Obedient Servant, T.W. Robeson.

ALS (No. 49) in DNA, RG 59 (State Department), Consular Despatches, Santa Marta, vol. 1 (T-427:1), received 12/4.

R[ichard] K. Crallé to Albert Smith, Commissioner, Houlton, Maine, 10/16. "I have the honor to acknowledge the receipt of your letter of the 5th inst., and to inform you, in reply, that an order (copy of which is annexed) was yesterday issued from the War Department, for the relief of the detachment of the Army serving with the commission on the North Eastern Boundary." FC in DNA, RG 59 (State Department), Domestic Letters, 35:2 (M-40:33).

From Tho[ma]s G. Clemson, Brussels, 10/17. In a six-page letter, Clemson informs Calhoun that he arrived in Brussels on 10/4. The

Belgian government is anxious to obtain a reciprocal trade treaty with the U.S., Belgium offering to the U.S. an exclusive 40 per cent discount on duties paid on cotton, tobacco, and other imports in return for an equal exclusive discount on linen and wool cloths, both pure and mixed. Clemson describes briefly his audience with King Leopold. The absence of the U.S. Consul at Antwerp [Francis J. Grund] from his post is harmful to the interests of the U.S. Clemson acknowledges Calhoun's despatches No. 2, 3, 4, and 6, "the latter being a copy of a Despatch to Mr. [Wilson] Shan[n]on[,] our Minister to Mexico." Instructions are requested for the proper way to ship nine unbound volumes containing the "annual expositions of the different departments of Belgium," received from the Belgian government. ALS (No. 1) with Ens in DNA, RG 59 (State Department), Diplomatic Despatches, Belgium, vol. 3 (M-193:4), received 11/25; FC (in Clemson's hand, dated 10/21) in DNA, RG 84 (Foreign Posts), Belgium, Despatches, vol. 4; PEx in Holmes and Sherrill, *Thomas G. Clemson,* pp. 71–74.

From Edward Everett

London, 17th October 1844
Sir, I availed myself of the first opportunity of the return of Lord Aberdeen to town, to seek a conference with him, on the subject of your despatch Nro. 102 relative to the instructions to the Colonial governors, as to the course to be pursued toward vessels from the United States having slaves on board, driven by stress of weather or brought by a mutinous crew into British ports. I adverted to the conversation which we had upon the subject last winter, as reported in my despatch Nro. 90, and repeated a portion of what had then passed between us.

Lord Aberdeen had a distinct recollection of our conversation on that occasion, and informed me that he immediately mentioned the subject to Lord Stanley within whose province the matter in the first instance lies. Lord Aberdeen would not, at the moment, undertake distinctly to call to mind what Lord Stanley had said to him at the time; and he was not aware that the subject had since been mentioned between them. He was inclined to think that, the instructions, being addressed to the British authorities, and not of course drawn up with a design of their being communicated to us, it may not have been deemed advisable by Lord Stanley to furnish a copy of them for that purpose. Should this prove to be the case, he should certainly concur with Lord Stanley; but as far as he was concerned, without of course pledging himself to the production of a paper which he had not seen, he could not imagine, whatever the instructions may have been, that he should object to their being communicated to the United States.

It should be borne in mind, Lord Aberdeen added, that any instructions which may have been given being prospective, must be general in their character. It was impossible to lay down rules before hand which would be sure exactly to meet the circumstances of individual cases. These must be dealt with as they arise; no doubt on general principles, in reference to which Her Majesty's authorities must be exclusively governed by the provisions of the law of England. In applying these provisions, Lord Aberdeen said, that one uniform rule would be observed by them toward all Countries. No other course would be adopted toward vessels of the United States, arriving with Slaves in a British Colony, than would be followed toward a vessel of any other nation under similar circumstances. A case in point had not long since happened in the Levant. A Turkish vessel with Slaves on board had been driven by stress of weather into one of the Ionian islands. The Slaves were instantly liberated. The master of the vessel remonstrated but in vain. The owners made repeated application through the Turkish Ambassador at this Court for indemnity, which had been refused.

I alluded to the liberal character of the observations made by Lord Ashburton in his correspondence with Mr. [Daniel] Webster on this subject, to which you refer in the last paragraph but one of your despatch. Lord Aberdeen was aware of the character of those observations, and admitted that it was such as I described it.

On leaving Lord Aberdeen he promised me that he would immediately speak to Lord Stanley again about the instructions, and I left him in the expectation that I should hear from him on the subject very soon. I am, Sir, with great respect, Your obedient Servant, Edward Everett.

LS (No. 195) in DNA, RG 59 (State Department), Diplomatic Despatches, Great Britain, vol. 53 (M-30:49), received 11/6; FC in DNA, RG 84 (Foreign Posts), Great Britain, Despatches, 9:13–16; FC in MHi, Edward Everett Papers, 50:167–170 (published microfilm, reel 23, frames 352–354).

From J[AMES] HAMILTON, [JR.]

Savannah, Oct. 17[t]h 1844

My Dear Sir, On my arrival at this place I had the gratification to receive your kind favor. Drop me a line on what day you will be in Charleston on your way to Washington & I will endeavour to conform if possible my movements to yours so that if in the range of possibility we may enjoy the satisfaction of a personal interview before you go to the Seat of Govt.

I have requested [Barnard E.?] Bee to send you a corrected Copy of my Letter to [Daniel] Webster, which [John A.] Stuart from not correcting the proof allowed his printer[']s devil most dreadfully to bedevil. You see that it is designed for the New York elections & *for the Northern Market.* [Silas?] Wright [of N.Y.] writes me that he regards his State for [James K.] Polk entirely safe. I hope it may be so for I have very serious misgivings of the Presidential vote of Pen[n]syl[vania]. She is so deeply tainted with the Tariff heresy that she can scarcely maintain her democratic adhesion. The truth is if Polk could be elected without the assistance of one tariff vote I should deem it far more desirable than that he should owe ["the" *canceled*] his election to the friends of the restrictive system.

I have written to Polk since our triumph in this State—and have taken occasion with much delicacy to inform him how much he owes to the Zealous & untiring support of your friends ["every" *canceled and* "who" *interlined*] were every where in the Band[?].

Be so kind to address me immediately to Charleston & believe me with esteem—My Dear Sir—faithfully & respect[full]y Your friend, J. Hamilton.

P.S. I presume Doneldson [*sic*; Andrew J. Donelson] has accepted his mission? I hope to meet him there early in Dec.

ALS in ScCleA. NOTE: This letter was addressed to Calhoun, "now at Pendleton." An AEU by Calhoun reads "Gen[era]l Hamilton."

From Wylie W. Mason, Eatonton [Ga.], 10/17. He asks that Calhoun send him, if possible, a "condensed treatise" on the duties of U.S. diplomats. "It affords me much pleasure to congratulate you upon the cheering prospects of our cause in the South & throughout the Union & I can but indulge the pleasing hope that the reign of Federal[ist] misrule is destined soon to come to an end." ALS in DNA, RG 59 (State Department), Miscellaneous Letters (M-179:105, frames 522–523).

From C[HARLES] S. TODD

Legation U.S. America
at St. Petersburg, 5/17 Oct. 1844

Sir, I have the honor to acknowledge the receipt of your Despatches Nos. 17 & 18, the first enclosing a copy of a recent letter [of 8/12] from the Department to Mr. [William R.] King our Minister at Paris and the other transmitting a copy of your letter of 10th Sept. to Mr. [Wilson] Shannon our Minister to Mexico; ["both" *canceled*] having reference to the interesting subjects of the Annexation of Texas and the proposed invasion by Mexico. As Count Woronzow Daschkoff is only Secretary of Foreign Affairs *ad interim* I have awaited the daily expected arrival of [Charles Robert,] Count Nesselrode to adopt whatever measures may be deemed prudent and practicable in giving effect to the wishes of the President. The Count arrived last evening and as soon as he shall resume the Foreign Portfolio I will take an early occasion to communicate with him.

I have the pleasure to transmit, herewith, a Copy of a note from the Secretary of Foreign Affairs, together with the Treatises referred to, in reply to the application for information as to the most authentic mode adopted in Russia for extracting gold from its ore. The subject shall be resumed by an effort to procure further details from the private sources offered to me. It is rumored that the Emperor has wisely determined to prohibit the further exploration on private account for Gold Mines in Siberia lest the increased quantity may depreciate its value. I have the honor to be, with high Consideration & Esteem, your ob[edien]t Ser[van]t, C.S. Todd.

ALS (No. 48) with En in DNA, RG 59 (State Department), Diplomatic Despatches, Russia, vol. 14 (M-35:14), received 11/25; FC in DNA, RG 84 (Foreign Posts), Russia, Despatches, 4406:227–228.

From Tho[mas] Barrett, Collector, New Orleans, 10/18. In response to a letter of 8/28 from P.C. Dumas asking confirmation of the American make and registry of the *Cyrus*, Barrett encloses a certificate of 10/18 stating that the *Cyrus* was built in Salisbury, Mass., in 1836, that register no. 119 was issued to the vessel in New Orleans on 12/9/1843, and that she cleared on 12/16/1843 for Havana, P.C. Dumas master and owner. FC with Ens in DNA, RG 84 (Foreign Posts), Great Britain, Instructions, 8:572–574; CC with Ens in DNA, RG 76 (Records of Boundary and Claims Commissions and Arbitrations), Miscellaneous Claims, no. 1887; PC with Ens in Senate Document No. 300, 29th Cong., 1st Sess., pp. 41–42.

From Geo[rge] M. Bibb, Secretary of the Treasury, 10/18. He reports the unexpended balances available to the State Department as of 9/30. He asks Calhoun to supply estimates of the probable expenses under each heading during each of the following three quarters and the probable unexpended balances that will be subject to being carried to the surplus fund as of 6/30/1845. LS in DNA, RG 59 (State Department), Letters Received from the Fifth Auditor and Comptroller, 1829–1862.

R[ichard] K. Crallé to Patrick J. Devine, 10/18. Devine is informed of his appointment as U.S. Consul for Sagua la Grande [Cuba]. An exequatur will be sought from Madrid. FC in DNA, RG 59 (State Department), Consular Instructions, 10:272–273.

From R[OBERT] M. HAMILTON

Consulate of the United States
Montevideo, 18th Oct[obe]r 1844
Sir, I have the honor to transmit herewith copies of sundry Official correspondence, which has recently taken place between, Brigadier General Don Manuel Oribe, Commander in chief of the Besieging forces, near Montevideo, Captain P[hilip] F. Voorhees in Command of the United States Ship "Congress," and this Consulate, from No. 1 to No. 8 inclusive, also copies of Statements made by the Captain, and Owner (Nos. 9 & 10,) of the American Barque "Rosalba" directed to Captain Voorhees; to all which I beg leave to respectfully crave your referrence for the particulars thereof.

It becomes my painful duty to inform you of the death of Commander [William D.] Newman, late in command of the U.S. Brig "Bainbridge," which occurred on the night of the 9th In[stan]t, and it grieves me to say, that in consequence of mental derangement, he hastened his death by drow[n]ing himself alongside his Vessel, on the morning of the 10th being missing his body was searched for, and soon found, in the Water near the Bainbridge; it was supposed that he jumped overboard about midnight, on the 11th In[stan]t he was interred at the British Cemetery with the honors due to his rank, and was followed to his grave by all the foreign Officers, as well as our own, on this Station. Com[mande]r Newman had been suffering with Dyspepsia for some time, & which preyed upon his spirits and caused a melancholly derangement of his mind, & to which may be attributed his lamentable and fatal act of self destruction.

The U.S. Ships Congress & Boston and Brig Bainbridge are near this Port, the Boston departs for Rio de Janeiro on the 20th In[stan]t. I am sorry to say that the Small Pox recently made its appearance on board the "Congress," there are at present some seventy or eighty cases, but all of exceedingly mild character, no deaths have occurred, and none anticipated, a Hospital has been established on shore near the Mount, where the Invalids receive all necessary attention, and it is believed the disease will disappear very shortly. I have the honor to be Sir, With profound respect, Your most Obedient, & humble Servant, R.M. Hamilton, United States Consul.

ALS (No. 92) with Ens in DNA, RG 59 (State Department), Consular Despatches, Montevideo, vol. 4 (M-71:4), received 1/2/1845. NOTE: A Clerk's EU reads "Respectfully referred to the Secretary of the Navy [John Y. Mason] for perusal, with a request that they be returned." Hamilton, a Marylander, had been appointed to his post in 1838 and was the only U.S. representative in what became Uruguay. He served until 1857.

From ROB[ER]T MONROE HARRISON

Consulate of the United States
Kingston Jam[aic]a, 18th Oct. 1844
Sir, The letter which you did me the honour to address to me under date of the 16th ultimo, has this moment been received; and in answer thereto, I beg leave to inform you that it has been stated in almost all the Papers of this city, that instructions have not only been sent out to the Governor to have all the Forts and Batteries repaired, and put in a complete state of defence; but also to have the Militia reorganised and placed in a fit state of discipline, in the event of their services being required.

These papers also further state, that a large body of marines are to be forthwith sent here to do Garrison duty in lieu of the regular troops, who are to be employed elsewhere. The Secretary of the Commissioners of Forts and Fortifications has this day given notice to that body to meet in the Council chamber to audit accounts, and transact other business.

Nothing has as yet transpired as regards the augmentations of the Naval and Military Forces on this station, but you may depend on my vigilance to inform you whenever there is the least appearance that such is likely to take place; even if I be compelled to employ a special messenger for that purpose.

In the meantime I pray you to accept the assurance of the great respect with which I have the honor to be Sir Your very ob[edien]t and most humble serv[an]t, Robt. Monroe Harrison.

LS (No. 304) and duplicate LS in DNA, RG 59 (State Department), Consular Despatches, Kingston, vol. 9 (T-31:9), received 11/29.

From F[RANCIS] W. PICKENS

Edgewood, [Edgefield District, S.C.] 18 Oct. '44

My dear Sir, Our elections are just over and the excitement within the last days was very great. The basest means were resorted to to defeat me [for the S.C. Senate]. They rode night & day & made the low appeal of the rich ag[ain]st the poor &c. Not within my recollection has there ever been such exertion made ag[ain]st any man as was ag[ain]st me. They even ["brought" *canceled and then interlined*] Whigs over from Augusta [Ga.] to vote in Hamburg ag[ain]st me—& locked men up & made them drunk to get a vote, & notwithstanding all, I beat [Francis H.] Wardlaw [by] 996 votes. I got more votes than any man ever got in Edgefield Dist[rict] who had any opposition at all, & I never left my house or went to a single muster or meeting of the people & he went to all. I rec[eive]d 1861 votes—& the whole ticket for the lower house is elected by 500 majority, devoted friends of mine, although they plumped[?] one or two supposed to be ag[ain]st me. Every Whig in the Dist[rict] voted of course ag[ain]st me. This opposition was instigated & counciled from Beaufort under a direct understanding for a Judgeship.

I see N[ew] Jersey has gone ag[ain]st us & Pa. for us by a small majority. Georgia is with us by about 3400 majority & will be increased in the Presidential election. I have letters from Nashville which ["state" *canceled*] speak confidently of about 4000 ["major" *canceled*] majority in Tenn: & also that we have high hopes of Kent[uck]y. I suppose you saw the publication in the Philadelphia papers purporting to give a conversation which you had in Charleston the day you arrived there & [which was] sent on immediately to Philadelphia & circulated just before the elections or on the day. Who could have been so lo[o]se as to retail your private conversation?

I see the Mercury takes ground ag[ain]st your ever *accepting any Federal office again.*

I think [James K.] Polk's election now certain, although if either Ohio or N[ew] York goes for [Henry] Clay it will yet make it a close race.

I take it for granted all will now be quiet in our State, & if Polk is elected we will wait & give his Adm[inistratio]n a fair hearing. If he is elected by a large majority I would not be surprised to see England change her [*partial word canceled*] course as to Texas & in relation to slavery. She cannot meet the issues of war in the present state of Europe, particularly of France. If Louis Phillippe [*sic*] should die it will be difficult to avoid a compulsion, & England cannot risk a Rupture with us at this juncture. If Polk is elected by a large vote, it will be the time to push our positions *boldly* & fearlessly.

I heard the other day from Mr. [Thomas G.] Clemson but suppose you got letters also. I understood from him that you would take charge of his plantation this Fall. Will you be so kind as to let me know within a few days when you will return through this place to Washington, in order that I may be at home, as I am often at my River place & am compelled to go with [my daughter] Susan [Pickens] to Charleston the first Frost? I should be very glad to see you & if you could bring [Martha] Cornelia [Calhoun] & Cousin Floride [Colhoun Calhoun] this far we would be delighted with a visit from them.

I shall go in Jan[uar]y to Ala: & if you have any business there to be attended to I will do so with great pleasure.

Our love to Cousin F[loride] & Cornelia. Very truly, F.W. Pickens.

ALS in ScCleA.

From THEO[DORE] S. FAY

Berlin, Oct. 19 1844

Sir, I have the honor to send, by Mr. [Theophilus] Fisk, ratified copies of the two Conventions for the mutual abolition of the droit d'aubaine & taxes on emigration, between the U.S. of America, on the one part, & the Grand Duchy of Hesse, & the King of Wurtemberg, on the other parts. A copy of the *Protocole*, exchanged with the minister of Wurtemberg, is enclosed. I am, Sir, with the highest consideration Y[ou]r Ob[e]d[ien]t Serv[an]t, Theo. S. Fay.

ALS (No. 22) in DNA, RG 59 (State Department), Diplomatic Despatches, Germany, vol. 3 (M-44:4), received 11/25; FC in DNA, RG 84 (Foreign Posts), Germany, Despatches, 4:157–158.

R[ichard] K. Crallé to C. F[rederick] Hagedorn, Bavarian Consul, Philadelphia, 10/19. "The enclosed copy of a letter [of 10/16] from [John Y. Mason] the Secretary of the Navy was received at this Department on the 17th instant, and is in answer to one communicating a copy of your note of the 30th of July last, to this Department, soliciting information upon the subject of Canal Steam Navigation, and particularly in relation to Lieutenant [William W.] Hunter's propellers." FC in DNA, RG 59 (State Department), Notes to Foreign Legations, German States, 6:98 (M-99:27).

From Ja[me]s H. Hey, "Athenian Hall," Athens, Ohio, 10/19. "The Athenian Literary Society of the Ohio University, fully assured of your zealous attachment to the interests of Literature and Science and to whatever adorns and en[n]obles the human character, have elected you an honorary member of that association." ALS in ScCleA.

From JOSEPH HUME

London, 19 Oct[obe]r 1844

Dear Sir, In 1840 I had the pleasure of sending you a Copy of the Report & Evidence of the Committee of the H[ouse] of Commons on "Customs Duties Imports" which has assisted to open the Eyes of this Commercial Community, & may lead to "Free trade" with all the World.

I had a Committee on the Tobacco Trade last Session & the Evidence at length you will receive, as important to the U[nite]d States as to G[rea]t Britain; & I now request your acceptance of two Copies of the Report I prepared as Chairman of the Committee—founded entirely on the Evidence before us, & I expected to have had it agreed to by the Committee: But the Ch[ancello]r of the Exch[eque]r was able to postpone all report, alledging that there was not time to discuss & consider it fully.

If the Govt. of the U[nite]d States would use their best efforts with Sir Ro[bert] Peel, I hope the object I have in view, the reduction of the Duty to 1 s[hilling]/p[e]r lb., instead of 3 s[hillings]/2 d. as at present may be effected, which would prove highly useful to both Countries.

Pleased to see your exertions in former days to prevent the *high tariff* I hope you may be able with the New Government to remove all protective & high duties on your imports; & give an example of wisdom to the World. I remain Your Obed[ient] Serv[an]t, Joseph Hume, M.P.

P.S. I have taken the Liberty to inclose in the same parcel Copies for some of your most distinguished men, & I hope you will allow them to be forwarded as directed & oblige J.H.

ALS in ScCleA. NOTE: The report enclosed by Hume is not found with this letter, but was doubtless the same as was printed under the title *Report from the Select Committee on Tobacco Trade. . . . Ordered, by the House of Commons, to be Printed, 1 August 1844.*

From THO[MA]S G. CLEMSON

Bruxelles, 20th of Oct. 1844

My dear Sir, Mr. [Joseph A.] Scoville has been kind enough to write me a long letter of news a part of which I am sorry to say has given me some anxiety, that concerning the sickness of Washington[.] We were very much grieved to hear of Mrs. [Elizabeth Morris] Crallé's severe indisposition & hope that you have escaped. We knew that if you left Washington you would do so to return, where from accounts there has been a good deal of sickness. We hope that James [Edward Calhoun] is recovered & that there have been no fatal cases at Fort Hill. We shall be exceeding anxious to hear from you now that we have been informed of the sickness of your two homes. Yours of the 14th 7ber came by last evening[']s mail & at the same time one from Mr. Mobley giving me an account of the doings at the Cane Brake. Accompanying this is an answer addressed to my worthy friend John Mobley Esq[ui]r[e] which you will oblige me by franking & forwarding.

Accompanying this I have written you a Despatch which I hope you will not find too long. As it contains the amount of what has transpired officially I shall say but little more to you on that subject, than call your attention first to the consideration of the Treaty[;] 2nd The Consulate at Antwerp. The absence of the Consul [Francis J. Grund] from his Post is giving rise to informalities & troubling me with that which I can not arrange at this distance from the residence of parties who complain & which business is altogether the province of the Consul.

I have already written you word concerning the clothes I have ordered to be sent you & I hope you will find them to your liking. They are the very highest priced articles that can be had[;] therefore there are none better. I could send you as good looking articles & probably for wear equally good but the first I wished to be of the very best.

I am happy to hear that the Alabama crop is so fine, it is much more than from accounts I can say of my own [in Edgefield District].

Mr. Mobley writes me of the continued health of my servants and of the great drought which will occasion a short crop[.] My cotton at best could not have produced a large crop as all the ground I had in was old & needed help which I was not prepared to give it.

The Box containing the clothes was sent to Mr. Beaseley [*sic*; R.G. Beasley] our Consul at Havre to be forwarded to Mr. [James Edward] Boisseau [in New York City]. It is no doubt on the Atlantic by this time.

I am happy to hear that the political prospect is so good. I was led to believe that [Thomas H.] Benton was defeated in Missouri but I judge from yours that such is not the case which I regret.

Anna [Maria Calhoun Clemson] is very well & the children [John Calhoun Clemson and Floride Elizabeth Clemson] have been equally so[;] however ["bad" *canceled*] Calhoun has been suffering from a bad cold & Anna thinks aggravated by worms. I sent for a Physician for him yesterday fearful lest a change of climate might by neglect make the matter more serious than I have reason to apprehend at this time. The little fellow often talks of you.

We have at length gone to House Keeping[.] We found it a difficult task at first to find a house, but at last succeeded; it is in a very agre[e]able position near to the Public walks & garden[.] We took the House already furnished & we pay for it about $70 per month. We have our two servants and have found them very good[.] Basil attracts a good deal of attention from his colour.

Anna prefers having our meals sent us to putting up with the trouble of marketing & having a cook in the House[.] Yesterday was the first day we commenced & therefore can not say how the thing will wear.

I have just this moment recieved [*sic*] a note informing me that the King [Leopold I] will recieve me on Sunday tomorrow a[t] 3 o[']clock & an invitation to dine at 6 in uniforme. This uniforme business is somewhat stiff and Anna laughs at me a good deal about it

& wishes that you were here to see me. She says she knows you would die laughing. It wears off when you are in company & see every body around you in the same kind of thing. I have a carriage at my service for the sum of about $70 per month which I find essential as all visiting is done in carriages. Both Anna & myself have written you frequently since our arrival in Europe which as you know was long time deferred. The trip was long but agre[e]able tho Anna was very sick during nearly the whole time. Even when the sea was as calm as a floor she was on her back.

My health is much better than before leaving home. My liver troubles me some little but the paroxysms are much less severe and a greater time elapses between them so that I hope to get the better of it.

All the Diplomatic corps have been very polite to me since my arrival & they all compliment me much upon the facilities I offer in the French way, which is certainly a very great pleasure to me & almost a sine qua non to one who pretends to see society.

Anna will write you in a few days again & expects to write her mother [Floride Colhoun Calhoun] by this opportunity. Your affectionate son, Thos. G. Clemson.

ALS in ScCleA.

From J[OHN] R. MATHEWES

At Home [Clarkesville, Ga.] 20 October 1844
My Dear Sir, Your ever welcome favour of the 14th I rec[eive]d in Clark[e]sville last week in the midst of Law Politics &c &c. It was court week—I foreman of the Grand Jury—no sinecure, but I had an orderly body to deal with. All of the Great Political leaders in these regions were Present—and such speaking and antagonistical reproaches I have not witnessed for a long time. Judge [Edward D.] Tracy from Macon presided[,] a very clever man in his office—a Whig—he of course made no political demonstration. Gen[era]l [William B.] Wofford an electoral candidate [and] Judge Dougharty [*sic*; Charles Dougherty] his opponent—Judge [William] Law[,] Mr. J[ohn] M. Berrien's particular friend & Legal partner in Savannah— Mr. Sam[ue]l Wales &c &c. Wofford took the skins of the eels off when [Howell] Cobb rec[eive]d & dress'd them for the people and such a feast I have seldom witnessed. Cobb will be an important man

in this State[,] he speaks con amore and gives universal satisfaction—
he called for replies[,] responses &c & not ["one" *interlined*] could or
w[oul]d be given altho these Whigs were present. They are done in
Georgia & the next Election I think will give Democracy 6,000 majority—a prominent Whig said to me yesterday that he was done with
the elections & w[oul]d go to business; but warned me that the next
question was to be Emancipation (I presume he spoke by the card or
Ex Cathedra) & then he would prove that he was a Georgian & Southern Born. I replied that it was no news to me as I had told my friends
25 years ago "to this complexion we must come at last" and had they
received my remarks with judgement they would not now be on the
verge of a precipice[,] "a stitch in time saves nine." A Democratic
member of congress also informed me that the Pen[n]sylv[ani]a
Demo[crati]c delagation at Washington said that if they carried the
State of Pen[n]syl[vani]a we the South must *for a while* compromise
& they w[oul]d ultimately fall into our Ranks. I replied compromises
h[ad] ruined the South—Missouri, and the Tariff of 1832. We must[?]
have no more compromises—"Caesar aut Nullus" must be our watch
word whether [James K.] Polk or ["Dallas" *altered to* "Clay"] was
President, otherwise we w[oul]d become as a sounding Brass & tin-
kling cymbal—he seemed struck with the remark & said he believed I
was right. The fact is if we do not under any circumstances strike
for our Salvation at the very opening of the Doors of the next congress
without fear or dread—we will be compromised by Southern Office
seekers & placemen; we must Clinch the Resolutions of the Baltimore
[Democratic] Con[ventio]n of '44 "in limine" of the next Session of
congress or the Loaves & fishes will draw the nails of our security—
no equivocation, no double dealing should avail—the question ["is"
interlined] to us freedom or Bondage, life or death—a final adjustment
of our differences must be had forthwith but not such a one as England promised Ireland. The New England States have hitherto compromised with ["us" *interlined*] as practical gamblers. They leave
everything to be fought over that they have hitherto relinquished
under the *compromises* of the constitution or by legislation. With a
lawless appetite to rule they pretend a hollow sympathy for our
wrongs, and to enslave us they appeal to the holy Union of Sheep &
Wolf—or sheep & Shears. Their opposition to Texas is to strip us of
power to cover that nakedness which the constitution alone deceit-
fully veils [*sic*; "us" *canceled*] from their meditated violence.

I have much to say to you tha[t this] letter can ["not" *interlined*]
contain. My carriage goes [to] Pendleton & will leave ["here" *interlined*] about the 30th Ins[tant] and if I can concentrate my busi-

ness in time I may be able to spend with you the night 31st or 1st Prox[im]o. I wish to be back in time for the succeeding Monday[']s election. When you arrive in Charleston I may not have got there or if I am before you—my plantation business may require prompt attention. The State Politics of So[uth] Ca[rolina] is not smoothly gliding—Whiggery is trying to jostle us & if some thing is not done previous to the meeting of the Legislature—ignorance, vanity and ambition, selfishness &c may introduce into our State Babelism, once more. Disunion of the South is a clover field to our Task Masters. I remain most sincerely & respectfully yours, J.R. Mathewes.

ALS in ScCleA.

From E[DWARD] PORTER

Consulate of the United States of America
at Frontera de Tabasco, October the 20th 1844
Sir, I have the Honour to wait on you with the Enclosed copy of a Letter handed to me during one of my Visits to our Citizen Prisoners in Tabasco Carcel. There remain now in Confinement the writer of the Original of the enclosed Letter to which Statement I beg to call your attention and a Creole of N. Orleans under age called Garcia who has Severely injured his own Head by beating it against the Iron Bars of the Prison in Delirium. The other is a Native of Philaddelphia of German or French de[s]cent named Louis Backman. The ballance of our Citizens taken in the [Francisco] Sentmanat Catastrophe has been Shot with the exception of the Sailors one of whoom perrished in Confinement. The Remainder of the Sailors were Liberated by the Favourable Report made by Mr. Patterson in their behalf asserting fearlessly that the Sailors and Many others knew no more of the intentions of the Expedition than he did and as a matter of Coarce They never did nor could not be compelled to bear Arms. I have the Honor to Remain Your Most ob[edien]t Humble Serv[an]t, E. Porter.

ALS with En in DNA, RG 59 (State Department), Consular Despatches, Tabasco, vol. 1 (M-303:1, frames 227–229), received 1/16/1845. NOTE: Porter enclosed a copy of a letter to himself from Franklin Newhall, datelined "Tobasco Prison, Sept[embe]r 27th 1844," in which Newhall described the attack upon the *William A. Turner*, and his capture and imprisonment by Mexican authorities.

From THEO[DORE] S. FAY

Legation of the U. States
Berlin, 21 Oct., 1844

Dear Sir, In connexion ["In"(?) *canceled and* "with" *interlined*] my private Letter of Oct. 3 announcing the intention of Baron [Heinrich] v[on] Bülow immediately to return a negative answer to our application that the time might be prolonged, in the matter of the Convention of 25 March, & stating the step I had ventured to take in order to prevent this premature abandonment of an important negotiation, I have now the pleasure to inform you that my mediation has been successful, & that the Convention at present stands exactly as it would have stood, had it not yet been submitted to the Senate, or had the time for the exchange of the ratifications been prolonged by the Zollverein States. Mr. Eichmann has just informed me that, in consequence of my conversation with Baron v[on] Bülow, it was determined to with[h]old the negative answer, then on the point of being returned. This course is equivalent to an affirmative, at the same time saving the *amour propre* of the States of the Zollverein, & leaving your future plans, as to the Convention, perfectly unobstructed.

I subjoin copy & translation of a confidential private Letter [of 10/21] addressed to Baron v[on] Bulow, at his suggestion, in which it will be perceived I have personally assumed the responsibility of my interposition, in case the Convention should be ultimately rejected. I have the honor to be, with the most respectful consideration, Dear Sir, Y[ou]r Ob[e]d[ien]t Serv[an]t, Theo. S. Fay.

ALS with Ens in DNA, RG 59 (State Department), Diplomatic Despatches, Germany, vol. 3 (M-44:4), received 11/25; variant FC with En in DNA, RG 84 (Foreign Posts), Germany, Despatches, 4:160–163; three CC's with Ens in ScCleA; CCEx with En in DNA, RG 46 (U.S. Senate), 28B-B11.

From FRANCIS HARRISON

Porto Plata[,] St. Domingo, 21st October 1844

Sir, Official intelligence has arrived in this place to day from the West and from the city of St. Domingo which states that the Black President [Philippe] Guerrier of the western part of this island is prepareing and organising his Black army to march on this or the Eastern end of the island to reconquer it from the proper inhabitants who drove the Haitiens out by force in the revolution of last March.

The campaign is to commence in December and this place is to be the first point of attack.

Judgeing the struggle of the people of this part to be a righteous one, a struggle of my own race to liberate themselves from the horrible bondage of the Blacks, as many of the people of this part of the island are white the population being similar to that of Mexico, I have aided them by supplying them as a Merchant with powder[,] balls[,] muskets and other munitions of war to liberate themselves from what I considered the horrible oppression of the Blacks of the West.

You are aware Sir as it is part of the history of the events of this year that in one month the people of the East had complete possession of their part and defeated the two large armies of the West that marched against them. At this time the Government of the West is decidedly one of the Blacks—there is more union among them and it is probable from great numerical force they may over come the people of this part.

I feel that I am personally obnoxious to the Blacks of the West. First as a white man a citizen of the United States, and second for having supplied these people here with the materials which destroyed the black army before Santiago, and have now put them here in a tolerable state of preparation by having imported since that battle every necessary article. I am also personally obnoxious to many of the officers of the Black army that is gathering in the Cape from the circumstance that in June 1843 I being attacked in the street by two of them, killed one of them in my own defence and put the other one to flight. The U.S. Brig Somers Lieut. Commanding [John W.] West called in here in July 1843 and by the energy of Lieut. West arranged that affair.

I have resided here as an American Merchant since 1836[,] have generally from my great reserve kept myself out of difficulty—but my sympathies being enlisted in the favor of the people of the East and having actively employed those sympathies—I feel that if those blacks[?] of the West should reconquer this part that possibly my property and person and the persons of my family would be in jeopardy.

The object of this communication is to beg of you Sir that an order may be given that one or more of our small gun brigs may visit this place and the city of St. Domingo—in the months of December and January—as I am now also establishing a mercantile house in that city.

I commanded from the years 1822 to 1825 the Ship General Wade Hampton as a packet from Philadelphia to Charleston. The Ship

Florian from 1825 to 1830 as a packet from Philadelphia to Charleston and from New York to Savannah and the Ship Helen Man from 1830 to 1833 in the same trade. I am known to most of the Gentlemen of Charleston and Savannah.

As a good citizen of the United States, a member of *your own* political family settled in this country to extend the lawful commerce of my own—I now claim the protection of the government of my country and address you sir as its Chief acting member and I trust I may feel the proud confidence that, that, protection will be afforded in the manner in which I request. I have the honor to be sir your most Ob[e]d[ien]t Serv[an]t, Francis Harrison.

ALS in DNA, RG 59 (State Department), Miscellaneous Letters (M-179:105, frames 528–530), received 11/11.

From WILLIAM R. KING

Legation of the U. States
Paris, 21st October 1844

Sir, I have the honor to transmit you, herewith, the copy of a communication (Appendix A.) addressed to me on the 11th inst. by [George de Tschann] the Chargé d'Affaires of the Swiss Confederation, at Paris, proposing to renew the negotiations formerly entered into with Mr. [Henry] Livingston, for the conclusion of a Convention regulating the rights of inheritance and "detraction" with regard to property acquired by the citizens of each country established within the territory of the other. These negotiations resulted in a Treaty which did not receive the approbation of the Senate of the United States, upon the ground that its stipulations conflicted with the legislation of several of the States. I have not been able to find in the archives of the Legation, a copy of this Convention, and I cannot therefore ascertain what were the objectionable clauses. Under these circumstances, and in the absence of instructions, I could promise the Swiss Chargé d'Affaires nothing more than a prompt transmission of his letter, with the assurance that the government of the United States was disposed to treat the citizens of Switzerland as favorably as those of any other nation. In his letter, Mr. de Tschann refers by designation and date to a number of treaties between the United States and other countries containing stipulations upon this subject, and particularly to those with Sardinia, Hanover and Portugal concluded

111

since the rejection by the Senate of ["the" *interlined*] Convention with Switzerland. These latter I have examined, and I find that they contain mutual concessions upon equal terms, for the disposal of personal property, by testament, donation or otherwise, and the right of selling real estate within a reasonable time and withdrawing or exporting the proceeds thereof without molestation, subject only to the dues paid by citizens. I take it for granted, therefore, that the United States will be willing to enter into similar arrangements with Switzerland, and I await your instructions to enable me to comply with the wishes expressed to me by the representative of the Swiss government. By referring to the Convention concluded with Mr. Livingston, in March 1835 you will be able to see in what respects its stipulations differ from those contained in the Treaties cited, and I presume that there will be no difficulty in authorizing me to contract with Switzerland engagements as liberal as those which regulate the rights of inheritance and "detraction" in our conventions with the most favored nations.

I have the honor to acknowledge the receipt of your despatch No. 7, with reference to the disposition manifested by the Swiss government to arrest and deliver up to justice the notorious Gerard Koster, and you will perceive by the concluding paragraph of my letter to the Chargé d'Affaires of the Swiss Confederation, (Appendix B.) that the instructions which it contains have been promptly executed.

Your Despatch No. 8 with the Commission of Gabriel G. Fleurot appointed Consul of the United States for the Island of Martinique has also been received, and application has been made to the French government for its Exequatur. I am, very respectfully your obedient servant, William R. King.

LS (No. 5) with Ens in DNA, RG 59 (State Department), Diplomatic Despatches, France, vol. 30 (M-34:33), received 11/25.

From George Stevens, "2d U.S. Dragoons," Fort Jesup, La., 10/21. Stevens informs Calhoun that he has conveyed the State Department despatches entrusted to him to Washington, Texas. Finding no U.S. diplomatic agent there, he deposited them with [Anson] Jones, Secretary of State of the Texas Republic, with instructions to turn them over to a U.S. diplomatic agent when one arrives. LS in DNA, RG 59 (State Department), Letters from Bearers of Despatches.

To J[ohn] A. Stuart, [Charleston?]

Fort Hill, 21st Oct[obe]r 1844

My dear Sir, I am glad you have noticed [in the Charleston *Mercury*] as you have, the statement of the Charleston correspondent of the U. States Gazette of Philadelphia, purporting to give a conversation, which I had on my way through Charleston. There is no truth in it, or semblance of truth, except that I expressed my opinion pretty confidently, Mr. [James K.] Polk would be elected to all my friends who made any enquiry on the subject. With that exception, I said nothing to justify, or any way to countenance the statement; & you are authorized to say so. I made no allusion to my remaining in the office I now hold, or that there was any understanding that I should continue in it. It would have been both indelicate & untrue to have done so. Nothing has ever passed between Mr. Polk & myself, directly or indirectly, on the subject. I neither know his views nor he mine on the subject. The whole was [a] base devise to influence the Pennsylvania election.

I congratulate you on [your] election [to the S.C. General Assembly]; and rejoice, that the tricks resorted to, in order to defeat or rather to distract the party in Charleston, have been so effectually counteracted.

In giving my opinion, as to the probable result of the Presidential election, while in Charleston & since my return, I spoke on the supposition, that the abolitionists could not be brought to vote for [Henry] Clay. Such was believed to be the case when I left Washington by all our friends. I fear, however, that the fact will turn out otherwise. The present indication is, that they will vote for Clay. In that event, I fear he would be elected. Should such be the case, we may look out for a fearful struggle the next four years, which we ["could" *canceled and* "can" *interlined*] not too soon prepare to meet. The first step should be to unite and organize the South. If that can be done, all will be well; otherwise, it is difficult to say what may come. With great respect yours truly, J.C. Calhoun.

ALS in ScU-SC, John C. Calhoun Papers; PC in Jameson, ed., *Correspondence*, p. 626; PEx in the Charleston, S.C., *Mercury*, October 29, 1844, p. 2; PEx in the Washington, D.C., *Constitution*, November 1, 1844, p. 3; PEx in the Anderson, S.C., *Gazette*, November 8, 1844, p. 1; PEx in the Greenville, S.C., *Mountaineer*, November 8, 1844, p. 1; PEx in the Pendleton, S.C., *Messenger*, November 8, 1844, p. 1. NOTE: The Philadelphia, Pa., *United States Gazette* of 10/7/1844 published an article under the heading "Highly Important to Pennsylvanians. The Voice of Warning." The article purported to be based upon a letter from Charleston dated 10/2. "The writer [of the letter] says that John C. Calhoun had just arrived there, and had informed his friends; 1st, that Mr. Polk will be elected; 2d, that the game playing in Pennsylvania and elsewhere, to make it appear that Mr. Polk is a *protectionist,* is well understood to be a kind of justifiable deception (we call it a gross *fraud,* a *cheat,* a most *un*justifiable deception) upon the people, by those who support him; 3d, that if elected, it will be regarded as a FREE TRADE triumph; 4th, that he (Mr. Calhoun) will hold on the office of Secretary of State; 5th, that the tariff will be, in all probability, repealed, and that the government will be strictly administered on the principles of FREE TRADE. This information from the great gun of Southern 'democracy' has created high hopes among his friends. It is understood, he says, by the Central Committee in Washington, that the Polk speakers are to fight for Polk in Pennsylvania as a *protectionist,* to secure the vote of that State as necessary to make him President; while his election is to be regarded as a *free trade* triumph. That, if they succeed now, they will be able, by means of the patronage of the government, to elect another President of the same stamp, and Mr. Calhoun is looked to as the man. That Mr. C[alhoun] will hold on to the office of Secretary of State, and be the master spirit of the Polk administration—President *de facto.* The two great and leading measures of the administration will be *the repeal of the Tariff of 1842,* and *the annexation of Texas.* These measures they are determined to force through if they can; but if they fail in this, they will *nullify* the Tariff, and the government, army, navy and treasury being in the hands of Southern disunionists, they will have nothing to fear: there will be no Gen. Jackson to threaten to hang them as high as Haman— aye, and carry his threats into execution, too. 'Young Hickory' is not 'Old Hickory.' " Stuart refuted these assertions in the Charleston *Mercury* of 10/18 in an article entitled "Slanders of Mr. Calhoun for Pennsylvania Elections."

R[ichard] K. Crallé to Rich[ar]d K. Call, Tallahassee, Fla. [Territory], 10/22. "In compliance with your request I herewith transmit copies of the explanations, received at this Department, in reply to the Charges preferred by you against Cha[rle]s S. Sibley, Attorney of the United States for the middle District of Florida." FC in DNA, RG 59 (State Department), Domestic Letters, 35:4–5 (M-40:33).

From ALLEN A. HALL

Legation of the United States
Caracas, October 22nd, 1844

Sir, Herewith you will receive the duplicate of a note [of 10/18] addressed by me to [Juan Manuel Manrique] the Secretary of State for Foreign Affairs on the subject of the claim of Mr. John W. Holding and others [relating to the *Good Return* affair]—referred to in your despatch of the 9th of August last. It is one of a class of claims held by certain citizens of the United States against the late Republic of Colombia which the States that formerly composed that Republic can have no just grounds whatever for refusing to pay, although the Government of the United States may not feel called upon, under the circumstances, to make a formal demand of payment, and to coerce it, if refused. The origin and nature of these claims are briefly these:

About the year 1818, a state of open and declared war then existing between the Banda Oriental and Spain and Portugal, and the Portuguese being actually in possession of Montevideo, [José Gervasio] Artigas, the recognized Chief of the Banda Oriental, commissioned a number of privateers, among which were several that were fitted out, owned and commanded by citizens of the United States. That at that time Artigas was as much the true, rightful and generally recognized Executive of the Banda Oriental as [Simon] Bolivar was of the Republic of Colombia, and that the former had just as much right to grant letters of marque and reprisal as the latter, I think, there cannot be the slightest question. Nevertheless, Admiral [Luis] Brion, then in command of the Colombian Navy, whose rendezvous at that period was the Island of Margarita, being greatly in want of funds and munitions of war could hit upon no better expedient for supplying his wants than to make prizes of the prizes which had been previously captured by the superior skill and enterprize of the Banda Oriental privateers, under the absurd and frivolous pretext that the Banda Oriental was not an independent State and had no regularly constituted Government, and that, commissions for privateering granted by Artigas could not in consequence be recognized and respected. Upon Admiral Brion's rendering an account of these proceedings to Bolivar, the latter addressed him a letter which he commenced by stating the difficulty he had in yielding credence to his, Brion's statements, and pertinently inquiring, if he, Brion, regarded the Banda Oriental privateers as pirates, as Brion pretended, how came he to dismiss in safety the so-called pirates while their prizes were retained? Bolivar then proceeds in the same letter indignantly to disavow Brion's proceedings—recognizes the Banda Oriental as an independent State—orders that, in future, privateers commissioned by Artigas shall be respected by the Colombian authorities—and concludes by directing the immediate restoration of the Banda Oriental prizes which Brion had seized. A certified copy of the letter of Bolivar's is in my possession. It is dated, Head Quarters, Angostura, February 24th, 1819. It reached its destination too late, however, to prevent the confiscation of several rich prizes, which proceeding constitutes the ground of reclamation in the class of cases above referred to.

It is worthy of remark that in each case the proceeds of the sale of these prizes were applied to the public service of Colombia, and no doubt materially contributed to subsequent successes of the Colombian arms.

At the Island of Margarita there was at that period a sort of a Court of Admiralty, before which the prizes in question went through a sort of a form of trial and condemnation. But when, several years afterwards, the question of the legality of their condemnation was brought before the High Court of Justice at Bogota, which had been established in the interim, that Court decided that for want of a law declaring what tribunal should take cognizance of maritime causes existing prior to 1821, the decisions of the Court of Margarita previous to that year could not be called in question or reversed.

I am well aware that these claimants have no right to demand the interposition in their behalf of the Government of the United States. They embarked, in a foreign service, on a not very creditable enterprise whose object was the commission of spoliations on the property of citizens of a Government with which we were at peace and against which we had no cause of quarrel; and if the question were now between the original captors and the original owners of the property, I am free to say, that my sympathies would be all enlisted in favor of the latter. But a third party has stepped in and recaptured the property, not for the generous purpose of restoring it to its original owners, but with the sole object of applying it to its own uses. On the part of Colombia it can be viewed in no other light than as an aggravated case of lawless plunder, for which, I confess, I should be glad to see due reparation exacted. As between the present claimants and the Government of Colombia there could not possibly arise a case calling more loudly for redress, or one, I conceive, more deeply involving the honor and justice of that Government. The Government of the United States may not deem it expedient, under the circumstances, formally and peremptorily to demand redress in these cases, but it might, with perfect propriety, it appears to me, cause this Government to understand the strong feelings of surprise and dissatisfaction with which it would regard a refusal to afford redress.

The case of the "Good Return," which I have put forward first, has one strong feature distinguishing it from the others of its class, and that is the fact, that the "Good Return" was a vessel belonging to citizens of the United States and sailing under the flag of the United States, and with the lawfulness of whose voyage or the contents of whose cargo, Commodore Joly had not the shadow of a right to meddle. Of the fact of her capture and detention by Joly—of his exacting a ransom of $28,000, and of the whole cargo (valued at $98,000) having been sacrificed at a forced sale at St. Bartholomews in order to raise the ransom money, there exists no doubt whatever. The evidence going to establish these facts is full and unquestionable.

Following the language of Mr. [John] Forsyth's instructions to Mr. [James] Semple, I have, in my note to Mr. Manrique characterized this particular claim as one for which "the United States have a right to hold the States formerly composing the Republic of Colombia accountable."

The aggregate amount of claims of this class exceeds half a million of dollars. I have the honor to be, Sir, very respectfully, Your ob[e]d[ien]t serv[an]t, Allen A. Hall.

ALS (No. 42) with En in DNA, RG 59 (State Department), Diplomatic Despatches, Venezuela, vol. 2 (M-79:3), received 12/2.

O[gden] Hoffman, U.S. Attorney, New York [City], to "J.K." [*sic*; Richard K.] Crallé, 10/22. Hoffman acknowledges Crallé's letter of 10/19 [*not found*] "with its confidential enclosure." He will attend to the matter. ALS in DNA, RG 59 (State Department), Passport Applications, 1795–1905, vol. 33, unnumbered (M-1372:15).

From H[ENRY] G. LANGLEY

Office of the Dem[ocratic] Review
8 Astor House N. York [City,] Oct. 22/44

Sir, We herewith enclose to you a Bill for you[r] subscription to this Journal for Two years ending with June 1845 now due.

As our Review now absolutely requires the encouragement of its friends, by the prompt payment of their several subscriptions, we are constrained to use this method of soliciting the same. Your attention to this matter will greatly oblige Very Respectfully Yours &c, H.G. Langley, per Dan[ie]l Noble Johnson.

ALS with En in ScCleA. NOTE: An enclosed printed bill, dated 11/1/1844 and addressed to Calhoun, is for $10. An endorsement on the letter reads: "Paid 19 Nov. 1844 by E. Stubbs."

R[ichard] K. Crallé to "Messrs. Ch[arles] H. Todd & Co., New York [City]," 10/22. Crallé acknowledges their letter of 10/8 concerning their claim on the Mexican government in "the case of the Brig Henry Leeds." In reply Crallé informs them of a pending convention between the U.S. and Mexico that might "enable you to obtain the redress which you seek much more expeditiously" than direct application to the Mexican government. If ratified, the convention "will be published for the information of Claimants on that Government generally." FC in DNA, RG 59 (State Department), Domestic Letters, 35:5 (M-40:33).

R[ichard] K. Crallé to Joseph C.C. Ellis, [St. Louis?], 10/23. Crallé informs Ellis of his appointment as U.S. Consul at Maracaibo and encloses relevant documents. FC in DNA, RG 59 (State Department), Consular Instructions, 11:289–290.

R[ichard] K. Crallé to Samuel H. Kneass, [Philadelphia], 10/23. Crallé informs Kneass of his appointment to be U.S. Consul at Cartagena and encloses documents relevant to the office. FC in DNA, RG 59 (State Department), Consular Instructions, 11:288–289.

Richard K. Crallé to Sam[ue]l McLean, U.S. Consul, Trinidad, Cuba, 10/23. McLean is informed that the announced appointment of a replacement for him was a mistake. The person announced was supposed to have been appointed Consul for the island of Trinidad. FC in DNA, RG 59 (State Department), Consular Instructions, 10: 273.

R[ichard] K. Crallé to Ramon Leon Sanchez, U.S. Consul, Cartagena, New Granada, 10/23. Crallé informs Sanchez that Samuel H. Kneass has been appointed to succeed him. Sanchez is to surrender to Kneass the archives and property of the consular office. FC in DNA, RG 59 (State Department), Consular Instructions, 11:289.

R[ichard] K. Crallé to Wilson Shannon, [Mexico City], 10/23. Crallé transmits the commission of Don Pedro de Regil y Estrada as U.S. Consul for Merida and Sisal in Yucatan. An earlier request for an exequatur for Regil y Estrada was refused on the ground that Yucatan was in a state of disturbance. That excuse has now been removed. Shannon is instructed to renew the request and to forward the exequatur, when it shall have been obtained, and the commission to Regil. FC (No. 8) in DNA, RG 59 (State Department), Diplomatic Instructions, Mexico, 15:322–323 (M-77:111).

From Tho[ma]s G. Clemson

Bruxelles, October 24th 1841 [*sic;* 1844]
My dear Sir, Since my arrival here I have been very busy[.] The
Cabinet & King [Leopold I] judging from what I have seen are very
anxious to conclude a treaty with the United States & at this time are
busy in preparing a copy of such an one as will give them pleasure to
accept. It will be a treaty of commerce & navigation[.] As soon as
recieved [*sic*] it will be forwarded to you[;] in the mean time I should
be happy to recieve your advice & instructions on the subject.

I hope you found every thing going on well at Fort Hill & that all
the family had recovered from indisposition. Fort Hill is so proximate
to the mountains that I should have supposed Mrs. [Floride Colhoun]
Calhoun & James [Edward Calhoun] would have been much benefitted by a trip to Zacharys. We were very anxious about yourself
for from what Mr. [Joseph A.] Scoville wrote us it must have been
very sickly even before you left.

We heard from our place [in Edgefield District, S.C.] & were very
much gratified that every thing on the place was well. But I fear my
crop will be very short. I am convinced of the futility of planting
cotton on my old fields without manure[.] The only thing that can
be done there is to [*one word canceled*] manure every hill that is
planted on old ground.

I am anxious to hear from you on the subject of the place & how
you found things there.

Anna [Maria Calhoun Clemson] & myself have been ta[l]king for
some time about your sending Pat[rick Calhoun] out as bearer of
Despatches. He might obtain a furlough or leave of abscence [*sic*]
& come out here & stay with me a year or as long as I remain with
great advantage to himself. He could stay with me without much
expense & I would make him Secretary to the Legation which would
give him great advantages. I would say as much for John [C. Calhoun, Jr.] but I fear that the Climate here would be unsuitable to
him, for it is very changeable & judging from what I have seen quite
severe. We are all suffering from Colds & poor [John] Calhoun
[Clemson] has been quite unwell. He is I think somewhat better
than he was.

I hope you will on your return either send Mr. [Francis J.] Grund
[U.S. Consul to Antwerp] to his Post or appoint some one to his
place. Our Despatch agent at London (Mr. Miller) informed me by
mail that he had forwarded to me ["through the consul at Antwerp"
interlined] a package from the United States some two weeks since

119

and I have heard nothing of it. When in Havre I left three trunks to be shipped to Antwerp for me—& have addressed the consul & can neither get answer or hear of my trunks.

I wrote you word that I had been visited by sailors & captains on business that did not regard me & which was owing to the abscence of the Consul.

Anna is well & sends much love to all. Your affectionate son, Thos. G. Clemson.

[P.S.] I have just this moment recieved the letter [*not found*] that I send you herewith. This is one of several letters that I have recieved[.] I have done all that I [*"could" canceled and "can" interlined*] & know that there is some thing wanting at Antwerp. This sailor is the one that came up twice to see me from Antwerp[.] I gave him a letter to the consul & urged upon the Consul to see justice done. I afterwards saw the Consul & spoke to him on the subject; when the man left me he professed himself satisfied with what I had done. Yours affectionately, Thos. G. Clemson.

ALS in ScCleA.

From L E V I J O N E S, T H O[M A]s F. Mc K I N N E Y, J A[M E]s L O V E, and J O N A S B U T L E R

Galveston, 24th October 1844

Sir, In the absence of Gen[era]l Duff Green, who remained here only long enough to appoint a Vice Consul, Col. E[lisha] A. Rhodes, but did not take time to possess himself of the official papers of the late Mr. A[rchibald] M. Green, or the Consular seal, we learn that both the papers and seal are most unwarrantably withheld by Mr. Stewart Newell.

It seems that he (Newell) is Consul for Sabine (where he never resided) and upon the death of Mr. A.M. Green took possession of the books, papers, &C, with the consular seal and proceeded to act as consul at this place.

When Gen[era]l Green arrived, he appointed Col. Rhodes to perform the duties during his absence in Mexico. Yet Newell, in a paper we have just seen, addressed by him to the Collector of this Port [William C.V. Dashiell], protests against the action of Col. Rhodes, and insinuates that he (Col. Rhodes) will not be recognised by the Govt. of the United States in consequence of some threatened but undefined charge against him during his incumbency in the Consulate before the appointment of Mr. A.M. Green.

Lest, therefore, any attempt should be made by Newell before the return of Gen[era]l Green, to represent any matters at your department, to the prejudice of Col. Rhodes, and at the same time to justify his own unwarranted proceeding, we, as citizens of Galveston have deemed it not improper to address you this communication; and we say to you that Col. Rhodes with his most estimable family has lived in this community since Galveston was settled (the greater part of the time, as Consul of the United States) and has always borne himself as the hospitable, amiable and upright gentleman, as well as faithful officer; for during the whole period of his official term (about four years) we fully believe he was no one day absent from the Island; and for his urbanity, correctness and faithfulness in discharge of the duties of his office, the entire community of Galveston, will most cheerfully avouch; indeed no little regret & surprise was felt here, when Mr. [Daniel] Webster in 1842 removed him from the office in which he had acted so worthily for himself and his country.

We would from our personal knowledge detail many instances of truest kindness and benevolence, as shewn by Col. Rhodes & his family to their sick and destitute countrymen found on our shores, and in cases too, where no official remuneration was sought or contemplated, but such would not be compatible with the object of this address, that[?] as before stated, is simply intended to protect Col. Rhodes against the effect of the false representations, with which he seems to be menaced, until he can be h[eard?] or until Gen[era]l Green returns.

As a communication of this kind might seem obtrusive or not entitled to consideration, when the writers are wholly unknown to, or not recollected by yourself, we beg leave to refer you to Judge [George M.] Bibb of the Treasury Department for any information you may desire as to the character of such as are personally known. When, Very respectfully, we are Sir Your Ob[edien]t S[er]v[an]ts, Levi Jones, Thos. F. McKinney, Jas. Love, Jonas Butler.

LS in DNA, RG 59 (State Department), Consular Despatches, Galveston, vol. 2 (T-151:2), received 11/18.

From H[aym] M. Salomon, New York [City], 10/24. "Please return to me the documents forwarded to your department which accompanied my Application for a foreign Consulate about three months ago." (An EU reads: "Such of them as were received from the President [John Tyler], returned to him Oct[obe]r 31st 1844.") ALS in

DNA, RG 59 (State Department), Applications and Recommendations, 1837–1845, Salomon (M-687:29, frames 171–172).

From Silas Wright, [Senator from N.Y.], Canton, St. Lawrence County, N.Y., 10/24. He recommends Egbert T. Smith, a "firm, active, and unwavering" republican, for appointment to be a despatch bearer to Europe. Wright is not acquainted with Smith, but respectable men whom Wright does know have recommended him. ALS in DNA, RG 59 (State Department), Applications and Recommendations, 1837–1845, Smith (M-687:30, frames 689–690).

[Richard K. Crallé to George M. Bibb, Secretary of the Treasury], 10/25. [As requested on 10/18] Crallé encloses to Bibb an "estimate for that Department." Entry in DNA, RG 56 (Secretary of the Treasury), Registers of Letters Received, 1834–1872, vol. 11, no. S437.

From H[enry] L. Ellsworth, [Commissioner of Patents], 10/25. "The patent fund is a special fund created by law for the Patent Office—hence the appropriation remains from year to year." As of 9/30, $159,093.77 constituted the unexpended balance in the Patent Fund. LS with En in DNA, RG 59 (State Department), Accounting Records: Letters Received from Departments and Bureaus.

From ROB[ER]T MONROE HARRISON

Consulate of the United States
Kingston Jam[aic]a, 25th Oct. 1844
Sir, Herewith I have the honor [to] enclose you a copy of my despatch of the 18th inst. per Brigantine Good Hope, since when no increase has taken place in the military or naval Establishment of this Colony, nor have any tenders for repairs of the Forts and Fortifications been advertised for as yet. With great respect I have the honor to be Sir Your ob[edien]t and most humble serv[an]t, Robt. Monroe Harrison.
P.S. 29th October.
The vessel which takes this having been detained, until to day, I am enabled to forward you a paper by which you will see the contemplated repairs to be put on Fort Charles the principal work of defence at the entrance of this Port; and I presume all other fortifications which may require repairs will be also attended to; but whether

on account of any meditated attacks from any enemy or otherwise, I cannot say. R.M.H.

LS (No. 305) with Ens in DNA, RG 59 (State Department), Consular Despatches, Kingston, vol. 9 (T-31:9), received 11/27.

Rich[ar]d K. Crallé to Thomas O. Larkin, U.S. Consul, Monterey

Department of State
Washington, Oct. 25, 1844
Sir, Your letters of the 20th June and 24th April, *not numbered*, have been received.

The information contained in the former relative to the Hudson Bay Company and their settlements in the Oregon, as also the dissatisfaction of the Emigrants to that Country, and their removal to California, is of an important & interesting character, and it is earnestly hoped, that you will continue to report to the Department, such facts as may come to your Knowledge touching the political condition of these Countries, especially if your communications can be made subservient to, or may effect the interest and well being of our Government.

An Exequatur having been obtained and sent to you, upon the Commission issued during the recess of the Senate, it was not necessary that the Commission subsequently sent, bearing the confirmation of your appointment by that Body, should have been accompanied by a like paper.

The Bond which you mention in your letter of the 12th April last, as having been sent to the United States to be filled up, and transmitted to this Department, has not been received. As it is probable, that it may have been miscarried, I enclose another blank form, which you will take immediate steps, to have executed & returned as directed in Art. 1st Chap. 1st of your General Instructions.

Mr. A[lbert] M. Gilliam appointed U.S. Consul for the port of San Francisco, has returned to this Country and resigned his office. No appointment will now be made in his place as it appears from your letter of the 24th April, that San Francisco is not a port of entry. Your Jurisdiction under your Commission as Consul at Monterey, extends to such ports as may be nearer to you, than to the residence of any other U.S. Consul.

The Return and Statement of Fees required by your General Instructions, have not been received. Forms for making them out by, were sent to you on the 1st of May 1843, and it is expected that you will in future transmit them punctually, at the expiration of each half year to the Department. I am, Sir, Respectfully Your obedient Servant, Richd. K. Crallé, Acting Secretary.

LS in CU, Bancroft Library, Larkin Papers; FC in DNA, RG 59 (State Department), Consular Instructions, 11:293–294; PC in Hammond, ed., *Larkin Papers*, 2:261–262.

R[ichard] K. Crallé to Pedro de Regil y Estrada, U.S. Consul, Merida and Sisal, 10/25. The Mexican government has refused to grant Regil y Estrada an exequatur since his appointment in 1843 because of the revolt in Yucatan. The request for an exequatur has now been renewed in Mexico City. Regil y Estrada should send to the State Department a copy of the protest in regard to the brig *Henry Leeds* and should henceforward correspond in English rather than Spanish. FC in DNA, RG 59 (State Department), Consular Instructions, 11:292–293.

R[ichard] K. Crallé to J[ohn] A. Robinson, U.S. Consul, Guaymas, [Sonora, Mexico]

Department of State
Washington, Oct. 25th 1844

Sir, Your letters Nos. 4, 6 & 7 have been received. No. 5 not having come to hand I will thank you to forward a duplicate of it. The Books requested in No. 4, it is regretted cannot be furnished you, there being no surplus Copies at the disposal of the Department. By the 9th Article of the Treaty between the United States and the United Mexican States, the Citizens of both Countries, respectively, are exempted from compulsory service in the Army or Navy; nor are they to be subjected to any other charges, or contributions, or taxes, than such as are paid by the Citizens of the States in which they reside. In case of the violation of this Article you will report the fact properly substantiated to this Department, in order that such instructions may be given to our Minister at Mexico, as may be necessary & proper.

There is no stipulation in the Treaty regarding the hoisting of Consular Flags, and if it be contrary to the Laws of Mexico for Consuls to hoist the Flags of their respective Nations, you will of course be compelled to abide by them—but, unless there be a Treaty stipulation to that effect, it is your duty to see that this privilege, is not denied to you, if extended to Consuls of other Nations.

No Returns or Statement of Fees have been received from you for 1843. The Statement of Fees for first half of 1844 enclosed in No. 7, is made out after a form long since abandoned. Copies of the forms now required to be used, are enclosed and I will thank you to preserve them in your office, and in future let your Returns & Statement of Fees be made out conformably to them. I am Sir &c, R.K. Crallé, Act[in]g Sec[re]t[ar]y.

FC in DNA, RG 59 (State Department), Consular Instructions, 11:295.

R[ichard] K. Crallé to C[harles] S. Sibley, U.S. Attorney for the [Middle] District of Fla. Territory, Tallahassee, 10/25. "I herewith transmit a copy of a letter to this Department from the Hon: D[avid] Levy [Yulee, Delegate from Fla. Territory], together with copies to which he therein refers, as requested by you, of certain letters of the Hon. R[ichard] K. Call." FC in DNA, RG 59 (State Department), Domestic Letters, 35:8 (M-40:33).

From JOHN A. STUART

Beaufort, S.C., Oct[obe]r 25, 1844

Dear Sir, You will confer a great kindness on me, if your important duties allow you time, to write me a letter defending the present mode of electing Governor and President [by the legislature] in this State against the proposed innovation. I made use of your suggestions, in a speech ["I made" *interlined*] before the meeting subsequent to our election in Charleston, and I think with some good effect; but as it is a matter I have much at heart, and which I wish to be fully prepared to discuss, I would avail myself if possible of your full argument on the question, when it comes up in the legislature—making my maiden, and, as I *now* purpose, *only* speech on that subject. Your letter if you write I will, unless you otherwise desire keep to myself, by way of *cramming*. If you can not spare time, say so, in five lines—and I will do my best for *old* South Carolina, God bless her! out of my own limited resources.

I would wish particularly to meet the proposal to get over the objection to General Ticket voting by ["proving" *changed to* "having"] the *people* vote by Districts. It would amount I think to the same thing—sacrificing the republican to the Democratic principle. They will propose that each District elect *one* elector, and the legislature *two*—and give it plausibility as the mode which *we* proposed in choosing delegates to the Baltimore convention. I wish to shew that the legislature is already chosen in the best mode for giving the voice of all classes of the State: and that had it been feasible we would have been content that the States sh[oul]d have chosen delegates to Baltimore through their legislatures. If you write give me a view of the whole ground.

Though you abstain from local politics, it may interest you to know that if we fail to elect our old friend [Whitemarsh B.] Seabrook Governor on the first ballot, some of us think of naming Rob[er]t W. Barnwell for Governor. He is in excellent condition, and it would be a brave blow for our good State to get him back at once into the political traces. I think [Robert F.W.] Allston's and Seabrook's friends will have to come to some compromise in caucus—for I am sure the Old Subs [*sic;* Submissionists?] are too cunning to split their vote, and will unite on [William] McWillie, or more probably on [William] Aiken, whose purse and good feeling will weigh—and who though a Democrat and assenting to all we say is under old union influences which he is too weak to rise above. Both Allston & Seabrook would prefer, I presume declining in favor of a new man, than either of the two to yield to the other. You will I know excuse my making this application—and believe me Faithfully and Affectionately Your Servant, John A. Stuart.

ALS in ScCleA; PC in Boucher and Brooks, eds., *Correspondence,* pp. 253–254. NOTE: An AEU by Stuart on the address page of the letter reads: "To be *forwarded* if Mr. Calhoun is not in Pendleton."

To JOHN HASTING[s], [former Representative from Ohio]

Fort Hill, 26th Oct[obe]r 1844

My dear Sir, I have received your letter enclosing the [New Lisbon, Ohio] Ohio Patriot, and have read your letter on the Tariff, which it contains with much pleasure. You take strong & sensible views on the subject.

I agree with you, that Democracy must give up its trim[m]ing &

place itself on principles to save itself from distruction. It is its trim[m]ing & departure from principle, which has raised the Whigs to their present power. They will continue to rise in strength untill they will utterly prostrate the democracy unless it shall return to its original policy & purity. Nothing else can save it.

Our papers are so taken up with the elections that I do not know whether any of them can find space to publish your valuable letter till the election and the bustle accompany[ing] it are over. With great respect yours truly, J.C. Calhoun.

ALS in ScCleA. NOTE: This is a finished autograph letter, found among Calhoun's papers, with the address leaf missing, so perhaps it was never mailed.

From "A SOUTHERNER"

Virginia, Oct. 26, 1844

To the Hon. John C. Calhoun, Secretary of State: To hear *unpalatable* truths from an *estranged* friend, is agreeable to no man; and to you, particularly must be irksome. But I will not forego a public duty, because in the discharge of it, I may disturb the serenity of a former political favorite; nor will the recollections of party alliance for a long series of years, deter me from the task. This letter will find you, probably, in the calm retirement of your home, and in the midst of those delightful associations which *ought* to make your troubled mind tranquil and contented. It may be a season for reflection, and I hope that it may reach you while you have leisure to think over its contents. Its author you may know. He never fawned upon or flattered you—he never begged you for office, nor never strove for your elevation, in order that he might obtain office. He is independent of you, in every sense, and, probably, has often heretofore, shown his friendship for you, when you were ignorant of his services—because they were *disinterested.* Can the "toads and frogs," that have squatted at your ear or leaped through your ante-chambers, since you have been at Washington this last time, say as much? I did not join in the chorus of congratulation when I heard that you were *appointed* Secretary of State. And when the news reached me that you had *accepted* the nomination, I felt as if it was the death knell of your fame. Whose Secretary did you become? Did you ask yourself the question? Did the degradation never present itself to your mind? Did the shame and mortification of true friends never present themselves to your imagination? The man of Iron Will [Andrew Jackson?] had made the Heads of Departments *his* officers, and the man of Treason and Perfidy [John Tyler] had; in this respect, followed the example. We know that in theory, in design, such an idea never entered into the heads of those who organized the government on its present foundations; but we also know, and our posterity will fearfully realize the awful nature of the change, that, in practice, the Secretaries have ceased to become responsible ministers of high trusts, amenable to the laws; and are only the tools and instruments of the President—his arms and mouths. And are you in a different attitude? Are you not, in one word, the minister of *John Tyler?* Can you consent for any *consideration,* to hold on to such a position any longer? Quit, then, I abjure you, by all the recollections of your former fame, the post you now occupy! What is past cannot be recalled—but there may be a "lower deep" in the future. This administration will be *blotted out* next March. I do not desire that the national spunge should be applied to *you,* along with the others who compose its *materiel.* Suppose, even, that Polk should be elected President—a very improbable supposition, I admit—and he should invite you to retain your present office—as he would do—would not your continuance in the enjoyment of rank and pay, under the circumstances, be every way unworthy of your former high character? I think so. I, who once cherished your political honor, as a precious jewel, think that for J.C. Calhoun to become the agent of James K. Polk, who is the agent of Gen. [Andrew] Jackson, would be *almost* as bad as to be the agent of John Tyler! And there are hundreds of others, South of the Potomac, who are not of the present parties that divide the country, who unite with me in opinion. You have *not* settled the Texas question; and you have *not* settled the Oregon question. Leave them both. Wash your hands of the men and things now about you. They whisper flattering hopes in your ears. Your want of knowledge of human nature, makes you, great man as you are, the dupe of the designing. Again, I appeal to you, to reflect calmly in your present retirement, upon your actual situation as a public man, and believe that the advice here given you is from a source, that you yourself have confidence in and respect for. I had intended to say more—but will pause until your return to Washington. [Signed:] A Southerner.

PC in the Alexandria, D.C., *Alexandria Gazette & Virginia Advertiser*, October 31, 1844, p. 2.

From A[lexander] de Bodisco, New York [City], 10/27. De Bodisco announces his arrival at New York City the previous evening and that he has resumed his duties as Minister of the Emperor of

Russia to the U.S. He recalls his good relationship with Calhoun during his first residence at Washington, when Calhoun was a U.S. Senator, and anticipates that their official relations will be cordial. LS (in French) in DNA, RG 59 (State Department), Notes from Foreign Legations, Russia, vol. 3 (M-39:2).

From J[OHN] F. H. CLAIBORNE

Natchez [Miss.], Oct. 27th 1844

My dear Sir, I take the liberty of enclosing a letter to a gentleman who is, I believe, a translator in your department.

I also send by this mail a newspaper [*not found*] in which I have replied to some of the calumnies heaped on your State & yourself. You will note the extracts from the N[ew] O[rleans] Herald & Jeffersonian. With high respect, Y[ou]r friend & Ser[van]t, J.F.H. Claiborne.

ALS in ScCleA. NOTE: Claiborne was a former Representative from Miss. The "translator" referred to was doubtless Robert Greenhow, since both he and Claiborne were historians. For Greenhow's career as an historian, see Clyde N. Wilson, ed., *American Historians, 1607–1865*, vol. XXX of *Dictionary of Literary Biography* (Detroit: Gale Research Co., 1984), pp. 102–107.

From JOHN W. FISHER

Consulate of the
United States of America
Island [of] Guadeloupe
Point a Petre, 27 October 1844

Sir, I have the honor at this time, of informing you of my arrival at my Station on 25th inst., and happy to state, the City of Point a Petre is rapidly recovering in appearance from that awfull storm w[h]ich twook[?] place 8th Febr[ua]ry 1843.

Our American Commerce commences here[?] the middle of November, at w[h]ich time I have many American Ships in Port, and continue so untill the middle of July. The last Season, I found, grate difficulty in getting home mutinious and run a way Sailors.

I have freaqueantly meat with some Difficulty in Carrying out my different Functions. This seams to arrise from my not being a *French* subject, *as I* am the first American born Citizen that ever held this Consulate So you may Suppose it is trying to my national feelings, at times. His Excellency the Governor, has ordered[?] to do a way with it but without Effect; he express his feelings in behalf of my Country. And often express his astonishment that no United States Ships of War, do not Visit the Island.

You will pleas[e] to allow me to request of the Department, to forward[?] a national ship of war, the Com[man]d[e]r of w[h]ich I should like[?] to be experienced. This ves[s]el I can assume, would support me in my official Character And do a way with many things that is [*sic*] trying to my feelings and degrading to our National Character. With Grate respect I am Sir Your Ob[edient] Se[rvan]t, John W. Fisher.

ALS with Ens in DNA, RG 59 (State Department), Consular Despatches, Guadeloupe, vol. 2 (T-208:2), received 11/29.

From Tho[ma]s G. Clemson and Anna [Maria Calhoun Clemson]

[*In the hand of Thomas G. Clemson:*]
Legation of U.S., Brussels
October 28th 1844
My dear Sir, Mr. [Theophilus] Fisk leaves this tomorrow & we avail ourselves of this occasion to send you[,] Mrs. [Floride Colhoun] Calhoun & [Martha] Cornelia [Calhoun] a few triffles [*sic*] by way of recollection.

A few days since I went to see a loom which is patented here & which appears to me to have very many advantages over all others that I have seen—upon that loom cloth[,] linen[,] silk[,] carpets[,] velvets can be made without difficulty—& a boy 12 years of age can do as much as five or six persons with the ordinary loom; there is little or no fatigue and the whole very simple. Ribbands of the narrowest kind can be woven & stuff of any width no matter whether linnen [*sic*,] silk, wo[o]llen or of any degree of fineness can be made with the same facility[.] I will endeavour to forward a description of it for publication[.] It strikes me that it would be an admirable thing to introduce throughout the South. I send you a pair of suspenders which I saw made & which are sold for less than 2 francs. Such suspenders in the United States cost two or three dollars.

I send you a cravat of Black silk which are the only cravatts [*sic*] worn here[.] Stock[s] are never seen. Anna says she finds it difficult to know what would please you. Most gentlemen smoke, chew or snuff & it would be easy to send a triffle suitable to those tastes. Myself I think cravatts much warmer & more comfortable than stocks.

By Mr. Fisk I send a despatch interrogatory & preliminary to the form of treaty the government will give me for your consideration. If you have time have the goodness to give me your view on the subject. Anna will add a Postscript. Your affectionate son, Thos. G. Clemson.

[In the hand of Anna Maria Calhoun Clemson:]

Dear father, Mr. Fisk came yesterday & goes tomorrow. We could not let him go direct to you without sending if only a trifle of remembrance & we have been out all the morning searching but between the hurry & the necessity of sending small things lest we should incommode Mr. Fisk I have made I fear indifferent choice but it is not the value of the things I know which you will all think of. For mother & sister there were a thousand things one might send but you are a man so utterly without *fancies* that it is hard to know what would suit you. The silk cravat therefore is absolutely the only thing we saw this morning which it would not have been ridiculous to have sent you.

I send mother a pair of cuffs of Brussells [*sic*] lace & a cashmere cravat both in the last style worn here[;] the other little cravat & the box containing a specimen of the beautiful ivory carving of Dieppe in France (which I bought in Havre for her) are for sister.

I wrote you two days ago so have nothing more to say save that we are all getting better of our colds & [John] Calhoun [Clemson] has recovered his appetite. Your devoted daughter, Anna.

ALS in ScCleA.

From Tho[ma]s G. Clemson, Brussels, 10/28. Clemson asks on behalf of the Belgian government if the U.S. is willing to give Belgium an exclusive 40 per cent tariff discount on woollen and linen cloth and thread imported into the U.S. in exchange for a similar exclusive tariff discount by Belgium on rice, tobacco, whalebone, and fish oils. The Belgian government wishes to sound out the attitude of the U.S. before attempting to form a treaty. Clemson encloses documents concerning U.S. trade with Belgium. ALS (No. 3) with Ens in DNA, RG 59 (State Department), Diplomatic Despatches, Belgium, vol. 3 (M-193:4), received 11/25; FC (in Clemson's hand) in DNA, RG 84 (Foreign Posts), Belgium, vol. 4.

From DUFF GREEN, "Private"

Mexico [City,] 28th Oct[obe]r 1844

My dear Sir, From Gov. [Wilson] Shannon's Official dispatch you will learn that he has as yet recieved [*sic*] no reply to his letter to the Mexican Minister on the subject of Texas. I learn that a reply is in the course of ["publication" *canceled and* "preparation" *interlined*] and that it may be expected in the course of a few days. Gov. Shannon now having determined to avail himself of the English Courier which leaves to morrow, I will remain a few days longer, that he may forward the reply by the Brig Lawrence which is now at Vera Cruz waiting his orders to convey me to Galveston.

I am convinced that it is *impossible* to obtain the consent of this government to the Cession to the United States of Texas, California or any part of the public domain of Mexico whatever. I proceed to give you my reasons for thinking so.

The policy of Santa Anna has been for years—since the time of Mr. [Joel R.] Poinsett [U.S. Minister in Mexico, 1825–1829], to foster a prejudice ag[ains]t the United States. His purpose has been to occupy the public mind of Mexico with the apprehension of an invasion from the United States, and make his countrymen believe that he alone can protect them and the interests of Mexico. The Mexicans are ignorant and jealous of all foreigners and especial[l]y of the North Americans, and all the measures which Santa Anna has taken against foreigners are popular in Mexico. He excited a national sentiment throughout the whole country, which is strengthened by the apprehensions of the Priests who fear that the whole country will be overrun by us & that the confiscation of the church property will follow. The fundamental law forbids the Executive to alienate any portion of the public Domain without the consent of Congress, and such is the state of parties that if either Congress or the Executive wished to alienate Texas, it would be opposed by the other and made the pretence for a revolution.

Indeed, Santa Anna, left here on the 12th of September for Mango de Clava, under a confident belief that the Army would pronounce against Congress and make him Protector for life. His partisans were divided, in opinion, many of them urging him to assume supreme power at once, but he feared that if he overthrew the Congress a counter Revolution would ensue, and he might ["pay the" *canceled*] forfeit his life. He has about ten thousand soldiers at Jalappa [*sic*] and Vera Cruz. That he might throw the responsibility on the Congress, he availed himself of the occasion of the death of his wife, to retire, and [Valentín] Canalizo a creature of his will was appointed President *ad interim*. The Government press & the partisans of Santa Anna every where denounced Congress for failing to make the necessary appropriations for the "War of Texas" and thus endeavored to make the failure to vote the means of prosecuting that ["war" *interlined*] the pretence for the over throw of Congress & declaring Santa Anna *Protector* for life. The Army is nominal[l]y 35,000 men. Congress had voted 30,000 more and had voted an ["special" *canceled*] appropriation of four millions of dollars for that war, to ["be" *interlined*] raised by a special tax. Of that tax a very small part had been collected, and the greater part, more than it is believed can be realised, had been anticipated by drafts of the Government in favor of favorite contractors. It was with great difficulty that funds could be raised from week to week to pay these troops on which Santa Anna relies for personal protection, and instead of marching men into Texas, they cannot find money to send troops into the districts where their presence is required to enforce the collection of the Taxes.

When I reached here it was believed that things had reached a crisis. ["Santa" *canceled*.] A Pronunciamento was daily expected. Santa Anna, his old wife, not yet one month in the grave, had married a young girl of 16, by proxy, and I met her on the way to Jalappa, under the charge of her God father (Canedo) where she was to meet her husband. The plan was for the Army to pronounce ["in f" *canceled*] against Congress & to call Santa Anna from his retirement who was to sacrifice his domestic happiness and, leaving his young wife, again to take upon himself the cares of state to save his country. In the mean time the opposition in Congress & throughout the country gained strength. The Senators and deputies became bolder. They had voted four millions for the war of Texas[.] Santa Anna demanded ten millions more. The opposition demanded an exhibit of the manner in which the four millions had been applied and ["made"(?) *canceled*] defended themselves upon the ground that the sum voted had been absorbed by the ministers and that they would vote no more without a change of ministers. Each party professing to wish the reconquest of Texas, and both using the Texas question as a means of masking their own movements. Both relying on the Army, not to reconquer Texas but to revolutionise the Government. Santa Anna has the advantage of being in power, and of having surrounded himself by men who are dependant upon him for their Commissions. He is without the means of paying his troops. The exhausted condition of the treasury and the unwillingness of the people to pay direct taxes, must soon bring a crisis. In one district a tax collector was killed ["by" *canceled*] and in another the people have refused to pay & troops left here yesterday to enforce the payment. It is well understood that [*one word canceled*] both parties are doing all they can to defeat the measures of ["the" *canceled and* "each" *interlined*] other and to throw upon their opponents the odium of the Revolution which both declare must soon take place. The opposition wish to drive Santa Anna to pronounce against & dissolve the Congress, hoping that the reaction in favor of the Constitutional Government & of Congress will enable them to effect a counter revolution. In which case Santa Anna & his principal advisers will in all probability lose their lives. On the other hand Santa Anna thinks that as things are getting worse and worse the country will soon call him to the exercise of absolute power, in which ["case" *interlined*] he will shoot his enemies.

In such a state of things—In the midst of a civil conflict where each party is seeking pretences to murder & confiscate the property of their opponents, & where the principle [prevails] that it is treason to sell any part of the public domain to the United States, it is worse than folly to suppose that either party can alienate any part of Texas or California.

I have ascertained too that the Mexican bond holders in England, hold a mortgage on the Californias to secure the payment of twenty six millions of deferred debt, which mortgage expires in 1847.

You will naturally ask if such is the condition of the country why is it the Mexican Government will not sell? As the Govt. is so much in debt & unable to raise money but by direct taxation why do they not disband the army, economise their expenditure and sell a part of their territory which they must soon lose by revolution?

The answer is that the arguments of the public interest & public duty, are in vain addressed to both parties. The purpose of Santa Anna & his party is to establish a military despotism, and hence they find an argument in the discord & disorganisation of the government. Both parties look to power as a means of enriching the official incumbents. The embarrassed condition of the Treasury enables them to purchase in demand against the Government at a discount, and the command of the Treasury enables them to pay the claims thus purchased in preference to all others. It is said a seat in the Cabinet with a salary of $6000 per annum enables a minister to realise $500,000 per annum. Santa Anna himself, it is said, makes a large sum by the sale of ["offices" *canceled*] Commissions in the Army & in the Customs— and besides he has large Haciendas on which he feeds large droves of cattle, which are sold to the Army at three times the usual market prices.

You will see that the war against Texas is the pretence on which both parties are seeking office & that the embar[r]assed condition of the Treasury is used as a means of enriching those who have possession of the Government. When to this you add the fact that the state of public opinion is such that any party, being in power, and selling Texas or California to the United States, would be driven from office & that the chances are as ten to one that their doing so would be used as an argument for shooting them & confiscating their property, you can then understand why I say that it [is] impossible to make any new arrangement with Mexico as to Texas or California for some time yet to come at least.

I believe that there is one way & but one in which all that our Government desire & much more than you ask for can be had, but I am not now prepared to submit my views to paper. I reserve them for a personal explanation, & until after I have visited Texas.

In the mean time permit me to call your attention to the Mortgage on the Californias. I am told that it contains a condition that if the money is not paid in 1847, the creditors shall take possession of the country. The British Consul Gen[era]l here is the agent of the creditors. I have endeavored to obtain a copy of the Deed, but cannot do it without paying fifteen hundred or two thousand dollars for it. Permit me to say that it is important that you should obtain this through our minister here or in London, as the possession of California will necessarily command the settlements on the Columbia [River].

The Tactic of the opposition is not to assail Santa Anna personally, [*one word canceled*] but his ministers. He has been compelled to sacrifice [*several words canceled*; Ignacio] Trigueros ["Minister of the Treasury" *interlined*] and others are expected to follow. Each removal adds to the list of his enemies, and as each new incumbent comes into office to play the game of his predecessor, & enrich himself & his ["friends" *canceled*] associates by plundering the treasury, the same opposition continues. Thus in the face of Governor Shannon's letter and the declaration that a war with the United States is inevitable the House of Deputies by a vote of 43 to 13 ["refused" *canceled*] a few days ago, refused the loan of ten millions demanded by Santa Anna. The present Government may therefore temporise, but we have nothing to hope from Mexico. [*Interlined*: "They cannot reconquer Texas but they will not sell Texas."] The revolution here may be delayed. It may not be a bloody or a protracted civil war, but to me it appears that a revolution is inevitable & that nothing but

135

an army can prevent a civil war. The army is said to be as much divided as the Congress. Yours truly, Duff Green.

ALS in ScCleA; PC in Jameson, ed., *Correspondence*, pp. 975–980.

From D[UFF] GREEN, "Private"

Mexico [City,] 28th Oct. 1844

My dear Sir, I promised to write to the President [John Tyler] & to Mr. [Richard K.] Cralle on the affairs of Mexico. I have taken the liberty to refer them both to my letter to you of this date.

I have also written to them both requesting that my name may not be sent before the Senate for the Consulate at Galveston, as my return there will depend on circumstances. I hope that you will bear this in mind and not permit my name to be sent in.

I have also written to the President that I have some important suggestions to make in ["the" *canceled*] relation to the Cherokees and hope that he will not permit that question to be concluded before I reach Washington. I hope my dear Sir that I am not asking too much of you when I bespeak your aid in this matter. The public welfare no less than my own private interest are concerned, and I am sure that when I see you I can satisfy you that most important measures depend upon it. I have examined my ground well, and I am sure that when I come to explain myself fully to you, my plans will meet your ["apr"(?) *canceled*] approbation. I beg you therefore not to permit this negociation to be closed until you see me.

The accounts from the United States seem to leave no doubt of [James K.] Polk[']s election and in that case you will necessarily exercise great influence over the future. You have taken already the initiatory steps and the measure I propose is one [of] the most important in the series which are to accomplish the great ends you have in view.

You will have to encounter much opposition. The efforts of [Thomas H.] Benton, of the tariff and manufacturing interests will be united against you. The effect will be to keep the tariff question open and to force Carolina on her reserved rights. The arrangements I propose will greatly strengthen you in more ways than one. I entreat you therefore to keep the question open until I return. Having delayed so long to act, and compelled me to come to Texas before it was concluded I may appeal to the assurances given to me by the

President and to the interest which my friend Mr. [William H.] Thomas has in the question for the delay I now asked [*sic*] for. I rely on your doing what you can to secure it for me. Yours truly, D. Green.

ALS in ScCleA. NOTE: An AEU by Calhoun reads: "Mr. Green. He desires that his appointment not to [*sic*] be sent in till he is heard from & that nothing definitive should be done in reference to the Cherokees untill his return." Green's "friend Mr. Thomas" was doubtless William Holland Thomas (1815–1893), a white North Carolinian who was a chief and an attorney of the Eastern Cherokees.

From ALLEN A. HALL

Legation of the United States
Caracas, October 28th, 1844

Sir, In my despatch of the 2nd of August, I advised you that order and quiet continued to reign in this country, and that the elections, so far as they were then heard from, had passed over without the occurrence of any of the anticipated popular outbreaks.

These elections were merely primary—held for the purpose of choosing Electors upon whom it would afterwards devolve to vote for a Vice President—for members of both houses of Congress and for the members of the Provincial Assemblies or State Legislatures. The various Electoral Colleges met in the Capitals of their respective Provinces on the 1st inst., and I am glad to inform you that the general result has been altogether favorable to the Government party—the party which I regard as the peace and order party. It is certain that the coloured people, as a class, were appealed to by [Antonio Leocadio] Guzman, Editor of the Venezolano, the most talented and influential leader of the opposition, and that to this cause the opposition were mainly indebted for the signal triumph which they achieved at the primary elections over the Government in the City of Caracas and in several of the other cantons of this Province. Many of the slaves were taught to believe that they would be liberated as soon as the primary elections were over. Some of them, I am credibly informed, subsequently called upon Guzman, and demanded the fulfillment of his promises—their immediate freedom!

As the Electors in this, the Province of Caracas, were eighty one in number, and a part of them unpledged, it was impossible to ascertain, until the College met, which party had the majority. Great anxiety and excitement prevailed as the day appointed by law for the meeting of the Electoral Colleges ["approached" *interlined*]. In the Electoral College of this Province, the election of their presiding officer by the Government party by a majority of ten votes demonstrated their superior strength. The Government in expectation of, had made due preparations for, a popular outbreak. On the second day of its session, the deliberations of the Electoral College were interrupted by cries and menaces from a crowd of persons of divers colours, characters, and pursuits, many of whom were in the Hall outside the bar, and a still larger number in the street fronting the building in which the Electors had assembled; whereupon, a member of the Government party rose in his place, and, addressing the mob outside the bar, warned them emphatically not to expect that they would be permitted to enact over again the scenes of the 9th of February, for—if necessary to protect the rights and independence of the Electoral College, the Government would not hesitate to resort to the use of the bayonet. The mob mistaking this threat of the conditional use of the bayonet for its actual and near approach, instantly dispersed in great alarm and confusion, some of them in their great haste even forgetting their mules: after which, the Government party succeeded in electing their whole ticket for Members of Congress, Members of the Provincial Assembly, and in giving a majority of six votes to their candidate for the Vice Presidency, Diego B. Urbaneja.

I am in possession of information which entirely satisfies me, that had the opposition proved to be the dominant party in the Electoral College of this Province, most serious disturbances would have followed immediately. For such contingencies the Government were better prepared than I had previously supposed their timidity and apathy would ever permit them to be. It required, however, the voice of General [José Antonio] Paez to rouse them from the supineness in which they were slumbering. He warned them that a crisis was rapidly approaching, and intimated that unless they adopted more energetic and efficient measures to meet it, he would sell out his possessions and abandon the country. I know from unquestionable authority, that *he* is of opinion, that the existing party dissensions *will* terminate in civil strife and bloodshed. For myself, I have not a doubt of it. Not, that the leaders or the respectable portion of the opposition contemplate or desire such a catastrophe. *Their* object, I am persuaded, is limited to the acquisition of power and place with the accompanying emoluments. But, being in a feeble minority, they, or rather their chief leader, Guzman, has unfortunately invoked to their aid an element fraught with all mischief, and which, when thoroughly called into action, will be far beyond his or their control.

He has enlisted in his support, and arrayed against the Government, with a few exceptions, the coloured part of the population, *as a class*. And this has been done at a time when, and in a country where, an anticipated collision between the two races is a common topic of conversation with every description of persons, old and young, male and female, black and white—in the kitchen no less than the parlour. The bare fact that so fearful a contingency should be the subject of common, every-day allusion, remark and speculation by both whites and blacks appears to me one of the signs not least ominous of a disastrous and bloody future for this country.

These considerations led me to watch with much interest and anxiety the progress and result of the late elections. After they had terminated no less favorably for the Government, than, as I conceived, propitiously for the welfare of Venezuela, I took occasion to call on President [Carlos] Soublette at his private dwelling, and to say to him, that though I had most carefully avoided, as was my duty, identifying myself, or interfering in the slightest degree, with either of the parties into which this country is now politically divided—nevertheless, as I regarded the recent elections as involving not merely a change of national policy or a party triumph, but the safety of the Republic itself, I had come to offer *him* my sincere congratulations on the result: I added, that in making due preparations for meeting the anticipated and still impending crisis, he had, in my opinion, acted most wisely and patriotically. The President was evidently much gratified, and after expressing the deep sense he entertained of the imminent dangers which menace the domestic tranquillity of the country and the very existence of the Republic itself, he proceeded to remark that though it was neither to be expected or desired that the United States should interfere in the internal concerns of Venezuela, still, any outward demonstrations of sympathy and good understanding between the two Governments at this time would be highly appreciated by him, while they might be of the greatest service to the Government of Venezuela. He particularly requested that, when our men-of-war touch at La Guayra (and I am quite sure he would be glad at their doing so as often as practicable), the officers, or as many of them as can conveniently leave the vessel, should visit Caracas.

You will be at no loss to understand the the [*sic*] object of the President in desiring these frequent visits from our naval officers; and believing myself that the effect which could not fail to be thereby produced, especially on a certain class of the population of this City, would be highly salutary and conducive to the best interests of both countries, I shall endeavor, whenever any of ["our" *interlined*] men-

139

of-war do touch at La Guayra, to have President Soublette's wishes in this respect complied with.

Taking into consideration the peculiar character of the dangers to which this country is exposed, and the effect, as well direct and immediate as remote and contingent, which a conflict here between the negro and white races would and might exercise on the interests of the United States, I think you will agree with me, that Venezuela is a point to which the earnest attention of the Government of the United States should be constantly directed.

I beg in conclusion to repeat a suggestion contained in my despatch of the 25th of May last, that "orders be issued to such of our men-of-war attached to the West India squadron as can conveniently touch at La Guayra, to do so as frequently as practicable." Prior to the meeting of the Electoral Colleges, on the 1st inst., the Dutch Consul General deemed the prospect of revolutionary disturbances so great that he caused a man-of-war to come over from Curaçao and lie at La Guayra, while the Electoral College of this Province was in session. I have the honor to be, Sir, with great respect, Your obedient servant, Allen A. Hall.

ALS (No. 43) in DNA, RG 59 (State Department), Diplomatic Despatches, Venezuela, vol. 2 (M-79:3), received 12/2.

From A [mbrose] D [udley] Mann

United States Consulate
Bremen, Oct[obe]r 28, 1844
Sir; Since I entered upon the discharge of the duties of this Consulate, in December 1842, I have been constantly impressed with the necessity that exists, for our Government to adopt some regulations, by which to prevent the migration of paupers, and persons charged with or convicted of crime, to our shores. It is most gratifying to my feelings to witness the immense number of valuable Emigrants, many of them sober and industrious, and some of them possessed of handsome sums of money, who embark at this Port annually for the United States to people our almost interminable forests—but, it cannot be denied that among them are many *utterly worthless and vicious individuals* whose residence amongst us occasions deplorable consequences, and should in justice to ourselves be prohibited. It is not only the mischief which they create in the region where they take up

their abode—or rather where they pass their vagrant and demoralizing lives—but they deter more substancial Germans, whose inclinations otherwise would lead them over the Atlantic, from accomplishing their wishes. In a tour which I recently accomplished through some of the emigrating districts of Germany, the remark was frequently made to me by farmers in affluent circumstances, "I should like to go to America but A. who lived in my neighborhood a notorious rogue went there last year, and B. a perfect vagabond has just started. As I am now rid of them I will keep out of their way, as much better as I am sure I could do with my means in Iowa or Wisconsin, or some of the new States." Hence we get too large a portion of the population of the *lees* of Germany, when it is in our power to secure its very *essence*.

But can this evil be remedied? To do so effectually will be exceedingly difficult. The first and most salutary step will, in my opinion, be to require the *brokers and agents, or owners* of ships, who secure emigrants for them, to establish to the entire satisfaction of the Consul, at the port from which they sail, and procure his certificate to that end, that no one of the passengers, who they are embarking, is a criminal, or has been charged with crime, or is a vagrant. Also the master before clearing should make a declaration, under the solemnity of an oath on the Consular Books, that to the best of his knowledge and belief he has no person of this description on board, and that he will receive none such.

It was proposed I believe by this Consulate, before it came under my administration, that the United States should require each emigrant to have a certificate that he sustained a good character in the country from which he expatriated himself. This would be an unnecessary tax upon him, particularly as the object can be as well accomplished in the manner I have proposed. The importance of the matter however, without pursuing it any further than merely to bring it before you, I leave to be examined by yourself.

It has been customary for the despatch Agent of the Department at New York [City] to send all Documents directed to this Consulate via Hamburgh. This practice should be discontinued inasmuch as there are vessels sailing every few days from the former Port to Bremen—at least twice as often as to Hamburgh.

The consular Seal which has been in use for about fifty years is at last worn out, and I would be obliged if you would have a new one forwarded. The U.S. Coat of Arms is also so old and so much defaced that another is needed. The one that is here seems to have been badly executed in the first instance. They should be made at least doubly as large as those heretofore furnished by the Department, in order to designate the Consulate more clearly. I have the honor to be with high regard Your ob[edien]t serv[an]t, A.D. Mann.

LS (No. 13) in DNA, RG 59 (State Department), Consular Despatches, Bremen, vol. 4 (T-184:4). NOTE: A Clerk's EU reads "Bring to the Sec[retar]y's notice early in the Session." Mann (1801–1889), a Virginian, held a variety of official posts in Europe from 1842 to 1853. He was Assistant Secretary of State during 1853–1856. During the Civil War he undertook several missions in Europe for the Confederate States, and he remained an expatriate until his death.

From S[tephen] P[leasonton], Fifth Auditor, Treasury Department, 10/28. He discusses at length the expenses incurred during 1840–1843 by Consuls for the care of destitute seamen and for sending them back to the U.S. He believes that a bill that he sketched under date of 11/2/1843 for Calhoun's predecessor [Abel P. Upshur], had some provisions that would reduce these public expenses and would amend advantageously the law of 1840 on this subject. FC in DNA, RG 217 (General Accounting Office), Fifth Auditor, Letters Sent, 5: 172–173.

From WILSON SHANNON

Legation of the U.S. of A.
Mexico [City,] Oct. 28th 1844

Sir, Your despatch of the 10th of Sept. last reached me on the 12th inst., and in compliance with your instructions I lost no time in addressing to the Minister of Foreign Relations of this Government [Manuel C. Rejon] a communication expressive of the views of the President of the United States [John Tyler], in relation to a renewal of the war, on the part of Mexico, against Texas, and to the manner, in which it is proposed to be conducted. Accompanying this despatch, you will find a copy of this communication, marked no. 1. I have received no reply, as yet, to this note, and can not say when one may be expected. President Santa Anna is at his Hacienda near Jalapa, and until he can be heard from, no reply will be given. The uncertainty of the time, when a reply will be received, has determined me to delay this despatch no longer.

At the date of my last despatch, having been here but a short time & having had but a limited opportunity of ascertaining the real intentions of this Government, or the true state of public opinion, in relation to a renewal of the war against Texas, the views, which I then expressed, were of course imperfect. Since then I have taken every means which I could with propriety to inform myself on both these points.

There is no room to doubt that Mexico some time since determined to renew the war against Texas and immediately commenced extensive preparations for that purpose. There are two great political parties in this country, one struggling to maintain, the other to get political power; both however united on this question, and each appear to be zealously in favor of a vigorous prosecution of the war. At the head of one party stands President Santa Anna, holding the administration of the Govt. in his hands; the centre of the other is the majority in Congress, around which all the opponents of the President and his administration rally. This party strife however was not merged in the great question of the proposed invasion of Texas. On the contrary each party, while making strong professions in favor of the proposed invasion, have been by no means unmindful of their own interests, or the means, by which their views on the Govt. were to be promoted.

It was supposed that, by a renewal of hostilities against Texas, Mexico would either subjugate the country, or force her into an alliance with England, under a guarantee from that power that she should in no event transfer her sovereignty to the U. States. It is the desire of Mexico, beyond doubt, if she can not reconquer and hold Texas herself, that the latter should constitute an independent power, and serve as a barrier Republic against the encroachments, which it is feared the U.S. desire to make on Mexican territory. It has been the policy of all parties here for years back to represent us as a dangerous and grasping neighbour, and that it was necessary for the safety of Mexico we should be held at a distance. Hence the hostility of this Govt. & people to annexation, and hence also the policy, which has been adopted and adhered to for years past, in utter disregard of all treaty stipulations, of preventing, by every possible means, our citizens from settling in Mexico and especially in the four northern departments, and also of driving those out of the country, who are located in it.

The army, at the time a renewal of hostilities was determined upon, nominally consisted of thirty five thousand men, but its actual numbers were far short of this. Congress with the avowed object of renewing the war against Texas, authorized an additional levy of thirty thousand troops, making the whole force that the administration was authorised to make for the prosecution of the war sixty five thousand. The levy of troops immediately commenced, & has been, & still is, going on. I have found it not only difficult but impossible to ascertain the exact number of available forces the Govt. now has at its command, but it may be safely stated at not less than thirty thousand, & this number is daily being increased by new recruits.

This force is distributed at various points throughout Mexico, but that portion of it intended to act against Texas is concentrated at Jalapa, Vera Cruz, San Luis Potosi, and in this city, making in all about fifteen or eighteen thousand strong, exclusive of the force under the command of Gen[era]l [Adrian] Woll, on the western frontier of Texas, the number of which I am unable to state. The force in Jalapa is eight thousand; in Vera Cruz about two; in San Luis Potosi between two & three; and in this city five, thousand.

The plan of the campaign is said to be to concentrate about ten thousand troops at Vera Cruz, & convey them direct from that place, by means of transports and steam vessels, to Galveston, with the view of taking that City & overrunning Eastern Texas; while the army under Gen[era]l Woll is to be strengthened, cross the Rio Grande, and invade Texas on the west and form a junction with the Eastern division of the army at some central point. In view of this plan of attack, Mexico sent her two steamers to New York to be repaired, and contracted for four additional ones, with some small crafts. These, it is said, are on the stocks and being finished in the U. States, but will not be ready for delivery for some time to come. She has also, it is said, a contract for the construction of several vessels in England, intended for the same purpose.

That this was the plan of the campaign originally adopted & intended to be carried out, & in view of which all the military preparations by the Govt. have been made, I have no doubt. Independent of the positive information I have received that such was the plan, all the movements of the Govt. go to confirm this information. The number of troops, you will perceive, collected at Jalapa and Vera Cruz is about ten thousand; & that this force can at any time be concentrated at the latter place in four days, & thence embarked at once for Galveston. If it had been the intention of the Govt. to assail Texas by the Rio Grande alone, the whole force of the invading army would have been concentrated at San Luis Potosi; but the force at and ready to be thrown on that point is by no means sufficient to justify an invasion of Texas. As to the plan of the campaign, then, I think you may rely with confidence on what I have stated.

Congress also made an appropriation of four millions, some time since, for the purpose of carrying on the war, & have been actively engaged in discussing for several weeks a loan bill, authorizing the additional sum of ten millions for the same purpose. There is a decided majority in Congress, as I have already stated, opposed to the President Santa Anna, and they are beginning to doubt the policy of placing such a large military force in his hands, with the pecuniary means to sustain it. Within the last two months this party has been gaining strength rapidly, and is now strong enough to have confidence in being able to overthrow the President. He is aware of the combinations against him, and keeps himself in the midst of his troops at Jalapa and Vera Cruz, and is actively engaged in preparing to crush his opponents & defeat their contemplated movements. In this state of party strife here, with the known views of the President of the U.S., in relation to a renewal of the war against Texas, I feel confident that that measure will be abandoned at least for the present; that the two parties will come to an open rupture, and that a revolution, to say the least, is probable. On the 22d inst. a final vote was taken in the House of Deputies on the ten million loan bill, and the measure failed by a vote of forty three against it and thirteen for it. This goes to confirm the opinion that the war, for the present, is to be abandoned. I will not at this time speculate as to the future. Things are rapidly coming to a crisis, and a short time will enable me to give results instead of opinions.

As many of our citizens ["who are" *interlined*] favourable to the acquisition of Texas, appear to be under the impression that the consent of Mexico to that measure might be obtained, and that that would be the best and most convenient mode of accomplishing the object our Govt. has in view, I have been induced, through confidential sources, to sound the leading men of both political parties on this subject. The uniform reply has been unfavourable—that public opinion would not sustain such a measure, & that neither party would be willing to risk their popularity, and, especially at this time, by proposing or agreeing to it. From everything I have been able to collect since I came here, I am convinced that it is useless to think of obtaining the consent of Mexico to annexation, or the sale of any portion of what she claims as belonging to her territory, until there is a change in public opinion. What change in public feeling, on this subject, a revolution may produce, or what the result would be, should the conviction become general that annexation is inevitable, it is difficult at this time to say. I know of nothing however that should lead us to hope for a favourable change in public opinion on this subject.

That a feeling of hostility should exist against us with this people is by no means strange, when we recollect that for years past oppo-

145

sition to the U.S. has been used by both parties as a lever by which to obtain public favour and political power. We have been represented as seeking to overrun all Mexico, and that, if not held in check, we would plant the American standard on the walls of the Capitol. Such has been the unjust and odious light, in which we have been held up to this people by the political men of all parties, until they have created a public opinion, which they cannot, if they were so disposed, easily resist or control. It is true that many intelligent Mexicans privately entertain & express opinions favourable to the amicable arrangement of the difficulties with Texas, & believe that the proposed invasion, if attempted, would result in no good to Mexico. But there are few, who have the boldness to express these opinions publicly, or who would be willing to stem the current of popular prejudice by undertaking to carry them out. I am not aware that these opinions prevail to any extent in the army, which is the great controlling power in the country. I think we must therefore rely on time and a new combination of circumstances to dissipate these prejudices against us, before we can reasonably hope to acquire by negociation any portion of the territory now claimed by Mexico, and I do not think we have any grounds to flatter ourselves that a favourable change in this respect will soon take place.

Nos. 2, 3, 4, 5 & 6 are copies of a correspondence with the Minister of Foreign Relations on the subject of the Retail law. From them you will learn the state of this question.

No. 7 is a copy of a note, which in pursuance of your instructions I addressed to the Mexican Govt., in relation to the order of the 14 July 1843, expelling all natives of the U.S. from California & the adjoining Departments. To this I have received no reply.

Nos. 8 and 9 relate to the recent passport regulations, copies of which have already been forwarded to you.

No. 10 is a copy of a note to Mr. Rejon, asking to be informed whether the crew of the Wm. A. Turner are still confined in Tabasco. In reply to this note and to frequent personal enquiries I have received no other than a verbal answer, that enquiry had been made of the Minister of War upon the subject; that the latter had written to Tabasco to ascertain the fact, and that as soon as a reply was received, I should be informed of it.

No. 11 is the reply of Mr. Rejon to my note in relation to the excessive charges in the case of Patrick McCarthy, deceased at Tampico. I have the honor to be Your ob[edien]t serv[an]t, Wilson Shannon.
[Enclosure]

Wilson Shannon to M[anuel] C. Rejon, Minister of Foreign
  Relations and Govt. of the Republic of Mexico, No. 1

Legation of the U.S. of A.

Mexico, Oct. 14th 1844

The undersigned, Envoy Extraordinary and Minister Plenipotentiary
of the U. States of America, has the honor to inform H.E. M.C. Rejon,
Minister of Foreign Relations and Govt. of the Republic of Mexico,
that the President of the United States has learned with deep regret,
that the Mexican Govt. has announced its determination to renew the
war against the Republic of Texas, and is now engaged in extensive
preparations with a view to an early invasion of its territory; and instructs the undersigned to protest, in the most solemn form, both
against the invasion at this time, and the manner, in which it is proposed to be conducted.

The orders of the Commander of the Army of the North, Gen[era]l
[Adrian] Woll, issued on the 20th of June last, and the Decree of the
Provisional President of Mexico of the 17th of June, 1843, leave no
doubt as to the manner, in which the war is to be conducted. The
decree makes the Generals in chief of division of the Army, and the
Commandant Generals of the Coast and Frontier responsible for its
exact fulfilment. It was under this responsibility, it would seem, that
General Woll, to whom the Texan Frontier was assigned, issued his
order of the 20th of June. After announcing that the war was renewed
against Texas; that all communications with it must cease; and that
every individual of whatever condition, who may have communication
with it, shall be regarded as a traitor, and as such punished according
to the articles of war; it states, that every individual, who may be
found at the distance of one league from the left bank of the Rio Bravo,
will be regarded as a favourer and accomplice of the usurpers of that
part of the national territory and as a traitor to Mexico, and, after a
summary military trial, shall be punished accordingly. It also states,
that every individual who may be embraced in the foregoing, and
who may be rash enough to fly at the sight of any force, belonging to
the supreme Government, shall be pursued until taken or put to death.

In what spirit the Decree of the 17th of June, which the order is
intended to fulfil, is to be executed, the fate of the party under Gen-
[era]l [Francisco] Sentmanat at Tabasco affords an illustration—Under it, they were arrested and executed without hearing or trial,
against the express provision of the Constitution and the Sanctity of
Treaties, which were in vain invoked for their protection.

If the Decree itself was thus enforced, in time of peace, against the subjects of foreign powers, some faint conception may be formed of the barbarous and inhuman spirit, in which the order of Gen[era]l Woll may be expected to be executed against the inhabitants of Texas and all, who may in any way aid their cause, or even have communication with them. It was under a decree of a similar character, issued on the 30th of October, 1835, but not so comprehensive or barbarous in its provisions, that the execution of Fanning [*sic*; James W. Fannin] and his party was ordered, in a former invasion. This decree was limited to Foreigners, who should land at any port of Mexico, or arrive by land, and having hostile intentions, or who should introduce arms or munitions of war to be used at any place in rebellion, or placed in the hands of its enemies. Highly objectionable as were its provisions, the order of Gen[era]l Woll intended to carry out that of June, 1843, goes far beyond it. It embraces every individual, who may be found east of a line drawn three miles east of the Rio Bravo, without distinction of age or sex; foreigners or citizens, condition or vocation. All of every description are to be treated as traitors. It proclaims, in short, a war of extermination. All are to be destroyed or driven out, and Texas left a desolate waste.

Such is the barbarous mode, in which the Government of Mexico has proclaimed to the world it is her intention to conduct the war. And here the enquiry naturally arises; what is her object in renewing, at this time, a war, to be thus conducted, which has been virtually suspended for eight years, and when her resources are known to be so exhausted as to leave her without the means of fulfilling her engagements? But one object can be assigned, and that is to defeat the annexation of Texas to the United States. She knows full well that the measure is still pending, and that the rejection of the Treaty has but postponed it. She knows that, when Congress adjourned, it was pending in both Houses, ready to be taken up and acted upon at its next meeting, and that it is at present actively canvassed by the people throughout the Union. She is not ignorant that the decision will, in all probability be in its favour, unless it should be defeated by some movement exterior to the United States. The projected invasion of Texas by Mexico, at this time, is that movement, and is intended to effect it, either by conquering and subjugating Texas to her power, or by forcing her to withdraw her proposition for annexation and to form other connections less acceptable to her.

The United States can not, while the measure of annexation is pending, stand quietly by and permit either of these results. It has been a measure of policy long cherished and deemed indispensable to their safety and welfare, and has accordingly been an object steadily

148

pursued by all parties, and the acquisition of the territory made the subject of negociation by almost every administration for the last twenty years. This policy may be traced to the belief, generally entertained, that Texas was embraced in the cession of Louisiana by France to the United States in 1803 and was improperly surrendered by the Treaty of Florida in 1819; connected with the fact that a large portion of the Territory lies in the valley of the Mississippi and is indispensable to the defence of a distant, ["weak" *canceled*] and important frontier. The hazard of a conflict of policy upon important points between the United States and one of the leading European Powers, since the recognition of Texas, has rendered the acquisition still more essential to their safety and welfare, and accordingly, has increased in proportion the necessity of acquiring it. Acting under the conviction of this necessity and the impression that the measure would be permanently defeated by a longer postponement, the President of the United States invited Texas to renew the proposition for annexation. It was accepted by her, as has been stated; is still pending; and here the question again recurs: shall the United States quietly stand by on the eve of its consummation, and permit the measure to be defeated, by an invasion by Mexico; and shall they suffer Texas for having accepted an invitation to join them and consummate a measure alike essential to her and their permanent peace, welfare and safety, to be desolated, her inhabitants to be butchered or driven out; or, in order to avert so great a calamity, to be forced, against her will, into other alliances, which would terminate in producing lasting hostilities between her and them, to the permanent danger of both?

The President has fully and deliberately examined the subject, and has come to the conclusion that honor and humanity, as well as the safety & welfare of the United States, forbid it, and he would accordingly be compelled to regard the invasion of Texas by Mexico, while the question of annexation is pending, as highly offensive to the United States. He entertains no doubt that they had the right to invite her to renew the proposition for annexation, and that she, as an independent state, had a right to accept the invitation, without consulting Mexico, or asking her leave. He regards Texas, in every respect, as independent as Mexico, and as competent to transfer the whole or part of her territory as she is to transfer the whole or part of hers. Not to insist on the unquestionable right of Texas to be regarded and treated, in all respects, as an independent power, on the ground the [*sic*] she has successfully resisted Mexico and preserved her independence for nine years, and has been recognized by other Powers, as independent; it is only necessary to recur to the Constitution of 1824 to show that she is perfectly entitled to be so regarded and treated. Under that Constitution she, with Coahuila, formed a separate state, constituting one member of the federation of Mexican States; with a right secured to Texas, by the Constitution, to form a separate state as soon as her population would warrant it.

The several states of the Federation were equal in rights and equally independent of each other; and remained so until 1835, when the Constitution was subverted by the Army, and all the States, which dared to resist, were subjugated and consolidated into one, ["except" *canceled*] by force, except Texas. She stood up bravely in defence of her rights & independence and successfully asserted them on the battle ground of San Jacinto in 1836, and has ever since maintained them. The constitution, then, of 1824 made her independent and her valor and her sword have since maintained her so. She has been acknowledged to be so by three of the leading powers of Christendom; and is regarded by all, as such, except by Mexico herself. She neither now stands nor ever has stood, in relation to Mexico, as a rebellious power or Department struggling to obtain independence after throwing off her yoke, much less as a band of lawless intruders and usurpers, without Government or political existence, as Mexico would have the world to believe. On the contrary the true relation between them is that of having been independent members of what once was a federal Government, but now subverted by force, the weaker of which has successfully resisted, against fearful odds, the attempts of the stronger to conquer and subject her to its power. It is in that light the United States regard her, and in that they had the right to invite her to renew the proposition for annexation, and to treat with her for admission into the Union, without giving any just ["cause" *canceled*] offense to Mexico, or violating any obligation by Treaty or otherwise between us and her.

Nor will our honour any more than our welfare and safety, permit annexation to be defeated by an invasion of Texas, while the question is pending. If Mexico has thought proper to take offence, it is the United States, who invited a renewal of the proposition, and not Texas, who accepted the invitation, who should be held responsible; and we, as the responsible party, cannot without implicating our honor, permit another to suffer in our place. Entertaining these views, our honor and interests being both involved, Mexico will make a great mistake, if she supposes that the President can regard with indifference the renewal of the war, which she has proclaimed against Texas.

But another and still more elevated Consideration would forbid him to regard the invasion with indifference. Strong, as the objections to it, of itself, are, in connection with existing circumstances, those to the manner, in which it is proclaimed it will be conducted, are still more so. If honor and interest forbid a tame acquiescence in the renewal of the war, the voice of humanity cries aloud against the proposed mode of conducting it. All the world have an interest that the rules and usages of war, as established between civilized nations in modern times should be respected, and are in duty bound to resist their violation, in order to preserve them. In this case that duty is preeminently ours. We are neighbours, the nearest to the scene of the proposed atrocities; the most competent to judge from our proximity, and for the same reason enabled more readily to interpose. For the same reason also, our sympathies would be more deeply roused by the scenes of misery which would present themselves on all sides; not to mention the dangers, to which we must be exposed in consequence of an invasion, so conducted, near a distant and weak frontier, with numerous and powerful bands of Indians in its vicinity.

If any thing can add to these strong objections to the manner, in which it is proclaimed, the war will be waged, it is the fiction, regardless of the semblance of reality, to which the Government of Mexico has resorted, as a pretext for the Decree of the 17th of June 1843, and the orders of Gen[era]l Woll of the 20th June last. Finding nothing in the conduct of the Government or people of Texas to justify their barbarous character and palpable violation of the laws of nations and humanity, it has assumed, in wording them, that there is no such Government or community as Texas; that the individuals to be found there are lawless intruders and usurpers, without political existence, who may be rightfully treated as a gang of pirates and outcasts from society, and, as such, not entitled to the protection of the laws of nations or humanity. In this assumption the ["Government of Mexico" *interlined*] obstinately persists, in spite of the well known fact, universally admitted by all except itself, that the colonists, who settled Texas, instead of being intruders and usurpers, were invited to settle there, first, under a grant by the Spanish authority to Moses Austin, which was afterwards confirmed by the Mexican authority, and, afterwards, by similar grants from the state of Coahuila and Texas, which it was authorized to make by the Constitution of 1824. They came there then as invited guests, not invited for their own interests, but for those of Spain and Mexico, in order to protect a weak and helpless province from wandering tribes of Indians; to improve, cultivate and render productive wild and almost uninhabited wastes, and to make that valuable, which was before worthless. All this they effected at great cost and much danger and difficulty, which nothing but American energy, industry and perseverance could have overcome; not only unaided by Mexico, but in despite of the impediments caused by her interference. Instead then of a lawless band of adventurers, as they are assumed to be by the Government of Mexico, these invited colonists became in a few years constituent portions of one of the members of the Mexican Federation, and since their separation have established wise and free institutions, under the influence of which they have enjoyed peace and security, while their energy and industry, protected by equal laws, have widely extended the limits of cultivation and improvement. It is such a people, living under such institutions, successfully resisting all attacks from the period of their separation nine years ago, and who have been recognized and admitted into the family of nations, that Mexico has undertaken to regard as a lawless banditti, and against whom, as such, she has proclaimed a war of extermination, forgetful of their exalted and generous humanity in refusing to exercise the just rights of retaliation, when, in a former invasion, victory placed in their hands the most ample means of doing so. The Government of Mexico may delude itself by its fictions, but it can not delude the rest of the world. It will be held responsible, not by what it may choose to regard as facts, but what are in reality such, and known and acknowledged so to be, by all save itself.

Such are the views entertained by the President of the United States, in regard to the proposed invasion, while the question of annexation is pending, and of the barbarous and bloody manner, in which, it is proclaimed, it will be conducted; and in conformity to his instructions, the undersigned hereby solemnly protests against both, as highly injurious and offensive to the United States.

The undersigned, while making this protest and declaration, has been instructed at the same time, to repeat to H.E. the Minister of Foreign Relations and Government of Mexico, what was heretofore communicated to him by the Chargé d'affaires of the United States, in announcing the conclusion of the Treaty, that the measure was adopted in no spirit of hostility to Mexico, and that, if annexation should be consummated, the United States will be prepared to adjust all questions growing out of it, including that of boundary, on the most liberal terms.

The undersigned avails himself of this occasion to renew to H.E. M.C. Rejon, Minister of Foreign Relations and Government of the

Republic of Mexico, the assurance of his distinguished consideration. (Signed) Wilson Shannon.

[Enclosure]

Wilson Shannon to M[anuel] C. Rejon, Minister of
    Foreign Relations &c &c., No. 7

Legation of the U.S. of A.
Mexico, Oct. 10th 1844

The undersigned, Envoy &c, in obedience to the instructions of his Government, embraces the present occasion to call the attention of H.E., M.C. Rejon, Minister &c, to an order dated on the 14th of July, 1843, addressed by the Mexican Secretary of War to the Governors of California, Sonora, Sinaloa and Chihuahua, in relation to the expulsion of citizens of the United States from their respective departments.

This order, in substance, directs that, it is not proper for natives of the United States of the north to reside in either of the above named Departments; that they shall quit the country within a reasonable time, to be fixed by the Governors of the respective Departments for that purpose; and that from the date of the said order, no individual belonging to the United States shall be permitted to enter either of said Departments. The Treaty of the 5th of April 1831, between the United States and the Republic of Mexico expressly provides, among other things, that "the citizens of the two countries shall have liberty to enter into the same, and remain and reside in any part of said territories respectively." The 14th article of this Treaty provides that, "both the Contracting parties promise and engage to give their special protection to the persons and property of the citizens of each other, of all occupations, who may be in their territories, subject to the jurisdiction of the one, or of the other, transient or dwelling therein, leaving open and free to them the tribunals of justice for their judicial recourse, on the same terms, which are usual and customary with the natives or citizens of the country, in which they may be."

The undersigned will not enter into an argument to prove that the order in question is in direct conflict with the Treaty stipulations above recited. No one can read the order in connection with the provisions of the Treaty without admitting that the former is a gross and palpable violation of the latter. It will be recollected by H.E. that this order led, at the time, to a correspondence between the predecessor of the undersigned (Mr. [Waddy] Thompson) and Mr. [José M. de] Bocanegra the, then, Minister of Foreign Relations &c, in which it was not attempted by the latter to defend or justify said order, under the existing Treaty between the two countries. The result of this correspondence seems to have been none other than an enlargement, or modification of the terms of the order, so as to embrace all foreigners, or such of them as might be deemed, by the Governors of the respective departments, vagrants or dangerous to the public peace. Although the predecessor of the undersigned (Mr. Thompson), on his own responsibility expressed himself satisfied with this modification of said order, the Govt. of the United States views the subject in a different light, and still considers the order, modified and enlarged as it has been, as conflicting with the existing Treaty and injurious to its citizens residing in said departments. The undersigned is unable to see how the subject could have been otherwise viewed. The order as modified still authorizes the Governors of the respective departments arbitrarily to fix the time, when those deemed obnoxious shall leave the country; to determine also who are vagrants and what persons are dangerous to the public peace, without affording to the suspected a trial of any kind, to enable them to vindicate their character, and establish their innocence. The Governor of a Department has only to determine that a citizen of the United States, residing within his jurisdiction, is a vagrant or dangerous to the public peace, to enable him, as the order ["now" *interlined*] stands, to issue his mandate, expelling him from the country. This, certainly, is not giving that protection to the persons and property of citizens of the United States, provided for by the Treaty of 1831. The original order complained of declares that no individual, belonging to the United States, shall be permitted to enter either of the said Departments. This is in direct opposition to both the letter and the spirit of the Treaty; yet the subsequent modification leaves this obnoxious provision in full force. As the order now stands and as understood by the undersigned, the residence of citizens of the United States within the four Departments named is virtually at the will & pleasure of the respective Governors. It can not be expected that the United States will consent that rights guaranteed to their citizens by solemn compact, should be made to depend on a tenure so uncertain; nor can they allow their citizens, induced to take up their residence within the territories of Mexico, under the solemn sanctions of a treaty, to be driven from their abodes without trial, or otherwise injured in their persons or property on slight and frivolous pretexts.

As it will not be claimed that the original order, as it emanated from the Secretary of war, was authorized by the Treaty, and as the modification, which it subsequently received, only in part removed its objectionable features, its unconditional repeal would seem to be demanded as well by what is due to Mexico herself as to the United

States. The undersigned will not permit himself therefore to believe that Mexico will hesitate to do an act, which is so obviously demanded by a sacred regard for her treaty stipulations and a sense of justice and good faith towards a sister Republic.

The undersigned renews &c &c the assurance of his distinguished consideration. (Signed) Wilson Shannon.

LS (No. 3) with Ens in DNA, RG 59 (State Department), Diplomatic Despatches, Mexico, vol. 12 (M-97:13), received 11/23; FC in DNA, RG 84 (Foreign Posts), Mexico, Despatches (C8.9); PEx with En in Senate Document No. 1, 28th Cong., 2nd Sess., pp. 47–52; PEx with En in House Document No. 2, 28th Cong., 2nd Sess., pp. 45–50; PEx with En in *Congressional Globe*, 28th Cong., 2nd Sess., Appendix, pp. 7–8; PEx with En in the Washington, D.C., *Globe*, December 6, 1844, p. 2; PEx with En in the Washington, D.C., *Daily National Intelligencer*, December 9, 1844, pp. 1–2; PEx with En in the Washington, D.C., *Madisonian*, December 12, 1844, p. 2; PEx with En in *Niles' National Register*, vol. LXVII, no. 15 (December 14, 1844), pp. 234–235. NOTE: The enclosure "No. 1" was the one printed in the published versions cited above.

From A[NGEL] CALDERON DE LA BARCA

New York [City], 29th October, 1844
As soon as the Honorable John C. Calhoun informed him in conversation of his desire that the Captain General of Cuba should recommend to the tribunals the observance of despatch and law in the judicial proceedings set on foot against some American citizens arrested upon a charge of conniving at the scheme of revolt of the colored people of that Island, the Undersigned, Envoy Extraordinary and Minister Plenipotentiary of Her Catholic Majesty, hastened to communicate the same to His Excellency, and acquainted him, at the same time, with the favorable opinion which the Secretary of State of the Union had expressed of his justification and upright intentions.

This was accordingly done, and, for the purpose of showing that the Honorable John C. Calhoun has not been mistaken in the good opinion which he has formed of General [Leopoldo] O'Donnell, the Undersigned has the honor to enclose to him an open copy of the reply of that Chief of the Spanish Colony, dated the 2nd of this month.

It seems to the Undersigned that it would be fair and just with a view to the due appreciation of the zeal with which the said Superior Chief labors to preserve and consolidate the existing relations of good understanding between Spain and the United States, that the Secretary of State of the Union should give it through the periodical press the publicity which it deserves; even if it were for nothing else than to refute the hostile calumnies and neutralize the unbridled slanders which, for a sinister design, the newspapers of other countries and even those of the United States themselves, incessantly propagate against His Excellency.

The Undersigned renews to the Honorable John C. Calhoun the assurances of his most distinguished consideration. A. Calderon de la Barca.

[Enclosure]

[Leopoldo O'Donnell to Angel Calderon de la Barca]

Havana, 2nd October, 1844

I am apprized by Your Excellency's communication of the 15th of August of the conference held by you with the Secretary of State, and of the language used by him in regard to the imprisonment of some Americans with reference to the plan of revolt of the colored people, and it is very satisfactory to me to know that that Minister reposes the greatest confidence in the prudence and rectitude with which that disagreeable subject is managed here. This very day I am answering a complaint which the American Consul residing in this place [Robert B. Campbell] has addressed to me upon the same subject, and I tell him, in substance that if indeed in the alarm ["produced in the minds of some inferior judges by" *interlined and* "which" *canceled*] the vast ramifications of that plot, and the guilt which immediately resulted from it, any one had been arrested, so soon as the proceedings were put into a regular train, the guilt of some was disproved and of others extenuated; and that I have the satisfaction to inform him that, at present, there is no American citizen under arrest, ["and that" *canceled and* "since" *interlined*] all had been set free pursuant to the requirements of justice in their respective cases; ["and that" *canceled*] notwithstanding bail had been exacted of Mr. [John] Thompson and some others, conformably to law. I am also informing him that this business is about being brought to a close, as he may see from the publications in the newspapers, and that the decisions of the tribunals who are charged with it, are impressed with the indelible seal of impartiality and clemency: and I have nothing more to communicate to Your Excellency upon the same subject, because, in answering the Consul, I have displayed the frankness and truth by which I am characterized, and the conviction that every thing has been done agreeably to the most impartial justice. God, &c.

State Department translations of LS and En (both in Spanish) in DNA, RG 59 (State Department), Notes from Foreign Legations, Spain, vol. 11 (M-59:13, frames 991–1001). NOTE: In addition to the letter from O'Donnell, Calderon de la Barca enclosed a clipping from the New York, N.Y., *Courrier des Etats-Unis* of 10/24 which referred to Cuba as "un immense *abbatoir*" and threatened English or U.S. intervention to prevent bloodshed and to halt the slave trade.

From BEN E. GREEN

Mexico [City,] Oct. 29th 1844

Dear Sir, Deeming it to be my duty to inform the Department of every thing that might go to show the purposes and view of the British Govt., in relation to Texas, I have in several of my despatches, spoken of conversations held with Mr. [Charles] Bankhead. I hope that it may not be necessary to submit those portions of my correspondence to the Senate, or that, at least, they shall not find their way into the public newspapers.

The publication in one of the Galveston papers of a letter of mine to Mr. [William S.] Murphy has made me more anxious that those parts of my correspondence with the Department should not be published. Since the publication of that letter, Mr. Bankhead has been much more guarded in his conversations with me; and although he has treated me with great kindness and we are still on terms of the most friendly intercourse, I know that he was not at all pleased with its publication. To be always on the watch as to what may have a bearing on the interests of his country, whether in private society or elsewhere is the duty of a diplomat; but to have correspondence of that character published is not only disagre[e]able to him personally, but materially impairs his usefulness.

In consequence of the difficulty about my pay as Chargé d'affaires, I have been compelled to have recourse to the kindness of a friend for an advance in anticipation of the appropriation, which will be made, I trust, at an early period of the coming session. The embarrassment, which I feel under the circumstances, must be my excuse for requesting you to urge an appropriation on the consideration of Congress, and you will much oblige me, if it could be included in the appropriation, which is generally made at the commencement of the session of Congress. I am Sir, very respectfully Your ob[edien]t Serv[an]t, Ben E. Green.

ALS in DNA, RG 59 (State Department), Diplomatic Despatches, Mexico, vol. 12 (M-97:13), received 11/23; draft in NcU, Duff Green Papers (published microfilm, roll 5, frames 838–840).

From JOSIAH C. NOTT

Mobile, 29th Oct. 1844

Dear Sir, I have been at work on an article for the Charleston Medical Journal on the *Comparative health* & longevity of Northern & Southern Seaports. The Statistics which I have procured & worked up, show results in favor of the South much stronger than I anticipated & I hope they may prove useful. The article will not be published before the January Number; & as the facts connected with a single point (the mortality of the Negroes &c) might be useful to you in some way before that time, I have concluded to give you a little extract from my notes. The facts may all be fully relied on as they are from published reports of the respective Cities.

"*Mortality of the Negroes.* The statistics of Charleston afford some curious & instructive information on this point. The influences of climate & social condition are both strongly illustrated here. The facts are proven by their Bills of mortality & ["are" *canceled and* "must be" *interlined*] admitted that the deaths amongst this class are double in Philadelphia, & treble in Boston, those in Charleston, however we may differ as to the causes operating to produce such a result. I gave reasons for believing, on a former occasion that this mortality was mainly attributable to the influence of cold on a race of beings who were created & intended for Tropical climates & my opinion has remained unchanged, though I have no doubt that the social condition of the negro at the North will account ["very" *canceled*] for a very large percentage, possibly half of this mortality. The negro by nature is indolent & improvident in all climates, & there can be no question that many die in the Northern cities, because they have neglected to provide those comforts which [are ne]cessary for protection against cold. The following tables of ["motl" *canceled*] mortality will speak for themselves. The Charleston table I have calculated with care from a recent report of the City Register & that of Philadelphia is taken from a Philadelphia Medical Journal as it stands.

Deaths of Blacks in Charleston		In Philadelphia
1830—One in 40.00	1840—One in 46.64	1821—One in 16.9
1 " " 37.93	41 " " 44.80	22 " " 21.5
2 " " 55.95	42 " " 47.85	23 " " 17.5
3 " " 55.75	43 " " 32.98	24 " " 17.5
4 " " 44.16	44 " " 43.36	25 " " 27.0
5 " " 66.44	45 " " 48.54	26 " " 26.1
6 Cholera 19.64		27 " " 18.9

7	"	" 46.79		28	"	" 20.8
8	"	" 33.00		29	"	" 23.7
9	"	" 39.00		30	"	" 27.2

The average for 16 years (excluding 1836 the Cholera year) ["in" *interlined*] Charleston shows a mortality amongst the Blacks of *1 in 44*, & the 10 years in Philadelphia 1 in 21.7. I have not as yet been able to procure recent tables from Boston, New York & Baltimore, but the mortality amongst the free Blacks of these cities I have seen put down by competent authorities at 1 in 15—one in 18, & one in 32. We have the authority for [*sic*] Dr. [Nathaniel] Niles for putting the mortality of the ["Free" *interlined*] Colored in Baltimore at 1 in 32 while the slaves give the proportion of 1 in 77!! There can be no question that if the Free Colored in Charleston were seperated from the slaves, a still less mortality than 1 in 44 ["b" *canceled*] would be exhibited.

No where in the reach of history, though we can trace them back at least 2000 years before the Christian era, have the negroes shown themselves capable of providing for their physical, to say nothing of moral wants—they are every where when left alone in[dolent?] & improvident & consequently subject to greater mortality than they should be. There is also a large proportion of *Mulattoes* in Charleston, which should be taken into consideration when estimating the influence of climate & social condition on the Colored Class. There are good reasons for believing that they are a degenerate *Hybrid race*, subject to much greater mortality, & lower average duration of life than either whites or Blacks.

To those who believe that the excessive mortality amongst this class at the North is attributable to climate alone, & who believe that the condition of the negro is capable of being improved by emancipation, I will say, without fear of contradiction, that if health, & longevity (& I might add hap[py] faces) are evidence of physical comfort, & content, they are in a better condition in Charleston (& the Southern States generally) than any laboring class on the face of the globe. It is a remarkable fact that this class in Charleston shows, not only a lower mortality than any laboring class of any country, but a lower mortality than the aggregate population, (including all classes high & low) of any ["population" *canceled*] country in Europe except England with which it is about on a par—(I have given tables of other countries to prove this farther back)—if we could seperate the Free Colored, the ratio would be lower than England, as it now is compared with her towns, apart from the Country.

Liberty & climate combined, in Boston are far more destructive to the negro, than slavery & Asiatic Cholera ["at the South" *interlined*]. This scourge, which in 1836 in Charleston fell most heavily on the negroes, raised the mortality for that year to 1 in 20, while in Boston it averages [1] in 15."

I have no question that the facts connected with this subject in Boston have been carefully suppressed for some years back. There is an octavo volume of statistics published in this city every year by authority & the tables of mortality &c are given with most admirable detail in every particular except this, & it is never alluded to once. I am trying however to get at them.

It was not with any political or sectional view that I commenced these investigations, but with a view to the question of Life Insurance. Nor do I desire to put you to the trouble of a letter. The facts I thought might interest you & I therefore have sent them. With the highest respect & esteem Yours &, Josiah C. Nott.

ALS in ScCleA. NOTE: An AEU by Calhoun reads "Dr. Nott."

From Tho[ma]s G. Peachy, Williamsburg, [Va.], 10/29. "The President of the U. States [John Tyler] having appointed me physician and surgeon of the Hospital about to be built at Key West, in Florida, I beg leave to resign my commission as Consul at Amoy in China." ALS in DNA, RG 59 (State Department), Consular Despatches, Amoy, vol. 1 (M-100:1).

From E[LISHA] A. RHODES

Consulate of the United States of
America at Galveston Republic of
Texas, October 29th 1844

Sir, General Duff Green when leaving this place for Vera Cruz, gave me a letter from the United States State Department, address'd to the late Hon[ora]ble Tilghman A. Howard, with instructions to open it, and communicate with the Government of Texas, upon the Subject of its Contents, so soon as he had been recognized as United States' ["Consul" *interlined*] for this port. It enclosed a "paragraph" to be appended to a Communication, addressed to the Hon[ora]ble Wilson Shannon United States Minister at Mexico. The Despatches transmitted thro' Lieut. George Stevens addressed to Mr. Howard, and

160

consisting in part, of that communication, were delivered by him to the Hon[ora]ble Anson Jones Secretary of State of Texas and forwarded to me upon my recognition as Vice Consul for this Port. I have furnished Mr. Jones with a Copy adding the "Paragraph" as instructed. Mr. Howard was also, instructed to *"Shew* to ["the" *canceled*] President [Samuel] Houston & to the Secretary of State," the copy of a Despatch address'd to [William R. King] the United States' Minister at Paris.

In the absence of a Minister from the United States to this Republic, (the distance of this place from the Seat of Government rendering it impossible for me to communicate personally with the Government) I was compelled either to With[h]old the Despatch addressed to Mr. King, altogether, for the present, or to furnish a Copy; and believing it to be the intention of the United States Government, to be full and explicit in her understanding with that of Texas, particularly at this Crisis, I have pursued the latter Course, and have also furnished Mr. Jones with a copy of the letter addressed to Mr. Howard No. 3 which accompanied the above named Despatches, as the information he was instructed in that letter to Communicate to this Government could not well be furnished in any other manner. Trusting this will meet with your Approval, I have the honor to be Your Obedient Servant, E.A. Rhodes.

ALS (No. 1) in DNA, RG 59 (State Department), Consular Despatches, Galveston, vol. 2 (T-151:2), received 11/18; FC in DNA, RG 84 (Foreign Posts), Records of the Texas Legation.

From E[LISHA] A. RHODES

Galveston, October 29th 1844

Sir, Having received from Gen[era]l Duff Green, the appointment of Vice Consul, for this Port, with instructions immediately on the recognition by this Government of himself as Consul, and myself as Vice Consul, to apply to Stewart Newell, the acting Consul, for the records[,] Seal &C of the Office: I did so, but he refused and still refuses to deliver them to me, for reasons which I presume he will state to the Department. The Character and Standing of Mr. Newell, have always been such as to preclude the ["possibillity" *altered to* "possibility"] of any friendly intercourse between us, and I may be permitted to State, that it was with a full knowledge of our respective Standing here, the appointment was given to me, unsolicited, for I had not the pleasure of Gen[era]l Green[']s acquaintance until the morning he sent for me.

Since my application to Mr. Newell for the records &c I learn for the first time that Charges have been made against me to the Department. I am wholly unaware of the nature of those Charges, the very fact of their having been made, having been kept studiously concealed from the knowledge of myself and friends; and I respectfully ["ask" *interlined*] from the Department that before any action is had upon the subject of them, or any opinion based upon them, to my disadvantage, Mr. Green may be allowed to investigate not only my Consular but private Accounts thoroughly & fully. I know with whom these Charges have originated, and that were Mr. Newell and his Associates ["were" *canceled*] as well known at Washington as here, it would be unnecessary for me to trouble you with this letter.

Mr. Newell has sent on a Bill upon the State Department certified by Mr. [John M.] Allen (Mayor). I am well acquainted with all the Circumstances of the transaction, but as the Object of this letter is to be allow'd to Vindicate my self, and not to make Charges against Mr. Newell, I would only respectfully Suggest that before the payment of that Bill, Gen[era]l Green be instructed to inquire into the nature and justice of the Claim.

In conclusion permit me to State that if I had ever received an intimation of the existance of Charges affecting my honor, integrity or Character in any way, I should immediately have demanded an investigation, tho' it is humiliating in the extreme to find myself compelled to defend my reputation from the secret attacks of those who have none to loose. Since my residence in Texas, I have been on terms of friendly intercourse with Gen[era]l [Samuel] Houston—Ex-President [Mirabeau B.] Lamar, and most of the leading men of the Country, and for my Character and Standing while a resident of my native State North Carolina, I beg leave to refer you to Gov[erno]r [John] Branch of Florida & Gen[era]l [James] Iredel[l, Jr.] of North Carolina who were my neighbours and friends. I have the honor to be Your Obedient Servant, E.A. Rhodes.

ALS (Private) in DNA, RG 59 (State Department), Consular Despatches, Galveston, vol. 2 (T-151:2), received 11/18. NOTE: A Clerk's EU reads "Ans[were]d."

From WILSON SHANNON, "Private"

Legation of the U.S. of A.
Mexico [City], Oct. 29th 1844

D[ea]r Sir, Your draft of a note you had the goodness to send me, I considered so entirely applicable to the present state of things here, that I made no alterations in it, except of a verbal character as you will see by my Dispatch [to Manuel C. Rejon dated 10/14]. It has produced quite a sensation in this city—its contents having been made known by the officers of the government. I have received no answer. I am told Santa Anna, to whom it was sent at Jalapa[,] has directed it to be transmitted to Congress and that it will be sent in tomorrow. I am also advised that he is not displeased with the document as he thinks he can turn it to his advantage by forcing Congress to take the responsibility of abandoning the Texas war. Neither Santa Anna nor Congress will think of renewing the war against Texas so long as it is believed that the U.S. will have to be encountered as well as Texas. Congress will now be compelled to act and provide the means to carry on the war or abandon it. The former they will not do for various reasons. In the first place they are determined to give Santa Anna no more money, and in the second place they have no sourse from which to raise the money without producing a revolution. The four millions appropriation will not produce more than two and a half and that is already exhausted and more than anticipated by drafts on the treasury. The people are now taxed beyond indurence and while I am writing the government is sending troops to the south to enforce the payment of this tax. Their [w]retched prohibatory system has nearly cut off all revenue from importations and the internal resourses are gone. I see it is predicted in some of the papers in the U.S. that Mexico will declare war against the U.S.; there is as much probability that the Emperor of China will do so. Gen[era]l [Duff] Green will give you the details of the political rumors and speculations here. I did not think it prudent to put them in my official Dispatch. His views and opinions of things here may, I think, be relied on. The U.S. Brig Laurence (Capt. [Joseph R.] Jarvis) is now at Vera Cruz waiting my orders. As my Dispatch and accompanying documents are highly important and should be in Washington city before the meeting of Congress I have transmit[t]ed them to Capt. Jarvis and directed him to go direct to Pensacola and to deliver my dispatches at that place to Lieutenant [Alexander M.] Pennock who is instructed to convey them to Washington by the nearest and quickest route. Considering the uncertainty of the mails this season of the year, and the possibility of the packages being miscarried or not reaching you in time I have thought it would best meet with your approbation to pursue the course I have above stated.

There has been a new minister of finance appointed in the place of Mr. [Ignacio] Trigu[e]ros who has been permit[t]ed to retire. The new minister is about issuing a general order suspending the payment of all drafts on the Treasury for the want of money. It is said and, I believe truly, that there is not a dollar in the Treasury. The next instalment due our citizens will be payable in a day or two but I do not think it will be possible for the government to raise the means to make the payment. It is said that exersions are making to raise the money but the belief here is so strong among the monied men that a revolution is inevitable that they cannot be induced, upon any consideration to advance the government money. Yours with great respect, Wilson Shannon.

ALS in ScCleA; PC in Jameson, ed., *Correspondence*, pp. 980–982.

From L[emuel] Williams, Collector [of Customs], Boston, 10/29. He forwards a statement of "certain vexatious proceedings" to which Capt. Francis D. Hardy of the U.S. brig *Silenus* was subjected [by British authorities] in Kingston, Jamaica. The U.S. Consul at Kingston [Robert Monroe Harrison] interfered in Hardy's behalf and assisted him in every possible way. LS with En in DNA, RG 59 (State Department), Consular Despatches, Kingston, vol. 9 (T-31:9).

R[ichard] K. Crallé to JOHN A. BRYAN, [U.S. Chargé d'Affaires to Peru]

Department of State
Washington, 30th October, 1844

Sir: The distance between the United States and Peru and the want of speedy and regular means of communication between Washington and Lima are calculated in no small degree to embarrass the relations, political and commercial, of the two countries, while they necessarily add to the responsibilities of the station to which you have been called by the President. Occasions not unfrequently occur when, to act efficiently, a minister must act promptly; and when, however desirable it might be to have special instructions from his government, delay would inevitably defeat the objects for which they were sought.

These embarrassments, incident to the relations of all countries widely separated from each other, are in the present case much increased by the actual condition of the government to which you are accredited. Peru, for many years convulsed by intestine commotions and ravaged by military bands under various and hostile leaders, appears, from recent events, to be on the verge of anarchy. In 1836 it was a member of the Bolivian Republic with General [Andres de] Santa Cruz at its head as Supreme Director. On the 28th of December ["of" *interlined*] that year Chile, jealous of the increased power of her neighbour, growing out of this Confederacy, declared war against Peru, and though a pacification was effected between them for a time, by the treaty of Paucaparta, concluded on the 17th of November, 1837, an invasion soon after took place, and on the 20th of January, 1839, the Peruvian forces were defeated and dispersed by the Chilean army under the command of [Augustin] Gamarra, Santa Cruz driven from the country and Gamarra proclaimed provisional President in his stead. In December, 1840, Colonel [Manuel] Vivanco, Prefect of Arequipa, was proclaimed by the army in that Department "Supreme Chief of the Nation," but this rebellious movement was soon quelled by the forces of the Republic.

In the autumn of 1841, President Gamarra invaded Bolivia for the purpose of suppressing the movements of the followers of General Santa Cruz, in that country; but fatally for himself; for in a pitched battle fought on the 18th of November of that year, his army was totally routed by the Bolivians and he himself killed, and the Chief Magistracy of the Republic passed into the hands of General Manuel Menendez, the President of the Council of State. His dynasty, however, was destined to be as brief as that of his predecessors, for in August, 1842, he was deposed by General [Juan Crisostomo] Torrico, in command of the military forces in Lima, who took possession of the government with the title of "Chief of the Nation."

He had hardly taken his seat at the head of affairs, when, in the effort to suppress a revolt in the southern portion of the Republic, he was defeated by General [Francisco] Vidal, at the head of the revolutionists, who, after driving him out of the country, assumed the supreme authority under the title of "Vice President of the Council of State, charged with the Executive power of the Republic."

Early in the year 1843, General Vivanco, who had accepted the situation of Minister of War under Vidal, headed a revolt of the military in the South of Peru. The forces sent against him by Vidal, having deserted, he himself resigned his situation and Vivanco entered Lima on the 5th of April, 1843, and took quiet possession of the government under the title of Supreme Director. On the 20th of October, following, General [Ramon] Castilla, who had refused obedience to his authority, placed himself at the head of 1500 militia in the Southern part of the Republic, and defeated the forces of Vivanco which had been sent against him and threatened the total overthrow of his government. This, however, was effected by other hands, for during the absence of President Vivanco, who was zealously engaged in the effort to quell the rebellion of Castilla, Domingo Elias, Prefect of the Department of War, suddenly threw off his allegiance to his government, and on the 17th of June, last, proclaimed himself "Supreme Director of the Republic," in the face of three competitors, Vivanco, Castilla and Echineque [*sic*; José Rufino Echénique], each at the head of his respective military command.

Such was the actual condition of this distracted country at the date of our last advices; and the events are adverted to with the view of drawing your attention to the line of policy adopted by the United States, in the history of the past, and which must be regarded as settling the course of our government in its future intercourse. During these various revolutions, our political relations, regulated by principles of the strictest neutrality, have remained undisturbed, and the intercourse between the two countries continued on the most friendly footing.

It is impossible to say which of the contending rivals, if either, may be, at this time, at the head of the government, nor, considering the line of conduct which it will be your duty to adopt, is it important to inquire. The United States claim no right to inquire into, or, in any manner to interfere with the internal affairs of other powers. In their relations with them they only look to the actual government, as it may exist, without undertaking to inquire into the means by which it has been established, the validity of its title or the tenure of its authority. Whoever may be in the actual possession and exercise of the supreme power, whether by the consent of the governed, or by force, must be regarded as the government *de facto* of the country, authorized to contract obligations in behalf of the community of which it is the head, and as such, liable for all injuries inflicted by its agents or citizens on the rights of others.

At the date of our last advices, Domingo Elias was, whether rightfully or otherwise, in the actual possession and exercise of the supreme power at Lima, the seat of Government and it appears that not only the civil and military authorities of the capital and other places had quietly submitted to his government, but that there had been no actual resistance on the part of the people at large. He must, therefore, under such circumstances, be regarded as representing the Supreme Directory of the Republic; and so long as he is in the actual exercise of the powers appertaining to it, his government must be treated as the government *de facto* of the country; nor can you, in your official character, rightfully question the mode in which he has acquired, nor the means which he may possess to maintain his authority. These questions belong exclusively to the people of Peru; and the United States, acting upon the well established principles of neutrality and non-interference, as respects the domestic institutions and policy of other states, assume no right to take cognizance of them.

It may be said that, during the disorders incident to revolutions like those we have witnessed in Peru, the rights of neutrals might be endangered and that to protect them, the diplomatic agents of Foreign Powers would be justified in employing the military or naval forces of their respective countries, either in aid of the government for the time being or independently of it. In such cases, the protection of the persons and property of their respective citizens might be strongly urged in favor of such interposition, but considered in reference to the general principles of National Law, and especially to those which have heretofore regulated the intercourse of the United States with foreign nations, its propriety may well be questioned. Such interposition does not seem to be compatible with those principles of neutrality and non-interference which lie at the foundation of that system of policy which the United States have uniformly regarded as of controlling influence in their intercourse with other countries. The Revolution of the 17th of June, last, which placed Elias at the head of the actual government of Peru, may have been in violation of the Constitution and laws of the Republic. It may, in effect, have subverted the whole frame of its government and substituted another in its stead, and in the convulsions and disorders to which it may have given birth, the rights of neutrals may have been endangered or suffered actual outrage. In either case the remedy is to be found in the responsibility of the State within whose jurisdiction or by whose agents the injury may have been inflicted. Governments are to be regarded as moral persons whose liabilities remain unimpaired through all the revolutions to which they may be subjected. No change of rulers or modifications of forms can exempt them from their liabilities, or bar the reclamations of the injured.

These principles, founded on natural equity, and sanctioned by the common consent of all civilized nations, apply with peculiar force to the only case of difficulty now pending between the United States and Peru. The commercial relations between the two countries were deemed by the United States to have been firmly established by the Treaty of the 30th of November, 1836, while Peru and Bolivia were united under a confederate Government, with General Santa Cruz as Supreme Director. This Treaty (a copy of which I herewith transmit to you) was negotiated, concluded and ratified with the usual forms and solemnities. But since the dismemberment of the Confederacy, the Government of Peru has exhibited some unwillingness to acknowledge it as the basis of our commercial relations. Your predecessor Mr. [James C.] Pickett has been instructed to represent to the Peruvian government that the United States regard the Treaty as still obligatory on the parties and that no change in the political relations of Peru and Bolivia can justly exempt either from the performance of its stipulations.

On the 17th of March, 1841, a Convention providing for the adjustment of claims of citizens of the United States on the Peruvian Government was signed at Lima and has since been duly ratified on the part of both governments. This Convention stipulates for the payment, by Peru, of three hundred thousand dollars in ten annual instalments of thirty thousand dollars each. The first instalment was due in January, last, but in anticipation of that period, the Peruvian government asked that the payment might be postponed for one year, to which Mr. Pickett assented, upon condition that twelve per cent interest should be allowed on the deferred payment. This arrangement was agreed to by the Peruvian authorities, and consequently on the 1st of January, next, two instalments of thirty thousand dollars each will be due, with two years interest at four per cent and one years interest at twelve per cent on the first and three years interest at four per cent on the second; making in the aggregate sixty nine thousand six hundred dollars. A power authorizing you as the agent of the United States to demand, receive and give acquittances for the amount, is herewith transmitted. If the payment should be made in dollars, pursuant to the 4th article of the Convention, you will remit the same in some national vessel, if possible, or otherwise you may make the remittance in a merchant vessel, the dollars to be deposited to the credit of this Department at the port of the United States where the vessel which brings them shall arrive. But as it will be your duty to make the remittance on terms the most advantageous to the parties interested, if good bills shall be preferable for that purpose, you will choose them, being careful that they are made payable to the order of this department.

It is possible that the Peruvian government may avail itself of the option granted by the 6th article of the Convention, by making the payments in orders on the Custom House at Callao. In that case you will not fail to require a sufficient amount of the orders to make good any depreciation to which they may be subject, and instead of sending them to the United States for distribution amongst the claimants, it would be advisable to convert them into cash or bills, so that you may make the remittance as above directed. If you remit specie, you will effect insurance on the amount, provided it can be done at a moderate premium by underwriters worthy of confidence, and you will deduct the amount of the premium and any other incidental expenses from the amount to be remitted.

Considering the forbearance shown by this government in the adjustment of these claims and its liberality in agreeing to the compromise embodied in the Convention, we have every reason to expect that the payments will henceforth be punctually made; and you will accordingly address such representations to the Peruvian authorities as may be proper to prevent any further disappointments. But if, contrary to all just expectation, the payment should not be made as agreed upon, you will lose no time in communicating the fact to this Department; informing the Peruvian government at the same time, that such neglect on its part cannot be regarded by the government of the United States but with marked dissatisfaction. There are some claims against that government which are not provided for by the Convention of March, 1841, and which you will find mentioned in Mr. Pickett's correspondence. The principal of these is that of Mr. S.F. Tracy, in regard to which you are referred to the instruction of this Department to Mr. Pickett, No. 13, of the 16th of November, 1842. You will omit no proper opportunity of bringing about an adjustment of these cases. I am, Sir, your obedient servant, R.K. Crallé, Acting Secretary.

FC (No. 1) in DNA, RG 59 (State Department), Diplomatic Instructions, Peru, 15:38–45 (M-77:130); incomplete draft in ScCleA. NOTE: The draft differs significantly in wording and content from the finished form of the instructions to Bryan. It constitutes an early, unpolished, version of the document. Both the FC and the draft are in the handwriting of William Hunter, Jr., a State Department Clerk.

R[ichard] K. Crallé to WILLIAM CRUMP, [U.S. Chargé d'Affaires to Chile]

Department of State
Washington, 30th October, 1844

Sir: Amongst the subjects which will claim your earliest attention after your arrival at the seat of the Chilean government, is the case of Thomas H. Perkins and others, citizens of the United States, who claim indemnity for spoliations committed under the authority of that government during its revolutionary struggles with the mother country.

The facts of the case seem to be these. In 1821, a cargo of merchandize, the property of Thomas H. Perkins and others, was shipped from Canton on board the brig Macedonian, captain Eliphalet Smith, for the western coast of South America. The vessel arrived at Tagna and a part of the cargo was sold for seventy thousand four hundred dollars. Captain Smith, taking with him this amount in money, and the remainder of the cargo, departed for Arequipa in the further prosecution of his voyage. He was intercepted on the public highway by an armed detachment of Chilean troops in the service and under the command of an officer of the government, and forcibly deprived of the whole amount of money in his possession, notwithstanding his solemn protest and offer to prove that it belonged to citizens of the United States. He was denied the privilege of introducing the necessary evidence in support of the fact except upon conditions more injurious to the interests of the owners than the loss of the money of which he had been forcibly plundered—and which was taken to the commander of the detachment, and by him distributed amongst his troops in discharge of the claims due them for military services from the Chilean government. It further appears that these facts were subsequently verified, in due form of law, by the bills of lading, the returns of sales, the evidence, under oath, of the merchant who shipped the goods at Canton, of Smith, the captain of the brig, of three individuals who were present at the time of the seizure, of Colonel Miller, by whose order it was made, and by the written statement of captain Balderana, made at the time.

This evidence, with the protest of captain Smith, was laid before the Supreme government of Chile, and by it transmitted to the proper legal tribunal, constituted for the trial and adjudication of prize cases, where it has remained ever since, without further action either on the part of the government or the Court.

In 1841, Mr. [Richard] Pollard, the United States' Chargé d'Affaires, was instructed to bring the case to the notice of the Chilean government and to urge the final settlement of the claim. Your immediate predecessor, Mr. [John S.] Pendleton, under similar instructions, has since pressed the subject with much zeal, but ineffectually, on the attention of the Chilean authorities. The correspondence between himself and Mr. Yramaraval [*sic*; Ramon L. Yrarrazaval] the Minister for Foreign Affairs, conducted, it is to be regretted, in a tone little calculated to secure an amicable adjustment of the matter in controversy, contains the views of the respective governments, and you are referred to it for fuller information in regard to the facts and circumstances of the case.

Mr. Yramaraval, in his correspondence with Mr. Pendleton, and subsequently in a note addressed to the Secretary of State of the United States (a copy of which is herewith transmitted for your perusal) justifies the course of his government in refusing to recognize the claim, solely on the plea of prescription, founded on the lapse of time between the date of the seizure in 1821, and the prosecution of the claim in 1841. It is true that, in his note to the Secretary of State, he says "his government has not placed the question upon this ground because it had no means of rejecting the claim upon its intrinsic merits": that it "was in possession of authentic proofs which, in its opinion, leave no doubt as to the legality of the capture." Still, these proofs, which go to the intrinsic merits of the case, are passed by, and the Minister, in behalf of his government, rests the whole case exclusively on the plea of prescription.

It is to be regretted that Mr. Yramaraval should have deemed it proper on the part of his government to withhold the testimony to which he refers, and which he assures us has so clear and decisive a bearing on the merits of the case. It would, perhaps, have enabled the two governments to adjust the matter in dispute without that labor of argument and asperity of feeling to which it has given rise. The claim itself, assumed to be founded on principles of natural justice, was the proper subject of such testimony, and eminently entitled to be decided upon its intrinsic merits; and it is much to be lamented, that neither in the correspondence with our Ministers in support of the course of his government, nor before the Judicial tribunals as preliminary to a sentence of condemnation, has any part of these authentic proofs been produced. They are known only to the government of Chile, and it does not become the government of the United States to express any opinion in regard to them. It must consider the case, so far as the Chilean government is concerned, as no longer open for evidence, as no longer resting on its intrinsic merits, but depending solely on an abstract and assumed principle of national law, alike arbitrary in its nature, and unjust in its operation.

The position assumed by Mr. Yramaraval, that a claim due from one government to another is barred by the lapse of twenty years, seems equally novel and untenable. The idea of an international act of limitations is entirely new, and so far as I am informed, has no support either in the opinions of any respectable Publicist, or the decisions of the prize courts of any civilized nation. Governments are presumed to be always ready to do justice; and whether a claim be a day or a century old, so that it be well-founded, every principle of natural equity, of sound morals, requires that it should be paid. The present case is one which addresses itself with peculiar force, not only to the justice, but to the honor of the Chilean government. It is not denied that the money was forcibly taken from the owners by the Chilean authorities, or that it was actually appropriated by them to the use and support of the government; neither is it pretended that the amount has ever been ["paid" *altered to* "repaid"]. It is plain, therefore, that if this new principle be admitted as a bar to the claim, it would only be to work acknowledged injustice, and it is to be hoped that on more mature consideration, the government of Chile will feel it due to its own character to repudiate at once a principle so extraordinary in its character and so unjust in its tendencies.

Mr. Yramaraval, in his correspondence with Mr. Pendleton, has dwelt with needless interest on the negligence of the claimants in the prosecution of their claim. He does not, it seems to me, do them full justice. Considering the distance between the two countries, the means of communication at the time, the unsettled condition of the Chilean government and the state of the relations subsisting between it and the United States, the nature of the evidence called for and the forms of judicial proceedings in the prize courts of the country, there does not seem to have been any extraordinary negligence or remissness on their part. They appear to have procured, with remarkable promptness, all the necessary evidence in support of their claim, and if there have been any unnecessary delay in the final adjustment of the matter, it is to be traced rather to the course of the captors and the courts of the country than to the claimants. To this day it does not appear that the captors have ever filed any libel in the case or that the courts have ever condemned the property seized as lawful prize, although it has been actually taken, without any judicial warranty and appropriated to the use of the Chilean government. The captors have, in fact, surrendered the claim, and the government, as the receiver of the fund, must be regarded as holding it in the character of trustee for the benefit of the owners.

These views you will take the earliest occasion to present, in respectful but firm language, to the Minister of Foreign Affairs. The President [John Tyler] cannot allow himself to doubt but that they will, on further reflection, meet with the concurrence of the Chilean government; and that the whole subject will be promptly adjusted without disturbing the amicable relations now happily subsisting between the two countries. If, however, he should be disappointed in this just and reasonable expectation, it is highly important that the fact should be communicated at as early a day as possible, so that he may be able to lay the whole matter before Congress during the ensuing session, with a view to such action on the part of that body as it may think proper to adopt. You will, therefore, after stating fully and clearly the views of your government in reference to the subject, request of the Minister for Foreign Affairs a prompt and definitive answer, which you will transmit by the first opportunity to this department. I am, Sir, very respectfully, Your obedient Servant, R.K. Crallé, Acting Secretary.

FC (No. 4) in DNA, RG 59 (State Department), Diplomatic Instructions, Chile, 15:56–61 (M-77:35).

R[ichard] K. Crallé to Vespasian Ellis, [U.S. Chargé d'Affaires to Venezuela]

Department of State
Washington, 30th October, 1844

Sir: So little change has taken place in the relations between the United States and the Republic of Venezuela during the mission of your predecessor [Allen A. Hall], that it is deemed necessary only to refer you to the instructions which from time to time have been given to him as containing the views and principles by which you will be governed.

He was directed to use his exertions to procure from the Government of Venezuela an acknowledgement of the claims of citizens of the United States upon the late Republic of Colombia, and advised to discuss the cases singly with the Minister for Foreign Affairs, beginning with that of the Brig Morris. He has accordingly pursued this course and effected with that functionary an arrangement by which Venezuela stipulates to pay eighteen thousand dollars in discharge of its liability in that case. The Congress of that Republic, however, having omitted, at its last session, to make an appropriation for the amount, it will be your duty to use all proper means for the purpose of having the omission supplied at the next session of that Body.

So long as the claim in the case of the Morris remains unsatisfied, it would not, perhaps, be advisable to press for an adjustment of the others; for no material progress in them could be reasonably expected during the pendency of this; while, on the other hand, the final settlement of the adjusted balance might be retarded. When, however, the appropriation in that case shall have been made and the money received, you will devote your attention to the settlement of the other claims. Their amount would scarcely warrant the conclusion of a formal Convention upon the subject, but if the Venezuelan Government should insist upon that course, the power with which you are provided will enable you to meet their wishes. The Convention should provide for the payment by Venezuela of a gross sum in discharge of all her liabilities on account of claims of citizens of the United States against the late Republic of Colombia, payable by annual instalments, with interest, the payments to be completed in from five to ten years; the Government of the United States assuming the distribution of the money among the claimants.

The accompanying copy of a Convention between the United States and Peru upon a similar subject, may serve as a form, to be modified according to circumstances. If, however, that Government should not insist upon a formal Convention, you may, in adjusting the remaining claims, pursue the course recommended to Mr. Hall by discussing the cases singly with the Minister for Foreign Affairs and settling them in the same manner by means of an agreement signed by yourself and that officer.

The trade between the United States and Venezuela is important and valuable to both countries; and it would probably be greatly increased in amount, and be far more advantageous to us, if the heavy duties which are charged upon the importation of our productions into that country, could be reduced.

Our tariff allows the importation of the principal staple of Venezuela, coffee, free of duty—and it is hoped that those liberal principles of reciprocity and enlarged views of commercial policy which mark the progress and the spirit of the age might be successfully urged upon the consideration of its government. Such a course, discreetly pursued, might possibly lead to some favorable modification of its restrictive system, and it may be well for you to take advantage of any occasion which may offer to effect so desirable a change in the policy of the Government, being careful not to render yourself liable to the charge of improperly interfering in the domestic concerns of the country.

You will keep the Department accurately and promptly informed upon the points referred to in your personal instructions and upon any others which may touch the interests of the United States. I am, Sir, your obedient servant, R.K. Crallé, Acting Secretary.

FC (No. 1) in DNA, RG 59 (State Department), Diplomatic Instructions, Venezuela, 1:50–52 (M-77:171); CC (misdated 1845) in DNA, RG 84 (Foreign Posts), Venezuela.

From Daniel P. King, [Representative from Mass.], Danvers, Mass., 10/30. He asks whether any information about the illegal seizure by the British government of the U.S. fishing vessels *Director* and *Pallas* has been received. Claims for indemnification were filed four years ago, and no news has since been heard of the matter. The owners of the vessels are citizens of Danvers's Congressional district, and he hopes that some information may be furnished to them. ALS in DNA, RG 59 (State Department), Miscellaneous Letters (M-179: 105, frames 547–548).

From Stewart Newell, [Galveston]

Consulate of the United States
at Sabine, Texas
October 30th 1844

Sir, I have the honor, to acknowledge receipt of your Letter, of 25th September, ult[im]o, and agreeable thereto, have been ready, to comply with the instructions of the Department, in handing over to Duff Green Esq[ui]r[e] the Archives, Seal &C of the Consulate, at Galveston, when called upon, by him, for the same, and continue in possession of them, until the Instructions of the Department, are received, or the arrival of Mr. Green, at his Post, and ready, to enter upon, the duties of his Appointment.

In my No. 7 from the Consulate at Galveston, Oct. 1st 1844, I advised the Department, of the manner of proceeding, on the part of Mr. Green, on his arrival here, and of his Appointment, of Elisha A.

Rhodes, as Vice Consul, at this Port, and requested the Department to inform me, *if* E.A. Rhodes, would be recognised by the Department, *as* Vice Consul, refer[r]ing the Hon. Secretary, to Letters 8 & 9 of the *late* A[rchibald] M. Green Esq[ui]r[e] relative to said Rhodes, but *omitted* calling the attention of the Department to Letter *No. 18*, upon reference to which, and the manner of his Appointment, I felt unwilling to deliver into custody of said Rhodes, the Archives, Seal &C, until further advised, by the Department, fearing with a knowledge of such, being recorded against him, and unknown to Mr. Green, the Department would censure me. The Duties of the Consulate, have not been interrupted however, in consequence of this, *until* the 21st inst., when the American Steamer "Republic," of New York, and from New Orleans, *also* American Ship "Star Republic," of, and from New York, arrived at Galveston. The latter, having encountered much Stormy weather, had a considerable portion of her Cargo damaged. The Master of the Latter, deposited his Ship[']s Papers, with me, as the Act[in]g Consul of the United States, and noted Protest, and received under Seal, *my* Consular Certificate of Deposit, of said Papers, which upon being presented, at the Custom House, in Galveston, the Collector [James H. Cocke] refused to permit an Entry, of said Ship, or vessel, until the Master, had deposited *said* Papers, in the Office of Elisha A. Rhodes, claiming to be Vice Consul, upon which, in order that the interests of the vessel, owners & Shippers, should not be interfered with, I immediately surrendered the Papers to the Master, and which were accordingly deposited with E.A. Rhodes, and the vessel entered. The Collector of this Port, having refused an entry to the Steamer "Republic," *her* Papers, were deposited with E.A. Rhodes also, but had not previously been handed to me, although the Master was excused by me, for not having done so, as *he* did not with[h]old them, from me wilfully.

On the 5th inst., the Brig "Reaper" from Baltimore, being in sight of the Port, and with a view of avoiding any dispute, if such, should be likely to arise, on her arrival, with permission of the Collector, *I*, placed a notice in a conspicuous part, of the Custom House, requireing Masters of vessels to deposit the Ship[']s Papers, in this Office, and appended an Extract of the Law &C, to the same. The "Reaper" arrived about 4 P.M. of the 5th, after the Collector[']s Office, had closed. On the 7th, about 12 M., I called at the Collector[']s Office, and *there* met the Master, ["of said" *canceled*] of said vessel, Samuel R. Breaton, who had previously, made an Entry of his said vessel & Cargo, without having delivered to me, his Ship's Papers. I called upon him, for the same, and was told by said Master, *he* had deposited them with E.A. Rhodes, as Vice Consul. He was then informed by me, of the Law, and Penalty, and requested to obtain and deliver to me, said Papers. I waited until next morning the 8th, and then, addressed a note under Seal, to said Master, requireing the Papers of said Brig "Reaper," to be delivered to me immediately, after which the Papers were carried by said Master, to the Collector of Customs, of the Port, and delivered to him, and where I received them, this being a direct, and apparently wilful violation of the Law of Feb[ruar]y 28th 1803, & Consular Instructions Sec. 4, Art. 29th, and which refusal, or neglect, is more apparent, by reference to Deposition of James G. Burnham Esq[ui]r[e] Dep[uty] Collector, and herewith enclosed. Said vessel sailed from the Port of Galveston, on the 28th inst., bound for Baltimore. Also came by said vessel, various Invoices of Merchandise, entitled to Debenture, and consigned to H.H. Williams & Co., a branch of a Mercantile House of Baltimore, Md. The whole Cargo has been landed, and part sold, and the Debenture Certificates signed by the Master and Mate, as the former told me, and before E.A. Rhodes, but not verified under Seal, as is the case I am told, with others p[e]r Steamer "Republic," and Ship "Star Republic" refer[re]d to in Certificate enclosed. May I, be permitted to ask, if said Certificates, not under Seal, will be received at the Treasury Department, as valid, and permit the Bonds for Duties, to be cancelled, by the Collectors, at the Ports whence Shipped. If so, the Door would be opened wide, for Frauds upon the Revenue. Cotton, Hides, Tallow, and other produce, is now being shipped from the Port of Galveston, on Brig "Reaper," to Baltimore, and on other vessels, to New Orleans, and New York, without application for Consular Certificate of value &C, as required by Law to be done.

On the 26th inst. Sch[oone]r "Oregon," an American vessel, arrived at the Port of Galveston from St. Jago, de Cuba, in Ballast, bound for Attakapas La., as stated in distress, and sailed this day, on her voyage, without having reported at my Office, but I understand had done so, to E.A. Rhodes, and I have not yet, learned further particulars.

On this day, arrived American Sch[oone]r "Lone Star," of, and from New York to Velasco, thence to this Port, also a small Sch[oone]r, from Calcasue [*sic*; Calcasieu] La. about 30 Miles East of Sabine, both of which, I am told, reported to Rhodes. Thus the Department will see, the confusion, and difficulty, consequent, upon the hasty, and unnecessary course, of proceeding on the part of Mr. Green, in thus appointing Mr. Rhodes, as Vice Consul, *and that*, before he Mr. Green, was qualified to Act, as Consul, his Commission to Rhodes, bearing date *Sep[tember] 30th,* the day upon which Mr. Green *arrived,* and *sailed,* from this Port, for Mexico, and whose Commission, did not leave Galveston, to be presented to the Secretary of Foreign Affairs, (Chap. 2d, Art. 2d, Consular Instructions,) for an Exequator, until some Hours after, Mr. Green had sailed. The Commission was transmitted by Mr. Green, through E.A. Rhodes, who received the Exequator, *addressed* to Mr. Green, had it published, and immediately took down, the notice, placed by me, in the Custom House, and replaced it, by one of his own, directing Masters of vessels, and others, having buisiness with the Office, to call upon him.

Finding Mr. Rhodes, disposed to throw such obstacles in the way, of the buisiness of the Consulate, as would prove to be, a source of litigation, and expence, to our Citizens, & Masters of vessels, I addressed him a Letter, upon the subject, a Copy of which, is herewith enclosed, and to which I most respectfully, ask the attention of the Department, as well as ["to" *interlined*] the other Documents, enclosed, in order that my views in the matter, may be properly understood, by the Department, and if right, I feel assured, of being sustained. If wrong, I submit, upon being so informed, under the circumstances, beleiveing, a total disregard of the Law, and Instructions, have been practised, by Mr. Green of Chap. 2d, Art. 2d, and Art. 4th, and did not acquaint the proper authorities of the place &C, of his Appointment &C, also Sec. 7th, Art. 41st, by not giving notice, to the local authorities, of the place &C &C.

Mr. Green having neglected, or failed, to comply with the Laws of the United States, first required, to be done, and Appointing a Vice Consul, at least 15 days before legally authorised *to Act,* in person, and at the time, *when qualified,* not in the Country, I could not feel, as if my duty, was discharged properly, to my Government, to know these facts, and acquiesce in such, without informing the Department, as a duty, and at same time, should the Department consider, *I* had in this case, been more cautious, than requisite, I can only say, that if vigilence, and honest desire for Public interest, is to be so considered, then *no* inducement is presented to the faithful Officer, but rather a Licence, to the dishonest, permitting the grossest excesses, would be the result. I have too high a sense, of my own, and my Country[']s honor, for one moment, to permit such thoughts, and I beg leave to add, that in a Treaty with this Country a condittion, defineing particularly, the rights, privileges &C of American Consuls, is essentially neccessary, to prevent the constant vexations, and harrassing interference ["of" *interlined*] the petty Courts and Attorneys, and a portion of the Citizens of this Republic, more particularly so, at the Ports on the Coast.

The Letter of 25th Sep[tember] from the Department, advises me, in relation to F[rederick] D. Howard, an American Citizen &C, "As we have no Treaty with Texas &C."

I beg leave to call the attention, of the Department, to a Notice to Texian Consuls, issued by the Govt. of Texas under date of Oct. 15th 1838, and to ask, of the Department, if the same, is understood by my Government, as it is, by many intelligent persons, in this Country, to be still, in Force and is as follows.

"By an arrangement entered into, between the Government of the United States, and that of this Republic, the Treaty of Amity, Navigation, and Commerce, existing between the former, and Mexico, is declared binding on the United States, and Texas, *till* a new one, shall *be concluded*, between them, by the stipulations of which, the Consuls of this Republic, will be governed, in the adjustment of all matters, relating to the regulation of our Commerce, with that Country, so far, as thier duties, may be concerned." Signed, R[obert] A. Irion, Secretary of State.

No new treaty, having been *concluded*, between the United States and Texas, I have continued to urge, when required, that as the Old Treaty, was binding *till* a New One, was concluded, then does a Treaty really exist[?] Although it may, by its own limitation, between Mexico and the United States, have expired, as to the Contracting powers, yet Texas had an interest in its continuance, for a longer period, and with consent of the United States, did make it, virtually a Treaty between them, which can only be broken, by a new one, being concluded, *or* the consent of both the contracting Powers, to its expiration, being publicly announced to the World.

This being a matter, not within the Consular Function, yet the reference in the Letter of Sep[tember] 25th, being so entirely opposite, to my former views of the Treaty, induced a reference to the Document itself, and finding it to be, as stated, induced me, to call the Attention of the Department, to the same, and trust I shall be excused the liberty, of having expressed my views, upon this subject, to the Department, and which was only induced, by the desire, that our Commerce and Citizens, should have the benefit of it. I have the honor to be Most Respectfully Your Ob[edien]t Servant, Stewart Newell, U.S. Consul.

Documents enclosed are

Duplicate *No. 21*, Consulate, Sabine

Copy of Letter [of 10/19] to E.A. Rhodes
Certificate of Refusal of Samuel R. Breaton to deposit Papers &
    Certificate J.G. Burnham Dep[uty] Coll[ector]
Letter S. Newell to Cap[tain] Breaton
    "   do.   "   J.H. Cocke, Coll[ector]
Certificates Cap[tai]n John R. Crane
    "   Stewart Newell
Protest of   do.   to Collector.

ALS (No. 27) with Ens in DNA, RG 59 (State Department), Consular Despatches, Texas, vol. 1 (T-153:1), received 11/23.

From W[ILLIA]M C. BROWN

Boston, Oct. 31, 1844

Dear Sir, The writer of the enclosed is Rev. Charles T. Torrey, now in a jail in Baltimore, charged with aiding slaves to escape from bondage; an act which would call forth your highest gratitude, were you a slave in Algiers, & were some philanthropic individual to effect your escape. Is it any less a virtue in Mr. Torrey's case? No candid man can show that it is.

The *Christian Citizen* is published at Worcester, Mass., & is edited by *Elihu Burritt*, the *Learned Blacksmith*, one of our *"white slaves."*

I have been taught, my dear sir, to look upon you as a man of great talents, & of pure character. Are the charges made in the enclosed, true? If not true literally, are they true in substance? Or are they totally untrue?

We look upon such things with great horror in the North. We cannot see that they are any less crimes than if done to white persons. The idea that color makes any difference, is too absurd for an argument.

I sign my proper name to this note. I have a brother [Simon Brown] in Washington city, attached to the Library of the H[ouse of] R[epresentatives] & an unflinching adherent to the Democratic party, who knows me well. Respectfully Yours, Wm. C. Brown.

[Enclosed newspaper clipping]

JOHN C. CALHOUN

PHILADELPHIA, Pa., March 30, 1844

[To:] Elihu Burritt, Esq., I notice that you speak of John C. Calhoun, in a recent paper, in terms of commendation in regard to the purity of his character. That Mr. Calhoun is the greatest man living, if *merely reasoning intellect* is the standard of greatness, I have long believed; not the less firmly from having had the opportunity to see and compare him with [James G.] Birney, [Henry] Clay, [Daniel] Webster, [John] McLean, [Silas] Wright, [James] Buchanan, [George] Evans, and other really eminent persons, in different parts of the country. I cannot hear that he ever was a gambler, or a lewd person, a profane man or intemperate. He is by no means a temperance man, however. Still I object to the commendation of his moral character. He holds a large number of human beings in bondage. He refuses them the *rite* and the *rights* of the MARRIAGE STATE. He keeps them in utter ignorance of letters and deprives them of their entire earnings. But even all this is not my strongest objection to your commendation of him as a man of "pure character." It is this: *Three years since he sold another man's wife for a harlot.* She was the wife of his coachman, a beautiful and pious girl, a member of the Methodist church. The purchaser was a planter in Alabama: the price $1400. Some months after the sale, the poor husband having been sent into the upper part of South Carolina with the coach, for a member of Mr. Calhoun's *white* family, took the opportunity to flee. He went to Alabama, sought and found his injured wife, and fled, in the night and on foot. After weeks of hunger and toil they reached the upper part of Maryland. The wife, a delicate woman, was taken sick and died. Three days the sorrowing man wept over her remains. At last, he buried her, with his hands, by the river side; and then toiled onward towards Canada. He is in a Canada city. I saw him some months ago a sad, gloomy, heart-broken man. Is the man who can perpetrate such a deed worthy of commendation? John C. Calhoun was not even educated in a community where such atrocities were lawful. He was a kind-hearted humane man in his youth. Slaveholding has debased him. If my evidence is not satisfactory in kind or degree, I will give you more and better!

Yours, for Christian citizenship, [signed:] C[harles] T. T[orrey].

LS with En in ScCleA; PC in the *Christian Citizen,* vol. I, no. 51 (December 21, 1844); PC in *The Liberator,* vol. 15, no. 1 (January 3, 1845), p. 4; PC with En in Boucher and Brooks, eds., *Correspondence,* pp. 254–256. NOTE: An AEU by Calhoun reads: "Mr. Brown[,] contains an article from the Christian Citizen[.] Answered 14th Nov[embe]r 1844."

From A[MBROSE] D[UDLEY] MANN,
"Unofficial—Private"

[U.S. Consulate,] Bremen, Oct. 31, 1844

Dear Sir; It is contended, and I doubt not honestly believed, by no inconsiderable number of the citizens of the United States, that Great Britain has no designs—either immediate or ulterior—upon Texas. In this is to be found the only justification for the rejection by the Senate of the Annexation Treaty. Mr. [Henry] Clay in one of his Letters says: "If any European nation entertains *any ambitious designs* upon Texas, such as that of *colonizing her, or in any way subjecting her, I should consider it as the imperative duty of the government of the United States to oppose such designs by the most firm and determined resistance, to the extent if necessary, by appealing to arms.*" This I am disposed to regard, as being a sentiment which prevails generally, amongst the party of which he is the acknowledged leader. Of course it cannot be in favor with the *nether end* of it—the Abolitionists and old Hartford Conventionists.

Now it is imperative, on every lover of his country, who is under the impression that "any European nation" "entertains ambitious designs upon Texas," to contribute all in his power to the establishment of the fact; and I, therefore, under a solemn sense of duty, transmit to you *my* testimony. About eight months ago a Treaty was concluded at Paris between the Hanse-Towns and Texas by their respective representatives, Baron von Romff [*sic*; Rumpf,] resident Minister there, and Col. [William H.] Daingerfield, accredited to the Hague and the Hanse-Towns. It was forwarded soon afterwards to Bremen and Hamburgh for ratification. The "Burgher's Convent" of the former City, before which it was laid for approval, accepted it and authorized the Senate to transmit it to the capital of Texas for the action of Congress, which assembles in December, which, as I learn from a high source, was accordingly done. An Exequator was then granted to the Consul for Texas. At Hamburgh the Treaty met with slight opposition, some of its stipulations not being altogether satisfactory, and it was postponed for future consideration. But no question, as I understand, was raised relative to the independence of Texas. Her *right to negotiate Treaties had been recognized by the Hanseatic Minister in his negotiations with the Texas Chargé at Paris.* It is proper for me to remark, that during the early stage of the pendency of this matter at Hamburgh, tidings reached Europe that an annexation Treaty had been concluded at Washington. British influence now commenced its wily operations, successfully but unseen, and final action ["was" *interlined*] procrastinated and avoided on the Treaty, so long, that about three weeks ["since" *interlined*] Col. Da[i]ngerfield who was staying at the Hague, suspecting that something was wrong, repaired to Hamburgh. Immediately after his arrival there the Mexican Consul General addressed a note to the Senate of Hamburgh, protesting against the ratification of the Treaty with Texas; and, as I am assured, subsequently refused to certify the papers of the ship "Najade," bound to Vera Cruz with merchandize, until he received from that body a satisfactory decision. The Treaty of "Navigation and commerce" between Mexico and the Hansetowns expired by limitation in August, and as the 12 months notice, required before it can expire, has not been given by either of the contracting parties, *Mexico now threatens if Texas is acknowledged by Hamburgh to make reprisals upon Hanseatic vessels.* I have no *positive* evidence of the truth of this latter statement, but for the last day or two, it has been currently rumored. The Senate of Bremen received a note, also, from the Mexican Consul at this place, making a similar protestation to that at Hamburgh. A question arose whether Bremen should recede from the position which it had taken and notify the government of Texas of this determination, previous to the meeting of Congress, or disregard the Protest utterly, with the risk of alienating itself from Hamburgh[,] the last of its confederates (Lubeck excepted) of the once powerful Hanseatic League? It was a most momentous one, and public opinion as far as it expressed itself, preponderated in favor of the former policy. Such a trial Bremen never experienced. While the excitement was at its heighth [*sic*], I was, unofficially, asked for a frank expression of my sentiments on the subject. As an American citizen (not as U.S. Consul)—as one who felt as if the immutable principles of justice had been grossly, wantonly outraged by the vile conduct of Mexico, urged on by England—I gave them fully, unreservedly. It is revolting to the feelings of humanity, to the philanthrophy [*sic*] which characterizes the age in which we live, that the civilized world should permit Mexico to raise a question touching the right of Texas to enter into Treaties at this late period. The battle of San Jacinto terminated the struggle between the two countries and the war waged since by Mexico, is merely a *quasi* one. I am now *confidentially* advised, from a high quarter, that come what may Bremen will adhere rigidly to her original purpose. At her head is the great *Burghermeister* [Johann] Smidt, not only the master spirit of the Hanseatic Republics, but one of the most distinguished personages in Germany—renowned all over Europe as one of the most talented members of the Congress of Vienna of 1815. And here allow me to ask the question, what stand would the United States assume, if, in consequence of the policy adopted by Bremen, one of her ships should be captured by a Mexican man-of-war while on a voyage to Galveston? It is known that Bremen has no Navy, whatever, to protect her commerce.

Hamburgh is an English City—almost as much under the control of the British Ministry, as Washington is under the control of the Federal Government. Its merchants derive their chief benefits, in Trade, from England. They are in reality English factors and the nation does every thing that it can to sustain and encourage them. The postage on Letters from London to Hamburgh, by the Royal mail, is only about one-third of that charged to Altona, when the distance to the two places is the same! If Great Britain had said to Hamburgh, I have recognized Texas long since; it is your duty to do so, it is idle to suppose that the matter would have been unnecessarily delayed for a moment. But unfortunately in her diplomacy, and in her general relations with the world—savage or civilized—she is actuated by no higher principle than *interest*. If she can cut off Texas from the German markets, she embarrasses in a pecuniary point of view its citizens, and puts them in a condition to accept such overtures as she may hereafter make. If she can prevent its recognition by other powers she creates additional objections in Europe against its annexation to the U. States. I have watched her stealthy movements so closely for the last two years that I can see through all her artifices. Hanover, whose King [Ernest Augustus] is one of her *subjects*, is ready to act any part which may be assigned it. Through him she has control of the Elbe, and uses it when necessary to tame any refractory spirit that may be evinced at Hamburgh.

The Mexican Consul General is said to be on terms of the closest intimacy with [G.L. Hodges] the British Consul General, a functionary who receives a salary four times as large as that given to you, in payment of the weighty duties discharged by you, and who no doubt uses it freely, in the accomplishment of important measures. Moreover I have been kindly permitted to read letters from English merchants in Hamburgh to their correspondents, expressing the greatest delight at the "bold stand," as they termed it, taken by the Mexican Consul.

The "Protests" of certain powers in Europe and the manifest opposition of others, against the annexation of Texas, should be regarded by our government in the light they are intended, as *mere scare-crows*. No nation dare go to war with us. Rothschild holds the purse-strings, and he will never untie them, for the purposes of war any where. His own safety forbids such a belief, for let any state become involved in war with America and revolution would succeed revolution in Europe. But the time may come when Great Britain will be immensely formidable to us. In the unsettled condition of Spain she may secure a foothold on Cuba, and through her machinations Texas, rather than come under the galling yoke of Mexico, may throw itself into her arms. Then, then indeed, she would no longer feel the dependence upon us for our Cotton, which now exists, and surrounding us by her armies and her fleets, she would humble us to the very dust of the earth. Would to Heaven that my countrymen could stand where I stand, and see what I have seen for the last two years, of British duplicity. With one voice they would exclaim to their rulers *"give us Texas if possible without a War, but give us Texas whatever the consequences."*

In a few weeks I shall forward to you a Report of the political condition of the "Deutsche Zollverein"—the production and consumption therein—(as well as in the other states of Germany &c. &c.)—of tobacco.

I enclose you, in a slip from the "Richmond Enquirer" of the 25th June a Letter which I wrote to the Editors over the signature of "Agricola." The opinions expressed in relation to *France*, from an intercourse with many people of that country during the summer, I am sure are not without the best foundation. You will perceive the necessity of regarding this note as *altogether private*; and believe me Your Friend Faithfully, A.D. Mann.

ALS in ScCleA; PC in Jameson, ed., *Correspondence*, pp. 982–986.

NOVEMBER 1–15, 1844

〇

Calhoun left home in early November and was in Charleston on November 7. By November 10 he was back in the federal capital and by the twelfth back in harness at the State Department. For the first time in many years, Mrs. Calhoun accompanied him to Washington, along with their younger daughter Martha Cornelia.

The forces of history were gathering for one of those decisive periods that now and then occur. The American elections came to a close with a victory for the Democratic Presidential candidate Polk, who would perhaps have a working House majority. The victory could not be called overwhelming, but it did provide a basis upon which to achieve Calhoun's first objective—to fix Texas to the Union. The inevitable intra-party maneuvering had, of course, begun the moment victory was certain. Texas had also had elections, and Anson Jones, something of an unknown quantity, would succeed Sam Houston as President in December.

The most portentous occurrences, however, were unfolding in the ancient City of Mexico. From there the American Minister, Wilson Shannon, wrote on November 12, though his despatch would not be received in Washington for several weeks. He had to report the complete failure of efforts to settle the many outstanding irritations between the sister republics. The rulers of Mexico, doubtless for their own reasons, had rebuffed American overtures with calculated insult. Shannon wrote to Calhoun, unofficially, at the same time: "The insolence of this Government is beyond indurence. . . . I am fully convinced we can do nothing with Mexico as to the settlement of any of the difficulties we have with her until we either whip her, or make her believe we will do so."

〇

DRAFT "Prepared for the President" by
R[ichard] K. C[rallé]

[Washington, *ca.* November 1844]
There has been no material change in our Foreign relations since my
last annual message to Congress. With all the Powers of Europe we
continue on friendly terms. It, indeed, affords me ["indeed" *interlined*] great satisfaction to state that, at no former period has the
peace of that highly enlightened and important quarter of the Globe
ever been, apparently, more firmly established. The conviction that
peace is the true policy of nations would seem to be growing, and becoming deeper among the enlightened every where; and sure[?] there
is no people who have a stronger interest ["for" *canceled and* "in"
interlined] preserving peace, or in cherishing the sentiments, and
adopting the means of giving it permanence that we have ["than those
of the U.S." *interlined and then imperfectly erased*]. Among these the
first and greatest, ["and" *changed to* "are"] no doubt the strict observance of justice; and the honest and punctual fulfilment of all engagements. But it is not to be forgotten that it is no less necessary, in the
present state of the world, to be ready to enforce their observance and
fulfilment in reference to us, than to observe and fulfill them on our
part in reference to others.

The negotiation in reference to the Oregon Territory was entered
on between the Secretary of State [John C. Calhoun] and the minister
of Great Britain [Richard Pakenham] as soon as practicable after the
["close" *canceled and* "termination" *interlined*] of the last session of
Congress. It has not yet been brought to a close; but it is to be hoped
it will be in time to communicate the result before the end of the
present session.

[*The following paragraph was added to the end of this document
and marked for insertion here*:] Other questions of importance, and
amongst them the ["interpretation" *canceled*] the Construction of the
[*blank space*] Article of the Treaty of Washington, (in reference to
the extradition of fugitives) growing out of the Florida [slave] case,
brought to the notice of Congress at its last session, have become the
subject of Correspondence between the two Countries; but which
have not yet, however, been brought to a close.

The Government of China has appointed a Commissioner to meet
and treat with ours [Caleb Cushing]. He had, by the last advices, arrived at Canton; and the negotiation was ready to be opened with, as
it was believed, a fair prospect of success.

With all the States of South America ["the most" *canceled*] our relations continue on the most friendly footing. Against nearly all of them our citizens have claims, which, for the most part, originated during the period of their revolutions. They have all been urged for settlement; ["during the present year," *interlined*] and some progress ["has been" *canceled*] made, but ["nothing has yet been, during the present year, definitively" *canceled*] no final adjustment has yet been effected.

With Mexico our relations remain without any material change. That Government has not yet agreed to the amendments proposed by the Senate to the Convention of the 20th of November 1843 for [*blank space*] nor has it repealed or modified its order ["against" *canceled*] in reference to the Retail Trade, issued in violation of the Treaty with the United States of the [*blank space*] day of [*blank space.*] On the contrary our citizens, engaged in carrying on trade within her territories, including inland as well as through her Ports, have been subjected to new vexations and injuries. It has, also, in the meantime, issued orders to renew the war with Texas, and announced its purpose to conduct it in a manner utterly inconsistent with all the usages of war amongst civilized nations. Against its renewal at this time, while the question of annexation between the United States and Texas is pending and undecided, and the mode in which it is proclaimed it will be conducted, I have deemed it to be the duty of the Executive solemnly to protest. It is to be hoped that the grounds on which this protest is placed may have the effect of inducing the Government to review its course in reference to Texas; and to adopt a line of policy; more consistent with the actual state of things, and the usages of civilized nations, as well as the laws of humanity. Towards Mexico no unfriendly feelings are entertained on our part. We wish her well, and would be glad to maintain with her the most friendly relations; but we cannot agree to ["forgo" *canceled and* "allow" *interlined*] the adoption of a measure of policy believed to be essential to our peace and safety, and not inconsistent with the rights of Mexico, to depend upon her assent or dissent.

With Texas our relations continue to be of a most friendly character. Questions growing out of the act of disarming the Texan forces under the command of Capt. [Jacob] Snively, by an officer in the service of the United States [Capt. Philip St. George Cooke], under the orders of our Government, and the forcible breaking open of the [Texan] Custom House at [*blank space*] by ["certain" *interlined*] citizens of the United States, and ["abstracting therefrom" *canceled and* "taking" *interlined*] the goods seized by [James Bourland] the Collector of the Port, ["as being forfeited under the laws of Texas," *interlined*] have been adjusted, as far as ["it is in" *canceled*] the power of the Executive extends. The correspondence between the two governments in reference to both subjects, will be found amongst the accompanying documents. It contains a full statement of all the facts and circumstances, with the views taken on both sides, and the principles on which the questions have been adjusted. It remains for Congress to make the necessary appropriation to carry the arrangements into effect; which I respectfully recommend.

I would also recommend to the serious and early attention of Congress a subject of deep and vital interest to the two Countries; I mean that of the annexation of Texas to the United States, which remained undetermined at the close of the last Session. Time and reflection have but served to strengthen my Conviction of the vital importance of the measure to both Countries; and of their perfect right to adopt it, without giving any just cause of offence to Mexico or any other Power. The events which have occurred since the close of the last Session have removed many of the objections which were taken to the measure, and which were most strongly urged against it. It has since been fully canvassed before the American People; and no reasonable doubt can now remain but that the ["popular" *canceled and* "public" *interlined*] sentiment is decidedly in its favour in a great majority of the States of the Union. The two Governments have already agreed through their respective organs on the terms of the annexation; ["and" *interlined*] I would respectfully recommend to Congress their adoption in the form of a joint Resolution or act, to be consummated and binding on the two Countries when adopted in like manner by the Government of Texas. In order that the subject may be fully presented, in all its bearings the Correspondence which has taken place in reference to it, since the adjournment of Congress, between the United States ["and" *canceled,*] Texas ["on the one side" *canceled*], and Mexico ["on the other" *canceled*], is ["herewith transmitted with" *canceled*] herewith transmitted, and will [be] found amongst the Documents accompanying this Message.

Autograph draft in ScCleA. NOTE: This document is an early draft of that portion of John Tyler's annual message to Congress dated 12/3/1844 which related to foreign affairs. The first paragraph of Crallé's draft appeared nearly verbatim in Tyler's message but the remainder of the message considerably revised and lengthened topics mentioned in the draft. However, a small part of the draft relating to Texas is reproduced verbatim in Tyler's message.

From W[illia]m Hogan

Boston, Nov[embe]r [1844]

Sir, A circumstance has occurred here during your absence from Washington, to which I beg leave to call your attention. It has led to consequences, which I did not anticipate. You are, no doubt, aware of the existence of several American republican associations throughout the country. Their immediate object is to check, or rather suppress entirely, all Irish repeal associations & foreign interference in the management of our Government; knowing better than others can possibly know, the designs of [Daniel] O'Connell—the parent of Repeal—& the Pope on the Institutions of the South particularly, I became a member of the American party and established a branch of it in this City. I knew you were opposed to Oconnel & thought you were also opposed to that *Arch Abolitionist* the Pope [Gregory XVI], & it seemed to me a duty which I owed to the South & to yourself its fearless friend to bring over if possible this great & growing American party to support you for the next Presidency in [18]48, presuming & hoping that you would never again, Sir, place yourself in the "hands of your friends" or submit to the possibility of being tricked out of your rights by a National Convention. Pardon me in requesting that you would throw yourself into the hands of American republicans, on whom I now look, as the true Democracy of the Country. They talk of Mr. [William S.] Archer of Virginia as likely to be their Candidate for the Presidency in [18]48. The party will unanimously support the man who pledges himself to oppose *foreign influence* & use his ["influence" *canceled and* "best efforts" *interlined*] in effecting a change in the present Naturalization laws. I believe, Sir, you would do both, and if—when the *tempora mollia*—shall arrive, you will say so, I think I can obtain for you the support of the American Party.

Soon after you left Washington, Mr. [Lemuel] Williams appointed me to an Office in the Custom House here, but the repealers & Papists knowing my sentiments, induced Mr. [George M.] Bibb [Secretary of the Treasury] to reject my nomination & so frightened Mr. Williams with threats of his removal that he acquiesced. The fact is, Sir, that the powers in Washington are jealous of you. Others expect the nomination in [18]48 & the expectants of Office here, could not fair so well, if you were nominated as they would if others obtained it, merely because you are said to be an honest man. They have opposed me for the last four years, because "it would not answer to talk of Calhounism in New England." This is an error, there is honesty in New England & you will reap the benefit of it, when these political loafers are got rid off. I have written to the Secr[etar]y of the Treasury in relation to my removal from Office here. I have the honor of enclosing it to you. He made no reply, an indication as I imagined, of his views of the policy ["of" *canceled*] to be adopted in [18]48 on the Presidential question. I also have the honor of enclosing to you one of the Native American papers, in which some mention is made of my removal from office. It has created an excitement of which I did not expect to be the hero. I shall have the honor of seeing you in Washington before long. In the mean time I am Very Respectfully, Wm. Hogan.

[Enclosure]
W[illia]m Hogan to [George M. Bibb]

Boston, Oct. 15th 1844

I have the honor, Sir, of enclosing for your perusal a paragraph, which has appeared in the *Olive Branch*, a Newspaper published in this City, having, as I am informed this day, twenty thousand subscribers. It is the organ of the Methodist Episcopal denomination, and has been always consistently democratic. It will show you, Sir, how unwise it may prove, to remove an individual from Office on account of his differing in religious opinions from Roman Catholics. Already Sir, the apparent & exclusive partiality of Mr. Robert Tyler, and consequently—as it is supposed—of his father [John Tyler] for Irish Roman Catholics, has arrayed against the Democracy & the friends of Mr. [James K.] Polk nearly every *native Republican* in the country ["nearly" *canceled*] all of ["whom" *interlined*] were & are, at heart, strong democrats. Witness the recent election in Philadelphia. Witness the proceedings of the natives in New York, and you will see that at the next election in this City every protestant democrat who belongs to the American Republican association in this State, will support Mr. [Henry] Clay, instead of Mr. Polke if President Tyler and yourself should deem it proper to remove me, one of their members, from Office for no other cause than differing in opinion from Papists. I will venture to add, Sir, ["that" *interlined*] neither of you has a friend in New England who does not believe that you both have been seduced into the commission of an outrage, which your better judgment & correct information on the subject, will induce you to undo. Can I, Sir, a Citizen of Georgia, advocate *Irish Repeal?* Can I, Sir, the friend of John C. Calhoun, have any connection with or feel any sympathy for the Irish Agitator, Daniel Oconnell who so grossly abuses the South & its Institutions? None whatever, Sir. All the Offices in the gift of the Government could not purchase me to support either Irish Repeal or Daniel Oconnell. Much less can I support the

191

Pope & his minions in this country. Read the *Bulls* & *Rescripts* in which he calls upon his *subjects*, to oppose slavery & shun heretics. The late Mr. [Abel P.] Upsher saw these things in their true colours & did me the honour of sending me to Mexico on a private Mission, with a view of ascertaining the extent of the conspiracy which he well knew existed to abolish slavery & place Texas in the hands of the British. My report to that good man on the subject of my Mission, is now filed in the Office of the Secr[etar]y of State, to which I would respectfully draw your attention. He intended sending me to Austria & to Russia, as may be seen by my private correspondence with him, or by referrence to Mr. [Charles H.] Winder his private Secr[etar]y who is now in the State Department, but unfortunately Mr. Upsher died a few days before my return to Washington. I know of no enemy I have except the pope[']s minions & ["a" *interlined*] man named George ["Roberts" *interlined*] who a few years ago has been let loose from the Hous[e] of Correction or Reformation, and who ever since up to the present moment inclusively, is keeping house for a woman who has been one [of] the most notorious prostitutes in this City & in New York where she has been also for some years. "Proh pudor [For shame]."

I should be much better pleased if Mr. Williams, the Collector, had given you a proper statement of some of these facts, but I fear he has scarsely nerve enough to meet the emergencies of our present political crisis. He is timid as a fawn & though friendly to Calhoun, we want no such men. We must be like Calhoun himself. We must fear nothing, but dishonor & treachery to the South. I am proud to hear that you are one of his warm friends. If so, Sir, & you find it necessary for *his* interest, to "cut off my head" hesitate not a moment to let the Axe fall & if my money also is necessary to advance *his* cause, you can have that too. I care not who is to be our next President if Calhoun is not to succeed him[.] I have the honour to Remain Sir Respectfully, Wm. Hogan.

ALS with Ens in ScCleA. NOTE: An enclosed newspaper clipping, headed "Sectarianism and Politics," deplores opposition of Catholic Democrats to Hogan's appointment, which opposition is attributed to his conversion to Protestantism. "Democratic native Americans," while differing from the Whigs, "would a thousand times prefer a Whig administration, to the ascendency of the mad bigots who head the Catholic political policy in the United States."

Account book of E[noch] B. Benson & Son with Calhoun family, [Pendleton, *ca.* 11/1]. This pocket-size volume contains 19 pages of journal entries for charges made during 1843 and 1844 against Calhoun's account, totaling $424.95. The charges are chiefly for purchases of small items of goods and provisions and for repairs to household and farm equipment. The account concludes with a notation of a payment made by Calhoun in the form of a draft on Charleston on 11/1, leaving $200 still due. Manuscript volume in ScU-SC, John C. Calhoun Papers.

Bill from E[noch B.] Benson & Son, [Pendleton, *ca.* 11/1?]. This document itemizes 13 transactions at Benson's "Tin Shop" for the purchase or repair of household items for John C. Calhoun. The transactions dated from 2/1 to 10/28 and totalled about $7.08. DU in ScU-SC, John C. Calhoun Papers.

From W[illia]m M. Blackford

Legation of U.S.
Bogotá, 1st Nov. 1844

Sir, I have been waiting, for some weeks, with much anxiety, to hear from the Department on the subject of the Brig "Morris," as well as to its decision with respect to my application for a leave of absence. The latest communication received is the Circular Despatch of the 1st April last, announcing your appointment.

Nothing further has been done in the case of the "Morris." About a month since, the Secretary [of Foreign Affairs, Joaquin Acosta,] asked me whether I would receive Twenty five thousand dollars, in full of the claim against this Government. I answered that I considered I had no right to entertain any proposition until I heard from the Department—but that I would take the responsibility of adhering to the offer I had already made, provided it were accepted before the receipt of any Despatch upon the subject. I pointed out to him, that the difference, between the sum he proposed & that which I was willing to take, was inconsiderable—and now, that his Government had abandoned the ground assumed in his Despatch of the 11th of December 1843, & was willing to pay a much larger amount than it therein proposed, I thought it might go a little further and accept my offer, which no considerations would induce me to abate in the slightest degree. He held out some hope of a speedy adjustment. Circumstances have come to my knowledge, which lead me to believe that the President [Pedro Alcantara Herran] and Secretary are both anxious to settle the claim, but are overruled by the Secretary of Home Affairs, whose influence in the Cabinet is paramount.

The Despatches of that gentleman have probably informed you of the imprisonment of Mr. [Thomas W.] Robeson, Consul of the United States for the port of Santa Martha, for a debt due this Government, on account of duties. I have been long aware of his embarrassments; and, on two occasions, within a year past, at his suggestion, have obtained indulgence as to time, in the payment of his bonds. He has represented to me that he offered obligations to nearly three times the amount of his debt, as collateral securities, besides surrendering all his personal effects. This offer was declined & he was informed that it was necessary for him to go to prison & there remain until the bonds were paid. As the debt due by him was more than covered by the obligations which he tendered, and as there was no probability of his leaving the place, I think, though the letter of the law may not have been exceeded, that, considering he was the consul of a friendly nation, he has been harshly treated, and I so informed the Secretary of Foreign Affairs.

I cannot but hope that this imprisonment of Mr. Robeson will serve to impress upon the Government the necessity of some reorganization, which may elevate the respectability, and increase the efficiency, of the Consular establishment. The Consuls of France & England, not being traders, cannot be imprisoned in this country. Though not inferior in talents or personal worth, our Consuls in Santa Martha [Robeson] and Carthagena [Ramon Leon Sanchez], from the fact simply of being merchants & not salaried officers, do not maintain with the local authorities the same relations, nor enjoy the same respect in society which the French & English Consuls do. The difference of their position is obvious, and mortifying to the national pride of every American who visits those ports. In all South American countries, it is important to have Consuls who besides being men of intelligence and prudence, can command the respect of the authorities and society of the place—this a trading consul can rarely do. His position is invidiously contrasted with that of the salaried officers of other nations, and he is regarded and treated as a functionary of an inferior order. I speak of the state of things which exists in this country, & which has become known to me, by personal observation or the representations of competent and unprejudiced persons—but I do not doubt the remarks, I have thought it my duty to make, are applicable to Consuls of the United States in all parts of the world.

In connexion with the case of Mr. Robeson, I beg leave to state, that he is a creditor, to a considerable amount, of Mr. Leoni, a citizen of the United States, whose treatment by this Government led to the correspondence, which ended in a demand for his Passports by [James Semple] my predecessor, and to the Special Mission to Washington of Col. Acosta, now Secretary of Foreign Affairs.

Hoping I might benefit Mr. Robeson, by presenting Mr. Leoni's claim for losses and damages sustained during his persecutions & wrongful imprisonment, I introduced the subject to the notice of the Secretary. He denied the charge that Mr. Leoni had been unjustly treated, and produced documents which go far to show his participation in the cause of the *Facciosos*, during the late attempt at revolution. Passing over the merits of the case, he said that he had, when in Washington, explained every thing connected with this transaction, and that the letter of Mr. [Daniel] Webster expressed the full satisfaction of the Government of the United States, and that he could not, in the face of this letter, entertain any negotiation about a claim for damages, founded upon the affair. I replied, that I had always supposed his mission had reference to the alleged discourtesy, with which my predecessor had been treated, and that I suspected Mr. Webster alluded only to the explanations touching that point. He said that Gen. Semple's despatches embraced the claim of Mr. Leoni for damages, and that Mr. Webster's expressions of satisfaction covered all parts of the transaction & barred any future claim based thereon.

I have never seen the correspondence to which the Secretary alludes. Nearly two years since, believing it important I should be acquainted with the issue of Col. Acosta's special mission, I applied in my Despatch No. 7 for information, but have never received any. Not having it in my power to rebut the Secretary's allegations, I must permit the claim to slumber until I am in possession of all the facts.

In previous despatches, I have expressed the opinion, that, whilst the abrogation of both classes of discriminating duties could not be obtained by Treaty, they would, ere long, be repealed by an act of Congress. I have studied with some attention their influence upon the commerce between the United States and this country, and am led to believe that the more injurious of the two is that, which a Treaty, upon the basis of the most favored nation, would abolish. I believe, moreover, that our making the abrogation of all discriminating duties an indispensable condition of a Treaty, has had, and will continue to have, a tendency to prevent their repeal by legislation. Some members, I have been assured, opposed the Bill last session—from the mistaken notion that it would be a concession to the United States, & from the belief that we were not content with the same terms, which satisfied France & England, but were endeavoring to extort peculiar privileges.

In my Despatches, Nos. 10 and 11—to which I beg leave respectfully to refer—I explained, at some length, the injurious operation of both classes of these duties. The one, we can at any moment, set aside by making a Treaty—the other, as I have said, will not be relinquished by Treaty stipulations, but will, I doubt not, be repealed, very shortly by an act of congress. Does not true policy dictate that we should, at once, relieve our trade of the more oppressive of these burdens, and trust to time & more enlightened views here, to remove the remainder? A very considerable impulse would be given to the commerce between the United States and this country by enabling our vessels to introduce American manufactures and produce, free of the 5 per cent discrimination—to say nothing of the equalization of the tonnage duties.

Fully impressed with the belief that we are losing many practical advantages by adhering to an abstract principle, and persisting in the demand for that which will not be yielded, I most respectfully request that, in case my leave of absence has not been granted, I may be authorised to make a Treaty on the best terms I can obtain. It is important I should receive this authority at the earliest possible date, as I believe I could obtain a more liberal Treaty from this Administration than from the one which is about to come into power.

The returns of the Presidential election have all been received. No election has been accomplished by the Colleges &, of course, the choice will devolve upon Congress—Generals [Tomas C.?] Mosquera & Borrero & Mr. Cuervo are the three candidates, whose names will be presented to Congress. The first wanted only a few more votes to ensure his election by the colleges. He is the choice of the larger portion of the people, and would beat either of his competitors, single-handed, by a large majority. It is by no means certain, however, that he will be the choice of Congress. I do not apprehend any commotion in the country, let who will be elected, though fears of the kind are entertained by some, should Mosquera be defeated. At present, he is not in the country, being Minister at Lima.

Some months ago, a gentleman informed me, that he had seen, a few days before, in the warehouse at Honda, five small, but very heavy, boxes addressed to me. As I had no advices and expected nothing at the time I was curious to know what the boxes contained. I wrote several times & got persons visiting Honda to make personal enquiries. The answers uniformly were, that none were there for me, & the Keeper persisting to say he had never seen such boxes as I have mentioned. I had forgotten the circumstance, when, a few weeks since, I was told that, about the time the boxes were seen at Honda, a large quantity of spurious dollars had been introduced into this country from England. I thought it possible my name and privileges might have been used to cover their importation, & immediately called on the Secretary of the Treasury to communicate what I knew. He, at once, adopted my suspicions, and took such measures as he deemed likely to lead to a discovery. The affair has made much noise here.

As exemption from duty of all articles, introduced for the use of Foreign Ministers, is here not a mere matter of courtesy, but provided for by law, the Diplomatic corps have been consulting as to the best means of preventing the abuse of the privilege. The returns called for, from the Custom Houses of Santa Martha & Carthagena, will, I do not doubt, show that many articles have been introduced under our names, of which we have never had any intelligence. I have authorised the detention of every thing addressed to me, which is not consigned to the care of the Consul.

The mail, hence to the coast, was robbed, on the night of the 4th ult. near this city, of about $24,000 in gold & silver, being near one third of the amount it contained. The news excited a great sensation from the novelty of the occurrence & the deep interest every one has in the safety with which specie can be transported, by mail, in a country where no other means of remittance exist. I am gratified to state that the robbers—eight in number—have been apprehended, and about $17,000 of the money recovered, and a clue to the remainder obtained.

That part of the Protocol, signed at Lima, by all the Foreign Ministers, resident there, which declares that Peru will be held responsible for spoliations, committed by any of the factions temporarily in the ascendent, has been disavowed by this Government, & Mr. Mosquera censured for giving his sanction to a doctrine, against which New Granada finds it to her interest to protest.

I have received the amount of the balance due the owners of the "Ranger," and am awaiting the instructions of Mr. [Frederick] Vincent, of Norfolk, Va., as to remitting the same. I have also received about two thirds of the sum, awarded to Capt. [John] Hugg, by the Convention, in the case of the "Henrietta," of the 22d April last. I have not heard from Capt. Hugg, nor has he been at Carthagena, which is his residence, since I settled the claim. Should I receive no news of him, I intend to remit the money to Mr. Sanchez, U.S. Consul of that port, to be held subject to his order.

I received, by yesterday's mail, a few Philadelphia papers of the 2d & 3d of Sept. which are my latest dates from the United States. I have the honor to be, with great respect Your Ob[edien]t S[ervan]t, Wm. M. Blackford.

P.S. I had scarcely signed the foregoing when I receiv[ed] a note from the Secretary inviting me to a conference at 12 oclock to day, on the subject of the "Morris." I attended—and was shown a copy of the clearance of the vessel from St. Jago de Cuba, obtained from Havana, and which arrived by the last mail. This was the document, the want of which has hitherto prevented him, as he has uniformly alleged, from settling the claim. It proved favorable to the "Morris," and, having no further pretext for delay, he accepted the offer made by me, at an early stage of the negotiation, and which is specified in my Despatches, Nos. 20 & 25, and a Protocol to that effect is now preparing.

I have much pleasure in thus announcing the adjustment of this long pending claim, upon terms which, I think, ought to be satisfactory to the claimants. If the sum obtained be not as large as they had a right to expect, and as strict justice would have authorised us to demand, it is as much, under all the circumstances, I am thoroughly convinced, as this Government in its present state of embarrassed finances, could, without coercion, have been induced to grant.

The closing of the mail will not permit me to go into any particulars. I must again refer you to the Despatches above cited for information as to the amount of indemnity obtained. Wm. M. Blackford.

ALS (No. 27) in DNA, RG 59 (State Department), Diplomatic Despatches, Colombia, vol. 10 (T-33:10, frames 273–281), received 1/4/1845; FC in DNA, RG 84 (Foreign Posts), Colombia, Despatches, vol. B4.

R[ichard] K. Crallé to E[dward] G.W. Butler, "near Bayou Goula," La., 11/1. "I have to acknowledge the receipt of your letter of the 9th ult. & to state that in compliance with your request instructions will be given to such of our Consuls as reside in countries where sugar cane is extensively cultivated, to send specimens of it to your agents in the manner pointed out in your letter. You will of course be expected to defray all expenses attending its transportation &c." FC in DNA, RG 59 (State Department), Domestic Letters, 35:10 (M-40:33).

From P[ETER P.?] MAYO, "Private"

Richmond, November 1st 1844

Dear Sir, I need not apologise for troubling you with a matter about which every friend of the Constitution must feel deeply interested. The Federal Constitution was framed and adopted by a virtuous agracultural [*sic*] people; for, of such was the great majority of the people when they ratified it; and of such is the a [*sic*] large majority now: but, the increasing and ["affilliated" *altered to* "affiliated"] Manufactures, Merchants, joint Stock Companies and all kindred Speculators, by combined and concerted action are exerting all their energies, and devoting their affluent means to wrest the Government from the hands of those whose right is to rule. The wicked devices of plundering and fanatical Combinations, must be checked or the Union cannot stand. The growth of the manufacturing and mercantile power, is daily undermining the palladium of our liberties and if not counteracted by some grand and powerful Organization of the Agracultural and other labouring Classes throughout the Union, the best and much the largest portion of the people will be enslaved. What, then, can be done? A Southern Convention would not be effectual. Something must be done, whether the Republican party succeed or not in the pending presidential struggle. My only hope is in the call of ["an" *altered to* "a"] Convention of the Agracultural and other labouring Classes from every State in the Union for the purpose of devising some plan to protect themselves against "The protective System" of their plunderers. The thought is worthy of your consideration. With Sentiments of the highest respect your fellow Citizen, P. Mayo.

ALS in DLC, Richard Kenner Crallé Papers.

From JOHN S. PALMER and Others

[Pineville, S.C., *ca.* November 1, 1844]

Sir, The Parishes of St. Johns Berk[e]ley[,] St. Stephens and St. James Santee have united to give a dinner at Blackoak on the 21st inst. to their immediate Representative [in Congress] the Hon[ora]ble I[saac] E. Holmes.

Your company on that occasion is most respectfully solicited. To declare that the lofty position which you now occupy in the councils of our Country is a source of hounarable [*sic*] pride to every Carolinian—and that your name is associated with every idea of Constitutional liberty, but inadequately expresses the sentiments of our community. Most respectfully your's, John S. Palmer [and] C.B. Snowden of St. Stephens, A.J. Harvey [and] H.F. Porcher of St. Johns B[erkeley], [and] Sam[ue]l J. Palmer of St. James Santee.

N.B. If not convenient to attend you will please inform the Committee through the P[ost] Office[,] Pineville S.C.

ALS in ScCleA. NOTE: Calhoun's AEU reads: "Invitation to attend a dinner to Mr. Holmes at PineVille."

From [Capt.] Foxhall A. Parker, Commanding U.S. East India Squadron, U.S. Frigate Brandywine, Boca Tigris, 11/1. He informs Calhoun that he has been unable to find a qualified person for the office of U.S. Consul at Hong Kong. The records of the Office are in the keeping of William P. Peirce, U.S. Naval Storekeeper at Macao. Parker encloses a copy of a "Report of the Board of Revenue at Peking (to the Emperor) on the Treaty with the United States." ALS with En in DNA, RG 59 (State Department), Miscellaneous Letters (M-179:106, frames 3–16), received 2/27/1845.

From Moses Taylor, New York [City], 11/1. Taylor asks that James J. Wright be appointed U.S. Consul at Santiago, Cuba, in place of the recently deceased Consul, Michael Mahon. Wright served as U.S. "Consular Commercial" Agent at Santiago from 1823 through 1826, at which time he resigned and removed to the interior of the island. Taylor considers Wright well qualified by experience, acquaintance with the island and natives, and personal character to fulfill the duties of U.S. Consul. LS and copy in DNA, RG 59 (State Department), Applications and Recommendations, 1837–1845, Wright (M-687:35, frames 159–164).

From HENRY A. WISE

Legation of the U. States
Rio de Janeiro, November 1st 1844
Sir, The last Government despatch from the U. States reached me about the 23d ultimo, and on the 26th ult[im]o the Emperor [Pedro II] granted me an audience, at which I presented to him the letter from the President of the U. States congratulating him on the marriage

of the Princess Donna Januaria. That Princess and her husband had, on the 24th, two days before, just departed in a French frigate for Europe. The Prince [Louis, Count of Aquila], it is currently rumored at court, did not part from the Emperor or the Empress, his sister, on the best of terms. The differences, however, were mere household bickerings. The Emperor is rather grave, studious and monastic in his habits, the Prince was gallant & gay & extravagant in his turn; and I suspect there were those in and about the Palace who did not try to cultivate the best understanding between them. But the Emperor received me most graciously of course, and made a very kind acknowledgment to the President for his letter. The Court is now in mourning for the death of the Arch-duchess of Russia, announced on the same day by Mr. Lomonosoff, who recommends to my *particular care* the enclosed letter for the Brazilian Minister at Washington.

I duly received the papers relating to the claim of Mr. [Joseph] Ray, and am giving them my earnest attention. I regret to complain that not a letter of mine respecting *claims* of our citizens has yet been answered. As soon as I read the case of Mr. Ray I ordered the Portuguese papers attached to it to be translated, and on Monday last had a personal interview with Mr. [Ernesto F.] França on that and other subjects. I told him without reserve that the U. States could not but feel dissatisfied with the manner in which their claims had been treated by Brazil. That the delays were unaccountable, and that the omission to explain even why they were not settled, was in itself a subject of just complaint. The change of Ministry was rung again, but I reminded him that it ought not to take as long as he had been in office or as long as I had been attending this Court to settle the whole budget of business of that sort with the U. States. He then said that claims required the action of the Council of State and he had not been able to get it together, and that he would again give notice for it to meet, and begged me to address him a note. I submit with all deference that an instruction to me, drawn in rather peremptory terms, and calling for prompt decision and settlement would have a good effect in favor of our claims, if based on some such flattering ground as a disposition to remove every obstacle to still closer relations with Brazil. I say this the more confidently, because the turn given to this conversation by Mr. França himself, more than intimated a wish for a stronger connexion with the U. States than any which has ever yet existed. I cannot in this letter detail our conversation fully, and I do not know that I exactly comprehend the precise end of certain enquiries he addressed to me. Besides other questions of less importance, he asked me directly: What the U. States would do, in conjunction with Brazil, for the protection of American interests and policy generally, and to prevent the intervention of Europe in American affairs? I replied that I was neither prepared nor instructed to answer any specific meaning of his question, if he designed it to signify any thing beyond general relations. But in the general, I was at all times prepared to say, both as an American citizen & Minister, that the U. States were always ready & willing, as they ever had been, to protect and cherish American interests and policy, both for their own sake and as opposed to those of Europe; and that to do so most effectually, the first precept of their policy was to enter into no entangling alliances. They had been eminently successful by freeing themselves from all treaties that would necessarily involve them in the differences and difficulties of other nations, or that would cramp their energies or contract their resources at home, and they had by wise internal regulations so strengthened & magnified themselves as now to have become by their very existence a strong defence of American interests and policy. And this course they would not fail to commend to every state in North & South America. They should first make themselves entirely free & independent of Europe—free from the bondage of their debts, from their treaties, their alliances & wars, and as independent as possible of their trade and the necessities of their social and political condition. That American states should favor each other in all respects, rather by interchange of good offices and by mutual regulations at home to unshackle trade, to encourage science, letters & the mechanic arts, to promote and even to *compel* peace among themselves, to insure & secure the just & prompt administration of their international rights, to encourage commerce, to facilitate emigration & immigration with the rights of expatriation, to protect the freedom of the seas, and to maintain neutral rather than belligerent rights, and to improve, at every expense & trouble, their own agriculture, and their own internal communication, and to encourage & foster their own industry. He immediately referred to the instance of the war now existing between Monte Video & Buenos Ayres, annoying every other nation & weakening themselves. He said Monte Video was so reduced as to be knocking at the doors of England & France for assistance, and asked whether the U. States would not unite with Brazil in putting an end to that war by force, if necessary, rather than permit England or France to interpose and acquire a dominant influence in the Platte country? I said that the U. States had long ago assumed & acted on the policy to prevent European intervention in the wars of North America, and they had once interposed to protect South American states; and I had no doubt but that they would approve of the same course on the part of Brazil in this instance, and would interpose their own good offices to arrest the war of Monte Video & Buenos Ayres. I added that I would ask for instructions what to say on the whole subject. Already has the blockade of Monte Video involved our Navy in the very unpleasant necessity of capturing the whole Buenos Ayrean squadron. The conduct of Capt[ai]n [Philip F.] Voorhe[e]s in that affair has not only been universally approved, but is rejoiced at here, so weak & irregular is the blockade, so futile ["are" *interlined*] the means to enforce it, so wanton is the whole war and so ridiculous & at the same time so uncivilized is the mode of conducting it. In fact it is a purely personal contest between [Juan M.] Rosas [Governor of Buenos Aires] & [Fructuoso] Rivera, of unmitigated revenge and unbridled ambition, equally injurious to American interests and dishonoring to the American name. It has no prospect either of speedy termination. Rosas would not be favorably impressed with the interposition of Brazil, because the latter is suspected, unjustly I believe, of a design to acquire Monte Video. England as the former mediator between Brazil & Monte Video is bound to guarantee the independence of Monte Video, and this guarantee is a basis for her intervention now, which Brazil is desirous to prevent. The U. States is, therefore, looked to as the power whose interposition would be regarded the most favorably by all parties, and would probably be the most successful. Indeed I have been appealed to from various quarters, to know why the U. States would not interpose their good offices, by remonstrance or otherwise, against this war. Rosas has formally disapproved of the conduct of the Commodore of his squadron, has exculpated Capt[ai]n Voorhe[e]s from all blame, it is said,* [*Asterisk*: "I am just better informed that this is a mistake."] and would listen gladly to terms for peace coming from the U. States. Mr. [William] Brent [Jr.] is there now and might be empowered to mediate. Or, as has been suggested, I might be instructed to accompany a special agent from this court. I seek no such additional duty, but if it is thought best to adopt that mode, in case any be adopted, I would cheerfully consent to take upon myself the mission. It would take but a short time, about forty days, to go down to the river, do all that could be done, and return. But these are mere suggestions which I submit to the better judgment of the Department. My main object is to impress the idea that a direct intimation has been made to me here, that the opportunity is now afforded for the U. States to manifest a leading interest in South American affairs, and the wish is openly expressed for them to do so much to their advantage. How far it is their policy to do so, and by what mode, the President will, doubtless, rightly judge.

The enclosed No. 1 is a copy of the letter of Mr. [Hamilton] Hamilton [British Minister to Brazil] relating to the Brig Cyrus, the papers concerning which case have heretofore been sent to the Department.

No. 2 contains the copies of the papers which were found on board the Brig Sooy, with all the information in possession of Mr. Hamilton respecting the capture and character of that vessel. No. 3 contains Mr. [George W.] Gordon's correspondence with Mr. Alexander H. Tyler at Bahia, and my correspondence with Mr. Gordon touching the same. These papers but too clearly show how the African slave trade is carried on in Brazil, and how shamefully the U. States flag is prostituted to its infamous uses. Our laws should be modified to meet this way of aiding & abetting the slave-trade by the sale of vessels here to be transferred and delivered on the Coast of Africa. Thus it is that our flag is made to protect a Brazilian vessel, with a crew and perfect outfit of slave deck, water casks, irons &c. &c. to the African Coast; and I venture to affirm that not a vessel of the U. States is sold in Brazil to be delivered at a port in Africa, without taking out a crew & such outfit for the slave-trade, and without the U. States Captain & crew, if not owners and consignees, wilfully & knowingly aiding and abetting that traffic; and I affirm further, that in all such cases the U. States Consul has reason to know & does know to a moral certainty that in every such case without exception, there is more or less preparation for and an intention to engage in the slave-trade, if opportunity favors the attempt, when any such vessel clears from his office in Brazil. But the Consuls say to me: What can we do? The owners or persons empowered have the right to sell and to deliver where they please. I have ventured to say to Mr. Gordon that there is a qualification to this right, and I beg to know whether, in case a Consul has good reason to believe, from the notoriety of the mode of carrying on this trade, and from his knowledge of the parties to the given transfer of vessel, that the flag of the U. States is about to be abused to the purposes of an infamous offence against the laws of the U. States, he may not refuse to clear the vessel? Ought not our Government to give immediately as strict and strong instructions, in a circular to Consuls on this subject, as its nature requires and as our laws of navigation & commerce will permit? What power have I to instruct & direct U. States Consuls in the jurisdiction of Brazil? If American Ministers have no power of controlling them, there ought to be a Consul General of the U. States allowed & appointed for this Empire forthwith. No fitter person could be found for such an office than George W. Slacum Esq[ui]r[e], late Consul for this port. Until instructed not to do so, I shall assume to call for information from and to direct the action of Consuls—and, in one word, to take any lawful responsibility for the suppression of the slave-trade carried on by citizens of the U. States under their flag. I therefore hesitated not to have sent to Mr. Consul Tyler at Bahia, the letter a copy of which is enclosed. He is, I am told, a clerk or subordinate in the house of Mr. John S. Gillmer, who, you will see by the letter of Mr. Gordon to me, is said to have actually sold the ship "Gloria" for the slave-trade. At all events you will see the names of the owners of the Sooy in the State of New Jersey, and of her Master & Mate. The exposure of the names alone of our citizens engaged directly or indirectly in this traffic, may go very far to arrest it. I beg to know of the Department whether my action in all these matters has been too strong, and, if it is not approved, I desire instructions for the future. If I felt fully empowered, and that I would be fully sustained in the prompt & decisive application of moral & physical means here, I would stake my reputation on the attempt to break up all participation in the slave-trade by U. States vessels and citizens, root & branch, in one year from the commencement of operations, and that too without any undue restrictions upon or obstructions to our lawful commerce. Frigates are not the ships of war to cruise upon this station. Station one here; and one at the river Platte to interchange frequently, and to visit Pernambuco and Bahia at *irregular* intervals. And near those places keep a regular force of two sloops of war and four brigs at least, to run into shoal waters on the Coast from Frio to St. Roque; and keep them & as many more small vessels as possible cruising from the Brazilian to the African Coasts between the parallels of 7 or 8 North, & 7 or 8 South of the Equator. Instruct the Consuls to inform the Captains & Commanders of these vessels immediately in all cases of a sale of a U.S. vessel in Brazil to be delivered in Africa or elsewhere, and instruct those Captains & Commanders to keep a look out for these vessels when sailing, and to examine their outfit, if suspicious, while under the American flag. Cause the Consuls to inquire the names of Owners, Consignees, Masters & Mates of such vessels so sold, and to have the same published in the U. States and in Brazil, and appoint such Consuls only as are men of high & firm character, and pay them well enough to enable them to live without engaging in any trade or traffic, or having any business connections in this country. I beg that the whole subject may be brought before Congress, and I refer to Mr. Slacum's correspondence already published for further information and, though I don[']t agree with the mode suggested by him of not allowing our vessels to trade from S. America to Africa, yet from his representations the nature of the evils may be seen and the remedy for them may be judged of.

No. 4 is the copy of a letter, the last addressed by me to Mr. França, touching the first operation or the introduction of their new Tariff. I have the honor to be with great respect Your ob[edien]t Servant, Henry A. Wise.

P.S. We have in the last few days, by the arrival of the Boston, received the melancholy news of the death of Capt[ai]n [W.D.] Newman by Suicide.

ALS (No. 7) with Ens in DNA, RG 59 (State Department), Diplomatic Despatches, Brazil, vol. 13 (M-121:15), received 1/2/1845; FC in DNA, RG 84 (Foreign Posts), Brazil, Despatches, vol. 11; CCEx in DNA, RG 233 (U.S. House of Representatives), 28A-E1; draft in Henry A. Wise Papers, Eastern Shore of Virginia Historical Society, Onancock, Va. (copies in NcU and ViHi); PEx's with Ens in House Document No. 148, 28th Cong., 2nd Sess., pp. 39–54.

From John Baldwin, "Mansion House," New York [City], 11/2. Baldwin asks whether the State Department has any knowledge in regard to the overdue installment to certain U.S. citizens for their claims against Mexico. ALS in DNA, RG 59 (State Department), Miscellaneous Letters (M-179:106, frames 18–19).

Rich[ar]d K. Crallé to A[lexander] de Bodisco, [Russian Minister to the U.S.], 11/2. Crallé acknowledges receipt of De Bodisco's note of 10/27, announcing his arrival at New York City and his resumption of diplomatic duties. "I will not fail to lay your communication before the Secretary upon his return to the seat of Government, from which he is now absent, and in the meantime beg leave to reciprocate, on his part, the very friendly sentiments you are pleased to express towards him." FC in DNA, RG 59 (State Department), Notes to Foreign Legations, Russia, 6:20 (M-99:82).

From Edw[ar]d K. Collins, New York [City], 11/2. Collins asks that James J. Wright be appointed U.S. Consul at Santiago, Cuba. Wright has been recommended by Moses Taylor, whose "commercial operations with Cuba, are not second to those of any other merchant in this country." LS in DNA, RG 59 (State Department), Applications and Recommendations, 1837–1845, Wright (M-687:35, frame 165).

From EDWARD EVERETT

London, 2 November 1844

Sir, I transmit herewith a copy of a note addressed to Lord Aberdeen, in compliance with your instructions Nro. 108, of the 25th of September, relative to the objects of the late Act of parliament "for the more effectual suppression of the Slave-trade."

There being no room to doubt the authenticity of a Statute published by the parliamentary printer and contained in the authorised edition of the laws, I thought it best to take that point for granted.

The act does not extend to British subjects in any Country by name, and its apparent object, the suppression of the African Slave-trade, would not indicate an extension of its provisions to the United States. That it might not, under these circumstances seem a gratuitous assumption on our part, to suppose that it was intended to apply to them, I thought it expedient to refer particularly to the letter [of 10/23/1843] of the English Consul at Charleston [William Ogilby], in which he speaks of the anxiety of British subjects in his Consular district to become acquainted with the provisions of the law.

As the circular letter of instructions to the Consuls of Great Britain, with respect to the state of Slavery and the Slave-trade are contained in the collection of parliamentary papers relative to the suppression of the Slave-trade for 1843, which have been already furnished from the Foreign Office and transmitted to the Department by me, I thought it unnecessary to ask to be furnished with them. They will be found in the collection of papers referred to (part D p. 1, 117), together with the replies of several of the Consuls.

In conversation with Lord Aberdeen a short time since, in reference to these enquiries, which I had not then seen, he said that they were not made with any specific object; but in conformity with the practice of this Government of collecting through their Consuls or special Agents statistical information upon all subjects of great public interest.

With reference to the Act of 6 & 7 Victoria Chapter 98, I am inclined to think its real object, was that which you ascribe to it in your instructions and no other. I have even heard it suggested, but not from an Official source, that it was in contemplation to exempt from its penalties such a transaction as the *bonâ fide* purchase of a Slave for domestic Service. If any such purpose was ever formed and abandoned, it was probably because such exemption would be giving a direct sanction to Slavery and also open a door for fraudulent evasion of the real objects of the law.

I intended to have some conversation with Lord Aberdeen on the object of the law before addressing you on the subject, and for this and other purposes shortly after the receipt of your despatch Nro. 108, I asked an interview; but he had made arrangements to leave town for his estate in Scotland, on the day for which I requested it. I am, Sir with great respect, Your obedient Servant, Edward Everett.

Transmitted with despatch Nro. 202.

1. Mr. Everett to the Earl of Aberdeen, 1 November, 1844.

2. A printed Copy of the "Act for the more effectual suppression of the Slave-trade" 6 & 7 Vict. Cap. 98.

[Enclosure]

Edward Everett to the Earl of Aberdeen

Grosvenor Place

1 November 1844

The Undersigned Envoy Extraordinary and Minister Plenipotentiary of the United States of America, has been instructed to acquaint the Earl of Aberdeen, Her Majesty's Principal Secretary of State for Foreign Affairs, that the attention of the President [John Tyler] has been called to the Provisions of an Act of parliament purporting to be the 98th chapter of the Statutes of the 6 & 7th year of Her Majesty's reign, and entitled "an Act for the more effectual suppression of the Slave trade."

Although the Government of the United States has no Official knowledge of the existence of the act in question, the Undersigned supposes that its authenticity as contained in the printed Copy accompanying the present note may be taken for granted. On this supposition, he has been directed to apply to the Earl of Aberdeen for those explanations of its objects and the means of carrying them into effect as far as the United States are concerned, which are rendered desirable by the apparent character of its provisions.

The act in question seems to be designed to extend the criminal jurisdiction of Great Britain, in all cases embraced within its provisions, to British subjects in foreign Countries. It is well known that there are in almost every part of the United States many natives of Great Britain, some of them temporarily resident and others permanently established as naturalized Citizens.

As the provisions of the Act referred to are without qualification, they would seem of course to extend to British subjects in the United States. This supposition is confirmed by some facts of public notoriety. It is stated in a letter of Mr. [William] Ogilby, the British Consul at Charleston, dated 23d October 1843 and found in the volume containing the correspondence with foreign powers relative to the suppression of the Slave-trade, (class D p. 129) that "great anxiety exists among the British subjects" resident in the United States to become acquainted with the provisions of the law in question; and Mr. Ogilby adds "I feel well assured that I shall very frequently be applied to, by subjects of Her Majesty residing in this part of the world, for an opinion as to the legality or illegality of certain acts connected with the subject to which the law refers, if done, or participated in by them."

For this reason Her Majesty's Consul at Charleston requests to be furnished with a copy of the law and of any opinions which may have been given by the law Officers of the Crown upon its enactments, and asks permission to publish the law in some of the newspapers of Charleston for the information and guidance of all British subjects residing within his Consular district.

A letter has appeared in ["in" *canceled*] some of the public journals of the United States, purporting to be a circular letter of Instructions to Her Majesty's Consuls, signed by Lord Aberdeen, dated at the Foreign Office 31 December 1843 and containing directions relative to the promulgation and contravention of the Act of 6 & 7 Victoria C. 98.

The precise objects of this law taken in connection with the 5th of Geo. IV C. 113 are as the enquiry of Her Majesty's Consul at Charleston shews not fully apparent, at least as far as the United States are concerned. The object of both as declared in their respective letters is the suppression of the Slave-trade, by which designation the African Slave trade is usually understood. Such unquestionably was the design of the original act of 5 Geo: IV C. 113. The 6 & 7 Victoria C. 98 appears to go further. As far as can be judged from the reported debates, on its passage through parliament, it would seem to be the design in which this act was framed indirectly to suppress the Slave-trade by prohibiting British subjects and British capital from being engaged in the purchase and employment of Slaves in Countries where the African Slave-trade is pursued, and thus to deprive that trade of a part of the stimulus, under which it is now carried on.

If such be the object of the law it must of course fail of application within the United States, where the African Slave-trade under the influence of a unanimous public sentiment and of the severest penal statutes, has long since ceased to exist. Notwithstanding this circumstance, however the impression evidently prevails as the Undersigned has shewn on the part of the individuals in the United States most concerned, that the act is designed to have a further operation. To remove all doubts on the subject, he is accordingly directed to ascertain, through the proper department of Her Majesty's Government, whether British subjects in the United States are intended to be embraced within the provisions of the Act; and if so, whether it is to be restricted to those who may be temporarily sojourning in the United States, without intending to become naturalized citizens; or whether it will be extended to all persons in the Union born within the limits of Her Majesty's dominions including as well those who have become naturalized citizens as those who have not.

If such an extension be given to the Statute, the Undersigned is also directed to ascertain whether any and if any what measures have been adopted or are proposed, to carry the provisions of the law into effect, as far as concerns the United States; and particularly what instructions, if any, have been given to Her Majesty's Consuls in the United States concerning the Acts of 5 Geo. IV C. 113 and 6 & 7 Victoria C. 98.

The Earl of Aberdeen will not be surprised that the information now asked for is desired by the United States. An Honorable member of the House of Commons is reported to have said on the passage of the law in question through that body, that "no man could enter into trade with any Country between Virginia and Brazil, who did not run the risk of falling under the penalties of the bill." The Undersigned is not advised whether this remark was made in reference to the provisions of the bill as it passed or to other provisions, which he understands were removed by way of amendment. Could such an effect be regarded as the designed or necessary consequence of the law in question, it would constitute a most serious and alarming departure from the rule of policy announced by Lord Aberdeen in his despatch to Mr. [Richard] Pakenham of the 26th December 1843 as the principle of Her Majesty's Government, in reference to the Slave-holding States: in virtue of which His Lordship remarks that "we have never in our treatment of them made any difference between the Slave-holding and the free States of the Union."

Higher considerations than those of Commercial interest make it the right and duty of the United States to be informed on a subject of this character. The Undersigned perceives from a circular letter of Instructions addressed by His Lordship to the British Consuls in all the American States entitled "Queries on the state of Slavery and the Slave-trade," that information of the minutest description has been sought by Her Majesty's Government as to the colored population of the United States of all descriptions and the laws which apply to that part of their inhabitants. If the laws of a friendly Government in

210

reference to its own citizens and subjects, over which Great Britain claims to have and can have no jurisdictional or legal rights are deemed a legitimate subject of enquiry by Her Majesty's Government, it will not be denied to be the right and duty of the United States to be promptly informed as to the nature and objects of foreign enactments, purporting to extend to large numbers of persons residing in the American Union, owing obedience to its laws and entitled to its protection.

The great principle of non-intervention in the concerns of other independent states has received the most efficient support in England. It has in fact been made, in no small degree through the influence of Her Majesty's Government, to decide the condition of Europe for the last quarter of a century. Experience has proved that all infringements of this principle are fraught with hazard to the good understanding of nations and the peace of the world; and Lord Aberdeen will not be surprised, that the Government of the United States who more than any other power have made it the basis of their foreign policy, should look with some jealousy on any thing which wears the appearance of a departure from it, as far as they are themselves concerned.

The Undersigned avails himself of this opportunity to renew to the Earl of Aberdeen the assurance of his high consideration. (Signed) Edward Everett.

LS (No. 202) with Ens in DNA, RG 59 (State Department), Diplomatic Despatches, Great Britain, vol. 53 (M-30:49), received 11/25; FC in DNA, RG 84 (Foreign Posts), Great Britain, Despatches, 9:33–36; FC in MHi, Edward Everett Papers, 50:233–236 (published microfilm, reel 23, frames 390–391).

From EDWARD EVERETT

London, 2 November 1844

Sir, In my despatch Nro. 195, I made report of what had passed between Lord Aberdeen and myself on the subject of communicating to the Government of the United States the instructions given to their Colonial Governors, in reference to the course to be pursued toward vessels having Slaves on board, brought into their ports by stress of weather or mutiny. I now transmit a short note from Lord Aberdeen, in which he declines making the communication, on the ground of the confidential character of the instructions.

I was in some degree prepared for this by a remark which fell from Lord Aberdeen on the occasion referred to and which was repeated in my despatch Nro. 195 vizt. that their character as private instructions addressed to their own Governors in reference to future occurrences, might be reason enough for not communicating them to a foreign power.

If they had been of a nature to satisfy the expectations of the Government of the United States as set forth in your instructions, as well as those of Mr. [Abel P.] Upshur, and Mr. [Daniel] Webster I have no doubt they would have been communicated to us; but it ought not perhaps to be inferred, that there are no considerations of a different character, which lead to their being with[h]eld from the public.

The position of the present Government in reference to all questions connected with Slavery is one of some delicacy. They are no doubt in substantial accordance with the public sentiment of England on this subject, which is powerful and unanimous to a degree perhaps unexampled. But on all practical questions and measures of detail they are of course obliged to have regard to those considerations which weigh with a prudent Administration, and which are apt to be wholly overlooked by private individuals engaged without responsibility in the work of popular agitation. While the individuals of this class as far as Slavery is concerned form a body in England too numerous and respectable to be overlooked, it is not to be inferred that the Government while it treats them with consideration, allows itself to be guided by their Councils.

It has occurred to me as not unlikely, that the instructions in question, though coming short of the principles which have been maintained on the part of the United States, may yet be of a character which the Government does not wish unnecessarily to subject to the criticism of the persons of the class alluded to. It ought, however, in justice to be stated, that I do not make this suggestion, in consequence of any thing which has fallen from Lord Aberdeen on the subject; but altogether from my own observation of the relation of the Government to public opinion on this question. I am, Sir, with great respect, Your obedient Servant, Edward Everett.

Transmitted with despatch Nro. 203.
The Earl of Aberdeen to Mr. Everett 21st October 1844.

LS (No. 203) with En in DNA, RG 59 (State Department), Diplomatic Despatches, Great Britain, vol. 53 (M-30:49), received 11/25; FC in DNA, RG 84 (Foreign Posts), Great Britain, Despatches, 9:36–39; FC in MHi, Edward Everett Papers, 50:236–239 (published microfilm, reel 23, frames 391–393).

From E D W A R D E V E R E T T, "(Confidential)"

London, 2 November 1844

My dear Sir, You will perceive that in my note to Lord Aberdeen of 1st November on the extension of the act of 6 & 7 Victoria C. 98 to British subjects in the United States, I have foreborn to adopt one of the arguments, adduced in your instructions on this subject. I refer to that which is expressed in the following words of your despatch Nro. 108:

"We hold that the criminal jurisdiction of a nation is limited to its own dominions, and to vessels under its flag on the High Seas; and that it cannot extend to acts committed within the dominion of another, without violating its sov[e]reignty and independence."

Although I have not had time to investigate the subject as thoroughly as I could wish, what research I have been able to make has led me to think, that this principle is too broadly expressed.

It is, of course, impossible for any power to exercise criminal jurisdiction within any other foreign State or over any persons while there. It is also, in point of fact, nearly impossible for any power in ordinary cases, to exercise criminal jurisdiction over its subjects, in reference to acts done within a foreign country, and after the persons doing them have returned home. The difficulty of proving the alleged crime would generally be insuperable.

Still, I imagine, the claim of jurisdiction in such cases exists on the part of all Governments.

With respect to Great Britain, it was enacted by 9 Geo. IV C. 31 § 7 that "British subjects may be tried in England, for murder or manslaughter committed abroad, whether within the King's dominions or without." I believe however that the person killed must have been an English subject, though this I think is not stated in the law, which passed 27th June 1828.

By an Act of Congress 14 June 1797, it was made penal for an American citizen, *without the limits of the United States,* to fit out a vessel to cruize against a friendly power. This would be almost of necessity an Act performed in a foreign jurisdiction.

An Act of 30th January 1799, makes it penal for an American citizen, whether in the Union or out of it, to correspond with a foreign Government for certain purposes.

The first section of the Act of 10 May 1800 prohibiting the Slave Trade, makes it penal for any American citizen to serve on board any foreign ship or vessel, which shall hereafter be employed in the Slave trade.

213

The Act of 20 April 1818 makes it penal for a citizen of the United States, without their limits, to fit out a vessel to cruize or commit hostilities upon citizens of the United States or their property.

The Act of 15 May 1820 makes it piracy and punishes it with death for a citizen of the United States to be engaged in the Slave trade on board a foreign vessel.

The Act of 3d March 1825 (cap. 276 of that Session) provides in the 5th Section, that a citizen of the United States may be tried at home for an offence committed on board an American vessel, in a foreign jurisdiction; with a proviso that if he has been tried for the same offence in the foreign jurisdiction, he shall not be subject to a second trial in the United States; thus expressly claiming jurisdiction over our citizens, in cases where the foreign jurisdiction is also admitted.

Mr. [Henry] Wheaton in his elements of international Law (Vol. 1 p. 158) lays it down, that the judicial power of every independent State extends

"1. To the punishment of all offences against the municipal laws of the State, by whomsoever committed, within the territory.

2. To the punishment of all such offences by whomsoever committed, on board its public and private vessels on the High Seas, and on board its public vessels in foreign ports.

3. To the punishment of all such offences, by its own subjects *wheresoever committed.*

4. To the punishment of piracy and other offences against the law of nations, by whomsoever and wheresoever committed.

It is evident (he continues) that a State cannot punish an offence committed against its municipal laws within the territory of another State, *unless by its own citizens*; nor can it arrest the person or property of the supposed offender within that territory; but it may arrest its own citizens in a place which is not within the jurisdiction of any other nation, as the High Seas, and punish them for offences committed within such a place, *or within the territory of a foreign State.*"

These authorities and instances seem to be so clear, that I thought it would not be safe, without submitting them to your reconsideration, to controvert the doctrine which they sustain. I am sure you will candidly appreciate my motives. I am, Dear Sir, with great regard, faithfully yours, Edward Everett.

LS in ScCleA.

R[ichard] K. Crallé to Geo[rge] Hubbard, Stonington, Conn., 11/2. Hubbard's letter of 10/21 to President John Tyler has been referred to the State Department. In reply Crallé states that the President is empowered to appoint a consul at Rio Negro, Patagonia, [Argentina], without the advise and consent of Congress, if it can be demonstrated that "the interests of our Commerce, and the protection of our Seamen, and Citizens would be promoted thereby." FC in DNA, RG 59 (State Department), Consular Instructions, 11:299.

R[ichard] K. Crallé to Amory Edwards, Buenos Aires, 11/4. Edwards is requested to turn over to his successor as U.S. Consul, Joseph Graham, the records of the consulate. FC in DNA, RG 59 (State Department), Consular Instructions, 11:300.

From John G. Floyd, [former Representative from N.Y.], Mastic, Suffolk County, N.Y., 11/4. He recommends Egbert T. Smith to be a despatch bearer for the State Department. Smith is a grandson of the late John Smith, who was a Senator from N.Y. ALS in DNA, RG 59 (State Department), Applications and Recommendations, 1837–1845, Smith (M-687:30, frame 691).

R[ichard] K. Crallé to Joseph Graham, 11/4. Crallé notifies Graham of his appointment to be U.S. Consul at Buenos Aires and transmits to him documents relevant to the office. FC in DNA, RG 59 (State Department), Consular Instructions, 11:299–300.

From JOEL W. WHITE

Liverpool, England, November 4th 1844
Dear Sir, On reading in the public journals, the an[n]ouncement of my appointment as Consul for Liverpool, I noticed the comments of some of the Washington letter-writers, who stated that you expressed much chagrin at my appointment. I could not but doubt this, unless it were for other considerations than that I was the successful candidate.

Now Sir, you could not have had a person appointed, who was a more fast friend or a stronger admirer of your honest and independent political course, than myself.

The only political act of my life, that came well-nigh destroying my prospects, was my adherence, to your cause at the breaking up of President [Andrew] Jackson's Cabinet, and my opposition to the measures of Mr. [Martin] Van Buren on that occasion.

But Sir I have persued the even tenor of my ways to support the cause of "equal rights" with an honest conviction, that at some future day, justice would be rendered you by the American people. By them one point has been most signally settled at the Baltimore Convention[.] That influence, which was used to head your prospects, by chaining public sentiment to the car of *self constituted dictators* under the influence of *packed* delegates with mocked instructions, will not soon be re-enacted. ["In" *canceled*] The discharge of the duties of consul ["it" *canceled*] is wholly divested of party consideration, being strictly national in its function. I am gratified on examining for four days in the office, there is nothing that appears intricate to render dif-[f]icult the discharge of its duties. So far as I possess the ability, every effort in my power will be brought into requisition to ["discharge" *canceled and* "perform" *interlined*] the duties of my new appointment for the honor of the U. States, the best interest of the public & creditably to myself.

Any act on your part to promote the confirmation of my appointment, by the senate will be most fully appreciated and the favor reciprocated whenever an opportunity presents[.] I have the honor to be with great respect Your Ob[edien]t Serv[an]t, Joel W. White.

ALS in ScCleA. NOTE: An AEU by Calhoun reads: "Mr. White[,] Consul at Liverpool." The important Liverpool Consulate was vacant from death of the incumbent. White's appointment was rejected by the Senate in 2/1845.

[Richard K. Crallé] to [Alexander de Bodisco], 11/5. "The Acting Secretary of State offers his respects to Mr. A. de Bodisco, Envoy Extraordinary and Minister Plenipotentiary of His Majesty the Emperor of all the Russias; and, in answer to his verbal inquiry of yesterday, has the honor to state that the President [John Tyler] will receive him in his official character, on Thursday next, at one o'clock, P.M., if agreeable to Mr. Bodisco." FC in DNA, RG 59 (State Department), Notes to Foreign Legations, Russia, 6:20 (M-99:82).

From Rob[er]t Monroe Harrison, U.S. Consul, Kingston, Jamaica, 11/5. He asks that his son, Robert Adams Harrison, be appointed U.S. Consul at St. Jago, Cuba, in place of the deceased Consul. Robert is a "strictly moral" youth and was brought up in his father's office; therefore, he is well acquainted with the duties of a Consul. He speaks French and understands Latin and Italian. Harrison hopes that Calhoun will recommend Robert to the consideration of the President [John Tyler]. LS in DNA, RG 59 (State Department), Applications and Recommendations, 1837–1845, Harrison (M-687:14, frames 756–759), received 12/2.

From H[enry] Bailey

Charleston, 6th Nov. 1844

My dear Sir, Some of our friends here are very anxious to have a personal interview with you prior to your return to Washington, and have directed me very earnestly to request that you would remain a day with us on your transit through our City, which we understand may be anticipated about the 8th & 9th inst.

I refer more particularly to [Franklin H.] Elmore & General [James] Hamilton [Jr.], both of whom have left town for a few days, but will be back on tomorrow, or the next day; and the object of the interview desired is to exchange views with you as to the course to be pursued by your friends under existing circumstances. The importance of beginning right, and of a general understanding of the line of action to be maintained, are so obvious, and the mischiefs likely to result from a mistake in the commencement, & a want of concert in our movements, are so numerous, that I hope you will feel the propriety of the request that we make, & that you will be induced to remain a sufficient length of time with us to afford an opportunity for a full conference.

I shall do myself the honor to wait upon you as soon as I learn of your arrival, & hope in the mean time that this communication may have the effect of detaining you if you had contemplated passing through without stopping.

The inclosed [*not found*] was handed to me this morning with the request that I would transmit it to you. I remain Dear Sir With the highest regard & esteem Very truly Your Ob[e]d[ien]t Serv[an]t, H. Bailey.

ALS in ScCleA. NOTE: This letter was addressed to Calhoun at the "Charleston Hotel."

R[ichard] K. Crallé to W[illiam] H. Freeman, Curaçao, 11/6. The government of the Netherlands has declined to approve a U.S. Consul at Curaçao. Therefore, Freeman's commission is revoked. FC in DNA, RG 59 (State Department), Consular Instructions, 12:101–102.

DELAZON SMITH to R[ichard] K. Crallé

Dayton (Ohio), Nov[embe]r 6th, 1844
Sir! I had the honor to receive your note of the 2d inst. informing me of my appointment by the President of the United States, as Special Agent to the Republic of Equador. I accept the appointment with cheerfulness and gratitude.

Owing to the illness of my little son it is impossible for me to fix, positively, the day on which I shall be able to enter upon the duties of the office conferred upon me; probably, however within ten days or two weeks at farthest. With profound respect, I am, Sir, Your obliged and willing Servant &c, Delazon Smith.

ALS in DNA, RG 59 (State Department), Diplomatic Despatches, Special Agents, vol. 13 (M-37:13, frames 82–83). NOTE: Smith (1816–1860) was a native of N.Y. and an Ohio Democratic newspaper editor. He became in 1859 one of the first U.S. Senators from Oregon.

T[homas] L. Smith, Register's Office, Treasury Department, to R[ichard] K. Crallé, 11/6. "You will receive enclosed, a statement of the balances of appropriations on the 30 June last, for the Contingent expenses of the Department of State, and of the balances in the hands of Edward Stubbs, agent for that Department, & of Edward Everett, Minister to Great Britain; prepared in compliance with your request of the 5 Inst." (A Clerk's EU reads "Statement to Congress[,] 5 Dec. 1844.") LS in DNA, RG 59 (State Department), Letters Received from the Fifth Auditor and Comptroller, 1829–1862.

R[ichard] K. Crallé to James J. Wright, "now at Belmont, Ohio," 11/6. Wright is informed of his appointment to be U.S. Consul at Santiago, Cuba, and is sent relevant documents. FC in DNA, RG 59 (State Department), Consular Instructions, 10:276.

From John H. Litchfield, Puerto Cabello, Venezuela, 11/7. He asks that he be considered to replace his uncle, the late Franklin Litchfield, as U.S. Consul there. Having lived at Puerto Cabello for 11 years, he is well acquainted with the people and customs and has extensive knowledge of U.S. commercial interests. ALS in DNA, RG 59 (State Department), Applications and Recommendations, 1837–1845, Litchfield (M-687:19, frames 496–499).

From Simeon Toby, President, Insurance Company of the State of Pennsylvania, Philadelphia, 11/7. Toby has given to Vespasian Ellis, recently-appointed U.S. Chargé d'Affaires to Venezuela, copies of documents relating to a claim against the Venezuelan government in the case of the *Josephine*. Toby requests Calhoun to instruct Ellis "to press this business to a settlement." He also inquires whether the State Department has received any information from William M. Blackford and Seth Sweetser, U.S. Chargé d'Affaires in New Granada, and Consul at Guayaquil, Ecuador, respectively, concerning those nations' obligations for the claim. LS in DNA, RG 59 (State Department), Miscellaneous Letters (M-179:106, frames 20–22).

From JAMES J. WRIGHT

Belmont, Belmont County, Ohio, November 7th 1844
Dear Sir, Under the auspices, and at the recommendation of my brother Benjamin G. Wright, who informs me that he is about to advise you of my pretensions to the Consulate of Santiago de Cuba, I take the liberty of addressing you. Circumstances prevent me from visiting the Capital at present, and therefore to manifest, that I at least possess a knowledge of the proper views, and the information necessary for my pretensions, I herein state them, in as concise a form as possible, in order not to intrude too much upon your valuable time. I undoubtingly believe that, the best, and truest policy of the United States at present, is to have maintained intact the statu quo, of the island of Cuba, and by a proper course to extend and confirm her actual well grounded influence there. Firstly, In order to preserve her commercial intercourse, as it is, Cuba as regards her commerce with this country, being both as to tonnage, and value of Imports and Exports the third in the list of nations. Secondly, In as much as no abrupt transition can be effected, without a sanguinary struggle between the whites, during which it is more than probable that, a servile war, promoted and aided by Great Britain, would emancipate the coloured population, And thirdly because in the latter event, British influence would become eminently paramount, and perhaps she might establish a protectorate, as it is undeniable that her efforts are directed to that end, for I know from other than public sources that the head of the late conspiracy at Habana was the British Consul General [David] Turnbull. I believe also that, a few of the past years, the actual present, and some years to come, form the great critical period for the statu quo of the island, involving the integrity of her institutions, political and domestic, to this belief I am led, firstly, From the

revolutionary spirit of the mother country, and the weakness, the instability, and the exhausted resources of her government. Secondly, From a political bias amongst the white natives of the island in favour of Independence, which was at its zenith some years ago, and is now gradually diminishing. And Thirdly, The probability of a war between England and France upon the demise of Louis Philippe, into which Spain will no doubt be dragged, when if she side with the latter, which she will do, if the present conservative rule then sway, on the Peninsula, England will leave no stone unturned in her attempts to revolutionize and St. Domingomize Cuba. In consequence of the foregoing, and other weighty reasons, I hold that, there is no quarter of the world, where it is more essential, or beho[o]ves this country more to fill her Consulates & Vice Consulates, with men of influence, capability, and sound political views than Cuba, Which are, Firstly, A good standing with the public authorities, and popularity with the people. Secondly. A positive practical knowledge of men and things, and lastly a steady and determined opposition to British encroachments and influence of every class, and under all phases. Now it becomes not me to say, in how far I possess the qualifications here specified, as in my opinion necessary for at [*sic*] American Consul at the port in Cuba, to which my pretensions are directed, and I must leave the establishment thereof in the hands of my friends who I presume will forward the necessary vouchers and recommendations to the Department at Washington. I remain with much consideration y[ou]r Ob[edien]t S[ervan]t, James J. Wright.

ALS in DNA, RG 59 (State Department), Applications and Recommendations, 1837–1845, Wright (M-687:35, frames 166–168). NOTE: A Clerk's EU reads "Not to be sent to the Senate."

R[ichard] K. Crallé to Daniel P. King, [Representative from Mass.], Danvers, Mass., 11/8. Crallé acknowledges receipt of King's letter of 10/30. In reply he states that no formal application has ever been made to the British government concerning the *Director* and *Pallas*, fishing schooners "alleged to have been seized some years ago by a vessel under the British flag." FC in DNA, RG 59 (State Department), Domestic Letters, 35:13–14 (M-40:33).

From J[OHN] P. SCHÄTZELL

Mexico, Matamoros, Nov: 8, 1844

Sir, With feelings common to the occasion, I have to advise the death of Rich[ar]d Heath Belt Esq[ui]re, Consul of the United States at this port, who died on the 11th Oct: of an Epidemic fever, which is still raging, and carrying off victims daily. I have with the approbation of several of the Am[erica]n Citizens taken charge of the Archives of the Consulate to await the orders of the Government or our Minister Mr. [Wilson] Shannon at Mexico [City], who has been addressed upon the occasion, of which I hand Copy herewith. Mr. Belt's private or personal Concerns are in the hands of Mr. Henry Breese, who will address his relations by this vessel, the first that has offered for the U. States, since the Demise of Mr. Belt. Mr. Belt was enter'd by his Countrymen privately, agre[e]able to a written request subjecting the further disposal of his remains to the wishes of his friends who reside at Baltimore.

Not doubting but Mr. Shannon, will order such steps as will serve intermediate the public interest; I await your disposition in due time of the Books, Papers &c, appertaining to this Consulate. I am most respect[full]y Sir, your ob[edien]t H[onora]ble S[ervan]t, J.P. Schätzell.

LS with En in DNA, RG 59 (State Department), Applications and Recommendations, 1837–1845, Schätzell (M-687:29, frames 417–419); duplicate LS with En in DNA, RG 59 (State Department), Consular Despatches, Matamoros, vol. 4 (M-281:2), received 12/16.

R[ichard] K. Crallé to Simeon Toby, President of the Insurance Company of the State of Pennsylvania, Philadelphia, 11/8. "I have to acknowledge the receipt of your letter of yesterday and to state in reply that all necessary instructions shall be given to Mr. [Vespasian] Ellis in regard to the balance due from the Venezuelan government in the case of the Josephine. No communication upon the subject has been received from Mr. [William M.] Blackford or Mr. [Seth] Sweetser since the date of the last letter to you from this Department." FC in DNA, RG 59 (State Department), Domestic Letters, 35:14 (M-40:33).

From Francis S. Claxton, Washington, 11/9. Claxton has heard from the Attorney General [John Nelson] that "several removals [are] about to be made amongst the clerks of the different Depts.," and he wishes to be considered for any vacancies that may be created in the

State Department. ALS in DNA, RG 59 (State Department), Applications and Recommendations, 1837–1845, Claxton (M-687:5, frames
441–442).

From JAMES L. ORR

Anderson [S.C.,] 9th Nov. 1844
Dear Sir, I regret exceedingly my disappointment in not having the
pleasure of a personal interview with you, prior to your departure for
Washington. I was very solicitous to ["you" *altered to* "hear"] your
views on public policy generally and especially your opinion as to the
position which the Legislature of S.C. should assume at its approaching session in the event of Mr. [Henry] Clay[']s election to the Presidency and if [James K.] Polk should be elected whether any movement should be made. Will you have the Kindness to write me and
give your views of the propriety of the States moving at all without
the Cooperation of other Southern States. I have the honor to be with
great respect your humble S[er]v[an]t, James L. Orr.
[P.S.] Please state in a N.B. whether your answer is intended for
my eye alone—or for such friends as I can confidentially confide it to
or for the press.

ALS in ScCleA. NOTE: James Lawrence Orr (1822–1873), a native of Anderson District, had left the University of Virginia in 1842. He was a lawyer and
was about to begin the first of several terms in the S.C. House of Representatives.
During the two decades after Calhoun's death, Orr was a major political leader
in S.C. and held a number of high public offices.

From JOSÉ M[ARI]A CASTANOS

Consulate of the U. States
Tepic [Mexico,] November 11th 1844
Sir, The Consulate [of San Blas] under my charge, supplied the American prisoners, who came from California in the year 1841—Mr. Pow-
hatan Ellis being minister plenipotentiary, the sum of one thousand
one hundred and fifty dollars, and though the government of Mexico
has given several orders to the custom house of S. Blas for the payement of this sum thus far, I have not been able to obtain the reimbursement of the money so advanced. I beg leave therefore to sub-

mit the subject to your consideration in order that you may take such measures as you may think proper so that I may not suffer further prejudices in addition to that which I have already sustained, by the delay of payement of this money—for so many years. Permit me to refer to the copies herewith of a portion of the correspondence on the subject which I had with Mr. [Waddy] Thompson [U.S. Minister to Mexico] previous to his depparture from Mexico. I am Sir Your most humble servant, José M[ari]a Castanos, Consul.

ALS with Ens and duplicate LS in DNA, RG 59 (State Department), Consular Despatches, San Blas (M-301:1), received 12/31.

From A[ndrew] J. Donelson,
[U.S. Chargé d'Affaires to Texas]

Galvezton, Texas, Nov[embe]r 11[t]h 1844

Sir, I have the honor to inform you that I reached this place yesterday on board the Steamer New York, having waited some days at New Orleans for her arrival and departure.

Meeting here General Terrill [*sic*; George W. Terrell], the newly appointed minister from this Republic to France, who informed me that both the President [Samuel Houston], and Secretary of State [Anson Jones], of Texas, were at this time absent from the seat of Government, I determined to remain a short time here with the Consul [Stewart Newell] who has charge of the papers and other articles belonging to this legation, for the purpose of examining their character and condition. A schedule of them, for which I have receipted to the Consul, is herewith enclosed. Of their contents I will give you a more particular report hereafter, barely remarking now that they appear to have been carefully preserved by the Consul in the order in which they were received by him. Among the bundles of promiscuous papers there is one of letters addressed to Mr. [Tilghman A.] Howard, which as they appear to be private I have thought it best to return to the Department to be forwarded ["to" *interlined*] his family. Their seals have not been broken.

It gives me pleasure to say to you that the tone of feeling manifested by the most prominent of the citizens of Texas, I have yet met with, is that of cordial friendship and good will to the United States. And I have no reason to apprehend that a different feeling animates the Government, although some of its late appointments and particularly that of Gen[era]l Terrill would seem to warrant some distrust. This Gentleman has frankly avowed to me his opposition to the policy of annexation, but he at the same time admitted that his views were not in accordance with those of any other member of the Cabinet.

I learn that the Chargés des affaires from France and England [Alphonse de Saligny and Charles Elliot] are soon to be here, and that every movement of our Government in this quarter is watched with much anxiety. At this place, which is the depot of three fourths of the trade of the Republic—a trade rapidly passing into European channels for the want of a commercial Treaty with the United States— it is natural that the advocates of the seperate independence of the Republic should have found most encouragement. Accordingly, among the merchants, it is not uncommon to observe this view of the subject maintained with all the plausibility which a reliance upon the advantage of a comparatively unrestricted trade is calculated to give. Against this position and the less apparent influence which the British Government may be expected to exert on the hopes of many of those who have embarked their fortunes here, I shall hope to oppose successfully the reasons which recommend annexation as a measure of safety and prosperity equally necessary to both Republics.

Guided by the spirit of the instructions you have been pleased to give me, and which devellope so clearly and fully the principles which lie at the bottom of this question of annexation I trust that my exertions will not disappoint you.

Tomorrow I shall proceed directly on to Washington[-on-the-Brazos], and will advise you promptly of what may be expected. I have the honor to be with great respect your obedient Servant, A.J. Donelson.

ALS with En in DNA, RG 59 (State Department), Diplomatic Despatches, Texas, vol. 2 (T-728:2, frames 394–398), received 11/27.

To Henry L. Ellsworth, Commissioner of the Patent Office, 11/11. "You are requested to transmit to this Department, to be embodied in a report to be made to Congress at the commencement of the ensuing year, a statement containing, with respect to the Patent Office, the infor[mation] required by the 11th Section of the act legalising and making appropriations for such necessary objects as have usually been included in the general appropriation bills without authority of law, and to fix and provide for incidental expenses of the Departments and offices of the Government, and for other purposes; approved 26th August, 1842." FC in DNA, RG 59 (State Department), Accounting

Records: Miscellaneous Letters Sent, 1832–1916, vol. for 10/3/1844–5/29/1845, p. 64.

From R[OBERT] M. HAMILTON

Consulate of the *United States*
MonteVideo, Nov[embe]r 11th 1844

Sir, I have the honor to acknowledge the receipt of your Letter under date 17th July last, stating that my Letters from No. 80 to No. 88 inclusive had been received, and likewise my notes on the "Political, moral, and Commercial condition of Paraguay" which you have been pleased to say, was read by you with much satisfaction, and submitted to the President, who has taken a like interest in them, permit me to say, Sir, that I feel most highly flattered, by this mark of approbation, of my feeble attemp[t]s, to augment the commercial interests of our Country; I avail myself of this occasion to transmit herewith, Copies No. 1 to No. 10 of Official Correspondence, which has transpired, between Brig[adie]r General Don Manuel Oribe, Commander in chief of the Beseiging Army near this city, Commander [Garrett J.] Pendergrast of the U.S. Ship "Boston," Captain [Philip F.] Voorhees U.S. Ship Congress, and this Consulate, in relation to certain property belonging to Citizens of the United States, which have been detained at the Port of Maldonado, in consequence of said Port having been closed against all Commerce, since December 1843, by order of General Oribe, and I am happy to say, that the united efforts of Captain Pendergrast, and myself, have produced the desired effect, that of releasing the said property, consisting of Hides, Horse hair & sundries, to the amount of Fifty thousand Dollars, from further detention, being now on its way to New York, referring you to said Correspondence, I have the honor to be Sir, With profound respect, Your most Obedient Servant, R.M. Hamilton, United States Consul.

ALS (No. 93) with Ens in DNA, RG 59 (State Department), Consular Despatches, Montevideo, vol. 4 (M-71:4), received 1/22/1845.

From W[illia]m H. Marriott

Baltimore, November 11, 1844

I congratulate you my dear friend, on your safe return to Washington, and the Glorious result of the Presidential Election. I think there can be no doubt of Mr. [James K.] Polk's election, and the entire prostration of the whig party, if our friends, shall act with wisdom and prudence.

During your absence I made the President [John Tyler] a visit, and had some conversation with him in relation to the subject of the office of Collector of this Port. He treated me with much kindness, and I inferred from his remarks that he would be likely to remove the now Incumbent [Nathaniel F. Williams], as soon as the Elections for President had terminated. I presented to him a letter voluntarily tendered to me by my old friend and acquaintance the Honorable Louis McLane. Now, that the Elections are over, and the result certain, I am very desirous that the attention of the President shall at *once* be called to the matter, and I respectfully ask, that you will do so for me, as early as practicable.

You will I hope, pardon me for this request, and further for saying that having been steadfastly your friend for thirty years, I feel that you will excuse me for any trouble that ["I may" *canceled*] I have or may give you in relation to my desire, to receive the office of Collector. I have never received from any administration, any favor. I have always been an undeviating Democrat of the *old School*, an old States Right Democrat. Old Federalists were elevated to office by Gen[era]l [Andrew] Jackson & [Martin] Vanburen; to the exclusion of old Democrats. *The new Democracy* received everything. I never applied to Jackson for office, nor to Vanburen except so far as the application or rather the mention of my name ["by you" *interlined*] to Vanburen for the office of Commissioner, if the bill *then* before Congress to establish a Board of claims, became a Law. The old Vanburen Clique *here*, your opponents as well as mine, & who continued to abuse Mr. Tyler from the time of his election, until he withdrew from the *Canvass* desire the appointment of Mr. [William] Frick, who was appointed by Vanburen, and all that they can do through *certain* Individuals will be done, and probably has been done, to effect their object, by preventing Mr. Tyler from making a change, during the residue of his term. *They* rely on Mr. Polk to restore Frick, and there is nothing they would not do to defeat your friends, and the friends of the President from obtaining any countenance, or notice from Mr. Tyler.

Now my dear Sir, permit ["t" *canceled*] me to say, that *this is the time* for you to serve me & I earnestly but most respectfully ask your immediate action in my behalf. If you will speak to the President and urge my appointment, I shall be successful. If not, I fear when Mr. Polk comes into office the Vanburenites will defeat me.

John V.L. McMahon mentioned to me this morning, that he would give me a letter to the President, and if necessary I can obtain it. Mr. [John] Nelson [Attorney General] expressed himself willing to serve me, and I must believe, that he will act with you. So soon as I hear from you, I will visit Washington if you deem it important for me to do so. I regret, that I am obliged to trespass on your kindness, & pray your forgiveness. Very Truly your friend, Wm. H. Marriott.

P.S. As my signature is not easily decyphered, I ask leave to write it in a different form. William H. Marriott.

ALS in ScCleA. NOTE: Marriott was nominated to be Collector at Baltimore by Tyler and confirmed by the Senate in 12/1844.

From Silas M. Stilwell, U.S. Marshal, [New York City], 11/11. "I enclose herewith copy of a letter received at this office on the 9th inst. The two witnesses therein mentioned [John Fairburne and James Gilliespie] have been temporarily committed, but having no legal process under which I can hold them, I have to request your directions on the subject." (Stilwell enclosed a copy of a letter, dated 9/18, to himself from Geo[rge] W. Gordon, U.S. Consul at Rio de Janeiro, requesting Stilwell to secure the two American seamen as witnesses to illegal slave trading and to request further instructions from the State Department.) LS with En in DNA, RG 59 (State Department), Miscellaneous Letters (M-179:106, frames 27–28).

From "A. A. A."

Boston, Nov. 12, 1844

Dear Sir, Having a firm reliance upon your generosity and charity I have the high presumption to offer to your notice a few suggestions for your consideration. You are well aware of the crisis to which our presidential election has approached and of the conflicting interests and feelings attendant upon it. The two parties are nearly balanced and the wreath of victory rests in the hands of your native State. Under the present aspect of affairs [James K.] Polk will undoubtedly be elected—but if South Carolina refuses to give her electoral vote for Polk and confers it upon her own worthy son (*of course without your interposition*) the *presidential chair* will be filled by a man ["of" *interlined and* "worthy" *altered to* "worth"] and ability instead of ["being filled by" *interlined*] one without merit or claim, to say nothing of the inevitable disgrace to the Country. Such a movement would meet the approbation of the majority of the Democrats and the unbounded applause of the entire Whig party. The Whigs have determined to alter the naturalization law and a word from you in favor of such a measure would influence them in their utter despair of [Henry] Clay's election, to cast their electoral votes for you. And allow me now to say, sir, that these suggestions are made with utmost kindness and friendship toward yourself and in the confident belief that such a movement would meet with success and almost universal favor. [Andrew] Jackson would denounce it—but he is your enemy and such a ["step" *canceled and* "event" *interlined*] would be a signal of triumph to his enemies throughout the Country and a pleasing consolation to Mr. Clay.

Allow me, to subscribe myself, with the highest respect and reverence for your Honor's high character, a Democrat & sincere friend, A. A. A.

ALI in ScCleA.

To T[homas] G. Clemson, [Brussels]

Washington, 12th Nov[embe]r 1844

My dear Sir, I arrived here on my return from home day before ["yesterday," *interlined*] accompanied by Mrs. [Floride Colhoun] Calhoun, [Martha] Cornelia [Calhoun], James [Edward Calhoun] & Eugenia Calhoun. We had a very pleasant journey, with fine weather all the way. I have taken lodgings for the winter at a new Hotel, between Gadsby's and the Deposite. James has come on to go to the Virginia University, and will leave in a few days. We left Willey [William Lowndes Calhoun] at Fort Hill, with Mrs. Ryan [*sic*; Margaret Hunter Rion] & her son James. Patrick [Calhoun] & John [C. Calhoun, Jr.] have not yet returned. I had a letter from John yesterday. They were high up on the Miss[iss]ippi, at Fort Leavenworth, but expected to leave for St. Louis in a few days. They will be with us shortly, unless they should return by Fort Hill. So much for the family news.

While at Fort Hill, I attended to all your business in that quarter. I paid and took up your note to the estate of [James C.?] Griffin, amounting, principal & interest, to $550. Paid James Lawrence $550 for Bill & took a Bill of Sale, accompanied by the consent of his mother & the agent of his brother, who is absent in Alabama. The papers were drawn by Mr. Harburton. Paid Dr. [Frederick W.] Symmes $48 & Dr. Taylor $21.87½ & Mr. [Alfred?] Fuller $10.25, & took receipts on their bills. Mr. [John S.] Lorton has a small bill ["on" *canceled and* "ag(ai)nst" *interlined*] you, he told me; I think of $7. I intended to pay it, as I came through on my way here, but he was not in the Village, but I directed Mr. Kirksey who acts as my agent in my absence, to pay it & take a receipt. The sum due to the estate of Griffin & for Bill were paid by drafts on Mathew[e]s & Bonneau. ["It" *canceled and* "They" *interlined*] some what exceeded the ["$2" *canceled*] balance left of the $2,500 which you left with me, when you were here, & which I placed in their hands, after meeting your bank debt, which will stand, as a debit on the proceeds of your cotton crop. The residue I paid out of the proceeds of the sale of your Iron & what was due by Miller. Mr. Fuller took the whole of your iron, but would not allow more than 4½ cents per pound. It amounted to $67.90. Miller gave me a due bill for ["what" *interlined*] he owed ($17), which Dr. Symmes took in part payment of what was due to him. The two amounted to $84.90 & which I paid, including Mr. Lorton[']s ["(say" *canceled and* "about" *interlined*] $87. It may be a few cents more or less.

I intended to visit your place from Edgefield on my return, and made my arrangement accordingly; but Col. [Francis W.] Pickens told me it was unnecessary; that he had made arrangements for the next year, & laid in all supplies; and that every thing was going on well. He will write you fully. He seems to take much interest in your affairs, and informs me, that Mr. Mosly [*sic*; John Mobley] your neighbour, was over every day. I would have gone any how, but I found, that he was so intent on having me to meet all of the gentlemen of the Village [of Edgefield] at the dinner he had made his arrangement to give me, the next day, that I had to yield to his wishes.

I consulted him on the point, whether it would be expedient to add to your force under ["existing" *interlined*] circumstances, and we both concluded, considering the price of negroes & cotton, & the prospect as to the future price of that article, that it would not be.

Negro women were selling at from $300 to 400, & men in proportion, notwithstanding the low price of cotton.

I received yours & Anna's [Anna Maria Calhoun Clemson's] letters from Paris before I left home, by the former Steamer. The letters by the last, among which there was one from you, ["after" *canceled*] written after your arrival at Brussels were forwarded to Pendleton, I learn since my arrival here, but had not reached there when I left, nor have they yet returned here, so that I have not yet got ["your's" *canceled and* "it" *interlined*]. Tell Anna I had much pleasure in perusing her letter, & that I will answer it by the next Steamer after this. I would by this, but this is the last day & I have not time in consequence of the crowd of business on hand from my absence.

The papers will give you the account of the decided defeat of [Henry] Clay, and election of [James K.] Polk. The election has been one of unequal interest, & excitement. All the questions of policy between the two parties were put fairly in issue, & the Whigs fairly beaten on their own ground. It is the end of the whig party. They have already dissolved at the North & taken the name of the native American party. It remains now to reap the fruits of the victory—a much more difficult part, than to win it.

Mrs. Calhoun has for several days been indisposed, but not seriously. The rest of the family, with us, are all well & all join in love to you, & Anna. I hope you are all well, & that [John] Calhoun [Clemson] & Floride [Elizabeth Clemson] are growing finely. Kiss them both for their Grandfather. Yours affectionately, J.C. Calhoun.

ALS in ScCleA; PEx's in Jameson, ed., *Correspondence*, pp. 626–627. NOTE: Eugenia Calhoun, a niece of John C. Calhoun, was a daughter of his brother William Calhoun and his wife Catherine Jenner de Graffenreid Calhoun.

From MARK A. COOPER, [former Representative from Ga.]

Athens Georgia, Nov[embe]r 12th 1844
Dear Sir, Our mutual Friend Dr. W[illia]m C. Daniel[l] is desirous of getting his son Tatnall F. [Daniell] in the Marine Corps. Lieut[enant Ferdinand] Piper was lost a few days ago in Pensacola Bay. This creates a vacancy. Will you do me the favour to aid him.

I presume we have carried the Election for Mr. [James K.] Polk. Our State did well. The Cherokee Country saved it. It seems I could do for Mr. Polk what we could not do for ourselves last year. You must not take last year as an evidence of what we can do for you. You are still the strongest man in Georgia. Last year Cherokee was not organized. Then being the candidate I had not a chance or time to organize. This year it has been done & see the result.

We are much interested to have you remain for the coming four years in the State departm[en]t. Will you not consent?

Who are likely to be called by Mr. Polk? Will he take Party Hacks—or Vigorous Working men? Will Georgia be looked to, to contribute?

I am on my way to my residence, at Mount Hope[,] Murray Co[unty]. My P.O. is Coosawattee.

It may be worth while to say our Friend Dr. Daniel[1] was amongst the first to express his reliance on President [John] Tyler. I remain with highest respect your obedient Serv[an]t, Mark A. Cooper.

ALS in ScCleA.

From DUFF GREEN, "Private"

Mexico [City,] 12th Nov[embe]r 1844
My dear Sir, I have been detained here much longer than I anticipated and refer you to Governor [Wilson] Shannon's dispatches for the causes. Benjamin's [Ben E. Green's] letters to you will have prepared you in some measure for events, here. They are now hastening to a crisis. There is great dissatisfaction with Santa Anna, persons speak against him openly and without restraint, but the press is afraid to speak and hence, as the country is large and rumor always magnifies or misrepresents events it is difficult for any one to ascertain the truth, and such is the want of confidence and tendency to change that if we could ascertain the truth today, no one could tell what may come up tomorrow.

This much I believe to be true, that a large majority of Congress are opposed to Santa Anna, that the opposition is organised, that it extends through all the northern provinces, that five or more of the principal northern commanders are pledged to take part—that Parades [*sic*; Mariano Paredes] & the Governor of Jalisco have already pronounced against Santa Anna, demanding that he shall be deposed, that another President shall be installed, and that Santa Anna and his ministers shall be held to account for the monies they have recieved [*sic*]—that in the south the Indians have cut off the right hands of the tax collectors, and many ["persons"(?) *canceled*] persons refuse to pay the tax for the war ag[ains]t Texas.

Canaliso [*sic*; Valentín Canalizo] has issued a proclamation saying that the tax was levied to enable the Govt. to reconquer Texas and calling on the people to pay it. The Government have requested Santa Anna to march against Parades and suppress the revolt in Jalisco, and he is now on the way with his Jalappa [*sic*] troops amounting to 7,500 infantry & 1500 horse with 20 cannon. In the mean time there is not a dollar in the treasury, and the resources of the country being dried up there is no means of obtaining but by forced loans and seizing the church revenues. There are two ways of doing this[,] one is the confiscation & sale of the property, the other is by forced loans. Santa Anna it is said argues that if the property is confiscated and sold, it will command but little, that the better way is to permit the church to hold the property & tax it—this he calls "milking" the church.

As far as I can learn there is no confidence in those who are opposed to Santa Anna. I have asked many who is to lead the opposition? No one can answer. I have asked what is the purpose of the opposition? No one can say, further than that it is opposition to Santa Anna. When I ask will you better your condition? The answer is—"I don[']t know." When I ask will those whom you are to put in office be more capable, or more honest, the answer is—more capable? No. More honest? No. When I ask what are you to gain by the overthrow of Santa Anna? The answer is—I don[']t know.

Therefore when you remember that Santa Anna is a man of decided talent—that he knows his own people well—that he has command of the Government and is at the head of the army, that altho Congress refuse to give him money & the resources of the treasury are dried up—you must remember that he has a body of dependant partisans, that his opponents altho organised as to the wish to oust him from office & to put themselves in his place, they are not organised on any plan which will give them greater resources of men or money than he has or ["as" *canceled*] to the country a better Government than he gives them, and taking into account the character of the people it ["is" *interlined*] obvious that the movement may enable him to overthrow the Congress and establish himself as Dictator, but I see no prospect of his overthrow.

I take it for granted that you will therefore have to deal with Santa Anna, and you may assume that such is the state of public opinion that any party coming into power on his down fall will be compelled to take as strong or stronger ground against the United States than he has done. What he has done and is prepared to do if he had the power you will see in ["the" *interlined*] public dispatches of our minister.

Indeed I am convinced that Santa Anna's object is to isolate Mexico from the rest of the world. His policy is to flatter the vanity and national pride of Mexico, and to make his people believe that he is indispensable to their protection against the encroachments of foreign powers & especial[l]y against the United States. That he does not wish for war with the United States, may be; but he wishes that our relations shall always be such as to furnish him with a pretence for keeping up an army, which he finds indispensable to keep himself in power.

You therefore cannot adjust the question of Texas by the consent of Mexico. He would not have that question adjusted if he could. If ["were" *canceled*] Texas were annexed, it might not lead to war. I doubt much if it would, because Santa Anna knows that he cannot sustain himself in a war with us, and therefore he would much prefer angry negociations which would serve his purpose, as a pretext for keeping up his army and levying contributions—["while it" *canceled*] & for driving all Americans out of Mexico. He fears contact with intelligence, [*one word canceled*] as the bigoted Catholic fears the bible and from the same instinct.

You cannot have peace with Mexico without a war. They have so long bullied and insulted and plundered us with impunity that they have lost all respect for us as a nation, altho they fear us as a people.

Their policy towards France & England has been of much the same character, and altho England has done much to aid in driving Americans out of the country that the trade may be left in the hands of Englishmen, such has been the war on ["all" *interlined*] foreigners that the Englishmen themselves would be glad to see them whipped into a proper sense of what ["is" *interlined*] due to other nations.

But upon all these matters I refer you to my son [Ben E. Green], who has many facts in confirmation of what I now say, and to Gov[er-no]r Shannon's correspondence. It seems to me that the Government of the United States have no alternative—that they cannot be content with the annexation of Texas. They must demand the withdrawal of the insolent charges & imputations contained in Mr. [Manuel C.] Rejon's notes, & an immediate adjustment of all our claims against Mexico. This will not be done and a war must be the consequence.

Gov[erno]r Shannon was at first resolved to demand his pas[s]-ports, indeed he had written his letter demanding them, & he was only prevented from sending it, by a belief that the course which he adopted would relieve the Government from the charge of wishing to place the United States in a position which would necessarily lead to war.

By suspending his official relations until he can recieve instructions from you, he enables the President [John Tyler] to throw upon Congress its just responsibility, and I cannot permit myself to believe that Congress will hesitate to sustain what Gov. Shannon has done. Indeed the time has come when we have no alternative but to punish Mexico and other nations into a proper respect for national character.

I have been told by two of the best informed men in Mexico that party spirit ran so high and that we are so much divided among ourselves that we cannot go to war, and you will ["see" *interlined*] in Rejon's letters that he relies on the opposition to President Tyler to take ["part" *interlined*] with Mexico in any question growing out of the measures of President Tyler[']s administration. Such is the impression which the British Legation here have endeavored to make, and I have it from a source that I cannot doubt that the British Minister has advised and approves the course which Mexico has taken in this matter. The policy of England is to bring Mexico & the United [States] into collision, because they think that the effect will be to leave the trade of Mexico in English hands. The foreign trade of ["Engla" *canceled*] Mexico is now almost entirely cut off. It is of little value and that little is chiefly monolopised [*sic*] by British subjects. As it is, the trade is lost to us. The treaty is a dead letter and serves as a snare to entrap our citizens. We have no means of regaining the trade of Mexico but by chastising them into decent behavior and the advantage of a war with Mexico will be that we can indemnify ourselves while by chastising Mexico, we will show other nations what we can ["and will" *interlined*] do and command their respect also. If you could go abroad as I have done you would feel that we have lost caste & that nothing but a war can regain the position we have lost. A war with Mexico will cost us nothing, and reinstate us in the estima[tion] of other nations. I need not dilate on th[is] subject to you. You know that I am for peace and that I would ["be" *interlined*] one of the last to advise a war, because I know the influence which it will have on the question of duties, but we have gone so far that I see no means of avoiding a conflict with Mexico, and I do not hesitate to give you my opinion. I do not express this opinion to others. I leave you to act as your own better judgment may direct. Your friend, Duff Green.

ALS in ScCleA; PC in Jameson, ed., *Correspondence*, pp. 991–995.

From DUFF GREEN

Mexico, 12th Nov[embe]r 1844

My dear Sir, I beg to refer you to my son [Ben E. Green] for much that I cannot write. I have matters of private interest to arrange which may require his presence in Washington and as Gov[erno]r [Wilson] Shannon had suspended his official intercourse with this Govt. until he can hear from you I concurred with Gov[erno]r Shannon in the opinion that his presence in Washington might be of service to the Government, more so than if he were to remain here. I will detain but a few days in Texas. I hope to be able to get all that I wish done, ["through" *canceled*] in a few days and will then hasten on to Washington.

The next few months will be important. I can not doubt your cordial approbation of the course Gov. Shannon has deemed it his duty to pursue. It seemed to me that he had no alternative but to demand his pas[s]ports or to discontinue his official intercourse. Some parts of his letter are strongly put, but how could he do less? He himself was disposed to demand his pas[s]ports and he was restrained by a wish to leave ["to" *canceled*] the President [John Tyler; "as" *interlined*] free to act, as he could do. One reason why he wished to demand his pas[s]ports was a sincere desire to serve you. He is an old, sincere and reliable friend and feeling that much may depend on the State of Ohio he was very anxious to be at home for the purpose of taking part in the new organisation of parties which he foresees must take place there. [William] Allen & [Benjamin] Tappan [Senators from Ohio] belong to [Thomas H.] Benton & [Silas] Wright. [Thomas L.] Hamer [former Representative from Ohio] is the partisan of [John] McLean & Benton, McLean & [Lewis] Cass will be aspirants for the Presidency in 1848. Gov[erno]r Shannon has written to many of his friends and among them to his brotherinlaw who is a man of talents and property and urged them to establish a paper at Columbus to sustain our views & principles.

I find him to be a man of great labor & of excellent jud[g]ment. He has been the leader of the State rights party of Ohio and his position there will, enable him to do as much or more than any one else to control that State, and it is apparent that if we can command Ohio we will command the whole North West.

Will not Ohio be entitled to a member of the Cabinet? And should Mr. [Charles A.] Wickliffe go to Austria or Mr. [William] Wilkins go out of the Cabinet, can you do better than to give the situation to Ohio? Is there any man in Ohio who is so well qualified or who has a better claim than Gov[erno]r Shannon[?] He has been with us in evil as well as in good report, and has borne the winter of our adversity as well as the summer of our prosperity. He has been tested & proved faithful.

He advises that Cass should be sent to England. [Edward] Everett ought certainly to be recalled, and Cass will no doubt be much gratified to go to England, & the Governor thinks will be gratified with the Vice Presidency.

You must understand all these matters better than I, but I give you my views—take them for what they are worth. Yours truly, Duff Green.

ALS in ScCleA.

From W[illia]m Hogan

Boston, Nov. 12th 1844

Sir, We have had, this morning, returns from nearly all the Counties in this State. A Whig Governor [George N. Briggs] & Electors, have been chosen by a large majority, say five or six thousand, over the last election.

I partly congratulate you, Sir, on the election of Mr. Polke [*sic*; James K. Polk] for the Presidency; I say partly, because I believe that the bell which announces this event tolls the death-knell of southern slavery. You will perhaps say—should you deem it worth your notice to give the subject a thought—that I am a dreamer or prejudiced, but I think I am neither & that time will bear me out in the truth of my observation. Mr. Polke has been elected by Irish, French, & German Roman Catholics, every man of whom—especially the former—is an abolitionist. The success of Mr. Polke is owing to a union between Papists & abolitionists—a union conceived in Hell & brought to partial maturity by the Pope [Gregory XVI] & his Agents in this country but this union—corrupt & infamous as it is—is as yet only in its C[h]rysalis state. It will soon unfold itself, it is taking wing, it will fly over your State & mine [Georgia?] too, carrying death & destruction in its train over all we value there. True, it is, we have gained a victory in the election of Mr. Polke; but look at the cost. We have paid dearly for it. We have given for it, at least the property of our children, probably their lives & their blood. We have now let loose amongst us, the bloodhounds of Abolition & mark what I tell you, Sir, in sorrow that causes will cease to contain or produce effects, if the Abolition of slavery—that darling object of England & the Pope of Rome—shall not be the consequence in less than ten years from the date of this scrawl. I see but one way of preventing it. Let the Natives unite as a body against foreigners & let them nominate a Southern man for the next Presidency. Let us narrow down the question for the next Presidency to *native* & *foreign* influence; this can & will be done. Whig, Democrat, Bank, Tariff will soon become obsolete in our political vocabulary. Let the great question be—& it will be—shall natives or foreigners rule this country: in other words shall Abolitionists trample under foot the Constitution of this country, or shall we give it up to the Pope and James Burney [*sic*; James G. Birney] to be remodelled or amended as such ["mis" *canceled*] political & ["religious" *changed to* "irreligious"] miscreants may think proper. Or shall we send for Daniel O.Connell to draft a new one & give us "an American Code of laws"?

Listen, Sir, I beseech you to the voice of an humble individual. Pause before you oppose the *native party* though many of them are Whigs. Much is expected from *you*; the powers of your mind are great; let your judgement have time to give them a proper direction & all will be well. I have been busy among the natives of this City, New York, & Philadelphia; they will in due time write to you to ascertain your views on nativeism & should they be what we expect, it will confirm us in our course & under your flag, the cause will triumph. Should you think differently a few more & myself may withdraw from the party, though I believe, as far [as] my judgment goes, the party ["will" *interlined*] triumph. You, Americans, know nothing of European Roman Catholics. All the energies & all the powers of the Romish Church, have, for twenty years & upwards been employed in trying to acquire an ascendency in this country. During all that time, I have been proclaiming the fact but never until now, did even the people of New England, believe me. During all that time, I have been trying to obtain from our Government a Mission to Austria & other Catholic countries, with a view of laying before it *facts* which would satisfy my fellow Citizens, that I was right, but some one who understood intrigue better, defeated me. But, Sir you never will know the intrigues of Catholic Europe through any other Agent than myself. If the facts were before their eyes they could not recognize them. They are always shrouded in symbolics with which Americans have no more acquaintance than they have with the ravings of the *latter day saints*. Had I a fortune, I would spend my days in travelling through Catholic countries with a view of evolving the schemes that are on foot for the overthrow of this Government; but I do not want that so much as I do the protection of this government, without which I could not travel in safety, even in cog. I tell you now, Sir, on the honour of a man, that when I departed from Ireland to this country as a Catholic Priest ["in" *and an illegible year canceled*] my instructions *were never to cease* in trying to abolish Slavery & [*partial word canceled*] overthrow this *heretical* government, nor is there now in the United States a single Catholic priest or Bishop who is not engaged in the same work[.]

Under all these circumstances I trust you will take some time to consider what party you will support[.] I have the honor to Remain Yours Respectfully, Wm. Hogan.

ALS in ScCleA; PC in Boucher and Brooks, eds., *Correspondence*, pp. 256–258.

From HENRY A. HOLMS

New York [City], Nov[embe]r 12th 1844
Sir, You may remember that early in the month of June last I had the honour of a personal interview with you at Washington. I was then about to undertake a voyage to Sisal in Mexico, in the Brig Henry Leeds, chartered and loaded by Messrs. Hale & Todd, then of Baltimore; since removed to this city, and continuing business under the firm of Charles H. Todd & Co.

I beg leave to address you on this subject, and to state that the result of the voyage was disastrous, owing to the effect of a prohibition on the part of the Provincial government of Yucatan, by which Breadstuffs & some other articles of the Cargo were excluded. The prohibition had very recently been enacted; so recently that no knowledge of it existed in the United States; nor was it known to the Mexican chargé d'affaires [Juan N. Almonte] whom I saw at Washington & consulted on the subject. Indeed I was told by him that all the articles I intended to take out were admissible, but I found it very different on my arrival at Sisal & Merida, where they threatened to confiscate both vessel and cargo, altho' there was no attempt at concealment or infraction of Law. I placed my affairs in the hands of Mr. [Pedro] de Regil y Estrada, the U.S. Consul there, and after some negociation the Government allowed the entry of the admissible goods on *condition* of their *being sold at the Nett cost in the U.S.* in barter for Logwood; the prohibited goods to remain on board. This was a pretty hard bargain for us, at a time when the admissible goods were saleable at a handsome profit; we were therefore cut off from the market and subjected besides to heavy charges. The contract for the sale of the Goods was made with one Dario Galera of Merida[;] was drawn up and witnessed by the Consul, Regil. The conditions regarding the quality and delivery of the Logwood were not complied with on the part of Galera, and there resulted a further and considerable loss.

I noted a Protest against the prohibition before Mr. Regil, who was to have forwarded the same to Washington but ["Mr. McLaughlin" *interlined*] the Bookkeeper of Messrs. Todd & Co. who was lately there, during your absence, learned that no such protest had been received.

When I left Sisal & Merida, to load at Rio Lagartos on the Coast of Yucatan, I placed in the hands of Mr. Regil the charge of my rights under the contract with Galera. These were infringed by the attempt to deliver us a bad quality of wood; so bad that I felt it my duty to reject it. I called a Survey on it by the Alc[alde?] who readily pronounced it unmerchantable, as it manifestly was and I had to procure the greater part of my return Cargo elsewhere. This Galera subsequently agreed to pay for in substitution of his o[wn?]. But there ensued a claim for 35 days Demurrage, & $60 expenses which I wrote to Mr. Estrada to insist on; he writes however to Todd & Co. that on final settlement with Galera, he relinquished this and all other claims under the Contract without either warrant or authority to do so.

I am now immediately returning to Sisal, in the Sch[oone]r Alleguash, chartered and loaded by Messrs. C.H. Todd & Co. and intend to assert and endeavour to recover these claims. I also intend to state to the provincial government of Yucatan that I have submitted the whole affair to the consideration of the Department of State at Washington.

I cannot say how far it were proper in [me] to ask it, but I think it would facilitate the recovery of an indemnity from the Government there, if you would be so kind as to give me a letter to that effect. The conduct of the authorities there was harsh and arbitrary to say the least. I must add that Regil y Estrada greatly neglected our interest intrusted to him, and in this case was far from affording us the protection and respect to which the flag of the United States entitles our citizens. He seems to have allowed the w[hole?] issue of the affair to have taken place, with the view most probably, of deterring American citizens from prosecuting the trade.

I should also be thankful to receive a letter from you to our Consul at Campeche, instructing him to forward my protest noted before him, and recorded in his books, relative to the Schooner Margaret Ann & Cargo, in which I was interested. I was bound to Laguna, but was captured and carried into Campeche, where ["under" *canceled*] I was subjected to a forced sale. Mr. [John F.] McGregor is cognisant of all particulars, which are noted in the Protest.

The vessel in which I am to go, will sail on *the 18th Inst[an]t.* I have the honour to remain, with great respect, Sir, Your most obed[ien]t Serv[an]t, Henry A. Holms.

[P.S.] Address care of C.H. Todd & Co. New York.

ALS in DNA, RG 59 (State Department), Consular Despatches, Merida, vol. 1 (M-287:1, frames 120–121). NOTE: A Clerk's EU reads "Mr. Regil written to Jan[uar]y 24."

From D[ANIEL] JENIFER

Legation of the U. States at Vienna
Rome, 12th Nov[embe]r 1844
Sir, In my last dispatch I advised the Department of a severe illness with which I was attacked at Trieste. Having gone there, the first of Sept. on the occasion of the visit of the Emperor of Austria [Ferdinand] with Prince Metternich and Court to that City—I was confined to my bed near four weeks which left me in so debilitated a state that my Phisicians advised, as soon as I recovered strength enough, to take a short sea voyage as the most speedy and effectual means of restoring me to health. There being then several American Ships in Port, one of which was about to sail for the Mediterranean, I embraced the opportunity and took passage in her and landed at Palermo on the Island of Sicily. The sea air and salt water bathing with the mild climate of Palermo soon restored me sufficiently to enable me to commence my return to Vienna. From Palermo I went by Steamer to Naples and am now thus far on my way with as much dispatch as the still delicate state of my health will permit.

Your dispatches No. 19 & 20 with the enclosures have been received. I have given to them my most earnest and anxious attention and will avail of every possible opportunity, as I have heretofore done to correct any misapprehensions which prevail to the prejudice of the U. States.

Great efforts have been made in England and some parts of the Continent of Europe to produce additional, and continue former prejudices against us. I have never permitted a moment to escape me, since I have been abroad, when I had it in my power, to do away the erroneous impressions created by the unjust and wilful misrepres[ent]ations of the public presses, and others from more authentic sources. I have had frequent conversations with the members of the Diplomatique Corps and others who have misunderstood our relations with Mexico and Texas, produced principally by the London and Paris papers. The Galignani of Paris and the Allgemeine Zeitung, printed at Augsburg, in Bavaria have a more extensive circulation throug[h]out Germany and the Continent generally than all other papers, and for years the Colum[n]s of each have been filled with denunciation and abuse against us. The extracts in the one from the most abusive and wreckless London papers—and the willful misrepresentations by an American Correspondent in the other, have produced more false impressions against the U. States than from all other sources. Aware of this fact, during the last Autumn I made a visit to Augsburg for the purpose of confer[r]ing with the Editors of that paper and to see if a stop could not be put to the insertion of such calumny as their correspondent furnished them with. I convinced the Editors that they had been imposed on and that they were accessory to rank injustice ["done to the U. States" *interlined*] and that their correspondent who wrote from Washington & Philadelphia was not entitled to credit. I ascertained that this writer, who calls himself an *American,* by which the greater injury was inflicted, was a *German employé,* then in Philadelphia and an applicant for an office under the Governm[en]t of the U. States. Since my visit to Augsburg I have been gratified to find, as then assured, that no similar abuse has been published in that paper. As far as I have been enabled to ascertain, and I have taken pains to be correctly informed, there is less prejudice, expressed or existing, against the U. States, in Austria than in any other Country in Europe. It may be that Foreign papers do not circulate to any extent within the Empire, but certain it is that none of its papers, as far as I have seen, either originate or copy such abusive articles as characterize those of other Countries. Whenever I have found it necessary to correct untrue or perverted statements I have always found the officers of State and others favourably disposed to a proper understanding, and a due appreciation, of our Character.

I shall now hasten my return to my official Post—as rapidly as my health will allow me, where no endeavours on my part shall be omitted to further the views of the Government. I have the honor to be Y[ou]r ob[edien]t S[ervan]t, D. Jenifer.

ALS (No. 25) in DNA, RG 59 (State Department), Diplomatic Despatches, Austria, vol. 1 (T-157:1, frames 299–300), received 12/23; draft and CC in DLC, Seth Barton and Daniel Jenifer Papers.

STEWART NEWELL, [Galveston], to R[ichard] K. Crallé

> Consulate of the United States
> Sabine, Texas
> November 12th 1844

Sir, I have the honor, to acknowledge receipt on 10th inst., of Letters from Department of State, dated 10th, 16th, and 29th Oct. ult[im]o, and beg leave, to return my acknowledgements, of the marked approbation, of the Department, of the manner, in which I, have discharged my duties, as refer[r]ed to in Letter from Department of Oct. 10th, and which approbation, is an honor, highly appreciated by me.

I have the honor, to report the Arrival at this Port, of the Steam Packet New York, from New Orleans, on the 10th inst. with Hon. A[ndrew] J. Donelson, Charge de Affaires of U. States, to Texas, and whose arrival in fine health, has revived, the almost expired hope, of Annexation, in the Citizens of this place, and I should judge, is a gentleman in every respect, well qualified, to increase the friendly views, of this Government, and poeple [*sic*]. Upon his arrival, I, immediately tendered, every facility in my power, to aid the Hon. Chargé, in entering upon his duties, by delivering into his Custody, all the Archives, Seals &C, of the Legation, at my Residence, and have afforded him, every hospitality, in my Family, that is due, to his Rank, and Station.

I beg leave to refer, to that portion of the Letter, of the Hon. Secretary of 10th Oct., relative to the payment of my Draft for *$100*— as compensation to ["Bearer" *altered to* "Bearers"] of Despatches, and trust the Hon. Secretary, will excuse the digression, to explain the cause, of my not having drawn upon the Department, instead, of the [New Orleans] Collector of Customs.

At the time of receiveing intelligence, of the decease of Hon. T[ilghman] A. Howard, I was at a loss to know, if the Department, would authorise such an expenditure, but deeming the matter of too much importance, in its results, to be delayed, I decided at once, to send the Despatch, and the Draft was made upon the Collector of Customs, for *Two* purposes. *First*, that the Bearers of Despatches, should receive thier [*sic*] pay on delivering the despatches, and without which, they would not, have carried them, being poor men, and exposed in a small open Sail Boat, *at Sea*, the compensation, would have been of less value, if delayed payment, until, my Draft, could have gone to the Department, and Money returned, and which Draft, could not have been, negotiated here, and I had not the Amount by me, and although drawn for only *$100*, this was accepted, with the understanding, that if my course was approved of, that a further reasonable allowance, would have been paid these Men, they having expended, the whole Amount, in Provisions, Towage up the Missis-[s]ippi, of the Boat with despatches, and detention in New Orleans, awaiting a favorable opportunity, to return to thier Families, at Galveston.

2d, Had the Department not, sanctioned the course adopted by me, in the matter, the draft being paid by the Collector, would have been a relief to me, until I could have returned the Amount to him, as I advised the Collector of my wish to do so, while what I deemed a sacred duty, to my Govt. had been performed, and the injury of a Protested Draft, having been avoided, all of which, uncertainty, was created by the sudden causes, and state of things, existing, and did not deem Chap. 9th, Art. 49th, Consular instructions, as applicable to this case, and no directions, from the Department, being in my possession.

In obedience to Instructions of Department, under date of 16th Oct., ult[im]o, I immediately notified E[lisha] A. Rhodes, of my readiness, to deliver to him, the Archives, and all property, belonging to the U.S. Consulate at Galveston, and agreeable thereto, have this day, delivered the same, and taken the receipt of E.A. Rhodes, therefor.

The Personal expences of Gen[era]l [William S.] Murphy, refer[r]ed to in the Letter of the Hon. Secretary of 29th Oct., ult[im]o, as embodied in my account, forwarded to Department, I beg leave to say, that a portion of them, seemed to bear so close an affinity, to his Funeral Expences, that I, was induced to forward the whole, that the Department, might if thought reasonable, allow such portions, as met approbation, and prevent the delay, which neccessarily [*sic*] would arise, in forwarding to the Family of Gen[era]l Murphy, an account, and the uncertainty of Ability, to refund any portion of it.

I have however, addressed a communication, and enclosed a Copy of accounts, to the Widow [Lucy Maria Murphy] of Gen[era]l Murphy, and hope the Amount will be forwarded to me. I have the honor to be, Most Respectfully, Your Ob[edien]t Servant, Stewart Newell.

ALS (No. 30) in DNA, RG 59 (State Department), Consular Despatches, Texas, vol. 1 (T-153:1), received 12/13.

From WILSON SHANNON

Legation of the U.S. of A.
Mexico [City], Nov. 12th 1844

Sir, I have the honor to transmit to you herewith the reply of H.E. Mr. [Manuel C.] Rejon, Secretary of foreign Relations, to my note of the 14th ultimo, a copy of which I sent you with my last despatch. The papers accompanying this communication, marked nos. 1, 2, 3 & 4, will put you in possession of all the correspondence that has taken place between this Legation and the Mexican Minister of Foreign Relations, on the subject of the renewal of the war on the part of Mexico against Texas & the mode, in which it is intended to be conducted since the date of my last despatch.

The note of the Mexican Minister, of the 31st ultimo, is so insulting, both in its language and charges, to the Government and people of the United States, and is such a flagrant breach of those rules of courtesy, that should characterize international diplomatic intercourse that I felt myself called upon to demand that it should be withdrawn. To this demand, a still more insulting and exceptionable note was received in reply, in language so grossly offensive to the Government and people of the United States, that if I had consulted my own feelings, I would have demanded my passports, but in view of the consequences, which such a course would involve, and not wishing to take any step that might appear rash, I thought it best to notify the Mexican Government that the two exceptionable notes (nos. 1 & 3) would be immediately referred to my Government for instructions, and that, unless they were withdrawn, all official intercourse between this Legation & the Mexican Government must cease, until those instructions were received. I have found myself placed in a position, which no person can properly appreciate, unless he was here and familiar with the circumstances, by which I have been surrounded. To see my Govt. insulted, and that insult made the subject of boast in the streets by the partisans of the present administration and used for the purpose of making political capital seemed to demand a more prompt and decisive course than the one I have adopted. On the other hand, had I demanded my passports at once, I might have been charged with acting with too much precipitancy and without a due regard to the probable consequences resulting from such a step. The course I have adopted leaves the Government entirely at liberty to take that course in the matter, which the honor, dignity & interests of the nation may demand, and I hope it will receive the approval of the President. I know it has been the policy of our Government to act with great forbearance with Mexico; but this, in my judgment, is a mistaken policy, and one that is not appreciated in this country by either the people or Government. The people and Government of the U. States are the objects of continual abuse by all parties here, and our forbearance is attributed to our party divisions, rather than to a sincere desire on our part to cultivate and preserve friendly relations with Mexico. The two notes of Mr. Rejon, of the 31st ultimo and 6th instant, were both sent to the press for publication, immediately after they had been received by this Legation. They were written for the purpose and with the view, of arousing the jealousies and exciting the prejudices of this people against the Govt. & Southern people of the U.S., and thereby to make political capital for the party in power. To accomplish this object, you will see that Mr. Rejon has not hesitated deliberately and purposely to misrepresent, in the most gross and palpable manner, both of my notes, and to charge the Govt. and southern people of the U.S., in language of the most exceptionable character, with acts and motives highly dishonourable. Under these circumstances, I thought I would not be doing my duty to the Government and people of the United States by permitting the two notes of Mr. Rejon to go to the Mexican people, calculated as they were to excite against us feelings of the most unfriendly character, without a reply, placing the Mexican Secretary and his two notes in what I conceived to be, their true character. See no. 4, accompanying this despatch.

The revolution, of which I spoke in my last as being probable, has actually commenced. General [Mariano] Paredes, who is said to be at the head of about two thousand troops at Guadalajara, in the Department of Jalisco, has pronounced against the Government. The Secretary of War [Isidro Reyes], a few days since, made a formal communication of this fact to the Congress now in session, asking at the same time for the necessary means to enable the Government to put down this revolution. This request will not be granted, as a majority of Congress are anxious for the success of the revolution and the overthrow of General Santa Anna. Gen[era]l Paredes is not alone in this movement. It is said that four of the neighbouring departments are cooperating with him and will pronounce against the Govt. in due time. The seeds of disaffection are wide spread and broad cast over the whole country, and nothing can save Santa Anna, but the scattered condition of his opponents, & a bold and rapid movement on his part, before they have time to concentrate their forces. He sees this and has set his forces in motion. Seven thousand infantry, with fifteen hundred cavalry and twenty pieces of cannon are now on the road from Jalapa to this place and are expected to reach here in a few days. President Santa Anna is at their head, and commands in person. It is said that General Paredes will be able to concentrate an equal force before Santa Anna can reach him. In the south there is a general rising of the people in opposition to the payment of the contributions levied to raise the four millions voted by Congress some time since to carry on the war against Texas. The officers of the Government charged with the duty of collecting these contributions have in many instances been arrested, their right hands cut off and in other respects cruelly treated. Large military forces have been sent by the Govt. to restore order and enforce the collections of the contributions. The malcontents in the south will cooperate with Gen[era]l Paredes and others against the Government. Such is the present condition of this country and the prospects for the future are still more gloomy. This revolution is a natural consequence resulting from the measures adopted to renew the war against Texas. A large army distributed at various points over the country, under different leaders, all ambitious to promote their own interest and selfish purposes, would at any time be dangerous to the ruling powers in this country; but at a time like this, when the country has been drained of nearly all of its resources, and the taxes and contributions levied on the people greatly increased, a revolution is the necessary consequence. Had the war against Texas been abandoned, the army reduced to about five thousand, the taxes diminished, a rigid accountability of public officers enforced, and a liberal foreign policy adopted, all of which might have been done, the present Govt. would not now be threatened with being overthrown.

When I say that this revolution is the necessary consequence of the measures adopted to renew the war against Texas, I do not wish to be understood as saying that the people of Mexico are opposed to that war. On the contrary they are unanimously in favour of it. For the reasons, which have induced the revolutionists to pronounce against the Government, I refer you to the Manifiesto [*sic*] of Gen[era]l Paredes, which I herewith send you.

Permit me to call your special attention to the claims of the citizens of the U.S. on this Govt. It will be recollected that a convention was concluded and signed on the 20th of Nov. 1843, by the accredited agents of the two Govts., which provided for the adjustment of the claims of our citizens on Mexico, and was submitted by the President to the Senate at an early period of the last session, by which it was approved, except as to the articles relating to the adjustment of the claims of the two Govts. on each other, and the designation of the City of Mexico, instead of Washington, as the place, where the board should hold its sessions. It therefore became necessary to refer this convention with these amendments back to the Government of Mexico for its approval. This was done early last spring, and Mr. [Ben E.] Green, the chargé d'affaires *ad interim*, pressed the subject on this Govt. and repeatedly urged its speedy action in the premises. Yet no action was had, and no steps have been taken, up to this day, by this Govt., in relation to this Convention and the two amendments proposed by the Senate. Mr. Green received no other satisfaction than delusive & deceptive promises and evasive answers. Shortly after my arrival in this city, finding that the time fixed for the exchange of ratifications had expired, I addressed a note, in obedience to my instructions, to the Mexican Minister of Foreign Relations, requesting the appointment of Plenipotentiaries to treat with me on this subject. Feeling anxious to conclude a convention in time to have it submitted to the Senate at its next session, I sought and obtained a personal interview with President Santa Anna, in which I urged on him also the early appointment of a minister to treat on this business. From both I received the strongest assurances that the subject should receive the immediate consideration of the Mexican Govt. I was induced to believe such would be the case, and that the business would be concluded in time for the action of the Senate at its next session. Having received no answer, on the 1st instant I addressed a second note to the Mexican Minister of Foreign Relations, calling his attention again to the subject, and requesting an early reply. ["(See no. 5)." *interlined.*] To this note I have received no answer. From these facts and other circumstances, which might be stated, I am compelled to believe ["that" *interlined*] it is the settled purpose of this Govt. to decline all action upon this subject so long as they can do so without incurring the risk of a war with the U. States. The very fact of baffling all efforts on our part to procure an adjustment of those claims will be made the grounds, by the party in power, for further demands on the confidence and support of the Mexican people. It would seem to me that when Mexico has refused even to talk upon this subject, it is time for Congress to begin to act, & vindicate the honor of the Country as well as the just rights of our plundered citizens. Until Congress takes hold of this subject, and gives this Govt. distinctly to understand that the claims of our citizens must be adjusted in a fair and just manner, I do not believe anything can or will be done. The whole tendency of things in this country is downward, and there is great danger, if these claims are postponed a few years longer, that they will be entirely lost to our citizens.

Our agent appointed to receive the Instalment due our citizens under the Convention of the 30th Jan. 1843, was directed to call at the proper department on the 30th ultimo, and demand payment of the Instalment that fell due on that day. He did so, and payment was refused on the alledged ground that there was no money in the Treasury applicable to such a purpose. He has called on two occasions since, but has not received any satisfactory answer as to the time when payment may be expected. Taking into consideration the revolution that has just commenced, the evident indisposition on the part of the Mexican Govt. to do justice to our citizens or Govt., the exhausted state of the national Treasury and the ruined condition of the country, I do not feel myself justified in giving you any encouragement as to the payment of the last or future instalments under the Convention of the 30th of January 1843.

My note, (a copy of which I sent you with my last despatch), protesting against the decree for the expulsion of citizens of the U. States from the four northern Departments, remains unanswered, and I do not believe any answer is intended.

No. 6 is a note [of 11/1] which I addressed to the Minister of Foreign Relations, requesting that our whaling ships may be permitted, as heretofore, to sell goods in the Ports of California to the amount of $500. The document, marked A, is a copy of a letter [of 8/1] from our consul in Monterey [Thomas O. Larkin], upon which this request was made.

No. 7 is a note [of 11/1] to the Mexican Govt. in relation to the conduct of the Governor of Acapulco towards one of our whaling ships, the Braganza, from the note itself you will learn the particulars of the case.

No. 8 is another note [of 11/5] to the Mexican Minister, in relation to the Crew of the W[illia]m A. Turner; & no. 9 is the reply [of 11/11] to that note this moment received.

The document, marked B, is the reply [of 9/6] of our Consul in Tabasco [Edward Porter] to the enquiries made by Mr. Green, in relation to this affair of [Francisco] Sentmanat and as to the truth of the rumours here in relation to [William] Patterson's connection with the expedition. I have the honor to be Very Respectfully Your Ob[edien]t serv[an]t, Wilson Shannon.

[Enclosure]
Manuel Cre[s]cencio Rejon to Wilson Shannon, No. 1, Translation

National Palace, Mexico, October 31, 1844

The undersigned, Minister of Foreign Relations and Government, had the honor to receive the note addressed to him, under date of the 14th instant, by the Hon. Wilson Shannon, envoy extraordinary and minister plenipotentiary of the United States, protesting, solemnly, by order of his government, as well against the invasion of the territory of Texas, which the government of the Mexican republic has determined to effect, as against the manner in which it is proposed to conduct that invasion.

As the object of the said note, which has revealed fully the duplicity with which Mexico has so long been treated, may be to cause the suspension of the hostilities projected against the colonists of that province who have risen in rebellion against her, whilst the work of annexing it to the United States is going on, the undersigned, in repelling this protest, finds himself under the necessity of examining how far it is founded on justice; and with that view, he must be permitted to lay down certain facts, which should be kept always present to the mind, in order to be able to decide with accuracy as to the right which the American government has to interfere in this affair.

The undersigned agrees that the first colonists of Texas established themselves in that territory, as well under grants from the Spanish government, confirmed after the completion of the independence of Mexico by the authorities of this republic, as subsequently by others of a similar nature, made by the State of Coahuila and Texas, which was fully authorized to make them; but he must at the same time strongly direct the attention of the Hon. Mr. Shannon to the very essential circumstances, that in the proclamation and act of independence of Texas, those who figured as the principal persons were almost all natives of the United States; that such was [Samuel Houston] the general, as well as the others composing the army, which fought under the standard of Texas in the action of San Jacinto; and that in many parts of the United States meetings were at that time publicly held, for the purpose of affording (as were in fact afforded) supplies of men, arms, and other materials and munitions of war and provisions to the so-called Texans, in order that they might sustain their cause; that if at that time it might have been believed that they united themselves to effect their independence of Mexico, it has since been clearly shown that they were endeavoring to separate that rich and extensive territory from its lawful sovereign, in order to annex it to the United States—a measure of policy which, as the Hon. Mr. Shannon expressly says in his note, has been long cherished, and has been deemed indispensable for the safety and welfare of the United States, and has accordingly been steadily pursued by all parties in that republic, and by all its administrations, for the last twenty years. Well, does not this open confession, united to the public and notorious facts which the undersigned has rapidly noticed, prove that the proclamation of the independence of Texas, and the demand for its annexation to the United States, are the work of the government and citizens of those States interested in effecting this acquisition, which they have for the last twenty years considered indispensable for the safety and welfare of that republic? And this being the case, can the right be admitted as just which they claim, to interfere in this question, by preventing the Mexican government from reconquering an interesting portion of its territory, whilst the question of its annexation to that republic is pending? In order to justify an intervention of this nature, it was necessary to recognise solemnly as existing, in each of the nations of the earth, the right to raise itself by means of the territories of its neighbors, by first peopling them with its own citizens, then causing them to withdraw themselves from obedience to the territorial authorities and to proclaim their independence, aiding them at the same time, in an effective manner, to sustain it; and, finally, to ask that the territory thus occupied be incorporated with that of the country to which those citizens belong. This is the position in which the United States stand with regard to the Texas question; and the North American government may thus far deceive itself by its fictions; but it will not be able to deceive the world, which, knowing the circumstances here mentioned by the undersigned, and taking into consideration the note of Mr. Shannon, (most important as it is to bring into relief the justice of the cause of Mexico in this affair) will see that the proclamation of the independence of Texas, made and sustained almost entirely by citizens of the United States, who were not repressed by their government, but, on the contrary, assisted by it, and by the southern States of that republic, was intended for no other object than to aggrandize the United States, by the annexation of that territory; thus endeavoring to give an honest appearance to the spoliation which is attempted against this nation, by supposed rights, to be founded on circumstances intentionally brought about by the southern people and the government of the United States themselves.

Who, indeed, does not see that this independence of Texas has been effected, and is now sustained with so much warmth and energy in the Hon. Mr. Shannon's note, only because it was agreed that the Texans should be made an independent and sovereign nation, in order to give them the right to conclude treaties, and thereby to annex themselves to the republic, of which the so-called President [Samuel Houston] of that Mexican province, as well as all the authorities governing it, are natives? The artifice, as well as the arguments founded on it, may surprise those who are unacquainted with the facts, and have not seen the note to which the undersigned has now the honor to reply; but those who know all the circumstances here mentioned, cannot but agree that by these means only has an appearance of justice been given to that, by which the law of nations, and the relations of good feeling between neighboring powers, are so deeply wounded. Did not President [Andrew] Jackson, one of the most extreme partisans of the annexation, and against whom has been brought the heavy charge of having sent General Houston to Texas in order to carry his designs into execution, confess, in deference to truth and justice, in a message which he addressed to the House of Representatives in December, 1836—and that when the question was only as to recognising the independence—that such an act would be regarded as one of serious injustice to Mexico, and that by it the United States would render themselves subject to the most severe censure, as the Texans had all emigrated from that country, and were endeavoring to obtain their recognition with the manifest intention of effecting their incorporation into the United States? This confession, being no less than that of the government of that republic, whilst it corroborates what has been already said—to wit, that the independence of Texas was effected by emigrants from the United States, with the object of annexing Texas to their country, affords clear proof of the assertion of the undersigned, that an attempt has been made to give to the occupation of Texas by the United States a course which should divest it in some manner of the odium of a barefaced usurpation; making it appear as if it had been obtained by the express consent of a people, who had succeeded in emancipating themselves from their mother country, conquering their independence by their own sword and valor.

Thus, as the Texans who proclaimed the independence of Texas were emigrants from the United States; as it could not be doubted that they were openly protected in the United States, in order to support their rebellion against the authorities of a country which received them with so much generosity; as it was public and notorious that the government of the United States, which affected so much respect for the opinion of the world, fearing lest its acknowledgment of the independence of Texas might be regarded as an act of serious injustice to Mexico, was the first to hasten to make such acknowledgment, while aware that the independence had been proclaimed with the

251

object of annexing that Mexican province to the northern republic; it being afterwards seen that this same government of the United States, and a large portion of its people, were openly, and without attempt at concealment, laboring with enthusiasm for the annexation of Texas to their territory, so far as to have solicited a renewal of the proposition for incorporation, when there was no necessity for such a demand, because the Texans and the people of the United States being one and the same, they all had, and still have, the same interests and tendencies; and, finally, as the history of this question between the two countries presents everything that could be desired, to prove that the independence of Texas is the work of the government and the southern people of the United States, and that they effected it only for the purpose of obtaining possession of those rich and extensive territories—how can this independence be represented as a matter in which they had no part?—and how can the foreigners who proclaimed it, be considered as having the same title which the Mexicans, the owners, by every right, of the soil on which they were born, had to their independence?

But it will be said that these foreigners, having been invited to establish themselves in that province, settled there under the federal system which then governed the Mexican republic; and that this system having been dissolved by armed forces, they had the right to separate themselves from Mexico, especially as the constitution of 1824 had given them the right to be an independent State whensoever they should possess the requisite qualifications.

In answer to this, it should be borne in mind that the citizens of the United States who proclaimed the independence of Texas, (with the exception, perhaps, of the first colonists,) went there, not to remain in submission to the Mexican republic, but with the object of annexing Texas to their own country—thereby strengthening the peculiar institutions of the southern States, and opening a new theatre for the execrable system of negro slavery; that they never subjected themselves to the laws of Mexico, but lived as they pleased; and that when they considered that they could erect themselves into a State of the confederacy, to regulate their affairs in their own way, they formed their constitution, which the general administration of the republic did not approve, because that act wanted the requisites fixed by the fundamental law. This, together with the decree for the suppression of slavery, and the means adopted to subject them to compliance with the laws which they contemned, irritated them, and disposed them to raise the standard of rebellion against the national authorities. They did, in effect, rise in rebellion; and then, finding a pretext in the variation of the federal constitution, (the dispositions of which they had never observed, except so far as suited their convenience,) they relied upon it to advance their movement—maliciously denying the right of the nation to vary its institutions whensoever it might be proper for its interests; then proclaiming their independence, and afterwards their annexation to the United States, which had been the real object of their coming to Texas, and the end to which all parties and all administrations in that republic have directed their efforts for the last twenty years, as the honorable Mr. Shannon declares in his note. And does not all this manifestly prove that a system of falsehood has been constantly pursued towards Mexico? Does it not destroy even those semblances of right by which it is attempted to justify the rebellion of the colonists of Texas? Moreover, was the independence promised to that province in the federal constitution such that it might separate itself from the republic whenever it should possess the qualifications required, and annex itself to a foreign nation? Examine that constitution with care, and it will be seen to promise no more than that the State should be independent in its internal administration; but not that it should be emancipated from the national sovereignty, which all the States were under obligation to acknowledge and respect. Besides, what has one nation to do with the institutions of another in its vicinity? Or, by what right can it take to itself the territories of another, in which its citizens have established themselves, because the constitutional forms of the people who received them have been varied?

Will it be also said that they have effected their independence, and that, possessing means sufficient to maintain it, they should be recognised as an independent nation having the right to conclude treaties, and thereby to annex themselves to another power, which may be more agreeable to them, and will admit them into its union? But here the undersigned will repeat what he has already said respecting the artifices by which the government and the southern people of the United States have brought on the actual situation of Mexico, in order to form an argument apparently solid, on which they might support the acquisition of that territory, which has been for the last twenty years "deemed indispensable *by all parties and successive administrations* of that republic." But those called Texans are not the persons who have effected the independence of that province, or who have the means to carry it through; the people of the southern States of the Union have done everything, not to make Texas an independent nation, but to annex it to their own territory, with some show of justice. The note to which the undersigned is replying is a proof of the insufficiency of those (so called) Texans; because, had their resources been adequate to sustain them against the power of the Mexican republic, there would have been no necessity for the honorable Mr. Shannon's government to place itself thus openly on their side, and to tear away at once the veil with which it has long sought to cover its intrigues and designs.

But proceeding now to the belief which is said to be generally entertained in the United States, that Texas was comprised in the cession of Louisiana made by France to that republic in 1803: the undersigned will ask, can it be sufficient to invalidate subsequent treaties, concluded with the proper solemnities? By the treaty concluded at Washington on the 22d of February, 1819, between the plenipotentiaries of the United States and of Spain, the Americans acknowledged the province in question to form part of the Spanish possessions; and if it be now said that this renunciation was improperly made, and it be pretended to found upon that belief a right superior to that given by the said treaty, what guarantee can there be to public conventions in future, when against all may be alleged some pre-existing right improperly renounced or stipulated? Could not Spain have adduced the same reason, with much better titles, for disputing the possession of Louisiana by the United States? Did she not, on retroceding Louisiana to France, (which sold that territory to the American government for eighty millions,) reserve to herself, by the treaty of October, 1800, the right of preference in case France should be about to part with it? And did the United States depend upon her previous consent to making this important recognition? Far from so doing, this business was entered upon without giving her any notice whatsoever; and when she became informed of it, she bitterly complained of this conduct, and refused for one year to approve the treaty of cession of Louisiana. What, then, would the United States have said if the court of Madrid, notwithstanding this solemn approval, should now come forward with a declaration that it had been given in an improper manner; and that this territory, clandestinely transferred to another, should be returned to her? Would they fail to adduce in this case the conventional right flowing from the treaty of approval, as a peremptory reason in opposition to the pretensions of Spain? Well, this is precisely what Mexico now does; she relies, not only on the treaty of Washington, of February 22, 1819, but on the treaty entered upon and concluded on the 12th of January, 1828, between the plenipotentiaries of this republic and the United States, and afterwards solemnly ratified by the two contracting parties. In both treaties it is agreed that the dividing-lines should be marked out; that Texas should not belong to the United States, but first to Spain, and afterwards to Mexico, as succeeding to the rights of Spain. In neither treaty will be found the reservations which could give to the American government the titles which it appears to found upon a belief contrary to solemn conventions, whilst both treaties contain express and positive renunciations of that territory in favor of Spain and this republic, as may be seen by reference to the 3d article of the treaty of Washington, and the 2d article of the treaty of Mexico.

As it is thus asserted that this belief that the territory of Texas belongs to the United States has existed in every part of the Union for the last twenty years, it is indeed surprising that in the year 1828 they should have agreed, by the ratifications of the treaties of limits with Spain, to acknowledge that province as an integrant part of the Mexican republic. If these reasons were then good, why did they not amend the defect in the first treaty, and at least make some reservation to support that right which now begins to be brought forward, and which they endeavor to make valid? It is equally surprising that it should be desired to found on the security of the United States the right to appropriate a vast and fertile province belonging to a neighboring nation, and recognised as an integrant part of its territory by solemn treaties. If this argument were good, few nations could rest secure and quiet in the possession of their respective territories, because the stronger would always have a reason for absorbing the weaker, on the grounds of their own security. Thus the United States, after taking Texas, might, by the same title, adjudge to themselves the other frontier departments of the Mexican republic, if they should not proceed at once with the territory comprehended between the river Bravo del Norte and the Colorado, which empties into the Californian gulf, and their respective sources.

Can Mexico, finding herself threatened by these new and overwhelming evils—especially as she sees a powerful reason for fearing them in the unworthy (*poco leal*) conduct of the government and the people of the southern States of the Union, as regards the Texas question—can she fail to avail herself of her right of security, founded on better titles than those which the honorable Mr. Shannon's republic can adduce, on the grounds of providing against the influence of Great Britain, which is considered as ominous of evil to the welfare and prosperity of the American people?—for whilst Mr. Tyler's government is seeking the security of his country, by seizing a territory belonging to another, the government of the Mexican republic provides for its own safety by endeavoring to retain a province which belongs to it by every right. Whilst the American government is endeavoring to avoid an inconvenient neighbor, the Mexican government, operating with the same object, also strives to preserve its other departments, and even its national existence, which are placed in jeopardy. Finally, whilst the one power is seeking more ground to stain by the slavery of an unfortunate branch of the human race, the other is endeavoring, by preserving what belongs to it, to diminish the support which the former wants for this detestible traffic. Let the world now say which of the two has justice and reason on its side.

The undersigned, coming to the charge made against his government as to the manner in which it proposes to conduct the war against the (so called) Texans, will say, that its severity has been occasioned by the policy of the government and of the people of the southern States of the Union, conformable neither with the relations of good neighborhood, nor with the respect due to the rights of a friendly nation. Because, if instead of fomenting the spirit of rebellion in the native citizens of the United States established in Texas against the government of that territory, they had been made to understand, in a decisive and effective manner, that they could in no case rely on the assistance of their own country in support of their undertaking; if the neutrality inculcated by President Jackson in his message of December 8, 1836, as a duty on the part of the United States in the civil struggle between Mexico and Texas, had been other than a vain formality, and he had effectually repressed what he then called strong temptations and powerful inducements to protect the Texans; it is almost certain that they never could have ventured to rise in insurrection, and still less to proclaim their independence. The war would not have arisen; and even though it should have broken out, as the noble and honorable conduct of the United States would, in justice, have inspired unbounded confidence, the struggle would not have been influenced nor have reached the extremity to which it was brought by the open co-operation of Messrs. Jackson and Tyler, and of the southern States of the Union. This has caused the Mexican government to see, as it now sees, a conflagration, the flames of which it has endeavored, and is endeavoring, to quench by every means in its power; and for all the evils of which, those should be responsible who have provoked them by acting in this dishonorable manner.

Besides, can the manner in which a government endeavors to restore to order one of its provinces which has declared itself independent, give to the government of a neighboring nation the right to prevent the former by force of arms from reconquering that territory, and on such a pretext to appropriate it to itself? The undersigned has said that the colonists of Texas, without the assistance of the government and of the people of the southern States of the American Union, would neither have risen in rebellion, nor have had the means to maintain their independence. Nevertheless, admitting the fact to be established, that the inhabitants of the province in insurrection could have succeeded in withdrawing from the dominion of the Mexican republic, and could have had resources adequate to place them in security against the attacks of this republic, should not the United States have limited themselves to the recognition of their independence? and, in case the war against them should have been conducted in a manner not conformable with the usage generally adopted, should they not have been content with interposing their good offices to have it carried on regularly, from respect to humanity, which is so little respected in the United States, and to prevent the evils which President Tyler affects to fear? Why not act in this case, as the other powers who acknowledged the independence of Texas have done, without endeavoring to prevent the Mexican government from availing itself of its rights over the territory in insurrection?

Is it because the government of the United States has pledged itself to the Texans to ask for their annexation again, and because, under this supposition, its honor does not allow it to see another suffer in its place? It is scarcely to be believed that a most serious fault should serve as a reason for committing another and a greater one, especially as there is no obstruction to saying so in an important document which is to be made known to the whole civilized world. If honor does not allow the American government to see another suffer in its place, neither does it allow it to acknowledge the independence of Texas, as declared in the President's message of December, 1836; and still less to invite the Texans to renew their proposition for annexation; failing so clearly in the honor and consideration due to a friendly and neighboring nation, and in respect to the repeated assurances of good faith, by means of which it has been attempted to tranquilize them.

But, admitting that the conduct of Mexico has not been strictly regular: why, instead of completing an act at variance with all morality, does not the American government recede, and give full satisfaction to the friendly power whose rights it has outraged; using its influence over that power, in an amicable manner, so as to calm her just irritation against rebels whom it has compromised; and negotiating to the effect that those rebels, by returning under the authority of their legitimate sovereign, may obtain indulgence and the passage of laws of exception in their favor, sufficient to satisfy their wants? Mexico has manifested the best disposition to do so; but as the object of the United States is to annex to themselves the province of Texas, the acquisition of which has been considered necessary and indispensable by all parties and all administrations in that republic for the last twenty years, nothing but that is wanted; and for that, a state of things has been brought about, to give an appearance of justice to an act which can in no way be justified.

Now, whether these proceedings have been honorable or not; whether the conduct of the two administrations, and of the people of the southern States of the Union, who have proposed to dismember the territory of the Mexican republic, is or is not conformable with the law of nations and the relations of friendship which the government of the undersigned has endeavored to maintain with them, the civilized world will decide; and the northern portion of the United States will also decide—that portion on whose honor Mexico relies, doing to it the justice which it merits, and which its own government endeavors to take from it, by representing it as an accomplice in a policy to which the nobleness of its generous sentiments is repugnant.

As it then appears, from what has been here said, that everything alleged by the American government to prevent Mexico from recovering the province of Texas is, upon analysis, a manifest violation of the law of nations, because it reduces itself to a demand that that government should be allowed to effect the usurpation of a large portion of the territory of a friendly power—to which end it has been laboring for the last twenty years—reserving to itself the faculty to do so, unless the object could, in the mean time, be attained by friendly negotiations; and the right of this republic to the said territories (the ownership and sovereignty of which have been solemnly recognised by the government of the United States) being unquestionable, the Mexican government neither can nor should cease its exertions to bring those territories back under its dominion. The undersigned, therefore, has orders to repel (*rechazar*) the protest now addressed to his government, and to declare to Mr. Shannon that the President of the United States is much mistaken if he supposes Mexico capable of yielding to the menace which he, exceeding the powers given to him by the fundamental law of his nation, has directed against it.

The government of the undersigned does not desire, nor has it ever desired, to interrupt the relations of friendship which it wishes, in good faith, to cultivate with that republic, notwithstanding the latter has so seriously failed in its duty on the point in question, so far as to declare plainly that it has been for twenty years deceiving Mexico by protestations of honor, whilst it has been, during all that time, desiring to seize, gradually or by force, one of her most extensive and fertile departments. Mexico therefore, at present, desists from saying more; but she does not desist, nor will she ever desist, from endeavoring to bring back into the national union a territory which, by every title, is her own; and if, on her using this right, which gives offence to no one, the government of the United States should proceed to carry into effect the threat uttered against her, by changing the existing relations between the two countries, the responsibility for the consequences which may result will rest upon them, and not on the Mexican government, which will confine itself entirely to repelling unjust and unprovoked aggression.

The undersigned repeats to the Hon. Mr. Shannon the assurances of his most distinguished consideration. Manuel Cre[s]cencio Rejon.

[Enclosure]

Wilson Shannon to M[anuel] C. Rejon, No. 2

Legation of the U.S. of America

Mexico, November 4, 1844

The undersigned, envoy, &c., has received, and read with surprise, the note of his excellency M.C. Rejon, minister of foreign relations of the republic of Mexico, of the 31st ultimo, which purports to be in reply to the note of the undersigned of the 14th of the same month, protesting against the proposed invasion of Texas at this time by Mexico, and the mode in which it is proposed to be conducted.

The undersigned can hold no communication with the government of Mexico, unless in terms respectful to himself, and to the government and people whom he has the honor to represent. The note of his excellency Mr. Rejon repeatedly charges, in terms the most grossly offensive, the government and people of the United States with falsehood, artifice, intrigues, and designs of a dishonorable character, and with barefaced usurpation. It also charges General Jackson with having, while President of the United States, sent General Houston to Texas, with the secret purpose and dishonorable design of exciting that people to revolt, with the view of procuring the annexation of that territory to the United States.

These charges are predicated, in part, on a misrepresentation of the note of the undersigned, so gross and palpable, and are so often repeated in language so offensive, as to manifest a purpose of deliberately insulting the people and government of the United States. To such charges, so unfounded, made in language so insulting, and for such a purpose, the undersigned can make no reply. He has, therefore, no alternative but to demand that the note be withdrawn.

As the undersigned proposes to send by a special messenger, to leave on the morning of the 10th instant, despatches to his government; and as the future relations to subsist between the United States and Mexico may depend on the representations which he may then make to his government, he requests an immediate reply to this note. The undersigned renews, &c., &c., Wilson Shannon.

[Enclosure]

Manuel Cre[s]cencio Rejon to Wilson Shannon, No. 3, Translation

National Palace

Mexico, November 6, 1844

The undersigned, Minister of Foreign Relations and Government, has received the note from the Hon. Wilson Shannon, envoy extraordinary and minister plenipotentiary of the United States of America, dated the 4th instant, relative to the reply given to him by the undersigned, on the 31st of October last, repelling the protest which the Hon. Mr. Shannon made against the invasion of Texas by the Mexican government, and the manner in which it was proposed to be carried on.

As the conduct observed by the government and the southern people of the United States, in the question respecting the said province belonging to this republic, has been very irregular, the undersigned is not surprised that, after the question had been placed in its true point of view, and freed from the intricacies in which it had been intentionally involved, the American minister should have been unwilling to enter upon it; and should give, as a pretext for not doing so, that he was not allowed to continue communications with this government, except in terms respectful to himself, and to the government and nation represented by him. In fact, to what else can be attributed this exclusive desire on the part of the Hon. Mr. Shannon to claim for himself, his nation, and his government—leaving aside the question at issue—that respect denied by him to the Mexican republic and its government, to which he has so often applied the term *barbarous* in his note of October 14. Is the government of the United States superior in dignity? or has its legation any right to be thus far wanting in respect for a government, to which it has refused the attentions due by courtesy to mere individuals?

Mexico may, with justice, claim reparation for these injuries, and would easily obtain it, if the American government, instead of endeavoring to cultivate friendly relations and amity with her, did not seek the occasion to change those relations, by provoking a rupture, which the government of the undersigned has endeavored, and is still endeavoring, to avoid.

The Mexican government might also have returned insult for insult, by openly using the same uncourteous language which characterizes the two preceding notes from the American legation; but it knows what is due to itself, after an attempt has been made to cover it with opprobrium before the whole world, in treating a question in which it has justice and reason on its side.

Mexico has been obliged to refer to important acts tending to prove the dishonorable conduct of two administrations, and of the southern people of the United States. No other resource has been left to her, in order to render obvious the justice of her cause, as well as the injustice of the attempt made to take from her an important portion of her territories, the acquisition of which has been judged necessary by all parties and governments of that republic for the last twenty years, as shown by the note from the American minister of the 14th of October last. Her government has, however, limited itself to what was absolutely indispensable to render its case clear, showing in the discussion all the consideration due to the majority of the American people, from whose representatives it hopes for amends for the excesses committed on this point by the actual President of that republic, whose Senate, composed of respectable and honorable men (such as [John Quincy] Adams [*sic*] and [Henry] Clay) has given to Mexico proofs of the justice of its character.

Thus the government of the undersigned, so far from withdrawing the note which it addressed to the American legation on the 31st of October last, is more and more convinced, after meditating on its contents, of the necessity of leaving it in the terms in which it was delivered; regretting, only, that no occasion has been offered to develop more completely the facts which have been presented, in order to demonstrate to the world the system of duplicity pursued towards Mexico for the last twenty years, as confirmed by the note from the American legation of the 14th of October last.

The undersigned, therefore, has orders to recapitulate what he has said in every point; and at the same time to repeat, that if, in case Mexico should use her rights, the relations of amity which the Mexican government has endeavored, and still endeavors to maintain, should be broken by the existing (*actual*) government of the United States, the Mexican administration will accept the hard conditions which are forced upon it, and will repel the unjust aggression committed against it; leaving the government of President Tyler responsible, in every way, for all the evils which may ensue from the change of relations.

The undersigned repeats to the Hon. Wilson Shannon the assurances of his distinguished consideration. Manuel Cre[s]cencio Rejon.

[Enclosure]
Wilson Shannon to M[anuel] C. Rejon, No. 4

Legation of the U.S. of America
Mexico, November 8, 1844

The note of his excellency M.C. Rejon, minister of foreign relations of the republic of Mexico, of the 6th instant, is of such a character as to leave the undersigned no alternative but to announce to the supreme government of Mexico that it, together with the note of his excellency of the 31st ultimo, will be immediately referred to his government for their further instructions; and that, unless they are withdrawn, all further official intercourse between the undersigned and the government of Mexico will be suspended until those instructions are received.

The undersigned has too much self-respect, and knows too well what is due to his government, to make any reply to the charges made in his excellency's note of the 31st ultimo, and reiterated in a manner so offensive in his note of the 6th instant, for the purpose of vindicating the honor or character of the people or government of the United States. During the 49 years that that government has been in successful operation, it has discharged its international duties, and performed its obligations both to its own citizens and to other nations, with a fidelity, honor, and integrity, that command the respect of all the governments of the civilized world. Its measures and policy in its intercourse with all nations have been open, frank, and undisguised, "demanding nothing but what is right, and submitting to nothing that is wrong." It stands self-vindicated in the purity, integrity, and fidelity which have characterized its brilliant national career, and command the confidence and respect of the civilized world. If the government of Mexico constitutes an exception to this truth, the government of the United States, (to whom the undersigned will refer the notes of his excellency Mr. Rejon,) knowing what is due to its own character, can and will correct the erroneous opinion (which is the misfortune of Mexico) by means more efficient than any written refutation by the undersigned, of the calumnies made and reiterated in the notes of Mr. Rejon, would be.

But, inasmuch as the undersigned is forced to believe that the misrepresentations of his note of the 14th ultimo, and the reiteration of the unfounded charges and unjust imputations against the government and southern people of the United States, contained in the notes of his excellency, are intended to mislead the public opinion of the people of Mexico, and to excite an unjust prejudice in their minds against the government and people of the United States; and inasmuch as his excellency, in his note of the 6th instant, endeavors to make the people of Mexico believe that the reason why the undersigned did not reply to these unfounded charges and imputations is not the reason alleged by the undersigned in his note of the 4th instant, but because they are true, and cannot be denied; the undersigned therefore avails himself of this occasion to correct his excellency's misrepresentations of his note of the 14th ultimo, and also to repel the charges and imputations contained in the notes of the 31st ultimo and the 6th instant—not for the purpose of vindicating the honor or character of his own government, but that the people of Mexico may be disabused, and the consequences of the discourteous and unjust conduct of his excellency Mr. Rejon in the premises may rest with the government and people of Mexico, who are responsible therefor, and that they may be without apology if they adopt and justify the same.

The undersigned is further induced to do this, because the publication of his excellency's notes of the 31st ultimo and the 6th instant, and the comments of the official newspaper thereon, leave no room to doubt as to the purpose for which they were written and published.

The undersigned, in his note of the 14th ultimo, said that the acquisition of Texas had been a policy long cherished, and deemed indispensable to the safety and welfare of the United States, and had, accordingly, been an object steadily pursued by all parties, and *"made the subject of negotiation by almost every administration for the last twenty years."* His excellency Mr. Rejon seized upon this declaration, and says that it has *"just revealed the falsehood with which Mexico has been so long treated;"* and this charge, which the records of his own government fully disprove, is repeated in all the phases which the most unfair and uncandid sophistry can give to it. Did not his excellency know that almost every administration of the American government for the last twenty years had endeavored to acquire the claim of Mexico to the territory of Texas? Does he not know that Messrs. Adams and Clay, of whom his excellency Mr. Rejon now makes such favorable mention, made two attempts to negotiate with Mexico for the acquisition of Texas—one in 1825, and the other in 1827? And does he not know, also, that the negotiation was afterwards renewed by General Jackson and Mr. Van Buren; and that President Tyler, after Mexico had lost her right of sovereignty, and Texas had become, *de jure* as well as *de facto*, an independent and sovereign power, sought by negotiation to acquire the same territory?

The undersigned repeats, does not his excellency Mr. Rejon know all these facts? and asks, how can he, knowing them, say that the reference by the undersigned to a fact thus known to all the world, and especially to the Mexican government and to Mr. Rejon himself, has "just revealed the falsehood with which Mexico has been so long treated?"

There has been no time, during the whole period mentioned, that the government of Mexico did not know, nor has the government of the United States, at any time during that period, attempted to conceal its desire to acquire Texas. This his excellency Mr. Rejon knows to be true; and yet he makes the charge, that the note of the undersigned of the 14th instant has "*just revealed*" it, and would persuade the Mexican people that the government and people of the United States have for twenty years entertained a secret purpose, and resorted to improper means, for the acquisition of Texas; and that to him belong the honor and the credit of having discovered the proof, and vindicated the rights of Mexico. And when told that such a charge is unjust—an unfounded misrepresentation of what the undersigned had said—the same charge is again repeated in the note of the 6th instant, in terms even more offensive. The undersigned cannot believe that his excellency does not know that the fact that the acquisition of Texas "has been made the subject of negotiation by almost every administration for the last twenty years," is no argument to prove that the government of the United States has treated Mexico with "falsehood," or attempted to acquire Texas by artifice or improper means; and he is, therefore, compelled to believe that the use which has been made of that fact, as stated in his note of the 14th, is a misrepresentation, intended to create a false impression on the minds of the people of Mexico, and to create a prejudice against the government and southern people of the United States; and he regrets to believe that his excellency finds in the present condition of the government or people of Mexico anything to justify a proceeding so flagrant and unjust.

The belief that the misrepresentations of the note of the undersigned were intentional, and that the charges and imputations founded thereupon were made for the purpose of creating an unjust prejudice in the minds of the people of Mexico against the government and people of the United States, is further confirmed by the manner in which his excellency has referred to President Jackson, and the fact that his excellency has made a false quotation (or, what is equivalent thereto, a palpable misrepresentation) of his official communication to the Congress of the United States.

His excellency asks if President Jackson, "in a message which he addressed to the House of Representatives, in December, 1836—and this, when it was proposed to recognise the independence of Texas—did not confess that such an act would be *'regarded as a grievous injustice to Mexico, and that the United States would be subject to the blackest censure for it, inasmuch as the Texans had emigrated from thence, and sought this recognition with the manifest intention of obtaining their incorporation with the United States?'* " The undersigned has examined the official documents, and can find no message of President Jackson containing the language imputed to him. Why does his excellency impute to President Jackson language which he did not utter? The answer is found in the character given to President Jackson, and the use made by Mr. Rejon of the false quotation. The purpose was to charge the United States with endeavoring *"to give to the occupation of Texas a turn which would take from it the odium of a barefaced usurpation,"* and to introduce President Jackson as a witness to prove the charge in its most odious aspect. To give greater weight to the language imputed to President Jackson, his excellency says that "he was one of the warmest partisans of annexation, against whom grave charges have been made of having sent General Houston to Texas to realize his designs;" at the same time saying that he was forced, "by a regard to truth and justice, to confess" that *"to recognise the independence of Texas would be regarded as a grievous injustice to Mexico, and that the United States would be subject to the blackest censure for it."*

Does not his excellency Mr. Rejon, by misquoting President Jackson—imputing to him that which he did not say, by way of giving greater effect to the charge which his excellency makes against the United States—furnish the most conclusive proof that he himself believes the charge, as made by himself, to be untrue? For who can for a moment believe that if his excellency could have sustained the charges made by him, by a fair and true quotation, he would have adopted one so unfair and incorrect? To believe this, would be to suppose that his excellency prefers to sustain the charges which he feels called upon to make against the United States, by falsehood rather than by truth—an imputation which the undersigned cannot make; and he therefore assumes that his excellency Mr. Rejon attributed language to President Jackson which he knew that President Jackson did not utter; because, under the peculiar circumstances in which he is placed, he believes that it is for the "interest" of the gov-

ernment of Mexico to make the unjust charges against the government and southern people of the United States, which are made in
the notes of his excellency; and because he knows that the truth will
not sustain the charges which it is the purpose of his excellency's note
to make. The undersigned is the more inclined to this belief, because
it is apparent that the purpose is to persuade the Mexican people of
the truth of the charges, to establish which this quotation was made;
and because few of the Mexican people, in the minds of whom it was
the purpose of his excellency's note to impress these charges, can, by
comparing the quotation with the messages of President Jackson, de-
tect the imposition thus practised upon them.

His excellency Mr. Rejon admits that "the first colonists established themselves in that territory by grants from the Spanish government; confirmed after the independence of Mexico by the authority of this republic, and afterwards by similar grants made by the
State of Coahuila and Texas, competently authorized to make them;"
and yet refers to the fact, that those who figured as principals in the
declaration and act of independence, who fought under the standard
of Texas in the battle of San Jacinto, were almost all natives of the
United States; and that aid of men, arms, and other munitions of war,
were furnished by citizens of the United States, to prove "the declaration of the independence of Texas, and the demand for its annexation
to the United States, to be the work of the government of the latter,
and its citizens interested in making an acquisition that for twenty
years they have considered indispensable to the safety and welfare of
that republic."

That the citizens of the United States had the right to emigrate to
Texas; and that, having emigrated, and become citizens of Texas,
they had the right to take part in any public proceedings, affecting
their rights and interests; and that those who did not emigrate, had
the right to furnish to those who did, arms, provisions, and other
munitions of war; and that all this might have been done in such a
manner as to furnish no ground whatever for the charge which his
excellency Mr. Rejon makes against the government of the United
States—his excellency knows, or ought to know. Not to know this,
would be to argue that he was ignorant not only of the laws and constitution of the United States, but of the law of nations, and of the
history of his own country, and of the aid in men, money, arms, and
munitions of war, which Mexico herself received from the United
States, and which contributed so much to achieve her independence.
To this branch of the argument, therefore, the undersigned will make
no reply; because the people of Mexico must be as ignorant as his

excellency Mr. Rejon affects to be, if they can be induced to believe it.

To that branch of this proposition which charges that, because those who figured as principals in the declaration of independence, and who conquered in the battle of San Jacinto, were natives of the United States, therefore the declaration of independence and the demand for annexation was the work of the government of the United States—it is enough to reply, that although they were natives of the United States, they had been invited to Texas, (as is admitted by Mr. Rejon himself,) first by the government of Spain, next by Mexico, and then by the State of Coahuila and Texas, competently authorized to do so; that Mr. Rejon knows, or ought to know, that the government of the United States contributed in nowise whatever to induce the governments of Spain, or of Mexico, or of Coahuila and Texas, to give that invitation; and that he also knows that the declaration of independence, and the application by the people of Texas to be annexed to the United States, were the consequence of measures adopted by the government of Mexico, over which the government of the United States exercised no control, and in which it had no agency whatsoever.

As well might his excellency argue that the government of Spain instigated the revolution in Mexico, because many of those who took part in that revolution were native Spaniards, or their descendants; or that the government of Mexico instigated the resistance made in Zacatecas and other States of the Mexican confederacy to the government of General Santa Anna, because those who took part in that resistance were native Mexicans, as to allege that the government of the United States instigated the independence of Texas, because those who made the declaration were natives of the United States.

The undersigned repeats, that to make such a charge argues an utter ignorance of the history of Mexico, or a deliberate purpose of making a false charge against the government of the United States.

The emigration from the United States to Texas, under the authority of Spain, which was afterwards ratified by Mexico herself, commenced in 1821. The resistance to the acts of the Mexican government, which led to their declaration of independence, may be said to have commenced in 1832, with the affairs of Anahuac, Velasco, and Nacogdoches; but it was a resistance to the usurpations of Bustamente [*sic*; Anastasio Bustamante]; and the undersigned does not believe that, much as his excellency Mr. Rejon is now interested in establishing the unfounded charge, he will venture to assert, in the face of the civilized world, that the government of the United States had any agency whatever in those proceedings. For the inhabitants of Texas, who took part in them, declared for General Santa Anna, whose avowed purpose was to support the constitution of 1824; and General [José A.] Mejia, who was sent by General Santa Anna to Texas for the purpose of restoring order, finding the "*constitution of 1824*" triumphant, and the whole people rejoicing in the downfall of Bustamente and the elevation of General Santa Anna, then the professed advocate of that constitution, and confided in as a friend of liberty, professed himself most agreeably surprised, and awarded his cordial approbation to all that had been done.

That there may not be further cavil on this point, and to prove that the government of Mexico, and not the government of the United States, is responsible for the proceedings in Texas which resulted in the declaration of independence, and the subsequent application to be annexed to the United States, the undersigned refers to the well-known facts of Mexican history; and to show the state of things on which the government of the United States recognised the independence of Texas, the undersigned refers his excellency Mr. Rejon to the report made by a special agent sent by President Jackson to ascertain and report upon the condition and facts in relation to the independence of Texas. The following are extracts from that report:

"The present political condition of Texas has been produced by a series of alleged aggressions upon the laws of colonization; a refusal upon the part of Mexico to protect the colonial settlements from the depredations of the Indian tribes; by laws excluding citizens of the United States of the north from admission into the country; by a refusal to incorporate this province into the federal system, as provided by the constitution; and, finally, by the establishment of a central or consolidated government, and the destruction of the constitution itself. Such are the reasons assigned by the old inhabitants, with whom I have conversed, for the separation of this State from Mexico.

"The history of the events leading to the revolution, as I find it in the public documents, is this: In 1824 a convention was held by representatives from all the provinces, and a federal system and constitution adopted, by which all Mexico became a republic. Texas at that time did not contain the required population to become a State, but was provisionally united with the neighboring province of Coahuila, to form the State of Coahuila and Texas, until the latter should possess the necessary elements to form a separate State for herself. This law was understood and intended to guaranty to the latter a specific political existence as soon as she should be in a condition to exercise it.

"In 1833, the inhabitants having ascertained that their numbers were equal to most, and exceeded several of the old States, and that the resources of the country were such as to constitute the required elements for a State, they held a convention, and formed a constitution upon the principles of that of the Mexican republic. This was presented to the General Congress, with a petition to be admitted into the Union. The application was rejected, and the delegate imprisoned.

"In 1834, the constitutional Congress was dissolved by a military order of the President, Santa Anna, before the expiration of its appointed term; and in the following year a new Congress was assembled, by virtue of another military order, which is said to have been aristocratical, ecclesiastical, and central in its politics. Numerous applications were made by meetings of the citizens, and by some of the State legislatures, to restore the constitution and federal government, and protests were presented against the subversion of the laws; but they were disregarded, and in many instances the author was persecuted and imprisoned.

"The central government deposed the constitutional Vice President without trial; elected another in his place; united the senate and house of representatives in one chamber, and, thus constituted, declared itself invested with all the powers of a legitimate convention; and under this assumption it abolished the federal constitution, and established a consolidated government.

"In September, 1835, General [Martín P. de] Cos invaded the province of Texas by land, with orders to disarm the citizens, and to require an unconditional submission to the central military government, under penalty of expulsion from the country. At the same time, all the ports were declared to be in a state of blockade; and a military force having been sent to Gonzales to require from the citizens a surrender of their arms, a battle ensued, which terminated in a retreat of the Mexicans.

"The Texans assert that this resistance was not because they even *then* wished to separate from the confederacy; but, on the contrary, because they were desirous to bring back the government to the terms of the constitution of 1824."

"They therefore held a convention at San Felipe, in November, 1835, composed of fifty-six representatives from all the municipalities, in which they declared that, as Santa Anna and other military chieftains had, by force of arms, overthrown the federal institutions of Mexico, and dissolved the social compact which existed between

Texas and the other members of the confederacy, they had taken up arms against the military encroachments of military despots, and in defence of the constitution.

"This was considered as an absolute separation from Mexico, and on the 2d of March, 1836, delegates from the people from all the districts declared Texas a free, sovereign, and independent State."

In communicating this report to Congress, President Jackson, referring to the recognition of the independence, and the application of Texas to be annexed to the United States, advised that the government of the United States should maintain its "then present attitude, if not until Mexico herself, or one of the great foreign powers should recognise the independence of the new government, at least until the lapse of time or the course of events should have proved, beyond cavil or dispute, the ability of the people of that country to maintain their separate sovereignty, or to uphold the government constituted by them."

Such was the language of President Jackson. The contingencies contemplated by him have been accomplished. The independence of Texas has been acknowledged by more than one of the great foreign powers; and eight years have elapsed, and Texas, during all that time, has proved, "beyond cavil or dispute, her ability to maintain her separate sovereignty." During the greater part of that time, her proposition for annexation was pending before the government of the United States; and yet, such was the respect for the government of Mexico, and such the desire to preserve its friendship and goodwill, that, although no one could believe that the government of Mexico could reconquer Texas, and although the acquisition of Texas has been "the subject of negotiation by almost every administration for the last twenty years," the government of the United States has forborne to agree to the proposition for annexation, until, in the progress of events, new circumstances, connected with the negotiations between the governments of England and Mexico, forbade any further delay.

For further proof that the declaration of the independence of Texas was the work of the government of Mexico, and not of the government of the United States, the undersigned refers to the admission made by Mr. Rejon himself, that the revolt (as he terms it) in Texas was occasioned by the refusal of the Mexican government to approve of the constitution adopted by the people of Texas, for the purpose of becoming one of the confederated Mexican States, and by the decree abolishing slavery, and the measures adopted by the Mexican government "to compel them to comply with laws which they despised."

His excellency admits that the government of Spain first invited citizens of the United States to Texas, and that the government of Mexico renewed that invitation by tendering large grants of land. These invitations were accompanied by pledges of protection of person and property; and the Mexican government should have foreseen that natives of the United States, well informed as to what their rights were, and accustomed to a government in which just laws and good faith prevail, would resist the attempt of the Mexican government to subvert the constitutional government and laws; and it is therefore manifest, from this statement of the case, that their removal to Texas, and their declaration of independence, was the work of the government of Mexico, and not of the government of the United States, as is unjustly charged by his excellency.

The undersigned refers to these facts as conclusive, not only to disprove the calumnies against the government of the United States, which it is the purpose of his excellency Mr. Rejon to impress upon the people of Mexico, but also to show that, in forbearing to accept the annexation of Texas for so long a period, when tendered by those who alone had the right to do so, and who had achieved her independence of Mexico, and in renewing the assurance "that it is now adopted in no spirit of hostility to Mexico, and that if annexation is consummated, the United States will be prepared to adjust all questions growing out of it, including that of boundary, on the most liberal terms," his government has given the strongest proofs of a desire to preserve the relations of peace and goodwill with the government and people of Mexico; and the undersigned takes this occasion to say, that should those relations be disturbed, or should the government of Mexico fail hereafter to receive the compensation which the government of the United States, for the sake of preserving those relations, would willingly have given for a territory over which Mexico does not now, and cannot hereafter, exercise a jurisdiction, the Mexican people must charge the loss which they will thus sustain, to his excellency Mr. Rejon and the government by whose order his notes of the 31st ultimo and the 6th instant were written.

His excellency makes an elaborate comment, the purpose of which is to induce a belief that the government of the United States is about to seize upon the territory of Texas, on the ground that "it was embraced in the cession of Louisiana by France to the United States in 1803, and was improperly surrendered by the treaty of

1819." In reply to all that his excellency has said on this subject, it is sufficient to say that the United States do not seek, and never have sought, the acquisition of Texas on any such pretence; and that the undersigned made the remark which his excellency has quoted, and of which he has made a use so unfair and uncandid, in connexion with the fact that "a large portion of the territory lies in the valley of the Mississippi, and is indispensable to the defence of a distant, weak, and important frontier," as a reason why his government seeks to acquire Texas—not by seizing it under a pretence of right under the treaty of 1803, as his excellency would persuade the people of Mexico to believe; but by negotiation, first from Mexico, and now from Texas. And the undersigned cannot forbear to express his surprise and his regret that his excellency, by quoting a part, and suppressing the material part of what the undersigned had said, and using the part thus unfairly quoted for the purpose of creating an unjust and unfounded prejudice in the minds of the Mexican people against the government and southern people of the United States, has given another proof, not to be misunderstood, of his desire to foment hostilities between the two countries; for his excellency must know that the remarks of the undersigned furnish no justification for the comment made thereupon. And the purpose of suppressing the material part thereof is palpable; for at the same time that his excellency labors to impress upon the people of Mexico a belief that the undersigned had admitted that the United States were about to seize upon the territory of Texas, under the pretence of a claim under the treaty of 1803, his excellency must have known that the remarks of the undersigned did not warrant the construction which his excellency endeavored to give to them; and he also knew that the United States set up no such pretence of claim as it was the purpose of his comment to charge upon them.

His excellency Mr. Rejon also states that the people of Texas were bound to submit to the form of government adopted by the other States; and, inasmuch as they did not do so, he claims the right in Mexico to treat them as rebels, and to urge a war of extermination against them. The undersigned is by no means willing to concede the proposition of his excellency Mr. Rejon, and much less to agree to his conclusion. It must be recollected that the Spanish provinces embraced in Mexico, declared and achieved their independence of the Spanish crown, and in 1824 established a confederation of States, similar in all respects to the United States. Coahuila and Texas formed one of the confederated Mexican States, and was sovereign and independent, except so far as she had delegated to the general government a portion of her sovereign powers. She was entitled to and enjoyed her own local legislature, and was only bound to the general government according to the express terms of the constitution of 1824. When the army, therefore, destroyed that constitution, the State of Coahuila and Texas was remitted to its original sovereignty; and the constitution of 1824, which bound the States together, being destroyed, and consequently Texas, owing no allegiance to that which had no existence, was left free to choose and adopt her own form of government, as best suited to her interests. The other States had no right to force upon her a form of government of which she did not approve; and much less had the army, without consulting the will of the people, the right to do so. It follows, therefore, that as Texas never agreed to the present government of Mexico, which was erected by the army on the ruins of the constitution of 1824, the present government of Mexico, in seeking to subjugate Texas, is now, and has been from the first, the aggressor.

His excellency complains that the undersigned has been wanting in courtesy; and, to justify that complaint, alleges that he applied the term "barbarous" to the government of Mexico. If his excellency will do the undersigned the justice to reperuse the note of the 14th ultimo, he will find that the term "barbarous" was applied to the manner in which it is proposed to prosecute the war against Texas, and not to the government of Mexico. Of that war, of the manner in which it is declared Mexico will carry it on, and of the reasons assigned therefor, the undersigned forbears to speak, because he could not do justice to his own feelings, and at the same time use terms sufficiently respectful to the government of Mexico.

The undersigned renews to his excellency Mr. Rejon the assurance of his distinguished consideration. Wilson Shannon.

LS (No. 4) with Ens in DNA, RG 59 (State Department), Diplomatic Despatches, Mexico, vol. 12 (M-97:13), received 12/13; FC in DNA, RG 84 (Foreign Posts), Mexico, Despatches; CC in DNA, RG 46 (U.S. Senate), 28A-E3; CC in DNA, RG 233 (U.S. House of Representatives), 28A-E1; PC with Ens in House Document No. 19, 28th Cong., 2nd Sess., pp. 5–32; PC with Ens in *Congressional Globe*, 28th Cong., 2nd Sess., Appendix, pp. 27–34; PC with Ens in the Washington, D.C., *Daily Madisonian*, December 20, 23, and 24, 1844; PC with Ens in the Washington, D.C., *Daily National Intelligencer*, December 20, 1844, pp. 1–2; PC with Ens in the Washington, D.C., *Globe*, December 20, 1844, pp. 1–2; PC with Ens in *Niles' National Register*, vol. LXVII, no. 17 (December 28, 1844), pp. 259–265. NOTE: The enclosures are transcribed from House Document No. 19, 28th Cong., 2nd Sess.

From WILSON SHANNON

Legation of the U.S. of A.
Mexico, Nov. 12th 1844

Sir, The importance of my present Dispatch (No. 4) together with the uncertainty of its reaching Washington City in a convenient time by the mail has determined me to forward it by Benjamin E. Green Esq. whom I have appointed bearer of Dispatches. I have been induced to take this course also, because it would seem from the last advises [*sic*] from Washington city some of the Dispatches of Mr. Green as Charge de affaires had not reached that place although forwarded long since.

Gen[era]l [Duff] Green goes on the Woodbury to Galveston, by whom I have forwarded to our Charge de affaires at Texas [Andrew J. Donelson] copies of the correspondence that has taken place between this Legation and the Mexican Government in relation to Texas. I thought it was adviseable that our Cha[r]ge at Texas should be informed of what had been done here in relation to this subject.

Owing to the importance of the events transpiring here, I have detained Gen[era]l Green up to this time and am greatly indebted to him for his aid and advise. Yours with great respect, Wilson Shannon.

ALS in DNA, RG 59 (State Department), Diplomatic Despatches, Mexico, vol. 12 (M-97:13), received 12/13; CC in DNA, RG 46 (U.S. Senate), 28A-E3; CC in DNA, RG 233 (U.S. House of Representatives), 28A-E1; PC in House Document No. 19, 28th Cong., 2nd Sess., p. 4; PC in *Congressional Globe*, 28th Cong., 2nd Sess., Appendix, p. 34; PC in the Washington, D.C., *Daily National Intelligencer*, December 20, 1844, p. 2; PC in the Washington, D.C., *Globe*, December 20, 1844, p. 2; PC in the Washington, D.C., *Daily Madisonian*, December 24, 1844, p. 2; PC in *Niles' National Register*, vol. LXVII, no. 17 (December 28, 1844), p. 265.

From WILSON SHANNON, "Private"

Legation of the U.S. of A.
Mexico [City], Nov. 12, 1844

My Dear Sir, The dispatch [of today] which I forward to you by Mr. [Ben E.] Green will inform you of the state of things here. Mr. Green will give you a full history of all that has transpired and of the present state and condition of the country. The insolence of this Government is beyond indurence and if it is submit[t]ed to in one case it will only give incouragement to its repitition. I think we should take high ground with Mexico and ["let" *interlined*] her distinctly to understand that she must retract her insults and do us justice in all matters of complaint which we have against her. I am fully convinced we can do nothing with Mexico as to the settlement of any of the difficulties we have with her until we either whip her, or make her believe we will do so. So long as she thinks we will confine our complaints to diplomatic notes she will treat them with an indifference amounting to insult. I think we ought to present to Mexico an *ultimatum.* My last note [of 11/8] to Mr. [Manuel C.] Rejon may appear rather severe but I think it was called for and that a more mild note would have produced no effect, on this people. I will wait with some solicitude your further instructions. Yours with great respect, Wilson Shannon.

ALS in ScCleA; PC in Jameson, ed., *Correspondence,* p. 995.

From R[OBERT] M. HAMILTON

Consulate of the *United States*
MonteVideo, Nov[embe]r 13th 1844
Sir, I had this honor on the 18th Ult[im]o, transmitting copies of sundry Correspondence from No. 1 to No. 10 inclusive, in relation to the Capture of an armed Schooner called the Sancala, by the U.S. Ship Congress near this port, since when, having received another Communication from Brig[adie]r Gen[era]l Don Manuel Oribe, on the same subject, I forward herewith a copy & translation No. 11 and my reply thereto No. 12, also copy of statement, of remarks 13 made by the Com[mande]r of the "Sancala," to two respectable Gentlemen while on a visit to the Congress & which clearly proves the outrage practised upon the Barque "Rosalba," that of firing *purposely* into said vessel, thus endangering the lives of the Crew on board, after committing this barbarous act, the Schooner ran off to, and communicated with, the Com[mande]r of the Argentine Blockading Squadron, and then commenced Cruzing again after Fishing-Boats, during all which time, she had the Oriental flag (an illegal flag) flying, and no other; Captain [Philip F.] Voorhees, and his Officers having observed, the unjustifiable, & outrageous proceedings, of the said Schooner, and the fact, of her having communicated with the Argentine

Commodore, determined the former, to resort to immediate retaliation, in the first instance, by the Capture of the Sancala, and in the second, by ordering the Argentine Com[modor]e and the Vessels under his command to strike their colors, considering them as aiders and abettors, of the illegal acts committed by the Sancala, under an illegal flag; after which, the Commander of the Congress, on finding some Fishermen prisoners, on board the Argentine Commodore's Ship, all of whom had been captured by the "Sancala," on the same morning under the same flag, liberated the said Fishermen, as having been illegally captured, and put them on shore near this City; he also found on board the Argentine Ship some five or six American seamen who claimed his protection stating that they had been prevailed upon to enter the service when in a state of intoxication, and that the time they agreed to serve had expired, but that they were still detained on board against their will and wished to return to their native Country, and after the requisite enquiries were made by Captain Voorhees, as to the facts of the case, he liberated the said seamen, and subsequently at their own request, they were sent to Buenos Ayres, for the recovery of wages due from the Government, these men would probably have been detained in the Argentine service, so long as the war lasted, had not Captain Voorhees, paid attention to their just appeal for his protection.

I would here beg leave to introduce a few remarks in relation to the Blockade of the port of MonteVideo, by the Argentine Naval forces, as to its mode of application.

The Buenos Ayrean Government, in the first instance, resolved upon a strict and full Blockade of this port, but a modification of the same, being proposed, by the Diplomatic agents of England, France and the Brazil, to the effect, that the vessels of their respective Nations, should be boarded by their own vessels of war, and be prevented from introducing into this port, fresh & Salt provisions and all other articles Contraband of war, instead of being boarded by the Argentine Blockading forces, which proposal was finally agreed upon, by the aforementioned agents, and the Argentine Government, but on receipt of the Notification of the same, Commodore [John B.] Purvis Commander in chief of the British Naval forces, refused to comply with the terms specified, stating that H.B.M. Ships of War were not stationed in the River Plate, for the purpose of assisting the Argentine Squadron, in Blockading the port of MonteVideo; and his non-compliance was subsequently approved of, by his Government, consequently the Vessels of all Nations, coming into this port, are subject to visitation, and detention, by the Blockading forces, with the exception of those of France & Brazil, by which arrangement the latter Countries, are likely to reap an advantageous trade in the article of salted provisions, as many of their Respective vessels, after having been boarded have been allowed to pass in with a supply of this kind of provisions for the market, when at the same time, our Merchant vessels of the United States, are fired at, and detained by the Argentine Squadron; Consequently our trade is not upon a fair footing with France & Brazil; and I crave your attention to the accompanying List of French, & Brazilian vessels, which have introduced provisions, after being boarded as aforesaid, No. 14, and altho' the quantity be not great, the principle is the same.

Captain Voorhees of the Congress, after mature consideration on this subject, believed it to be his duty, in the protection of our Commercial and Neutral rights, to notify the Com[mande]r in chief of the Argentine Squadron, that "unless he boarded the vessels of all Nations, alike which traded to the port of MonteVideo, he (Captain Voorhees) would not permit the vessels of the United States to be boarded, or molested, going in, or coming out of said port," and did send a note to the Commander to that effect under date 22nd Ult[im]o, and received for answer, that the Merchant Vessels of the United States, should not be boarded, until he the Commander received instructions from his Govt. on the subject; thus matters remained until the arrival of Commodore [Daniel] Turner, in the "Raritan" Frigate, on the 30th Ult[im]o, when on the 3rd Inst. the Commodore thought it expedient to notify the Argentine Com[mande]r, that he recognised the Blockade (which had been interrupted by Captain Voorhees) and that "it would be respected by the Squadron under his Command, so long as it was respected by all other nations"; on the receipt of which note, the Argentine Com[mande]r dispatched a Circular dated the 3rd October to the surrounding Ships of War, advising that the Blockade was in force again, under the same forms, and conditions as heretofore.

The fact is Sir, that this is nothing more or less, than what is termed a "paper Blockade," as a proof of which, but a short time has elapsed, since a few Gun Boats sallied from the Harbour of MonteVideo, and drove the Blockaders from their station near the port, since when, they have not ventured nearer than seven, or eight miles of the harbour, rendering the Blockade useless, Several vessels having come in with cargoes of live cattle unmolested.

The War between the Argentine & Oriental Republic is likely to be maintained for a length of time to come, to the serious injury of our Citizens, Merchants of this City, whose outstanding debts are to a very large amount, without the slightest probability of recovering any part of the same, until the war ceases. The Oriental Govt. pressed for pecuniary resources, to sustain its garrison, after having disposed of the Customs Revenue for the years 1844 & 45 have recently sold the first six months Revenue for 1846, by which means, it will be enabled to support the Troops, the defenders of the City, for the next eight months. Gen[era]l Oribe besieges the place with about five thousand Men, and about the same number defend it; with a line of about seventy heavy Guns mounted; this market is superabundantly supplied with provisions of all descriptions (safe [*sic*] fresh Beef,) and any attempt of the enemy, to drive the Garrison to subjection under the present system of Blockade, is truly preposterous.

The Hon[ora]ble William Brent Jr., Charge d'Affair[e]s for Buenos Ayres, and family, and Commodore Turner, have arrived at Buenos Ayres. I have the honor to be Sir, With unlimited respect, Your most Obedient Servant, R.M. Hamilton, United States Consul.

LS (No. 94) with Ens in DNA, RG 59 (State Department), Consular Despatches, Montevideo, vol. 4 (M-71:4), received 2/3/1845.

From C[HARLES] J. INGERSOLL, [Representative from Pa.]

Philad[elphia,] Nov. 13, '44

Dear Sir, I see by the Newspapers your return to the seat of government, where the late Elections encourage me to expect to find soon begun a system of simple administration divested as far as practicable of all artificial and factitious contrivances. But habits, prejudices and what will be deemed vested rights will like the feudal system be hard to overcome and I think should not be too roughly handled. Mr. [John] Tyler has been very fortunate in most of his measures and Mr. [James K.] Polk will succeed to easy popularity if prudent and moderate while resolute & progressive. I perceive nothing in our domestic affairs which will not do well almost by itself. I wish to see the duties on wines and silks reduced. They are now clumsy and excessive. What public will may be in the tariff States generally it is yet rather too soon to say: but I believe the cotton [manufacturing] interest is overprotected, and that the iron is about to assume much more local independence of tariffs than it now enjoys and demands. The difficulty is not so much with manufacturers as with mechanics. One and all, or nearly so, now acknowledge that coin currency is indispensable and well nigh sufficient. Next year's reaction however will probably be felt at the custom house as much as the action of this year. I doubt whether the Tariff will ever again be a party question. There is in truth very little difference between revenue and protection.

Our foreign relations may be rendered by increase of the exports of cotton, raw and wrought, iron, coal, rice, meat, grain and other products the best pacifier of the Tariff controversy. Such arrangements as the German treaty, why can't they be extended largely?

Our party triumph I trust secures the Texas business. I was very glad to learn from Mr. [Isaac E.] Holmes [Representative from S.C.] the basis on which the Executive will present it to Congress. I have more than performed the promise left at Washington as to propagating this seed. I am reelected on that postulate and I have no doubt that as far north as the Delaware if not the Hudson public sentiment is as unanimous as it need be. I have been striving to make some impression on the northern members of Congress who proved so impracticable last Session and I have ventured to caution Mr. Speaker [John W.] Jones [Representative from Va.] as to the distribution of his power next month. My fate last winter was continual frustration and mortification. I think that no measure should be disappointed of at least committee presentation to the house for its consideration.

The party triumph is marvellous. When I was alone saved from the wreck hereabouts I felt in doubt whether to be sorry or glad. In the fine sentiment of Seneca, partibus jam fractis, nihilominus inter publicas ruinas erectum, a position which if twenty years younger I w[oul]d prefer to any other. But as we have succeeded I am easily reconcileable to the quieter honors of majority. I am very truly y[ou]rs, C.J. Ingersoll.

ALS in ScCleA. NOTE: The Latin in the penultimate sentence is a paraphrase of a passage in Seneca's *De Providentia*, II:9, which refers to the noble spectacle of Cato, after his party had been several times defeated, still standing upright amid the ruins of the commonwealth.

From W[illia]m H. Marriott

Baltimore, November 13, 1844

My Dear Sir, It gives me much pleasure to Introduce to you my friend John Kettlewell Esquire of this City, who visits Washington, and wishes to make your acquaintance.

Mr. Kettlewell is one of our most respectable Citizens, and a distinguished member of the Democratic party. He was a member of the late Democratic Convention for the nomination of President and Vice President, and the President Elect Col. [James K.] Polk, is as much, if not more indebted to him for his nomination, than to any other member of that body.

Mr. Kettlewell is better known to the members of the Democratic party here, than any other member of it—no one has greater popularity, and none knows so well their opinions and feelings. I am sure you will be much pleased with him. With regard your Friend & O[bedien]t Se[rvant,] Wm. H. Marriott.

ALS in DNA, RG 59 (State Department), Letters of Introduction to the Secretary of State, 1820–1849.

To J[ohn] Y. Mason, Secretary of the Navy

Department of State
Washington, Nov. 13, 1844

Sir: The enclosed communication [from Francis Harrison, dated 10/-21] has been submitted to the President [John Tyler], who thinks it advisable to despatch some vessel of war to the Port designated [Porto Plata, Santo Domingo] as soon as may be, if there be any that can be spared for such service. I would thank you, after perusing the letter to return it to this department. I am, Sir, very respectfully your ob[edien]t Serv[an]t, J.C. Calhoun.

LS in DNA, RG 45 (Naval Records), Letters from Federal Executive Agents, 1837–1886, 7:144 (M-517:2, frames 618–619).

From R[ICHARD] PAKENHAM

Washington, 13 November 1844

The Undersigned Her Britannick Majesty's Envoy Extraordinary and Minister Plenipotentiary, transmitted in due season to Her Majesty's Government the Note which He had the honor to receive on 23d August last, from the Hon[ora]ble John C. Calhoun, Secretary of State of the United States, in reply to that of the Undersigned of the 27th April, relative to the course pursued by [Joseph Mattison] the Commander of the United States Brig "Bainbridge" in the case of the two Individuals [Samuel S. Thomas and Joseph R. Curtis] charged with the Murder of the Captain of the English Merchant Ship "Naiad" at Gonaives in the Island of Haiti.

Her Majesty's Government, having considered with attention the statement contained in Mr. Calhoun's note, have instructed the Undersigned to make to the Government of the United States the following observations respecting the case therein referred to.

The Circumstances of the case are admitted to be peculiar, the Master of the English Vessel had by the unfairness and temerity of His own conduct brought upon Himself the fatal punishment which was inflicted upon Him. The Island of Haiti was also in a state of insurrection and anarchy, and notwithstanding the already long imprisonment of the Persons charged with the Murder, there seemed to be no present prospect of their being brought to trial. Under these circumstances Her Majesty's Government must admit that there was much to extenuate the conduct of the Commander of the "Bainbridge" in demanding their surrender to Him.

The Secretary of State also in His reply to the Representation of the Undersigned of 27th April, distinctly admits the principle asserted on the part of Her Majesty's Government that Independent States possess alone Jurisdiction over offences committed within their respective Territories.

This being the case, and as it seems moreover that no power exists in the United States of bringing to Trial in this Country Persons charged with Murder under the circumstances in which the two Individuals in question were placed, Her Majesty's Government are unwilling in the present instance to press a demand which it may be impossible for the United States to satisfy.

In notifying this forbearance in this particular case to the Government of the United States, The Undersigned is instructed at the same time to state that it is the just and fixed determination of the British Government, for the future, not to consent that officers of the

United States shall carry off, and withdraw from trial before the legal and proper Tribunals American Citizens charged with the commission of Murder, or of other offences against British Subjects.

The Undersigned takes advantage of this opportunity to renew to Mr. Calhoun the assurance of His high Consideration. R. Pakenham.

LS in DNA, RG 59 (State Department), Notes from Foreign Legations, Great Britain, vol. 22 (M-50:22).

From JOHN W. SERJONE[?], "(Confidential)"

New York [City] 13 Nov. 1844
Esteemed Sir, Excuse a Stranger from addressing You a few lines; the recent Election and the Calculations of the presumed Victors, are no ways backward of making there [*sic*] views known, to there friends political; the writer of this met a leader [*Interpolation:* "The Tam(m)any author Joshua L. Pell an att(orne)y of little moment who made the above declaration"] of Tam[m]any, who was overjoy'd in the success of *Mr. Polk* to the *Presidency* remarked "If Georgia, Main[e], Missi[ssi]ppi went right they would[,"] as he express[e]d himself *Tumble John C. Calhoun* "to the *Devil*." But says I to him, suppose You do not have sufficient number of Votes without South Carolina[?] We will promise him all untill we get the Vote then clear him out. Thus far does Tam[m]any feel for the Hon. J.C. Calhoun. I presume your honour is as well, if not better acquainted, with those Virtuous Tam[m]any men. I beg I may be Excused I write this through pure motives of friendship to your honour. I am Ever truly Your friend & Ob[edien]t Humble Ser[van]t, John W. Serjone[?], A Friend of the Hon. J.C. Calhoun who will visit Washington for the first time this winter.

ALS in ScCleA.

From [NATHANIEL] B[EVERLEY] TUCKER, "Private and confidential"

Williamsburg Va., Nov. 13, 1844
I beg that Mr. Calhoun will pardon the liberty I am taking. The importance of the subject of this letter must plead my excuse, as there is no other person to whom I could so properly present it.

When the Missouri question was agitating the Union, I was an inhabitant of that State, holding a high judicial office, in intimate communication with the first men of the country, and exercising, in my own person and thro' them, an extensive influence among the people. Having a large and fixed interest there, and animated by an ardent zeal for the rights of the States, and especially of the south, it was not less my inclination than my duty to study the subject, to endeavour to acquaint the people with their rights, to rouse them to resist the purposed wrong, and to bear an active part in the controversy. Of that affair then I may say "pars fui." I did much of what was done, & was privy to all that was done by others, and fully understood the reasonings which prevailed with the people to assert and maintain their rights.

They were these.

By the Treaty of 1803, France, in ceding the Country to the United States had stipulated that the inhabitants should be admitted into the Union *on the same footing* with the other States, whenever they should be in condition for admission. Hence it was denied that Congress had the right to refuse admission to Missouri, because of a feature in her Constitution which was found in the Constitutions of nearly half the existing States.

Moreover it was contended that all the other States had come into the Union as free[,] sovereign and independent States; that Missouri had a right to be admitted on the same footing, which could not be, if any power out of Missouri should presume to dictate to her in the highest act of Sovereignty—the formation of her own constitution.

The idea that Missouri was already a Sovereign State was at first startling to men whose habits of thinking had been influenced by the tameness manifested by other new States. But it was corroborated by an appeal to the Constitution, which was a compact freely entered into by States fully established in all the rights and functions of Sovereignty ["that," *canceled*]. In inviting Missouri to make a Constitution for herself and to apply for admission into the Union, Congress had virtually and most effectually established her in a state of complete independence; because in no other state could she exercise that freedom of will necessary to a binding consent to the obligations imposed by the Constitution of the United States. Had not the treaty then stipulated for her admission *on the same footing with the other States*, it would have made no difference. It was enough that she was to be admitted, as she could not possibly be admitted on any other footing.

It is a striking instance of the authority of precedent, not only over the judgment, but over the feelings and conduct of men, that when the claim of Missouri for admission was first laid before Congress, these ideas were all overlooked; the thing passed *sub silentio*; and she was rejected without debate, and almost without thought. Her delegate [John Scott] wrote home that there was reason to believe that Congress would admit no more slave States, and this letter was published without comment in a paper edited by Col. [Thomas H.] Benton. A fortnight passed away before a word appeared to assert the right of Missouri to decide that matter for herself. The reason was that they who afterwards led in the contest were in an obscure corner of the State attending a distant court. As soon as they reached St. Louis they drew their pens on behalf of Missouri, and strove to enlighten the minds of the people, to rouse their spirit, to check the influx of Yankeys, and to awaken the whole South to their common interest in the controversy. How they succeeded you know. An article embodying the ideas set forth above was published by myself, and is believed to have exercised a decisive influence on the minds of the People of Missouri. I enclosed a copy of it to Mr. [Henry] Clay, to whom I was then a stranger, and he did me the honour to write me a long letter expressive of his approbation of my views. I afterwards had the satisfaction to find that they were adopted by our Southern friends, who saw that the very fundamentals of the Constitution were involved in the controversy, and acting together as one man, in defence of the rights of the South and the Sovereignty of the States, drove the spoilers from their prey.

Meanwhile Missouri had organized her government, and was administering it under her own laws. Her competency to do this was made a question before me by certain factionists. It was fully discussed by the whole bar, and decided to the satisfaction of the profession generally, that she was and of right ought to be, and, from the necessity of the case must continue to be a Sovereign State & *until* Congress should admit her into the Union would be no otherwise connected with the U.S. than N[orth] Carolina was connected with the other States until she adopted the constitution. The correctness of this opinion no one has ever presumed to question, tho' many are, to this day interested to do so. Much property was then sacrificed under Executions issued in the name of the State of Missouri, and not, as before in that of the U.S. which are utterly void if that decision was wrong.

I have made this statement with a view to proposing to Mr. Calhoun the consideration of this question. Assuming that the whole of the Country between the Rio del Norte and the Mississippi was embraced in the cession made by France to the U.S. wherein does the situation of Texas now differ from that of Missouri then? Is Texas an independent State? So was Missouri. Is it to be said that in 1819 The U.S. ceded Texas to Spain, in derogation of the rights of the people of Texas, and in disregard of the plighted faith of the U.S. to France? What is this plea but an attempt to take advantage of their own wrong? If the U.S. were bound to admit the people of Texas into the Union, they could not free themselves from this obligation by their own act. They wrongfully and faithlessly surrendered Texas to a foreign despot. The people of Texas shake off his yoke, and come again to the U.S. demanding the long deferred fulfilment of their pledge to France. Can any argument be framed to justify them in refusing this demand?

This view of the subject is new, but not more so than was the same view when presented for the solution of the Missouri question. It satisfied the people then. Why not now? I have, of late, presented it to very intelligent and devoted partisans of Mr. Clay, who admit that they can see no answer to the argument. I offer it to Mr. Calhoun that if he think favourably of it it may be used for what it is worth by those who have to manage this important question.

But it may not be enough that Mr. Clay and others of his school have said that Texas is part of Louisiana. Is there any other proof? There is, ample and precise proof in the French bureau of foreign affairs. About 1762, just before the cession of Louisiana by France to Spain the Rio del Norte was established as the boundary by treaty. The subsequent cession made that treaty of no consequence, and it was forgotten. But mean time a copy had been furnished to the vice-regal government of Mexico, where Branch Archer told me, in 1835, it had been seen by many persons of his acquaintance during the connexion between Texas and Mexico. But Jos[eph] M. White, about the same time assured me that a *copy* of *the article* had been *furnished him* by the *French Minister* of foreign affairs.

Now when France ceded to the U.S. "by the same boundaries by which Spain had ceded to her" (these are the words) Spain having ceded to France "by the same boundaries by which France had at first ceded to Spain," France came under an obligation to furnish any evidence in her power to show what those boundaries were. She has it. It ought to have been demanded then. The very words show the existence of some known boundary, and France, if properly called upon, is bound to produce, and will produce the treaty of boundary.

But the Texan debt? It is properly the debt of the U.S. incurred by the Texans in defending themselves from dangers to which the bad faith of the U.S. had exposed them. It was as much the duty of ["Texas to d" *canceled*] the U.S. to defend Texas as Florida, and she has the same right to reimbursement of any expense incurred because of the default of the U.S. as the people of Florida.

But what does Texas want but to have the debt secured? Let Texas be admitted to the Union, and the Texas creditor will ask no better security than a pledge of the nett revenue of the ports of Texas to the payment of the debt. Will this take a cent from the people of the U.S.? Certainly not.

Knowing these things, soon after the battle of San Jacinto and the recognition of Texas by the U.S. I purchased lands and sent slaves there, nothing doubting the final reannexation. Were Mr. Clay, whose expressed opinions on this matter influenced me and so many others, now President of the U.S. and I should present a memorial demanding the assent of the U.S. to the application of Texas for admission, what answer could he make me?

I have said that these thoughts are offered, to be used for what they are worth, by those to whom it belongs to adjust this important interest. But I have another object. My acquaintance with the subject, my deep interest in it, my knowledge of individuals in Texas, and the knowledge of me by many there from Missouri whom I never saw, seem to make it my duty to offer myself for a mission to Texas. Not now. At Mr. [John] Tyler's hands I would not receive it. As his minister I could have no weight. A private letter from Mr. [James K.] Polk expressing his approbation of my person and views would be far more efficacious ["than" *canceled*] for all purposes of usefulness, than any credentials Mr. Tyler could give. I do but offer this suggestion to Mr. Calhoun. If he approves of it, and the ideas set forth above, he will act upon it. If not, he will take no notice of this letter, and this, like other attempts to serve my country, will come to nothing. Mr. Calhoun will know how to sympathise with one whose honourable ambition is condemned to that fate. He will not rank in the [*partial word canceled*] despicable class of office-hunters one who sought none, when his most intimate friend [Abel P. Upshur] was Secretary of State, and the Presidential chair was filled by one [John Tyler] he had helped to place there.

It would be folly to deny that in this matter I am not influenced by my own large interest in Texas. But it should be remembered that while this enhances my desire for justice to that country, it would decide me to leave the management of her interests to others, if, on full reflection, I did not feel assured of my ability, as well as my disposition to advance the common interest both of Texas and the U.S. It is clearly best for me that the negotiation should be placed in the most competent hands.

I do not presume to dictate the use Mr. Calhoun shall make of the ideas set forth in this letter. He will cast them from his mind, and me from his memory; or use both as he shall think best for the public good. With Mr. Polk I have no acquaintance, and I cannot even claim the merit of a partisan. In the late election I did not even vote. I am a States Right Man. No more—No less. My admiration of Mr. Clay could not reconcile me to his open renunciation of principles, of which he [*mutilation*] has sometimes seemed to think favourably, & I never have brought myself to support the [Democratic] authors of the [anti-Nullification] Proclamation and force bill or their adherents.

Retaining these sentiments, it is almost of course, that I cherish for Mr. Calhoun a very high respect, and am his obed[ien]t Serv[an]t, B. Tucker.

ALS in ScCleA; PEx in Boucher and Brooks, eds., *Correspondence*, pp. 258–262.

From HENRY A. WISE

Legation of the U. States
Rio de Janeiro, Nov[embe]r 13th 1844
Sir, My last despatch notified you of my letter of the 30th ult: to [Ernesto F. França] the Minister of Foreign Affairs, respecting the new rate of duties upon goods &c. *imported* into Brazil *prior* to the 11th inst. and *despatched* from the Custom house *after* that date. The inclosed copies contain Mr. França's reply, dated the 4th inst., and my answer dated the 8th inst. To the latter clause of my last, respecting a modification of their new Tariff, suggested by me, I beg to call your particular attention. Such a clause in their Tariff regulations, it strikes me, would essentially favor the trade of the U. States; and it might conduce to some successful arrangement, if the Department will take up the new Tariff of Brazil, examine its provisions, and give me some definite instructions on the whole subject. Our trade in flour is not injuriously affected, but it is certainly the policy of the U. States to obtain, by some modification or movement, an increase of exports to Brazil, to make up for the balance of trade now existing

against them with this country. It is true that difference is partly diminished by the profits of navigation in our favor, but those profits from their nature do not tend directly to diminish the rates of exchange against us. We, by all means, should make the effort to introduce here more of our manufactures, provisions &c. &c.

I cannot conjecture what will be the answer to the suggestion which I have ventured already to make.

I inclose also a copy of my letter to the Minister of Foreign Affairs respecting the claim of Mr. [Joseph] Ray. Every sort of excuse has been given for returning no answers to my frequent communications, oral & written, respecting our claims. The Minister was sick—the Council of State had not assembled—they would be notified—but still weeks & weeks elapse without any other than a verbal reply in the case of the [ship] John S. Bryan, that the Executive would have to wait for the appropriation for payment in that case by the Legislature. Thus all kinds of business is delayed in the public offices of this Empire. And daily we hear the rumor that Mr. França is to retire from the Office of Foreign Affairs, and a change of the Minister will leave the business to commence de novo. So it has gone on for years & years, until good claims are stale & so seriously impaired, that now, perhaps, they will never be paid. The President [John Tyler] in his Annual Message to Congress, dated Dec[embe]r 6th 1842, said: "The Empire of Brazil has not been altogether exempt from those convulsions which so constantly afflict the neighboring republics. Disturbances which recently broke out are, however, now understood to be quieted. But these occurrences, by threatening the stability of the Govts. or by causing incessant & violent changes in them, or in the persons who administer them, tend greatly to retard provisions for losses and injuries suffered by individual subjects or citizens of other States. The Govt. of the U. States will feel it to be its duty, however, to consent to no delay, not unavoidable, in making satisfaction for wrongs and injuries sustained by its own citizens. Many years having in some cases elapsed, *a decisive & effectual course of proceeding will be demanded of the respective Govts. against whom claims have been preferred.*"

Notwithstanding this message, no decisive and effectual course of proceeding has been authorized in respect to claims upon Brazil. From conjecture, founded on the only data in the office of this Legation, those claims amount to not less than half a million of dollars. I have proposed a Convention. What more shall I do in case there be, on the part of Brazil, continued silence and delay?

Within the last few days I have received from the Department of State a box containing the following vols. of books: American Archives, fourth series, vol. 4th 1775–1776, and id. vol. 5th 1776–Senate Journal 3d Sess. 27th Cong: 1842–1843–House Journal 27th Cong. 3d Sess. 1842–1843–Senate Documents 1st, 2d, 3d & 4th vols. 3d Sess. 27th Cong. 1842, 1843–Reports of Committees, 1st, 2d, 3d & 4th vols. 3d Sess. 27th Cong. 1842, 1843–Executive Documents, 3d Sess. 27th Cong. vol. 1st, 2d, 3d, 4th, 5th, 6th, 7th, & 8th. By my receipt heretofore transmitted, the Department will see what books are wanting or missing in this office.

I have this day drawn on Messrs. Baring Brothers & Co. for the sum of £212.9.4d, worth here $1000.00 cts. Spanish Dollars. The bill was drawn in favor of Maxwell, Wright & Co., and I will soon send my account in full for outfit, salary & contingencies, stated up to the 16th day of this current month, when the 3d quarter of my accounts will expire.

We have heard nothing certain from Monte Video lately, but the rumor is that the blockading squadron having admitted English, French & Brazilian vessels with the understanding that they were not to take in contraband articles, Capt[ai]n [Philip F.] Voorhe[e]s notified the Buenos Ayrean Commander that he was no party to such understanding and would not consent to a partial blockade. That, if French, English & Brazilian or any other merchant vessels were admitted, those from the U. States should be allowed to enter. And, insisting upon & enforcing this point, the U. States Merchantmen were admitted and the blockade was consequently broken up. The rumor is, also, that the blockading squadron having fired at a boat of the frigate Congress with the U. States flag hoisted, whilst fishing, Capt[ai]n Voorhe[e]s fired in return two of his guns at the vessel aggressing. A letter from Mr. [Harvey M.] Watterson to me, dated Oct[obe]r 24th, says that there is no more prospect of a termination of that war in the Plata than when he first set his foot on the shores of S. America. He adds "it is a most savage struggle and conducted in a most savage manner," and no one can form a correct opinion as to what the result will be. Mr. [William] Brent [Jr.] had not then arrived [at Buenos Aires]. The Corvette Boston is now here. With the highest respect & esteem, I have the honor to be, Sir, Your ob[edien]t Servant, Henry A. Wise.

ALS (No. 8) with Ens in DNA, RG 59 (State Department), Diplomatic Despatches, Brazil, vol. 13 (M-121:15), received 1/11/1845; FC in DNA, RG 84 (Foreign Posts), Brazil, Despatches, vol. 11.

From ———

New York [City] 13d Nov. 1844
Sir, As it is now assertained[?] that Mr. [Henry] Clay can not be our next President, You certainly can now be elected, if the States which are known to be in your favour, will cast their Votes for you & the Whig States will of course do it, in case your friends will give their Votes for Mr. [Theodore] Frelinghu[y]sen for Vice President. Or if your States will Vote for you this will prevent Mr. [James K.] Polk[']s election & will carry it into the House [of Representatives] & there of course the Whig States will vote for you. I am Sir Very Respectfully Y[ou]r ob[edient] S[ervant].

ALU in ScCleA. Note: An AEU by Calhoun reads "Anonymous. A base attempt to seduce me to defeat the will of the people in their choice of Chief Magistrate."

To W[illia]m C. Brown, [Boston]

Washington, 14th Nov[embe]r 1844
Dear Sir, I have received your note [of 10/31] enclosing an article from the Christian ["Advocate" *canceled and* "Citizen" *interlined*], headed John C. Calhoun, and Written by the Rev[eren]d Charles T. Torrey as you state. The Rev[eren]d Author states; that "three years since, he (John C. Calhoun) sold another man's wife for a harlot. She was the wife of his Coachman; a beautiful and pious girl; a member of the methodist church. The purchaser was a planter in Alabama: the price $1400. Some months after the sale, the poor husband having been sent into the upper part of South Carolina, with a coach, for a member of Mr. Calhoun's white family, took the opportunity to flee. He went to Alabama, sought & found his injured wife, & fled in the night on foot. After weeks of hunger and toil they reached the upper part of Maryland. The wife a delicate woman was taken sick and died. Three days the sor[row]ing man wept over her remains. At last he buried her, with his hands by the river side, then toiled onwards towards Canada. I saw him some months ["afterwards" *canceled*] ago, a sad, gloomy, heart broken man."
You have been taught, you say, to look on me as a man of great talents & pure character, and ask me "are the above charges true? If

not true litterally, are they true in substance? or are they totally untrue?["]

Believing, ["that" *canceled*] your motive for making these enquiries, ["to" *canceled and then interlined*] originate in friendly feelings and a desire to know the truth, I will answer you. They, then, are not only not true, either litterally or in substance, but are totally untrue, and without a shaddow of foundation; and have been fabricated by some artful runaway[?] to attrack sympathy or acquire distinction, or with some one else for ["a" *interlined*] still baser purpose. My character, as a master is, I trust, as unimpeachable, as ["I hope" *interlined*] it is in all the other relations of life. I regard my relation to those, who belong to me, in the double aspect of master & guardian, and am as careful to discharge the duties appertaining to each, as I am those, which appertain to the numerous other relations in which I am placed.

How far the Rev[eren]d Author stands justified before God & man, for ["fo"(?) *canceled*] publishing the base & unfounded charges he has made against me, or ["for" *interlined*] violating the laws of the land in perpetrating the act for which he is imprisoned, I ["am" *canceled*] leave it to others to decide. With respect yours & &c, J.C. Calhoun.

[P.S.] If I am ["cor" *canceled*] right as to the motives which induced you to address me on the subject, you will of course you will [*sic*] take steps to have this published in the journal through which the slander was propagated. I will thank you, if you will forward the paper containing it.

ALS (retained copy) in ScCleA; PC in the *Christian Citizen,* vol. I, no. 51 (December 21, 1844); slightly variant PC in *The Liberator,* vol. 15, no. 1 (January 3, 1845), p. 4; PC in Jameson, ed., *Correspondence,* pp. 627–629. NOTE: An AEU by Calhoun on the ms. reads: "A draft of a letter to W.C. Brown in reply to the false charges published in the Christian ["Advocate" *canceled*] Citizen." The *Christian Citizen* of December 21, 1844, denounced the story they had previously published as an "entire fiction" and published Brown's letter of October 31 to Calhoun and Calhoun's reply of November 14 with the advice that "we would respectfully exhort our anti-slavery friends to be chary of their credence to all the harrowing narratives that are related by fugitives from slavery."

From R[ichard] K. Call, Tallahassee, [Fla. Territory], 11/14. Call acknowledges receipt of copies of letters and papers submitted to the State Department in defense of Charles S. Sibley against charges made by Call. "The Indictments prefer[r]ed against me by the District Att[orne]y [Sibley], will be disposed of during the first week in December, after which I will proceed to lay before you conclusive proof of the charges made by me against this officer." ALS in DNA, RG 59 (State Department), Applications and Recommendations, 1837–1845, Sibley (M-687:30, frames 301–302).

CIRCULAR to U.S. Consuls

Department of State
Washington, Nov[embe]r 14, 1844

Sir, I subjoin a copy of a letter [of 10/9] addressed to the Department by Mr. E[dward] G.W. Butler, of Louisiana, who states, that many of the Sugar planters of that State are desirous of obtaining specimens of the Sugar cane raised in foreign Countries.

If you can conveniently comply with the wishes of these Gentlemen I will thank you to do so. Mr. Butler designates the manner in which shipments may be made, and he will, of course, be expected to defray all expenses attending such shipments. I am Sir &c, J.C. Calhoun.

FC in DNA, RG 59 (State Department), Consular Instructions, 12:104–105; PC in DNA, RG 59 (State Department), Circulars of the Department of State, 1:96. NOTE: Butler's letter was appended to the above circular and sent to U.S. Consuls "at Canton, St. Thomas, Santa Cruz, Batavia, Manilla, Teneriffe, Guayama, Mayaguez, St. Johns, Ponce, Cardenas, Baracoa, St. Jago, Matanzas, Havana, Malaga, Cayenne, Guadeloupe, Antigua, Barbadoes, Kingston Ja[maica], Turks Island, Nassau, Demerara, Bermuda, Calcutta, Singapore, Brazilian ports & the Islands in the Pacific."

From EDWARD EVERETT

London, 14 November 1844

Sir, I transmit herewith a copy of a note addressed by me to the Earl of Aberdeen, in obedience to the instructions contained in your despatch Nro. 101, acknowledging the kindness and hospitality manifested to Mr. [Caleb] Cushing [U.S. Commissioner to China] and his suite, and to Commodore [Foxhall A.] Parker and the Officers of the Brandywine, by Sir George Arthur, Sir Robert Oliver, and the other British Authorities at Bombay and Poonah and elsewhere, throughout the progress of Mr. Cushing to his destination.

The trust expressed in your despatch on behalf of the President that these good offices of the British Authorities would, when an opportunity presented itself, be reciprocated by the Officers in the Service of the United States, has already been justified by the event. The last overland mail from the east brings intelligence, that on occasion of some recent outrage attempted or menaced by the populace at Canton against the foreigners there, and particularly the Americans and English, recourse was had to [Capt. Isaac McKeever] the Commander of the St. Louis for protection, which, in the absence of any British vessel of war on that Station, was effectually rendered by that Officer. This service was amply acknowledged in the printed accounts and letters from China; and though it is with extreme reluctance, on all occasions, that any thing creditable to the United States is noticed by the London press, the friendly conduct of the Commander of the St. Louis in this instance was duly mentioned in all the Journals.

Having made this remark, justice requires that I should add, that I do not ascribe the unfriendly spirit of the press towards the United States, to a corresponding feeling on the part of any very large portion of the English people. I have not perceived any indications of such a feeling during my residence in the Country, although my opportunities for observing it, had it existed, have certainly been considerable. As far as manifestations of good will go, on the part of public assemblies of every description, the opposite inference might safely be drawn.

The unfriendly tone of the press, I am inclined to think, is mainly prompted by those who have suffered by their investments in American Stocks. Great bitterness of feeling is very naturally felt by individuals, and they are numerous, of this class. Many of them have by these investments lost all the earnings of active life and the fund on which they relied for their support in old age. That this feeling should find vent in the public papers is natural. In addition to this an opinion has been formed here, that nothing is so likely to lead the States to redeem their Credit, as strong and unanimous condemnations of default on this side of the water; and the more indiscriminate these censures, the more likely are they, in the opinion of their authors, to produce the desired effect.

These I think though certainly not the only are the chief sources of the growing bitterness toward the United States, which has characterized the press, since my residence in this Country. I do not as I have already said believe that it reflects, in this respect, the feelings of the mass of the enlightened community; though I cannot conceal from myself the fact, that extreme discredit has fallen upon us in consequence of the failure of so many of the States and especially Pennsylvania to keep faith with their creditors.

The material injury which has thus accrued to the Country is, in all essential respects, that of a general bankruptcy. At a time when capital is so abundant that the three per cent Stocks of England are above par, it has been made impossible to obtain a loan on any American basis, at any rate of interest or with any prospect of gain however well founded. Projects of the most interesting character for developing the vast mineral wealth of the United States are offered in vain to the co-operation of the European Capitalist. The public works undertaken by the authority of the States are, from the same cause, left in a condition of hopeless incompleteness. Every proof which the general prosperity of the Country and the restoration of its Commercial activity affords of the unimpaired exuberance of its resources, serves but to point with new keenness the reproaches against the insolvent States, as shewing (in the European apprehension) the want not of means but of will.

I have allowed myself to be led by the natural association of ideas into this train of remark, not because the subject matter is directly within the province of the General Government, but because I am aware of the interest taken by the President and yourself, in a subject so closely connected with the prosperity and good name of the Country. Any state of things which, besides being in itself morally discreditable, produces the effect of cutting off from the public service and from the private wants of the Country, all the benefits which would accrue from the free application to both of the surplus capital of Europe, must be regarded as a calamity of no ordinary magnitude; an evil so enormous, that the discovery and application of an adequate remedy is a subject second to no other within the range of patriotic American statesmanship. I am, Sir, with high respect, Your obedient Servant, Edward Everett.

Transmitted with despatch Nro. 209;
Mr. Everett, to the Earl of Aberdeen, 14th November, 1844.

LS (No. 209) with En in DNA, RG 59 (State Department), Diplomatic Despatches, Great Britain, vol. 53 (M-30:49), received 12/12; FC in DNA, RG 84 (Foreign Posts), Great Britain, Despatches, 9:50–56; FC in MHi, Edward Everett Papers, 50:320–325 (published microfilm, reel 23, frames 434–436).

From JOHN H. HOWARD

Columbus, Geo[rgia,] Nov[embe]r 14th/44

Allow me to congratulate you upon our triumph over Federalists & Federalism. I think it a greater triumph than that of 1800 since there were more inducements in the way of bribery & rewards offered to the people to seduce them from their honesty than was held out at that day. Mr. [James K.] Polk now has it in his power to bring the people back to a proper view ["the" *altered to* "of"] the limited powers of our government if he will only pursue a strait forward undeviating course. Although the issues were not fully unfolded by the whigs in every section, yet they were sufficiently known & understood by the people, for us to be satisfied that we have won the election upon the popularity of the strict construction principle, and therefore it is not now a difficult task to retain power in the hands of the democracy by a *rigid* adherence to the principles which gave us the majority. I hope you will accept the offer which we presume will be made to you, to retain your place in the cabinet, and if you should do so, I can but believe that the President will receive such council, as will result beneficially to the country. Some of the Northern democracy is as sound as I could wish it, but a portion of the Northern section regard men, & office more than measures, another portion are unsound upon some of the great measures which have been agitated. It is the duty of *all* the sound democracy to come up earnestly to the task of confining the action of congress strictly within constitutional limits, and thus learn, to the unlearned of the country the true principles of our government. Great good may be done ["by" *altered to* "in"] four years by an *able* and *just* administration, of the govt., upon our construction of the powers granted to ["the genl govt." *canceled and* "it" *interlined*]. The South and the *sound* democracy of the north will be disappointed if the Tariff should not at once be brought to a strictly revenue standard, with discriminations for revenue only. The democracy may not be able to effect this, because of the disagreement of a whig Senate but the Representatives should at any rate make the modification, and the bill for that purpose should be as near perfect, as the best & wisest counsellors can frame it.

If we do all that we can do earnestly & honestly & the whigs prevent us from carrying into effect our measures, upon them rests the responsibility & upon them I think will fall the denunciation of the people, at least the Southern People. I do hope the democrats will make no appropriations which are not indispensible to an economical

administration, and that they will vote against all ["which may be"
interlined] either extravagant or of doubtful propriety. The *commencement* of Mr. Polk[']s administration is the proper era to *begin
again* and confine the action of congress to its constitutional power.
You will have great responsibility resting upon you personally as you
will share much of the credit or the blame of the measures recommended. If this Administration should compel a return to our own
["& old" *interlined*] principles you I think will be considered as the
author of the beneficial change and will enjoy ["almost" *canceled*]
as much glory as if you were the President. The first message is the
important document and if it should be full upon all important points,
and correct too, firmness afterwards is the only requisite for perfect
success during the four years. Texas I should suppose would be considered as necessary now as it was during the canvass and that therefore another treaty will be presented to the Senate provided it can
now be made with the Texan Government. The whigs say "now that
the election is over we shall hear nothing more of Texas." I hope
they will be disappointed ["&" *canceled*] by another treaty, proving
to the world, that annexation was a subject of greater importance
than a mere electioneering ["hobby" *interlined*] as it was charged to
be. You will I hope excuse me for all this freedom as I should not
have troubled you with my opinions, had I not been requested to
write in behalf of an applicant for the Post office in this place, and
for the collectorship of Ap[p]alachicola [Fla. Territory]. Mr. Guerry
of this place desires the appointment of Postmaster, and if Mr. Biddle
[*sic*; G.W.E. Bedell] is to be removed I should be pleased to see him
appointed. Mr. Toney[?] wishes to be appointed collector in place
of Mr. [Hiram] Nourse of Ap[p]alachicola. Both Guerry & Toney
are competent and if removals are to be made I should be pleased,
to see them appointed to the places they desire. But I told these
gentlemen that I was opposed to removals unless for incompetency
or remissness of duty or some cause more just than for opinion[']s
sake, and that although Biddle is a violent & active whig and received
his place for partizan services in 1840, yet he is a good accommodating
postmaster. Nourse I know nothing about, but that my application
in their behalf must be upon condition that these gentlemen were to
be removed & that I would not apply for their removal. I have long
believed, that our republican system would tumble into anarchy &
finally into monarchy when it became the settled practice to yield to
the doctrine that "To the victors belong the spoils." If this doctrine
should generally obtain & find its way into our system as an approved

political axiom, a nation of freemen will soon be made subservient to a band of aspiring office seekers. If I were the President I should remove no man who discharged his public duties with fidelity. And I should rejoice to see a democratic administration set the example of retaining all the *good* officers, without regard to their politics, or the clamors of those ["who" *interlined*] want their places. Then we should have a government for the People and not one for Placemen. I repeat that you must excuse me for obtruding my opinions, as I should not have expressed them but for the application of these gentlemen, that I should write. I told them that I must express my opinion *against* removals but if the usual course was resorted to, then I would advise their appointments, and they accepted the condition I imposed. I am very respectfully & Sincerely, your friend, John H. Howard.

ALS in ScCleA. NOTE: An AEU by Calhoun reads "Col. Howard[,] Mr. Young[?] desires the place of Post Master at Columbus & Mr. Toney of Collector at Appalachicola."

From J[OHN] Y. MASON, [Secretary of the Navy]

Navy Department, November 14, 1844
Sir, I have the honor to acknowledge the receipt of your letter of the 13th inst. and to state in reply that orders were given several days since by Commodore [David] Conner for one of the vessels of his squadron to proceed to the island of Hayti.

Commodore Conner has also directed the Commander of the U.S. Brig Somers [James T. Gerry] to go to Cape Haytien, to enquire into the outrage committed on the Master of the Schooner Baltimore, of Philadelphia. The Somers will touch at other ports in the island.

Agreeably to your request, the letter from Francis Harrison Esq[ui]r[e] is herewith returned. I am very respectfully Your Obed[ien]t Serv[an]t, J.Y. Mason.

LS in DNA, RG 59 (State Department), Miscellaneous Letters (M-179:106, frame 36); FC in DNA, RG 45 (Naval Records), Letters Sent by the Secretary of the Navy to the President and Executive Agencies, 1821–1886, 5:54 (M-472:3, frame 69).

To SILAS M. STILWELL, U.S. Marshal, [New York City]

Department of State
Washington, 14 Nov[embe]r 1844

Sir, Your note of the 11th inst. with its enclosure has been received, and in reply to it I have to request that you would immediately wait upon the District Attorney of the U. States, Mr. [Ogden] Hoffman and obtain his instructions in regard to the two witnesses [in an illegal slave trading case] sent on by the Consul at Rio de Janeiro [George W. Gordon]. Copies of the Depositions &c forwarded by the said Consul to this Department, will, in a few days, be transmitted to Mr. Hoffman with instructions upon the subject. In the mean time you will keep the witnesses in custody. I am &c, J.C. Calhoun.

FC in DNA, RG 59 (State Department), Domestic Letters, 35:26 (M-40:33).

From [NATHANIEL] B[EVERLEY] TUCKER

Williamsburg [Va.,] Nov. 14, 1844

My young friend and pupil Mr. [Archibald C.] Peachy has been so good as to charge himself with the delivery of this and the accompanying letter [from me to you, dated 11/13]. I have no right to expect that my bare recommendation of Mr. P[eachy] would be at all regarded by Mr. Calhoun. Yet I cannot permit myself to doubt that my testimony will have all due weight, when I speak of him as one I have known almost from infancy, as a ripe and good scholar, of various[,] extensive and accurate knowledge, and as a gentleman, by birth, education, and manners, above all reproach. Brought up a States-Right man of the straitest sect, and bound to Virginia by a lineage which makes the names of his ancestors a part of her history, his devotion to her honour, her interests, and her peculiar institutions is unsurpassed. In all things in which Mr. Calhoun may have occasion to engage the services of such a man, he will find Mr. Peachy farther suited to his purpose by habits of sobriety, steadiness, order and application, with a total exemption from those vices which often so sadly deform the characters of our most brilliant young men. I have conversed with him unreservedly on the subject of the accompanying letter. Should the ideas contained in it seem to Mr. Calhoun worthy of a second thought, and of farther elucidation, Mr. P[eachy] will be at no loss to supply any thing I may have omitted, or to explain whatever may be obscure.

In conclusion, I beg leave to add, that, should the suggestion I have made be acted upon, I should wish to be accompanied by Mr. P[eachy]. My success might depend on the cooperation of one whose kind and courteous demeanour cannot fail to make friends, and whose ability might be relied on to supply what might be deficient in myself. I beg leave again to assure Mr. Calhoun of the very high respect of B. Tucker.

ALS in ScCleA. NOTE: Tucker endorsed the cover of this letter: "Politeness of A.C. Peachy esq."

From Jesse E. Dow, Washington, 11/15. He notifies Calhoun that "Gen." Vincent G. Barney is seeking appointment to be the U.S. Marshal of the Northern District of N.Y. Barney is "a democrat" and a "gentleman of high standing and correct principles" whose appointment would gratify the "unflinching democracy of the Empire State." ALS in DNA, RG 59 (State Department), Applications and Recommendations, 1837–1845, Barney (M-687:1, frames 708–709).

From Geo[rge] W[illia]m Gordon

Consulate of the United States
Rio de Janeiro, 15th Nov[embe]r 1844
Sir, I take the liberty to enclose herewith a Translation of Articles 20th and 21st of the Decree of the Government of Brazil No. 376, dated 12th August 1844.

Article 20th authorises the Government of Brazil to impose upon the Goods of any foreign nation which may put a heavier duty upon Brazilian Merchandise than on Goods of a like nature from any other country, a differential duty equal to such additional duty.

Article 21st provides that a like differential duty "*shall be collected*" upon the Merchandise of those nations which levy or require greater duties upon Goods imported into their ports in Brazilian Vessels, than are collected upon Goods imported in their own Vessels.

As the operation of these provisions depends upon the character and execution of the revenue laws of other nations, a correct construction and right understanding of our own laws in regard to duties on goods imported into the United States in Brazilian vessels, becomes highly important to American Merchants having intercourse with this country, and especially to those resident therein.

It is with the object of obtaining information on this subject, that may be considered official, and for the purpose of presenting to your attention the provisions of the Decree of this Government, just referred to, that I now address the Department.

By the 11th Section of the Tariff Law of the United States of August 30th 1842, it is enacted, that an addition of 10 per centum shall be made to the several rates of duties by this act imposed, in respect to all goods, wares and merchandise, which shall be imported in ships or vessels not of the United States—*Provided*, that these additional duties shall not apply to goods, wares and merchandise which shall be imported in ships or vessels not of the United States, entitled by treaty, or by any act or acts of Congress to equal privileges in regard to duties with American Vessels.

According to the 9th Section of the same Law, Coffee is exempt from duty, *"when imported in American Vessels* from the place of its growth or production.["]

There is not, at present, any Treaty of Commercial reciprocity existing between the United States and Brazil; and I am not aware that there exists any Act of Congress, or that the President has issued any Proclamation, as he is authorized by the Act of 7th January 1824, to do under certain circumstances, suspending the assessment and collection of the discriminating duty of 10 per centum imposed as above, on goods imported into the United States in Brazilian Vessels.

If therefore it be the fact that there is no such Treaty, Act of Congress or Proclamation of the President existing, are not the provisions of the Act of 1842 imposing discriminating duties of 10 per centum on goods, wares and merchandise imported in Foreign Vessels, in force in relation to all goods imported into the United States in Brazilian Vessels?

And if this be the case, does not the Decree of this Government under consideration, authorize and require the assessment and collection of the differential duty on all goods imported into Brazil in American Vessels?

Information on these subjects, particularly in regard to what duties would be required on goods imported into the United States in Brazilian Vessels, has been asked of me by merchants of this City. In responding to the requests, I have limited myself to pointing out the laws on the subject, and stating orally my individual views. In this manner I have represented that although the United States' Government may have the right by existing laws to exact discriminating duties on goods imported in Brazilian Vessels, authority, on the other hand, is vested in the President to suspend and discontinue by proclamation the collection of such duties when, and for so long time, as such exemption is, and shall continue to be, reciprocal. And that, although I knew that the opinion prevailed among merchants here, that such discriminating duties would be collected on Coffee and other merchandise if imported into the United States in Brazilian Vessels, and that they had, from prudential considerations on this point, declined in several, certainly two cases within my knowledge, to charter Brazilian Vessels, when offered, for the purpose of transporting merchandise to the United States, I was still not aware of any case in which such additional duty had been exacted; and referring to the well known liberal policy of our Government, should a case occur for the operation of the law, I presented as a reasonable doubt, whether such discretionary duties would be enforced by the United States so long as Brazil omitted to collect additional duties on goods imported into her ports in American Vessels.

And from this view of the subject I have argued against the propriety and right of this Government to assess and collect any differential duties on merchandise imported into Brazil in American Vessels by virtue of this Decree; and contended that as no instance of the collection by the United States of any discriminating duty on merchandise imported in Brazilian Vessels, was known or had been cited, no ground existed for the collection of any differential duty on the part of Brazil; for in fact there existed no "inequality" to be "counteracted" by such a measure. And that it is upon the existence of such "inequality" alone that these provisions of the Decree, are founded, and that under no other circumstances can they rightfully be enforced.

And I have also advised that should this Government, at any time, exact on goods imported into its ports in American vessels, the differential duty provided by the Decree of August 12th, that such duty be paid under protest, until the action or decision of the Government of the United States in relation to discriminating duties on goods imported in Brazilian vessels, shall be obtained.

This Decree became Law, and went into effect on the 11th of the present month ["and" *canceled.*] The language of the 21st Article is *commandatory.* As yet, however, this Government have not enforced the provisions of this Article in regard to merchandise imported in American Vessels; and I do not apprehend that, in their enactment, they were aimed in any degree at American Commerce. And it is, moreover, most probable that they will not be thus enforced, unless it should be ascertained by this Government, that our laws imposing discriminating duties on goods imported in foreign Vessels have been, or apprehended by them that, should a case occur for their application, they would be enforced on goods imported into the United States in Brazilian Vessels.

But under all the circumstances that exist, if I may be allowed, I would most respectfully submit, whether it would not be advisable, for the purpose of rendering our merchants secure in regard to any future exactions by this Government under the provisions of this Decree, and to relieve them from all apprehensions and solicitude on the subject, that an Act of Congress be obtained, or the necessary Proclamation issued, suspending, so long as such suspension shall be reciprocal, discriminating duties on merchandise ["shall be reciprocal" *canceled*] imported into the United States in Brazilian Vessels. The language of the Decree of this Government is conditional, and it would appear, therefore, that such suspension on the part of the United States, would suspend also the differential duty imposed by said Decree on merchandise imported into Brazil in American Vessels.

It is unnecessary for me to make any remarks to show that the collection of these discriminating, or as they are here termed, differential duties by both Nations, would be greatly to the disadvantage of American interests; the commerce ["of" *canceled*] between the two countries being almost wholly carried on in American Vessels. I have the honor to be, Sir, with great respect, Your Obedient Servant, Geo. Wm. Gordon, Consul of the United States.

ALS (No. 13) in DNA, RG 59 (State Department), Consular Despatches, Rio de Janeiro, vol. 7 (T-172:8), received 1/11/1845. Note: A Clerk's EU indicates that this despatch was referred to the Secretary of the Treasury.

From WILLIAM R. KING

Legation of the United States
Paris, 15th November 1844

Sir, I have the honor to acknowledge the receipt, since my last communication, of your Despatches Nos. 9, 10, and 11. The first which came last, having been received but a few days ago, has been already referred to in my despatch of the 6th of last month. I shall not fail to expose and to press the able considerations which it presents, on all suitable occasions and in all proper quarters. The Texas question seems to awaken little or no interest here at present, nor can I perceive that it has assumed any new aspects. Its fate is considered to be very much involved in the Presidential contest, the result of which may revive that solicitude which is now permitted to slumber. In my conversations here, I have ever sought to treat it as a national rather than a political or party question, dependent for its solution upon personal or temporary considerations. In taking this elevated and, as I flatter myself, patriotic view of the subject, events will soon prove whether I am right, or whether I have over estimated the sensibility of the great mass of the American people to considerations of national dignity and power. Perhaps the recent difficulties between the French minister [Baron Isidore Alleye de Cyprey] and ["the" *canceled*] Mexico, have rendered this government ["less" *canceled*] more insensible to the supposed rights or wrongs of the Mexican Republic. Be this as it may, as long as the *action* of France is not hostile, or does not lend itself to the unfriendly designs of England towards the United States, we have no right to complain of her sentiments with regard to Texian independence, however much we may wish that they were more politic for herself, and more favorable to us. The avowed policy of the King of the French [Louis Philippe], is peace, and non-intervention as the best means of securing peace; therefore, even had I not his declarations and those of his minister, I would not easily apprehend that so wise and wary a monarch would permit himself to be en tangled in the meshes of a knotty question, and one altogether profitless, ["at"(?) *canceled*] with the certainty of alienating the American people, the "natural allies" of France, by such wanton interference. Upon his favorite topics of peace and non-intervention, His Majesty dwelt emphatically in a late interview, when he expressed sentiments and opinions which though not uttered with reference to the United States, Mexico and Texas, were strikingly applicable to the existing relations of the three republics.

The map of Texas from the Topographical Bureau, which accompanied the copy of your Despatch [of 9/10?] to Mr. [Wilson] Shannon is of opportune interest.

In accordance with your instructions I have purchased a copy of the work upon Oregon and California by Mr. Duflot de Morfras [*sic*], for the Library of the Department of State, and it shall be transmitted by the first eligible opportunity. Immediately upon the receipt of the letters of felicitation of the President to the King of the French upon the birth of the son of the Duke de Nemours, and of the daughter of the Prince de Joinville, I requested an audience for the delivery of the originals to His Majesty, which, I suppose will be shortly accorded. I am, very respectfully your obedient servant, William R. King.

LS (No. 6) in DNA, RG 59 (State Department), Diplomatic Despatches, France, vol. 30 (M-34:33), received 12/23. NOTE: Eugène Duflot de Mofras's "work upon Oregon and California" was *Exploration du territoire de l'Orégon, des Californies et de la mer Vermeille, exécutée pendant les années 1840, 1841 et 1842* (Paris: A. Bertrand, 1844).

From Hen[ry] C. Murphy, [Representative from N.Y.], Brooklyn, 11/15. "A few days since I requested of you passports for two of my Constituents, J. Sullivan Thorne M.D. & Philip R. Underhill—they came to hand signed by Mr. [Richard K.] C[r]allé Act[in]g Sec[re]-t[ar]y of State. My Friends are anxious on account of your well known name to have your autograph to their passports. Again as the description of their persons is written in two different styles of writing they fear it may cause them some difficulty with the French Police. To quiet their uneasiness will you be kind enough to have new passports made out for them and enclosed to my address—if you desire it the others will be returned to the Department." ALS in DNA, RG 59 (State Department), Passport Applications, 1795–1905, vol. 33, nos. 2624–2625 (M-1372:15).

To JOHN S. PALMER and Others, [Pineville, S.C.]

Washington, 15th Nov[embe]r 1844

Gentlemen, I greatly regret, that it will not be in my power to attend the dinner to be given the 21st Inst., at Black Oak, by the Parishes of St. Johns Berk[e]ley, St. Stephens & St. James St. [*sic*] Santee to their Representative in Congress, the Hon. I[saac] E. Holmes. My publick engagements forbid.

Were it in my power, I assure you, that it would have afforded me much pleasure to meet you and those you represent with your worthy & faithful Representative on the occasion.

For the kind terms, in which you have tendered the invitation, I return you my sincere acknowledgement. Never did a publick man owe a heavier debt of gratitude to his Constituents, than I do to the people of South Carolina. So uniform, steady and warm have been their confidence & support during the long period I have served them, and the trying scenes through which I have passed, that were I to live a thousand years, I could make no adequate return. With great respect, I am & &, J.C. Calhoun.

ALS in ScSpW; slightly variant PC in the Charleston, S.C., *Mercury*, December 4, 1844, p. 2. NOTE: The other addressees include C.B. Snowden, A[rnold] J. Harvey, H.F. Porcher and Sam[ue]l J. "Porcher" [*sic*; Palmer].

From F[RANCIS] W. PICKENS

Charleston, 15 Nov. 1844

My dear Sir, In a conversation just now with [John A. Stuart] the Editor of the Mercury he insists that I write you to send me the outlines of just such a report as you think the Legislature ought to pass, and I will take it & write it off as confidential. I merely write as he requests it. You know I doubted the policy of saying anything which might be construed by your opponents into a desire on the part of your immediate friends to take control in advance of the Adm[inist]r[ation] &c, which would embarrass you. I think your position a beautiful & a powerful one—*masterly inactivity.* If [James K.] Polk moves ag[ain]st you in the organization of the Cabinet then we know what is to come, & if for you (*as he will do*) then [Thomas H.] Benton & [Silas] Wright fire at you through the Adm[inist]r[ation], & it gives us all the Southern Whigs in the future. I think it due to So[uth] Ca[rolina] to have a quiet modest session of the Legislature— it will increase her moral weight abroad, & keep us all perfectly united. But if you think we ought to move then if you will drop the outlines it shall be attended to *confidentially.*

Stuart seems to think you are for decided action and for doing something at any rate. I did not so understand you.

We had great enthusiasm here on the news of the Election. I go up in the morning. *Write me* to *Columbia* by the 23d inst.

My love to Cousin F[loride Colhoun Calhoun]. Yours truly, F.W. Pickens.

P.S. I have written [Thomas] Ritchie fully & freely. I will see what he is at. F.W.P.

ALS in ScCleA.

"Memorial" of John Shiels, Washington, 11/15. Shiels, who claims to have been in the U.S. Navy for 36 years, says he was a gunner's mate in 1841 when he was detained in a Naval hospital on a "frivolous" charge for four months. After that, he was discharged as a seaman and paid reduced wages as such. He asks Calhoun's aid in obtaining "such relief as he is justly entitled to." (A Clerk's EU refers this to the Secretary of the Navy [John Y. Mason]. An AEI by Mason reads: "This man is insane.") ADS in ScCleA.

From J. Irwin Sterett, Williamsport, Md., 11/15. Sterett asks that Calhoun grant him employment as a Clerk in the State Department. Although Sterett exercises the most strict economy, his present salary of $250 per year is not adequate for the support of a young wife and an aged mother. "Knowing your reputation as a Statesman, Philanthropist and gentleman, I have been induced to believe you would interest yourself in my behalf." ALS in DNA, RG 59 (State Department), Applications and Recommendations, 1837–1845, Sterett (M-687:31, frames 261–263).

From DAN[IE]L B. TALLMADGE

New York [City,] Nov. 15th 1844

Dear Sir, I will call to your mind that I had the honour of a formal introduction to you last summer, at Washington, by my friend *Senator* [Robert J.] *Walker* [of Miss.]. A similarity of opinions with yourself, as to men and measures is my apology for now addressing you[.]

I have, from the first agitation of the question, been a decided advocate for the annexation of Te[x]as[.] I gave a most cordial and hearty support to the election of Mr. [James K.] Polk[.]

I have examined the official returns for the city of New York and if there be no falicy in my mode of examination, I prove most conclusively, that over *seven hundred of Mr.* [*Martin*] *Van Buren[']s friends* in this city, who voted for [the Democratic candidate for Governor, Silas] Wright, not only abandoned Polk, *but actually voted for* [Henry] *Clay.* The same result will be shewn, and in the same ratio, when we get the official returns for the *State*[.] This matter is becomeing a subject of News paper discussion[.]

The *Utica Observer* ventured to express a doubt upon the good faith with which Van Buren[']s friends supported Polk, and the Evening Post of last evening made a most savage reply[.] I thereupon, to day, sent to the Utica Observer my speculations in regard to this city, to embody in his reply to the Post[.]

I requested him to forward you a copy[.]

For the *present* I desire not to come openly in collision with the friends of Mr. Van Buren, and therefore wish my name, as connected with this discussion, not to be made public[.] I have this day sent to the President [John Tyler] my calculations and argument to prove the bad faith of Mr. Van Buren[']s friends in the late election[.]

I doubt not but that the official returns of the State will shew that five thousand of Mr. Van Buren[']s friends who voted for Wright, also voted for Clay—many also of his friends staid from the polls[.] In my opinion they intended to defeat Mr. Polk[']s election[.]

Herewith I send you my proofs of the treachery of Mr. Van Buren[']s friends in this city[.] With great respect yours &c, Danl. B. Tallmadge.

[Appended]

The result of my calculations upon the vote of this city, satisfies me, that at least *seven hundred of the principal Van Buren democrats* of this city, *abandoned Polk* and *voted for Clay*[.]

Now to my proofs[.]

Wright has 29220 votes
Polk has— 28388
Difference 832 votes

Wright then has 832 votes more than Polk. This difference be-twene the vote for Wright and Polk, does not arise from any number of voters casting their votes for governor *only*, without voteing for presidential electors; because, the ag[g]regate vote for presidential electors, and the ag[g]regate vote for governor, are the same e.g.

Presidential votes	*Governor* votes
Polk—28388	Wright—29220
Clay—26571	Fillmore—25834
Birney— 98	55054
55057	

This comparison shews that *every* elector that voted for governor, *also voted for presidential electors;* and that Wright[']s excess of 832 votes over Polk, did not arise from any omission by voters, to cast a presidential ballot[.] Of the 832 votes, Mr. Wright could not have received over 100 from the whigs[.]

You must bear in mind that in voteing in this State, we had but *two* ballots, one for *Presidential electors*, and the other for *State officers*—on the State ballot are printed the names of the candidates for Governor, Lieut[enant] Governor, Senators, members of Assembly, &c &c &c[.] A whig, therefore, intending to vote for Wright for governor, and the residue of his own whig ticket, would, from his own whig ballot, strike out the name of [Millard] Fillmore and substitute

Wright[']s in its place[.]   The difference then, betwene Wright[']s
vote for Governor, and his associate [Addison] Gardiner for Lieu-
t[enant] Governor, will shew the number of *whig votes* cast for
Wright e.g.

  Wright[']s vote is 29220
  Gardiner[']s   29117
  Difference   103

But if we compare Fillmore[']s vote for governor, with his associate [Samuel J.] Wilkin[']s as Lieut[enant] Governor, it will indicate a less whig vote cast for Wright e.g.

  Wilkin[']s vote   25875
  Fillmore   25834
                      41

I have however assumed the difference betwene Wright and his
Lieut[enant] Governor, as the whig vote cast for Wright.   It is not
to be supposed that at such an exciting election as we have just
passed through, any considerable number of *whigs* seperated from
their party on so important a candidate as governor; and more especially that they did so to support the father of the sub treasury and
the boosom friend of Mr. Van Buren[.]   Beyond all question the
candidate for Lieut[enant] Governor, of each party, received the *fair
party vote*[.]

Compareing then, the ["candidate" *canceled*] vote of either candidate for Governor, with the vote of his own associate for Lieu-
t[enant] Governor, it is manifest that the whig vote cast for Wright
did not excede 100.   It follows then, that Mr. Wright[']s excess over
Polk beyond the 100 whig votes given him (say 700) is the vote of
Democrats given to Wright—and *not merely withheld from Polk,
but cast for Clay*[.]

If we take Lieut[enant] Governor Wilkin[']s vote, as exhibiting
the true whig vote, and deduct it from Clay[']s vote, it shews the
same result—about seven hundred votes for Clay beyond the whig
vote e.g.

  Clay['s] vote   26571
  Wilkin[']s vote 25875
                     696

Thus it is apparent that about seven hundred of Van Buren[']s
friends ["who voted for Wright" *interlined*] *abandoned our candidate Polk* and *voted for Clay*!

ALS with En in ScCleA.   NOTE: An AEU by Calhoun reads: "Talmage[,]
Shows that many of the Democrats of N[ew] York City voted for Mr. Clay."

Enclosed is an undated and unidentified clipping giving the breakdown of New York City votes for President, Governor, and Lt. Governor by wards.

From H[ENRY] WHEATON, "Private"

Paris, 15 Nov. 1844

My dear Sir, I have used the discretion reposed in me by your official leave of absence [from Berlin] by protracting my stay here somewhat longer than I had intended. But as our affairs in Germany have suffered no injury from my absence, & as I have had an opportunity here of explaining, with the aid of your despatches, our policy in respect to the affairs of Mexico & Texas, in quarters where it was important that it should be correctly understood, I doubt not you will entirely approve of the course I have adopted. I shall, however, soon return to my post, & shall be ready to execute your further instructions with zeal, industry, & perseverance, & with whatever ability I may possess—should you still continue in office, as I have no doubt you will.

I trust the new Prussian minister [to the U.S., Friedrich von Gerolt] will be instructed to explain to you the views of his Govt. in respect to the Zollverein treaty, & I cannot help indulging the hope that the Arrangement may still be carried into effect, either in that shape or some other, as there can be no doubt that the Prussian cabinet, acting in the name of the associated states, will be disposed to ratify if we do so.

When the Treaty of extradition, & the minor conventions relating to the droit d'aubaine are completed, I shall have completely gleaned the Prussian field, & I think the public interests will best be promoted by my transfer to some other field of action. I hope you will not think me importunate if I again suggest how very important it is to me, on every account, to be informed, as soon as ["soon" *canceled*] as [*sic*] possible, what is to be my future destination. I know of no other post likely to be soon vacant, except Vienna, ["which would suit me" *canceled*]—& I trust you may be able to arrange it for me in case of Mr. Jennifer's [*sic; Daniel Jenifer*] asking for his recall, as he doubtless will do if Mr. [James K.] Polk is elected. I flatter myself the Senate would readily confirm my nomination to any diplomatic post, & cannot believe there would be any serious difficulty as to the outfit. I am at present in a very uncomfortable situation, as I cannot remove my family from here until I know to what post I am to be assigned.

I am sure you will readily excuse me for reverting to a subject so interesting to me, especially as I ask nothing but what I firmly believe will promote the public interest. The warm & constant friendship with which you have so long honored me induces me to open myself with a degree of confidence on which I could not venture with any other man. You will know how to appreciate this frankness. I believe I have acquired some advantages from my ["my" *canceled*] long experience in this line of public life over other men, my superiors in other respects, & from the knowledge I may be supposed to have acquired of men & things in Europe from my long residence in this part of the world, without, I trust, having abated the ardour of patriotism & zeal for my Country's interests. What I ask is that my attainments & aptitudes, whatever they are, may be utilized for the public service in the sphere of greatest importance to which the confidence of Government may call me. I am, my dear Sir, ever truly your faithful friend, H. Wheaton.

ALS in ScCleA.

NOVEMBER 16–30, 1844

◫

While James Edward, his fourth son, settled in at the University of Virginia, Secretary of State Calhoun settled down to the relentless business of his office. There was the inevitable flow of claimants, applicants, and foreign ministers. There was the necessary preparation for the session of Congress soon to commence. President Tyler's friend, Henry A. Wise, the American Minister in Brazil, was busy seeking to break up and punish the activities of American merchantmen who were engaging in the outlawed slave trade between Africa and Brazil. This required a prosecutorial follow-up in the United States.

Most pressing and most difficult was the need to comprehend and capitalize upon the strange and alien contours of Mexican politics, about which there were always conflicting reports and rumors and in which sudden changes were the norm.

Within a more limited and less violent context, American politics were just as volatile. There was now a President-elect, James K. Polk, who kept his own counsel, at least as far as Calhoun was concerned. The legislature was meeting in South Carolina, giving an opportunity for untold and sometimes embarrassing and divisive maneuvering. Calhoun's correspondents kept him informed of the situation in many states, each of which was a part of the bigger picture. The bigger picture seemed to indicate clearly the dissolution, after less than two decades of life, of that strange entity, the Whig Party. As to the victorious Democratic party—divided between the "friends" of Polk, Calhoun, Van Buren, Benton, and others, the picture was rather less clear.

◫

To A[NGEL] CALDERON DE LA BARCA

Department of State
Washington, 16th November, 1844

Sir: I have the honor to acknowledge the receipt of your note of the 30th ultimo, respecting the Queen's confirmation of the appointment of Vice-Consuls, by the Spanish Consul General, for the ports of Wilmington, North Carolina; Portsmouth, New Hampshire; and Savannah, in Georgia—and to inform you that, as soon as the commissions of these officers shall be communicated for the President's inspection, and for record in this Department, the usual exequaturs will be granted. In the mean time the Secretary of the Treasury [George M. Bibb] will be informed of the fact, and requested to extend to the persons named, all proper facilities.

I feel highly gratified at the contents of your note of the 29th ultimo, in reference to the prompt manner in which His Excellency General [Leopoldo] O'Donnell has met the views of this Government, in the case referred to; but some difficulties are presented as to the form in which his communication should appear; and in order to their removal, I have concluded to await your arrival at the seat of Government, when I may have the pleasure of a personal interview. I take this opportunity to renew to you assurances of my distinguished consideration. J.C. Calhoun.

FC in DNA, RG 59 (State Department), Notes to Foreign Legations, Spain, 6:114–115 (M-99:85).

From EDWARD EVERETT

London, 16 November 1844

Sir, I observe in one of the morning papers a movement of some interest in reference to the duty on Cotton imported into England; vizt. the adoption of a memorial to the Lords of the Treasury by the Chamber of Commerce at Manchester setting forth the impolicy of the duty and recommending its repeal. I shall endeavor to procure a copy of the memorial in a separate form, to be transmitted with this despatch for your information.

Although the duty amounts only to five sixteenths of a penny per pound, the Chamber of Commerce considers this as equal to ten per Cent, taking three pence halfpenny (seven cents) as the price at New

Orleans of the quality of Cotton most largely used in England. They add that the American manufacturer, by contiguity to the Cotton growing region, lower freight, saving in time, and economy in other charges, possesses a farther advantage over the English manufacturer of at least seven sixteenths of a penny per pound, making in the whole 24 per Centum, which "on all the American Cotton used in Great Britain will amount, according to last year's consumption, to upwards of a million and a half sterling, clearly establishing advantages in competition against this Country, which neither ought to be nor ever can be permanently sustained."

The memorial proceeds to state, that "since the close of the great European war of 1815, the tendency to enter into the pacific pursuits of trade has been evident on the part of every civilized nation; but the extension of the Cotton trade in the United States of America is the most extraordinary; as the spinners of that Country are now consumers of Cotton to a greater extent than were the British in 1815: therefore this rapid progress has become evidence to which your memorialists refer, that foreign competition may arise to a ruinous extent."

There is no doubt, I presume, that a vigorous effort will be made at the approaching session of Parliament to obtain a reduction of the duty on Cotton; but the success of the attempt will depend on nearly the same considerations as those to which I have invited your attention, in my despatch Nro. 207 [of 11/11], in reference to the repeal of the duty on tobacco. I am, Sir, with great respect, Your obedient Servant, Edward Everett.

LS (No. 211) in DNA, RG 59 (State Department), Diplomatic Despatches, Great Britain, vol. 53 (M-30:49), received 12/12; FC in DNA, RG 84 (Foreign Posts), Great Britain, Despatches, 9:62–64; FC in MHi, Edward Everett Papers, 50:332–334 (published microfilm, reel 23, frames 440–441).

To OGDEN HOFFMAN, U.S. Dist[rict] Attorney, [New York City]

Department of State
Washington, 16 Nov[embe]r 1844

Sir, I enclose you herewith copies of a communication [of 9/18] received at this Department from [George W. Gordon] the U.S. Consul at Rio de Janeiro, and of the affidavits accompanying it. They may

313

be necessary in case of the arrest of [Jason L.] Pendleton should he return to New York.

I have referred Mr. Stillwell [*sic;* Silas M. Stilwell] the Marshal of the District to you for instructions as to the proper course to be pursued in order to secure the attendance of the witnesses [to illegal slave trading] now in his custody. I am &c, J.C. Calhoun.

FC in DNA, RG 59 (State Department), Domestic Letters, 35:19 (M-40:33).

From R[ober]t Tyler

[Philadelphia,] Nov[embe]r 17th [1844]
My Dear Sir, The writer of the enclosed letter is a warm political friend of yours. He is a worthy man. He stands in the lead of the German Entent[?] in N. York. His wishes expressed in the within letter should be gratified if practicable.

I congratulate you on the result of the late Canvass. Very tr[ul]y Y[ou]r fr[ien]d & ob[edien]t S[ervan]t, Rt. Tyler.

ALS in DNA, RG 59 (State Department), Applications and Recommendations, 1845–1853, Albers (M-873:1, frames 417–418). NOTE: Exactly what letter was enclosed is not certain, but from the file in which Tyler's letter is located, it is clear that his letter refers to the candidacy of John H. Albers for appointment as U.S. Consul at Elberfeld, Rhenish Prussia. The "warm political friend of Calhoun" may have been John A. Stemmler who was also an endorser of Albers.

From Francis Wharton

Philadelphia, November 17th 1844
My dear Sir, Paradoxical as it may appear to the old leaders, Pennsylvania would have been lost to Mr. [James K.] Polk had it not been for the energetic action of the anti-tariff republicans. A very false game was played in the tariff districts. The tariff of 1842 was admitted to be perfect, & a question of fact was raised as to who passed it. That question was determined against us, as was very natural, in a majority of instances, and had the true state of the case been known better, the State would have been gone. In the northern tier of counties, however—where, by the way, ["the" *canceled*] several of the most influential men, who were brought up at the feet of old

Judge [David?] Scott, profess to be your friends—we gained largely, because we met the issue fairly. Your late letter [of 10/21 to J(ohn) A. Stuart], as published in the Mercury, went a great way to give to your friends, & to those who agree with you in opinion, energy in support of the republican nominations.

The whig party is breaking up with a rapidity that justifies your prediction that when Mr. [Henry] Clay was gone the party would dissolve. The great question is, where is it to go? The native American Coalition has been fatal to both of the uniting elements; and the leading Whigs here, Mr. [John] Sergeant, particularly, are backing out of nativeism with all quickness. But it is the impression of many of the most discerning politicians that a coalition between Whiggery & [Thomas H.] Bentonism is by no means improbable. Whether you remain in the cabinet or return to the Senate, it is clear Mr. Benton will not brook your superior genius when supported by the more intimate relations you will bear to the administration. The Bentonites here say that Mr. Benton will not follow your lead. I suspect that Texas will be used again, as it has been already, to be ["held out to the country as" *interlined*] the wedge which has produced the split which, in fact, has arisen from the political & personal jealousy of the chief intriguer. I only trust that the Texas negotiations will be conducted in such a way as to rob the mal-contents of much of their supposed strength.

Would it be agre[e]able to you for me to prepare an article for the Dem[ocratic] Review on the Texas treaty, as a diplomatic effort? I think the literary & diplomatic character of the correspondence has not been yet examined, and it seems to me that the unjust attacks on one or two of your letters require notice. If it should please you that such should be given, and you can send me the papers connected with the treaty, I will be much honoured in executing the Commission. My professional engagements are now rapidly increasing, but whatever I have, whether of time or labour, I most cheerfully put at your feet. If there are any other ["litery" *canceled*] literary points in which I can be of use to you, I hope you will give me your commands.

Let me ask you, in your goodness, to let me know what is the situation of Judge [Edward] King's nomination [to the Supreme Court] before the senate, & whether it is now so far out of the president[']s hands as to make its withdrawal out of the question. Judge King is a man of consummate ability, & ["of" *canceled*] a lawyer of remarkable accomplishments, especially on the equity side. He is, by our peculiar system, the chancellor of the eastern district of Pa., as well as the presiding judge of an important common law court. Do let me press his claims upon your attention, as I am sure I can safely do, as he is already nominated, & only waits confirmation. He has saved us lately, by his manly & bold conduct during our late melancholy disturbances, from much danger; and I cannot but believe that he will be an ornament to the Supreme bench. It is a matter of great importance to the bar here that a satisfactory judge should fill the vacant seat, and I am sure you excuse my importunity. Judge King is with us in politics.

Let me know whether I may be of service to you about the Texas correspondence, as I will be able, before the Jan[uar]y term sets in, to put it to press. Yours most truly, Francis Wharton.

ALS in ScCleA; PC in Boucher and Brooks, eds., *Correspondence*, pp. 262–264.

From Levi Woodbury, [Senator from N.H.], Portsmouth, N.H., 11/17. He introduces John T. Tasker, who desires a position as teacher of Mathematics in the Navy. ALS offered for sale as item M-2143 in *The Collector* (November, 1948), p. 251.

To George M. Bibb, Secretary of the Treasury, 11/18. "I have the honor to refer to you a letter [*not found*] which was addressed to me under date the 15th instant by Mr. Richard S. Coxe, complaining in behalf of himself and others interested, of the delay in receiving from Mexico the money paid by that Government under the convention of the 30th of January 1843." Coxe erroneously supposes that the payments are managed by the State Department. Calhoun believes that the U.S. agent at Mexico is under instructions from the Treasury Department. Calhoun encloses to Bibb a translation of a note of 9/2 from [Manuel C. Rejon,] the Mexican Minister for Foreign Affairs to [Wilson] Shannon, affirming that the payments due from Mexico on 4/30 and 7/30 have been made. FC in DNA, RG 59 (State Department), Domestic Letters, 35:20–21 (M-40:33).

From A[NDREW] J. DONELSON, *"Private"*

Houston, Texas, Nov[embe]r 18[t]h 1844

D[ea]r Sir, I refer you to the enclosed letter to the President [John Tyler], having nothing yet official to communicate to the Department. Since writing the enclosed I learn that there is some possibility that the Secretary of State [of Texas, Anson Jones] may have gone to Galvezton by the coast route. But there is no doubt of President [Samuel] Houston's being now on his way to Washington [Texas] and that he will reach there about the time I will.

Gen[era]l Duff Green was looked for at Galvezton when I left. The prisoners who have been liberated from the castle of Perote report that they saw no preparation for the threatened invasion: and they are of opinion that none is seriously contemplated by Gen[era]l Santa Anna.

The further I advance into this country the stronger is the evidence of the anxiety of the people for incorporation into our union. Much is said about the activity of the British & French parties to defeat our policy. But I shall not trouble you with the probabilities in relation to such overtures until I present my credentials, and have an interview with the President who will doubtless disclose to me all that has passed between this and other Governments.

My attention is directed to the Topographical and Geographical features of the count[r]y, and the effect they will have upon the population. My object will be to be prepared to anticipate the action of the people in the alternative of Col. [James K.] Polk's defeat, and to judge as correctly as I can of the policy which is best for us in that event. Whether it is worth the effort to make another trial for annexation in case of Mr. [Henry] Clay's election will be a grave question. So strong is the attachment of the great body of the Texans to our Union, that I am not sure they might not be induced to stand the hazards of another war with Mexico, rather than take independence with a condition imposed by Great Britain against annexation at any future day.

President Houston has been on the frontier this fall and has concluded Treaties I learn with several of the Indian tribes. No one has spoken of difficulties growing out of the acts of the Indians within our limits: and I therefore take it for granted that the occasion for the requisitions authorised conditionally by my instructions will not ["arise" *interlined*], or rather, has not, arisen.

You shall hear from me fully and constantly as soon as I have an interview with the President. Y[ou]rs truly and respectfully, A.J. Donelson.

[Enclosure]
A[ndrew] J. Donelson to President John Tyler, "Private"

Houston Texas, Nov[embe]r 18[t]h 1844

D[ea]r Sir, Thinking that you would not be unwilling to hear from me, as I approach the seat of Government of Texas, even before I have any thing official to communicate, I take the liberty of addressing you a few lines from this place. The want of communication from Galvezton to the interior compelled me to wait there a week: and now after my arrival here I find no direct conveyance to Washington [Texas]. The earliest mode will be that of the mail wagon which it is said will depart tomorrow; and upon which I may place my baggage, going on horseback myself. No public inconvenience however, results from the tardiness of my progress, in as much as President Houston is yet absent, and has been for several weeks, from Washington: and so also has been the Secretary of State [Anson Jones]. President Houston will probably be at Washington about the time that I reach it.

It was my hope, when I left home, to have been able to communicate something, before the meeting of our Congress, in relation to the views of this Government on the subject of annexation; but, from the causes mentioned this will be impossible. From present appearances I shall not be regularly accreditted before the 25[t]h of this month; and the Department therefore cannot be apprized of the effect of my presence at this Government for some weeks after this letter will have reached you.

From the observations, I have already made, of the expectations of the people of Texas in regard to the future course of their Government, no fears should be entertained of the fate of the annexation question, if the elections now decided in the United States are favorable to the Democratic candidate. The people of Texas desire annexation with such unanimity, that the Government, if so disposed, can scarcely thwart their will. At Galvezton and some other commercial points where the merchants have opened a direct trade with Europe there is some effort to reconcile the country to the idea that the seperate existence of the Republic is preferable to Union with the United States, but this will be vain, if reasonable assurances are made that our people have sanctioned the policy of annexation. The hardy spirits here that are familiar with the dangers of the position— that intend to follow the pursuits of agriculture; and that desire the blessings of equal laws for their posterity—will cling to the hope of protection from our flag until it is apparent that its withdrawal is the result of a settled determination to extend no further "our area of freedom."

You might be led to suppose from the opinions avowed by Gen[era]l Terrill [sic; George W. Terrell], recently attorney General for the Republic, and now minister to France: and also from the similar ones which will be expressed by Mr. Riley [sic; James Reily] the newly appointed minister to our Government, that I bespeak too much for the people of Texas when I say that the object dearest to their hearts is annexation to the United States: and that the support of it will overrule any combination that may be formed against it. My explanation of these apparently opposite convictions is that they indicate only the policy which may be adopted in case the hope of annexation is precluded by the elections in the United States and by the action of our Government thereupon. In that event aspiring men here will contend for the lead in such alternative measures as are necessary to secure independence to the Republic: and as these measures necessarily look to foreign aid it is but natural that the front ground in projects for their execution should be already occupied. But the order of position in the policy of the Republic, depend upon it, will be this—first, annexation to the United States—second, independence and peace with Mexico—third, if Mexico perseveres in her present attitude, *war*, and a further extension of Texan territory so as to take in Mexican provinces sufficient to cripple Mexico forever.

But I forebear to speculate on the probable consequences to result from the failure of the United States to give to these brave and hardy people the boon they have so long asked. I will defer the task until the necessity arises, which I trust will never be. Allow me, however, to congratulate you upon the assurance which may be safely made that your country will soon be almost unanimous in thanking you for your patriotic exertions to obtain this valuable addition to our Territory; and the equally certain one, that if it shall have been lost, those instrumental in the fatal error will not be able to drag you to the level of their shortsighted and condemned policy.

The more I see of Texas, the more satisfied am I of its paramount importance to all the sections of our union. It is necessary not only to give us strength—but to save these brave and patriotic people from the hazards of more and doubtful struggles for liberty & independence. May we not say that Texas lost to us under all the circumstances which bear upon our sympathies and interests in the course of her cause, will furnish an occasion to the friends of monarchy to rejoice at our weakness—or may we not go further and say that the enemies of Republican Government will hail the event as the harbinger of the presence in our system of a defect which will dissipate the boasted theory of popular sover[e]ignty?

I send this letter to the care of our consul at Galvezton [Elisha A. Rhodes], to be forwarded by the first safe conveyance to New Orleans.

Wishing you health & happiness and a fortunate meeting with

Congress on the subject of annexation and all other national interests, I subscribe myself very truly & sincerely your obliged Servant, A.J. Donelson.

ALS with En in ScCleA; PC in Jameson, ed., *Correspondence*, pp. 996–997.

From H[enry] L. Ellsworth, [Commissioner of the] Patent Office, 11/18. In response to Calhoun's request of 11/11 for a report of the sums of money paid to Patent Office employees during "the present year," Ellsworth asks whether the year is to be considered ended on 7/1 or on 12/31. If the former, Ellsworth will report expenditures from 1/1 through 6/30, the previous half-year having already been reported. If the latter date is meant, he cannot fully comply with the request until 1/1/1845. "I should not have hesitated had not congress changed the fiscal year." (A Clerk's EU indicates that this letter was answered on 11/19.) ALS in DNA, RG 59 (State Department), Accounting Records, Letters Received from Departments and Bureaus.

From F[RANKLIN] H. ELMORE

Charleston, Nov. 18, 1844

My Dear Sir, I cannot tell you how much I regret not seeing [you] on your way to Washington. I was most anxious to have your views of what we were to do here at this session of the Legislature. Something will be expected either formally or informally. If not in the Legislature, by private association & organization. If you can spare the time I would be glad to hear from ["you" *interlined*] as fully & specifically as you can give me your ideas of our line of action. Much will have been known to you since your return which will enable you to come to clearer conclusions of the actual condition of affairs & you will no doubt be better prepared for the proper course for us to pursue. If we do not have some aid from you I fear we will be at some loss & in some danger of distractions.

The final result of this contest has been most disastrous to the Whigs. I trust it may prove as fortunate for us as it is ruinous to them. I suppose Mr. [James K.] Polk will soon be casting about for his Cabinet & I can hardly doubt he will give you the option of remaining. You said when I saw you last that if he did you would remain upon his agreeing to such conditions as would justify you.

I doubt my Dear Sir if it will not be unwise to be exacting—if any conditions are indispensible, of course your honor & usefulness are above office or that position—but if they are not, I think you may safely rely on your own weight & powers, if one of his Cabinet, for all you could desire. Mr. Polk *cannot* go through what is before him without some strong man to lean on—and if you are offered that post ["& you accept without conditions," *interlined*] he will be as much, *I think more,* under your influence than he would be if you stipulated before hand for terms. It does seem to me that if there is the least disposition to pass you by, the requiring conditions may be used successfully as the pretext to do it—or if acceded to, they will render Mr. Polk less confiding & your influence more precarious. He must dread [Thomas H.] Benton & his set. He cannot face them so well under any other auspices as yours & very little while will be required to cement your power.

I know you will excuse my intruding these opinions & therefore I do not hesitate to express them for what they are worth.

I shall be at Columbia early in the Session. Will you also inform me if you have yet heard any thing from Russia on the process for smelting the gold ores? The value & extent of these mines are every [day?] becoming wider & more known. Yours truly, F.H. Elmore.

ALS in ScCleA.

From O[gden] Hoffman

United States Attorney[']s Office
New York [City], 18th November 1844
Sir, I have the honor to acknowledge your letter of the 16th inst., together with copies of a communication, received at the Department of State, from [George W. Gordon] the U.S. Consul at Rio de Janeiro, and of the affidavits accompanying it. I will adopt all necessary measures, to procure the arrest of [Jason L.] Pendleton, should he return to this port, and I have given, the requisite instructions to the Marshal of this District [Silas M. Stilwell], to secure the attendance of the witnesses, now in his custody. I have the honor to be Sir, Very Respectfully Your obed[ien]t Serv[an]t, O. Hoffman, U.S. Attorney.

LS in DNA, RG 59 (State Department), Petitions for Pardon, 1789–1869, Tyler Administration, no. 110.

From WILSON LUMPKIN, [former Governor of Ga.]

Athens [Ga.], Nov. 18th 1844

My dear Sir, I have my full share of gratification in the result of the late Presidential election. But much remains yet to be accomplished, before the strife between the *Tax payers* & *Tax consumers* are set-[t]led & adjusted.

I discover already, that the old *office seeking* faction are in the field, and unless the patriotic portion of the Republican party are on the alert, they ["(the selfish)" *interlined*] will do mischief, & destroy the harmony of the friends of the President Elect [James K. Polk].

A great effort will be made ["to" *canceled and* "by" *interlined*] the *faction*, or *clique* to whom I refer, to gain a controuling influence in the new administration. And as one means to accomplish their object, they are disposed to detract from your merit. I felt it my duty to say this much to you, on hearing of some of the expressions of [Howell] Cobb (re-elected from this Dist. to Congress) who was so devoted to Mr. [Martin] Van Buren & the [Washington] Globe, that he very reluctantly, was forced into the support of Mr. Polk.

They have no specific charges against you, but deal in loose sayings, intended to disparage.

As soon as the members of Congress begin to arrive at Washington—the faction to which I allude, will commence their work of mischief, & covertly, if not openly sow the seeds of strife & discord amongst the dominant party. Unfortunately we have in our ranks *spoils men*, whose only object is the *loaves & fishes—pil[l]age & plunder*. May God in his mercy, deliver the country from the controul of selfish & bad men. Every true patriot who may be at Washington, should be on the alert. The destiny of the coming in administration, & the prosperity of the Country, depends mainly on the events of a few weeks to come.

My solicitude & anxiety will not cease, until I see the complexion of the new administration. I have great confidence in Mr. Polk, but I foresee the difficulties, ["by" *canceled and* "with" *interlined*] which he will be surrounded. In haste as Ever Y[ou]r friend, Wilson Lumpkin.

ALS in ScCleA; PC in Boucher and Brooks, eds., *Correspondence*, p. 264.

From JOHN McKEON, [former Representative from N.Y.]

New York [City,] 18 Nov[embe]r 1844
My Dear Sir, The result of the election which has just taken place satisfies me that the people of this country are anxious to abandon the protective policy now fixed upon us in the present tariff. Free trade has been endorsed by the people. It now remains for the legislative & Executive branches to take the necessary steps to perfect the work. No man in this country stands in advance of yourself as the friend of liberal commercial principles and I believe no one would do more than you to accomplish commercial liberty. I am satisfied much can be done by selecting as our agents abroad not only in our diplomatic but in our Consular situations gentlemen who have information on the subject of trade and who can by their talent & address return information to this country & satisfy the American people that freedom of trade is essential to the national prosperity. Since the reduction of the British Tariff in 1842 a new era has arisen in our commercial relations with England. Articles are now exported to Great Britain from the United States which articles no one ever dreamed could be ever advantageously sent to England. The article of leather has been exported by my friend Mr. James Fiora of this City and I have no doubt will afford (if proper attention be given to the preparation of the article so as to suit British taste) profitable returns. The experiment is a hazardous one but there is every prospect of its success.

Mr. Fiora is a mechanic of this City who has for years devoted himself to the study of political economy. During the late political campaign I have listened with delight to his speeches and I confess I envied him his facility & clearness of illustration. He has a thorough knowledge of his subject & understands the practical workings of the protective system. He went to England at some expense & has taken great pains to learn what articles can be sent from the United States to England. He is anxious to obtain an appointment as Consul either for Hull or Leeds in England. His object is to hold some situation the emoluments of which will indemnify him for the expense of residing abroad while he opening [*sic*] new channels for American industry. Such a man would be of great service to us not only by giving his own countrymen useful information on which they could act but also in enlightening the British people to their true policy with this country. He is acquainted with [Richard] Cobden & all the great champions of free trade in England.

Of Mr. Fiora as a man it gives me great pleasure to say that his private character is without stain. He is a man of great industry & enjoys the respect of all who know him.

Mr. F[iora] will be sustained by some of our most respectable citizens in his application. His success in the present application would be a service to a great cause & would oblige many of your friends and particularly Your Obed[ient] Ser[van]t, John McKeon.

ALS in DNA, RG 59 (State Department), Applications and Recommendations, 1845–1853, Fiora (M-873:28, frames 94–96).

From JOHN D. VAN BUREN

New York [City,] Nov. 18 1844

Sir, I take the liberty to enclose to you an application to the President signed by several mercantile firms (my own, Aymar & Co. among the number) and individual merchants for the appointment of Mr. Henry Adolphus Wappaus as Consul of the United States at Angostura [Venezuela].

We can speak with entire confidence of Mr. Wappaus' fitness for the station having known him well in this city while a resident merchant here for several years and since; and can safely promise his faithful and diligent attention to the duties of his office.

No United States Consul has ever been appointed to reside at Angostura and indeed the trade there with this country is of such a nature as would not yield fees of office to warrant its acceptance by any but a person residing there for other purposes. The intercourse between this and Angostura is mostly kept up by vessels of that country: American vessels are, however, occasionally employed and the services of a Consul might at times be of serious importance: the nearest Consul [*one word altered to* "in"] the Republic of Venezuela being at Laguayra which is several days' journey from Angostura.

I have not deemed it necessary to forward you any farther testimonials of Mr. Wappaus' fitness than those with which this is accompanied—should additional proofs be required they can be furnished.

Begging your favorable consideration of the matter I am with great respect Your Obedient Servant, Jno. D. van Buren.

ALS in DNA, RG 59 (State Department), Applications and Recommendations, 1837–1845, Wappaus (M-687:33, frames 535–537). NOTE: John Dash Van

Buren (1809–1883) was a native of New York City, an attorney and merchant. He was not related to Martin Van Buren and the Van Burens of Kinderhook, N.Y.

From FRANCIS WHARTON

Philadelphia, November 18th [1844]
My dear Sir, I am afraid that in the hurried letter I wrote to you on Saturday, I did not dwell as earnestly as I ought on the importance of Judge [Edward] King's confirmation. I am sure you will pardon my mentioning the subject twice to you when you reflect upon the personal interest felt by every lawyer in the circuit in the appointment. If Judge King, at the time of his nomination [to the U.S. Supreme Court], presented high claims, such is much more the case now. If, at that time, his consummate abilities as a chancery judge, and his long and successful common-law experience, made his appointment desirable, the events which have since taken place should make his confirmation certain. On the court in which he presides fell the whole brunt of the responsibility brought out by the late [anti-Catholic] riots. Had *he* flinched, lynch-law would have become the common-law of the district. Had the mawkish sensibility which has been invading other courts pervaded his own—had the terror which struck other portions of the community seized the judiciary—I do really believe that the Secretary of War [William Wilkins] would long before this have issued orders to the head-quarters in Philadelphia. I send you a copy of Judge King[']s charge to the grand-jury— a charge delivered at a time when even the profession was bowing its head in submission to the monstrous doctrine of mob-supremacy— which I am sure you will recognize as putting forth, with singular ability & in full force, positions as necessary to the safety of society, as they were then forgotten or combatted. What can be gained for the party by Judge King[']s rejection? Nothing, probably, but the contingent elevation of one of that little clique of politicians who surround Mr. [James] Buchanan, and who, like him, have swung from anti-war federalism to pro-tariff democracy. I confess I should be proud to see the vacant seat filled by abilities so signal, character so strong, learning so extensive, & experience so successful, as ["those" *canceled and "are" interlined*] brought forward by Judge King.
I would not have troubled you on the subject had not there been a prospect of the appointment being defeated in the senate by a coali-

tion of infuriated Whigs, who are anxious to caricature democracy by exaggerating its policy, and of mistaken democrats, who think that by keeping everything for Mr. [James K.] Polk, they are best serving the interests of the party. Yours most truly, Francis Wharton.

ALS in ScCleA.

To Richard S. Coxe, Washington, 11/19. "I have to acknowledge the receipt of your letter of the 15th instant upon the subject of the delay in receiving from Mexico the monies paid by that government under the Convention of of [*sic*] the 30th of Jan[uar]y 1843; and to inform you that it has been referred to the Secretary of the Treasury, who is by law charged with the business." FC in DNA, RG 59 (State Department), Domestic Letters, 35:21 (M-40:33).

C [HARLES] J. INGERSOLL to [Richard K. Crallé?]

Philad[elphia,] Nov. 19 [18]44

Dear Sir, I think it w[oul]d be very useful to publish in the [Washington] Madisonian of about the 3, 4, or 5th of December an improved and if need be corrected edition of all that Mr. [Charles H.?] Winder published in that paper sometime last spring explaining what the late Judge [Henry] Baldwin said of Mr. [John Quincy] Adam[s]'s dealings with Mr. Rufus King, Mr. Timothy Pitkin and whoever the others were, on the subject of Texas—stopping at the Sabine when we might have gone to the Colorado.

It is obviously important to meet Congress with all possible information on that subject—and if, as Mr. Winder here assures me, documentary proof may be vouched in support of Judge Baldwin's revelations that Mr. Adams with[h]eld from the Senate, the Cabinet and probably the president [James Monroe] his—Mr. A[dams]'s— concert with the Eastern Gentlemen for shortening our extension South, his late elaborated defence by speeches at home may be fully overcome.

I do not trouble Mr. [John C.] Calhoun with this letter because you can probably do what I desire (if he and you approve it) better than he. But shew it to him if you choose, and believe me very truly y[ou]rs, C.J. Ingersoll.

ALS in ScCleA.

To John C. Williams, 11/19. Calhoun notifies Williams of his appointment as U.S. Commercial Agent for the Navigator's [Samoan] Islands, encloses standard instructions, and discusses Williams's previous claim for compensation for aid rendered to destitute American seamen. FC in DNA, RG 59 (State Department), Consular Instructions, 11:307–308.

From HENRY A. WISE, "Private"

Rio de Janeiro, Nov[embe]r 19th 1844

My dear Sir, I am informed that charges have been or will be preferred against Mr. [Amory] Edwards, our Consul at Buenos Ayres, involving very serious specifications of mal-versation in his office. I am told that the impressions of our Navy officers and merchantmen, particularly the opinion of Capt. [Philip F.] Voorhees is very strong against him. He is accused of selling the real & personal effects & estate of a U. States citizen, a Mr. [Andrew] Thorndike dec[ease]d, in virtue of his official character of adm[inistrato]r, and of appropriating the proceeds to his own use. He is said to have sold the real estate without authority, and the only assets which the heirs at law or persons entitled to the distribution & inheritance of the estate, have been able to recover have been the amount derived by compromise on their part with the venders of the real estate improperly sold and conveyed by Mr. Edwards. He is represented as a man of gambling & dissipated habits and as having squandered these funds upon his vices. I know nothing of the case whatever except from hearsay, but that is so strong here against him that the supposition is confidently entertained that he will be removed.

In that event, and without meaning at all to mingle in the accusations against Mr. Edwards, I beg that Llewellyn Jones Esq[ui]r[e], who has just been removed by operation of the last naval law from the office of Naval Store Keeper here, may be appointed in his, Mr. Edwards's place, as Consul at B: Ayres. Mr. Jones was appointed, I know, at the instance of your predecessor who placed the highest confidence in him: a confidence which Mr. Jones' conduct in his office has more than fully justified as you will see by Com[mo]d[o]re [Daniel] Turner's report of him lately sent to the Sec[re]t[ar]y of the Navy [John Y. Mason] & President, praying that he may be retained in the public ["service" *interlined*] in some capacity or other, and averring the reason that the diligence, faithfulness and business tact of Mr. Jones had saved the Govt. at least $10,000 in the short time he has been in place here. He is now to be superseded by a Master's Mate in the Navy, having been allowed but $1500 p[e]r an: from the time he entered upon the duties of his office here—a sum upon which I know he could not live, and from which too he had to pay his expenses out & his sacrifices of business in leaving home. I am sure that the day he turns his present place over to his Successor that he will be loser by his faithful service of the Govt. from $1000 to $2000. This ought, certainly, to be repaired in some way. There is no easier way than to give him this Consulate at B. Ayres. He has a most interesting family of a wife & two children, and Mrs. Jones' health requires that she should, if possible, remain in this climate. Mr. Jones is poor, and he now has not the means of taking his family back to Comfort in the U. States. He is here in proximity to B. Ayres and may be ordered immediately to his post, where, I assure you, an honest, firm & faithful consul is especially required. With the highest respect I have the honor to be Yours truly, Henry A. Wise.

ALS in DNA, RG 59 (State Department), Applications and Recommendations, 1837–1845, Jones (M-687:17, frames 526–530), received 1/9/1845.

To ——

Washington, 19th Nov[embe]r 1844
My dear Sir, As I expect to see you shortly, I write simply to say, that I have received your letter & concur in most of the views you take; and that your election has been highly gratifying to your numerous southern friends, and to none more than myself. When we meet we will go over all the points touched on by your letter. Yours truly, J.C. Calhoun.

ALS in ScU-SC, John C. Calhoun Papers; transcript in DLC, Carnegie Institution of Washington Transcript Collection.

From M [ARIA] D [ALLAS] CAMPBELL

Phila[delphia,] Nov[embe]r 20th 1844
I have waited My good friend, untill that certainty which now seems to have reached the rejoicing hearts of the true democracy, should

permit me to remind you, that I *have not* untill *now*, asked any thing of that friendship, which you have so often assured me, I should never find wanting.

As no *political* ["capital," *interlined*] is required at this *immediate* time I conclude my request may meet with fewer obstacles. I have an old friend, (whose parents were excellent and cherished friends of my *father's* [Alexander J. Dallas's]) whose worth, education & attainments, would make him competent to fill any situation with credit to any administration, whose health has become feeble, & whose acquirements & industry are consequently less efficient, than they would otherwise be to the support of a wife & family. He [Dr. Robert M. Patterson] is by profession a Physician & held for a term of two or more years the chair of Professor in the University of Virginia, & was compelled by ill health to vacate that advantageous position to the great regret of the Students & Professors; he is by birth a Philadelphian. I have never suggested to him, my present intention to apply to you, *he* therefore will feel no disappointment, should you not have it in your power to confer a *Consulship* to some mild & genial climate, & I shall be very sure that you would not refuse to *me* a request you could conscientiously acquiesce in. My motives are entirely, as you will perceive *unselfish*, & those, ["in" *canceled*] which I am persuaded would meet your own. "He is ho[*mutilation*] & capable"; by birth & education a gentleman, & a man of both science, & general literature. He & his wife are both conversant with the French & Spanish languages.

Will you consider this as *entre* nous, & let me hear from you as promptly as is convenient to you whether you think it possible to give him such a situation as may meet his views, & my earnest wishes.

As I hope to see you in Feb[rua]ry I will reserve the expression of my satisfaction at the great triumph of our glorious political principles, & of the hopes which are nourished & encouraged therefrom.

Mr. [Alexander] Campbell unites in kind regards to you & believe me now as ever your unchanged & sincere friend, M.D. Campbell.

[P.S.] Direct [your reply] to Mrs. M:D: Campbell, Girard Square, No. 349 Chestnut St:

ALS in ScCleA. NOTE: Maria Dallas Campbell was the sister of Vice-President-Elect George M. Dallas. She married Alexander Campbell in 1813.

From THEO[DORE] S. FAY

Legation U. States
Berlin, November 20, 1844

Dear Sir, I have felt a certain embarrassment in asking, from Baron [Heinrich von] Bulow & M. [Franz August] Eichmann, further admissions in the affair of our proposed Convention with the Zollverein, believing they have given me all in their power, & that I have no authority to add anything to what I have stated. But in a slight Conversation with Mr. Eichmann, he intimated their intention to instruct the Baron [Friedrich] de Gerolt (who must now be at Washington) more particularly on the subject; in doing which, I suggested, no time should be lost. In my communication to you of the first conversation I had with Baron Bulow, I stated his wish that I should express to you the surprize of the Prussian Government at the claims advanced by England &c to all the advantages which, it was supposed, the Convention secured to the Zollverein exclusively. M. Eichmann incidentally made a similar remark, but as he had alluded ["to Instructions" *interlined*] intended to be sent to B[aro]n de Gerolt, I thought it better to abstain from farther interference.

In connexion, however, with the assurances contained in my Letters, 3 & 21 October, I will merely repeat my impression that Mr. ["de" *interlined*] Gerolt will be directed to require information as to the real right of other nations to share the advantages conceded, by the proposed Convention, to the Zollverein.

The report of the death of M. Consul [John] Cuthbert, at Hamburg, was an error, but he is in a precarious state of health. When he dies, the country will lose a most worthy man. I have the honor to be, with the highest regard & respect, Dear Sir, Y[ou]r most ob[e]d[ien]t Serv[an]t, Theo. S. Fay.

ALS (Private) in DNA, RG 59 (State Department), Diplomatic Despatches, Germany, vol. 3 (M-44:4), received 12/23; FC in DNA, RG 84 (Foreign Posts), Germany, Despatches, 4:164–165.

To Henry A. [Holms], "Care Messrs. C.H. Todd & Co., New York [City]"

Department of State
Washington, 20 Nov[embe]r 1844

Sir, I have to acknowledge the receipt of your letter of the 12th instant. In answer to that part of it which relates to the case of the brig Henry Leeds, a copy of a communication addressed by this Department on the 22nd Ult. to Messrs. C.H. Todd & Co. of New York is herewith transmitted.

This government cannot with propriety apply to the authorities of Yucatan for redress, that province constituting only a part of the Republic of Mexico, which is responsible in the last resort for all injuries, which the judicial tribunals may have neglected or may have been incompetent to redress.

Letters have been addressed by this Department to the Consuls of the United States at Sisal [Pedro de Regil y Estrada] and Campeachy [John F. McGregor] upon the topics to which you advert. I am &c, J.C. Calhoun.

FC in DNA, RG 59 (State Department), Domestic Letters, 35:22 (M-40:33). Note: The FC is erroneously addressed to "Henry A. Holmes."

From R[obert] M. T. Hunter

L[l]oyds[,] Essex C[ount]y [Va.] Nov[embe]r 20th 1844

My dear Sir, Some time since I wrote to inform you of the proceedings of your friends at the Dem[ocratic] Convention at Charlottesville in Sept[embe]r last. They then determined to appoint a committee (of which I am a member) to see Mr. [Thomas] Ritchie immediately after the election to ascertain his course in reference to yourself and in the event that he refused to commit himself to you, the committee was empowered to call a convention of your friends to take steps to start a paper at Richmond at once and to place your name before the people should that convention so determine. Although not approving of such steps so early in the action, yet I found that in order to keep up the spirits of our friends it was necessary to seem to be doing something, and I relied upon your interposition should it become necessary to prevent hasty and premature *action*. I received a letter from [James A.] Seddon by the last post who thought it his duty to write to some of our confidential *friends* on the subject, and although he seems to think we ought to do nothing just now, he urges me to go on to Washington to get your opinion on the subject. As it can be as well managed by letter and the trip just now would be exceedingly inconvenient, I write by the first mail which has occurred since the receipt of S[eddon]'s letter and hope you will find it convenient to give me an early response. Should you think it necessary for me to come on to Washington I will do so, but if it is as convenient for you to write, it will save me from a trip which just now would be exceedingly inconvenient. The proposed step would be mischievous in several respects. Mr. Ritchie would say it is too soon to meet that question and probably he would say that it must be decided by a convention whose salutary agency recent events have demonstrated. The election being now over we should have all the disadvantages in the split. As no election of consequence is pending we should be less feared now than at a later period and he would rely confidently on the hope of killing us off before an election could occur in which we could be felt. I think I may say that I know he would give no such absolute pledge even should he secretly prefer you. We have acquired advantages in the late canvass which we should thus destroy. This is not all. Mr. [James K.] Polk and his friends would probably regard this movement as hostile. The arrangement of his cabinet and the conduct of his administration would thus probably be thrown against us. Here too we should throw away the advantages of our position. We have [Thomas H.] Benton on the hop—Polk owes his election mainly to yourself and your friends, there is no prominent influence to detach him from us save [Silas] Wright[']s, which I confess is formidable. There is yet a third objection ["wh" *canceled*] to any movement at present. The whigs may possibly disband, it is at least probable that they will lose much of their strength in the South. This event would I think strengthen us. But they would regard such a movement as evidence of an approaching split in the ranks and they would hold together under the expectation of receiving a portion of the Rep[ublican] party as accessories, and subordinates. But if we ["keep our" *canceled*] remain quiet and keep our own counsels avoiding all appearance of a split, we shall I think control Ritchie, [*partial word canceled*] acquire some strength by accessions from the whig ranks and have a chance at least for assistance from the new administration. Our line it seems to me is to keep up a correspondence with our friends and to push those measures of which you are regarded as the truest exponent and upon which the new administration will come into power—I mean Texas and a revenue Tariff. We must claim the popular verdict on these measures and whilst we avoid the [*partial word canceled*] threat of extreme remedies ([*partial word canceled*] which some of our Southern friends have imprudently made) we must firmly push our principles and measures. It is easy now to get up a public sentiment in the party which will loudly demand these measures and whilst you are in position to advance with the tide, it leaves Mr. Wright behind. His only chance of success in such a direction of popular opinion (as it seems to me) will be in his withdrawal ["of" *canceled and* "from" *interlined*] Federal politics and the difficulty which will thus be found in ascertaining his "whereabouts" from time to time. Our friends in congress will be cautious I trust in ["say" *canceled*] making known their ultimatum on the Tariff at this session. That question I fear will have to be settled again by a compromise upon mixed principles. And if a creditable compromise can be made, I wish you could have the credit of it. But my speculations upon that event are not worth much I know, but still I hope you will give this subject some reflection as it will be one of the difficulties I know.

If you think with me that our proposed action is premature please write me at once, or rather let me know what you desire to be done as your opinion will be decisive either way.

What will probably be Polk[']s feelings toward yourself? Our friends have asked me the question where ever I have been, and I have been unable to answer it except by saying that he would be singularly ungrateful unless kindly disposed. Your friends have fought this battle. They have whipt not only the whigs but they have whipped in the recusants of our own party. I wonder what Mr. [Henry] Clay thinks of the "Texas humbug" and its victims just now? His violence[,] indelicacy and I fear something worse have met with a just retribution at last. Yours most truly, R.M.T. Hunter.

ALS in ScCleA.

From JOHN A. MORRILL, "Private"

New York [City,] Nov. 20th 1844

Dear Sir, I think by writing to the Hon. Charles H. Hall of our City who was formerly the confidential partner of the late Mr. Thomas H. Smith who was so largely engaged in the China trade[,] he will give you much information in relation to the same. I informed him this morning that I should address you on the subject & he stated that he would give you much information in detail. Yours humbly & with great respect, John A. Morrill.

ALS in ViU, Crallé-Campbell Papers.

From J[OHN] L. O'SULLIVAN

New York [City,] Nov. 20, 1844
My dear Sir, Permit me to introduce to your acquaintance Mr. William H. Tracy, our Consul at Gu[a]yama, who, being on a visit to this city, is desirous of the honor of paying his respects ["to you" *interlined*], and who, as a gentleman of high character and intelligence, and a merchant of greatest respectability, is highly worthy of your regard. Very Respectfully & Truly Yours, J.L. O'Sullivan [Editor of the *United States Magazine and Democratic Review*].

ALS in DNA, RG 59 (State Department), Consular Despatches, Guayama, Puerto Rico, vol. 2 (M-76:23).

From V[ICT]OR ROUMAGE

New Orleans, Nov[em]ber 20th 1844
Sir, Some years since I placed in the hands of the Government, my Claim against the Republic of New Greneda and Venezuella, for indemnity for the illegal seizure and Condemnation of the Brig Sarah Wilson of New Orleans, She being my property. As I have no information for some time past in relation to this claim, I have, and do hereby Constitute and appoint James W. Breedlove of this City my agent to attend to the adjustment of said claim in such way as he may deem most advantageous to me, trusting that you will afford him all the information necessary. I have the honor to remain Sir Your most ob[edien]t Ser[van]t, V[ict]or Roumage.

ALS in DNA, RG 76 (Records of Boundary and Claims Commissions and Arbitrations), Miscellaneous Claims Records: Colombia, 1818–1825.

From AARON SARGEANT, "Private"

N[ew] York [City,] the 20 Nov[embe]r /44
Hon. Sir, Another Plan on foot[.] The vote of New York[,] Pennsy[l-
vani]a[,] New Hampshire & Maine is to be offered to Mr. [James K.]
Polk on Condition he pledges himself to not touch the Tariff nor An-
nexation of Texas[;] this is purely friendship to your honor (& strictly
Confidential) from your Friend & Ob[edien]t Hum[ble] Ser[vant],
Aaron Sargeant.

N.B. My letter of 13 Nov. I trust [h]as reached your honor.

ALS in ScCleA.

To FRANCIS WHARTON, [Philadelphia]

Washington, 20th Nov[embe]r 1844
My dear Sir, Judge [Edward] King's nomination [to the Supreme
Court] will, if my memory serves me, have to be renewed, according
to the usage of the Senate.

I must say, that your letter places his character in a light, [in]
which I have not heretofore regarded it. I had taken the impression,
that although a man of talents, his political association connected
him with a set of politicians of a very objectionable character, which
subjected his to doubt. Under this impression, I was disinclined to
his nomination, without, however, taking any part against it, while
before the Senate. It is due to the occasion to say, that the impression
made on my mind, has, I am inclined to think, been made on that of
many others; so much so, that his nomination will be in great danger,
unless it should be well sustained from the respectable portion of your
bar and the City, especially, if your two Senators [James Buchanan
and Daniel Sturgeon] should be opposed to him. I take it, that the
wing of the party, usually opposed to the nominations of the President, will be against him, which would certainly cause his defeat;
unless he should receive the support of the better portion of the Whig
party. If, however, your two Senators will support him, I should
think that his prospects would be fair. Without it, there would be
great difficulty in obtaining the confirmation of his nomination. I
write in confidence, and only for your own eye.

I regard the defeat of [Henry] Clay and the election of [James

K.] Polk, under all circumstances, as a great political revolution. Great events may grow out of [it], if the victory be used with prudence and moderation. There is much to be done to bring things right, and save the Government, but in order to be successfully done, it must be done gradually and systematically. I say, save the Government; for to my mind it is clear, that it cannot go on much longer, as it has for the last 15 or 20 years, and especially the last 8.

I am of the impression, an article, such as you suggest for the [Democratic] Review, is very desirable, but that it ought to be delayed untill several other papers, I have prepared, since the close of the session, make their appearance, which will be during the coming session. My two letters to Mr. [Richard] Pakenham were intended but as the beg[inn]ing of a long correspondence with the British Government which in its progress would involve all the subjects embraced in her course in reference to our country on the question of slavery. In that, I was disappointed, as no reply was made to my second letter to Mr. Pakenham; but much, which I intend to bring out, has been brought out on other questions.

PC in Jameson, ed., *Correspondence*, pp. 629–630.

From FRANCIS WHARTON

[Philadelphia,] Nov. 20th [1844]

My dear Sir, Do let me at once remove the impression which I see you have most mistakenly received in relation to Judge [Edward] King. Belonging, originally, before his 18 years judicial tenure began, to the old republican party, ["before" *canceled and* "at a time when" *interlined*] that party was ["not" *interlined*] steeped in latitudinarian dyes[,] his associations, as far as judicial dignity w[oul]d allow him to have any associations at all, have been with the republican leaders. But I do assure you that so far from being connected with the low agrarian, demagoguical, agitators who lead the grosser portion of the democratic party, his stand, judicially & personally, has been of a character most energetic & conservative. I do solemnly believe that if he had pandered, ["during the late riots," *interlined*] as he might have done just as well as every body else in the community, to either the native feeling, on the one side, or the low Irish, on the other, we would be now in civil war in this county. I say this, not because it is an instance, but because it is an index, of ["the" *canceled and* "his judicial" *interlined*] character. You ask about the bar. The bar will answer for itself, before long, in an ["almost" *interlined*] unanimous address, signed by ["almo" *canceled and* "all" *interlined*] parties, *except, perhaps, the very party to which you allude*, pressing his confirmation. I know that Mr. [Charles] Chauncey, whose mature experience, & whose great reputation, you already know—Mr. [Joseph] Randall, Mr. [Henry] Clay[']s organ here, & an eminent lawyer—Mr. H[enry] D. Gilpin—Mr. [John K.] Kane—Mr. [Garrick] Mallory, one of the oldest & wisest & most distinguished of the profession—Mr. Richard Rush, from whom I learn that he will write to you soon—are not ["no" *canceled*] only interested, but actively engaged in pressing the appointment. I should really not think, myself, honoured as much as I have already been by your kindness, to encroach upon your time by saying any thing more; but I am provoked and vexed that so low & local a conspiracy should have shot up so high. Mr. [Daniel] Sturgeon [Senator from Pa.] will support the nomination; if Mr. [James] Buchanan makes good his word, he will do so also. You will soon have sufficient indications of professional feeling here, and when you know how jealous the bar is of a judicial appointment so high, you will place great weight on the endorsement. You must pardon my writing to you so earnestly, but I feel, though not personally involved, most deeply interested in the result of a struggle in which I see character, & worth, & ability, on one side, & nothing at all but ["ambitions" *canceled and* "intrigue" *interlined*].

Do let me have the treaty papers as soon as possible, & oblige Yours ever, Francis Wharton.

ALS in ScCleA.

From James Wise, Richmond, 11/20. "Allow me the liberty of introducing to your acquaintance my friend Mr. [John P.] Merrill. Mr. M[errill] is a gentleman of high respectability & a Superior Artist. He is in bad health and wishes to procure a passport to Cuba. Any assistance you can render him will be thankfully received by him and highly estimated by your friend . . . ." ALS in DNA, RG 59 (State Department), Passport Applications, 1795–1905, vol. 33, no. 2664 (M-1372:15).

From J[OHN] S. BARBOUR

Catalpa [Culpeper County, Va.,] Nov[embe]r 21st 1844
My Dear Sir, The election is over & whether for weal or woe is yet not entirely certain.

Should Colo[nel James K.] Polk close up his ears to all evil counsellors—reduce the expenditures—bring down the tariff to those expenditures—keep the patronage for principles, & not for partizans; hold the appointing power, as a trustee for wise & virtuous ends; divorce the Treasury & the Banks ["d"(?) *canceled*]—divorce the patronage from party, & throw reform chiefly on retrenchment, then his election will be a blessing. If however this great effort of patriotic ardour shall end only in like results with that of 1829, the publick heart will grow sick under disappointment, & will languish into stagnant & putrid quiescence, which ["will" *interlined*] render it wholly incapable, of any [*one word canceled and* "future" *interlined*] effort of disinterested patriotism. It will have spasm & convulsion; but its healthy action is gone forever. That you will be in the Administration is the expectation of every manly spirit of every party. The Whigs as well as the Republicans, throw their expiring & their kindling hopes on you.

I dread the influence of Gen[era]l [Andrew] Jackson in this particular. Were it a private matter exclusively with you & he, the old man w[oul]d follow the better impulses of his wiser thoughts. But he is impressed with the belief, that persevering injustice to you, is necessary to preserve his place, in the page of history. Without recollecting that the Historic muse, knows neither love nor fear, he cannot be disencumbered of the thought, that he is to be as puissant when in his grave, as when wielding his vast power through his vast popularity.

Mr. Polk should know, first, that his election is the effect of moral causes. That personally he has not a feather's weight of power in the deliberations of the publick. That to his principles mainly is he indebted for his election—and to that moral power which So. Carolina & Virginia, ["alone" *interlined*] carried to his aid.

Of South Carolina I need not say a word. Without your friends in Virginia, the election w[oul]d have gone for [Henry] Clay almost without a struggle. The party was a *Caput mortuum*, until the spirit of life, was breathed into it, by the Calhoun party. *They* fought the battle from the blue ridge to the Capes of Virginia; & from the Kentucky & Ohio borders through & over the Alleghanies. If the President elect offer you a seat in his Cabinet, I am justified in saying that your friends wish you to accept it, clearly understanding ["in advance" *interlined*] the principles on which the Government is henceforth to be conducted. Without this preliminary ["apprehension" *canceled and* "understanding" *interlined*], they think you w[oul]d prefer private life, & with it, they believe that your sense of public duty will prevail over private inclinations. As these are the views of your sincere & disinterested friends in every quarter of Virginia, that I have heard from; I feel myself at leave to write them to you. The fact that you have taken lodgings at one of the public taverns (for so the papers announce) leaves a painful suspense just now, on the minds of many, as to the part you will act, in the new administration. With profound Respect & true Regard Y[ou]rs Sincerely, J.S. Barbour.

N.B. The only unknown vote of any State, is that of Tennessee. A patriot might find cogent reasons for the wish that it has fallen into the urn[?] of the enemy, as we are safe without it. J.S.B.

[P.S.] *You see my haste.*

ALS in ScCleA; PC in Jameson, ed., *Correspondence*, pp. 997–998.

From EDWARD EVERETT, "(Confidential)"

London, 21 November, 1844

My dear Sir, Your instructions Nro. 99, relative to the refusal of the local authorities at Nassau to surrender the fugitive slaves charged with the murder of Mr. [John H.] Geeren, reached me in due course. I immediately commenced the preparation of a note to Lord Aberdeen on the important and delicate question raised on that occasion, and which forms the subject of your despatch.

Having however, after the note was nearly ready to be despatched, adverted more particularly to the wish expressed by you to be possessed of the views of this government before the Session of Congress, I was led to doubt, whether the discussion of the subject in a note to Lord Aberdeen was the surest way to effect that object. Apart from the delay which usually occurs in the receipt of answers to notes on important subjects, I thought it possible that a communication relative to this case, which pertains to occurrences that took place in the Bahama Islands, would in the usual routine of business be sent to the Colonial Office, and thence referred to Nassau, for a report from the local Authorities.

I determined therefore, in the first instance, to bring the subject before Lord Aberdeen at a personal conference, although I was sensible that this course also would be attended with some delay. You are aware that the season of the year immediately following the close of the session of parliament is regarded in this Country as one of general vacation. A few days after I received your despatch Nro. 99 Lord Aberdeen went with the Queen to Scotland. The visit of the King of the French immediately followed during which he was at Windsor. On his return to town I lost no time in asking an interview; but he had made arrangements to start for his estate in Scotland on the day named by me for that purpose. While he was absent I had a conversation with Lord Canning on the subject of the fugitives at Nassau, and though speaking as he said without authority, he expressed decidedly the opinion that the comments of the Colonial Court on the provisions of the Statute of 6 & 7 Vic. C. 76 were unsanctioned by instructions from home. On Lord Aberdeen's return from the north he immediately left town again to meet the Queen at Burleigh. While he was there I addressed a note to him requesting an interview at his earliest convenience, which was accordingly appointed, on his return to London, for the 20th, when the conversation took place, which is reported in my despatch Nro. 216.

Although these details have not seemed to me of a nature to form a part of a public despatch, they are of course proper to be communicated to you privately, by way of accounting for the delay which has taken place in carrying your instructions into effect.

I take this opportunity while addressing you confidentially to mention another subject vizt. the care proper to be observed in communicating the correspondence of foreign Ministers to Congress. I can best convey what I wish to suggest by referring to the document on "Rough Rice," printed by order of the House of Representatives at the past Session. I conceive that the objects of the call would have been all answered by communicating the notes exchanged between Lord Aberdeen and myself, with perhaps the case submitted to Counsel and the opinion of Counsel thereon.

Most of the extracts from my letters to the department had better, I think, have been spared. Some of them are mere matters of business reference conveying no information of value to Congress; proper and even necessary in their place, but as extracts sent in reply to a call, breaking up the document into scraps, and diverting attention from its important parts. Others of the extracts from my correspondence containing suggestions and opinions proper to be made to my own government, are calculated when published and thus brought back here, to prejudice rather than advance the claim. This is so decidedly the case, that the parties interested here thought it advisable neither to reprint the document nor in any way to call public attention to it, though the material portions of it might have rendered them service.

I am sure you will not be offended with the freedom of these remarks. I know the pressure of business on the gentlemen of the department and I gratefully acknowledge the degree of care which has been taken, in reference to such portions of my correspondence as have been published, to omit what is not well calculated for the public eye. I am only desirous to strengthen the impression of the necessity of great watchfulness in this respect and a careful reference to the effect of the publication upon the interest of the question abroad and the position of the Minister. I am, Sir, with the highest respect, faithfully yours, Edward Everett.

LS in ScCleA; FC in MHi, Edward Everett Papers, vol. 50:359–363 (published microfilm, reel 23, frames 453–455).

From H[ENRY] GOURDIN

Charleston, Nov: 21st 1844

Dear Sir, I enclose for your perusal a letter which I have received from my friend and fellow townsman, Mr. Geo[rge] L. Lowden, in relation to a claim on the Government of Denmark, in which he is interested, as one of the heirs of John Paul Jones. I need say nothing in relation to the justice of this claim, for the subject came under your notice the last spring, and I doubt not that you are much better informed in relation to their character than I am. The object of Mr. Lowden's letter is again to call your attention to the subject through his friends here, being unwilling to trouble you himself, and I would most respectfully suggest that it be brought before Congress in the President's Message, or in such manner, as will obtain for it some definite action. Of this you are the best judge, but I feel persuaded that you will place the business in as speedy a course for settlement as possible.

The claim on the Danish government is in the State department, but that on the American government was some time since referred to the Committee on revolutionary claims. The accounts of John Paul Jones, Mr. Lowden is desirous to have referred to the Treasury department for investigation, he tells me that Mr. Broadhead [*sic*; Richard Brodhead, Representative] of Pennsylvania, who has examined into the matter, is in favor of this course, and has a joint resolution prepared for both houses which he proposes to bring forward. ["If" *altered to* "Should"] you approve of this course Mr. Lowden will be greatly obliged by your lending your aid to accomplish it.

I hand annexed a list of other parties interested in these claims, the most of them of this State. Mr. Lowden has met with some reverses in business in the last few years, but he has conducted himself with fortitude throughout. He maintains an unblemished integrity, and is respected by every one, who knows him. The recovery of this Claim, which he believes to be just, will be of the greatest importance to his family, and while it will benefit him, it will be a gratification to his friends. I am Dear Sir, Very resp[ectfull]y Your ob[edien]t S[er]v[an]t, H. Gourdin.

[Appended:]

The Heirs of Nathaniel Ingraham
    "   "   " John Mayrant
    "   "   " J.W. Linthwaite
    "   "   " Spencer
    "   "   " Robert Coram
    "   "   " Richard Wall
    "   "   " Russell
    "   "   " John Paul Jones

All of these were volunteers on board the Bon Homme Richard, and Alliance, the heirs of whom are in Carolina. The Morse family of Philadelphia are also interested in these Claims.

I send a pamphlet, printed, containing the Certificates in relation to the Accounts of John Paul Jones, to which request your reference. Resp[ectfull]y, H.G.

ALS with En in DNA, RG 59 (State Department), Miscellaneous Letters (M-179:106, frames 70–73). NOTE: Gourdin enclosed a letter to himself from Lowden, dated 11/18, giving a history of the claim.

From Charles J.M. Gwinn, Baltimore, 11/21. Gwinn seeks employment from the State Department as a despatch bearer in order to undertake a sea voyage for health reasons. He has been injured in a fall, and his physician has suggested a voyage to recover his health. Although a graduate of Princeton and a member of the Baltimore bar, Gwinn does not have the financial means to pay for such a voyage. If appointed, Gwinn would seek only payment of his necessary expenses. ALS in DNA, RG 59 (State Department), Applications and Recommendations, 1837–1845, Gwinn (M-687:13, frames 757–760).

From R[occo] Martuscelli, [Consul General of the Two Sicilies in the U.S.], New York [City], 11/21. Martuscelli reminds Calhoun of his letter of 9/27 [*sic*; 9/17] seeking "une reponse decisive" from the Secretary of the Treasury concerning the claims of Martino and Dacorsi. If he cannot obtain a quick decision Martuscelli requests the return to him of documents presented in the case. Martuscelli hopes to resolve this claim before he departs for Europe on his leave of absence. LS (in French) in DNA, RG 59 (State Department), Notes from Foreign Legations, Two Sicilies, vol. 1 (M-55:1).

From H[ENRY] S[T]. G[EORGE] TUCKER

University [of Va.] Nov[embe]r 21, 1844
My dear Sir, I have received your letter by your son [James Edward Calhoun], who safely reached here two days ago, and who has been busily engaged in the arrangements, first of his room and boarding house, and then of the schools he is to attend. Upon conversation with him, we concurred in his selecting the ancient Languages, Mathematics, and Natural philosophy. I apprehended no difficulty except in the mathematics, but on consulting Mr. Courtney [*sic*; Edward H. Courtenay] it appears his junior class are just entering on a new and independent subject, so that he will not be embarrassed by his late arrival even in that school. He seems very zealous, & I shall with great pleasure consult your wishes, in looking to him with that solicitude, which is due to the son of a friend of nearly thirty years['] standing. Having fixed himself, he will dine with me to day, that I may introduce him to my family, whom I expect him frequently to visit. My house indeed is open to all the young gentlemen every Evening, & I shall have peculiar pleasure in seeing him often at my fire side.

We have been much disappointed in your not coming. You would have been received very cordially by all, & *we* had our rooms prepared to receive you. We feel deep interest as to your course, and hope you will continue where you are on the same independent foot-

343

ing on which you accepted the office. I am Dear Sir most truly yours, H.S.G. Tucker.

ALS in ScCleA.

To JOHN D. VAN BUREN, New York [City]

Department of State
Washington, Nov[embe]r 21, 1844

Sir, Your letter of the 18th Inst: enclosing an application to the President [John Tyler], signed by several Mercantile Firms of New York, for the appointment of Henry Adolphus Wappaus, as Consul of the United States at Angostura [Venezuela], has been received.

In 1834 a Consul was appointed to Angostura, who returned in 1837 and resigned, because of its limited Commerce with the U. States, the most of which was carried on by Vessels of that Country. Since then it does not appear that the Trade has at all increased, and it is deemed inexpedient at this time to make another appointment there. But for the proper protection of the little trade that exists, the United States Consul at La Guayra [John P. Adams], will be authorized to appoint Mr. Wappaus, should he think it proper as his Consular Agent at Angostura, to correspond thro' him with the Department; and it is hoped that this arrangement may be satisfactory. I am Sir &c, J.C. Calhoun.

FC in DNA, RG 59 (State Department), Consular Instructions, 11:309–310.

From JAMES J. WRIGHT

Belmont Ohio, November 21st 1844

Sir, I have the honor to acknowledge the receipt, of your despatch bearing date, 6th of present month, being a notification that, I had been appointed Consul of the United States, for the port of Santiago de Cuba, and of the various documents specified therein as transmitted.

The Consular bond will be executed without delay.

I was born in Ireland, and became a Citizen of this country by the naturalization of my father, while I was a minor, but I have resided nearly thirty years in Cuba.

I shall leave this, on the opening of the rivers in the spring for Santiago, and meanwhile, my partner Richard Stephens Esq., who acts in virtue of authority from the late Consul, will continue to perform the duties of the Consulate.

I shall endeavour to fill the Office, with which I have been honored, so as, to maintain the interests of the citizens of the United States, and the honor, influence, and popularity of the Government thereof. With the highest consideration I remain Sir Your Ob[edien]t S[ervan]t, James J. Wright.

ALS in DNA, RG 59 (State Department), Consular Despatches, Santiago de Cuba, vol. 2 (T-55:2).

To John P. Adams, U.S. Consul, La Guayra, [Venezuela], 11/22. Calhoun informs Adams that Henry Adolphus Wappaus, a merchant at Angostura, has been recommended for a Consular post at that place. Although a Consulate is not warranted at Angostura because of limited commercial activity, Adams is at liberty, if he thinks it advisable, to appoint Wappaus as his agent there. FC in DNA, RG 59 (State Department), Consular Instructions, 11:310–311.

From EDWARD EVERETT

London, 22 November, 1844

Sir, I transmitted with my despatch Nro. 193 of the 17th of October a copy of a note addressed to Lord Aberdeen on the use of the term "mis-statement," in connection with the President's Message to Congress at the opening of the Session of 1842–1843. I now forward the accompanying reply which was yesterday received from Lord Aberdeen.

You will perceive with satisfaction, that I had not erred, in supposing that this use of the term in question was without his knowledge or approval. Lord Aberdeen admits it to have been incorrect and improper and regrets that it should have found a place in a document destined for publication.

But though I was confident that a term so indecorous could not have been used with Lord Aberdeen's sanction in reference to the President's Message, I was fully aware that he was dissatisfied with the manner in which the President had described the course pursued by the Government of the United States in reference to that part of the treaty of Washington which provides measures for the suppression of the Slave-trade. Believing that Lord Aberdeen's impression, though sincerely entertained, was unfounded, I took the opportunity in my note of the 15th October to make a few observations calculated to remove it, in which I think I have not been altogether unsuccessful. He admits that the extent of his objection to the statement in the President's Message was that it had a tendency to produce a misconception and that this tendency was unintentional.

I cannot suppress the conviction founded on circumstances which have come to my knowledge though not of course derived from official sources, that on this and other occasions the most unfriendly interpretation of the language and conduct of the American Government was made by Mr. [Henry S.] Fox in his correspondence with the Foreign Office. That his feelings toward the United States were most unkindly I have good reason to believe. I think I do not err in the opinion that these feelings habitually, however undesignedly, gave a color to his official communications. I am, Sir, with great respect, Your obedient Servant, Edward Everett.

Transmitted with despatch Nro. 214;
Lord Aberdeen to Mr. Everett, 21 November, 1844.

LS (No. 214) with En in DNA, RG 59 (State Department), Diplomatic Despatches, Great Britain, vol. 53 (M-30:49), received 12/23; FC in DNA, RG 84 (Foreign Posts), Great Britain, Despatches, 9:68–71; FC in MHi, Edward Everett Papers, 50:346–349 (published microfilm, reel 23, frames 447–448).

From WILLIAM GARRETT, JR.

Hamburg South Carolina, Nov. 22d 1844

My Dear Sir, In July last I removed my family back to my native district (Edgefield), but contrary to my expectations I have been thrown out of business—principally on account of my getting here too late. I have my family boarding at this time, and am under a severe press. *My relations* will not assist me, particularly, my old Uncle, on account of my politicks.

I am the only one of the family who has thrown himself upon the the [*sic*] Republican party. I often am taunted with following you (by the whigs in this Dist.) but this has no influence on me. I follow my own lights, and if you accord with them, I feel proud.

If you can, in any of the Departments or Beuareaus [*sic*] give me imployment, until the 4th March, my disposition is to repair to Washington *immediately*. My family are *somewhat*, in distress, but I can leave them in tolerably good quarters for a month or two, if I can make something in Washin[g]ton to support them during my absence.

If I can get, even, temporary employment at Washington during the winter, it will be doing better than lying on my oars and doing nothing. You have ["have" *canceled*] it in your power to assist me, and I most sincerely invoke it. A Week to me, on account of my situation, seems like a month; therefore, write me, at this ["place" *interlined*] at your earliest convenience. Congratulating ["you" *interlined*] most heartily, on the elections, I am devotedly & Sincerely Your friend & Ob[edien]t S[er]v[an]t, William Garrett, Jr.

ALS in DNA, RG 59 (State Department), Applications and Recommendations, 1837–1845, Garrett (M-687:12, frames 235–236). NOTE: A Clerk's EU reads "(File under head of 'Clerkships.')."

From Geo[rge] W[illia]m Gordon

Consulate of the United States
Rio de Janeiro, 22d Nov. 1844

Sir, Referring to my Despatch No. 8 enclosing the deposition of two American seamen, John Fairburn & James Gillispie, in regard to the Brig "Monte Video," which seamen I sent as witnesses to New York in the Barque "St. Joseph," which left this port on the 18th of September last, I now hasten to inform you that said Brig "Monte Video" has since been sold and delivered at Cabinda on the coast of Africa; and that her late Master, Jason L. Pendleton, with his officers and crew, arrived at this port several days ago, and presented themselves at this Consulate for the discharge of the seamen, & the delivery of the Vessel's Register.

And I have at this time briefly to state, that in consequence of the statement contained in said deposition, confirmed in many particulars, and contradicted in none, by the Vessel's papers; and after having advised with His Excellency Mr. [Henry A.] Wise, Minister of the United States at this Court, and with Commander J.G. [*sic*; Garrett J.] Pendergrast of the United States Ship "Boston," the former of whom had been unofficially, (by memorandum,) informed ["by" *interlined*] His Excellency the British Minister [Hamilton Hamilton], that there had already been landed at Cape Frio on this coast, from the said Brig "Monte Video," 780 Africans, I caused on the 20th inst., the arrest of Captain J.L. Pendleton, late Master of said Brig, Robert Baker, 1st Mate, James Robertson, 2d Mate, and two seamen, named Charles Douglas & George alias Ezekiel Norton, all certified American Citizens, also three others, Charles Martin, John Johnson & Edward Jones, foreigners, on the charge of having violated the Laws of the United States for the suppression of the African Slave Trade. And the said persons are now held in custody for further examination, on board the United States Sloop-of-War "Boston," Com[mande]r Pendergrast, lying in this port. A copy of my letter to Com[mande]r Pendergrast on sending them on board, is herewith communicated. An account of all proceedings that may be had in this case, and of all the evidence that may be taken, and copies of all papers in relation thereto will follow in due course. According to the vessel[']s Register, Alexander Riddell of New York was the late owner of the Brig "Monte Video."

I have also to communicate that on board the Brig "Sea Eagle" of Boston, Captain [Gilbert] Smith, which arrived at this port on the 14th inst. from the coast of Africa, came passengers (in addition to Captain Pendleton,) the late Master, Hiram Gray, officers and crew of the American Brig "Agnes" recently sold and delivered also at Cabinda.

The late owner of the "Agnes," according to her Register, is John H. Price of New Castle, Del[awar]e. The Master, Gray, and his chief mate William M. Ruhl, gave depositions before me yesterday in the case of the "Monte Video," and have taken passage in the "R.H. Douglas" bound for Baltimore, which vessel was to have sailed this day. I would remark that both these persons appeared to be very "unwilling witnesses," and I would respectfully suggest that they be secured & detained by the Government for further examination. They were both on board the "Sea Eagle," lying at anchor in the harbor of Cabinda, at the time of the arrival and delivery of the "Monte Video" at that place, and also when that vessel sailed with a cargo of 800 Africans on board, an important fact that they did not disclose in their depositions taken yesterday. And as they afterwards accompanied Capt. Pendleton to this City their intercourse with him must have been constant & intimate since early in September last, if not for a longer period. Capt. Gray resides at Wilmington, Delaware, and Mr. Ruhl in Pennsylvania. I have the honor to be, Sir, With great respect, Your Obedient Servant, Geo. Wm. Gordon, Consul of the United States.

ALS (No. 14) and 2 duplicate LS's with Ens in DNA, RG 59 (State Department), Consular Despatches, Rio de Janeiro, vol. 7 (T-172:8), received 1/30/1845.

From J[ames] B. Mower, New York [City], 11/22. Mower recommends that W[illiam] B. Taylor be appointed Despatch Agent for New York City. Taylor was appointed to that post when Martin Van Buren was Secretary of State and held it for six years. "Were the Secretary of State to see the operation as at present conducted [by Fernando Wood], I feel confident he would be satisfied of the great importance of making the change as suggested." ALS in DNA, RG 59 (State Department), Applications and Recommendations, 1837–1845, Taylor (M-687:32, frames 109–111).

From A[ndrew] J. Donelson

Washington, Texas, Nov[embe]r 23d 1844
Sir, I reached this place on the evening of the 21st, but am still unfortunate in finding here neither the President [Samuel Houston] nor any member of his cabinet. The President is daily expected, being, when last heard from, on the Trinity river, about one Hundred and Twenty miles distant. As soon as he arrives I shall lose no time in presenting my credentials and in entering upon the task assigned me.

In my communication [of 11/11] from Galvezton which should be numbered (1), I adverted to the appointment of Gen[era]l Terrill [*sic*; George W. Terrell] as minister to France, with his open avowal of opposition to the measure of annexation, as a circumstance calculated to warrant some distrust of the designs of the Executive portion of this Government. Other circumstances lead me to fear that this distrust may be justified by a nearer view of what has been done in the course of the summer. These circumstances are, first, the uniform expressions which are to be traced to those in the confidence of the Government, of doubts as to the policy of the measure of annexation—second—the fact that such doubts do not appear to be entertained by the mass of the people—third—the reserve manifested by those subordinate officers here who are in charge of the public records, when questioned in respect to the future relations of their country to England, France, and the United States—and lastly—the absence of all excitement in regard to the threatened invasion by Mexico, which does not appear reasonable unless there be assurances connected with Gen[era]l Terrill[']s mission calculated to create a sense of security.

It is to be hoped that in a day or two I shall have the opportunity of measuring fully the force of these appearances; and that official intercourse will enable me to see whether any project has been started in the nature of a Treaty with Great Britain and France which will have the effect to defeat or embarrass our policy.

Whether the fears I now entertain be well or ill founded, it cannot be doubted that our Government should take the most prompt measures to give practicability to the question of annexation. The measure to be adopted, if in the shape of a law, embodying substantially the provisions of the late Treaty, could it be known here before the adjournment of the Texan Congress, would be doubtless met by corresponding Legislation referring it to the people for their approbation and sanction. But it is useless for me to make you a suggestion on this branch of the subject. The scope of my observation in relation to it is to bring to your view the necessity of speedy action. Every day's delay is adding strength to the hands of those who are playing the game for the ascendency of British influence in this Republic. Not that the people are averse to union with us, or are willing to obtain their independence by the sacrifice of any of the principles which are recognized as essential to the American idea of liberty; but that tired of war and panting for repose, they may be led to believe that annexation to the United States is not necessary to their prosperity, or not so necessary as to justify the hazards of continued hostility with Mexico. In this state of feeling, without forecast to unravel the real designs of Great Britain—without information to penetrate the motives of those who tell them that Texas can be a great state, and a happier one, out of our union than in it—it must be expected that delay will increase the difficulties already in our way, if it does not make them insurmountable.

It is my duty to mention to the Department that I received this evening from the hands of Mr. D.T. Crumpler a bundle of papers, said to be those left by my Predecessor Gen[era]l [Tilghman A.] Howard, containing his commission, instructions & official correspondence. His papers and effects of a private nature (including his money) remain at the house of his death, in the hands of the Gentleman to whom they were entrusted, and will await the order of those legally authorised to receive them. He did not bring with him to this place the Record books of the legation and of course his instructions and correspondence are unrecorded. These, with the arrearages already existing, which are referred to in Mr. A[rchibald] M. Green's communication of the 19th July last, will throw a good deal of labor on my hands.

I find that Gen[era]l Howard, although here but a few days, made a most favorable impression on the inhabitants, who speak of him with great admiration and love. I am very respectfully y[ou]r ob[edien]t Ser[van]t, A.J. Donelson.

[P.S.] I send this despatch to our consul at Galvezton [Elisha A. Rhodes], to forward it by the first conveyance to [New] Orleans.

ALS (No. 2) in DNA, RG 59 (State Department), Diplomatic Despatches, Texas, vol. 2 (T-728:2, frames 398–400), received 12/28.

From E D W A R D E V E R E T T

London, 23 November, 1844

Sir, The receipt of your despatch Nro. 99 of the 7th of August, relative to the refusal of the Authorities at Nassau to surrender the Slaves charged with the murder of Mr. [John H.] Geeren of Florida, and demanded as fugitives, has been already acknowledged. Believing that a personal conference with Lord Aberdeen afforded the means of learning with the least delay the ground intended to be taken by this Government in reference to the questions raised on occasion of that refusal and discussed in your despatch, I availed myself of the earliest opportunity for the appointment of an interview for that purpose. After some delays not easily avoided at this season of the year, it took place on the 20th instant at Argyll House.

I introduced the subject with a general statement of the facts of the case, as set forth in your instructions just mentioned. I called Lord Aberdeen's attention to the argument by which the judges at Nassau defended the supposed requirements of the Statute of 6 & 7 Vict. C. 76; and to the inference naturally to be drawn from their language. I observed to him that I had been led by various considerations, to doubt whether the Court on this occasion had rightly interpreted the views of Her Majesty's Government. That if it were so, I was instructed strongly to contest them, but that being desirous of ascertaining the principles adopted by Her Majesty's Government on this subject without the delay incident to an elaborate discussion, I had thought it better to bring the question before him in this way, in the hope that he would be able to furnish me at once with a satisfactory explanation.

I then read to Lord Aberdeen that portion of your despatch Nro. 99, in which the facts of the case are related, and the inference naturally to be drawn from the language of the Court at Nassau is commented on.

As soon as I had done this, Lord Aberdeen observed that he found no difficulty in saying that of the extract from the opinion of the Court at Nassau given in your despatch, the only portion which he adopted, as the language of the Government, was the first part, in which it is stated that an indictment is not of itself, under the Act of parliament for carrying the treaty into effect, sufficient ground for giving up a fugitive. But the same answer would have been given by Her Majesty's Authorities had the persons demanded been free. The argument contained in the other part of the passage quoted in your instruction was no doubt intended to enforce the view taken by the Court of the expediency of the provisions of the Statute; but the answer to the application was perfect without it, and he felt no hesitation in saying, that the argument or illustration of the Court was not adopted by him. Consequently, as far as the Government was concerned, no inference like that dwelt upon in your letter should be drawn from it.

I told him that the notorious fact that the technical crime of murder was the same in all parts of the United States and in England left little room for doubt, that when the Court stated that "what may constitute the crime of murder in Florida may be very far from doing so according to the British laws or even the laws of the northern States of America," they must have alluded to the case of Slaves, and have intended to say that evidence which would establish a charge of murder against a free man might not establish it against a Slave.

Lord Aberdeen admitted that this was a fair inference as far as the Court was concerned, but repeated that it was merely language of argument or illustration for which the Government was not responsible.

He then remarked that he thought, as far as the present case was concerned, this must be considered a satisfactory reply to the enquiry contained in your despatch. The surrender of the fugitives was refused, because the application was not supported by the evidence required by the Statute; and it would have been of necessity refused, for the same reason, had the application been made in any part of the United Kingdom and had the fugitives been free white men.

He did not however, mean to say that in no case whatever which might arise hereafter, would the result of an application for the surrender of a fugitive charged with murder, depend in any degree upon the question whether he was a Slave endeavoring to escape from his master. By the laws of all Countries the same act of killing did or did not constitute the crime of murder, according to the circumstances of the case, which were often matters of very nice discrimination; and he could very well conceive that in cases which might arise, the fact of a person's being a Slave might materially affect the question of his guilt on a charge of having committed murder. Her Majesty's Government must reserve to itself the liberty of dealing with cases of this kind when they present themselves and of being governed by circumstances which cannot be foreseen nor provided for, in any general regulations. He was, however, free to say that he did not share the opinion of those who hold that Slaves as such cannot commit a crime. He regarded them as moral agents, and of course to be regarded in that light on a demand for extradition, leaving the consideration due to their condition as such to be decided by the circumstances of each individual case.

In reference to my observation, that the legal crime of murder was the same under the laws of both Countries, Lord Aberdeen said that in arranging the provisions of the extradition treaty with France, they had experienced some difficulty on that point. It was found that the words "murder" and "meurtre," in the two languages respectively would not without further qualification technically describe the same crime; and it had been necessary to add the words of definition, "comprehending the crimes designated in the French penal code by the terms assassination, Parricide, Infanticide, and Poisoning."

In the course of the interview I stated to Lord Aberdeen, that the Government of the United States considered that an Indictment or a duly authenticated copy of one, was by the treaty a sufficient ground for demanding the extradition of fugitive criminals, and that the statute in requiring the depositions or copies of depositions on which the indictment was founded, (if it did so require them, which was matter of some doubt) went beyond the treaty which neither party to that contract was competent to do. I added that I made this remark not now by way of entering into discussion on that point, but to prevent an inference being drawn from my silence.

Such is the substance of our conference on this subject, from which taken in connection with what has fallen from Lord Aberdeen on occasions where it has been less formally alluded to, I am disposed to infer that the instructions given to the Colonial Authorities, in reference to slaves whose surrender is demanded as fugitive criminals, are of a very general nature and such as would require, in cases of any difficulty, a reference to the Home Government for its decision.

That no instructions have been sent to refuse the surrender of Slaves as such is, I think, clearly implied in the remark of Lord Aberdeen, that in his view they are to be regarded as moral Agents capable of committing crimes. His distinct disavowal of the argumentative statement by the Court as to the grounds of the statute provision, which is supposed to require the production of the evidence laid before the Grand Jury who find the indictment, may be considered as proof that no instructions had been sent to the Court authorising such a statement.

As it appears from the observation of Lord Aberdeen that an indictment will in no case of itself be considered as a sufficient ground of surrender, I shall as soon as possible, address a note to him on that subject. I am, Sir, with great respect, Your obedient Servant, Edward Everett.

LS (No. 216) in DNA, RG 59 (State Department), Diplomatic Despatches, Great Britain, vol. 53 (M-30:49), received 12/23; FC in DNA, RG 84 (Foreign Posts), Great Britain, Despatches, 9:73–80; FC in MHi, Edward Everett Papers, 50:351–358 (published microfilm, reel 23, frames 449–453); CC in DNA, RG 233 (U.S. House of Representatives), 28A-E1; PC in House Document No. 114, 28th Cong., 2nd Sess., pp. 7–9.

From Ch[arle]s Hecker, Elberfeld, [Prussia], 11/23. Hecker applies for appointment to the now-vacant post of U.S. Consul for Rhenish Prussia. He has performed the duties of U.S. Commercial Agent at that post for three years and hopes that his experience will "counter balance" the fact that he is not a U.S. citizen. CC in DNA, RG 59 (State Department), Applications and Recommendations, 1837–1845, Hecker (M-687:15, frame 53).

From Henry A. Holms, New York [City], 11/23. "I am honoured with receipt of your esteemed favour of 20th respecting the Mexican claim, from the tenor of which you must have misunderstood the object of my visit[,] the letter which you had previously given me having been of great Service to me (to the U.S. Consul). Being now on the eve of departure for Yucatan I must postpone the further explaination, till I have again the pleasure of an interview with you." ALS in DNA, RG 59 (State Department), Miscellaneous Letters (M-179:106, frames 80–81).

To J.B. Lacey, "Appointed" U.S. Consul at Nuevitas, Cuba, 11/23. Lacey is sent copies of various documents pertinent to his official duties. His commission and exequatur will be forwarded to him when received from Madrid. FC in DNA, RG 59 (State Department), Consular Instructions, 10:277–278.

From EUSTIS PRESCOTT

New Orleans, 23d Nov[embe]r 1844

My Dear Sir, Thanks to the indomitable spirit of the Democracy of the South and West, lead by the little band of States rights men—who altho often vanquished, are never discouraged, we have obtained a victory as splendid, as unexpected—in the early part of the campaign.

Our opponents have not yet recovered their astonishment, and attribute our success to all manner of frauds, they do not reckon *the people*, the great mass of *consumers*, who can discover their own interest as keenly, as the great Manufacturers, and petty traders—nor did they recollect that little noble band who surrounding you my dear Sir—their leader, as a band of brothers for near fifteen years, entered into this contest with a determination, which neither the abuse of some, or the lukewarmness of others could appal—and their disappointment is the more intense. I have never witnessed in any previous contest the same violence and bitterness which has characterized this—friends have been separated—ridiculed and proscribed, and the bitterness does not yet abate, they do not appear to comprehend a contest for principles, and measures, which we deem paramount to all else.

I regret to say that many of the leading friends of Mr. [Martin] V[an] B[uren] both in New York and this city—I speak from my own observation, have stood aloof from the contest, or given us but their votes, and I am informed that the same course has been pursued in New Jersey and Ohio, yet they will be among the first to claim all the honor and profit; they are a selfish sett of politicians, and I trust that the President elect [James K. Polk] will learn their true character.

Already do we discover our old opponents gathering under a new name—"American Republican," and looking to a union with the Abolitionists of the north under Dan[ie]l Webster as their leader. I understood when last in Boston that such a movement would be made, but these people do not yet understand the character of the masses, no party can be formed on an isolated question of policy—which is that of an amendment of the naturalization laws, if defective, the Democratic party—when in power, will no doubt so amend them as to guard against frauds.

355

I hope and trust that the new Administration will bring forward some measure for the permanent settlement of the vexed questions of Tariff and Currency. I am satisfied that it can be done with a spirit of compromise—such as you have always manifested. I have heard many high tariff men say that an interest which required more protection than 33⅓% ought not to receive any, more, I feel confident that in a re-adjustment of the tariff an "accidental" protection of 25 to 30% on such articles as would appear most deserving of it, would eventually satisfy all parties. Even the Sugar interest of our own State, would I think be satisfied with a permanent revenue duty of *one and a half cent*, provided Salt was reduced to the same, Iron and other articles of their consumption to a similar ad valorem rate. I have always admired the plan pursued by the Br[itish] House of Commons on all questions of revenue, in calling before them intelligent men of business, and soliciting their advice & opinions.

The question of Currency is I think more difficult, but for some years I have come to the conclusion that it is probably best left to regulate itself, the Government doing her own business thro the Treasury Department, and the various Collectors of Impost, and Receivers of Sales of public lands. Our State Banks are under better regulations than formerly, and an intelligent Officer could always discover when it was prudent to receive, or reject the paper of certain Banks.

The Cotton interest is now in a sinking condition, the growth exceeds consumption, for this, I see no remedy but a diminution of cultivation, and the production of all articles for food and wear on the plantation. On the Mississ[ippi] bottoms Hemp might I think be cultivated profitably. This interest as well as many others might receive some aid from treaties of reciprocity with our neighbors of South America, Germany, Spain, Holland &c[;] with England I suppose such a thing impracticable. Spain and Mexico are taking much larger supplies of Cotton from us than formerly, and I am confident that Germany may be encouraged to do the same, we are too completely in the power of the "Manchester men" as regards the sale of our Cotton.

Your friends here my dear Sir look with great anxiety to your continuance in the Office you now hold under the ensuing Administration—unless you prefer the Treasury Department, and I assure you that our late opponents are equally anxious that you should do so. For ulterior objects we shall wait the movements of Virginia—which we understand that Mr. [Thomas] Ritchie has promised. Your friends here are always ready.

Excuse my dear Sir the great freedom with which I address you, and believe me to remain with great sincerity Your friend & Obed[ien]t Serv[an]t, Eustis Prescott.

ALS in ScCleA.

From ———, "Confidential"

Detroit Michigan, Nov. 23rd 1844

Sir, Presuming that an intimation of what may transpire on the Michigan chessboard may not be unacceptable, I take the liberty of writing you. Whatever of consequence the present movements or the contemplated plans may possess, it seems to me had better be known, at the right point, in season; at all events, I doubt not they will be received as they are given—as precautionary suggestions—and showing the commencement of more extensive operations in the future.

Although the great political contest of 1844, has yet scarcely closed, yet, strange as it may seem, the battle of 1848 is already mooted here. The cliques of two of the expected candidates are already in motion; they would feign suppose the contest will ["lie" *altered to* "be"] between the East and the West—and yet, with no little apprehension, they seem to be some-what restive in view of your Continuance in the state department. The administration of Mr. [James K.] Polk, it is anticipated, will be popular and should you be prominently identified with it, they fear that it would give you considerable advantage—that the success of the administration would be calculated to obviate whatever prejudice may exist against you in the north. Indeed I have heard such remarks from many of our respectable Citizens who are not regarded as active politicians but who heretofore entertained partial prejudices against you.

The hunkers expect that the recent election of Mr. [Silas] W[right as Governor] of N.Y. in addition to the influence he and his friends may have with the administration in taking care of *his friends*, will be sufficient to fortify his ["friends" *canceled*] position and place the Gen. [Lewis Cass] in the back ground.

On the other hand the friends of the latter are *already* in motion for his election to the U.S. Senate—the success of which is deemed of paramount importance. This they expect, will be calculated to produce a great effect in the other States, as well as enable him to form necessary associations while in the Senate, and though *last not least,* procure a large portion of the patronage for his friends throughout the Country. Thus, it is anticipated he will be able to compete with yourself and Mr. W[right]. There are several of the hunker clique, will pretend, I am satisfied, to be the friends of the Gen. for the purpose of obtaining his influence, for their own purposes. The position of men it is apparent, should therefore be cautiously watched and carefully considered.

It is rumored that you will retire to private life, while your friends are exceedingly anxious that you should not. They hope, if consistent with your own judgment, you will continue in the conspicuous position you now occupy—a contrary course, it is manifest, would afford your rivals and their friends the utmost satisfaction.

But I shall not continue these speculations at present. Your friends are determined on fair play, and I doubt not, will watch the progress of events with solicitude. Whatever of importance may fall under my observation shall be carefully noted.

As I have no confidence in the conduct of the post office here, I will not add my name, but which you may consider as the person who wrote you on the 11th inst. [*not found*], and which I sent by a friend to Buffalo to be mailed there.

ALU in ScCleA. Note: An AEU by Calhoun reads "Anonymous, relates to the Presi[dentia]l election."

From A[ndrew] J. Donelson

Washington Texas, Nov[embe]r 24[t]h 1844

Sir, I have the pleasure to state to you that President [Samuel] Houston reached this place last night; and favored me with an interview in less than fifteen minutes after his arrival.

In order that you may see the character of his views, I will give you a narrative of our conversation, very much in the order in which the topics arose, and were disposed of.

Adverting to the situation of Texas he dwelt with satisfaction on his success in defeating the schemes of many adventurers, who had found their way into Congress and other Departments of the Government: and declared that if he had not been disturbed by the *Texan certifiers* (alluding to those who furnished evidence of the desire of the people for annexation) he would have accomplished the measure himself. His idea was, that, England and Mexico encouraged by the hope of defeating the policy of the United States—and the United States alarmed, in their turn, by the fear of English intrigue—gave him a lever on the question which it was his intention to use, so as to restore Texas to our union, whenever he found it practicable. He denounced, in his peculiar manner, those who forced him to abandon his policy, and shew his hand before it could be played with success. He blamed Messrs. [J. Pinckney] Henderson and Vanzant [*sic*; Isaac Van Zandt] for signing the Treaty without obtaining a fuller guarantee from the Executive of the United States [John Tyler] to defend Texas, should the proposition for annexation provoke a renewal of hostilities on the part of Mexico, or otherwise expose her to injury.

I told him in reply that so far as the Executive of the United States was concerned there had been, and was, every disposition to befriend Texas, and even to defend her in the manner suggested, but that he was aware of his limited powers, and of the consequences which would have resulted from a disagreement between him & Congress in the exercise of an act which might have been deemed warlike. The Executive, with no Congress to sustain him, would necessarily have failed; and thus the cause of annexation would have received a prejudice far greater than it did from the course adopted. I also brought to his recollection that the remedy for all such cases in the United States was in an appeal to the people—that this appeal had been made, and the issue of the Presidential election just closed, if favorable to Mr. [James K.] Polk, would prove that the course of Mr. Tyler in regard to the policy of annexation had the popular sanction.

He said, that he was far from censuring President Tyler or his Cabinet—that he accorded to Mr. Tyler all praise for his patriotism and vigilance; and that he requested me to say to him in his judgement, of all the Presidents since Mr. [Thomas] Jefferson[']s day, he was the only one to be compared with Gen[era]l [Andrew] Jackson: and further that whatever might be the fate of Texas, in, or out, of the union, her people would soon be rich, and that they would erect a monument which would perpetuate their gratitude to Mr. Tyler.

I returned him my thanks for these generous and noble sentiments, and hailed them as evidence that the cause of annexation was still dear to the hearts of the brave people he had so signally served: and further remarked that I trusted nothing had been done to commit Texas to a policy inconsistent with the speedy consummation of the measure. That from the open avowal Gen[era]l Terrill [*sic*; George W. Terrell] had made of opposition to the policy of the United States on this subject, and from the concurrence in such sentiments generally manifested by the subordinate officers of his Government, I had been led to fear some line of conduct had been adopted which would render the contest in the United States abortive.

He replied that he was not in the habit of committing himself—that "leaky vessels would not hold water long"—that he had much to say on this subject (here some of his friends were present). As soon as they retired he insisted on my remaining with him. I did so. He then resumed the conversation by observing, that he could conceal nothing from me, acquainted as I was with his trials and sufferings thru life, and coming as I did from the Hermitage.

I replied to this, that Gen[era]l Jackson was still alive, and took an interest in his conduct, at this critical period, which he could imagine much better than I could express it—that he looked upon the annexation of Texas as the great question of the day, as having a greater influence on the affairs of this continent than any that had occurred since the Revolution: and he was anxious that his friend Houston whom Providence had made the prominent actor in it thus far, should maintain his elevated position to the close, and show that he comprehended the results which were to flow from its influence on the fate of free institutions—that he feared the path of his duty might be observed by the arguments which would be addressed in favor of the seperate existence of the Republic, and by the plausibility which would be given to the idea of making Texas a nucleus for the formation of new states, extending to the Pacific, affording a refuge for the oppressed of all nations, and rivalling the United States—that yielding to such a prospect, so tempting to ambition, and so natural to the spirit of adventure already too much aroused by the course pursued by Mexico and the United States in postponing so long the settlement of their boundaries, Gen[era]l Jackson, feared his friend might overlook what was due to the more sober injunctions of wisdom and experience.

No—no—no—was the reply. Tell Gen[era]l Jackson that his counsels influence my spirit—that his words are treasures—that the young sergeant who profitted so much by his advice in his early career has only learned to value that advice the more as time and adversity have strengthened his faculties. Tell him that Sam[ue]l Houston though distant from him in the wilderness, and abandoned to the chances of a merciless contest with Mexicans and savages, has not lost sight of the measure of annexation. He continued to remark in reference to the fear expressed concerning the purport of the instructions given to Gen[era]l Terrill, that I might dismiss it. He said it was true he,

[James] R[e]ily, and a few others were opposed to annexation, but that this was no indication of the course of the Government—that Gen[era]l Terrill was not authorised to conclude a Treaty—that he had sent him to England and France to see what bids they would make, what boot they would give—that he was not authorised to commit the Government, and power, to do so, would not be given to him.

I told President Houston here, that I was truly gratified at this frank declaration of his views and sentiments and more than happy to find them so favorable to annexation—that as soon as my credentials were received I would take pleasure in laying before him the views of my Government on that great question; and that I trusted he would not take ground on that part of the topics of his valedictory message, until I had an opportunity also of exhibiting to him the aspect of the opinion now existing in the United States on the subject— that I felt sure when he came to reflect on the views of my Government he would find them so reasonable and just as to command his respect and support.

To this he replied that he was glad the U.S. Government had made me the organ of their views; and that he would be proud to see annexation accomplished during my connection with the Government— that the Secretary of State [Anson Jones] was expected tomorrow, but if he did not arrive he would give a temporary appointment to some one else to hasten my official presentation.

I remained with the President nearly all night, there being nothing but a door to seperate our apartments, which are open log cabins. He was unreserved and cordial, and as far as I can form an opinion, determined to adhere to the idea of annexation as long as there is a hope of effecting it on terms of honor and justice to his Republic.

It is, perhaps, due to the President that I should not omit to state, that, in the course of our free and general range over the many topics suggested by the examination of the relations of the two Republics, among which, suggested by myself, was the prominence that annexation would assign to him as a citizen of the United States, he uniformly repelled the idea of personal political views. He declared it to be his intention to retire to his plantation on the Trinity river and devote the remainder of his life to the pursuits of agriculture and the education of his son. He said no inducement should tempt him from this retirement after the establishment of the independence of the Republic—that his ambition was satisfied—he had made no money and had no means of support except what would arise from the improvement of his lands, yet he hoped to have enough to pay the expenses of a pilgrimage to the Hermitage next spring, after which he would bid adieu to all other expectations save those which would centre round his own domicil.

This frame of mind, seeming to me to harmonize with a calculation of interest dependent upon annexation, is worthy of notice as an interpreter of his policy, perhaps as reliable as any of the impressions referred to. The stability which would follow the extension of the laws of the United States over this Republic, having the power which our flag would have to banish all apprehension of invasion or disorder, foreign or domestic, would at once raise the value of these lands, and in many other respects increase the wealth and population of the country—a consequence which must be seen by President Houston.

I have thus, Sir, laid before you a random view of my first conversation with the President, at the risk of fatiguing you with details which ought not to have a place in a public document. In my next despatch I shall give you what passes at my presentation, and endeavor to possess something in an official form which will be more pointed and explicit. In the mean time I have the honor to be with great respect Your ob[edien]t Servant, A.J. Donelson.

ALS (No. 3) in DNA, RG 59 (State Department), Diplomatic Despatches, Texas, vol. 2 (T-728:2, frames 400–404), received 12/28.

From J [AMES] HAMILTON, [JR.], *"Private"*

Pennyworth Island [Ga.], Savannah River, Nov. 24[t]h 1844

My Dear Sir, I have been so much occupied on my Rice Est[ate]s on this River where I found large Crops, that I have had scarcely a moment to spare to devote to other objects.

The victory is [*sic*] been won very much by our *moral* force and it remains to be seen how Mr. [James K.] Polk will use it. I received a few Days ["th" *canceled*] since the enclosed Letter [of 10/31] from him which I deem of no great moment beyond the indication of good feeling[,] good temper and moderation. As he has invited my correspondence I shall in the course of a few Days write him very fully on public affairs and the tone of the South, on those great issues on which he has been elected. I will send you a copy of my Letter, and

I trust whilst I shall aim on all public Questions to combine firmness with moderation, and candor with a respect due to Mr. Polk[']s own character and distinguished station towards yourself in my communication I shall maintain that delicacy which comports so entirely with your own reputation & self respect.

In a few Days we shall have [Governor James H.] Hammond[']s message [to the S.C. General Assembly], which will enable me to decide what influence my counsels have had over its tone. I have endeavoured to convince him that any blustering violence or indication of separate action, on the part of the State ["what"(?) *canceled and* "would" *interlined*] not only be the worst possible *policy* but in the worst possible *taste*, after obtaining by our own party a right to a fair participation in the Govt. of the Country. [George] McDuffie's advance may countervail all that I have done.

I sincerely hope, that Polk may have the sagacity consulting alone the best interests of the Country and his own to invite you on terms highly complimentary ["to yourself" *interlined*] into his Cabinet. I have no doubt that every base & malignant influence will be brought to bear on Gen[era]l [Andrew] Jackson to induce him to persuade Polk of the expediency & wisdom of reconstructing his Cabinet on a new basis and that the pretext will be suggested that he could not retain you in your present post without giving offence to the rest of Mr. [John] Tyler[']s Cabinet. If he takes this course I am resolved ["in advance" *interlined*] it shall not be adopted without a distinct intimation, that of all men at the South you are the individual with whom she would be pleased should represent her interests in the Govt.

Without looking at all to ulterior results I wish for you the renown of annexing Texas, adjusting the Oregon & Slave Questions with Great Britain and procuring through a reciprocity Treaty with her a modification ["of the Tariff" *interlined*] which shall bring it down to the Revenue Standard. [*One word canceled.*] If ["this" *canceled and* "such a" *interlined*] Treaty is defeated in the Senate the ["effect will be to" *interlined*] unite the So[uth] & West in determined & effective hostility to the whole Protective system.

I believe these objects can be accomplished by yourself with the agents[,] diplomatic & Legislative[,] capable of comprehending your views & with a Zeal ["perseverance & a" *interlined*] friendship ["& perseverance," *canceled and* "towards yourself" *interlined*] which shall gratify ["you" *canceled and* "them" *interlined*] for carrying them out.

You will permit me to request that no allusion be made to the

possibility of my employment in any public capacity—as such an intimation would impair my influence in giving a right direction to the
public sentiment & public measures of So. Carolina. I have not the
smallest idea that Polk[']s Northern allies from my known devotion
to yourself would allow me [to] occupy a station where it might be
possible for me to do any thing for your public repute however indifferent they might be to *what little* I might do towards my own.
Besides I have borne with too much severity on ["("Thomas H.) Benton" *canceled and* "the Whig" *interlined*] members of the Senate and
those of the Democratic party ["who acted with them on the annexation Question" *interlined*] to render a confirmation of ["any"
canceled; "my nomination of" *interlined and then canceled*; "my
nomination to" *interlined*] any high station probable even if Mr. Polk
was likely to make it.

Besides I understand that President Tyler desires the pageant to
St. James to gratify with its *eclat* the pride of his young wife [Julia
Gardiner Tyler]. I do not see very well how Polk can get *round* him
and still less *yourself.* Therefore My Dear Sir if you should be called
to share in the Govt. do not embarrass yourself with me or "my affairs" past[,] present & to come. I can return without a sigh to my
Cotton fields and leave the spoils to others.

It is quite true that nothing would gratify me more than to van-
quish under your orders the tariff ["even if the Battle Ground should
be" *interlined and* "at" *canceled*] the Court of St. James & speak in
reference to interests of the South in the terms fitting one of her *own*
Sons. But I have reached the temperate Zone of human hopes[,]
wishes & passions and can rest in the shade without a passing regret.

I send you a Copy of my Letter to the Nashville Committee, which
I wish you to read because they ["tell" *canceled and* "write" *interlined*] me ["from that place" *interlined*] it has done more to unite
Tennessee to So. Carolina than any public Document which has appeared since the election of Gen[era]l Jackson.

You see I have thrown down the glove to Benton. If he crooks his
finger at me, I will bring him up to tow[?].

If you write me on or before Friday the 29[t]h direct to this
place[;] after that to the Oswichee P.O. Ala. for which I leave on
Wednesday the 4[t]h Dec. After remaining ["a day or two" *canceled
and* "a week or ten Days" *interlined*] at the Bend I shall then proceed
to Texas *via* New Orleans where I hope to aid Doneladson [*sic*; Andrew J. Donelson] most essentially in effectuating your views. In the
mean time be assured My Dear Sir of the esteem with which I am
faithfully & respect[full]y Yours, J. Hamilton.

P.S. On Thursday night the 28[t]h the Georgians have a grand celebration on ac[count] of the Great Democratic Victory. They have invited me to address the Citizens from the monument of [Casimir] Pulaski in the City Square. I will endeavour to make the most of the occasion—and before I leave will send you the particulars.

[Enclosure]

James K. Polk to Gen. James Hamilton, Savannah, "Private"

Columbia Tenn., Oct. 31st 1844

My Dear Sir, I had the pleasure some days ago, to receive your very acceptable and friendly letter of the 13th Inst. giving returns of the Georgia election—for which I thank you. I had learned from numerous other sources—the fact which you state, that Mr. Calhoun and his friends had given a very cordial support to our ticket, throughout the canvass, and need not say to you that I am much gratified that is so. A few days more will decide the great contest in which we are engaged, and it would be useless to indulge in speculations as regards the probable result. I will say however, that our prospects for success, as I learn them from my numerous correspondents, are of a cheering character. My friends in New York—write to me most confidently that they will carry that State. Great efforts are however now being made by the Federal leaders to unite the *Natives* & *Abolitionists* with the *Whigs party proper.* If these efforts shall be successful—such a complete union shall be effected between these factions and the Whigs, the contest in New York will be close and the result doubtful. If we carry New York the contest will be settled. If we loose [*sic*] her, and carry any one of the six closely contested States of Connecticut, New Jersey, Maryland, N. Carolina, Ohio or Tennessee, I think we will still succeed. All our information in this State justifies the confident belief that we will carry her, though by a close vote. I shall be pleased my Dear Sir, to hear from you again, whenever your leisure may permit. I am Very faithfully & Truly Your friend, James K. Polk.

ALS with En in ScCleA.

From J[OHN] D. GARDINER

Sag Harbor[N.Y.,] Nov. 25th 1844

My very Dear Friend, The mighty contest is over and the battle is won. Victory perches upon the Republican Standard; and a proud victory it is. In this State the st[r]ife has been fierce; and without a parallel.

On the part of the political foe, every artifice, and every influence which money could command, and ["every artifice which" *canceled*] inginuity could devise, have been put in requisition. A combination has been arrayed against us, which for, a time, rendered the result of the struggle, in the Empire State, somewhat doubtful. But thank Heaven the Democracy has triumphed, and the Country is safe.

On such an occasion permit me to tender to you my heartfelt congratulations. I know you will rejoice with me, in the success of our cause, and the triumph of our principles. There is cause for joy and rejoicing; throughout the Land. The enemy has been completely routed and put to flight, overwhelmed with defeat, chagrin, and despair. On such an occasion, what friend to freedom, and equal rights, what Patriot, what Republican, nay what Christian, can refrain from demonstrations of gratitude and joy? This victory, like that of 1800, will form a new era in our political History. It will constitute one of its brightest pages, which, I trust our children, and our children's children, will read with delight.

This place being the Strong hold, the very focus of Modern Whiggery and old Federalism, strong in wealth and numbers we had to contend here with every sort of opposition. No pains, nor arts, nor money, nor efforts, were spared to put us down.

The hiss of derision and the fingers of scorn, were directed against the Republicans of this port, with a view to intimidate and dishearten them. Tho' their numbers and resources were comparitively small, they met their opponents, with that determined spirit, which conscious rectitude seldom fails to inspire.

We all did our duty; and "pushed on the Column." While the County of Old Suffolk is, and ever has been truly Republican in her principles, this place, I regret to say, is one of the most bitter and vindictive holds of Federal Aristocracy in the State or Country. The office holders are all of this stamp and used every means to carry the election. The Collector & Post Master were idle but arrayed themselves and their influence in direct opposition to us.

My Son Samuel [L. Gardiner], with other members of the Young men's Polk & Dallas Club, met them at every point, with boldness, and contended, like Heroes for every inch of ground. Knowing his invincible spirit, he was often called upon to address Democratic assemblies in different places; and he did so by night & by day, pleading their cause and advocating their principles; and at the same time, showing up the principles of his opponents in no very favorable light.

And while the elder son was thus engaged here in organising[,] encouraging and strengthening the Republican Ranks of the place and the neighboring towns, my younger son a member of the University, was heard pleading the cause of Democracy in the midst of thousands assembled at Tammany Hall in the City of N. York.

I mention these things not because I am vain but because I am happy to say, that all my five sons, are arrayed, by the side of their Father in the support of Republican principles. I am pleased to state that my youngest Son Calhoun [Gardiner], has taken the deepest interest in the progress and termination of the great struggle With the buoyant spirit and ardor of youth, he has watched the various movements of the contending parties with a degree of interest, vigilance, and solicitude seldom witnessed in a boy of his age. His confidence of success was never seen to waver, and when the result was announced his eyes glistened with Tears of joy, which for a time he could not express.

To shew you the feelings of my son Abraham S. Gardin[er] at the University, in the City of New York, when the news came that the State had gone for Polk & Dallas, I send you the letter which he then wrote to his Father. It was prompted you will perceive, by the overflowing joy of a youthful heart and shews his attachment to Democratic principles. I mention these little things because I know you can duly appreciate such trifles, as contributing, in no small degree, to make up the sum of Parental enjoyment.

In point of mind Calhoun is quite equal, and I think superior to either of his brothers. Nothing, but opportunity is wanting to make him shine. With reliance for aid to prosecute his Education, upon your kindness, and "the determination of the President to give my Son Samuel the appointment of Collector of this place," as you informed ["me" *interlined*] in your last, he will go on with his Studies, under a ["last" *altered to* "lasting"] sense of his obligation to you for the distinguished favor. Please to favor me with a line when convenient; and to excuse me for troubling you with this Letter, prompted by the wish to mingle my feelings of Congratulation with yours, on the achievement, of so splendid a victory, over our political opponents. With great respect & esteem I am your sincere friend, J.D. Gardiner.

ALS with En in ScCleA. NOTE: Gardiner sent to Calhoun, enclosed with the above, a letter from his son, A[braham] S. Gardiner, dated 11/7, which expressed fulsome delight in the election of Polk and Dallas and that the Democratic party had gained a majority of votes in N.Y.

From "Hamden" [Jabez D. Hammond], Otsego County, N.Y., 11/25. In this public letter to Calhoun, published in a pamphlet of 34 pp., the author sets forth in great detail the reasons for his opposition to the annexation of Texas to the U.S. He identifies himself as a N.Y. Democrat who declined to vote for James K. Polk in the recent Presidential election, and also as one who has been personally acquainted with Calhoun for a quarter of a century and who has "great admiration" for Calhoun's talents, integrity, and patriotism. He addresses Calhoun as the author of the Texas annexation treaty, but the bulk of his pamphlet is devoted to opposing the arguments not of Calhoun but of Robert J. Walker, Andrew Jackson, James K. Polk, Martin Van Buren, and others. "Hamden" is opposed to territorial expansion in general as tending to undermine the Union. He is opposed to the annexation of Texas because it will extend the viability of slavery. He believes amalgamation of the two nations is unconstitutional. He argues against assumption of the Texas debt, and he believes that, contrary to proponents of annexation, the admission of Texas will be deleterious rather than helpful to the economic welfare and defense needs of the Union. He is willing to support the slave states in their existing rights, but believes that the admission of Texas will constitute a greater concession to them than is justified. PC in "Hamden," *Letter to the Hon. John C. Calhoun, on the Annexation of Texas* (Cooperstown [N.Y.]: printed by H. & E. Phinney, 1844).

From BETSEY HAWLEY

South Norwalk Conn., Nov. 25th, '44

Sir, I am much surprised, after your promising me that my business should be "promptly" attended to, that it should have been so long delayed—especially, as I informed you it was so *very* important to me that it should be done as soon as possible. I really hope sir, you will be so kind as to inform me if any thing has intervened to cause the delay.

Please address Miss Betsey Hawley, South Norwalk, Fairfield County, Connecticut. I have the honor to be, sir, with high respect, Your serv[an]t, Betsey Hawley.

ALS in DNA, RG 59 (State Department), Miscellaneous Letters (M-179:106, frames 83–84). NOTE: An AEU by Hawley on the address sheet reads: "This letter is to be opened by Mr. Calhoun in person and *not* by any Clerk at the Department of State." Hawley sought information from the State Department concerning a claim of the estate of her brother, Capt. Isaac P. Hawley.

From ALBERT SMITH

Boundary Line
Moose River [Maine]
Nov. 25, 1844

Sir, I have a large party still in the woods, but trust they will have completed the work assigned them in ten days.

To be able to meet their Compensation & other expenses, I shall require the balance of the appropriation for the Boundary survey—(["$" *interlined*] 7,500) & I most respectfully request that *that* sum be placed to my credit in the Merchants Bank at Boston.

It is the intention of the Commissioners to complete the whole Line during the next season. To enable them to do this, at the lowest estimate I can make, the American Commissioner will require an appropriation of seventy five thousand dollars. I have the honor to be Most respectfully Your ob[edien]t Ser[van]t, Albert Smith, U.S. [Boundary] Com[missione]r.

ALS in DNA, RG 59 (State Department), Letters and Accounts from Despatch Agents at New York and Boston, vol. for 8/1840–11/1847; CC in DNA, RG 233 (U.S. House of Representatives), 28A-D30.6.

UNKNOWN PERSON to Cha[rle]s ——

Philad[elphia,] 25 Nov. 1844

Dear Chas., The name signed to the Charleston letters [published in the Philadelphia *Gazette*] in relation to Mr. [John C.] Calhoun is James M. Crane. He says in a letter to Mr. [Joseph R.] C[handle]r not published that the Editor of the Mercury [John A. Stuart], proclaimed openly & every where, free trade & Texas or disunion & that if Mr. [James K.] Polk was elected Mr. Calhoun would be Secretary of State. He mentions the address of Mr. [Henry L.] Pinckney as being in the same strain; that they had nullified once & would do so again, & a long letter of same tenor. He says Walter Forney Esq. wrote a similar letter to Hon. C[ornelius] Darragh at Pittsburg.

There were letters of this character simultaneously published at Balt[imor]e by the Intelligencer &c. Mr. Chandler's name *is not to be used*, in this investigation. If the Hon. Mr. Forney did write such letters, a clue to the whole matter might be found. The writer of the letters is not an educated man. He says—"put this in—as you *chuse.*"

Mr. C[handle]r thinks that his correspondent has appended a false name; & that certainly his zeal has run ahead of truth. Mr. C[handler] is so much dissatisfied with the course of the whig party during the late campaign, that he threw out for remark by me, the suggestion that he had better cease politics: he could not work with a good will, under the domination of such leaders as controlled the movements of the party in this State. He in common with many others fears, that Mr. Calhoun's open, unsuspecting course, can not match the secret cunning & intrigue of the [Thomas H.] Benton & [Martin] Van Buren parties who will leave no means unassayed to sow between him & Mr. Polk the seeds of discord & dissension. It will be a marvel, if by the 4th March next, Mr. Polk has not received, every insinuation & charge, which malice, fraud & cunning can suggest, ["to the in"(?) *canceled*] why Mr. Calhoun should not remain in his cabinet. They know full well, that it would be impossible for the relations of President & Sec[retar]y of State to subsist between these Gentlemen, without Mr. Polk's being firmly impressed, with the frank sincerity & open[n]ess of Mr. Calhoun; & that his counsels would be potential; besides which Mr. C[alhoun] would probably have the opportunity of doing eminent service to his country & credit to himself by his diplomacy on the Texas & Oregon questions.

Ms. in ScCleA. Note: An AEU by Calhoun, on this document among his papers, reads: "Gives the name of the author of the letter to the [Philadelphia] Gazette." Possibly the addressee was Charles J. Ingersoll.

From James T. Brady, New York [City], 11/26. He approves all that John McKeon wrote to Calhoun on 11/10 about James Fiora, who is not a political spoilsman and is highly recommended for a Consulship in England. ALS in DNA, RG 59 (State Department), Applications and Recommendations, 1845–1853, James Fiora (M-873:28, frames 100–102).

From D[ABNEY] S. CARR

Legation of the U.S.
Cons[tantino]ple, 26th Nov. 1844
Sir, I have the honor to acknowledge the receipt of your Despatch
No. 13 covering a copy of your admirable despatch No. 6 to the
Hon[ora]ble Wilson Shannon, our Minister at Mexico. I trust that,
by this time, the result of the President[i]al Election has given it the
popular sanction. I have the honor to be with sentiments of the high-
est respect, Your very Ob[e]d[ien]t Serv[an]t, D.S. Carr.

LS (No. 23) in DNA, RG 59 (State Department), Diplomatic Despatches,
Turkey, vol. 10 (M-46:12), received 1/27/1845; FC in DNA, RG 84 (Foreign
Posts), Turkey, Despatches, G:148.

From GEO[RGE] W[ILLIA]M GORDON

Consulate of the United States
Rio de Janeiro, 26 Nov. 1844
Sir, I have reason to suppose that R.S. Gough late 2d Mate of the
Brig "Agnes" and whom I consider an important witness in the [Afri-
can slave trade] case of [Jason L.] Pendleton and others, has in a
private manner left this City. Mr. Gough first came to this port as
Master of the Schooner "Sarah Ann" of Newport R.I. arrived 1st June
1843. He shipped as second Mate of the "Agnes" ["at this port" *interlined*] in March 1844 before that Vessel left for the Coast of Africa,
and was attached to her until she was sold by Capt. [Hiram] Gray.
I have reason to believe that while on the Coast, he lived a great deal
on Shore at Cabinda, and is probably better acquainted with what
took place there in regard to the Monte Video, than any other individual.

He is an intelligent man kept a Journal of what took place on the
Coast while there and as I have remarked, I consider his examination
very important in the case of Pendleton. I suspect that he secreted
himself on board the "R.H. Douglass" and left in that Vessel with
Captain Gray and Mr. [William M.] Ruhl for Baltimore.

The Certificates of Gough and Ruhl appear in the case of the Brig
"Cyrus" Capt. [P.C.] Dumas. His (Gough's) residence in the United
States I do not know. I have the honor to be Sir With the greatest

371

respect Your obedient Serv[an]t, Geo. Wm. Gordon, Consul of the United States.

LS (No. 15) and 2 duplicate LS's in DNA, RG 59 (State Department), Consular Despatches, Rio de Janeiro, vol. 7 (T-172:8), received 1/30/1845.

From HENRY SAVAGE

Guatemala, Nov[embe]r 26th 1844

On the 20th inst. I received a note from [Manuel Francisco Pavon] the Secretary of State of the Government of Guatemala, [a] copy of which you will find enclosed, in which the Executive of this State [Rafael Carrera] manifests a disposition to enter into negotiations to conclude a treaty of commerce and amity with the United States.

This note is the duplicate of that addressed to me in November 1843 on the same subject, and of which, I transmitted a copy to your department in December last year. The object of this note, is to communicate to the Government of the United States, the unchanged sentiments of the State of Guatemala in this particular.

I trust it will be unnecessary to recommend this subject to your attention. A treaty of Commerce with Guatemala is essential to the security of Citizens of the United States, prosecuting their lawful pursuits in this country; and it may prove the means of extending the intercourse with the United States, which is so much to be desired.

A convention of Peace was signed at Quesada on the 5th August ult[im]o by Commissioners of Guatemala and the Supreme Delegate; it reestablishes the friendly relations between the States of Guatemala and S[an] Salvador. The ratifications were exchanged on the 8th of October in this City.

Guatemala is not however, free from internal commotions. On the evening of the 20th September last, a revolt of the Garrison in this City, took place, which was happily put down, but not until after a few shops under the Portal, and several booths in the Public square had been sacked. The following morning, three of those said to be the principal ringleaders, were shot without any trial.

On the whole, the political condition of Central America is truly deplorable: the City of Guatemala is under continual alarm, through apprehension of a revolutionary outbreak, attributed to the general disaffection of parties against the Government. San Salvador and Honduras while overwhelmed with difficulties to suppress their intestine dissention, are struggling to repel the aggressive forces of Nicaragua, sent to subvert the administration of those States. With great respect I am Your Obed[ien]t Serv[an]t, Henry Savage.

ALS (No. 15) with En in DNA, RG 59 (State Department), Diplomatic Despatches, Guatemala (M-219:4), received 5/2/1845.

From ROBERT WALSH, "Private"

Paris, Nov[embe]r 26, 1844
Dear Sir, My friend Ashbel Smith Esq[ui]r[e], for the three or four years past Chargé d'Affaires of the Republic of Texas, [*one word changed to* "with"] French & British governments, is about to visit the United States & will visit Washington on his way to Texas. The excellent opportunities & superior intelligence of this gentleman have provided him with an ample fund of curious and instructive matter relating to the politics and men of Europe. You will naturally take great interest in the discourse of so able an observer and reporter. He is well acquainted with my humble opinions & with the general sources of my information, and if they should seem to deserve your attention, he will state what he has heard from me in our familiar communion.

I transmit to you herewith [*not found*] various articles which I have cut from British Journals & which contain statistical facts or political views of more or less importance for American interests. Allow me to direct your attention in particular to the essay of the eminent Spanish author, [Manuel de] *Marliani,* on the question of ["French" *canceled and* "foreign" *interlined*] influence in Spain. It abounds with truth eloquently & fearlessly expressed. I have just borrowed for him the volume which contains your Speeches. He had long wished to read those in which you treat the subjects of Free Trade and Tariffs. With the utmost respect, your ob[edien]t Serv[an]t, Robert Walsh.

ALS in ScCleA. NOTE: Marliani's pamphlet mentioned by Walsh was probably his *De la influencia del sistema prohibitivo en la agricultura, industria, comercio, y rentas publicas* (Madrid: J. Cuesta, 1842).

From FRANCIS WHARTON

[Philadelphia,] Nov. 26th, 1844

My dear Sir, I am very much gratified at the letter I received from you by yesterday[']s mail. I had previously made some enquiries in relation to Judge [Edward] King's early political history—the point to which your first letter was directed—and I am really most glad to be able to exhibit to you the true facts in the case in time to enable you to make up your unbiassed judgment. Judge King, in connection with a few others, whom you may remember as being concerned in the [Philadelphia] Franklin Gazette, [*"as"* canceled and *"was" interlined*] distinguished, to the period when he went on the bench, as being one of your most ardent political supporters. He was, in fact, one of the main-springs of that paper; & he was among the most reluctant & tardy of the little band, who, at the time of the junction with General [Andrew] Jackson in 1824, were [*partial word canceled*] assigned away, under Mr. [George M.] Dallas' lead, & with your consent. The last act of his political career was to vote, in 1828, as a presidential elector, for yourself & General Jackson. Such are Judge King's "political associations" down to the time when he ceased to have, very properly, any political associations whatever; and I am very much rejoiced at being able to assist in warding off a blow, which, under Mr. [James] Buchanan's wily management, may be meant to strike deeper than it at first appeared. Judge King's confirmation [to the U.S. Supreme Court] will not only defeat an intrigue of the lowest order, but it will fill the vacant seat with talents, energy, business character, & public worth, of the highest grade. Yours most truly, Francis Wharton.

[P.S.] I have kept back my letter to mention a point which has just been brought to my notice by a letter from a legal gentleman of Maryland of the highest authority. You are aware of how great importance it is to the Southern States that a man should fill the vacant seat whose views will be orthodox on the great question of slavery. The abolitionists have been howling about Judge King's path ever since he has been on the bench, in consequence of his energetic enforcement of the Constitutional provisions in reference to fugitive slaves, as declared in the great case of Comm[onwealth] of Pa. v. Prigg. ["Since the death of Judge (Joseph) Hopkinson," *canceled*] Judge King has been almost invariably resorted to by the owners of slave property in emergency; and he has sustained the constitution, as is a matter of record, with ["ener" *canceled*] uniform promptness and energy. Of how much importance it is that the vacant Judgeship should be filled by a man orthodox on that great question, I leave you to judge.

I have just heard that it has been rumoured in Washington that it would be Judge King's first act, if confirmed, to remove Mr. [Francis] Hopkinson from the C[ircuit] C[ourt] Clerkship, & appoint Joel B. Sutherland. It is not so; and I understand that Judge King has openly told Mr. Hopkinson that he would do all in his power, as he did on a previous occasion, to secure him in his position.

ALS in ScCleA. NOTE: An AEU by Calhoun on this letter reads: "Mr. Wharton[.] Relates to Judge King."

From JAMES [EDWARD CALHOUN]

University of Va., Nov. 27th 1844

Dear father, To the many arrangements I have had to make and the knowledge of Judge [Henry St. George] Tucker's having written shortly after my arrival here, you may attribute my perhaps seemingly long delay. I have therefore taken this opportunity of informing you that I reached this place the day after leaving Washington; and upon introducing myself to the Judge by the means of your letter desired him to aid me with his advice in selecting the tickets he thought I could most advantageously pursue, finding his selection to agree precisely with the ones selected by myself, viz: The mathematical[,] philosophical and classical tickets[,] the latter comprising both the Greek and Latin languages; In mathematics[,] philosophy and Greek I have taken the Junior classes not being prepared to enter the highest class and prefer[r]ing it to the intermediate, while in Latin I have entered the Senior thinking either of offering for graduation upon it at the close of the session in July next or drop[p]ing it altogether and taking in its place some other ticket.

As you have never visited this place I cannot consider it amiss to give you a brief description both as to its location and the course of instruction.

It is very pleasantly situated on an elevation at the foot of a chain of the Blue-Ridge mountains known as the South-Western chain and singularly laid out into ["four" *interlined*] ranges—the two extremities receiving their mames [*sic*] from their situation viz: the eastern and western ranges and the two middle from the side of the lawn upon which they are respectively situated namely the Eastern and western

375

lawns. Upon the former lawn I have very comfortably settled my self in a room the dimensions of which are twelve feet by ten having a fire place and a cheap carpeted floor which adds much to its appearance and comfort making it serve both as a dormitory and a sitting or studying room.

The course of instruction here, is as you may have noticed in the circular principally by the means of lectures[,] a system which I cannot conceive as being preferable to that adopted in most colleges since it renders the course far mor[e] difficult and causing [*sic*] a student to dispense almost entirely with the text-books which he is required to purchase of the Professors at the most extravagant prices and often in great numbers. While I think of it I will be much oblige[d] to you for pricing two books that will be very much needed by me here but can only be obtained in Charlott[e]sville at a price that I would not be willing to give unless they are not to be had at other places lower[?]. They are *Lieber's Encyclopedia Americana* and [Hugh] *Murray's Geographical Encyclopedia.* Also I would like you to get Mr. [Joseph A.] Scovill[e] to price a cloak for Rob[er]t Maxwell who is not willing to purchase here at the present prices. Ask Mr. S. [*ms. torn; word missing*] suit himself as to size and color and let me know about them in your answer to this letter. I believe I must close this letter as it is near the time for lecturing. Give my love to all ["and" *canceled*] tell Sister [Martha Cornelia Calhoun] and Mother [Floride Colhoun Calhoun] to write me and send me the papers after you have finished reading them. Excuse this letter since it has been written in great haste and I have not had time to look over it. Your affectionate son, James.

ALS in ScCleA. NOTE: An EU in an unidentified hand indicates that the *Encyclopedia Americana* (13 vols.) could be bought for $28 or $25 and that Murray's *Geographical Encyclopedia* (3 vols.) could be bought for $8.50.

From H[ENRY] L. ELLSWORTH

Washington City, Nov. 27, '44

Sir, As Chairman of the Committee of the Colonization Society I deem it my duty to lay before the Hon. Secretary of State a copy of a Communication rec[eive]d from Liberia a few days since.

For the Colony of Liberia the United States has cherished the kindest feelings. The ground now assumed by Great Britain is new, and unexpected & must if yielded to compel the Society to give up its parental control and consent to its immediate independence. The Society have thought it just & proper to establish for the Colony with their own consent a Tariff to aid in reimbursing the expenses of the Colony; if this must be abandoned the burden will fall so heavy upon the Patrons of the cause as to impede, if not to frustrate the grand objects in view—first the providing a home for the free people of color in the United States with their own consent, and secondly, the political & religious improvement of the Western Coast of Africa & thus prevent by moral suasion the continuance of the Slave trade from that Coast.

The situation of the Colony is now perilous. It has been founded in the purest philanthropy; it has been watered by tears of gratitude; for its prosperity the good have prayed, and for its defence many have laid down their lives. If it is soon to be destroyed the Executive Committee would deem it censurable in them to withhold any information which will avert an evil if such it should be considered.

Invoking for the Colony all the aid you can with propriety recommend I have the honor to subscribe myself Yours most Obediently, H.L. Ellsworth, chairman of Executive Commi[ttee].

LS with Ens in DNA, RG 59 (State Department), Miscellaneous Letters (M-179:106, frames 37–51). NOTE: Ellsworth enclosed a copy of a letter from W. Jones, Commander of the British African Squadron, to the governor of Liberia, dated 9/9/1844. Jones denied the authority of Liberian officials to impose customs rates and regulate trade among British subjects on the coast of West Africa. Ellsworth also enclosed a copy of House Document No. 162, 28th Cong., 1st Sess., relating to Liberia.

From J. Fr[anci]s Hutton

New York [City,] Nov[embe]r 27th 1844
Sir, The bearer Mr. [James] Fiora one of our most active, zealous, and influential free trade democrats is about to visit England for the purpose of organizing a new business in connection with some gentlemen on this side of the water, and our free trade men well knowing the great importance it will be to the cause, to have a man of talent, character, and discretion abroad, are desirous of having this gentleman appointed to a Consulship in some port near the scene of his opperations.

It gives me great pleasure to say that the friends of Mr. Fiora generally have urged upon him to become an applicant as much for the advancement of the principles of free trade as a desire to see him placed in a situation of advantage to himself, and if in the distribution of your foreign appointments you can find a place for him, you will confer a great benefit upon a large number of your fellow citizens in this city—friends of free trade—and ["though" *canceled*] upon Yours very respectfully, J. Frs. Hutton.

ALS in DNA, RG 59 (State Department), Applications and Recommendations, 1845–1853, Fiora (M-873:28, frames 97–99).

From S[ETH] T. OTIS

United States Consulate
Basel, Switzerland, Nov[embe]r 27/44
Sir, I beg leave to call your special attention to a statement of abuses that I have been most credibly informed exist, in the sending of Goods from this Confederacy to the United States—and their Entry at the different Custom Houses of the same—particularly in the City of New York.

You are doubtless aware that a very large amount of Silk Goods & watches are manufactured in Switzerland, and sent to the United States on commission. Many of the manufacturers of these Goods, contrive by various stratagems to have them Entered Illegal[l]y. This is done (*as I believe*) in some instances to Defraud the Revenue, and in others, probably only with the intention to save the Consular Fee of a Certificate at each Shipment as required by Law. In some instances it is their Custom to make shipments for several months together without a certificate (their Agents Entering into Bonds as prescribed in such cases) and at the End of 6 or 12 months make a *condensed Invoice* of the whole, and get it Authenticated by some Consul without their allegiance—knowing that I will not authenticate any such Documents.

In other instances (I am told by a Gentleman from N. York) that the Agents of these manufactures being regarded as highly respectable men are permitted to Enter the Goods without any Certificate *Ever being required.*

And again in some of the Cantons of this Confederacy, the manufacturers obtain the Certificate of two persons residents of their place, & in some manner get their Goods Entered by it; They assuming the Ground that each Canton in the Confederacy is a seperate Governm[en]t & as no U.S. Consul resides in their Canton, they have the right to adopt such a course.

You will readily perceive that all these evasions of the Law, are intended to enrich the manufacturer & Injure the interests of the U.S. and their Consuls, and so far as this last custom is concerned, it is of course perfectly unjustifiable, as the U.S. Government sends her Consuls to *Switzerland*, & not to Either of the Cantons Composing the Swiss Confederation, and the High Government of Switzerland alone grants their Exequaturs, & requests each Canton to sustain, & protect the Consul &c &c.

I have now resided in Switzerland for about one year, & have seen & heard so much of these abuses that I have deemed it my duty to inform your Department of them, to the end that the Custom House officers may be instructed to be more vigilant, & the Revenue of the U.S. not be diminished in such a manner—as also that Consuls may not be deprived of their legitimate business and trod (as it were) under foot by a set of mercenary & unscrupulous Foreign manufacture[r]s who are amassing immense wealth by their trade with the U. States.

By the recent resignation of the Consul at Zuric[h; Henry Mahler] I am left the only U.S. Consul in Switzerland, and it is believed the President [John Tyler] will not increase the number, as he has been advised by some of our Consuls & Ambassadors now abroad, that one Consul is enough for all pra[c]tical purposes. I have endeavored thus far to faithfully perform the Duties of my office, but I find this mercenary & Domineering spirit of the manufacture[r]s always opposing me, and if these abuses that I have named, cannot be checked at the Custom Houses my efforts will be useless—but if I can be *promptly* aided by their officers, I shall hope that the Revenue of the United States will be benefitted, and something like justice, & a respectable living, be gained by myself.

Hoping Sir, that you will immediately bring this subject to the notice of the Collectors in such a manner, as will prevent future abuses—I have the Honour to be with high Consideration Your Ob[edien]t Serv[an]t, S.T. Otis, Consul.

ALS (No. 10) in DNA, RG 59 (State Department), Consular Despatches, Basle, vol. 1 (T-364:1), received 12/24; CC in DNA, RG 56 (Secretary of the Treasury), Letters Received from Executive Officers, Series AB, 1844, no. 47.

From F[rancis] W. Pickens, "(Confidential)"

Columbia [S.C.,] 27 Nov: 1844
My dear Sir, I found great confusion and some excitement here. The Gov[ernor's; James H. Hammond's] Message as you see throws a firebrand out, and treats unjustly the Northern Senators who voted with us on the Texas question &c. It passes over in contempt the recent election &c. I now am satisfied that there is a deliberate & concerted movement ag[ain]st you & the true position of the State. Under these circumstances I was compel[l]ed to introduce resolutions immediately upon the reading of the message which you will see. I saw that a few ultra men, unsound in feeling & disappointed, were reckless and that they had control of the papers the [Charleston] Mercury & [Columbia South-]Carolinian. I therefore determined to move, and make them take the responsibility of a rupture by a counter move. I am sure if the vote had been taken in the Senate yesterday my resolutions would have *passed unanimously—* such was the evident feeling from both extremes. The opposite gent[lemen] caucused last night & I do not know the result. Mr. Stewart [*sic*; John A. Stuart] said to Mr. [Robert W.] Seymour a rep[resentative] from Charleston yesterday that "we were to decide whether the State was to lick your toes forever." Similar language is held I hear by the Gov:—and by *others* who are near to you. I think it my duty thus to speak freely. I conscientiously believe that it is a deliberate desire of some (but very few I think) to force us into such a position as to drive you from the Cabinet hereafter, and from all control over the current of events.

I have seen it in the Mercury for months & I believe the feeling has existed for years. I thought so in Congress & I ["thought" *canceled and* "think" *interlined*] so still.

You will see by my resolutions I pay no adulation to [James K.] Polk. I [*one word or partial word canceled*] do not rely upon the Rep[ublican] party in Congress finally—but have guarded the wording of the Resolutions on that point and I do not threaten but distinctly announce[?] that the State in her sovereign capacity has the power to protect her citizens in any emergency, & that we do *not waive that right* by waiting *events* at present. It strikes me that it is the exact thing & so our friends think here. I drew it alone & without the slightest consultation with any one, and it took the Senate by surprise. I found if I consulted all would suggest & there would be confusion. You see [William] McWillie sustained it fully—although I did not advise at all with him.

The calculation was to get the run of public opinion with the message & the press & to do all the harm in advance, & then to smother every thing by the committees, as both presiding officers are in their hands, ag[ain]st [*one or two words canceled*] three fourths of both bodies as far as these matters are concerned.

I think perhaps the expression of the Legislature will be so decided & unanimous finally that every thing may blow off with[out] [har]m[?].

Be so kind *as to write me.* In haste but truly, F.W. Pickens.

ALS in ScCleA. NOTE: Pickens's five resolutions, introduced on 11/26, which he evidently designed to head off the Blufftonites, affirmed that the annexation of Texas was essential to the Union, that because of British abolitionism annexation was a "paramount" question to the people of South Carolina, that the recent election of James K. Polk and George M. Dallas encouraged the hope of annexation, that the tariff of 1842 was unconstitutional, and that "by waiting events at present" the State did not waive the right to exercise her sovereign capacity in the future "should we be disappointed in our just expectations." With slight amendment the resolutions were adopted by the Senate and, several weeks later, by the House of Representatives.

To Stephen Pleasonton, Fifth Auditor, 11/27. "In addition to the Statement called for in the letter from this Department of the 5th instant, I have to request that you will cause to be made out, and transmit to me as soon as practicable, one, of the disbursement of the fund for the Contingent expenses of all the missions abroad, (other than that made by E[dward] Stubbs, Agent of the Department,) from the 1 July, 1843, to 30th June, 1844; to be laid before Congress in compliance with the 2d Section of the Act making appropriations for the civil and diplomatic expenses of Government, approved 9th May 1836." FC in DNA, RG 59 (State Department), Accounting Records: Miscellaneous Letters Sent, vol. for 10/3/1844–5/29/1845, p. 85.

From THOMAS SCOTT, "Private"

Chillicothe [Ohio,] November 27, 1844
Dear Sir, The tract [*sic*] is now clear for your entrance upon the Presidential Course. This is an event which for the last twenty five years I have most earnestly desired, having during that whole period preferred you to all others, not excepting even General [Andrew] Jackson. Although, in your written controversy with the General

you triumphed over him, yet, the influence of his military achievements were for the time being overwhelming. That influence is not now felt as it then was. Your talents and patriotic services are now duly appreciated and begin to be generally acknowledged. And permit me to assure you that, I would highly prize the honor of having your permission publickly to announce your name as a candidate for the next Presidency. I have often declared to my friends and political opponents that I knew of no man in the advocacy of whose election I would be willing again to take the stump except yourself.

I hope to have the pleasure of seeing you in the course of two or three weeks and shall communicate some facts and circumstances which may possibly be by you turned to account. It requires no extraordinary sagacity to perceive that, if General [Lewis] Cass, Mr. Buchannon [sic; James Buchanan] and Mr. [Silas] Wright are selected by President Polk as part of his Constitutional advisers, the Country will be constantly agitated by the intrigues which will be carried on at Washington in order to secure the succession to one or the other of those distinguished individuals. Already the political elements in this part of Ohio are considerably agitated in favor of Mr. Wright. Our Van buren friends are already urging the claims of Mr. Wright. If they fail as to him their next choice is Mr. [Thomas H.] Benton. At the head of these movements is Mr. Senator [William] Allen, whose influence will be exerted to have all the offices in this State filled by men whose influence will be exerted in favor of one or the other of those individuals. If they can secure the election of either, the ancient proscriptive policy and cliques will be revived. Yours truly, Thomas Scott.

ALS in ScCleA. NOTE: An AEU by Calhoun reads "Mr. Scott of Ohio." Thomas Scott (1772–1856) was a native of Va., had been Republican candidate for Governor of Ohio in 1812, and had been a judge of the Ohio Supreme Court.

From KER BOYCE

Senate Chamber [Columbia,] Nov[embe]r 28th 1844
My dear Sir, You will see that Stewart [sic; John A. Stuart] has broke ground against you as well as the Governor [James H. Hammond]. You are denounced as going wrong in order to give you another chance for a canvass for President, and those resolusions which have been offered by [Francis W.] Pickens is [sic] also denounced by Stewart and I have no doubt but the [Charleston] Mercury will make

a stand to go for convention and denounce every one that does not follow and that two parties will be raised in our State[,] one a [Robert Barnwell] Rhett and the other a Calhoun party. I am happy the signs of the times are that the former will be but a small minority. Now my dear Sir I wish you to be on your g[u]ard in Washington and not allow Mr. B. Rhett to get President [John] Tyler to remove Mr. Graysin [*sic*; William J. Grayson, Collector of Customs at Charleston] and put his brother B.R. [*sic*; Benjamin S.] Rhett in that place as that would give them great strength in Charleston as many of the minor appointments is [*sic*] with the Collector and In fact you must be careful not to allow Mr. Rhett to get any appointment from the President as any appointment given his friends will weaken yours. Tomorrow will show you how we have meet [*sic*] the Governor[']s Message which you will see not from the Mercury but from some other paper. The [Charleston] Courier will have a true statement of the action. I shall be glad to hear from you as often as your time will permit. Y[o]u[r]s Most Sinsarely Y[o]ur obedient Servant, Ker Boyce.

ALS in ScCleA.

From F[RANKLIN] H. ELMORE

Charleston, 28 Nov. 1844

My Dear Sir, Our friend Mr. Gourdine [*sic*; Henry Gourdin] called a day or two ago with Mr. Geo[rge] L. Lowden one of the Representatives of the late Com[modore] John Paul Jones to confer with me on the best course to be adopted by the parties who represent him for the prosecution of their claims ag[ains]t Denmark. It was my opinion that they had better do nothing until you had first been consulted & then that such a course should be taken as would best second & strengthen the action which I see the Government has taken in the case. I advised Mr. Lowden to possess Mr. [Isaac E.] Holmes [Representative from S.C.] fully with his case & also Judge [Daniel E.] Huger [Senator from S.C.] & through them to confer with you as to the measures best to be adopted. I doubted if it would now be best for the President to notice the matter in his annual Message, nor would it be worthwhile to bring the matter by memorial before Congress again, if the negotiations were in a proper train. I thought perhaps it might be that the *spontaneous* action of the House, by a call or

383

some such movement might be made to strengthen your hands, if the negotiation hung with the Govt. of Denmark, by showing that the popular Branch of the Legislature was taking a decided interest in the affair.

The parties interested here embrace some of our worthiest citizens—some of whom would experience in the recovery of this claim a most seasonable relief. They have greater confidence in your efforts than any other & are perhaps somewhat more anxious to avail themselves as early as possible of it for fear you may not continue in the Department. They are not people to be importunate—on the contrary they have been patient under long with[h]eld justice & are now waked up to greater activity from some new evidence & their great hopes from your energy. I am sure My Dear Sir you cannot give your aid to those who have stronger claims from justice or who are more deserving or who will be more grateful to you for it. I am faithfully Y[ou]rs &, F.H. Elmore.

ALS in DNA, RG 59 (State Department), Miscellaneous Letters (M-179:106, frames 88–89).

From CHRISTOPHER HUGHES, "Private"

The Hague; 28th November; 1844
My dear Mr. Calhoun, All our relations[,] interests & concerns are on the best footing; & every thing goes on well & *comfortably*—in our affairs—in this Country & at this Court.

The King [of the Netherlands, William II] is in perfect health & Boyish activity & spirits; he has plenty of *money*; a pretty good share of popularity; thinks himself a *very* Great Man; and *I do not*; (this, my opinion of him—is sincere & *true*; but, don't repeat it, if you *do*—I'll *deny* it: Sheridan's morality—perhaps justifiable—as the world goes). He is as afraid as *Death*, of his Brother in Law—the Emperor of Russia [Nicholas I]; He *dare* not go to France—& he is dying to do so—for these three years. He *dared* not give his Daughter to Prince of Joinville, which, the Girl would have preferred to her *ugly* Cousin—a Petty Duke of Germany (Saxe Weimar). In fact—H.M. trembles when he thinks of the Czar; but many other monarchs *do that*—by the way! ["Even" *interlined*] England has a sort of *awe* of H.I.M. & France allows & has allowed him—since 1830—to bully her! & they all *overrate Nic[h]olas's* power & resources; & *underrate* his *home* difficulties; for there is the *pinch* with the Emperor; and a Devil of a job he has to keep things orderly & obedient within his vast dominions—& with his brutal subjects! *This, I know!* and I further know—that Russia was so shaken—in the Polish Revolution—that if England—instead of acknowledging & paying a doubtful Debt—to the Emperor—to stave off a Row (some ["£" *interlined*] 3 millions—Russo-Hol[l]ando[?] pretensions of Russia) if England had kept one million herself (which she *wants* with all her wonderful resources & prosperity; & these are immense! I have *just* been in England—& in *Ireland* too! ! !)—had given one Million, to be applied & used by Gen[era]l La Fayette—as *he* would have known *how* to use it—in the Polish Cause; & given the *third million* to the most avaricious man (his crying sin) that ever sat on a throne—my late venerated & loved *Friend* & the late King of Sweden—to engage him to cooperate, Charles John might have landed in Finland—with 30,000 Swedes—reconquered Finland & its almost 1½ millions ["woul(d) have joined him;" *interlined*]—who are *Swedes* still in their *hearts*—marched up to, & taken, St. Petersburg (where there were not 10,000 troops—they were all at *Warsaw*) & thrown *back* the Great Giant of the North at least half a century—in his colossal March & Growth! All this—I thought; I may say *knew*; & I *told* it—*tête à tête*—to Lord [Charles Grey, Earl of] Grey in London! adding—"We say in the North—My *Lord*—that you are afraid of Russia—& overrate her power!" Upon which, the Premier seized the Poker—not to knock me down—happily—but to *poke* the fire & hide his almost confusion. "Mr. Hughes"—said He—"it may be all true—but it is now *too late.*" & so *it was.* Let me stop this Rigmarole!

You will consider the few first sentences of this letter—touching our *direct* concerns—with Holland, as having all I possibly ["good" *canceled and* "could" *interlined*] say—if I were to take "Fools"-cap paper, & indite you a formal despatch—with official seals—& other forms! I prefer a private letter to you—my dear Sir—and I write it with my assuetudinal freedom; perhaps flippancy! N'importe! I cannot & I *will not*—come what may (& I *know* the *News* by the Great Western—and that my friend & *favourite*—Mr. [Henry] Clay is "*floored*")—I will not change my manner of writing & of speaking—*now* I am in my 60th year! T'an't[?] worth the while! Do *you* think it is? I don[']t!

I have just had a visit from Baron Wahrendorff—an old Friend—Swedish Chargé d'Affaires here, & *at Brussels!* He tells me that Mr. Clements [*sic*; Thomas G. Clemson] has had the most perfect & *complete* success—in establishing himself—in the good opinion & gaining

385

the kind favour & feelings of *everybody,* at Brussels; Court—Corps—& Society; & that they all consider him *un homme distingué*—to use Baron W's (an old friend of mine ["I say" *interlined*]) *own* words. Now, Sir, tell this to the President [John Tyler]; & *this*—in *no* case— will *"I deny."* Do me the honour also to tell the President—that *I* had the most thorough Success in my late short trip to England—& to Ireland! In the latter, I found his old Friend Col. Sam Moore—grievously affected—at first meeting—but the sight of me, & my presence for 8 days—did him *wonderful good*! His health & spirits are better! He comes to see me & my Daughter, his adopted child, in April *here*; & He returns to Baltimore, & for good, in May, 1845!

I enclose a Letter for my friend Mr. Joseph R. Ingersoll! Mr. Markoe will take charge [of] it! I recommend it to your usual kindness.

Being in Ireland (Londonderry) I thought I'd return by Dublin; the sea passage is now only ⅓ of the time—*that* way compared with the [route] via Derry[?] & Liverpool. I was 26 hours *going* to Ireland: & 9 hours & a half from Dublin to Liverpool; In "The Iron Duke"—13 miles an hour! I stopped a few days in C[ount]y Down— at Mt. Stewart—the Estate of some old Friends of mine—The Marquis & Marchioness Londonderry—and their Son, Lord Castlereagh. Lord L[ondonderr]y is my Biographer; in his published work of Travels "in Russia & *Sweden*"—he has made very flattering mention of me & of my humble merits! His Estate of Mount Stewart—& his people— tenantry—& the general condition of that part—the North of Ireland— is admirable & *equal* to that of any part of Europe; & in *all* respects! The estate is a great one & descends to Castlereagh—25,000 acres— 22,000 £ Revenue; not 1,000 back[?] rent *due*! One town of 8,000 & another of 2,000 on the property & no *Beggars*! since the new poor Laws; Mt. Stewart is near Belfast; & Belfast is the most flourishing Town—the *Liverpool* of Ireland!

At Dublin—I was Most Graciously received by the Lord Lieutenant—the Ulysses of Britis[h] Diplomacy; Lord Heytesbury—formerly Sir W[illia]m A-Court: & by the Sec[retar]y [Edward Granville Eliot,] Lord Eliot; his wife is Lady Jemima Cornwallis—Grand Daughter of *our* old Revolutionary friends. They forced me—at their *own* dinner Table (Pho[e]nix Park)—to consent to stop a day longer—at their first Ball—in short—"I capitulated" to the Cornwallis— but it was ["to" *interlined*] a *Woman*! I must stop writing: the last moment for Steamer of 4th Dec[embe]r has come! In England—I received the most marked—& *remarkable* proof of continued kindness—confidence—& respect—from Sir Robert Peel—& in an Autograph

Letter—of the most friendly & flattering kind! Had a most affectionate meeting—& *tête à tete* of an hour—with my old friend—Mr. [Henry] Goulburn[,] Chan[cellor] of Exchecq[uer] & of Short Celebrity; & from all others of note & power. I never was *more* Successful.

Do tell all this to the President; if any one calls this, "bragging," I call him "an Ass." My Lord! what are these *people?* They are mere *men!* & *I* am *a man*; & I never felt flattered—nor honored—by the intimacy of *any* man (I except the Sex: I haven't said *mankind*) in my Life!) unless it were—as token of Success—with the truly Great—by virtues & abilities! And *such* are these men! Ask the President if he requires *another pair* of Link-Buttons? I hope *not!* I am sure he has not *forgotten* me! You may say *to him* (as I say *to you*) that if *ye* want *to finish* well in your great trust & high Power—let one of your *last* acts be—to name & make me—Minister at Vienna; & *at once!* All Europe will approve; & so will *all America!* If not, make me Minister at Russia (St. P[eters]burg) where Count Nesselrode *wishes* to see me: has said [*Marginal interpolation*: "Mr. Bloomfield, Brit. Minister at Petersburg (now in London) said this tother day publickly."] it over & over to many—& also *to me!* Ask [Alexander de] *Bodisco* [Russian Minister to the U.S.]! It is *true!* But tho I will *accept* ["Petersburg" *interlined*]—yet the North will *kill me!* I prefer Vienna; & it is cheaper by one half! There is the *double Buttons* for the President—["viz." *interlined*] Vienna *or* Petersburg; I'll take *either half*; but I *prefer Vienna!* I have a *right* to Promotion! I *have* done "the State some service"—in my 30 years employ! & I *can* & I *will* do it service; & *no* discredit wherever—I may be employed—*in Europe!* I would not accept anything in S. America! But, seriously—I *ask* the President—to consummate his *adoption* of me (when I made his acquaintance—in 1841) by *one classic act*—of Independent & discriminating selection & power; by making *me his* Minister at Vienna. If not—*why*—at Petersburg—instead of [Charles S. Todd] the Art*less* "*Todd*"ger—who is better at home—or any w[h]ere—but in Diplomacy! Upon my Soul I think you will *both* gain applause & credit—by *closing* your *present* power—by some such noble & spirited act! The United States will *approve you!* If you should rather prefer to *close my present power* & *place*—by *recalling me*—why *do it.* I do *not* say ["it" *canceled and* "this" *interlined*] *flippantly*; but I say it *Manfully*; & I shan't break my heart about it—I assure you. Respectfully & truly Y[ou]rs, Christopher Hughes.

ALS in ScCleA.

From H[aym] M. Salomon

New York [City,] Nov. 28, 1844

Dear Sir, I would have occasionally troubled you with a letter as heretofore on miscellaneous matters but your long abscence from Washington and your active occupation which I presume ensued on your return induced me to refrain.

I enclose you a few scraps [*not found*] showing matters in their relative position north & south regarding substantial credit and currency.

In respect to personal political matters I have attached to this ["a" *interlined*] paper cut from a morning Journal—see further in our New York Aurora which daily gives farther and more proof of the duplicity and venality of Northern Van B[uren] democrats.

Of this fact I can assure once more that had Van B[uren] been up he would have lost this State by scores of thousands. But still with the fact well known to them He and his friends were determined that no prominent man like yourself—[Lewis] Cass—or [Richard M.] Johnson—should be put up, fearing *they* could be elected and their official influence cease. Having opposed all of these they contrived to place [James K.] Polk as the candidate whose vicinity to Gen[era]l [Andrew] Jackson gave them a hope that if chance elected him they could continue to act some part of their drama. In which object 'tis said that [Benjamin F.] Butler visited the parties months before—as [Churchill C.] Cambreleng & [Martin] Van B[uren] did with [William H.] Crawford on a former day to elect Jackson on condition of Stifling Mr. Calhoun.

Whether they have gained their object Time will shew. But who dare deny that they are uniformly opposed *to all men* of good principles. Already they claim the next nomination for Mr. [Silas] Wright whom I think would disappoint them after all if he were to become President. It is probable he will ruffle them a little too, now he is the Elected *Governor*. [Thomas H.] Benton is a man truly of their Gang[?]. Resp[ectfull]y &c &, H.M. Salomon.

ALS in ScCleA; variant PC in Boucher and Brooks, eds., *Correspondence*, p. 265.

From CHA[RLE]S A. SECOR and
ELIJAH F. PURDY

New York [City,] Nov. 28, 1844
Sir, Having seen it officially announced in the journals of the day that the Port of Manchester, Gt. Britain, has been made a Port of Entry, the undersigned ["has" *altered to* "have"] taken the liberty to recommend a gentleman from this City for the office of Consul which will doubtless be demanded by this change. Mr. James Fiora is the person alluded to—a gentleman peculiarly fitted for this station by education, experience, the highest order of business talent and possessing a character in every particular irreproachable.

During the late campaign Mr. Fiora was one of our most efficient friends and laborers in the work of reform. His speeches upon the subject of the Tariff were among the ablest delivered, and drew forth the warmest commendations from all who had the pleasure of listening to them, marked as they were by an ability seldom surpassed.

It may not be amiss to state that Mr. Fiora has twice visited England with a view to the introduction into that Country of certain of our commodities which have hithertoo been overlooked in our business operations in that part of the world, and with success.

While there, his superior knowledge of upon [*sic*] the subject of American trade, brought him in close intimacy with the most eminent of the members of the Corn League Club but particularly with Colden [*sic*; Richard Cobden] & [*blank space*].

If from these considerations (of the correctness of which you can soon be convinced by a conversation with the gentleman in person) you can make the appointment, you will not only consult the public benefit, but confer additional favors upon the Democracy of this City, and particularly on Your Ob[edien]t S[er]v[an]t, Chas. A. Secor, Elijah F. Purdy.

LS in DNA, RG 59 (State Department), Applications and Recommendations, 1845–1853, Fiora (M-873:28, frames 103–104).

From [Col.] N[athan] Towson, P[ay]M[aster] G[eneral, U.S. Army], 11/28. "Mr. [Marcus C.M.] Hammond's letter and the papers recommending him for the appointment of Paymaster, together with your note of this morning, have been placed, with previous recommendations, on the files of this office and will be brought to the notice of the President [John Tyler] and Secretary of War [William

Wilkins], when a vacancy occurs in the Pay Department." FC in DNA, RG 99 (Paymaster General), Letters Sent, 25:429.

To [GEORGE M. BIBB, Secretary of the Treasury]

Nov. 29th 1844

Mr. Calhoun's compliments to the Hon: Mr. Bibb, and transmits for his perusal the enclosed document communicated by the Portug[u]ese Minister [to the U.S., J.C. de Figaniere e Morão], a portion of which refers to Mr. B[ibb]. Mr. Calhoun will thank Mr. B[ibb] to return the paper after perusal.

[Enclosure]

Extract of Dispatch No. 27 of the 21 August 1844 addressed by H[is] Ex[cellenc]y the Secretary of State [of Portugal, Joachim José Gomes de Castro] to the Portuguese Minister.

"Your Lordship's Dispatch No. 21 of the 18 ult[im]o was laid before Her Majesty. The favorable decision of our claim against the clause of the Act of 30th August 1842 which infringed the stipulations of article 3d of the Treaty of 1840, was received with satisfaction. The Secretary of the Treasury, Mr. Bibb, in his letter to Mr. Calhoun of the 12th of the said month of July, elucidated the question with great impartiality and rectitude, which does honor both to his learning and discernment, developing with great precision the principles by which the Government of the United States is to be guided in the interpretation of its treaties with other nations. Her Majesty's Government highly appreciate such principles of honor which have, also, ever guided it in its relations with the United States, to whose Government Your Lordship will communicate these expressions, and that the Queen's Government properly estime this act of justice."

LU with En in DNA, RG 56 (Secretary of the Treasury), Letters Received from Executive Officers, Series AB, vol. 1844, nos. 43, 44.

From W[ILLIA]M M. BLACKFORD

Legation of U.S.
Bogotá, Nov. 29, '44

In a Postscript to my Despatch No. 27, I had barely time to announce the settlement of the claim of the Brig "Morris." I have now the honor to enclose a copy of the Convention, signed on the 5th Inst. by myself and [Joaquin Acosta] the Secretary of Foreign Relations.

Referring to previous Despatches for my views of this case, I may now only reiterate the remark that, if the amount of Indemnity obtained be not such as the claimants expected, or as strict justice would have authorized us to demand, it is quite as large a sum, in my opinion, as this Government could have been induced to pay, without the employment, by ours of some measures of a minatory or coercive character—which from your loud silence with respect to the suggestions contained in my Despatch No. 25, I had reason to believe were considered inexpedient at present.

I have secured indemnity for the full value of the Brig and all the American property on board, with damages, in the shape of Demurrage, to the amount of five Thousand dollars, with interest on the whole until paid. Any thing like vindictive damages was out of the question. I hope the claimants will be satisfied. I have acted precisely as if the claim were my own. The amount to be paid by New Granada will, including interest, be somewhat more than Twenty eight Thousand Dollars.

On the 10th Inst. a letter from our consul at Carthagena [Ramon Leon Sanchez] informed me that the U.S. Brig Oregon had landed Mr. [Edward] Dixon, a Bearer of Despatches for this Legation, who left there on the 18th ultimo for Bogotá. Mr. Sanchez also informed me that Mr. Dixon had with him the Leave of Absence, which I asked of the Department. I have subsequently received a letter from Lt. Commandant [Arthur] Sinclair, of the Oregon, stating that he had been ordered to await my arrival at Carthagena to convey me to Norfolk.

For this attention to my request I beg leave to tender my most grateful acknowledgments.

Although forty two days have now elapsed, since Mr. Dixon left Carthagena, he has not yet arrived, nor have I had any intelligence of, or from him. The high state of the waters of the Magdalena, for the last month, led me to expect that his voyage up the river would be retarded—but it scarcely accounts for his detention for a period double that which the mail takes to perform the same distance. I am, therefore, very apprehensive that he has been taken ill on the River.

It gives me great pleasure to say that the moral effect of the news of a special messenger, with Despatches for this Legation, being landed from a vessel of war, which was placed at my disposition, has been most striking & salutary. It has greatly enhanced my importance in the eyes of this Government and of my Diplomatic colleagues. The character of the despatches on the way has, of course, given rise to no little speculation. I learn that the cabinet is exceedingly apprehensive of the adoption, by by [*sic*] our Government, of a new line of policy in regard to the claims.

Unwilling to lose so favorable a season for negotiation, I brought to the notice of the Secretary the case of the Schooner "Yankee." This is a claim against New Granada, and is based on circumstances of injustice & outrage, which have no parallel, even in the narratives of spoliation and robbery with which the archives of this Legation abound. I have the honor to transmit copies of my communication to the Secretary, of his answer & of my reply.

The case admits of no defence, nor—to do him justice—has the Secretary attempted one. He appears anxious that the case should be immediately adjusted, but fears he has not sufficient documents, at present, to justify him in acting upon them. I have fortunately found, however, an authenticated copy of the sentence of the court of Carthagena, which I have transmitted to him, & which I think is all that is necessary. As far as I can judge from the conversation of the Secretary, the claim will be settled. An extraordinary council is summoned to meet to day. If the decision be favorable, it will be owing less to the justice of the claim, than to the salutary fears inspired by a Bearer of Despatches being on the way.

I hope to leave here within a few days after Mr. Dixon's arrival, unless I be detained by the character of the Despatches which he brings.

I have the honor to enclose the Receipt of Mr. [William] Gooding for the 12th & last Instalment of the "By Chance" money, which I omitted to send with my last Despatch. I have the honor to be with high respect Your Ob[edien]t S[ervan]t, Wm. M. Blackford.

ALS (No. 28) with Ens in DNA, RG 59 (State Department), Diplomatic Despatches, Colombia, vol. 10 (T-33:10, frames 281–293), received 1/13/1845; FC in DNA, RG 84 (Foreign Posts), Colombia, Despatches, vol. B4. NOTE: According to the Ens relating to the *Yankee*, that vessel was damaged and its captain imprisoned in 1838 because of a dispute with a local customs officer over "six bags of pease."

From DUFF GREEN

Galveston [Texas], 29th Nov[embe]r 1844
My dear Sir, I wrote to you from Mexico. There are a few additional facts, ["which are" *canceled*] worthy of your consideration. The contest in Mexico is a struggle on the part of Santa Anna to place himself at the head of an absolute despotism. He has labored to create a state of things in which the friend[s] of order, would give him absolute power as the only means of escaping the consequences of anarchy. The opposition consist of all the elements of disaffection, and as far as I can learn are without concert or plan. ["They" *canceled*.] Some want power as the means of enriching themselves. Others have a vague ["notion" *canceled*] notion that if Santa Anna is overthrown, things may be better but cannot be worse. Some are for a confederation, but all agree that the United States are dangerous neighbors and that which ever party comes into power must reconquer Texas.

The British Minister is openly supporting Santa Anna. Parades [*sic*; Mariano Paredes] has offered to reduce the duties one half, and ["has" *canceled*] will no doubt command the Ports on the Gulf of California. Mr. [Charles] Bankhead [British Minister in Mexico] told me that he had notified the Consul Gen[era]l that the British Govt. would not recognise any payments made to Parades, and afford no protection in case Santa ["Anna" *interlined*] enforces a repayment.

I understood from a Mr. West, formerly British Consul at Vera Cruz & now a large manufacturer at Jalappa [*sic*] that Mr. Packenham [*sic*; Richard Pakenham] was authorised by his Govt. to guarantee a loan of twelve millions at 5 per cent, on a pledge of one half the *additional* revenue in case three millions was applied to indemnify the Mexican manufacturers, and the protective tariff was repealed. He showed me a copy of a letter ["from" *canceled*] addressed to Santa Anna by certain influential manuafacturers, renewing the proposition and I saw a letter from Mr. Bankhead to him, saying that he had no instructions but pledging himself to cooperate all in his power to accomplish it. And, the British Frigate Spartan, left, on the same day that I left Vera Cruz with despatches which I have no doubt had reference to this, and the present crisis in Mexico.

Santa Anna can do nothing until he overthrows Congress and gets absolute power, because such is the state of parties that congress will agree to no proposition coming from him & he will agree to nothing which congress proposes. In this category it is the interest of those who wish a reduction of the tariff, (and this ["proposition comes from the" *interlined*] manufacturers & is sustained by the commercial interest,) to favor Santa Anna's projects, as when he has overthrown Congress and clothed himself with power he will be the Govt. and, the parties have an interest in securing the guarantee of the British Govt. because they rely on that guarantee to secure the fulfilment of the arrangement in case of a counter revolution. I was told by a Mr. [Charles B.] Young, an English man, a partner & the business man of the House of Hargous & Co. of Vera Cruz that Santa Anna had been consulted on the arrangement and that he had pledged himself to carry it into effect in case he came into absolute ["power" *interlined*]. This confirms what Mr. West told me at Jalappa.

I believe that this is Santa Anna's only hope of maintaining himself in power. That he will prevail in the present struggle with Parades I entertain scarce a doubt. (Nothing but accident, I think can prevent it.) Mr. Bankhead told me that the trade with England was reduced to 600,000£ per an[num]. The whole customs duties I learn from an authentic source are less than $4,000,000. The current expences including the army and usury, exceed $30,000,000. The experiment of the contribution of 4,000,000$ for the Texas ["war" *interlined*] will admonish Santa Anna that he cannot rely on direct taxes to pay the army and he knows that he cannot retain power without the means of paying his troops. This measure will enlist England more in *his* support and as his war upon foreigners has been the pretence upon which he has made his way to power, he will modify his measures thus far as a means of getting money and conciliating England.

He relies on Vera Cruz as his Point de appui. He always falls back there, and makes his movements from thence. He has erected two powerful batteries in aid of the Castle, and manned them with Paix[h]an guns, carrying 96 lb. balls, and has furnished them with a large supply of ball &c.

I can give you but little news about Texas. I refer you to my son [Ben E. Green] for many additional details in relation to Mexico. Yours truly, Duff Green.

ALS in ScCleA; PC in Jameson, ed., *Correspondence*, pp. 1000–1002.

From DUFF GREEN, "Private"

Galveston, 29th Nov[embe]r 1844

My dear Sir, I enclose you a memo., which contains what seems to me important facts. It is not for me to advise, but I do not believe that you can accomplish any thing with Mexico, unless you seize upon Vera Cruz, and my opinion is that the best way of taking the fort is to take the town, and that this may be done with a very small force if it is done promptly. Santa Anna is an able man, and he has resolved to fall back on Vera Cruz, & this fort, but he is compelled to call off his whole force to meet Parades [*sic*; Mariano Paredes] and cannot supply ["their pla(?)" *canceled*] new troops for some two or three months. If we take the town & fort they should not be given up, as they are the keys to the commerce of Mexico.

I hope to reach home in January and must beg the favor of you to permit Benjamin [E. Green] to remain until I can get home as I have some important family arrangements which require his presence, and cannot well be carried into effect without him. And besides I find that his time in Mexico is a sacrifice which nothing but the most urgent necessity can justify, and I hope to have it in my power to make it his interest to resign. I trust that you will recognise my claims to this favor. His remaining until I reach home at least is so important that [I] must insist on it, & especial[l]y as I am sure that you will find his presence in Washington more important to the Govt. than his return to Mexico. I do not like to take the responsibility of asking him to resign until I know what else can be done, but I am most unwilling for him to return to Mexico for many reasons. Yours truly, Duff Green.

P.S. I wrote to the President [John Tyler] and to Mr. [Richard K.] Crallé requesting that my name should not be sent before the Senate until I got home. I have no expectation of wishing ["to" *canceled*] a confirmation. I send you a copy of a note from the new Texan President [Anson Jones] that you may see what he says of your letter to Mr. [William R.] King &c. Yours, D. Green.

ALS with En in ScCleA; PEx in Jameson, ed., *Correspondence*, p. 1003. NOTE: The "memo." mentioned by Green is probably a ms. translation (in ScCleA) in Ben Green's handwriting, of Mariano Paredes y Arillaga's *Manifesto a la Nacion*, dated 11/2/1844 and published at Guadalajara, Mexico. In this *Manifesto*, Paredes urges the Mexican people to rebel against the illegal dictatorship of Santa Anna in order to depose him and restore the government of Mexico to the conditions prescribed by the Constitution of Tacubaya. He details Santa Anna's failures and oppressions and attacks his Texas policy as a pretext for consolidating his power and obtaining money instead of being a true policy of reconquest. The copy of a note from Anson Jones mentioned by Green in his last sentence is not found among the Ens. However, the original is found among Green's papers. Dated 11/2/1844, from Jones to Green, and marked "Private," it states: "I was much pleased with the letters from the State Department to Mr. King and Governor [Wilson] Shannon and think them among the ablest papers which I have ever seen. They must have a salutary effect upon the governments to which they were to be addressed." ALS in NcU, Duff Green Papers (published microfilm, reel 5, frames 846–847).

From WILLIAM R. KING, "Private"

Paris, Nov[embe]r 29, 1844
My Dear Sir, I have just received the gratifying intelligence that New York, Virginia, and Pen[n]sylvania have cast their vote for [James K.] Polk & [George M.] Dallas. This must render the triumph of the Democracy certain; saves us from the dictatorial rule of Harry of the West, and ensures as I hope, & believe, the prosperity of our country. To ensure this last however, it is of the utmost importance that Col. Polk should surround himself with able counsellors. You will I trust continue in the State Department, and use your influence to keep down all ultraism. To cause the administration to be national, not sectional. If this is done, Whiggery can never raise its head again. The news of Col. Polk[']s election has created no little excitement in England; and the papers, particularly the [London] Times, has a long article abusive of the Democratic Party, & speculating freely on the prospect of a war with the United States on the Texas question. Here all is quiet. I saw Mr. [F.P.G.] Guizot yester[day], having dined with him, and from his conversation have no reason to believe that the views of this Government have, or will undergo any change on that subject. Mr. Guizot seemed to be rather pleased at Col. Polk[']s election as it held out a prospect of a modification of the Tariff, which would be favorable to the commerce of France; which I did not fail to impress upon him; adding should we reduce our duties, we shall expect the French Government to adopt a similar policy. To which he replied take the first step, and we will follow suit. Since I have been in Paris I have had an opportunity of becoming intimately acquainted with Mr. [Henry] Wheaton our Minister at Berlin, and I have come to the conclusion that he is decidedly one of the ablest of our Diplomatic agents. His long experience, and great

industry, peculiarly fit him for a representative of his country abroad. [Daniel] Jenifer [U.S. Minister to Austria] will I suppose ask for his recall; in that event would it not be well to transfer Mr. Wheaton to that Court. I take the liberty to make the suggestion, because I real[l]y think the public interest would be promoted by it. Of that however you & the President are the best Judges; and I must ask pardon for having made it. Mr. [Thomas G.] Clemson wrote me a few days past that his little son [John Calhoun Clemson] had been quite sick, but was recovering. Mrs. [Anna Maria Calhoun] Clemson & himself were in excellent health, and pleased with their situation. I presume however he keeps you informed of every thing relating to him. I still write with difficulty; and much fear, that I shall find my sufferings aggrivated during the winter. La Belle France, has an execrable climate; and could I have foreseen the effects it would produce on me, I should never have ["have" *canceled*] exposed myself to them. Continued suffering, with twisted fingers, is paying dearly for the honor of my position. When your leisure will permit I should [be] gratified to hear from you. Present me respectfully to Mrs. [Floride Colhoun] Calhoun. With the highest respect I am faithfully your ob[edien]t Ser[van]t, William R. King.

ALS in ScCleA; PEx in Boucher and Brooks, eds., *Correspondence*, pp. 265–266. NOTE: An AEU by Calhoun reads "Mr. King, Sees no reason for believing that the views of Mr. Guizot has or will undergo any change in reference to the position of France on the subject of Texas."

From ROBERT WALSH, *"Private"*

[U.S. Consulate] Paris, 29 Nov[embe]r 1844
Dear Sir, You must not think me too much of a scribbler if I offer you something like gossip, in addition to mere official communication. As the election of Mr. [James K.] Polk is deemed certain, it is presumed that you will continue in the Department of State. You may not, therefore, be loth to receive such matter as my various journal-reading and social intercourse enable me to furnish.

The day before yesterday, I was one of a large party, at dinner, at the hotel of the Minister of Foreign Affairs [F.P.G. Guizot]. I went early, supposing that Mr. Guizot would wish to converse with me about the result of your elections. This proved to be the case. He took me aside and asked several questions relating to the characters of men, the probable composition of the cabinet, & the construction of which the new American events were susceptible. I gave him such explanations and opinions as would naturally be entertained and expressed by one who has confidence in the patriotism and capacity of the elect of the American people, & who would imbue, if he could, all the foreign world with the same sentiment. It occurred to ["him" *canceled and* "Mr. Guizot" *interlined*] that your external policy would consist chiefly in resistance to foreign Abolition schemes, & to British aggrandizement in the Western hemisphere so far as this is resistible without war. He expected changes in the Tariff more extensive and radical than seem to me practicable or advisable. On the subject of *Texas* he expressed roundly his wish & aim that the Republic should remain independent. On this head, the *entente cordiale* between Mr. Guizot & Lord Aberdeen is, I believe, perfect; & I fear that a like understanding exists between them with regard to American negro-slavery. The governments, or at least, the present cabinets of Great Britain and France, require a complete fraternity, for their very existence. They know each other's dangers, & the necessity of mutual aid: they will not separate, or practically disagree, about views & measures that affect only foreign countries. The dinner was given in honor of Marshal [Thomas-Robert] Bugeaud [de la Piconnerie] whose commanding person, energetic eye and general carriage correspond to the scene and nature of his exploits. Mind, body and bearing give assurance of his fitness for future various public service abroad and at home. He relished my remark to him, that I regarded as one of his best achievements, the masterly repulse which he gave to the French Abolition Society who called on him to abolish the slave trade and slavery in the new French African empire. The company at the dinner table consisted of eminent Conservatives, with all of whom, as well as with the Minister, he manifested strong political sympathies. Mr. [Francois-Adolphe] de Bourqueney, the French ambassador for Constantinople, with leave of absence, was among the guests. This government ranks him with the ablest of the diplomatic corps. He chatted with me, apart, for a half hour; mentioned the entire accord between him and the British envoy near the Porte [Stratford Canning], on all points, & his belief in the *vitality* of the Ottoman power; and signified some regret at the comparative backwardness & inaction of the United States, at Constantinople, considering the magnitude of American commercial interests in the East, and American pretensions with regard to Christianity and the propagation of the Gospel. I observed that you could not associate or meddle with the politics & proceedings of the Five Powers whose concerns & plans are exclusively their own, while, however, you might, certainly, co-operate with them when objects common to the great Christian & mer-cantile nations were to be defended or promoted. The French Chambers will meet in the last week of December, but not transact serious business until after the holidays. The opposition is to be marshalled under [Louis A.] Thiers, who will play, more directly than heretofore, the antagonist to Mr. Guizot, with reference to the British connexion. The ministry are confident of being able to maintain themselves, with the resolute aid of the King [Louis Philippe], throughout the Session, which will last until July.

This government appointed a commission to investigate and revise the Consular system of France: Monsieur Génié, the Chairman, & chief of Mr. Guizot's private bureau, informs me that the work is done, & his ample Report will soon be published. As soon as the Report & new arrangements appear they shall be transmitted to your Department ["for the use of" *interlined*] the Committee of the House of Representatives on the Consular subject. My own comprehensive memoir, prepared from an examination of all the European systems, & most of the author[it]ative treatises, will soon be ready for your approval. My predecessor in office, Mr. [Lorenzo] Draper, returned to Paris on the 4th in[stan]t; he has not yet appeared to enquire how its *materiel* was delivered over to me; without having the slightest reason for complaint against his successor, he has kept himself entirely aloof. I have been obliged to part with the incompetent and unmanageable person, Mr. Barnett [*sic*; Charles Burnet], to whom he committed the whole business of the Consulate. I could bring the deputy to no terms whatever, & having material grounds of objection to him, I rejoiced in fact that my efforts failed. I venture to annex to this letter, copies of a communication & proposals made to him, which indicate what there was of irregularity & remissness on his side. They may serve to explain & defend my conduct in case in any grievance should be alledged. The substitute whom I have chosen—a respectable Irish gentleman thoroughly acquainted with the French language, and invariably sedulous—answers my official & personal ends. I could find no American, disposed and qualified for the clerkship. A Vice-Consul I have no legal power to create. Every day since I entered on the functions of Consul has satisfied me more and more, of the propriety of the suggestions which I have heretofore ventured to offer for the correction of gross abuses. Between a hundred & two hundred thousand dollars might be gained for the revenue of the United States by stringent laws and regulations.

Excuse these topics again, and believe that I return to them only from a sense of patriotic duty. I am, Dear Sir, with perfect respect, your faithful Serv[an]t, Robert Walsh.

ALS with Ens in ScCleA; PEx in Jameson, ed., *Correspondence*, pp. 999–1000. NOTE: Enclosed with this letter are copies of a letter of 10/22/1844 from Walsh to Burnet; of a memorandum by Walsh, in which he sets forth terms on which he is willing to retain Burnet's services as a Vice-Consul; and of a letter of 11/7/1844 from Walsh to Burnet informing him that his services as Vice-Consul are no longer required.

From J[OHN] S. BARBOUR

Catalpa [Culpeper County, Va.,] Nov[embe]r 30th 1844
My Dear Sir, I wrote you a hasty, careless, & frank letter, three days ago in relation to my second son [James Barbour]—and I wrote it with so little restraint or reserve that I may have exposed my vanity, in the hopes which paternal anxiety nourishes with more tenderness, than reason & judgement. This you w[oul]d I am persuaded excuse, without this apologetic note. The object of my son is to settle himself where he may diligently & successfully follow his profession—until he has secured by industry & thrift a perfect independency in wealth. He has no other wish or aspiration, but in his profession. The inquiry that engages my mind is where can he most wisely settle with that single & isolated purpose before him. And it is to this end I ask the assistance of your Counsels. A rough society he could not bear, & a wicked one w[oul]d make his life a load of misery. His education has been the best which our institutions could afford—and besides being a graduate of our University [of Va.], he attended a course of Judge [John T.] Lomax's Law lectures in Fredericksburg. His license as a Lawyer was signed by three Judges to whom he is personally known, without asking a question, or subjecting him to any examination. So that if I estimate him highly, I am not without example, in the opinion of Judges [John] Scott, [Richard H.] Field, & [Philip N.] Nicholas, of our Gen[era]l Court.

In Virginia political power, is following the tide of White population, and the country beyond the blue Ridge, will rule us for some time to come. At least until our population is more dense & until it presses so closely on the means of subsistence, as to render ["necessary" *interlined*] a resort to our Rivers & Bays, for that supply of ["peculiar" *interlined*] food which those waters [*one or two words can-*

400

celed] yield. In some respects it is a duty of patriotism to infuse into those regions of the State, the better doctrines of eastern Virginia, & especially on questions of constitutional law. These considerations combine to induce a preponderance on my judgement for western Virginia. And I am then met with a further inquiry, as to Winchester & Wheeling in the north west, & Staunton & Abingdon in the South west. Having troubled you already too much, I forbear to add to what I have said, more than a renewed request for such advice as you can give me.

My Son Calhoun [Barbour] who was for ["nearly" *interlined*] a year ["or more" *canceled*] at West Point, was withdrawn last March; & is now at our College of W[illia]m & Mary (Williamsburg) where he is diligently & profitably pursuing his collegiate studies. In great haste Y[ou]rs Truly, J.S. Barbour.

ALS in ScCleA.

From W[ILLIA]M BOULWARE

Legation of the United
States, Naples, Nov. 30 1844

Sir, I have delayed writing to the Department, a very long time in the hope of being able to transmit something definite in reference to the French treaty. When I last had the honor of writing to you, and for some months previous, the negotiation was suspended, the French Ambassador [Francois-Eugene, Duc d'Harcourt] awaiting instructions from Paris. The instructions have now arrived and he has given notice to the Neapolitan Commissioners, that he is ready to resume the negotiation. The contents of the instructions have not transpired.

The negotiation is one of much interest to the representatives of all the Powers at this Court, for they are all anxious for Commercial treaties and all await the action of France. England has again sent here Mr. Woodbine Parish to aid Mr. Temple; the regular Minister in his efforts to bring to a conclusion the long exertions she has been making to effect a new commercial treaty.

It is generally believed here that His Majesty [Ferdinand II] will accede to the demands of France. Indeed one of His Commissioners has given some very decided intimations to that effect. In addition, it is well known that there is nothing on which His Majesty piques himself so much, as independence; and so long as the present treaty with France continues his hands are tied.

Another and powerful reason for a change is found in the fact, that in the last year there has been a considerable failure in the revenue arising from the customs. The general exclamation is that something must be done for the commerce of the country. Nearly all seem convinced that their old system has been a bad one, that there must be a revision and reduction of their tariff, and that first of all they must be relieved from the obligations of those old treaties with the three Powers; then, treaties with all the world connected with the changes in their customs.

I have been and I am still exceedingly anxious to make a treaty with this government before I leave here. I still hope it may be possible. But I wish to return to my country in the spring, unless I should be then occupied in a negotiation. I hope the President will be willing to grant me the permission to retire upon these terms. I am exceedingly anxious to leave here in the first days of March. Under these circumstances, I trust you will find it convenient to ["respond to" *interlined*] this request immediately, as this will probably be necessary to enable me to receive the permission in time for my object.

The Mission of the United States at this court was instituted, in accordance with a suggestion, made to Mr. [Auguste] Davezac, or Mr. [John] Nelson, at the time, that one or the other of these gentlemen was here, occupied with the indemnity demanded for the spoliations of [Joachim] Murat. If I mistake not, we were invited to enter into a commercial treaty. Indeed Mr. Davezac was absolutely engaged in the negotiation, when this government must have known perfectly well that neither we nor any other Power would make a commercial treaty with this country, so long as the English, French and Spanish nations enjoyed the exclusive advantages which old treaty stipulations secured to them. These advantages were of course unknown to us. My impression is that their object was simply to amuse our Minister and our government, and by that means, obtain some delay in the negotiation for the indemnity. Mr. [Enos T.] Throop my predecessor, upon his arrival, entered into various consultations with the Minister of Foreign Affairs upon the subject of a treaty and at length learned from him the obstacles which existed in the secret stipulations with the nations before named. But negotiations had then been commenced with the view of a release from these impediments, which negotiations have been continued ever since. They have been successful with England. As to France you are aware of their present state. With Spain, there will be no difficulty, I presume for there is no commerce, literally none. Under such circumstances, this Mission originated and has continued, now eight or nine years. During all this time no minister has been sent by His Majesty to Washington. Is it consistent with the respect due to ourselves to continue it under such circumstances? The state of things may be changed, if I obtain a treaty before my departure. It might be then necessary to have some one here to see it carried into effect, and His Majesty might then perhaps think it worth his while to send a Minister to Washington. But if I should not, should we send another, a third representative here to attend upon His Majesty and wait an opportunity of effecting a treaty? Should we not rather wait for him to make the next movement? Is it not due to ourselves that the Mission should cease after so long a continuance without any reciprocation?

I take the liberty of throwing out these suggestions for your consideration; but at the same time I would not have it thought that I deem a mission, at this court, unimportant. Far from it. This is much the most important state of Italy. We have a considerable commerce with Sicily, the exports amounting to something less than a million of dollars. And under a different state of things, with such a tariff as would be adapted to the circumstances of the country, indeed with such changes as we now anticipate soon to take place, our commerce would be largely augmented. In addition this city is the resort of many of our countrymen it being the usual conclusion of the classic tour of Italy, and they often need such protection and assistance as can only be afforded by a representative of our country. Under these circumstances I consider a mission here highly important, if it can be continued consistently with our own dignity and self-respect.

In Brazil, His Majesty has only a Chargé d'Affaires although the Emperor has married his sister and has here a Minister Plenipotentiary. It is now a subject of complaint on the part of Brazil and it will not improbably lead to the withdrawal of the Minister. My impression is that in this case, and in our own, the reason of the King is simply parsimony. It may be also that the fact that our relations are merely commercial, and in addition that we are not connected with the political systems of Europe, take no part in their combinations, in general, and are not likely to participate in their wars; it may be and probably is true that these considerations have their influence.

There being practically no Minister of Foreign Affairs here, the incumbent being a mere cypher, we can obtain no information on such a subject, as this without addressing to him a formal note, which would be submitted to the King for an answer. This being a question of delicacy, one of courtesy, I have been unwilling to demand explanations or say any thing on the subject, although ever since my arrival, I have felt much in regard to it and have been anxious to learn from an authentic source the cause of this neglect. But I do not doubt that I have assigned the true causes. But if you deem it important as connected with the continuance of the mission and think it proper to ask an explanation, I will have no hesitation in making the demand.

On the 25th Ultimo, His Royal Highness the Duc d'Aumale was married to D[uchess] Mariah Carolina Augusta Bourbon daughter of His Royal Highness the Prince of Salerno Uncle of His Majesty. I do not deem it necessary to say any thing of the various ceremonies, festivities &c which attended this Union.

I have had the honor of receiving despatch No. 15 from your Department with its enclosure. I am with the Highest Consideration Your Ob[edien]t Ser[vant], Wm. Boulware.

ALS (No. 24) in DNA, RG 59 (State Department), Diplomatic Despatches, Two Sicilies, vol. 1 (M-90:2), received 1/27/1845. NOTE: Boulware was a Va. planter appointed to his post in 1841 by John Tyler.

From John R. Brady, N[ew] Y[ork] [City], 11/30. "Allow me to introduce to you James H. Suydam Esq. of this City formerly one of the Calhoun Committee and a member of assembly from this city." ALS in ScCleA.

From R[ICHARD] K. CRALLÉ, A. T[HOMAS] SMITH, and RUFUS DAWES

Washington, Nov. 30, 1844
Sir, A religious Society of the denomination of Christians known as the "New Jerusalem Church," beg leave respectfully to present to your notice, as Chaplain of the Senate, the Rev[eren]d Rich[ar]d De Charms a minister of that Church.

The Society asks this favor, not on account of the emoluments connected with the situation only, but that an opportunity may be secured of advantageously proclaiming views of Religion and Philosophy, not only new to the world, but of deep and momentous interest to mankind. The Church professes to be that spoken of in the Apocalypse of St. John—and all that it asks is that the *reasons* of this belief may be impartially weighed.

404

Superadded to this, the Society justly appeals to the impartiality of the Senate of the United States. The various Christian Churches amongst us have all received the notice and respect of Congress in the appointment of Chaplains, *except that of which they are members.*

Is it therefore asking too much in requesting that we may not be ostracised by the authorities of our Country? With high respect we are your Obedient Servants, R.K. Crallé, A.T. Smith, Rufus Dawes, In Behalf of the Society.

LS in ScCleA. NOTE: Smith was the Chief Clerk of the Navy Department. Rufus Dawes, a poet and former editor of a Baltimore newspaper called *The Emerald*, published in 1839 *Geraldine, Athenia of Damascus, and Miscellaneous Poems.*

From CHA[RLE]S HENRY HALL

New York [City], November 30th, 1844
Dear Sir, I have had the honour to receive your favour [*not found*] asking information relative to the Trade carried on between this Country and China, and do not hesitate a compliance with your request; but, fear, the flattering mention of me to you by Mr. Morrell [*sic;* John A. Morrill] may have led to an anticipation of facts, and of experience, beyond the actual truth, or within my power to impart: such knowledge however, as I am possessed of, will be given in detail, as well as the future Policy which in my opinion ought to be pursued in the Commerce with China, in order to remain upon good terms with the singular People, and Government of that Country.

In order to give a full view of the Trade in question it will be necessary, not only, to give in detail the direct interchange of commodities, but the indirect communications, by and through other Countries, and setting forth also, dealings in Specie, and Exchange by means of Bills of Credit.

The direct Trade up to the year 1824 was limited almost wholly to the export of *Specie* and of Ginseng to Canton—and the amount of Capital varied from $80,000 to $150,000 according to the size or capacity of the Ships. The returns, were in *Teas* of various grades and qualities, *Silks* in variety, *Blue* and *Yellow Nankeens*, Cinnamon, Cassia, Sugar, Sugar Candy; (the three first articles the bulk of the Cargoes) and some other fancy articles of Chinese manufacture. From the above *period of time*, an entire change took place in the trade, as *experience* proved that *other Countries* were pursuing a profitable interchange of *commodities,* without the aid of *Specie,* more than for balances of Trade, or for expediency in the purchase of goods, at times, at low prices with Dollars in hand.

It was found, that the British East India Company carried on the China Trade by the export principally of *Woollen* Goods, of peculiar fabrics of various Colours, and qualities, and also, those of Cotton of various grades, of *Lead, Iron, Cochineal, Camblets, Long Ells,* Chintz, *Blankets,* Furs; (vizt. Beaver Skins, Sea Otter &c, &c) *Knives,* Bottles, *Cornelian* Stones, Tin, Cloves, Sandal Wood, Cotton H[and]k[er-chie]fs, & many other articles, of less consequence. These articles were taken generally in the direct Trade from England to China. The indirect Trade from the former went through the Colonies in the East Indies, and to very large amount in value. The principal articles of Traffic were *Surat Cotton* to an immense extent—*"Opium"* to an extent almost beyond belief, and which article finally led to the late abominable War in China. To show you fully the Trade, of a single ["Year" *interlined*] by 19 Ships from England direct, & via, India, & the returns home, I enclose Copies of their Cargoes, for your information.

You will perceive on examining these Invoices of great value, that not *one* ["specie" *interlined*] *Dollar,* was employed in the business. I make this remark, ["in consequence of" *canceled*] having been called upon by a Member of Congress in the Year 1826 for information relative to the Trade ["in question" *canceled*] in consequence of a question having arisen about the *Taxing of China* Silks and other articles, with the view of *Curta[i]ling* the *export of Specie,* and that Body, actually laid on an *extra duty on Silks* from around the Cape of Good Hope, in order to favour European Silks, and thereby curtail the export of the precious metals. How preposterous! one would imagine that Congress must have thought Specie was confined solely to our own Country. Our rule was at the time, if Dollars ruled high *here* (and they sometimes bore a Premium of from 5 to 7 p[er] Cent) to call at Cadiz or Gibraltar, where Dollars could usually be obtained at *par,* and proceed thence to China. This measure had an almost immediate effect of stopping the importation of *Silks* from Canton, the greatest in value and altogether the most profitable, of any commodity brought from thence to this Country, especially to the fancy articles in imitation of *French Patterns,* which, were Consequently driven out of our market. Still, some Silk goods come from China, notwithstanding the extra Duty, as they find a Sale being preferable in quality to any brought from England or France. This extra duty, in my opinion should be taken off, in justice to the Government of China, as well as of ourselves. Why give support to France and England, the bitterest enemies of the Republic! and why do a wrong to a Country that will by good management become one of the best customers for our *Cotton, Lead* and *Manufactures*, within a very limited space of time.

From the time before stated to the present moment, the American Trade with China has been placed upon a different footing, and the almost exclusive remittance in *Specie* abandoned, by the substitution of *Woolen Goods*, our *own Manufactures* of *Cotton*; the shipment of *Lead, Cochineal, Iron*, as well as the Manufactures of *England*, and *Germany*, such as are prepared for the China Market from those Countries. The Goods from the ["former" *interlined*] Country have been already mentioned; of the latter, the fabrics are of Wool, Flax, Hemp & Cotton such as are transmitted over Land in the *Russian Chinese* Trade, with the North of China, at "Kiachta," and there interchanged for the Commodities of that Country. The *Furs* also, to an immense amount of money the produce of Germany & of Russia are passed into China by the above route. We likewise of this Country followed out the same mode of remittance of Furs brought hither through the North West Company, as well as those procured on the Northwest Coast of America, and the Islands of the Pacific Ocean, and thence to Canton. The most profitable Trade to China of Mr. [John Jacob] Astor grew out of his former monopoly in Furs; he was however driven out of the Trade by the superior skill of those following the example of the East India Company in supplying Manufactured Goods, & other articles before named. Of these Woolen manufactures of England and of Germany, we shall labour under disadvantage in the Trade, owing to the necessity of importing them until our *own* fabrics can be substituted at a price that may under sell them in China. We now have the vantage ground in *Cotton Goods*, in *Lead, raw Cotton* (owing to its superior quality over that of *Surat*) & in Ginseng. There are other articles of minor import sent from hence that serve to make up a Cargo to China of some consequence.

Mr. [Henry] *Wheaton's Treaty*, with the *"Zoll Verein"* League, may lead to a successful interchange of Commodities for the China Trade the produce of Germany [*sic*], to enable our Merchants to undersell the East India Company, especially so, in manufactures of wool; and this matter, is I think, of importance to be considered.

The *Raw Silk* of China is exported in *great quantity* to England for Manufacturing, and the East India Company strive to monopolize it: this system should in my humble opinion be counteracted, by

our Government allowing the article to come in *free* of Duty, in order
to encourage our home manufactures, and at the same time, a *Bounty*
on the article of *home produce* might be found to be advisable, as this
article promises to become a Staple of our Country, of great National
importance.

I would here further remark that owing to the high Duty on
Manufactured Silks from China the importation of them has been almost abandoned, saving in some staple articles, Consequently, lessen-
ing the Capital employed in the China trade, as that, is now only
transmitted to an extent to purchase returns in Teas, Cassia and some
other articles of nominal importance. Of Nankeens, (*Blue*, and yellow) formerly of large importation, are now of very limited extent,
having been driven out by our own Manufactures of Cotton.

The traffic in the article of "Opium" I never engaged in, owing to
its having been prohibited introduction by the Chinese Laws; but I
regret to say, there *were*, and *are*, Merchants of our Country that
follow *British example* in this *unlawful* Trade, much to their own
personal dishonour, as well as of their Government. This article it
is well known is the produce of *Hindostan* subject to the Iron rule
of the East India Company (that of Turkey being of limited import
into China) and raised by compulsory means by the unfortunate
People of India, and when prepared, is taken from them at prices
dictated by the Agents of the abominable monopoly—thence it goes
to China and is there *smuggled* into the Country, by most unjust and
dishonourable means. For a time, the British Agents confined the
business to themselves solely, and very secretly, ["and" *canceled*]
until the Mandarins of the Country discovered their modes of operation; then remonstrated, and *threatened* cutting off all trade with
them: the next step was to engage Persons of other Countries to *participate* in their unlawful dealings by the furnishing of *receiving
Ships*, which should ply off, and on the Coast, as smugglers, and now,
and then, to anchor at "Lintin" and hold intercourse with the smugglers of the Country who would take ["of" *canceled*] the "Opium"
from time to time, in small quantity, and pay for the same, in Specie.
Thus matters went on until the Emperor ordered all *Opium* to be
seized found in the hands of the British Agents, and others, and then
destroyed. Then came the late war, on which it is unnecessary to
enlarge. You will naturally enquire, who were those who participated in this smuggling business with the Englishmen? I am constrained to say mostly Americans, and I believe all of them from a
Latitude higher than that of 40^D 40^m North—they ["may" *interlined*]

be known by their riches, and almost Eastern magnificence of parade, & living.

This matter the Government ought to take in hand unflinchingly and firmly, not only for their own honour, but from sound policy in holding an intercourse with the Government of China. To suppress this infamous traffic effectually, it will be necessary to dismiss all *Agents* of the *Government* employed in China, or at *Manilla*, or at Hong Kong, who may have directly, or by implication, be identified in the buying and selling of Opium—and to identify such, is an easy matter.

It was matter of surprize to many, and to me especially so, that our late Embassy to China was sent out in such haste, and the Plan of it, so crudely digested. Had a little *time* been employed in gaining information, and giving *instructions* to the Ambassador [Caleb Cushing] *how* to proceed in his negotiations with the most subtle and wary Nation upon Earth, we should not have to lament the loss of ["the" *interlined*] *"Missouri,"* or ["of" *canceled*] the *"Brandywine"* being [*"at Bombay,* and" *interlined*] *Hong Kong*; or, the *acceptance* of a Treaty, *based* upon that of the *British*. The first intercourse with the Chinese should have held out the proffer of the suppression of the Traffic in *Opium* by *Americans*, under a severe penalty, and then an offer of aid in suppressing it on the Coast in the environs of the *Port* at which we might be allowed to Trade, (and an *exclusive one* should have been requested), to prevent all intercourse with the British Traders, and to prevent collisions from National jealousies.

What have we witnessed? our Ambassador proceeding on his mission, *via Gibraltar, Cairo* (where "Opium" grows) *Suez, Bombay* (where the Opium of India is shipped to China) and Hong Kong! One would suppose him to be a travelling Super Cargo, rather than an agent of high grade from his Country. At any rate, he might gain much insight into the *Opium* trade. Then the Secretary of Legation! he went Passenger in a Vessel built by a Mr. [Robert B.] *Forbes* of Boston (*Brother* of [Paul S. Forbes] the *American Consul* in China) and Nephew of Thomas H. Perkins, late, or now in the China Trade, and whose Partner Mr. [John P.] *Cushing* of Boston was, or now is, in it, & the *Kinsman* of the Ambassador. This is, a pretty close alliance. Then the vessel in question; when fitted for sea, a trip was made by her from Boston to Norfolk and back, to try her powers of sailing, & in her went as one of the Passengers a Mr. Thos. H. Perkins. The result (by the account of the Public Prints) was, that the vessel proved an *"unusual fast sailer,* and *would stow a certain number of*

Chests of *Opium*," and that she was intended for the "China Trade." Thither, the vessel proceeded with Mr. *"Fletcher Webster"* on board; but, whether via Bombay, or not, I am uninformed of; it is however stated, this vessel is now employed from that port, in the Trade with China.

The late news from Canton I think alarming, as it appears our Countrymen have come into collision with the Chinese from the necessity of fighting the Battles of the *English* growing out of their usual insolence in all foreign Countries. I repeat, we ought if possible, obtain from the Government of China, a Port, exclusively for our Commerce, otherwise, we shall ever have quarrels with British Seamen and Traders. Besides, until our Capital in the Trade may be as large as that of the English, a preference will be given them in the purchase of merchandize, and especially so, in the quality of Teas, unless we are apart from them.

Twenty years since we employed from Thirty to Forty Vessels in the China Trade of the burthen of from Three to Five hundred Tons, and the *Capital* employed, rising Six millions of Dollars. A Statement of the Trade at that time I send you, showing that rising Four millions of Dollars in *Specie* was employed, and rising Two millions in exports ["in" *altered to* "of"] merchandize. Since that time, the Trade has varied not only in the export of Specie, but, in the returns; as Teas, Cassia and China Ware, are now the principal articles, and Silks[,] Nankeens &c, abandoned, owing as before stated to high Duties, on Silks, and Nankeens going out of use, owing to the growth of our manufactures. Hereafter our own products and manufactures, will be the exports, to the exclusion of but a limited amount of Specie.

The immense Commerce of China with various Countries in the Indian Ocean by means of her large Junks will probably become an outlet for our Manufactures of Cotton and Woollen goods, as well as of *Lead* and other merchandize to, an extent not at this time to be estimated; therefore, this Trade, ought to be fostered and encouraged by the Government, by every possible means. Coupled with this Trade is that of *Manilla*, the *Sandwich Islands*, Peru and the Northwest Coast of America, for the interchange of the goods of China for sandalwood, Sea Otter and seal skins, Copper and all the various kinds of Furs obtainable on the Continent.

This Circuitous Trade from this Country has been very profitable in the hands of those well acquainted with it in our Eastern Ports, whence Cargoes were sent suitable for the Trade of South America, with the Indians on the Western Coast, and the Sandwich Islands;

thence to Canton with Copper, Specie, Furs and sandalwood. This Trade will hereafter become of great competition between the English and American Traders; the *former* however, will have the *vantage* ground, owing to [*one or two words canceled*] having almost exclusively the *possession* of the northern Bank of the *Columbia River*, together with Trading Posts upon its borders; all growing out of— what shall I say? ignorance, stupidity, *cowardice*, or dishonesty—of *our* negotiators of the *Treaty of Ghent*, who had the temerity to admit a *right*, never before thought of, or contemplated. The Rivers of Oregon had all been explored even to the mouth of the Columbia River, an *American trading Post* had been *established* upon the right Bank of its entrance into the Pacific Ocean, then *captured* in war, and never surrendered, in compliance with the *intent* of the terms, on which hostilities should cease. This is but the beginning of the story—where will it end? Relative to *Credit*, in carrying on the China Trade the Englishmen have greatly the advantage of our Countrymen, and by it sometimes great benefit arises by the fluctuation of Exchange between China, Bombay, Madras, Calcutta and London. When I was in the business, the House had acquired the necessary *Credit* to be enabled to negotiate Bills through all of the above places mentioned, and sometimes entire Cargoes were obtained at Canton, sent hither, ["sold"(?) *canceled*] sold, and remittance made to London before the Bills drawn had reached, and matured in London. This matter of Currency, or Credit, it will probably take some time to regain; it depends solely however, upon the merchants themselves. Having been sometime out of the China Trade, I have sent to some friends now in it, and should any matter further be elicited, I shall without delay transmit it to you.

Should any of my remarks in your opinion, bear too hard upon public Men, or of their measures, I trust you will pass them over lightly, as the ebullition of the mind of one, jealous of the rights, and honour of his Country. I have the honour to be, Dear Sir, With the most profound respect, Your obedient Servant, Chas. Henry Hall.

ALS with Ens in DNA, RG 59 (State Department), Miscellaneous Letters (M-179:106, frames 95–108). Note: Hall enclosed extracts from the invoices of nineteen cargoes shipped to and from China in British vessels during a one-year period. He appended to the extracts: "I send Copies of these Nineteen Invoices, that the usual course of the British Trade may be understood—it never varies, saving at times in the amount of *Cotton* or of *Opium*, according to a good or bad season or fluctuation of the market in China." Hall also enclosed a printed abstract, dated 1/18/1826, of the China trade of the English East India Company and an abstract of U.S.-China trade at Canton in 1823–1824.

From JOHN P. HELFENSTEIN, "Private"

Milwaukie W[isconsin] T[erritory,] 30th November 1844
Dear Sir, I now take great pleasure in congratulating you on the
happy Success of correct principles thus far, and hope before exersions [*sic*] cease to see them fully established. When I assumed the
boldness to invite your attention to President [John] Tyler[']s Administration immediately after his induction to Office, I felt confident,
if you gave assistance to his Affairs, a ground work could be laid to
put aside the dangerous leaders of the Democratic party, and effectually destroy Whig and other Combinations as united in 1840—under
[Henry] Clay[']s] influence.

You yet have an important task before you—before Col. [James
K.] Polk takes the Chair of State, care should be taken that the verry
[*sic*] men we have been fearful of in our party do not introduce
themselves so as to mould Col. Polk and his leading friends according
to their Views, thereby upsetting all we have been contending for—
for Years.

From this letter you learn I am in the extreme N[orth]west, my
family near me—A part in Chicago—a part in Milwaukie.

I was in Washington City on ["or about" *interlined*] the 1st Oct.
You were absent—I left my card. The object of my visit accom-
plished, I returned—(I offered for, in association with another in
Chicago, and obtained the right to supply the Army at the different
Stations on the lakes) to Wisconsin.

The North west will be, in the next Presidential Election highly
important in the scale of operation. Consequently care should be
taken who receives Gover[n]mental favour. Has not New York, or
East too large a Scale of favour in this quarter? As regards men it
is all one; but care should be taken that Northern Views don[']t get
too great a preponderence.

I have here, the entire confidence of the German and Irish population. They comprise about the one half of this district. You know
they are generally Democrats. I am with Sentiments of real friendship Yours &c., John P. Helfenstein.

P.S. I have ["ever" *altered to* "always"] been with you in feeling
and views, and have from the period I wrote you, continued till I
found my aid no longer wanted with the President.

ALS in ScCleA.

To [ROCCO] MARTUSCELLI, Consul General of the Two Sicilies, New York [City]

Department of State
Washington, 30th November, 1844

Sir: I have the honor to acknowledge the receipt of three notes from you, dated on the 21st instant, the two former, stating that, being about to avail yourself of a leave of absence for six months, the duties of your Consulate would be committed to the charge of the Chev[a-lier] L[uca] Palmieri; and, communicating the original and copy of a letter of ceremony from the King of the Two Sicilies. The letter will be laid before the President, and his answer sent, as usual, through the Legation of the United States at Naples.

I was absent from Washington when the communication referred to in your third note, on the subject of a "decisive reply" from the Secretary of the Treasury, in the case of Captain Dacorsi, &ca., was received—which will explain the reason why it has not been noticed earlier. In reference to it, I have to remark that, your note of the 17th of August was returned for the purpose of affording you an opportunity of representing the claim in question, in courteous and proper terms. Although your note of the 30th September, regarded as an explanation, is not entirely satisfactory, either in manner or matter, yet, if you continue to be dissatisfied with the decision already given, and desire that the case should be revised—I have no objections again to refer it to the Treasury Department, with that object; but it can only be done at your request, and upon stating the points with which you are dissatisfied, in language of courtesy and decorum.

In compliance with your wishes, I transmit, enclosed, certain documents which accompanied your note of the 25th December last; which constitute all the papers respecting this case, on file here. I am, Sir, with due consideration, Your obedient Servant, J.C. Calhoun.

FC in DNA, RG 59 (State Department), Notes to Foreign Legations, Italian States, Greece, and Turkey, 6:73–75 (M-99:61).

From Orr & Wyatt, [Anderson, S.C.], 11/30. This firm bills Calhoun for $4 for a subscription for 18 months to the Anderson *Gazette.* Receipt of payment is acknowledged by John B. Sitton. DU in ScU-SC, John C. Calhoun Papers.

To A[LPHONSE] PAGEOT, [French Minister to the U.S.]

Department of State
Washington, Nov[embe]r 30, 1844

Sir: I have the honor to acknowledge the receipt of your note of the 1st of October last, in which you inform me that Jean Baptiste Demerlier, a naturalized citizen of the United States, has applied for letters of naturalization in France, and that your Government desires to know what relation this individual bears to the authorities of this country; and whether, if his application be allowed, he would be absolved from all allegiance to the United States.

In reply I have to state, that, as regards your first inquiry, the Constitution and laws of the United States make no distinction between naturalized and native born citizens, except as to eligibility to office in some few cases.

As to the second inquiry proposed in your note, I have to remark that, under our naturalization laws, a citizen or subject of any foreign State, before he can acquire the rights of citizenship here, must, amongst other formalities, make oath or affirmation that he will support the Constitution of the United States, and that he absolutely and entirely renounces and abjures all allegiance and fidelity to any foreign Power, Potentate, State, or Sovereignty whatever, and particularly by name the Power, Potentate, State, or Sovereignty whereof he was before a citizen or subject.

From these provisions it would seem, by necessary implication, that our laws presuppose a right on the part of citizens and subjects of foreign Powers to expatriate themselves and transfer their allegiance; and although the abstract right has not, to my knowledge, been settled by any authoritative decision, I feel no difficulty in expressing the opinion that the United States, acting upon these principles, in reference to the citizens and subjects of other countries, would not deny their application to cases of naturalization of their own citizens by foreign Powers, and, of course, to the case of Demerlier, who, if he should be naturalized by France, would, on this view of the subject, be absolved from his allegiance to the United States. I have the honor to be, with high consideration, Sir, your obedient servant, J.C. Calhoun.

FC in DNA, RG 59 (State Department), Notes to Foreign Legations, France, 6: 84–85 (M-99:21).

From WILSON SHANNON

Legation of the U.S. of A.
Mexico, Nov[embe]r 30th 1844

Sir, I have the honor to transmit to you herewith two additional notes which I have received from the Mexican Secretary of State [Manuel C. Rejon] since the date of my last dispatch. No. 1 is in reply to my note of the 8th inst., in relation to a renewal of the war on the part of this Government against Texas. No. 2 is in relation to the retail trade.

Since the date of my last dispatch, congress has impeached Mr. [Isidro] Reyes, the Secretary of war which for the time being suspends his official powers. The main charge prefer[r]ed against him, is the appointment of Gen[era]l Santa Anna, the constitutional President of Mexico, to the command of the army intended to act against the revolutionists. By the constitution of Mexico the President is prohibited from taking command of the armies of the republic. It is also provided in the same instrument, that the constitutional President can not absent himself from Mexico, more than fifteen days at a time without the consent of congress and the appointment of a President to act *pro tempore.*

Early in September last President Santa Anna, asked and obtained leave to retire to Manga de Clavo, for the avowed purpose of recruiting his health but for the real purpose of placing himself in a situation that would enable him to receive the command of the army without being charged with a flagrant and palpable violation of the constitution. He at that time saw that a revolution was inevitable, in the event of which he desired to command the army in person. [Valentín] Canalizo his firm friend, was appointed to act as President during his absence. It is now claimed by the Government that inasmuch as Gen[era]l Santa Anna is not in the actual occupancy of the office of President, that he does not come within the above constitutional prohibition and can therefore legally receive the command of the army; while on the other hand the opposition claims that Santa Anna is the constitutional President of the Republic and therefore is expressly prohibited from taking command of the army. This is the question, involved in the impeachment of the Secretary of war. The opposition in congress are so strong, that they can carry any measure they propose by a large majority. The impeachment of the Secretary of war is intended to cripple the administration and suspend, for the time being a firm and reliable friend of Santa Anna[']s, from office, and at the same time vindicate the constitution. Mr. [Ignacio]

415

Basadre has been appointed to the office of Secretary of war in the place of Mr. Reyes impeached.

Gen[era]l Santa Anna at the head of his forces reached Queretaro some days since. This is one of the revolutionary cities that had pronounced against the Government. Before his arrival in that place he required the citizens to take back their pronunciamiento against the Government, within twenty four hours, and in case of refusal declared his determination to send them to the castle of Perote. The citizens, instead of receding from their former position, reaffirmed their pronunciamiento against the Government. The news of these transactions reached this city on yesterday morning and produced much excitement in congress. The senate immediately passed a resolution calling on the ministers to appear in person before that body and respond to the question whether Santa Anna was acting by orders of the Government or not. Although this is a customary mode of calling on the ministers they refused to attend, the consequence was the impeachment, by the senate, of all the ministers. Both houses of congress are, now in Secret Session on the question of impeaching the ministers and no doubt is entertained but that the measure will be carried. Should that be the case we will have an administration composed entirely of new men. This change however will not for the present at least, produce any change in the policy of the Government. The revolution has arrived at that stage where it is morally certain that congress must either overthrow Santa Anna or he must overthrow congress. They both cannot exist in power together. The result may be set down as doubtful.

It is said that Gen[era]l [Mariano] Paredes who commands the revolutionary army, and who had advanced in this direction, some distance from Guadalaxara is about falling back on that city, not being sufficiently strong at present to encounter Santa Anna.

There are many rumours in the city as to pronunciamientos against the Gover[n]ment in various parts of the country. The rumors, however that we hear, are so uncertain and so often incorrect, that I will not trouble you with them. No doubt some of them are true. Indeed the whole country is in an unsettled state and I see no prospect of a change for the better. The revolution must take its course, and until one or the other party obtains the entire mastery, we cannot expect any stability in public affairs in Mexico.

Richard H. Belt U.S. consul at Matamoros died in October last. The books and papers of that consulate are in the possession of Mr. T.P.S. Chalyell [*sic*; John P. Schatzell]. It is desirable to have the vacancy filled at as early a period as practicable. I have the honor to be yours with great respect, Wilson Shannon.

[Enclosure (Translation)]

M[anuel] C. Rejon to Wilson Shannon

National Palace

Mexico, November 21, 1844

The Undersigned, Minister of Foreign Relations and Government, has examined the note addressed to him on the 8th instant by the Hon. Wilson Shannon Envoy &c declaring that unless the Undersigned should withdraw the notes, which he sent to that Honorable gentleman on the 31st of October, and the 6th of the present month, all official intercourse between the Government of Mexico and the American Legation, must be suspended, until he should have received instructions from his Government, to which he had submitted the notes in question.

An attempt having been made to justify the annexation of Texas to the United States, on the ground of the right which a part of a nation has, to seperate itself from the remainder, with which it previously formed one, and to unite itself to a foreign nation which may be more convenient to it, and [one word canceled] may choose to admit it into such union, The Undersigned showed, that the said Mexican Province, had been taken away from this Republic, by native citizens of the ["said" canceled] United States, assisted by the Southern people, and the Government of those States; and that the intervention announced by the Cabinet of Washington to prevent Mexico from reconquering that territory, until the question of its annexation to the United States should be decided, could not be defended, without acknowledging solemnly the right in any one of the Nations of the earth, to elevate itself, by appropriating the territories of neighbouring nations first peopling them with its own citizens, then causing them to withdraw from obedience to the territorial authorities, and ["finally asking for the incorporation of the territory thus occupied, with that to which the said citizens belong, territorial authorities and" canceled] to proclaim their independence, assisting them in an effective manner to maintain that independence, and finally to ask for the incorporation of the territory thus occupied, with that of the country to which the said citizens belong.

Assertions such as these absolutely indispensable to prove the right of Mexico to repel the said intervention, have been considered by the Hon. Mr. Shannon as grave calumnies, on his Government, and on the Southern people of the United States: when the American

417

Press has afforded to the world so many proofs of the certainty of those charges, and when on the other hand, official communications afford their support to the facts, adduced by the Undersigned.

Among many facts which might be cited in proof, the Undersigned will only mention the enlistments, made by [Samuel] Houston in Tennessee, when he invited volunteers by the Public press in March 1836; and the loans of armed vessels sent from the Balize, near New Orleans, in the end of 1835. The Mexican Legation called on the American Government, to exert its vigilance, to remedy these wrongs, against the laws of the United States and the relations of friendship between the two nations; and what was the result? The American Government contented itself with protestations of honour, offering to fulfil the duties thus imposed on it; but subsequent facts have shown that these were vain formalities.

For this reason, the respectable John Quincy Adams, in a discourse pronounced by him at Braintree on the 17th of February 1842, remarking on the want of conformity between the words of one of President [Andrew] Jackson's messages, and his conduct, said that the orders given to the District Attornies of the Union, were, to proceed without regard to persons, wherever indications warranted, against all who should attempt to violate the neutrality; notwithstanding which, whole regiments of inhabitants were daily going to Texas, in order to sustain the liberty of that Country, without the district Attorney's having discovered any indications, on which to found proceedings, until the battle of San Jacinto had shewn what was going on; and the petitions for the recognition of the ["Country" *canceled*] Independence of Texas, had afforded sufficient proofs, of the sort of neutrality, which was proclaimed, and which induced the majority of Jackson's party in that legislature, to adopt resolutions at variance with the protestations of honour inculcated in the message of the 8th of December 1835.

The Undersigned will therefore ask Mr. Shannon, can his ignorance be such, that he is entirely unacquainted with events which are publick and notorious, in his country, and which prove the open cooperation of the Government and southern people of the United States, in support of the Independence of Texas? Whether the miserable and insignificant assistance, given clandestinely by some private individuals, to the Mexicans, who were struggling for the emancipation of their country, can be compared with that which was publickly afforded to the so called Texians? Whether the spirit which animated the United States, in the war of the Independence of Mexico, be the same, which exhibited itself so energetically with respect to the colonists of Texas? Whether there can be any analogy, between the character of the population which proclaimed and supported the emancipation of Mexico, from its ancient masters, and that which has seized upon Texas and its rich lands, and drawn them away, from the authority of their legitimate Sov[e]reign?

If the Hon. Mr. Shannon will reflect on this last circumstance, he will soon see, what little force there is in the reflection, which he has made, in throwing back the argument advanced by the Undersigned, when he represented the independence of the Department in question, as the work of native Citizens of the United States, assisted by the Southern people, and the Government of that Republic. In fact, how can the independence of Mexico be attributed to the few Spaniards, who took part in it, with the same reason, with which the Texan Independence is attributed to the people of the United States, established in that Department? In the latter case, all or nearly all who proclaimed and supported the independence, were persons drawing their origin from the Hon. Mr. Shannon[']s Republick, who came with the idea of annexing Texas to their native country, and were animated by the sentiments of the people of the Southern States of the Union. In the revolution of Mexico, appeared an immense majority of Mexicans, by birth, who though sons of Spaniards, had not the less right to the soil where they were born, as heirs to the property of their aboriginal ancestors on the other side—And can the Hon. Mr. Shannon produce the same titles to the Territory of Texas, in behalf of those citizens of the United States, who have seized on that province, and who immediately after effecting its independence, established a constitution forever excluding the descendants of Indians, and consequently nearly all the Mexicans, from the name, the prerogatives, and the rights of citizens? The fellow Citizens of the Undersigned, will hereby see at once, the weakness of the reflections by which it is attempted to refute his note of the 31st of October; and they will also remark, that the object is not only to strip them of their territory, but also to proscribe their race.

And after this, can the Hon. Mr. Shannon complain with justice, that the Undersigned should hasten to make these and other important revelations to his fellow citizens, by printing his notes, accompanied by those from the American Legation, in order that with the full knowledge of every thing adduced by each party, they may see what they have to expect, or to fear, in this serious question, in which even the national character of their country is jeopardized? It is certainly strange, that the minister of a nation which boasts of having required nothing unjust, during the sixty ["nine" *interlined*]

419

years of its political existence, should now expect that a government, from which it is attempted to take away a considerable portion of its territory, should remain silent, and so recreant to its duties, as not even to inform the people, of the dangers to which they are exposed.

But the American Legation will say, as it has already said that in this, it has been treated with injustice, by presenting its arguments in an odious light, mutilating its expressions, and even making false citations to mislead the Mexican people, very few of whom can compare them, with the words attributed to Jackson. The Undersigned will dispel these charges, by rapidly recurring to them, and will present for judgement, the conduct of the American Government during the Presidency, not only of that General, but also of [John] Tyler, by adducing the literal text of the Message, which he has cited and which the Undersigned is charged with disfiguring.

On the first point, relative to the confession made by the Hon. Mr. Shannon, that the acquisition of Texas was a measure long cherished, and deemed indispensable for the security and welfare of the United States, and which had therefore been invariably pursued, by all parties in that Republic, and made a subject of negotiation by all administrations, for the last twenty years—Of what effect in destroying the Argument founded by the Undersigned, on this confession, and on the facts adduced by him, is the question of the American Legation, whether it be not true, that the Archives of this Department of the Government ["do not" *canceled*] prove that negotiations had been carried on, even since the year 1825, for the transfer of Texas by the Mexican Government, to that of the United States?

Are ["we" *canceled*] on this account less certain, the facts, shewing that whilst waiting to see whether or not, this cession would be made, the Government and the southern people of the United States were taking measures to seize by force, the interesting Territory in question, in case Mexico should refuse to cede it? The repugnance of Mexico was regarded as invincible, from the date of the answer, given to a note, of July 26 1832, in which Mr. [Anthony] Butler, after announcing the ratification of the treaty of limits, proposed the conclusion of another treaty defining a line of seperation more natural, and precise, meaning probably thus to give greater weight to the arguments alledged [*sic*], against the Spanish Government, to shew that the limits of Louisiana extended to the Rio Bravo del Norte, as they had before been made to extend to West Florida. Notwithstanding the answer given by the Mexican Government, to that Gentleman, on the 4th of February 1843, he did not lose courage; he repeated the same on the 22d of June following; but no answer having been given to him, he again repeated his proposition on the 6th of September, always soliciting the settlement of other limits, for which he proposed the conclusion of another treaty. The Department now under the charge of the Undersigned, repeated to Mr. Butler on the 20th of that month, what it had already told him, in February preceeding [*sic*]; and then, after this sad removal of all doubts, it became necessary to adopt the artifice of producing the Independence of Texas, through the citizens of the United States established in that province, who were aided thereto; to seek out reasons in justification of their rebellion; and to give to the affair such a turn as to afford some appearance of justice, to what is in reality a pure usurpation let it be viewed in any light whatever. Is it at all strange, that the Undersigned should have said, that this open confession of the American Legation, respecting the twenty years, during which it ["is" *canceled*] desired to acquire the territory of Texas, together with the facts which he rapidly presented, and which he now reproduces, had dispelled any doubt which might have remained, as to who were the real authors of the Independence of Texas, and what were the designs with which it was proclaimed, and supported by the assistance of the Government, and the southern people of the Hon. Mr. Shannon[']s Republic? Is not all this moreover, confirmed by what is said in the note, to which the present is an answer, as to negotiations having been made formerly with Mexico, and now with Texas, for which latter object, it was necessary first to give to Texas, the character of an independant nation.

It was thus necessary, in order to arrive in this way, at the acquisition of the said Territory, to trample under foot, all the principles which had been constantly pursued in cases of a like nature, by the Government of the United States, and had obtained for them the reputation mentioned by the Hon. Mr. Shannon. Observe in proof of this, what Jackson, when President of that Republic, said in the message addressed by him to the House of Representatives on the 22d of October 1836, and compare his Doctrines, with the conduct which he subsequently observed on this subject and which the present Chief Magistrate of that nation has pursued.

With regard to the Independence of Texas, at that time, General Jackson used these words; "The acknowledgement of a new State as independent, and entitled to a place in the family of nations is at all times an act of great delicacy, and responsibility, but more especially so, when such state has forcibly seperated itself from another, of which it had formed an integral part, and which still claims dominion over it. A premature recognition under these circumstances, if not looked upon as justifiable cause of war, is always liable to be regarded as a proof of an *unfriendly spirit* to one of the contending parties. *All questions relative to the government of foreign Nations whether of the old or new world, have been treated by the United States as questions of fact only,* and our predecessors, have cautiously abstained from deciding upon them, until the clearest evidence was in their possession, to enable them not only to decide correctly, but to shield their decisions from *every unworthy imputation."*

Continuing in the same spirit, he uses the following words, "It has thus been made known to the world, *that the uniform policy and practice of the United States, is to avoid all interference in disputes, which merely relate to the internal government of other nations,* and eventually to recognize the authority of the prevailing party, *without reference to our particular interests, and views, or to the merits of the original controversy."*

Now were these equitable and just principles, which guided the American Government in the recognition of Mexico, and other Spanish American Republics, the same which have been followed, in acknowledging the independence of the Department of Texas? Did not that Government hasten to afford a place to Texas in the family of nations, within a few weeks after it had been asserted in the said message, that the so called Texans, had not secured their independence; as Mexico appeared to rely on her resources, as sufficient for reconquering it, and had not renounced the right of restoring it to her union? How much time had passed, between the said message in which was inculcated, the necessity of waiting until the independence of that Province should have been evidently assured, and the recognition by the American Government for so sudden a variation to have been produced in the circumstances of Mexico, and of Texas, that the former should have become impotent, and the latter so powerful and robust as to be able to sustain herself.

Besides, may the Undersigned ask, in what manner was this recognition effected? At the close of the session of Congress, and of the Presidency of Andrew Jackson, says the circumspect Adams, and when the report of the committee on the subject of the recognition of Texas ["had" *canceled*] as an independent state ["had" *interlined*] not been received, a member from the south moved an amendment to the general appropriation bill, providing for the salary of a Diplomatic Agent, to be sent to the said Mexican Province, so soon as the President of the United States should have received satisfactory information, that Texas was capable of sustaining her sov[e]reignty. The amendment having been approved and communicated to the

Government, Jackson immediately sent to the Senate, the appointment of a chargé d'Affaires, for Texas, by the approval of which, the independence of a Department belonging to a friendly Republic was recognized. And was this proceeding with the circumspection and caution recommended in the said message, in an act so delicate and involving so great a responsibility? Is conduct like this amicable and honorable and above all conformable with the principles of probity and good faith, inculcated in the above mentioned document?

On the other hand, has it not been, according to Jackson, the uniform policy and practice of the United States, to treat all questions relating to foreign nations as questions of fact only, avoiding all intervention in them, and never to recognize the independence of new states, until *their capacity to maintain themselves had been fully established, and the danger of their being again reduced to subjection had entirely passed?* Why then, has this line of conduct been abandoned in the Texas question, by assisting the Colonists to effect their independence, not only furnishing them with arms and am[m]unition, but also with men, who were publickly enlisted for that object, in the southern States of the Republic, and thus openly infringing the laws, of which, ["if" *interlined*] the Hon. Mr. Shannon is unacquainted with them, the Undersigned will have the pleasure to send him Copies? How, after having thus inculcated the laws of nations, which the gentleman now charged with the American Legation at Mexico, either does not understand, or ["interprets" *interlined*] in his own way, was the independence of Texas thus hastily acknowledged, at a time when the colonists, without the assistance afforded to them, would never have been able to effect it, nor would now be able to sustain it, if the American Government had not so openly placed itself on their side? How, in fine, has the question between Mexico and Texas been treated only as a question ["of fact" *interlined*] while examining minutely the right of the colonists of that province to seperate themselves from the remainder of this Republic, and entering seriously into the merits of the original controversy? The proof of this truth, among many others, which could be presented by the Undersigned, is found in the note now answered. In that note, the American Legation, referring to the intemperate report of the commissioner, appointed to ascertain the situation of Texas, and to make that country appear to have the elements necessary to constitute an independent State, and thus to give it the right of being annexed to the United States, endeavors to demonstrate, that the Colonists had the unquestionable right, to seperate themselves from Mexico, as it did not protect them from the depredations of the barbarous Indians, as if they, when they came to establish themselves in the Country, could have been ignorant, that they were about to fix themselves in deserts, overrun by those people, and as if the people of the United States, in penetrating through all the frontiers, did not unite to defend themselves, by forming themselves into regiments, well armed, like those which have entered the Department of California, scandalously infringing the regulations of the Country. In the said report, it is also alledged, that the so called Texans had not had granted to them, the right to become a state of the Confederacy; forgetting that they neither had the population required by law, as their [*sic*] amounted to scarcely Twenty thousand souls, whilst the smallest State in the Republic had at least sixty thousand; nor had the laws reserved to them the right to determine as to their own fitness to become a State, but to the general Congress, with the approval of three fourths of the members present in both ["houses" *canceled*] chambers, subject to ratification, by an equal number of the Legislatures of the other States of the Confederacy. The variation of the Federal Constitution is also cited as a just ground for the independence of Texas, though ["thought" *canceled*] that Constitution did not exist, when the first colonists established themselves in that Territory, and neither they nor the last colonists, ever submitted to it, but lived as they pleased, conforming always with the laws and practices of the United States, from which they drew their origin. But even though that code had been observed, and they had regulated their conduct by it, the right on their part, to seperate from the Union which had so generously received them, in consequence of a variation of the said code, could not be recognized without also allowing to foreigners, who may establish themselves in the United States, or in France, England or Russia, the same right to secede from those nations, whenever institutions should be adopted, different from those held by themselves.

But, returning to the comparison between the message ["and" *canceled*] above quoted, and the conduct observed by the Government of the United States, the Undersigned will repeat the question, why, as it had been the constant policy and practice of the United States, not to interfere in disputes relating to the internal administration of foreign countries, have they now engaged in that between Mexico and Texas; carefully devoting themselves to the examination even of the merits of the original contest? Why this inequality, as regards the Mexican Republic, ["an" *interlined*] inequality most odious, which the American Legation would in vain endeavour to justify, by citing these sixty ["nine" *interlined*] years of honorable conduct, during which the United States have always complied with their obligations and duties towards the other nations of the earth?

The Undersigned however finds it necessary to pass on to observations of a more serious nature. The Hon. Mr. Shannon's Government has said, that with regard to recognizing the independence of other nations, not presenting the circumstances in which the Department now in question is placed, it had always proceeded with caution, regulating its conduct according to the principles laid down by it, so as to shield its decisions from *unworthy imputation*—that is to say—from a charge of injustice towards the nation—the dismemberment of which it recognised. Now this charge would be very serious, as regards the recongnition [*sic*] of the independence of Texas, which had thus been entirely condemned, unless the rules of neutrality should have been most vigorously observed. This indeed was felt and was said, in that message, shewing that the recognition of Texas by the United States, as an independent State, would be regarded as a serious injustice to Mexico, and that the United ["States" *interlined*] would thereby be subject to the blackest censure, as the Texans were citizens of that Republic, and were seeking their recognition, with the evident intention of effecting their incorporation with it. This is exactly what the undersigned asserted, that General Jackson had said; and the American legation has nevertheless denied it, declaring that it had never used this language as if the ideas expressed in the said document were not the same which the undersigned had reduced to a few words, coinciding with the extract made of them by Adams, in censuring the inconsistencies of Jackson. But see the literal text of the part of that message, relating to the subject, and then say, which has been wanting in truth—the Mexican Ministry, or the American Legation.

"In the contest," says the message, "between Spain and her insurgent colonies, we stood aloof, and waited not only until the *ability of the New States to protect themselves was fully established, but until the danger of their being again subjugated, had entirely passed away.* Then, and not until then, were they recognised. The same policy was observed in the disputes growing out of the emancipation of the Spanish American States in their struggles with the mother country, with which they had been united under one form of Government. We acknowledged the separate independence of Venezuela, New Granada, and Equator [*sic*] only after their independent existence was no longer a subject of dispute, or was actually acquiesced in by those, with whom they had been previously united. It is true, that with regard to Texas, the civil authority of Mexico has been expelled, its invading army overthrown, the chief of the Republic himself captured; and all the power of Mexico in that Department to destroy the Government recently organized therein, is completely annihilated. But, on the other hand, there is, in appearance at least, an immense disparity of physical force, on the side of Mexico. The Mexican Republic is rallying its forces under another Executive power, and with another chief is threatening to recover its lost dominion. Taking into consideration, this imminent invasion, the independence of Texas may be regarded as suspended; and were there nothing peculiar in the relative situation of the United States, and Texas, our recognition of its independence at such a crisis, could scarcely be regarded as consistent, with that prudent reserve, with which we have hitherto considered ourselves obliged to treat such questions."

"But there are circumstances in the relations of the two countries, which require us to act, on this occasion, with even more than our wonted caution. Texas was once claimed as a part of our property, and there are those among our citizens, who, always reluctant to abandon that claim, cannot but regard with solicitude, the prospect of the reunion of the territory to this country. A large portion of its civilized inhabitants are emigrants from the United States; speake the same language with ourselves; cherish the same principles, political and religious and are bound to many of our citizens by ties of friendship and kindred blood; and more than all, it is known that the people of that country have instituted the same form of government with our own, and have since the close of your last session, openly resolved, on the acknowledgment by us of their independence, to seek admission into the Union, as one of the federal states. This last circumstance is a matter of peculiar delicacy, and forces upon us considerations of the gravest character. The title of Texas to the territory she claims is identified with her independence; she asks us to acknowledge that title to the territory, with an avowed design to treat immediately of its transfer to the United States. It becomes us to beware of too early movement, as it might subject us, however unjustly, to the imputation of seeking to establish the claim of our neighbors to a territory, with a view to its subsequent acquisition by ourselves. Prudence therefore seems to dictate that we should stand aloof, and maintain our present attitude, if not until Mexico itself, or one of the great foreign powers, shall recognize the independence of the new government, at least until the lapse of time, or the course of events shall have proved, *beyond cavil or dispute*, the ability of the people of that country to maintain their seperate sovereignty, and to uphold the government constituted by them." Now does not all this shew, that Jackson considered that the acknowledgment of the independence of Texas at that time might appear, an act of serious injustice to Mexico, as those who proclaimed it, were citizens of the U. States, and had done so with the object of annexing that Department to the territory of the U. States? And is it not certain, that in making the acknowledgment, the American Government did not wait for the recognition by Mexico herself, or by any other power, nor for time to put beyond question, the capacity of the colonists to maintain their sovereignty themselves. He then says, that it might subject the United States to the imputation, though unjustly, of hastening to give to Texas a place in the family of nations, in order afterwards to appropriate her territory to themselves. Now can it be said unjustly, that Texas was recognized in a premature manner, and at variance, with all the principles which, hitherto guided the American Government, in its conduct towards the other nations of the old and, the new world; thus adjudging to itself that territory, the acquisition of which, has been considered necessary to the well being and security of the United States, by all administrations, and parties in that Republic, for the last twenty years? And can it after this be denied, that the independence of Texas, effected and maintained, as it was, almost entirely by American citizens, who were not repressed but are on the contrary assisted by their Government and by the Southern States of the Union, was intended for no other object, than the aggrandizement of the United States, by the annexation of that territory, endeavoring thus to give to the affair a turn, which should deprive it, in some measure of the odium, of a barefaced usurpation.

But the same weakness presented in this point by the answers of the American Legation, is found in that given to the undersigned, respecting the belief entertained in the United States, that the territory of Texas, is comprised in the territory Louisiana, ceded by France to that Republic in 1803. The Hon. Mr. Shannon says that the United States, do not attempt and never have attempted, to acquire Texas under that pretext; that their argument has been, that a large portion of that territory is within the valley of the Mississippi, that this circumstance rendered its acquisition necessary for the defence of a distant weak and important frontier, and that this being the principal basis of his reflexions on this point, he is surprised at its omission, whilst the belief is brought forward, in order to prejudice the minds of the Mexican people, against the Government, and the Southern States of the Hon. Mr. Shannon's Republic. The undersigned must observe that there was a time, when a pretension was advanced to extend the limits of Louisiana to the Rio Bravo del Norte, and thus to take from the Spanish Government several provinces now belonging to the Mexican Republic; consequently in the statement of that belief as advanced by the American Legation, on the 14 of October, the Undersigned saw a revival of this old pretension which he immediately repelled, because, if this was not adduced as the foundation of a right, the Undersigned knows not for what object it could have been brought forward. But besides—does the Hon. Mr. Shannon suppose, that he can tranquilize the Mexicans, by the other part cited by him, and presented as the principle title to justify the Government of the United States in the violent acquisition by them, of the territory of Texas? Can the circumstance, that a large portion of that Department lies in the valley of the Mississippi, give to the United States, the right to take it to themselves, in defiance of the most solemn conventions? On the other hand, the argument founded on the security of that Republic occasions much more alarm, than the one respecting the extent of Louisiana because by the latter, some limits are placed on the pretensions of the American Government, while on the contrary, the other argument, opens the door for the absorption of the whole continent, and even of the whole world, by that Republic.

But it will be said, that the Administration of the United States has abstained from acceding to the proposition of annexation, until in the course of new events, circumstances connected with negotiations between the Government of Mexico and Great Britain, no longer permitted further delay. The Undersigned in answer to this, must declare, that his Government has never yet thought of concluding treaties with any power, to dispossess itself of its absolute dominion over that territory; and that the supposition here presented by the American Legation, is wholly gratuitous. As regards the very discourteous language, with which the Mexican Government has ["been" *interlined*] treated, the Hon. Mr. Shannon[']s excuse must seem very unsatisfactory, to any impartial person; for he who tells another he has acted barbarously, calls him barbarous, and this is what Mr. Shannon has done, frequently in his note of the 14 of October last, without having had any neces[s]ity to make use of so harsh a term, in support of his right; as there were others, by which he might have explained his meaning without failing in the consideration due by every Foreign Legation to the nation near which he is accredited. The manner in which the Mexican nation has made war on the fellow countrymen of the Hon. Mr. Shannon, disguised under the name of Texans, was occasioned as the undersigned said on the 31st of October, last, by the conduct so far from honourable of the southern people and Government of the United States, who in place of preserving a vigorous neutrality, in the contest between Mexico and the colonists of Texas, had openly formented the rebellion of the latter, affording them every species of supplies, and endeavoring to enervate the powers of this Government, for the re-conquest of that important territory. The undersigned nevertheless has shown, that his Government had the strongest disposition to treat them with the greatest indulgence, by allowing them the exceptional laws, which their interests and necessities required, provided they should recognise their legitimate sovereign. The Hon. Mr. Shannon however leaves aside this answer, presenting anew his argument in the same terms in which he had before presented it, as if no answer had been made to him on this point; and the undersigned here takes the liberty to say, that in his opinion, nothing can satisfy the American Legation, except leaving their Government to seize upon the territory of Texas, for which the manner of making war on that country is nothing more than a pretext; because as the Hon. Mr. Shannon has already said the acquisition of that Department has been considered necessary, and believed to be indispensable to the well being and security of the United States, by all parties and Administrations in that Republic for the last twenty years.

Not to extend this note further, the Undersigned will say in summary, that the facts related in his preceding notes, having proved that the independence of Texas is the work of citizens of the United States, assisted by the Government and the southern people of those States, that it was undertaken so soon as there was evidence that the Mexican Administration would not submit to yield that vast and fertile Department, to the United States; that the Government of the United States acknowledged that independence, in contravention of the principles by which its conduct had been always guided in similar cases, for the sole object of acquiring that province, which had been considered indisp[en]sable for the security of their country, for the last twenty years, by all administrations and parties in that Republic; and that these circumstances having been adduced only in the most moderate terms, and with the object of establishing the right of the Mexican Government to repel the injustice with which the American Government pretends to prevent the reconquest of a country, belonging to Mexico, by every title, the Undersigned has orders from His Excellency the President ad interim, to repeat to the Hon. Mr. Shannon, the contents of the notes of the 31 of October last, and the 6th of the present month; and at the same time to declare to him that if in consequence of the use by Mexico of her right, without regard to

429

the insulting intimation of the American Government, the relations between the two countries should be altered, the responsibility for the evils which may ensue, will rest on the present minister of the United States, in this country, and his Government, which has determined to provoke a rupture, to justify its ends, overstepping the powers granted by the Constitution of their Country, because in consideration of the peculiar circumstances of the case, it is believed to be "to their interest."

Whilst making this communication to the Hon. Mr. Shannon, in answer to his note of the 8th of this month, the Undersigned repeats to him the assurances of his consideration.   M.C. Rejon.

LS (No. 5) with Ens in DNA, RG 59 (State Department), Diplomatic Despatches, Mexico, vol. 12 (M-97:13), received 1/2/1845; FC in DNA, RG 84 (Foreign Posts), Mexico, Despatches; CC in DNA, RG 46 (U.S. Senate), 28A-F1. NOTE: The second enclosure, a 13-pp. letter of 11/22 from Rejon to Shannon, is a reply to Shannon's letter of 10/25 questioning the Mexican decree of September 1843 "restricting foreigners from carrying on the retail trade." Rejon contends that the commercial treaty of 1831 between the U.S. and Mexico speaks of "commerce in general" and never specifically mentions the retail trade in any way.   In addition, he feels that Shannon is incorrect in asserting that the treaty established "perfect equality" in trade between the two nations; it instead asserted the "most favoured nation" principle in trade.   Any further interference by the U.S. in these internal affairs of Mexico will be regarded as a sign of hostility and an attack on Mexican sovereignty.

From THEO[DORE] S. FAY

Berlin, November, 1844

Sir, A verbal enquiry has been made me, by the Prussian Government, whether Mr. Louis Mark be yet in the public service? I was obliged to reply that I had received no official notification on the subject. I have the honor to be, with the highest consideration, Sir, Y[ou]r Ob[e]d[ien]t Serv[an]t, Theo. S. Fay.

ALS (No. 24) in DNA, RG 59 (State Department), Diplomatic Despatches, Germany, vol. 3 (M-44:4), received 12/23; FC in DNA, RG 84 (Foreign Posts), Germany, Despatches, 4:163–164.

DECEMBER 1-15, 1844

⫴

On December 2 the Twenty-Eighth Congress convened for its last, "lame-duck" session. The head of an executive department could expect for the next three months to be immersed in urgent business. Besides the large though normal activities in regard to reports and appropriations there were two major diplomatic measures pending before the Senate, quite aside from any questions of Texas, Mexico, and Oregon.

These were the first American commercial treaty with the ancient and distant land of China and another unprecedented commercial treaty with the German Zollverein. Both of these had been concluded at great pains. The China treaty would eventually be ratified. The Senate at its preceding session had declined to act on the Zollverein Treaty. In a message early in the session, the President informed the Senators that he had reason to believe that the German states would still be willing to accept American ratification, even if the deadline were past. He could make this assurance because of the careful efforts of the Secretary of State and the American representatives in Prussia to keep the option open. Once more, however, the Senate refused to vote the treaty either up or down.

As to more pressing matters, closer to home, the President disclosed to the Congress the unfortunately tense relations between the United States and Mexico and the intent if not the ability of Mexico to reduce Texas to subjection. As to Mexico he made no recommendation, but as to Texas he urged the Congress to move ahead with the matter of annexation, which would seem to be the mandate of the elections just concluded.

In the Senate George McDuffie of South Carolina introduced a joint resolution to admit Texas to the Union as a state, upon the terms already agreed upon in the treaty concluded and rejected earlier in the year. This would bypass the process of treaty ratification. A bit later a similar bill was brought forward in the House by Charles J. Ingersoll of Pennsylvania, Chairman of the Foreign Affairs Committee. Thomas H. Benton was ready immediately with a complicating diversion—a bill to reopen diplomatic negotiations with Texas and Mexico. Still other proposals were floated. It would take some

431

weeks to formulate a proposal that could carry an effective majority. Of Benton Calhoun said: "He covers and protects the whigs by his course."

Party politics aside, the underlying conflicts referred back inevitably to that cluster of sectional antagonisms for which the South's domestic institutions were the symbol. On the second day of the session, the aged John Quincy Adams introduced a motion in the House of Representatives to repeal the 25th rule of the standing orders—the "gag rule" which automatically tabled abolition petitions (a method of dealing with the question of which Calhoun had never approved). Adams's motion passed 108 to 80 on a sectional vote which created serious tensions within both parties.

On the other side of the issue, the Spanish Minister took the occasion to renew the demands of his government for satisfaction in the case of the Amistad. A friend of Calhoun's at home wrote: "We at the South must not look back. . . . if we do not put our shoulders to the Wheel—we must expect the Devil and all his Works, in which I include John Quincy Adams, to overcome us in the midst of our righteous joy & triumph."

Ⅲ

"MEMORANDA" [by ROBERT J. WALKER]

[Washington] December, 1844

On my arrival here had long interview with Mr. Calhoun, being the second on this subject. He still insists that the plan by treaty was best, adheres to provisions for annexation on terms proposed in the rejected (treaty), and thinks it best if a treaty impossible to have these terms proposed to Texas by joint-resolution of Congress. If this cannot be done, would take my bill with following amendments: 1st, Let it be done by joint resolution of Congress, instead of by Act of Congress as in my bill. 2nd, In third clause in my bill where Texas cedes North of 36°.30, to the U.N. [*sic*] the soil and jurisdiction, insert "Subject to the Constitution of the United States and the decision in this and all other of the N.S. [*sic*] of all questions relating to slavery by the Supreme Court of the United States." 3rd, Strike out reannexation and insert annexation. Mr. Calhoun is vehement on this subject, and says it is an implied censure of Mr. [James] Monroe and all his cabinet in relation to the Florida Treaty. To the two first suggestions of Mr. Calhoun I cheerfully assented. To the 3rd I objected as weakening our position before Congress and the Country, and as approved by the historical records. Mr. Monroe himself, as well as Mr. [Thomas] Jefferson, Mr. [James] Madison, and even Mr. J[ohn] Q[uincy] Adams admitted and proved as shown by me that Texas was once ours, under the Treaty of 1803, and it was conceded by the Spanish Minister on his return home in 1821 after negotiating the Florida Treaty; to get Texas again then is clearly re-annexation. Nevertheless, the word must be yielded; rather lose the measure. Mr. Calhoun approves decidedly of the six States, and the equilibrium, as secured by my bill. He says if the whole South would vote for it in both Houses of Congress, it would succeed, but fears that party will be stronger than patriotism and will divide the South. Thinks the united South could accomplish anything it ought to ask.

PC in Lyon G. Tyler, ed., *Letters and Times of the Tylers*, 3:152. NOTE: The date of this interview cannot be determined, but Walker was in Washington in early and late December, making a trip to Nashville during the middle part of the month. The original of this ms. material published by Lyon G. Tyler has not been found.

From W[ILLIAM] W. IRWIN

Legation of the United States
Copenhagen, 1 December 1844

Sir; I have the honor to acknowledge the receipt of your Despatch No. 13, dated the 12th September last, covering a Copy of that addressed by you, on the 10th of the same month, to the Honorable W[ilson] Shannon, our Minister at Mexico.

Owing to the misrepresentations which have been industriously circulated for a considerable time past by the British press, instigated, doubtless, by government influence, the grossest ignorance has prevailed throughout Europe with regard to our course on the Texas question, and our relations with Mexico generally. We have been vilified with all the zeal and pertinacity which the malice of the enemies of our republican institutions could invoke to their aid. We have been represented to the civilized world as regardless of the laws of nations, as wanting in good faith towards Mexico, and as determined to despoil her of her just rights. Under these circumstances, knowing the falsehood of the accusation, and convinced of the justice of our cause, I have considered it my duty, whenever the question of annexation has been introduced, in my presence, in the diplomatic circles here, to justify the course of my government as demanded by every principle of public justice and political expediency, by the laws of humanity, and the civilization of the age in which we live. In conversation, too, with the King [Christian VIII] and the Minister of Foreign Affairs [H.A. Criminil-Reventlow], I have taken especial pains to remove any erroneous impressions which may have been made on their minds, and to vindicate the conduct of the United States by a plain statement of the truth in relation to this matter. I flatter myself that my efforts in this respect have not been fruitless, but I am glad that you have authorised me effectually to encounter the appeal made by Mexico to Foreign Powers. Your despatch to our Minister in that country must, I am sure be conclusive to every dispassionate mind, and I shall not fail to embrace every fitting opportunity of availing myself of its convincing arguments.

I have also the honor to acknowledge the receipt of your Despatch dated the 13th September last (likewise numbered 13) in relation to the Sound Dues.

The information which you require shall be procured, so far as the same may be practicable, as speedily as possible, but I fear that, with regard to some portion of it, there may be considerable delay; particularly, as I am not authorised to make a formal application to this Government on the subject. I shall, however, spare no pains to comply with your wishes, but if it is contemplated to give the notice requisite to terminate our Treaty of 26 April 1826 with Denmark, and a resolution of Congress to that effect should be desired at this Session, I would respectfully recommend to our government not to wait for the Statistical details sought for. Every thing moves so slowly here that I fear Congress will adjourn before I can have fully performed the duty assigned to me, and the result be made known to you. I am sure I shall be able to convince you that the Sound Dues have become more onerous to our Commerce than to that of almost any other country. This Toll was for the first time (indirectly it is true) recognised by us in the treaty of 1826. However desirable that treaty may have been, at the time of its ratification, we have ceased to derive any peculiar advantages from its provisions, and as the period of its duration can now be safely terminated, it is time that we should seek for some new arrangement more favorable to our trade in the Baltic. I have the honor to be, Sir, very respectfully Your ob[edien]t Ser[van]t, W.W. Irwin.

LS (No. 36) in DNA, RG 59 (State Department), Diplomatic Despatches, Denmark, vol. 3 (M-41:5), received 2/22/1845; FC in DNA, RG 84 (Foreign Posts), Denmark, Despatches, vol. 1843–1847:[152–154].

From [JOHN R. MATHEWES]

[near Charleston, S.C.?] Dec[embe]r 1, 1844
My Dear Sir, We may say that the Storm of dispair [*sic*] has blown over, & with the Duke of Glouster [*sic*] exclaim "Now is the Winter of our discontent made glorious summer by" the defeat of [Henry] Clay. We are not however yet in Summer, nor over the blighting winds of March; if we are to reap we must sow, tis not the soil alone makes the Crop, however good the former may be. There is seed required—there is skilful husbandry required—to make the most rank spot in the valley of the Mississippi become converted from a howling wilderness into a garden of comfort & wealth. So is it in the Election of J[ames] K. Polk—he is the soil, before the seed is sown, it must be prepared by a good husbandman, and as Nathan said unto David so say I unto you—"Thou art the man." We at the South must not look back. So far God has help'd us & if we do not put our shoulders to the Wheel—we must expect the Devil and all his Works, in which I include John Quincy Adams, to overcome us in the midst of our righteous joy & triumph.

It is not to be expected that you should make yourself the Target or Drum upon which our enemies are to aim their blows; but we must prepare for another Battle, if we go into Winter Quarters or if we compromise or ask for Peace we are as we were. A Bold stand must be made & *New* England put at defiance. Europe is with us if we are instructive & true to ourselves—half way measures will not do against the invitation of our New England bretheren [*sic*] to proscribe us from the alters [*sic*] of our Christian forefathers and to teach the world that we are little better than can[n]ibals—and all this too for the *sake of the Tariff*. The Thief crying Stop Thief to evade detection.

South Carolina as I have frequently remark'd is looked to with wonder[,] solicitude & trembling, and more caution & determination is to be observ'd by her for the next 2 years than most people are aware of—no blustering, vapouring or idle gasconade, but sober serious reflection. We have scotched the snake not killed him; this was our error in faith if not foolery on the election of Gen[era]l [Andrew] Jackson—we had the game in our hands but a bad partner lost it for us. We have it again & will win it—if we do not ["again" *interlined*] suffer our adversaries, to flatter[,] bribe, intoxicate and divert our Delilah.

The Governor of So[uth] Ca[rolina] is important. The message of the President if bold & concise will be effectual. If legislating for British taste and the African Slave trade—Bah!—I had a long conversation with the British Consul the other evening. I remarked how profoundly ignorant Mr. [Robert] Peel & his Government were as regards their true interests in this Country &c &c &c. He replied you will soon be undeceived. They are looking more closely into the truth of what is now going on than they have been, or that you are aware of, & concluded with observing—["]What an immensely rich country So[uth] Ca[rolina] would be with a trade with the World— it would be the richest spot in the World &c &c." Now we must push our foreign embassies. [Edward] Everett must come home—he is [Daniel] Webster's Creature turn him which way you will like 96 he is the same & you cannot make more of him. His namesake ought to be President of our college. The president now in office is ruining its success. I do not know him but I know the effects of his controul— 'tis no business of mine but I love my native State. I repeated these remarks to a Senator a few days ago in the presence of a third person. The reply was "but will it not offend Mr. [Robert] Henry to displace him." My answer—"Was the College of So[uth] Ca[rolina] instituted for individual emolument or ambition, or was it for the credit & character of the rising generation?" You are right says the third party and he ought to be turned out—and Mr. Senator said he at once saw into the propriety of the observation. I have no son at ["it" *interlined*] nor probably ever shall have. We must now show no variableness nor shadow of turning. J.K. Polk must abide by the Baltimore Resolutions in toto. Governor [James H.] Hammond[']s Message to the Legislature is bold[,] manly & fearless. The Tariff & the State bank he deals with in candour and in prospective truth. The military & financial resources of the State are opportunely pourtrayed. The whole is excellent—to some it may be too pungent but it is as well at an early period to exclaim we are "wide awake" as after the enemy has us, to exclaim that we were surprised at an unguarded moment. This may be flattering to us as usual but has never lessened one atom of our burthens nor one measure of their exactions. Mr. [Francis W.] Pickens' resolutions may however ameliorate these irritating expressions and do good with those they are intended for but altho' I never did like Hammond yet this message does him great credit. The papers say Webster & Clay are to occupy seats in the Senate—if they do the former is to Echo from the House J.Q. Adams, [Anacharsis] Clootzism; and the latter to keep his Charlies in the traces. Poor Webster can he not be put ["on" *canceled*] one side—can not a Sop be thrown to him as Gen[era]l [Andrew] Jackson did by sending a more distinguished man [John Randolph] to Russia whom he knew other wise w[oul]d never let him be at peace. Webster is needy & the loss of the U. States Bank has been a total one to him—he has never been a Statesman, but a feed advocate all his life. Adams, Webster & Clay—Slipshod politicians—will keep up a continued row—they cannot go far but by noise & constant motion—they can disturb the deliberations of the most august assembly in the world—but the Democrats will have to throw them off of their guard & make them at an early period of the Session expose their intentions and principles. The sooner they are unmask'd the less masquerading will they perform at any rate against the South upon the Slave and Tariff questions. We should have a general Tract society, sending off to every State in the Union pamphlets, papers, information, Speeches, enlightening the Farmer, the Mechanic, the Merchant, tradesman, those citizens whose days are too recent to know the polit[ical histor]y up to the period of the Whiggery & Federalism of the Elder [John] Adams—publishing information as extracted from Works that it would take an age with a close reader to obtain otherwise. The People North & South and I may add West are ready for such a Synopsis and, if properly arranged, the humblest cabin would read[,] mark, learn, & inwardly digest. Foreign nations too should be made Missionary ground and all other of our own States except Massachusetts the Disunion State. I would be willing to bare [*sic*] my proportion of the expence and I have no ["doubt" *interlined*] by proper efforts a handsome sum could be raised at the South and by friends at Washington & where can there be a more patriotic undertaking. Call it any thing but a (Clay) Club. I repeat it if we sleep our Victory had better never been won. The Zol[l]verein Treaty should ["be" *interlined*] raised from the filthy covering of last year[']s Senate—and again forcibly spread before the people—it is the entering wedge to the destruction of the Tariff. New England ["knows it" *interlined*] if Old England does not, & if the latter makes wry faces at it invite her consideration to the shameful breach of the treaty in making a discrimination 'twixt slave & free productions as regards Rice, Sugar &c. and in time, if submitted to, Cotton and all other of our Valuable Staples. If we act with determination at home depend

437

upon it Strangers will not think the worse of us—no time is to be lost—prudence & Wisdom—we must go ahead. I see Gen[era]l [Samuel] Houston has done you justice in his letter, and the Southern Review in the Article "Annexation of Texas"—has broadly advocated the Position you took in the Packenham [*sic*] letter. I am here cut off from all but weekly information.

I see Post Marks 12½ c[en]ts to this Post office, which has been recently made nearer to Charleston, by at *least* 6 miles when to ["there" *canceled and* "Jacksonboro 6 miles further" *interlined*] it used to be I think 10 Cents—the distance is not more than 25 miles. I will look more fully into this matter & write Mr. [Charles A.] Wickliff[e]—C'est un[e] Bagatelle—and is only here mentioned in confirmation of what I had previously remark'd to you—That the Post Office with probably the best intentions was suicidally promoting the progress of its ["un" *interlined*] popularity by its extortionate charges—every one who wishes to write either foregoes the pleasure by mail or seeks every means to escape ["the" *interlined*] Post Office Tariff—hence the creation of letter smuggling com[pan]ies on R[ai]l Roads in open defiance of the department and [*one or more words missing*]ing court aiding and abetting this Poaching upon the Post Master General[']s department. [*Manuscript ends here.*]

ALU (incomplete) in ScCleA. NOTE: This letter has no place of composition in its dateline, but would appear to have been written at Mathewes's plantation, Bear Island, St. Bartholomew's Parish, Colleton District, on the South Edisto River.

From J[AMES] S. SMITH, [former Representative from N.C.]

Hillsboro [N.C.,] Dec[embe]r 1st 1844

D[ea]r Sir, I think that you may feel some surprise at this letter. The great political battle has been fought and fairly won by the democratic party. My old fr[i]end [Henry] Clay is beaten. I went for the man from my knowledge of him and his long services & high & noble independence[,] His services in the late war & the Missouri question. His personal claims were great. I never agreed with in in [*sic*] his system of Internal improvement[,] his high tariff opinions nor his latitudinous construction of the Constitution. I always have been at heart a State rights man. I have not concur[r]ed either with the democratic party on all their measures so that I am now in a position to support such men & such measures as I deem best for the country.

I have had my preference formed ["ye"(?) *canceled*] Two years ago for the next Presidency after [James K.] Polk ["or" *canceled*]. I determined and so expressed it that whether Mr. Clay succeeded or not my next choice was for John C. Calhoun as haveing [*sic*] claims preeminent over any other man & that if my life was spared I should vote for him if he could be brought before the people. This is the reason why the whig party drop[p]ed me as an Elector. Be it so I am content. I also supported my son [Sidney Smith] on the democratic ticket[.] He came within Two votes of being elected running an hundred votes ahead of his ticket[.] He has long learned from me to admire Mr. Calhoun. He is yet a boy.

The object of this letter is to say to you as an old personal friend that great [hopes] are now entertained here ["that" *canceled*] by the Ultra whigs that Gen[era]l [Andrew] Jackson will proscribe you & that President Polk will be influenced by his ["consel" *canceled*] council [*sic*] & that the party will split in to a Benton-Van Buren wing & the Calhoun wing and that you will not have a place in the Cabinet. I hope these hop[e]s and conjectures will fail & that you will be called to aid in the new Administration & that you will not find it against your inclination to perform such a duty if it should be tendered you. Even the strong whigs say that if you should oc[c]upy that station the administration will be able—& its foreign relations conducted with wisdom & firmness.

The time is at hand in my opinion when the Southern States will have to consult their safety & that union in sentiment and action will be found the only shield against the combined influence of old & New England. In this we should not deceive ourselves. Every month brings new developments of [*one word missing*] policy of England. And that the age of [Louis Philippe] the King of the French will make him timid & that he will look to his family interests alone—which will give a compleat [*sic*] preponderance to the co[u]ncils of the British government.

I mean no flat[t]ery when I say that your aid is immensely important to the great slave holding interests in the present st[ate of] affairs. I think the time is coming when [you] will oc[c]upy your old place in the [*one word missing*] of the old North State. I hope to [live to?] see it and have it in my power to give you my feeble aid.

I hope you will will [*sic*] view this communication as coming from an old friend who altho he has differed from you never was heard to derogate from your abil[i]ty[,] great moral [wo]rth and pure patrio-

439

tism & [*one or more words missing*] never could hear the denunciations [of] others with complacency or without being dissatisfied.
Would like to here [*sic*] from you so far as delicacy of your situation
might permit. With much respect I am &c &c Your Humb[le] Se[r-
van]t, J.S. Smith.

ALS in ScCleA. NOTE: Dr. James Strudwick Smith had been Representative
from N.C. during 1817–1821.

From J[AMES] W. ZACHARIE, "Private"

[New Orleans, *ca*. December 1, 1844]
Dear Sir, Although not personally known to you, feeling a deep interest in the annexation of Texas to the U. States while on the subject of
Mexico, I would remark that the Ex President Gomez Farias who was
expelled by St. Anna is now here and is receiving by every vessel from
that quarter invitations from his different partizans opposed to St.
Anna to return, but has candidly acknowledged to me that without
means he could do nothing as St. Anna Understands the Mexican
Character so well that with his wealth he generally gains his victories (in fact nearly all subject to be bribed) and the most honest
are subject to treachery. Could he be furnished with Two hundred
thousand Dollars an army of opponents to St. Anna might be raised
on the borders of Texas which could be marched to the City of
Mexico, and were such things known as secret money by our government I think that it could not be better applied as it would Insure us
Texas without apparent interference and from my intimacy with
Mr. Farrias [*sic*] I think the matter could be accomplished through
me without the least publicity. My standing for respectability &
credit [as a merchant] I believe is known to many persons at Washington & our [La.] senators & representatives. Respectfully Yours,
J.W. Zacharie.

ALS in DNA, RG 59 (State Department), Applications and Recommendations,
1837–1845, Farias (M-687:11, frames 42–43). NOTE: Clerks' EU's read
"Farrias—Ex President of Mexico. Recommended for Secret Service" and
"Rec[eive]d Dec[embe]r 16, 1844."

From F[ITZWILLIAM] BYRDSALL, "Private"

New York [City,] Dec[embe]r 2d 1844

Dear Sir, I am highly gratified at the result of the presidential election, and my gratification would be without alloy if we had gained Tennessee or Maryland, for then James K. Polk would be president without the Vote, or over and above the Vote of New York. I do not like any president to be indebted to any one State for his election, and besides the game that has been played in this State ought not to give her politicians that influence with the coming administration which the fact of her vote being absolutely necessary to our success would seem to deserve; for our success was not *their* work.

It was proclaimed at an early day by the partizans of Mr. [Martin] Van Buren that "justice to the cause and to the man" demanded his nomination, "that a victory with any other chief would be no victory at all." This was significant to the knowing ones, but not so, thank God, to the Democratic people. A secret circular was got up professedly in opposition to the annexation of Texas, but what was this but a mode of collecting and combining the adherents of Mr. Van Buren and his letter on the Texas question? The result of this move is the fact that Mr. [Silas] Wright's majority in the State is about double the majority of Mr. Polk. Upon this point the great personal popularity of Mr. Wright is set forth as the cause of the difference, together with the State policy as to the public debt. But how comes it that the canal commissioners ["are" *canceled and* "have" *interlined*] also nearly double the majority of Mr. Polk? What has Mr. Wright or the canal commissioners to do with the State policy more than Mr. Polk? Not a whit—the honor belongs to Michael Hoffman and the legislature of a former year.

Whatever claims the democratic people of the State of New York have on the regard and consideration of Mr. Polk—her politicians of the Regency regime have none. The enthusiasm of the Young Democracy carried the Democratic people along. The exertions of Mr. Collector [Cornelius P.] Van Ness effected that Union here which carried the city and saved the State. The great Union meeting was got up by him; ["and" *canceled*] all the Calhoun men—[John] Tyler men—[Lewis] Cass men—[Richard M.] Johnson men—[Charles] Stewart men—cordially united on James K. Polk and not a man of them but rallied to his support. Not so all the friends of Mr. Van Buren. The Democrats who voted for Wright and the canal commissioners, but not for Mr. Polk, who were they?

And yet there is now scarcely a prominent office that friends of

Mr. Van Buren are not candidates for. It is becoming evident every day that they are going for a restoration of the old set as far as they can get at it. They want the removal of Van Ness or his transfer to the bench in order to get the controll of the custom house as a lever for 1848. There are secret organizations at work for this and the other great offices under the general Government in this city. The only and in point of fact, just policy for the appointing power to pursue, is to bestow its best considerations on the young democracy, in other words the States Rights Democracy. By the bye it is rumoured here that Ogden Hoffman will be soon an ex-U.S. Attorney. If you have any influence with the President, let James T. Brady be his successor. He is respectable every way—talented[,] capable—honest and is more than any other Lawyer in this city, the favorite of the Young Democracy. I could say much as to what he deserves from you but I refrain because I believe you are governed by higher considerations than those of a personal nature. A better appointment could not be made for the office in this city.

I confess that I am politically interested and that too in the highest degree as to the the the [*sic*] Collectorship—Surveyorship—Naval office—U.S. District attorney[,] Marshall and some others of lesser note in this city because I know their important bearing upon the contest of 1848. The one of 1844 is only the beginning of what 1848 must finish.

I can always give you correct information of our politicians here and you may depend upon it that I shall never suffer my private friendships here to induce me to attempt to mislead you. Very improper appointments are often made for want of that knowledge which should be previously obtained. In [Thomas] Jefferson's time, "is he honest—is he capable?" might have ["been" *interlined*] sufficient, but now a days—will he bring strength to the administration and its policy, is equally a necessary question.

And now my dear Sir you will permit me to express my views in relation to yourself. You will I hope remain in Washington the ensueing four years, if not as Secretary of State, at least as Senator from your own State. In my opinion Mr. Polk should call you to the office you now hold, and you should accept it. Throwing even proper personal considerations as regards ["your" *interlined*] future life out of the question, the true constitutional policy of this government requires your presence in Washington for such a policy is absolutely necessary to the stability of the Government itself. We want Statesmen—Constitutional Democrats at Washington and not truckling politicians.

I return you thanks for the Rhode Island Report. I should be much pleased to know your views with regard to the course the liberal democracy should pursue in this city. When, and under what form we should rally ourselves I am at a loss to determine. Will you drop me a few lines upon the future course and policy of the friends of Constitutional principles? Yours with the highest regard, F. Byrdsall.

ALS in ScCleA; PC in Jameson, ed., *Correspondence*, pp. 1003–1005.

To H[ENRY] GOURDIN, Charleston

Department of State
Washington, 2nd Dec[embe]r 1844
Sir, I have received your letter of the 21st Ult. (enclosing one from Mr. [George L.] Lowden); & that of Mr. Ellmore, [*sic*; Franklin H. Elmore] of the 28th Ult. relating to the claim of the heirs of the late Jno: Paul Jones. Mr. Lowden is well aware of the steps taken by this Government, & of my disposition to do every thing that can be done to effect the settlement of a claim so meritorious & of so long pendency.

Since the Communication to Congress of all the information on this Subject, which the Department possessed, in answer to a Resolution of the House of Representatives of 22nd April last, nothing further has been received. I have therefore, this day addressed a despatch to Mr. [William W.] Irwin, a copy of which I transmit; for the satisfaction of those interested, which it is hoped will stimulate him to new & successful exertions in the case.

And any new evidence which the parties may have that bears upon the subject, will of course be sent by them directly to Mr. Irwin, who has been in correspondence with Mr. Lowden respecting it. I am &c &c, J.C. Calhoun.

FC in DNA, RG 59 (State Department), Domestic Letters, 35:31–32 (M-40: 33); PC in Jameson, ed., *Correspondence*, pp. 630–631.

From O[GDEN] HOFFMAN

U.S. Attorney[']s Office
New York [City], 2nd Dec[embe]r 1844
Sir, In pursuance of the instructions contained in your letter of the 16th ult[im]o, I adopted the necessary proceedings for the committal

of John Fairburn and James Gillespie, to appear as witnesses on the part of the United States, against [Jason L.] Pendleton, master of the Brig "Montevideo," for being engaged in the Slave trade. I have adopted all the means, within my power to procure the arrest of Pendleton, but he has not arrived at this port, and, from all I can learn, his arrival is very uncertain. The Grand Jury, for the Nov[embe]r Term of this Circuit, are now in session, and have been, for ten days past; They are now nearly through their labors, and will be dismissed by the Court, on Thursday or Friday next. I have thus long detained Fairburn and Gillespie, in the hope, that Pendleton might arrive, during the session of the Grand Jury, but, now, there being no prospect of his arrest, and the detention of the witnesses, being attended with such expense to the Government, I would respectfully ask your instructions, to have them discharged.

I would have him indicted, upon the testimony now within my control, but you are aware, that for offences committed upon the high seas, there is no jurisdiction, except in the District, where the party "is first brought or apprehended." I have the honor to be very Respectfully Your obed[ien]t Serv[an]t, O. Hoffman, U.S. Attorney.

LS in DNA, RG 59 (State Department), Petitions for Pardon, 1789–1869, Tyler Administration, no. 110. NOTE: Clerks' EU's read "answered 4th inst." and "Tell him under the circumstances to discharge the witnesses."

Tho[mas] M. Hope, [U.S. Marshal], Springfield, [Ill.], to R[ichard] K. Crallé, 12/2. Hope attests to his adherence to State rights principles and his support for Calhoun as his political "first love." He requests Crallé to ask Calhoun to intercede with President-elect James K. Polk to prevent Hope's removal from office by Ill. supporters of Thomas H. Benton and Martin Van Buren. ALS in ScCleA.

To W[ILLIAM] W. IRWIN, Copenhagen

Department of State
Washington, 2nd December, 1844

Sir: You will perceive by the enclosed papers, which are copies of letters recently received, that the heirs of the late Commodore J. Paul Jones, believing the present to be a favorable time for urging upon the Danish Government a speedy settlement of their just and long neglected claims upon it, have again solicited the interposition of this Department.

In answer to a Resolution of the House of Representatives of 22d April last, I communicated to that Body copies of all your despatches upon the subject, in reply to the instructions you had received from this Department. I enclose a copy of the printed document containing this correspondence. There is reason to believe that a call will be made upon the Government this session, for further information. And your attention is thus early invited to the matter, to afford the opportunity to transmit the results of your application to the Government of Denmark, in behalf of the claimants, in time to meet any inquiry that may be made, before Congress adjourns: If no further steps have been taken by you in the premises, since your last despatch, No. 18, you will, without delay, address an earnest note, on this subject, to the Minister of Foreign Affairs, in which it may be expedient to mention the interest which the House of Representatives has taken in the case.

Your despatches, Nos. 30 and 31 have been received. I am, Sir, respectfully, Your obedient Servant, J.C. Calhoun.

FC (No. 14) in DNA, RG 59 (State Department), Diplomatic Instructions, Denmark, 14:45–47 (M-77:50); PC in Jameson, ed., *Correspondence*, p. 631. NOTE: In an appended "List of papers and documents, &ca., sent" Calhoun recorded the materials sent to Irwin. These included copies of the letters of Henry Gourdin and Franklin H. Elmore to Calhoun, dated 11/21 and 11/28 respectively, a copy of a letter from George L. Lowden to Gourdin, dated 11/18, and printed Congressional documents relating to the John Paul Jones claim.

From Juan Man[ue]l Manrique, [Venezuelan Minister of Foreign Affairs], Caracas, 12/2. When Allen A. Hall, former U.S. Chargé d'Affaires to Venezuela, took leave of his post, he presented to Manrique a letter from Calhoun, dated 10/15, informing Manrique of Hall's departure, and expressing the friendly feelings of the U.S. for Venezuela. Manrique praises Hall for the performance of his duties and reciprocates the friendly feelings of Venezuela towards the U.S. LS (in Spanish) in DNA, RG 59 (State Department), Notes from Foreign Legations, Venezuela, vol. 1 (T-93:1), received 2/14/1845.

From F[RANCIS] W. PICKENS

Senate Chamber [Columbia, S.C.], 2d Nov. [*sic*; Dec.] 1844 My dear Sir, I have just re[ceive]d a letter from my old friend Judge [John] Fine of N. York, and he informs me that [Silas] Wright will not and cannot accept any seat in the cabinet—it was so understood in the canvass [for Governor], and he an[n]ounces[?] it to me. He also takes it for granted you will be in the cabinet. He also says if any cabinet appointment is to be given to New York, it must be [Azariah C.] Flag[g] of Albany now Comptroller Gen[era]l, & it will be P[ost] M[aster] Gen[era]l &c.

He also begs that our senators will vote to confirm the appointment to the U.S. court of Chancellor Walsworth [*sic*; Reuben H. Walworth] of N. York. *Do see to it.* He speaks highly of his moral character & "strict construction doctrines."

[George] McDuffie has written from Charleston the most extraordinary letter to [William F.] Colcock & beg[g]ed him to shew it to me. He is for the Legislature taking decided steps & for no expression with reference to the Rep[ublican] Party &c. He denounces my resolutions as yielding every thing &c. Now I yield nothing. In fact I do not look with confidence to the Democratic Party, but my resolutions are very peculiarly guarded[?]. And I immediately consented to saying "unconstitutional" instead of "*ag[ain]st the whole* spirit of the Constitution"; and they are so amended. But I said expressly that I considered the or[i]g[i]n[a]l expression strange as it suggested the idea that there was a remedy *through the Political Tribunals, if not* through the courts. There is on a struggle to do much *harm in the Legislature,* I assure you & dead ag[ain]st you & your *future position.* In haste but truly, F.W. Pickens.

[P.S.] My resolutions will pass the House by large vote.

ALS in ScCleA. NOTE: Both the postmark and the events recounted leave no doubt that the correct date of this letter is 12/2 rather than 11/2.

From S[tephen] Pleasonton, Fifth Auditor, 12/2. As requested in Calhoun's letters of 11/5 and 11/27, Pleasonton encloses statements of what sums have been disbursed through his office from three appropriations: for contingent expenses of the State Department during 6/30/1843–6/30/1844; for contingent expenses of foreign intercourse, 12/1/1841–3/31/1844; and for contingent expenses of all missions abroad during 6/30/1843–6/30/1844. LS in DNA, RG 59 (State Department), Letters Received from the Fifth Auditor and Comptroller, 1829–1862; FC in DNA, RG 217 (General Accounting Office), Fifth Auditor: Letters Sent, 5:184–185.

To [PUBLISHERS of Five Washington Newspapers]

Department of State
Washington, 2nd Dec[embe]r 1844
By the 21st section of an act of Congress, approved the 26th of August 1842, the Secretary of State is required to cause to be published, the laws and resolutions of Congress, treaties and amendments to the Constitution of the United States, "in not less than two nor more than four of the principal newspapers published in the City of Washington for Country subscribers, giving the preference to such papers as have the greatest number of Country Subscribers and the most extensive Circulation."

Will you be pleased to inform this Department of the number of permanent subscribers to your paper. I am &c &c, J.C. Calhoun.

FC in DNA, RG 59 (State Department), Domestic Letters, 35:31 (M-40:33); PDU (blank form) in DNA, RG 59 (State Department), Form Letters and Circulars to Publishers. NOTE: A Clerk's EU on the FC indicates that this circular was sent to the publishers of the Washington, D.C., *Globe, Madisonian, Constitution, Daily National Intelligencer,* and *German National Gazette.*

To C[HARLES] H. RAYMOND, [Acting Chargé d'Affaires of the Texas Republic]

Department of State
Washington, 2nd December, 1844
Sir: In a note which I had the honor to address to Mr. [Isaac] Van Zandt, late Chargé d'Affaires of Texas, dated the 14th of August, last, in relation to the outrage alleged to have been committed by certain citizens of the United States in the collection District of Red River, I requested that, in order to a final adjustment of the difficulty, this Department should be furnished with [" 'all" *interlined*] the evidence which may be required to establish, authentically, the facts of the illegal introduction of the goods, their forcible seizure [from the Texas Collector of Customs, James Bourland,] and taking away by the citizens of the United States and the amount of damages suffered in consequence, to be transmitted by the President to Congress with his Message."

In Mr. Van Zandt[']s reply, dated the 16th of the same month, he observes "The testimony referred to as necessary to be transmitted to

447

Congress with the message of the President of the United States will be furnished at the earliest day possible."

Congress being now assembled, I respectfully invite your attention to the subject, and request that the evidence referred to, if it has been received, may be communicated to this Department in order that the same may be transmitted with the President's Message to-morrow. I have the honor to be, with high consideration, Sir, Your obedient servant, J.C. Calhoun.

FC in DNA, RG 59 (State Department), Notes to Foreign Legations, Texas, vol. 2–1/103, p. 7; CC in Tx, Records of the Texas Republic Department of State, Copybooks of Letters Received from Texan and Foreign Representatives, vol. 2–1/103, p. 7; CC in Tx, Records of the Texas Republic Department of State, U.S. Diplomatic Correspondence.

From CHA[RLE]S H. RAYMOND

Legation of Texas
Washington, Dec[embe]r 2nd 1844

Sir, In reply to your note, of to day, requesting that the evidence establishing, authentically, the facts of the outrage alledged to have been committed by certain citizens of the United States in the Collectoral District of Red River, if in my possession, might be communicated to your Department, in order that the same might be transmitted, to morrow, with the President's message to Congress, I have the honor to inform you that the evidence alluded to has not yet been received, but there is every reason to believe it soon will be, when I will lose no time in furnishing you with it. With assurances of my very distinguished consideration I have the honor to be Your Obedient Servant, Chas. H. Raymond.

ALS in DNA, RG 59 (State Department), Notes from Foreign Legations, Texas, vol. 1 (T-809:1); FC in Tx, Records of the Texas Republic Department of State, Letters and Dispatches Sent by the Texas Legation in Washington, 2:18; FC in Tx, Records of the Texas Republic Department of State, Copybooks of Letters Received from Texan and Foreign Representatives, vol. 2–1/103, p. 7; CC in Tx, Records of the Texas Republic Department of State, U.S. Diplomatic Correspondence.

From BERNARD ADAMS REYNOLDS

Carlow[s]ville, Dallas County [Ala.,] December 2d 1844
Dear Sir, I take the liberty of sending you a Mobile paper containing my reply to Col. [William C.] Preston's letter to Col. [David J.?] Mc-Cord, relative to the declaration made by him of a conversation with Mr. [Henry] Clay at the White Sulphur Springs in Virginia, some years ago. My main object was to shew that whether Mr. Clay did or did not make the assertion attributed to him, yet it is manifest, that Col. Preston did say as much in his speech in the S. Carolina legislature in 1830—so that there is no escape for him, as Col. McCord has re-asserted his statement of Preston's declaration, and produced the certificates of the gentlemen to whom reference was made in that statement.

As the extract from Col. Preston's speech gives a pretty faithful sketch of the tariff system, the publication of my letter may be important just at this time, when a reduction of the duties upon imports, must be made to appease the staple States. With sentiments of high respect, I have the honor to be &c., Bernard Adams Reynolds.

ALS in ScCleA.

From SAM[UE]L R. THURSTON, *"Private"*

Brunswick (Me.), Dec. 2d 1844
Dear Sir: You will recognise, from my signature, that I am the person who addressed you a note, a year or two since, enquiring after some of your confidential fri[e]nds with whom I could safely correspond. Without any preamble, you will allow me to say, that there was a strong push made in this State in your favor, but in this State, as in most others, the systematic organization of the old office holders, under Mr. [Martin] Van Buren, was effectual in packing caucuses, and carrying the delegates to the national convention in his favor. Without stopping to trace the history of those times farther, I am frank and happy to say, that Mr. Van Buren got thrown off the track; and why I am so is, that if nominated, he could not in any event have been elected. The more immediate cause of his overthrow, when he had so nearly attained a renomination, was, as no one knows better than yourself, his remarkable & unexpected position upon the re-annexation of Texas. I think I have the honor (for honor I call it to

449

be in favor of any step which would promote the glory of my country) of being the first man in this State who came out in print in favor of this important move. And when the Veteran [Thomas] Ri[t]chie, in revolt from Mr. Van Buren[']s ranks, sent his thunders over the union, and the [Portland] Eastern Argus of Me., conducted by one of Mr. V[an] B[uren]'s office holders, came out & informed Mr. Ri[t]chie, that there was no man in this quarter in favor of immediate annexation, and that no man in favor of it could carry this State for President, I immediately drew up a peti[ti]on praying the immediate ratification of your Treaty with Texas, and in one hour, in this little village, procured the signatures of 50 or 60 good & substantial names & forward[ed] the petition to Washington.

It would be idle for me to apprise you, how the whigs of the north have made, and did make this question, their for[e]most engine of war in the late Campaign, in this State—and for the reason that there are, in Me., a quite a large number of Abolitionists. We were pushed hard & we met it like men. And I think I know some what of the feelings of the people in Maine upon this question. For, every day, except Sunday, for the 3 or 4 weeks next previous to the Sept. Election, when *our* great battle was fought, I addressed the people from four to seven hours p[e]r day, and in every case, the whigs made the question of Texas their hobby horse to ride over the Democracy. The brilliant result of the battle in maine, you know. Me. is for re-annexation, immediate & unconditional; and no influence can make her otherwise. Therefore, now that the great battle has been fought upon this ground, and the whole country has spoken in its favor, the enquiry is now being made, if something is not to be done about Texas. I therefore write to you, with as much frankness, as tho I had enjoyed your acquaintance for years, and remind you, that no step of yours could be more acceptable to the Democracy, than to take a high handed, honorable, but energetic cou[r]se upon this subject. We always have to lay our plans according to the means we have. Now if any step, made in the path of duty, could bring over such a *rash* (certainly rash in this particular if no other) man as Mr. [Thomas H.] Benton, why it should be made. Depend upon it, Sir, let Texas once be annexed, and he who effects it will live always in the hearts of his countrymen. I will not, cannot, suggest ways & means to you of effecting this, but you must allow me, nevertheless, to exhort you to bring it about, if it is within the reach of honorable possibilities. One thing, however, allow me to say. It would be good policy, in all correspondence which may come to the public eye, to advocate it as a great national question, and not as being about to be, in the event of its success, ["more" *interlined*] favorable to one section than another. If this be a fact, it can be made known to those particular sections, through other channels. Also it would be policy not to advocate it on the ground that it would make secure southern slavery. If it would, that can be made known through other channels. You cannot look upon the abolition move with more disgust than I do, but we have to survey the lay of the land after all, in cou[n]ting up Presidential Elections. My sheet is failing me. I could hope you will be Mr. [James K.] Polk[']s Secretary, for the safety of this question at least. Prudence would forbid me to ask any reply to this note. But if at any time, you would like to know the tide of popular feeling on this or any other question, let a confidential of yours address the enquiry ["and you shall be correctly informed" *interlined*]. Excuse me, Sir, for being thus open, and taking this liberty, and believe me your sincere friend, Saml. R. Thurston.

ALS in ScCleA; PC in Boucher and Brooks, eds., *Correspondence*, pp. 266–268. NOTE: Thurston (1816–1851) moved to Iowa about 1845 and became the Delegate of Oregon Territory to the U.S. Congress in 1849.

To President [JOHN TYLER]

Department of State
Washington, December 2nd, 1844
To the President of the United States.

Sir: In obedience to your instructions, I have the honor herewith to transmit copies of a correspondence with the governments of Mexico and Texas, growing out of the proposed annexation of the latter to the United States, and also of the correspondence with the Texan authorities in relation to the disarming of a body of Texan forces under the command of Major [Jacob] Snively, by a detachment of United States troops commanded by Captain [Philip St. George] Cooke, and the forcible entry and taking away from the Custom House on Red River, of sundry goods and merchandize by certain citizens of the United States.

By a note [of 12/2] recently received from the Honorable C[harles] H. Raymond, Acting Chargé d'Affaires of the Republic of Texas, I am informed that the evidence referred to in my note to Mr. [Isaac] Van Zandt of the 14th of August, last, has not yet been received by him.

All which is respectfully submitted. J.C. Calhoun.

LS with En in DNA, RG 233 (U.S. House of Representatives), 28A-F1; FC in DNA, RG 59 (State Department), Reports of the Secretary of State to the President and Congress, 6:117–119; PC with Ens in Senate Document No. 1, 28th Cong., 2nd Sess., pp. 19–112; PC with Ens in House Document No. 2, 28th Cong., 2nd Sess., pp. 19–110; PC with Ens in the Washington, D.C., *Daily National Intelligencer*, December 7, 1844, p. 2; PC with Ens in *Niles' National Register*, vol. LXVII, no. 15 (December 14, 1844), pp. 230–235; PC in Crallé, ed., *Works*, 5:321. Note: Enclosed with the LS is a 3-pp. list of the papers that accompanied Calhoun's letter of 12/2 to Tyler. Tyler transmitted this report to Congress with his annual message of 12/3.

From JAMES R. WYLY

Clark[e]sville [Ga.,] 2nd Decem[ber] 1844

D[ea]r Sir, Be so good as to attend to a small portion of business for me, that is there resides in the County of York[,] State of Pen[n]sylvania a gentleman by the name of Andrew Wallace who holds a Small legacy left to my wife about two hundred dollars. I have written to Mr. Wallace to call on you in the City of Washington and you would receive the money for me and give him the necessary receipt. You will confer a favour on me by doing so and send me your draft on some of the banks in Charleston or Augusta. D[ea]r Sir your attention to the above will confer on me a favour which I shall not forget. I wish you to give me any information you have relative to Mr. [Thomas G.] Clemson, whether he got safe to Belgium, or what would be necessary for me to know relative to the times. Your friend Mr. [John R.] Mathew[e]s is now in Charleston. His family here are in good health except his lady [Elizabeth Jenkins Whaley Mathewes] who has been very Sick but is now on the mend. He is expected to return in a few days. I am as usual your friend and humble Serv[an]t, James R. Wyly.

ALS in ScCleA. Note: An AEU by Calhoun reads "Mr. Wyly. Received from A. Wallace $195 & transmitted a not[e] 64 drawn by Mr. Stubbs on the Bank of America, New York. Mr. Wallace paid $195 11th Feb. 1845."

From EDWARD EVERETT

London, 3 December 1844

Sir, In my despatch No. 211 of 16 November last I made mention of a memorial addressed to the Lords of the Treasury by the Chamber of Commerce at Manchester in favor of the repeal of the duty on Cotton wool. I now transmit the memorial *in extenso.*

The reasoning of the memorial has been adopted by the most respectable portion of the press, and the subject will unquestionably be brought before parliament in a very imposing form, at the approaching session.

I shall endeavor, by anticipation, to ascertain what course the government is likely to take, although great reserve will probably exist on this point till the moment arrives for a public avowal. I am, sir, with great respect, your obedient servant, Edward Everett.

Transmitted with Despatch 221.

Memorial of the Chamber of Commerce at Manchester on the repeal of the duty on cotton wool.

LS (No. 221) with En in DNA, RG 59 (State Department), Diplomatic Despatches, Great Britain, vol. 53 (M-30:49), received 12/23; FC in DNA, RG 84 (Foreign Posts), Great Britain, Despatches, 9:88–89; FC in MHi, Edward Everett Papers (published microfilm, reel 23, frame 468).

From G E O [R G E] W [I L L I A] M G O R D O N

Consulate of the United States
Rio de Janeiro, Dec[embe]r 3d 1844

Sir, Respectfully refer[r]ing to my despatches Nos. 14 and 15, I have now the honor to enclose herewith copies of the depositions of Zebiner H. Small Jr., one of the crew of the Brig "Sea Eagle"; & Patrick Kane, late of the crew of the Brig "Agnes." It will be seen on perusal that these depositions contain evidence not only against Capt. [Jason L.] Pendleton and others of the Brig "Monte Video," but also against Capt. Hiram Gray and William M. Ruhl, late of the "Agnes," and one R.S. Gough, implicating them in aiding & abetting, in a most positive manner, the Slave Trade. And I hasten to place the same in your possession that they may be arrested under the laws of the United States for the suppression of that trade. I have in addition, a large amount of other evidence to sustain this charge, which it is impossible to have copied in time for this Despatch, but which will be forwarded in due ["time" *canceled*] course.

Presuming that the correspondents of Captain Gray in this city, will communicate to him information of the evidence that I have obtained against him, Ruhl and Gough, by this conveyance, and fearing that they might consequently become alarmed and make their escape,

I have with the concurrent advice of His Excellency Mr. [Henry A.] Wise, addressed communications to the District Attorneys of New York, New Jersey, Pennsylvania, Delaware and Maryland, requesting the immediate arrest of said parties, if to be found in their respective districts, and that they be held in custody for your instructions; which course I trust will meet with the approbation of the President. A copy of my letter to the District Attorneys is herewith enclosed.

The investigation that is now taking place before me, is developing the existence of a state of things, in regard to the manner of prosecuting the Slave Trade upon the coast of Africa that is truly astonishing; and will enable me to lay before the Department a mass of testimony on the subject, particularly in regard to the connection of American Citizens therewith, and the use and prostitution of the American Flag in furtherance thereof, that in my apprehension will warrant a rigorous enforcement of the Laws of the United States for the suppression of that inhuman traffic; and probably render apparent also the necessity of further legislation on the subject.

I have already taken, with great minuteness, the depositions of twelve persons on this subject, and have eight others in waiting to give theirs; to which I hope to add also the depositions of American Merchants resident in this City. I have the honor to be, Sir, With great respect, Your Obedient Servant, Geo. Wm. Gordon, Consul of the United States of America.

ALS (No. 16) and LS with Ens in DNA, RG 59 (State Department), Consular Despatches, Rio de Janeiro, vol. 7 (T-172:8), received 1/29/1845. Note: A Clerk's EU on the ALS indicates that copies of Gordon's En, dated 12/2, addressed to several U.S. District Attorneys, were sent to them from the State Department on 1/30/1845 and "their particular attention asked to it."

To [John Y. Mason, Secretary of the Navy], 12/3. "The enclosed [*not found*] is from a highly respectable citizen of Carolina, now at Paris." This citizen wishes his son, Robert Oliver Gibbes, to be placed on the list of applicants for a Midshipman's warrant. Photostat of ALS in DLC, Charles C. Hart Autograph Collection.

To JONATHAN STODDARD, U.S. Dist[rict] Attorney, New Haven, Conn[ecticu]t

Department of State
Washington, 3rd Dec[embe]r 1844

Sir, The object of this note is to call your attention to a communication addressed to Mr. [Charles] Chapman, your predecessor by this Department on the 16th Nov. 1843, to which no reply has yet been received, on the subject of a complaint made by the Portuguese Govt. through [J.C. de Figaniêre e Morão] its Minister here, against John Holdridge master of the American Whaler Romulus of Connecticut, for feloniously carrying away from the Cape dé Verd Islands a certain negro, named Pedro Timas. The Portuguese Minister has repeatedly applied to this Department to learn what had been done under the instructions that had been given in the case. I have now to ask your prompt attention to this case, the particulars of which will be found in the documents that accompanied the instructions of this Department above referred to. I am &c &c, J.C. Calhoun.

FC in DNA, RG 59 (State Department), Domestic Letters, 35:32–33 (M-40: 33).

From J[AMES] W. ZACHARIE

New Orleans, December 3d 1844

Sir, I beg leave to hand you a letter just received under cover from my friend John P. Schatzell Esq. of Matamoros, announcing the death of Richard H. Belt Esq. American Consul at that Port. Mr. S[chätzell] says in his letter to me "I enclose you a letter to the Secretary of State the Hon[ora]bl[e] John C. Calhoun announcing the death of Mr. Richard Belt, our Consul. You can read it, and see that I do not solicit the appointment, if I am appointed in consequence of your former application, I will act, but it is an Office without Emolument, therefore no stimulous for Patriotism as times go, but to serve Mr. [James K.] Polk if elected, I shall work for nothing and find myself—so do your best in the cause of economy & promote his success." You will find on file in your Department, a recommendation by all the Merchants trading to Mexico from New Orleans, handed in by the Hon. J[ohn] J. Crittenden, an intimate friend of his, who although an opponent in Politics, will bear testimony of his being one of the most highminded & intelligent men, & in every way suited to the appointment. Through his instrumentality a great many Texians, who were unfortunately taken Prisoners at Mier & other places, & among them [George B. Crittenden] the son of Mr. C[rittenden], were delivered from the greatest distress, so much so as to call from the Texian Congress, a resolution of thanks. Very Respectfully Your Ob[edien]t Serv[an]t, J.W. Zacharie.

LS with Ens in DNA, RG 59 (State Department), Applications and Recommendations, 1837–1845, Schätzell (M-687:29, frames 415–419). NOTE: Zacharie enclosed Schätzell's LS to Calhoun, dated 11/8, and an LS, marked "Copy," of Schätzell's letter of 10/16 to W[ilson] Shannon announcing Belt's death.

From [ANGEL CALDERON DE LA BARCA]

Washington, 4th Dec[embe]r 1844
The epoch of the meeting of Congress, appears to the Undersigned, Envoy Extraordinary and Minister Plenip[otentiar]y from Her Catholick Majesty the Queen of Spain, a most seasonable opportunity for reminding the Hon[ora]ble John C. Calhoun, Secretary of State of the Union, of the urgent necessity for bringing to a decision an affair already too prolonged—that of the Scho[o]ner Amistad.

It would be superfluous for the Undersigned to enter into the particulars of this claim, concerning which there is but one opinion in the minds of all intelligent and thinking men, ["when" *altered to* "who"] are directed in its examination by good faith and impartiality. Its merits may ["be" *interlined*] briefly reduced to two questions—1rst Whether the treaty concluded in 1795 between the United States and Spain, the stipulations which it contains and those which emanate from it, continue in force or not, and 2dly whether these can be infringed or interpreted by one alone of the contracting Parties, or by any authority in the United States, without violating the most sacred precepts of the law of nations. Spain cannot agree that either the one or the other is lawful.

The Committee on Foreign Affairs [of the House of Representatives] in the Report presented last April to Congress, has made evident the irregularities in the proceedings, the infractions of the above mentioned treaty, and the gratuitously cruel persecutions against inoffensive subjects of Her Catholick Majesty, of which an example, fortunately rare in the annals of civilized nations, has been exhibited in the confiscation of the Amistad—its sale—and the arbitrary confinement in public prisons of the two respectable Spaniards escaped from the murderous dagger of the negroes who had inflicted a violent death on the Captain and crew of that ill-starred vessel.

In this Report the Government of Her Catholick Majesty has been gratified to perceive the most estimable proofs of noble frankness and of an intrepid love of truth, and it flatters itself that the conviction which it must necessarily produce in all enlightened minds will hasten the favorable termination of this vexatious question.

Moreover as the Hon[ora]ble John C. Calhoun must be aware and as the President himself observes in his message of yesterday [to Congress] that *the injury inflicted by delays* in the *settlement of these claims falls with severity upon the individual claimant,* the Undersigned cannot doubt that His Excellency will shortly adopt those measures which he shall judge most conducive towards the reparation of the wrongs suffered by the owners of the Amistad and towards vindicating the disregarded principles of the supreme law of civilized nations.

That His Excellency will adopt this course, cannot for a moment be doubted, without a supposition injurio[u]s to him, after the memorable words yesterday pronounced by His Excellency and which have gone forth to be circulated throughout the whole wor[l]d *"An interference of one in the affaires of another is the fruitful source of family dissensions and neighbourhood disputes; and the same cause affects the peace happiness and prosperity of States. It may be most devoutly hoped that the good sense of the American people will ever be ready to repel all such attempts, should they ever be made.["]*

The Committee on Foreign Affairs in the before mentioned Report recorded opportunely the sound principle that *"offences perpetrated on board of a Spanish vessel* (in Spanish seas and by Spanish subjects) *could only be tried by Spanish laws in a Spanish Country.["]*

The Undersigned could adduce nothing capable of defining with greater clearness the nature of the case in question nor which could point out more precisely the resolution dictated by justice and by the principle proclaimed by His Excellency the President as the fundamental one of the Government of the United States *"the strict observance of justice and the honest and punctual fulfillment of all engagements."*

The Undersigned avails himself of this opportunity to renew to the Honor[a]ble John C. Calhoun the assurances of His most distinguished consideration.

457

State Department translation of LS (in Spanish) in DNA, RG 59 (State Department), Notes from Foreign Legations, Spain, vol. 11 (M-59:13, frames 1008–1015); PC of translation in House Report No. 753, 29th Cong., 1st Sess., pp. 2–3. NOTE: The House Committee report referred to above is printed as House Report No. 426, 28th Cong., 1st Sess. and as an enclosure in House Report No. 753, 29th Cong., 1st Sess., pp. 4–17.

From A[NGEL] CALDERON DE LA BARCA, "Very private and confidential"

[Washington, December 4, 1844]
My dear Sir, I here enclose my note upon the Amistad. I have tried to be conciliating and to make use of neither word nor idea which might possibly be taken amiss. I have nothing so much at heart as to see this claim favorably settled. It would do you honor to contribute to this desirable result: it would prove to Europe that the consideration of having money to pay is not always an obstacle in America to obtain justice; it would be gratifying to the southern republican gentlemen—with no one of whom I have spoken of the case who has not expressed himself in strong language against the wrong inflicted upon us: it would confirm the sincerity and soundness of your arguments in an analogous, although no[t] so clear a case; it would prevent irritation in Spain, the necessity of a protest and of referring to the Cortes; it would above all be just and in fact it would be a meritorious and praiseworth[y] act of your and Mr. [John] Tyler's administration. I am sincere I assure you in what I say.

I am perfectly persuaded that you concur with me—in this case—in views and feelings. But my dear Sir there is a Spanish proverb, which I cannot refrain from quoting as applicable in the present instance

Quien da luego da dos veces,
He gives twice who gives at once.
Should my note have the good fortune of meeting your ap[p]robation let it take its course. Should the contrary be the case, have the goodness to write me a line and I shall do myself the pleasure of waiting on you—to confer about [it]. At all events I should be very much gratified to hear from you. I remain dear Sir Sincerely yours, A. Calderon de la Barca.

ALS in ScCleA.

From THEO[DORE] S. FAY

Legation U. States
Berlin, Dec. 4, 1844

Dear Sir, Contrary to my intention, I am obliged to address you again on the subject of our Convention of 25 March. I last evening had a long conversation with Baron [Heinrich von] Bulow, in the course of which I perceived that, in my endeavors to save this Convention, I had undertaken a difficult & delicate task. He said the circumstances had somewhat changed since he last spoke with me, that several "important voices" had been raised against ["it" *canceled and* "the Treaty," *interlined*], that some Govts. of the Zollverein began to think "the terms not good enough," & that the embarrassment of his position was increasing. I called his attention to the fact that, although I had given no positive promises on the part of our Government & made none, of an unqualified nature, for that of Prussia, yet, upon the strength of my several interviews with His Excellency & Mr. [Franz August] Eichmann, I certainly had advised, on our part, the measures necessary to carry the convention into effect. He replied, I had "done quite right," but that he had *since* found all was not so smooth as he then thought. I asked if he meant to say the Treaty would not be ratified by the Zollverein, & whether I should write you the conversation. He said I need not write you, as he did not consider the result certain, but only more doubtful. To my enquiry whether the claim of England &c were the principal objection, he said it was one objection, but not the only one.

If the interpretation given, by Sir Robert Peel, to our Treaty with England, (&, perhaps, a report that our Tariff is about to undergo a great reduction) be satisfactorily explained, the other obstacles, I hope, would not be insurmountable, & I was at first apprehensive that a Statement of this interview might embarrass you with inferences more serious than were intended, but, notwithstanding the suggestion of Baron Bulow, I have felt it my duty to communicate his remarks to you.

I did not leave him without expressing a hope that Baron [Friedrich] de Gerolt might be instructed to communicate frankly with you in the matter, in the propriety of which he acquiesced, but did not appear yet certain of his arrival in Washington.

News of the result of the Presidential elections reached here four days ago, & have possibly changed the prospect of our Convention. I have the honor to be, Dear Sir, with the greatest regard, respectfully, Y[ou]r Ob[e]d[ien]t Serv[an]t, Theo. S. Fay [Secretary of Legation].

ALS ("Private & Confidential") in DNA, RG 59 (State Department), Diplomatic Despatches, Germany, vol. 3 (M-44:4), received 1/28/1845; FC in DNA, RG 84 (Foreign Posts), Germany, Despatches, 4:165–167.

To O[gden] Hoffman, U.S. Dist[rict] Att[orne]y, New York [City], 12/4. "I have to acknowledge the receipt of your letter of the 2nd instant, relative to the [African slave trade] case of [Jason L.] Pendleton, Master of the Brig 'Montevideo,' and as you state that there is no prospect of the arrest of Pendleton, and as the detention of the witnesses, would be attended with much expense to the Government, you are authorized under the circumstances to discharge them." LS in DLC, John Davis Batchelder Collection; FC in DNA, RG 59 (State Department), Domestic Letters, 35:33 (M-40:33).

From B[asil] Manly

University of Ala. [Tuscaloosa,] Dec. 4, 1844
Sir, I have the satisfaction to acknowledge the reception of 18 Volumes of the Documents of the 3rd Session of the 27th Congress; intended for the use of the Library of the University of Ala.

Please accept the thanks of the University.

I cannot forbear to renew the assurance of my hearty approval of the leading doctrines in Government which it has been the business of your life to illustrate and establish; and of my warm admiration of your public character and services. In these views I have known no change, except that of greater intensity, from the period when I first became acquainted with them. I expect to die with them—popular or unpopular.

This testimony can have no other value than that it comes from a man who has nothing to desire of you; who scarcely expects ever to be recognized by you in this world. With the highest esteem, most truly yours, B. Manly, Pres[ident,] Univ[ersity of] Ala.

ALS in ScCleA.

From R[occo] MARTUSCELLI, [Consul General of the Two Sicilies]

New York [City,] December 4 1844

Sir—I have received the letter, with which you honoured me, under date of the 30th ult.; and I hasten to address to you my most sincere thanks, for the obliging offer made by you, to accede to my request, by once more submitting to the Secretary of the Treasury [George M. Bibb], for his decision, the claim of Messrs. [Sebastian] Dacorsi and [Francois] de Martino; thus inducing me to hope, that this decision may be such as is desired. Although in my preceding notes, I have demonstrated, as clearly as was possible, the right of the claimants, yet in order not to tresspass too much on your complaisance, I will present a short summary of the principal points of the question, in the hope, that through your kind intervention, this affair will be terminated definitively, to the satisfaction of the parties concerned.

Messrs. Dacorsi and De Martino, have protested against the valuation made by the appraisers of the Custom house of New York, on macaroni coming from Naples, because they considered it irregular: for if the valuation were made on the price current of another market, it could not shew the real value of the article; if it were made on the price current of Naples, it must be recollected, that this price current, was of a much later date, and at a time, when there was a momentary increase, ["of" *altered to* "in"] the price of corn in the Naples market, which necessary caused all kinds of pastes to become dearer. And moreover, no case had ever before occurred at the Custom house, of so high a valuation of pastes. Messrs. Dacorsi and de Martino hope that the Department will consider it just, to refund the fine, which they have been obliged to pay. It is a simple question of fact, and may I doubt not be easily determined, if you Sir will support my reasons by your influence with your Colleague. I have the honour Sir to assure &c, R. Martuscelli.

State Department translation of LS (in French) in DNA, RG 59 (State Department), Notes from Foreign Legations, Two Sicilies, vol. 1 (M-55:1). NOTE: An AEI on the LS reads "Translated by R[obert] G[reenhow]."

From H[AYM] M. SALOMON

New York [City,] Dec[embe]r 4 1844
Dear Sir, I am much obliged for your kindness in letting the C[hief]
Clerk [Richard K. Crallé] give me the information asked.

Now once more to the state of the Country and you personally[.]

It appears to me certain that if you can *for ever* be prevented a
nomination for the Presidency by the acting [Martin] Van B[uren]
Demo[cratic] Leaders at the north it will be done as I have previously for many years given you the intimation—simply because you
are quite *too honest* for *their* principles of action[.] They have had
the same objections to [Lewis] Cass and even to poor [Richard M.]
Johnson. They firstly *use* every body then *sacrifice* every body[.]

Now hereafter about yourself. I am one of those who wished to
see both you and [Henry] Clay rewarded with the Presidency for
your giant like support of the principle of the late war with England.
His exclusive *friends* have tried their exclusive plans of consummat-
ing *their* wishes—they have been repeatedly and ["finally" *interlined*]
forever foiled.

As to myself I wish you for the sake of the Country a better fate
altho I must say that after the Presidential Chair was disgraced in
the person of Van B[uren] the high honour formerly so properly attached to it is greatly diminished in my humble opinion[.] I here
submit my intended operation cogitated for the moment in my arm
chair by a good coal fire in my bed Room at 11 P.M., with this preface
of by gone facts[.]

And here I owe it to my consistency to remind you ["of some facts"
canceled] that after your election to the V[ice-]P[residenc]y with
[Andrew] Jackson against [John Quincy] Adams & [Richard] Rush—
And notwithstanding your antagonistical position to the anti Jackson Party having myself knowledge of the integrity of your feelings
and disposition, on my own responsibility I called on the owners of
the five great daily papers on the anti Jackson side and made such
representations to them of what *I* considered your true sentiments
that they not only ceased a war against you but became neutralized
and Friendly.

My next project was after the ill usage of Van B[uren] to make
you their Candidate against the 2d term ["of Jackson" *interlined*] &
it must I humbly suggest have fully succeeded—but, when I went to
Washington and submitted my idea to Gen[era]l [Duff] Green—that
of your being the President and the eastern "Notion" the Vice President—no! no! I will not consent to [Daniel] Webster—doubtless he

["Green" *interlined*] being a new man in part at Washington (and unacquainted with *strength* and depth of northern Van Beuren ["Rogery" *canceled and* "Roguery" *interlined*] and manoe[u]vering) thought that he could get a southern feeling strong enough to make head for yourselves without any obligation to the Adams' portion of the people.

The anti Jackson men were told to take [William] Wirt &c but it evidently was of no effect[.]

And as to the subsequent reign of Van B[uren] it is no new story[.] Then came the General revolt of the people against *his* plundering government by the election of an Honest Farmer ([William H.] Harrison[)] &c[.]

No one can hate the abolition and ultra tariff views of the Northern men more than myself[.] Still If I could flatter their pride so much as to procure a great good to the country without giving them the power to do an essential ["injury" *interlined*] I think one ought to use his exertions for such an object.

My plan therefore is That without consultation with Parties I mean Either Mr. Calhoun or Mr. Webster to propose to [James Watson] Webb of the [N.Y.] Courrier—and to [W.B.] Townsend of the Express the two main and leading papers—That the anti Van Beuren party—Shall think of no other Candidates to present to the people than Calhoun for Pres[iden]t and *Webster* for Vice President. ["I would thus gild the pill they would have to swallow" *interlined.*] As to the latter, he will from my old knowledge of him (although Gen[era]l Green would not credit me) ["will" *canceled*] take *any thing* he can get by way of ["honr"(?) *canceled*] Honour & *salary*[.]

If the party who supported Clay ineffectually would nominate you without propounding any question at all but take you up on your past merits, well, if not and they will propound questions—Then I would make a new era in answers. Which if they did not like you might say to them as the shop keepers do—"Gentlemen no harm done I hope."

Yes. I would let the answer amount to this which cannot Compromise the most honourable of men—[George] Washington—[John] Adams & [Thomas] Jefferson and [James] Madison were asked *no questions.*

"That if Elected you would endeavour to execute its trusts to the best of your Abilities and for the General good of the nation—as they have perceived in your management of the senate for a period of 8 years heretofore as V[ice-]P[resident]. That you calculate on ["aid from" *interlined*] the United Wisdom of the two branches of the national Legislature and ["that you are aware" *interlined*] of the Solemn obligations of the oath necessarily to be taken by the Incumbent of the high trust contemplated by the Constitution."

I would refrain from every kind of pledge if your nomination can be contemplated from the side alluded to and if *so* nominated without pledge what is to hinder the whole Country from falling into it. The few radicals you may say as was done in [William H.] Crawford[']s Case—but your old friends below Mason's line would be unanimous.

However you may already think I have ["already" *canceled*] trespassed too much so [I] will conclude as ever Your sincere friend & Servant, H.M. Salomon.

P.S. I forgot to remind you at one of my visits that had your matters been trusted in efficient hands last summer—your nomination might have been effected but Mr. [John A.] Morrill ["who may be an honest man" *interlined*] allowed the whole summer to pass, without getting a meeting up as he promised me. The best time for action was lost—he went to a country place to pass the summer[.]

I had no orders nor means—had I been in possession of the smallest patronage I would have risked my own unauthorised movements and paid the expences[.]

Would have had respectable and honourable men as I had in '32 to act on such occasions[.]

You had a man ["one (Joseph A.) Scoville" *interlined*] at Washington sent perhaps by our friend Morrill but ask Mr. [Sereno E.?] Dwight about him. Mr. Dwight is again at Washington[.]

ALS in ScCleA. NOTE: Haym Moses Salomon (1785–1858), a New York City merchant, was a tireless seeker of compensation from the U.S. government for the Revolutionary services of his father, Haym Salomon.

From Ch[ARLES] Serruys, [Belgian Chargé d'Affaires], "private and confidential"

Washington, 4 Dec. 1844

Dear Sir, My predecessor, *Baron* [Desiré] *Behr*, was recalled [in 1837] upon the demand of Mr. [Martin] Van Buren, for reasons well known in your Department. However, he impressed upon the mind of my government that it was *exclusively* on account of his Treaty, which had not been ratified by the King [Leopold I], and he was backed by Mr. [Louis Barbe Charles] *Serurier* and Mr. [Alphonse]

Pageot [former and present French Ministers to the U.S.], at that time in Belgium, who had been the constant and warm friends of Baron Behr in this country, and very nearly in the same odour.

I am indirectly informed, that it is intended to remove my [*sic;* me] to Denmarck [*sic*], because my Treaty having fallen to the ground, it is supposed in Belgium that *for the same reasons,* I must be very obnoxious in the United States and not in a situation to render any service.

I leave these considerations to your Judgment and that of the President, hoping, if I must not be placed here upon the same footing as my predecessor, you will have the kindness to seize an *early opportunity* to have these *very strong impressions* of my government corrected by Mr. [Thomas G.] Clemson. I remain with the highest regard Dear Sir, your very obliged Serv[an]t, Ch. Serruys.

ALS in ScCleA.

To "Messrs. Bartlett & Wilford, Booksellers, New York [City]," 12/5. "Mr. [Robert] Greenhow[,] the Librarian of this Department[,] having shewn me your letter of the 30th Ultimo, relating to two volumes of Spanish Manuscripts, entitled 'Documents para la Historia Civil y Ecclesiastica de Texas,' which formed part of the library of the late Lord Kingsborough, and are now for sale in London, I hereby request you without delay, procure those volumes for this Department at the price stated in your letter[,] namely fifty five pounds sterling in full of all expenses." FC in DNA, RG 59 (State Department), Domestic Letters, 35:34–35 (M-40:33).

From ANNA [MARIA CALHOUN CLEMSON]

Brussels, Dec. 5th 1844

My dear father, The Hibernia brought us more letters than we have yet received, & good tidings in all, & you don[']t know the happiness contained in those few words, to one so far from home as we are. We received at once your letter to Mr. [Thomas G.] Clemson, of the 12th of Nov., Sister's [Martha Cornelia Calhoun's] of the same date, & mother's [Floride Colhoun Calhoun's] of the first, written after you had all arrived safely in Washington. I am much pleased you are all together, & think "A winter in Washington" will be of service to both mother, & sister. You should prevail on sister to go more into society.

It will do her good, & she will be surprised how much better she can hear, & enjoy what is going on around her, when she gets the habit of attention, which she has at present entirely lost. She is somewhat in the position I was when I first came here. From not expecting to understand anything, I did not listen, but I soon found this would not do, & now by diligently listening, I have become able to understand almost everything I hear said. I have besides commenced to-day to take lessons in French & shall try very hard to learn, both for my own pleasure, while here, & that I may be the instructress of my children, & prevent them from feeling the awkwardness, & encountering the difficulties, I have since my arrival in Europe. In this travelling age of the world, the knowledge of one, or more, modern languages is much more essential, than the ancient, & I entreat you to cause James [Edward Calhoun], & Willy [William Lowndes Calhoun], to take every opportunity of perfecting themselves in French, at least.

I suppose I must first tell you of Calhoun's [John Calhoun Clemson's] health for it has been the object first in our minds for three weeks past. You will have seen from our last letters how sick he has been, & how much he has suffered. Thank Heaven! he is now tho' not entirely well, & still not well enough to go out, except in the carriage, so much better, as not to give us any farther uneasiness, save that as the inflam[m]ation has not yet quite left the eye, we are still a little anxious, lest there should be a relapse, & the eye sight be affected at last. He is much reduced, & disfigured, but if he only continues well, that will all mend soon. You may imagine how Mr. Clemson & I felt, when he was so sick, especially as every one was strange to us. I always wish to see you enough, heaven knows, but when he was so sick, I thought I would have given the world to have mother with me, & felt so lonely, to think there was no one in Brussels I could send for to ["give" *interlined*] me any counsel or assistance. But enough of our troubles. I hope they are happily over now, & will think of them no more.

Calhoun's sickness has of course prevented me from going out much, which I did not at all regret, for I find it very irksome, after being so long independent of all these forms, & trappings, to be obliged to return to them again, but I suppose use will soon make them easy again, if not agreeable, for I find there is a positive necessity for going out much more than I could wish, & even then I shall be considered as a very quiet, & unsocial person, for among the thousand of idlers, in Europe, whose only *business* is society, & ceremony, there is no conception of any other method of employing, at least certain portions of the day, ["save" *interlined*] in these *grave* occupations, & spending an evening alone, is considered equivalent to being a hermit. Now, tho' I care not what anyone here thinks of me, & did we come as private persons should laugh at such nonsense, still as these matters are of primary importance, & the declining an invitation, without a very special excuse, such as sickness, &c &c a personal insult, I am forced to be content whenever I can, with the least shadow of a reason, frame a suitable excuse ["to" *interlined*] get off, & go out the other times with as good a grace as I can, & you know me too well to suppose, I don[']t find ample amusement when I take the trouble to go. The most serious objection to the matter ["is," *interlined*] that this going out requires, even at the plainest, some dress, & this dress, even at the cheapest some money, which we can ill spare, for it will be as much as we can do to live on the salary, even if we can do so, tho' we use the greatest economy, I can assure you.

There is not the difference between society here, & with us, that people wish us to believe. There is more show in some things, not so much in others. The persons forming society are better educated, & more stupid, & twice as ugly, with better manners, that is to say in this, as in every thing else, nature has done more for us, art more for Europe. As to all the etiquette, ceremony, show, & *nonsense*, connected with royalty, it is the most ridiculous & childish business you can imagine, & makes me ashamed for humanity, & this is especially the case in these little second rate courts. In the palaces of the Tuilleries, or St. James, where every thing is on a so much more magnificient [*sic*] scale, the scene *may* borrow grandeur from the accompaniments, just as the Catholic religion is a much more imposing affair in one of these solemn cathedrals, ["from what" *canceled and* "than" *interlined*] it is in one of the two penny concerns in America, but it is foolish enough at best, I must say. I am pleased to find that I am a genuine republican, & only love my country the more, the more I see of the excellencies & defects, of other countries.

I do not think this an effective government. The king [Leopold I] is a sensible man, but seems to have as little to do as possible with the government, at least I should judge so, as he is scarcely ever in Brussels, & is very inaccessible when here, never being visible save on state occasions, or by particular audience. In this respect he forms a striking contrast to his father in law, Louis Phillipe [*sic*], who is ["almost" *interlined*] as easy of access as our President. This man here seems to be & consider himself a mere state puppet, & he has not even the liberty, I believe, which we allow our Chief Magistrate, of choosing his Cabinet, but they are chosen for him by the Chambers, tho' I believe they cannot force on him any one positively disagreeable. The Ministry now in, is tottering; Indeed one of them told Mr. Clemson, he did not think they would go through the session & this makes it more difficult to do anything with them, so Mr. Clemson gets on but slowly about the treaty but he is very anxious to do all he can & can do as much as any one could I suppose, for he is a general favourite. The British Minister here, Sir Hamilton Seymour, a very sensible, pleasant man, told Mr. Clemson he did not know how the American government fared in other courts, but here, from their not understand[ing] french, & being obliged to resort to him on all occasions, Mr. [Virgil] Maxcy, & Mr. [Henry W.] Hilliard, put whatever secrets there might be, completely in his power, & of course in that of his government, for almost every paper was submitted to his examination. He spoke particularly of Mr. Maxcy I believe. There really should be some regulation requiring the Ministers to continental courts either to understand french themselves or have a confidential secratry who does for we cannot afford to make England acquainted with our policy in this way. Am I not quite a politician still? The fact is the election of [James K.] Polk gives me some hopes of the country again which I confess I had almost entirely lost. His election was so entirely on principle & so free from the disgusting electionaring [*sic*] tricks so mortifying in the preceeding canvasses that it gives one hopes of better times.

I must stop & truly I am ashamed to send this letter it is so badly written but I have been much interrupted & the children have been plaguing me all the time. I am delighted Eugenia [Calhoun] is with Sis. My best love to mother, sister, & Eugenia. The children send kisses. Mr. Clemson will write to you & I shall probably write mother or sister by the steamer which carries this. You say you heard from Patrick [Calhoun] & John [C. Calhoun, Jr.,] but don[']t mention how they are. Your devoted daughter, Anna.

ALS in ScCleA.

From C[HARLES] A. CLINTON

Newyork [City,] December 5th 1844

Dear Sir, The bearer of this letter, Mr. James H. Suydam of this City, now holding the office of navy agent, will explain his business to you. He has requested a letter from me, and altho not in the habit of acceding to such requests, I am satisfied that his excellent character and good standing in this community entitles him to this civility at my hands. Mr. Suydam is a respectable member of the Democratic party and has represented this City in the Legislature. He assures me of the high respect that he entertains for you, both personally and politically, and has expressed himself in such high terms of your exalted character, that I should not feel justified in refusing a compliance with his request in the present instance. With esteem I have the honor to be Sincerely your friend, C.A. Clinton.

ALS in ScCleA. NOTE: Charles A. Clinton was the eldest son of Governor of N.Y. and 1812 Presidential candidate DeWitt Clinton.

From A[NDREW] J. DONELSON

Washington [Texas,] Dec[em]b[e]r 5[t]h 1844
Sir, You will receive herewith copies of my address [of 11/29] to the Secretary of State [Anson Jones] on presenting my credentials, and his answer [of 11/29]: and also my address to President [Samuel] Houston on the same occasion. The reply of the latter will be furnished as soon as he writes it out.

I transmit also, herewith, a copy of my communication [of 12/2] to this Government in relation to the complaint against the collector at Sabine in Texas, for the exaction of Tonnage duties from the United States schooners, Louisiana, and William B[r]yan. To this communication I have not received a reply but hope to obtain a satisfactory one before President Houston retires from the Government. In a conversation with the Sec[retar]y of State on the subject it was suggested that in as much as the collector was understood to have acted upon the orders of the President, it would relieve his successor of some embarrassment, perhaps, to have the subject disposed of before the new administration was organized. As soon as the answer is received it will be forwarded to you.

Since the date of my despatch No. 3 of Nov[embe]r 24, to the date of my presentation by the Secretary of State, Nov[embe]r 29th, I was employed in cultivating an acquaintance with the members of Congress and in ascertaining the state of the public feeling in relation to the great cause of annexation. The President was not in a situation, as previously intimated, to make an *ad interim* appointment, and I was therefore obliged to wait until the arrival of the Sec[retar]y of State. You will see from my address to President Houston that I touched only those points on which we are to rely, for the conciliation of the people of Texas, when the question of annexation is submitted to them, as it has been to those of the United States. Had I have known the result of our elections I might have been a little less reserved, but could not have elicited a more favorable expression from him than I did.

I found the Sec[retar]y of State as frank and cordial as could have been expected. He is the particular friend of President Houston, and struck me as possessing in a high degree the qualities which are needed to administer this Government.

The assurances made to me, by President Houston in the interview described in my despatch No. 3, respecting the scope of the powers given to Gen[era]l Terrill [*sic*; George W. Terrell], were renewed by Mr. Jones; and you may rely upon them as an indication not to be changed of the determination of this Government to adhere to the policy of annexation as long as there is a reasonable prospect of its receiving the support of our's. Your instructions to Mr. [Tilghman A.] Howard, and to our Ministers at Mexico & Paris [Wilson Shannon and William R. King], have been shewn again to both of those Gentlemen, and they express themselves as satisfied with their justice and soundness.

I have not felt it my duty to address an official communication to the Department of State here, embodying the considerations which authorise us to regard the question of annexation as not lost by the rejection of the late Treaty, but as still pending before Congress, with every prospect of success, consequent [*with the first "e" interlined*] upon the popular sanction manifested by the recent elections. The full force of these considerations and those which should incline Texas to prefer annexation to the United States, to any advantage that could probably result from commercial Treaties or other alliances with Great Britain & France, has been developed in conversation, and will be otherwise kept before the public mind. No practical answer could now be given to those considerations by this Government, which would not be calculated to embarrass it. I think it wiser, therefore, to rely on the unofficial assurance I have received that no such Treaties or alliances will be formed, in the present posture of affairs, than to obtain one in an official shape which would necessarily be qualified so as not to offend or disturb the friendly understanding existing between Texas & those powers.

All that we can desire of this Government, is, that it should maintain its present attitude, until the measure of annexation can come to it in some practicable form, from the Government of the United States. The revulsion of feeling produced by the rejection of the Treaty is subsiding, and the election of Col. [James K.] Polk is awakening the natural love which binds the people to their mother land. In a short time I doubt not the force of this affection will be strong enough to place the question of annexation on as good a footing in Texas as it has ever occupied—so strong indeed that no leading men in the Republic would hazard an opposition to it, if nothing unfavorable grows out of the effort to consum[m]ate it in the United States.

I had written thus far, when Gen[era]l [Duff] Green announced himself as the bearer of despatches from Mr. Shannon, our minister to Mexico. He brings important information which you will of course receive by his son [Ben E. Green], who has gone on to New Orleans with a full communication of the state of feeling produced by the correspondence between Mr. Shannon and the Government of Mexico—which I take it for granted will be followed up by a termination of all diplomatic intercourse on our part with that Government. I shall lay the correspondence before this Government tomorrow as evidence of the faithful adherence on the part of the President of the United States ["of"(?) *canceled*] to the line of policy declared to Texas when she was invited to sign the Treaty of annexation. Texas cannot but appreciate, as she ought, the frank avowal of the principle that the United States are justly bound for all the injury which may result to her from an acceptance of the overtures for annexation: and the temper in which it has been received by Mexico will have a salutary effect on the public mind here in reestablishing kind feelings towards our country.

I have stated to you in a former despatch that the measure of annexation will be endangered by delay. Texas can avail herself of the mediation of England and obtain the recognition of her independence by Mexico whenever she chooses. She can obtain this without being restrained by any stipulations on the subject of slavery, *even, without an agreement to reject another overture for annexation from the United States.* Such are the impressions which I derive from conversations with leading men here, and they are too reasonable to be set down as fanciful.

If the recent elections in the United States have given us the political power necessary to carry the question of annexation, the only hope of opposing it with success, would be a movement founded on the immediate self interest of Texas, so aimed as to demonstrate to the people that the advantages of union with us, are counterbalanced by those of seperate independence, obtained without any further expenditure of either blood or money. Suppose that England & France propose to put into operation Treaties with Texas, whereby she would have the benefit of an unrestricted trade for a series of years, and that this proposition should be pending, when our Congress adjourns, having failed to pass the joint resolution offered by Mr. [George] McDuffie; can we still expect to control the question? Can we trust the force of a wily diplomacy luring the people of Texas by the benefits of such a trade, and taking advantage of every opportunity to estrange them from the United States, knowing as we do that these opportunities will be of frequent occurrence on the Sabine & Red rivers? It is too much to leave to doubt.

To guard against this danger, our course is speedy action—not, however, if it loses the question. It is better to run the hazard of delay, deplorable as it would be, than to have direct evidence that the question is again lost. We might still say to Texas that one more appeal to the people who yet have representatives to elect would furnish the requisite political power: and those charged with the Government here might be led by great considerations of patriotism ["and forecast" *canceled*] to postpone yet longer a step which would not fail to prove disastrous to the cause of free Government.

I write in haste, having but a few hours since the arrival of the Gen[era]l, to make up this despatch so as to reach the Revenue cutter before she sails for New Orleans. I shall enclose with it a copy of President Houston[']s message to Congress. I am very respectfully Y[ou]r ob[edien]t ser[van]t, A.J. Donelson.

[Enclosure]
"Address of Mr. Donelson, on delivering his
    Letter of Credence to the Secretary of State"
                    [Washington, Texas, November 29, 1844]
Sir: It gives me pleasure to meet you on this occasion; and, in addition to the assurances expressed in the letter of credence which I have the honor to present to you, of the sincere desire of the President of the United States [John Tyler] to improve and render stable, the good understanding now existing between the two republics—to offer those I am authorized, personally, to give; and these are, Mr. Secretary, all that can arise from a thorough conviction that the interests of the two countries are the same, and ought to be cemented by every tie of friendship.

In the performance of my duties, I shall be regulated by the wish to promote the friendly objects of my government, in a manner satisfactory to yours; relying on that frankness which is the result of good intentions, and which cannot fail to be appreciated in a republic whose citizens, having a common origin with my own countrymen, are identified by the same pursuits, and cannot anticipate a different destiny in the effort to preserve the blessings of freedom.

It is gratifying to me to know, Mr. Secretary, that your agency in creating and maintaining the present amicable relations between our two countries, instead of being withdrawn, is to be continued in the more responsible station of the Presidency of the Republic: and, allow me to add, that your efforts to watch over and promote the lasting interests of the brave and patriotic people who have conferred this honor upon you—crowned, as I trust they will be, with complete success—can produce no more heartfelt joy, than that which will be felt by the Government and people of the United States.

[Enclosure]

"Reply of Mr. [Anson] Jones"

[Washington, Texas, November 29, 1844]

Sir: I cannot receive without the expression of feelings of unfeigned satisfaction the accredited Representative of that great country from whose bosom so large a portion of the citizens of Texas have sprung—and it is with peculiar pleasure that I meet on this occasion one whose life and history are so distinctly associated with that of the man who above all others, out of our own country, has been the warm and untiring friend of this young Republic [Andrew Jackson]. The people of Texas can never forget the warm grasp of him, who, as the executive chief of your country, first hailed her as a nation, nor his later efforts in her behalf.

The sameness of the origin and interests of the two countries to which you have so kindly alluded, has led the people of this, on all occasions, to desire the maintenance of the most friendly relations; and, if the hope which they have sometimes indulged, that these considerations might lead to the accomplishment of a common destiny, should be disappointed, I trust they will not be lost in their influences upon either country, in the preservation of those paramount principles which they hold in common keeping.

You certainly do me no more than justice in believing that it has been my constant desire in the discharge of the various duties heretofore devolved upon me as an officer of this government, to strengthen the relations best calculated to promote a durable friendship; and if I have been selected by my countrymen to fill the vacancy which will in a few days occur in the Executive chair, I can only assure you that the increase of my responsibilities and trusts will be attended with a corresponding desire on my part, not to disappoint their just expectations in preserving the relations, as they now subsist between the two countries, in harmonious accordance with the public will.

[Enclosure]

"Mr. Donelson's Address To President Houston, on

being presented to him by Mr. Jones, Secretary of State"

[Washington, Texas, November 29, 1844]

Sir: In appearing before you as the Chargé d'Affaires of the United States, I feel that I can scarcely add any thing to the warm expressions of good will and friendship, contained in the letter of credence which I have had the honor to present, and which are so cordially felt by the President of the U. States for the President and people of this Republic. Assurances of these feelings were eloquently conveyed to you by my predecessor, Gen. [Tilghman A.] Howard, whose untimely death, deplored by his own country as a national loss, was equally regretted here, because there were here, among your estimable citizens, many who knew him in his native land, and could testify to his high moral worth.

In taking the place of such a citizen, I cannot conceal the emotions of sadsadness [sic] produced in my own bosom—recollecting as I must, that under circumstances like the present, it was his painful lot also to recur to the similar fate which had befallen his predecessor [William S. Murphy], and to lament that the hopes of the U. States to improve the relations of the respective countries, by the good offices of a resident Minister here, had been so often disappointed. But I derive consolation from the reflection that these dispensations of Divine Providence may contain a salutary chastening for those who survive in the service of the two Republics; and that rightly understood, they may not be ineffectual in their influence on the prosperity of each. They have prepared the two Governments for a more thorough consideration of their mutual interests. They have given time for a more perfect development of those causes which are at work in their internal structure, as well as external relations, to harmonize their progress, if not to unite their destiny, in the great effort to increase the securities of freedom, at the same time that the principle of sovereignty in the people is strengthened. In this point of view, there is occasion for gratitude to the Giver of all good, even when we lament those strokes of His Providence which blast our personal efforts and force us to see that diplomatic agency is, at best, but a frail reliance in promoting the prosperity of nations.

Suffer me, Mr. President, in turning from this melancholy retrospect, to assure you again, that the President of the United States in confiding to me the office of Chargé d'Affaires, has been actuated by the most ardent desire to continue with Texas the good offices which are called for by a deep interest in her welfare, and by the anxious hope that nothing will ever occur to weaken the chain which holds the interests of the two Republics together. To keep this chain bright and strong, is not only his object, but I may safely say, it is that the people of the U. States, who claim, in their kindred and descendants here, an identity of interest, of patriotism, and of devotedness to the success of free institutions.

To the satisfaction springing from the discharge of duties thus directed, could any more be added, it would be that of meeting here so many of my personal acquaintances and friends, among whom, I trust, it will not be presumptuous or inappropriate in me, on this occasion, to claim your Excellency as one.

I look back, Sir, with delight to the early honors you received from my native State, when you were there, as you are here, identified with the cause of the people: and I rejoice that in the severe tests to which you have been since subjected in the fields of war and peace, that you have proved yourself equal to every crisis, and are now about to retire from the service of your countrymen, blessed with proofs of their love and gratitude, and distinguished by the common consent of the world, for the heroic manner in which you have conducted them through an eventful revolution, to a respected rank in the family of nations.

Among such a people I cannot feel as a stranger. I cannot but look upon them as brothers, who in their struggle for liberty and independence, have proved that they are the worthy descendents of the heroes of Bunker Hill and Yorktown. I must salute the "lone star" which they have set up in this hallowed sky of their victories, as a light which is to blend its rays with those that hang over my own loved Union, and which are, I trust, never to be extinguished.

ALS (No. 4) with Ens in DNA, RG 59 (State Department), Diplomatic Despatches, Texas, vol. 2 (T-728:2, frames 406–421), received 1/2/1845. NOTE: The "addresses" above were enclosed as printed in the Washington, Texas, *National Vindicator*, November 30, 1844, p. 3. The letter of 12/2 from Donelson to Jones reiterates the U.S. position that the duties attempted to be charged on the U.S. schooners *Louisiana* and *William Bryan* by the Collector of Customs at Sabine [William C.V. Dashiell] are illegal. Donelson feels assured the Texan government will cancel the bond required in these cases and issue instructions preventing future occurrences of the kind.

From W[ILLIAM] O. GOODE, "Private & Confidential"

Boydton, Mecklenburg [County], Va., Dec[embe]r 5, 1844
My Dear Sir, I have determined to break the long silence which we have observed. I did not continue our correspondence in 1843, because in the spring of that year, almost every thing in Virginia, moved "in a wrong direction", and I could find no pleasure in writing. After the course of our Democratic Friends here at that time, I came to the conclusion, that, the wisest conduct which could be persued by your friends, would be, to retain themselves in position to render the Country most efficient service in the state of things which has now come to pass. I think the time has come when we should take some action—and, I hope, the circumstances are propitious. I should be happy to know your own views as to the whole plan of the next campaign. What is the best line of conduct to be adopted, by those, who hold as *vital* those great principles, with which your name has become identified, & who believe that, to ensure the triumph & permanent ascendancy of those principles, it is important that you should be placed at the head of the Govt. Perhaps you may deem, that for one who has done so little to manifest his regard, I am bold to challenge so great a confidence, but [Robert M.T.] Hunter will tell you, that with the exception of himself you have no friend in Virginia, or perhaps any where, who would derive a higher gratification from your greatest success. He will further inform you, that no matter what may happen your confidence will never be betrayed. Tell me then what will your friends do every where—and what should they do in Virginia. With the most sincere esteem & regard Truly Your Friend, W.O. Goode.

ALS in ScCleA. NOTE: Goode had been Representative from Va. during 1841–1843.

From GEO[RGE] W[ILLIA]M GORDON

Consulate of the United States
Rio de Janeiro, 5th Dec[embe]r 1844
Sir, Respectfully referring to my despatches Nos. 14, 15, 16 & 17, copies of which are herewith enclosed, I have now the honor to enclose herewith a copy of the deposition of Peter Martin, late of the crew of the Brig "Agnes."

This Peter Martin, together with Patrick Kane, also late of the crew of the "Agnes," and Zebiner H. Small Jr., late of the crew of the "Sea Eagle," whose depositions accompanied my despatch No. 16, have been detained in custody ["in custody" *canceled*] on board the Brig "Bainbridge" now lying at this port, as witnesses for the Government against both [Jason L.] Pendleton and others of the "Monte Video," and [Hiram] Gray and others of the "Agnes," and will soon be sent to the United States in that capacity. I have the honor to be, Sir, most respectfully Your Obedient Servant, Geo. Wm. Gordon, Consul of the United States.

ALS (No. 18) with Ens in DNA, RG 59 (State Department), Consular Despatches, Rio de Janeiro, vol. 7 (T-172:8), received 2/19/1845.

From P. GWINNER, *"Private"*

Newtown[,] Bucks County Pa., Decem[ber] 5th/44
Dear Sir, I hope you will not consider me obtrusive, in addressing you on this occasion. I am prompted probably, more from a desire, than the ability to do ["you" *interlined*] a service. I cannot forget the hospitalities of your mansion, as well as other manifestations of your kindness to me, twenty years since, during the time Gen[era]l [Thomas J.] Rogers, was one of our Representatives in Congress, which you may long since, have forgotten, but still remembered by me. I felt then, what I now feel, an interest in your political career, a privilege which cannot be denied me. I feel it, a duty to myself, to apprise you of the movements as I conceive, of certain mercenary politicians in our State. Old federalists, *white-washed by Gen[era]l [Andrew] Jackson* & now the leaders of the democratic party, whom you can as readily identify, as if I named them to you, although you may not be familiar with their primary movements, to effect their purposes, which I have gathered from their political operators, not only in this County, but in the City, who are industriously urging, as the best policy for Mr. [James K.] Polk, to form an entirely new Cabinet, unconnected with the present administration, which is, as I conceive a thrust, aimed at yourself—and also to secure the Custom house appointments for their friends. The [James] Buchanan Clique may be willing to retain [*Calvin*] *Blythe* [Collector of Customs at Philadelphia] as he is in their interest. Your personal & political friends in this State (who are numerous) would consider your exclusion from the Cabinet, in the present juncture of affairs, a national misfortune. To give you

477

an idea of the malignaty of some of the political demagogues in this quarter, an intelligent, though violent partisan, was heard to declare within a few days, that "If Gen[era]l Jackson had hanged C[alhoun], Haine [*sic*; Robert Y. Hayne] & [George] McDuff[i]e, as he ought to have done, the Country would now be quiet." Notwithstanding such silly denunciations, you would be quite as safe in our State, as in South Carolina.

I was pleased with the President[']s [John Tyler's] views, contained in his messuage, in relation to Texas. I believe annexation, as important now, as was the purchase of Louisiana in 1803, and if it cannot be effected peaceably I think it worth the cost of a seven years war, to possess it. In case England should become possessed of Texas & ["prob"(?) *canceled*] indeed Cuba—which is within the reach of probability she would hold the lock & key to our Country, a state of things truly to be deplored.

As regards myself I have been out of politics, for some time. I committed the unpardonable sin in 1832, in not voting for Jackson, for which I hope I may be forgiven hereafter, if not in this world, of wo[e]. The only favour I am indebted to the dear people for, is my election in 1840, to the magistracy, an office I held ["for" *canceled*] eleven years, preceding, by appointment. In conclusion I will add, all that I have said may not be worth your perusal. If however you can profit by any suggestion I have made, I shall be gratified. If not all I ask is to receive it with the like spirit, in which it is sent, & consign it quietly, to oblivion. Very Respectfully & truly y[ou]rs, P. Gwinner.

ALS in ScCleA.

From J[ohn] B. Jones, [Editor of the Washington, D.C., *Madisonian*], 12/5. "In reply to your letter of inquiry of the 2d inst., I have to state that my list of subscribers, at this time, amounts to 3500." ALS in DNA, RG 59 (State Department), Miscellaneous Letters Received Regarding Publishers of the Laws.

To W[ILLIE] P. MANGUM, President Pro Tempore of the Senate, and J[OHN] W. JONES, Speaker of the House of Representatives

Department of State
Washington, 5 Dec[embe]r 1844
The Secretary of State, in obedience to the 20th Section of the Act, entitled "An act legalizing and making appropriations for such necessary objects as have been usually included in the general appropriation bills, without authority of law; and to fix and provide for certain incidental expenses of the Departments and offices of the Government, and for other purposes"; approved 26th of August, 1842; and the Act making appropriations for the civil and diplomatic expenses of the Government for the year one thousand eight hundred and thirty six, (2d Section) has the honor to submit to Congress the following statements; viz:

One marked A. shewing the manner in which the Contingent fund of the Department of State has been expended, so far as disbursements have been made by the agent of the Department [Edward Stubbs] during the fiscal year ending on the 30th of June 1844.

Another, B. shewing the manner in which disbursements have been made from the same fund, during the same period, by others than the Agent of the Department, as stated by the Fifth Auditor [Stephen Pleasonton].

Another, C. shewing the amount of all former appropriations for the same object remaining in the Treasury, and in the hands of disbursing Agents, on the 30th of June 1844.

Another, D. being a copy of a precise and analytical statement, made by the Agent of the Department, of all moneys disbursed by him during the fiscal year ending 30th June 1844.

Another, E. being a statement of the Contingent Expenses of Foreign Intercourse, paid by the Agent of the Department from the 1st of December 1843, to 30th November, 1844.

Another, F. being a statement of expenses from the same fund, from 1st Dec[embe]r 1841 to 31st March 1844, made by others than the Agent of the Department, as stated by the Fifth Auditor.

Another, G. being a statement of disbursements from the fund for Contingent expenses of all the missions abroad, by the Agent of the Department, from 1st July 1843 to 30 June, 1844: and, another, H. being a statement of expenditures from the same fund, paid by others than the Agent of the Department, on accounts stated by the Fifth Auditor during the same period. J.C. Calhoun.

LS (to Mangum) with Ens in DNA, RG 46 (U.S. Senate), 28A-F1; LS (to Jones) in DNA, RG 233 (U.S. House of Representatives), 28A-F1; FC's in DNA, RG 59 (State Department), Accounting Records: Miscellaneous Letters Sent, 1832–1916, vol. for 10/3/1844–5/29/1845, pp. 101–104; PC (to Mangum) with Ens in Senate Document No. 4, 28th Cong., 2nd Sess., pp. 1–37; PC (to Jones) with Ens in House Document No. 10, 28th Cong., 2nd Sess., pp. 1–28.

From J[ohn] Y. Mason, Navy Department, 12/5. "I have the honor to acknowledge the receipt of your letter of 3d inst. with the one accompanying it, & have directed the name of Mr. R[obert] O. Gibb[e]s to be entered on the register of applicants. Under the restrictions however of the Act of Congress of 4th August 1842, no more midshipmen can at present be appointed. There is moreover another obstacle to the success of Mr. Gibb[e]s' application: he is too old for admission into the Navy in the rank of Midshapman [sic]." LS in DNA, RG 59 (State Department), Miscellaneous Letters (M-179: 106, frame 127); FC in DNA, RG 45 (Naval Records), Miscellaneous Letters Sent by the Secretary of the Navy, 34:250 (M-209:13).

[Pedro] Santana, President of the Dominican Republic, to [John Tyler], 12/5. Santana describes the successful revolution of "the ancient Spanish portion of St. Domingo" from Haitian rule and introduces Dr. José M. Caminero, Envoy from the Dominican Republic to the U.S. "We doubt not that the Government of the United States will be disposed to extend to this new political Society all the attention which is to be expected between individuals who conduct and keep in view the great interests of their nation and the welfare of the human race." (Santana enclosed a letter of credence for Caminero, dated 12/5.) State Department translation of LS with En (both in Spanish) in DNA, RG 59 (State Department), Notes from Foreign Legations, Dominican Republic, vol. 1 (T-801:1); PC with En in Senate Executive Document No. 17, 41st Cong., 3rd Sess., pp. 25–26.

From JOHN TOMLIN

Post Office
Jackson, Tennessee [*ca.* December 5, 1844]
My dear Sir, In writing you now, I cannot do otherwise than to recall to my mind, one previous expression of your good will. A remem-

brance like this, sinks deep into my heart, and no time can rob it of its feeling. That I am not, and will not be ungrateful for a favor rendered me, time alone will show.

I am now Post Master at this place, and have been for the last four years. That the Office is no sinecure, any one at all acquainted with the daily routine of duties in a small country village, will most clearly perceive. With a small salary of four hundred Dollars, and a constant daily labor, life is worn out by the toils, without any promise of a *sunshiny day* on to-morrow.

You will please observe that some short time ago, I had the honor of addressing to his Excellency, John Tyler, President of the United States, a letter, disclosing to him these grievances, and most graciously beseeching him to remove them, by the bestowal on me of a more lucrative appointment. Since then he has been most silent on the subject.

In addressing you now, I do it ostensibly to secure your aid in this matter, and that you will serve me I have every reason to believe. In the Cabinet Departments, or in the one under your immediate supervision, offices vacated, I believe can be filled by myself with entire satisfaction to the head of the Bureau. A good Consular appointment, or a Secretary-ship of Legation would be prefer[r]ed, but the other however, would be gladly accepted.

To W[illiam] Gilmore Simms, the annalist of Carolina, and I[srael] K. Tefft, Corresponding Secretary of the Georgia Historical Society, I refer you, for my competency to such a task.

With a sincere wish that you may remain in your present Berth, under the Presidency of Mr. [James K.] Polk, I am with every consideration of respect, very faithfully, and most cordially, Your Obliged Servant, Jno. Tomlin.

ALS in DNA, RG 59 (State Department), Applications and Recommendations, 1845–1853, John Tomlin (M-873:87, frames 47–50). NOTE: This undated letter bears an EU indicating that it was received in the State Department on 12/12.

From JAMES M. WAYNE, [Associate Justice of the U.S. Supreme Court]

Washington, December 5th 1844

Sir, Mr. William Hogan having informed me that he was an applicant for the vacant Consulate at Trinidad, it gives me pleasure to say from my knowledge and acquaintance with him, that I think he would be an efficient representative of the U. States at that point. I have known Mr. Hogan for several years and write this letter very cheerfully at his request. I am Sir most respectfully Your Ob[e]d[ien]t Serv[an]t, James M. Wayne.

ALS and two CC's in DNA, RG 59 (State Department), Applications and Recommendations, 1845–1853, Hogan (M-873:40, frames 421, 426–428, 434–435). NOTE: An AES by I[saac] E. Holmes on the ALS reads "I concur with the Hon[ora]ble James M. Wayne that Mr. Mr. [sic] Hogan would make an efficient representative of the U. States at Trinidad."

From W[illia]m Wilkins

War Department, December 5, 1844
Sir, I respectfully transmit herewith copies of reports just received from General [Mathew] Arbuckle and Capt: [Nathan] Boone which it is believed may be interesting to your Department. Very respectfully Your Obed[ient] Serv[an]t, Wm. Wilkins, Secretary of War.
[Enclosure]
M[athew] Arbuckle to [Roger Jones],
    Adjutant General of the Army
Head Quarters, 2d Mil[itary] Dept.
Fort Smith [Arkansas], Nov. 15, 1844
Sir: In communicating the instructions received from your office, dated Sept[embe]r 17th, requiring the Commanders of Forts Towson and Washita to place their commands in readiness for service in the field, they were directed to report as to the disposition of the border tribes of Indians towards the United States and the Republic of Texas. Major [George] Andrews states in reply—"I have conferred with several of the leading and most influential men of the Choctaws and Chickasaws, and I am assured by them, that neither of their nations will, or have any idea of meddling with Texas or any other foreign nation. My own personal knowledge of these tribes, confirms me in their peaceful, and contented disposition towards the United States, and all other nations. It is barely possible that a few discontented individuals of the Caddoes and others in the vicinity of Fort Washita may cross the boundary of the United States." Colonel [William S.] Harney Com[man]d[in]g Fort Washita reports, "that from all the information that I have been enabled to procure I am con-

vinced that there is any thing but friendly feeling existing between the border Indians towards the Texans, and should any opportunity offer, such as an invasion by Mexico, they would soon join the Mexicans."

I think little apprehension need be felt in regard to the conduct of the great body of the Indians who have been located on our frontier by the Government. Some few of several of these tribes, roam about the borders, and are ever ready to en[g]age in any scheme of depredation; Kickapoos, outlawed Cherokees and others of the latter tribe who have been driven out of Texas, may be named, but their number is small. It is not so easy to form an opinion as to the disposition of the wild prairie Indians. They are a roving, thieving class, and of course little dependence ought to be placed on their engagements. We have treaties with most of them, viz: the Comanches, Kiaways, and Wichetaws, (four bands,) and as far as I am informed they have committed no depredations on our citizens, traders, or others, since those treaties were entered into. I have the honor to be, Sir, Your Obed[ien]t Serv[an]t, (Signed) M. Arbuckle, Bvt. Brig[adie]r Gen[era]l.

[Enclosure]
Nathan Boone to [William Wilkins], Secretary of War
Fort Gibson, C[herokee] N[ation]
November 12th, 1844

Sir, In conformity with instructions received from the Head Quarters of the 2d Military Dept. dated Fort Smith, September 20th, 1844, I set out on my mission to the council on the "Towacana Creek," in Texas, on the 25th September, 1844, taking with me for my guidance the instructions received from the War Dept., dated Indian Office, 31st August, 1844.

Previous to my arrival on the Tawacana Creek, at the Council Ground, I was informed that the place of meeting had been changed to the Falls on the Brazos River, about 20 miles S.E. of the Towacana. I therefore took the direct route for the Falls, leaving the Towacana, eight miles to my right.

On arriving at the Council Ground on the 13th October, I found ["that" *interlined*] the Council between the Citizens of Texas and the Indians, had broken up three days previous to my arrival, and the Commissioners and Indians had dispersed.

On the next day I set out for the Towacana Trading House, the place first designated for the Treaty, and where the Citizens thought the Camanches might make some little stay. On my arrival at the

Trading House on the 15th, I found that the Indians had proceeded directly for their hunting grounds, without making any delay whatever.

After conversing with several individuals on the subject of the possibility of reassembling the Indians, I declined making the attempt, as every one with whom I conversed gave it as their opinion, that the Indians could not be collected under two months, and that if they did come ["in" *interlined*] at all, that they would expect large presents, and these I did not feel myself authorized to make.

As far as I could ascertain from the citizens who attended the Council, there were but few of the wild Tribes who attended. One small band of Cammanches, and a few Towacanas, the greater portion present consisting of Cadoes and Delawares—the latter reside on the Missouri river when at home.

Although but few Indians attended, and but little was done, I have but little doubt but that it will be of much benefit to the citizens of Texas, and serve as a stepping stone to a General Treaty with the Cammanches and others.

Considering it entirely useless to attempt reassembling these Indians on the Prairie, I set out on my return march on the 16th October, and arrived at this post, on the 6th November, 1844.

Permit me here to express an opinion in regard to treating with the wild tribes of Indians residing in the neighbourhood of ["the" *interlined*] Red River, either in the Republic of Texas, or within our own limits, as several of these tribes reside north of the Red River and within the territory of the United States, and others again live south of the Red River, and in the Republic of Texas, who rove and hunt north of the Red River probably one half the year, and the other half are roving to the south. These roving tribes have no stated villages, or at least raise no provender, but depend entirely on game for a subsistence. I am of opinion that the whole of these Indians might be brought into Council by meeting them somewhere in their own Country, as they *"themselves"* consider it; and were such a plan adopted, I should say that the most appropriate place would be on the Red River, near the old Towash village—it would not matter on which side of the river. This is the great thoroughfare of these Indians as they travel north or south; this point would be central for all the tribes in that section of the Country.

In the year 1834, when out there, under Colonel [Henry] Dodge, we had several thousand Indians in a few days around us, viz: Wakoes, Towa-ash, Kiaways, Kichus, Witchetaws, and several bands of Cammanches. I am of opinion that if Col. Dodge had been authorized and had gone, with the view of treating with those Indians, that all living in this section of the Country might have been brought together in a few weeks.

The Towa-ash village here alluded to, is situated, about sixty miles higher up the Red River than the mouth of Cash Creek. A short distance above Cash Creek sets in what is now called the Witchetaw mountains, which extend up the Red River 40 or 50 miles, where they are seperated from a Chain of mountains which lay higher up the Red River, by a prairie valley six or eight miles wide, which leads from the large prairies south of the Red River to those north of it, and through this valley is the great thoroughfare for travel. I am, Sir, with great respect, Your obedient Servant, Nathan Boone, (signed) Capt. 6th Reg[imen]t Dragoons, U. States Commissioner.

ALS with Ens in DNA, RG 59 (State Department), Miscellaneous Letters (M-179:106, frames 128–133); FC in DNA, RG 107 (Secretary of War), Letters Sent by the Secretary of War Relating to Military Affairs, 1800–1861, 25:425 (M-6:25).

From GEORGE WILSON

National Anti Corn Law League
Manchester, 5 Dec[embe]r 1844
Dear Sir, I am desired by the Council of the National Anti Corn Law League, respectfully to request your acceptance of the enclosed Copy of the 1st Vol. of the league as a testimony of their esteem, and admiration of your able and consistent advocacy of Free Trade with all nations. I have the honor to be With sincere respect Sir Your mo[st] ob[e]d[ien]t Ser[van]t, George Wilson, Chairman.

ALS in ScCleA. NOTE: The En has not been found, but was doubtless the 1843–1844 volume of *League; The Exponent of the Principles of Free Trade, and the Organ of the National Anti-corn-law League* (London).

From J[OHN] D. GARDINER

Sag Harbor [N.Y.,] Dec[embe]r 6th 1844
My very Dear Friend, I received your kind letter of the 15th of Aug[us]t last in due time; in reply to mine ["address" *altered to* "addressed"] to you in June previous. Of that reply the following is a

copy; which I beg leave, under existing circumstances to submit to your friendly consideration.

"State department, 15 Aug[us]t 1844 My Dear Sir, It affords me great pleasure to state, that the President has determined on appointing your Son Samuel [L. Gardiner] Collector of the Port of Sag Harbor, which I hope will put you at your ease in reference to the Education of your youngest son Calhoun [Gardiner]; I trust he may one day do honor to you & the name he bears. With great Respect, yours truly, J.C. Calhoun. Rev[eren]d J.D. Gardiner."

Be assured the receipt of the above gave me great pleasure, in as much as it put me to rest respecting the Education of Calhoun, the highest object of my desire. I relied, with full confidence on the fulfilment of the President[']s determination in respect to the appointment of my Son Samuel &c. and no further means were deemed necessary to obtain it.

But I have learned to day with much surprise & regret that this appointment has be[en] given to another man [John H. Dayton]—With surprise because I had no reason to expect it, and with regret, because it has cut of[f] the only resource, and extinguished the last hope of educating Calhoun. It is this that gives the disappointment peculiar poi[g]nancy. Calhoun, when he ["heard" *interlined*] the fact shed Tears, and despair was depicted in ["his" *interlined*] Countenance.

I fear the President has acted in this matter under the influence of misrepresentation or mistake. As the appointment has not been confirmed, perhaps some thing may yet be [done]. I write in pain & grief, and will say no more, but commit all to you as my old & faithful Friend, with the request that I may hear from ["you" *interlined*] on the ["subject as" *interlined*] soon as convenient; that I may know what course to pursue in respect to your Name Sake. I shall wait to hear. I beg you will excuse my troubling you on this subject. What can be done—["by" *canceled*] your sincere friend, J.D. Gardiner.

ALS in ScCleA. NOTE: An AEU by Calhoun reads "Mr. Gardiner[,] relates to his Son." John D. Gardiner had been at Yale College with Calhoun. He was an Episcopal minister and the cousin of Julia Gardiner (Mrs. John) Tyler.

From J[ames] H. Hammond, Executive Department, Columbia, S.C., "Private," 12/6. Hammond transmits a printed copy of his Governor's Message No. III, which includes the report and resolutions of the S.C. House of Representatives of 12/5 relating to the visit of Samuel Hoar, Agent of Mass., to S.C. to gather information on the enforcement of the Colored Seamen's Act of 1835. In its report and resolutions, the S.C. House regarded Hoar's visit "as part of a deliberate and concerted scheme to subvert the domestic institutions of the Southern States, in plain violation of the terms of the national compact, and of the good faith which ought to subsist between the parties thereto, and to which they stand solemnly pledged." The resolutions determined that Hoar was an agent of sedition and affirmed the Governor's authority to expel him from the State. PDS in DNA, RG 59 (State Department), Miscellaneous Letters (M-179:106, frames 137–138).

From Will[ia]m Hogan, Washington, 12/6. "I have the honor to apply for the Consulate, now vacant at the Island of Trinnidad. The enclosed testimonials of my fitness for that Office, will I trust be satisfactory to yourself and His Excellency the President of the United States." [Hogan enclosed a letter addressed to Calhoun from James M. Wayne, dated 12/5.] ALS with En in DNA, RG 59 (State Department), Applications and Recommendations, 1845–1853, Hogan (M-873:40, frames 419–421).

From J[ohn] B. Jones, [Editor of the Washington, D.C., *Madisonian*], 12/6. "Since my note of yesterday I have agreed to furnish my country paper to the permanent subscribers to [Amos] Kendall's Expositor, which paper is to be discontinued. This will add 3000 to the number mentioned yesterday." ALS in DNA, RG 59 (State Department), Miscellaneous Letters Received Regarding Publishers of the Laws.

From H[ILLIARD] M. JUDGE

Tuskaloosa [Ala.,] 6th Dec[embe]r 1844
Dear Sir, It gives me pleasure to inform you, that after an arduous struggle, it is settled that your friend D[ixon] H. Lewis is to retain his seat [in the U.S. Senate] for the unexpired term of Col. [William R.] King.

The opposition [in our legislature] came from the old friends of Mr. [Martin] Van Buren, assisted by the whig members en masse.

The former regard you as the destroyer of Mr. Van Buren & the latter think, that you decided the late controversy for the presidency in favor of Mr. [James K.] Polk.

The opposition used the name of Col. King, supposing that his aspirations to the Vice-presidency, would ensure permanent opposition on his part, to yourself. An old letter of his, written from Paris, when he supposed that Mr. [Henry] Clay would be elected, expressing a desire to return to the Senate, was the pretext under which his name was introduced. A caucus was held last night to settle the conflicting claims of the Candidates, at which Lewis received nearly nine tenths of the party, over Col. King & Mr. David Hubbard his two opponents for the Seat. The election will take place in a few days at farthest. Your friends hail this result, as a demonstration in favor of your peculiar views, over those in our party, who differ with you. The Whigs & the malcontent democrats regard it in the same light.

We expect also, unless policy forbids it, to place a States right man, in the gubernatorial chair. The Northern part of the State claim the right from custom, to fill the chair & are presenting two very unworthy candidates to us, neither of whom we will take, unless absolutely necessary to preserve harmony in the party.

The whigs are unrelenting in their hostility to you, and regard the whole South as swept away from Mr. Clay, through your influence. I hope this will subside after the first burst of disappointment, as there are still many in their ranks, entertaining opinions not foreign to our own, on the subject of the tariff, & on the annexation of Texas.

There is a great deal of speculation on the subject of the Cabinet to the next administration. The whigs and "Hunkers" are exceedingly anxious to have your place filled by [James] Buchanan or some one entertaining views hostile to the "Chivalry," as they are pleased to denominate those entertaining opinions in common with yourself.

I have spun out this letter to a length, to which I did not intend when I began. I will now conclude, hoping that you will attribute the liberty I have taken in writing to you, not to any presumption on my part, but to its proper motive—a disposition to communicate to you, what I thought would be both agreeable & interesting. Very Truly Your friend, H.M. Judge.

P.S. My address if you should require it is at, Eutaw[,] Greene County, Ala.

ALS in ScCleA; PEx in Boucher and Brooks, eds., *Correspondence*, pp. 268–269.

From J[ohn] K. Kane, Philad[elphi]a, 12/6. Kane transmits to Calhoun a letter to himself, dated 12/4, from M[ary Warder] Cresson, mother of Warder Cresson, formerly appointed U.S. Consul at Jerusalem. Kane "should rejoice very much to be instrumental in effecting the object they [the Cressons,] have in view." Mrs. Cresson seeks Kane's assistance to have her son's Consular commission sent to him "according to the promise of Mr. Calhoun" despite a recent communication informing her that her son had been dismissed from office. Cresson has already established himself as U.S. Consul at Jerusalem and expended large sums in travel and equipment for his post. ALS with En in DNA, RG 59 (State Department), Miscellaneous Letters (M-179:106, frames 140 and 142–143).

From F[RANCIS] W. PICKENS

Senate Chamber [Columbia, S.C.,] 6 Nov: [*sic*; Dec.] 1844
My dear Sir, I enclose back the letter and have only to say that I have enquired from all quarters to ascertain as near as possible what was the popular vote in this State in favour of [James K.] Polk &c.

The result is that all agree that the aggregate vote of the State is fully 58,000 and that in no calculation can they give [Henry] Clay more than 6,000—so that would leave Polk a majority of 52,000. I think this is about right.

I have not heard a word from you. [George] McDuffie has written a letter to the Speaker [William F.] Colcock denouncing my resolutions, and urging immediate & decided steps. What is his precise idea as to the mode of action I am not aware as he does not state it in his letter to Colcock. But Judging from what those very few violent men, who seem to feel with him and are shewing his letters, say and do I should infer that cessession [*sic*; secession] is the remedy.

I have no idea that such a course will meet with any approbation. My resolutions will pass the House, I am now informed by a large majority. Some of the Union men desired me & beg[g]ed me to agree to withdraw the last resolution, but I would not consent to the slightest modification, and told them if they were to split, they must take the *Responsibility*, and the consequence is that they will now vote it. Some extreme men make the House a very combustable body. You have no idea how exciteable they are, & how little knowledge they have of general politics.

I wish you to know and recollect that I present the name of *Col. Eldred Simkins* [Jr.] now of Florida—as applicant for the Marshal of Middle Florida. You recollect he is the son of John Simkins & the nephew of Col. [Eldred] Simkins. He is a Gent[leman] of education & of the highest standing. This is the only favour on earth I desire from Mr. Polk. I have written him about it. Do be so kind as to recollect this matter, as you would do a great favour to and [*sic*] old & devoted friend.

You see that we have unanimously expelled old [Samuel] Hoar from Charleston. It will present a delicate point.

Present me affectionately to Cousin Floride [Colhoun Calhoun]. In haste but Truly, F.W. Pickens.

ALS in ScCleA; PEx in Jameson, ed., *Correspondence*, p. 990. NOTE: Presidential Electors were chosen in S.C. by the General Assembly, and there was no popular vote. Pickens's second paragraph above is an estimate of what the popular vote would have been in the election of 1844.

From G.U. Sage, Washington, 12/6. "In answer to your note of the 2nd inst. in reference to the number of permanent subscribers to the German 'National Gazette,' I have to state that the number is at present between 14 and 1500. I also take the liberty to state that Mr. [J.G.] *Klenck*, former editor of the 'Philadelphia Democrat' has lately purchased from me the establishment of the Germ[an] 'National Gazette,' under whose management the paper will in future be published. Mr. Klenck will arrive in this city in a few days." ALS in DNA, RG 59 (State Department), Miscellaneous Letters Received Regarding Publishers of the Laws.

From CHARLES T. SHELTON

New Haven Conn., Decem[ber] 6, 1844

My Dear Sir, I inferred from a short conversation with the Chief Clerk of your Department [Richard K. Crallé] that an effort had been made to remove [John W. Fisher] the Consul at Guadaloupe. He is a relative of mine by marriage and being absent would naturally expect me to interest myself to prevent (if possible) such a result. I cannot suppose that *political* reasons are assigned for his removal because he is now and always has been a democrat.

If not inconsistent with the rules of the Department I should be glad to know who the applicant is, and the reasons urged for Capt. Fisher's removal, and hope no action will be had in the matter until he has an opportunity to be heard.

The appointment of Mr. [Jonathan] Stoddard as District Attorney so far as I can learn gives general satisfaction. I shall in a few days send on the necessary papers to secure his *confirmation.* I am Sir your Friend & Humb[le] Serv[an]t, Charles T. Shelton.

ALS in ScCleA.

From JONATHAN STODDARD

State of Connecticut
New Haven, December 6 1844

Sir, I have Just received your communication of December 3d 1844— "Calling my attention to a Communication addressed to Charles Chapman my predecessor by the department on the 16th November 1843 to which no reply has yet been received—on the Subject of a Complaint made by the Portuguese Government through its minister here—against John Holdridge master of the American Whaler Romulus of Connecticut for feloniously Carrying away from the Cape De Verd Islands a certain Negro named Pedro Timas" and "asking my *prompt* attention to this Case."

I shall communicate with Mr. C[hapman] tomorrow on this subject and in the Course of the ensuing week devote to it personally prompt and Cordial attention. I am Sir Respectfully Your Obedient servant, Jonathan Stoddard.

ALS in DNA, RG 59 (State Department), Miscellaneous Letters (M-179:106, frame 139).

To Prof[esso]r [NATHANIEL] B[EVERLEY] TUCKER, [Williamsburg, Va.]

Washington, 6th Dec[embe]r 1844

I have been much engaged, since my return from a visit home, in bringing up the business, which had accumulated in my absence, which will explain why Prof[esso]r Tucker's letters have not been answered earlier.

I am very favourably impressed, as to the character of Dr. [Thomas G.] Peachy, and would be glad to favour his wishes, should an opportunity offer.

The Texian Mission was filled before Prof[esso]r Tucker's letter [of 11/13] was received. I highly appreciated at the time his course in reference to the Missouri question, and still do. If the South had taken the course it ought *then*, and resisted, with your brother ["(Mr. [John] Randolph)" *interlined*] all compromise, it would not *now* be exposed to the danger it is. The North might easily have been forced *then* to surrender at discretion; but she found a protector in Mr. [Henry] Clay. It was he, who extricated her from the Caudine Fork[s] by *his compromise.*

If what you state be so, it would be proof conclusive, that Texas to the Del Norte, formed part of Louis[i]ana, at the time we purchased it; but, I fear, there is some mistake. Jos[eph] M. White placed all his papers after his return from Europe in the hands of Mr. [Robert] Greenhow, Liberan [*sic*; Librarian] to the Dept.; and he assures me, that there was nothing in the whole collection like the article, of which he told you a copy had been furnished him. He ["(Mr. G[reenhow])" *interlined*] has been long engaged in examin-[in]g with great care all the documents in relation to Texas, which can be found. His investigation is brought down to 1763; The result has not been favourable to our claim beyond the Sabine. With great respect I am & &, J.C. Calhoun.

ALS in ViW, Tucker-Coleman Papers. NOTE: In 1839 White published a two-volume collection of laws, charters, and ordinances of the European powers relating to Spanish cessions. The work was the fruit of his European researches.

From D[ABNEY] S. CARR

Legation of the U.S.
Cons[tantino]ple, 7th Decemb[e]r 1844
Sir, I send herewith a Copy of a Circular recently addressed by me to all the Consuls and Vice Consuls of the United States within the Turkish dominions. Copies of it were sent by me to the minister for Foreign Affairs of this Government, to be forwarded by him to each of our Consuls, and a Copy, in French, unsealed, to apprize the Ottoman Government of their contents. You will find attached to the Copy I send you, a Copy of the Communication from the Porte, on which the Circular was grounded. The Turkish Government has manifested on various occasions, since I have been here, and had done the same under my predecessor, a disposition to vex and harrass the American religious missionaries within its dominions. This has not proceeded from any particular hostility, on the part of the Turks, to these in-

dividuals or their religion, for they are very tolerant of both, so long as they keep clear of interference with the believers in the Prophet: but it has arisen from the jealousy of Christian sects here, and the foreign Agents of others, hostile to protestantism; who have stimulated the Sublime Porte, by false statements and alarms. The request of the Porte seemed to me to afford a good opportunity to set this Government right in regard to the American missionaries, and I trust I have executed the task in such a way as to have a happy influence on it, and to meet the approbation of my own Government. I learn that there is an individual at present at Jerusalem, who calls himself "Warder Cresson, Consul of the U.S. at Jerusalem," and who has assumed to perform certain acts in that character. Among other things, he is giving papers of protection to Jews and others, not Citizens of the U.S. The impression of a seal which he has recently sent to the American Vice Consul at Jaffa—taking from him the one he had always previously used which was "U.S. Consular Agency for Jaffa & Jerusalem"—I herein enclose. Now, Sir, this man has sent me no evidence, of his appointment, and I have received none from the State Department; nor has the Turkish Government been applied to, or granted him any *Berat* or Exequatur. From all that I can learn of him he is deranged, and as his conduct is altogether irregular and outrageous, and calculated to injure us with this people, and bring us into ridicule with every people, I have disclaimed to the Porte all knowledge of him, and my belief that he is an imposter, and written to the American Consul at Beyrout [Jasper Chasseaud] to like effect. I have written also to the character himself, forbidding him to do any other or further act as Consul, while unrecognised by the Turkish Government, and to inform him that if he did, I should ask the Government here to send him out of its dominions. I have the honor to be Your very Ob[edien]t Serv[an]t, D.S. Carr.

LS (No. 26) with Ens in DNA, RG 59 (State Department), Diplomatic Despatches, Turkey, vol. 10 (M-46:12), received 1/27/1845; FC in DNA, RG 84 (Foreign Posts), Turkey, Despatches, G:152–153. NOTE: Carr enclosed copies of a circular of 8/4/1844 from the Sublime Porte at Constantinople to the foreign diplomatic corps in the Ottoman Empire, complaining of foreign consuls and vice-consuls exceeding their jurisdictions by issuing "patentas" or letters of protection to Turkish subjects. Carr also enclosed his own circular of 11/26 to U.S. Consuls and Commercial Agents in the Empire condemning such issuances but affirming U.S. interests in the welfare of all Christians within the Empire.

From JOHN DUNHAM

St. Clairsville [Ohio], Dec[embe]r 7 [1844]
Dear Sir: Not knowing the rules appertaining to your department, in relation to the public printing or the publication of the laws of Congress, would you be pleased to communicate them to me, & if you have not already disposed of the matter, so far as Ohio is concerned, I would be glad to forward any testimonials required by the department, to secure the above object. In conversing with our mutual friends here, on this subject, I have concluded to take this method of announcing my views. With sentiments of high regard, I remain, D[ea]r Sir, Yours &c, Jno. Dunham, Ed[itor,] St. C[lairsville] Gazette.

P.S. Enclosed is a note to Gov. [Wilson] Shannon [U.S. Minister to Mexico] which I wish to have sent by the earliest conveyance, & oblige, &c, J.D.

ALS in DNA, RG 59 (State Department), Miscellaneous Letters Received Regarding Publishers of the Laws.

From GEO[RGE] W[ILLIA]M GORDON

Consulate of the United States
Rio de Janeiro, 7th Decem[be]r 1844
Sir, I have the honor at this time to state that the papers of the American Brig "Sea Eagle" Smith, Master, belonging to Boston, which vessel sailed from this port on the 5th inst. for the Coast of Africa, were detained by me, against the formal protest of the Master, for three days, for the purpose of completing an examination, already begun, of said Smith, his officers and crew, in regard to their knowledge of the acts and doings on the Coast of Africa of Capt[ai]n [Jason L.] Pendleton and others of the brig "Monte Video" charged with having violated the laws of the United States for the suppression of the Slave trade, and now detained here by my order—and of their knowledge of the acts and doings of Capt[ai]n [Hiram] Gray and others of the Brig "Agnes" supposed to have been engaged in violating the same laws, and also for the purpose of ascertaining if there were probable grounds to suppose that the Master and others of the "Sea Eagle" were legally implicated in aiding and abetting in the slave trade.

The "Sea Eagle" arrived at this port from Boston, under command

494

of Capt[ai]n Gilbert Smith, on the 26th day of June last. Soon after her arrival she was chartered by Manoel Pinto da Fonseca, of this City on a monthly Charter at 900 Dollars per month to take to the Coast of Africa an assorted cargo of Merchandize, and was consigned there to a Mr. Cunha, Agent of said Fonseca at Cabinda. By the terms of the Charterparty, as I understand, the Vessel was to take such passengers to and from Africa as the Charterers might choose to put on board of her, they the Charterers finding stores &a for said passengers. The "Sea Eagle" cleared from this port for the Coast of Africa on the 20th day of July with a Cargo as follows, to wit[:]

70 pipes of Aguardente, 318 Sacks of Farinha, 6 Sacks of Beans, 15 Casks Rice, 75 packages Jerked beef, 30 Casks Biscuits, 12 dozens Cinnamon planks, 1 dozen pine joists, 6 Casks Bacon, and various other articles not enumerated on her manifest and having on board as a passenger Capt[ai]n Hiram Gray, Agent and former Master of the Brig "Agnes" which Vessel was then on the coast of Africa in command of William M. Ruhl, and under charter to the said Fonseca, and also 13 other passengers all of whom were either Portuguese or Brazilians.

The "Sea Eagle" arrived at Cabinda with the Cargo and passengers aforesaid on the 9th day of August last, when the 13 Portuguese passengers left her, and the Cargo was discharged, Capt[ai]n Gray still continuing to live on board, as will appear by the depositions of Capt[ai]n Smith and others, which will be forwarded to the Department in due time.

After the arrival of the "Sea Eagle" at Cabinda, as aforesaid, Capt[ai]n Gray sold the "Agnes" or carried into effect a preconcerted sale of her, to said Cunha, Agent of Fonseca, and the American Master and crew of said Vessel came on board the "Sea Eagle," and returned in her with Capt[ai]n Gray as passengers to this Port, the Portuguese passengers or a part of them taking charge of the "Agnes," which vessel immediately took on board and sailed with a Cargo of 400 or 500 Negroes, which were soon after reported to have been landed on this Coast. Before the "Sea Eagle" left Cabinda, the Brig "Monte Video" was sold at that place by Capt[ai]n Pendleton, or delivered in conformity to a previous sale, to said Cunha, Agent of Fonseca, and sailed also on the same day with a Cargo of about 800 Negroes, under a Portuguese Master and crew. Capt[ai]n Pendleton and crew at the time, or soon after, the "Monte Video" was sold or delivered, embarked on board the "Sea Eagle" and came passengers to Brazil. The "Monte Video" landed her Cargo of Negroes soon after at Cape Frio.

The "Sea Eagle" soon after the sale and delivery of the "Monte Video" as above sailed from Cabinda, and arrived at this port, after touching at the small port of Victoria, in the province of Espirito Santo, on the 14th day of November last. Immediately after her arrival she was rechartered to proceed again to the Coast of Africa for the Sum of One thousand Dollars per month. This second charter, however, was not made to the noted Fonseca, the previous charterer, but to one Joze Antonio de Souza Basto and Capt[ai]n Smith declared in his deposition made before me that he refused to recharter his vessel to said Fonseca *on any terms,* in consequence of his present knowledge of his character, as being a notorious African slave trader, and his belief that the "Sea Eagle" while under charter to him was, without his previous knowledge or ability to prevent at the time, used in furtherance of the slave trade—and that had he known at the time what he now knows he would not have engaged in a charterparty with him at all.

On the 23d day of November, I commenced taking the depositions of Capt[ai]n Smith and the crew of the "Sea Eagle" and while progressing in that duty, Capt[ai]n Smith, on Saturday, the 30th ult[im]o reported his vessel ready for sea, and demanded his papers and clearance. This was refused, as I have stated, until I had completed the examination of himself and crew. At the same time I asked to have exhibited to me his Charterparty with Bastos, and manifest of Cargo—a copy of both which Capt[ai]n Smith readily furnished to me; and by which it appears that he is not required to take passengers back from Africa to this port, but is to take a Cargo of Merchandize, and three passengers to Africa, and return to this port in ballast, a copy of said Charterparty and manifest is herewith enclosed. Having completed my examination of Capt[ai]n Smith and crew and received a copy of his manifest and Charterparty as aforesaid, On the following Tuesday, the 3d instant, (Monday being a holy day) I furnished him with his papers and clearance, after having first taken from his vessel[,] as witnesses against Gray and Pendleton[,] Zebiner H. Small Jr., one of his original crew who was with him on his first voyage to the Coast of Africa, and on board the "Agnes" while that vessel was shipping her Negroes, and Patrick Kane and Peter Martin, two of the crew of the "Agnes" before she was sold, and who were also on board of her on or about the time the Negroes were being shipped, and who had engaged in the "Sea Eagle" for her present voyage—all of whom had also witnessed the shipping of the Negroes on board the "Monte Video." These three seamen are now on board the "Bainbridge" and will be sent home as witnesses for the Government in the cases of the "Agnes" and "Monte Video."

Perhaps I should have been justified in detaining Capt[ai]n Smith also as a witness, but as nothing in connection with his present Charterparty or Cargo appeared of itself to be illegal, and as his detention would probably have broken up his present voyage, and been the occasion of large pecuniary damages and loss to his owners, and as I considered that I had besides his personal testimony, a sufficient number of witnesses in custody against Gray and Pendleton, I did not deem it necessary or expedient to incur the responsibility of his detention, and he was accordingly permitted to proceed to sea as aforesaid. He previously however represented to me, that he should be back to this port in about three months, and promised to be in the United States in five, or at farthest within six months, and would then and there be ready to give testimony in the cases of Gray and Pendleton, and of his general knowledge of the manner that the slave trade is conducted on the Coast of Africa, so far as it has and shall come under his observation or notice, if called upon by the Government so to do; and I would remark that he would undoubtedly prove a valuable witness on these subjects. Before leaving he gave me his deposition in great detail and placed in my possession the original notes in the handwriting of R.S. Gough giving instructions to him in regard to the discharge of his Cargo, while at Cabinda, shewing very conclusively that said Gough acted as Agent or Clerk of said Cunha at that place, all of which will be sent home to be used by the Government should they be needed.

I have thus given an account of the "Sea Eagle" so far as her course of procedure since her first arrival at this port in July last has come to my knowledge, without dwelling upon those of the "Agnes" and "Monte Video" beyond what was necessary to that end.

How far Captain Gray and others of the "Agnes," and Captain Pendleton and others of the "Monte Video" are implicated in the charges that I have preferred against them will appear from the evidence that has already been forwarded, and that will follow so soon as it can be obtained and prepared.

Hoping my ["course" *interlined*] and acts in regard to the "Sea Eagle" as well as in the cases of Pendleton and Gray will meet with your approbation, I have the honor, Most respectfully to be, Sir, Your Obedient Servant, Geo. Wm. Gordon, Consul of the United States of America.

LS (No. 20) with Ens in DNA, RG 59 (State Department), Consular Despatches, Rio de Janeiro, vol. 7 (T-172:8), received 1/25/1845.

To Miss Betsey Hawley, South Norwalk, Conn., 12/7. "Your several letters of the 25th August last and 25th Ult[im]o—were duly received. My other engagements have not hitherto allowed me leisure to attend to them. No document of the character mentioned in your letter of the 25th August, last, was received at this Department between the 1st of August and 12th of October, 1825, nor has any information upon the Subject of Captain Isaac P. Hawley[']s effects been received, which has not already been communicated to you." FC in DNA, RG 59 (State Department), Domestic Letters, 35:39 (M-40:33).

From WASHINGTON IRVING

Legation of the United States
Madrid, 7th December 1844

Sir, I returned to this city a short time since much recruited in health and nearly freed from the malady which has so long harassed me. Since my return I have received your Excellency's Despatch No. 37 [of 10/25] enclosing the commission of Patrick J. Devine [as U.S. Consul at Sagua la Grande, Cuba].

In applying for the Royal Exequatur I have taken occasion to follow your instructions in protesting against the tax levied by this Government on similar documents. I enclose a copy of such part of my note as relates to the subject and shall follow up my written remonstrance by personal representations.

You will have seen by the public papers that the late revolutionary attempts in various parts of the Peninsula have been promptly quelled and rigorously punished. They do not seem to have been sympathised in by the people at large, who in fact, are tired and exhausted by past agitations and troubles and are desirous of peace at any price. The party in power rules with a strong hand and having the army at its command and having disarmed the national militia, feels confident of retaining its stern domination. Having managed the elections so as to ensure the almost unanimous vote in the parliamentary bodies, the measures of reform are nearly completed and will leave the Constitution so modified as vastly to increase the power of

the Throne and to render the matrimonial question almost independent of the will of the Cortes.

By the way I have just received private information which if true
will cause new perplexities as to this all important question. It is
said that an arrangement formed under the auspices of the Queen
Mother [Maria Christina] had nearly been completed for the marriage of the young Queen [Isabella II] with her uncle [Francisco,]
the Count Trápani; that the Pope had with much difficulty been pro-
pitiated and was about to grant the necessary dispensation, (the
parties being within the forbidden bounds of kindred) when the
Austrian Ambassador suddenly interposed, and, in the name of his
Sovereign [Ferdinand I] "forbade the bans." The tidings of this
untoward event, it is said, have completely disconcerted the plans of
the Palace. The chances of Trápani are at an end: indeed I am told
they had never received the countenance of [Joaquin Baldomero]
Narvaez. It is added that a new candidate for the hand of the Queen
will be brought forward in the person of the Archduke Frederick,
nephew of the Emperor of Austria, who, is said to be about twenty
seven years of age, well educated and accomplished, of manly character and who has distinguished himself before Beyrout. His pretensions, it is said, will receive the support of England. If this be true
it will bring the diplomacy of France and England in arduous competition at this Court. From some recent symptoms the french influence would seem to be endangered with the ruling party. Spanish
pride has been ruffled by certain articles in the french semi-ministerial
paper "the Journal des Debats" strongly animadverting on the recent
measures of the Spanish Government. Recriminations have appeared
in the Ministerial journals of Madrid. The Heraldo particularly
resents the remarks of the Journal des Debats on the military execution of the son and brother in law of [Gen. Martin] Zurbano and observes: "The Spanish Government ought to investigate whether the
journal countenanced by the French Government speaks from its own
inspirations or under the inspirations of others. If the first, contempt
is all that is merited by language dictated by the most petulant arro-
gance or the grossest ignorance: if the second; this incident will serve
to make our Government regulate its conduct according to the proofs
of amity shown it. For our own part we are not accustomed to mingle
with passion or acrimony in the affairs of our neighbors; we respect
ourselves too much to repay, in the same money, the good offices of
the Journal des Debats; but we feel assured that if the Spanish Press
should meddle in so strange a manner in the acts of the French Gov-

ernment, and *should reveal certain transactions* ("hechos") and should be less circumspect and generous, in such case the damage received by our neighbors would be more serious than any that could be caused to us by the shots of the Journal des Debats. *If decidedly they throw us the gauntlet, they may be assured we will not suffer it to lie on the ground."* The passages which I have underlined in the above extract are extremely significant, especially as they are said to have been written under the dictation of Gen[era]l Narvaez. They do not speak well for the cordial understanding between the two Governments. As far as our own interests are concerned it may perhaps be more to our advantage that the influence of France should predominate over that of England in the Peninsula; especially as it regards colonial questions; though it is much to be desired that Spain could be free from all foreign influence and have the independent management of her own affairs. Gen[era]l Narvaez continues to be the master spirit of the present Government. He is prompt, sagacious daring and domineering. Under his military rule Justice is more apt to make use of her sword than of her balance; the latter being considered too tedious of adjustment for the exigency of the times. The vigor with which he acts, however, and the severity with which he punishes political offences have created for him many deadly enemies among those opposed to him in politics; while the eclát with which he moves, lavish ostentation with ["which" *interlined*] he lives and the degree of state with which he surrounds himself, create rankling jealousy and envy among ["his" *canceled*] military rivals in his own party. He is, therefore, in continual danger from secret perfidy more than from open violence. His life has been repeatedly attempted and almost miraculously preserved, while his death would be likely to throw all things here into confusion.

Various capitalists in Madrid interested in the prosperity of Cuba are attempting to arouse the attention of Government and of the public to the State of Affairs in that Island and of the Colonial Affairs of Spain in general. A weekly page of the Ministerial paper, the Heraldo, has been secured for the purpose; in which articles will appear, calculated to set the statistics of Colonial Trade in a proper light. I have conversed with a gentleman who takes a leading part in the measure, and, who, having resided for some years in the United States is well affected to our country and well acquainted with the nature and extent of its intercourse with the Spanish Colonies. I have promised to furnish him with any information on the subject which I might meet with in American newspapers and public documents. I am in hopes that this may prove a favorable channel for conveying facts to the Spanish Government and people calculated to give them a right understanding of our commercial relations, to convince them of the loyalty of our intentions towards their colonial possessions and to put them upon their guard against the invidious policy of any other power. I am respectfully your obedient servant, Washington Irving.

LS (No. 56) with En in DNA, RG 59 (State Department), Diplomatic Despatches, Spain, vol. 34 (M-31:34), received 2/22/1845; FC in DNA, RG 84 (Foreign Posts), Spain, Despatches, 2:117–121; PC in George S. Hellman, *Washington Irving Esquire, Ambassador at Large from the New World to the Old* (London: Jonathan Cape, 1925), pp. 310–313; PC in Aderman et al., eds., *Complete Works of Washington Irving, Letters,* 3:844–847. NOTE: Irving enclosed a copy of his note of 11/29 to Francisco Martinez de la Rosa, Spanish First Minister of State, protesting fees imposed by Spanish authorities for the issuance of exequaturs.

From JA[ME]S D[E] P[EYSTER] OGDEN

New York [City], 7th Dec. 1844

Sir, I have been instructed by the Chamber of Commerce to address your Department upon the subject of the overland communication with China.

It has been reported that the English Government has made a treaty or concluded some arrangement with the Pascha of Egypt, for the exclusive conveyance of mails through that country and its possessions.

The trade of the U. States with China and India is daily enlarging, and likely to increase still more in extent and importance, under the treaty, recently concluded by Mr. [Caleb] Cushing, the advantage, nay absolute necessity of having equal means of early information with other Commercial nations, becomes manifest.

I have accordingly been directed to bring this subject to the notice of your Department, particularly in relation to the rumor that prevails of the conclusion of this arrangement between England and the Pascha granting exclusively to one nation facilities which we think should be equally afforded to all friendly powers; and, at the same time, respectfully to ask that such measures may be taken as you may deem best calculated to accomplish the object of making the U. States to avail of the same medium of communication and thus share in the same benefits that are understood to have been granted to Great Britain. I have the honor to subscribe very respectfully,

501

Your obed[ien]t Ser[vant], Jas. DP. Ogden, President of the Chamber of Commerce of New York.

ALS in DNA, RG 59 (State Department), Passport Applications, vol. 33, unnumbered (M-1372:15). NOTE: An AEU by Calhoun reads "From the Chamber of Commerce."

F[RANCIS] W. PICKENS to J[ames] Edward Colhoun, Calhoun's Mills, Abbeville District, S.C.

Columbia, 7 Dec[embe]r 1844

My dear Sir, I calculated certainly that you would have been down here before this as I heard you were to attend the meeting of the R[ail] Road &c. This is the reason I did not write before.

I now write principally to inform you that I am to be married on the 9th Jan[uar]y to Miss [Marion Antoinette] Dearing in Charleston, and shall be more than happy to have you there on the occasion. I hope you will certainly come to Edgewood & go with me down on the 7th. I have invited Judge [Andrew P.] Butler—Arthur [Simkins] & John [C. Simkins]—& one or two young Gent[lemen] to attend me— and my Aunt Mrs. Hayne & Susan, & this will be all. It will be private and I will return on the 10th to Aiken.

Your beloved wife [Maria Simkins Colhoun] advised me on her death-bed to get married and said it was ["a" *interlined*] duty I owed myself and my children, and since her death I have had no female relation to whom my children could look with confidence as they rise up into life. The lady I have selected has been educated & raised in the best manner by worthy & pious parents, and she has all that diffidence and retiring softness to which I have been so much accustomed in life.

As to politics you see that the move of the Gov: [James H. Hammond] and the clique was to place this State in such a position as to drive Mr. [John C.] Calhoun out of the Cabinet & the power & control his admirable position was so well calculated to give him. I think I have turned their works, & my resolutions have passed the Senate unanimously & will pass the House also. [George] McDuffie has denounced them—he being for disunion immediately, but he has lost his weight. Mr. Calhoun has written the best of letters to [Franklin H.] Elmore & it has *annoyed his professed friends* very much. Be careful of [James] Gadsden. I told you years ago I doubted him. He is wrong at heart—& deeply involved. Your member [Armistead] Burt was here & he is at bottom ag[ain]st Calhoun to[o]. I never saw it clearly[?] before. [John A.] Stuart now openly says he wishes to know "if the State is to lick Calhoun['s] toes forever?"—the same is said by the Gov:—& their clique upon the floor of the House—"ask if he is to hold So. Ca. in his hands to offer her in market to the highest bid[d]er"?

We must have a split. We have bought out the [Charleston Southern] Patriot & will start a new paper called the So. Ca. Republican with good editors ["true" *canceled*]. In great haste but affectionately, F.W. Pickens.

ALS in ScU-SC, Francis W. Pickens Papers.

From Ch[arle]s H. Todd & Co.

New York [City], Dec[embe]r 7th 1844
Sir, We had the honour of addressing you on the 8th Oct[obe]r last, on the subject of a claim we have on the Mexican Government, and have since been favoured with the reply of the Acting Secretary, Mr. [Richard K.] Crallé, under date of the 22d idem, stating that there is a Convention between the U.S. and Mexico, soon to be held, before which our claim had better be laid.

We shall be duly prepared to bring the claim before this Convention, and in the mean time, we beg leave to transmit to you to be placed on file, Copies of the Invoices, and statement shewing the loss we sustained by being excluded from the market, in addition to the positive loss entailed by the disability of selling at a higher rate than the Nett Cost in the U.S.: a disability enforced by the Provincial Government [of Yucatan] as a condition of entry, under threat of confiscation.

It was in vain that Capt[ai]n [Henry W.] Holmes contended with the authorities at Merida, that he consulted the Mexican chargé at Washington, as to the admissibility of the articles composing the Cargo of the Henry Leeds, and was assured they were admissible; the recent enactment was taken advantage of to condemn the Cargo, or insist on its being sold at a positive loss.

It appears to be a peculiar feature of the Mexican Government to pay very little regard to the rights of Citizens of the U.S. Our property is often seized and sequestered in the most arbitrary manner, and on the most frivolous and unwarrantable pretexts, and it would appear to be the duty of our Government to insist on a rigid indemnity, and a proper respect for our Flag. We have the honour to remain, with great respect Sir, Your obed[ien]t Serv[an]ts, Chs. H. Todd & Co.

P.S. The Invoices are in the name of Hale & Todd, Baltimore. We have since closed our House there, and transferred the interest here, where the persons composing the firm are the same. Chs. H. Todd & Co.

LS in DNA, RG 76 (Records of Boundary and Claims Commissions and Arbitrations), Records of U.S. and Mexican Claims Commissions.

From F[RANCIS] M. DIMOND

Washington, 8th Dec[embe]r 1844

Sir, I had the honor previous to my leaving Vera Cruz, to receive your letter, asking for information respecting the capture and condemnation of the Schooner Vigilant.

That vessel was brought into Vera Cruz for an alleged violation of the Yucatan Blockade. It appeared by the protest sworn to by the master and crew, that said vessel sailed from New Orleans with a cargo of flour and corn bound for Baliz[e] Honduras, and that the day after her departure she run against a floating log, which caused her to leak badly, and which induced the Captain to make for the first port in the Gulf, and after making the coast of Yucatan, was captured, by a Mexican man of war and sent into Vera Cruz.

The ostensible reason however, for sending her in was, that she was suspected of having on board contraband of war.

But according to the statement of the Captain, I felt perfectly sure she would have been given up after she was examined, as he had sworn, that he had no knowledge of the Blockade, neither had the Vessel any contraband of war on board.

There was nothing found on board, of that nature, and the vessel and cargo, would have been given up had they not discovered in the Log Book written by the Mate of the vessel, setting forth that the day previous to their capture, they had been spoken by a Mexican man of war and ordered off.

And to get over this statement of the mate the Captain and the mate himself declared, to me, that when the mate came on deck to take charge of ["the" *canceled*] his morning watch, he understood the Captain to say "he had been spoken, and ordered off" and made the corresponding record in the Log book. On this proof the vessel was condemned.

But in my communication to the tribunals, I observed, if Commodore Lopez would declare that this vessel, had been informed of the Blockade and ordered off by any of his Fleet, I would give up that point, but *should* then most assuredly claim for *this* v[e]ssel that hospitality ceded by all christian nations, of offering shelter and aid to those who by stress of weather, had been driven on the coast, and that they were morally bound to render such assistance as the exigency of the case required. Nevertheless, she was with her cargo condemned and confiscated. A claim might be sustained on the evidence of distress, which I will make out as strong as I can, on my arrival at Vera Cruz. I have the honor to be Sir, most respectfully Your Ob[edien]t Serv[an]t, F.M. Dimond, Consul U.S. Vera Cruz.

ALS (No. 150) in DNA, RG 59 (State Department), Consular Despatches, Vera Cruz, vol. 5 (M-183:5); copy in DNA, RG 76 (Records of Boundary and Claims Commissions and Arbitrations), Records of United States and Mexican Claims Commissions. Note: A Clerk's EU reads "Copy sent to Mr. [William] Bevan Dec[embe]r 13th."

From Duff Green

Washington [Texas,] 8th Dec[embe]r 1844
My dear Sir, I have now been here several days and have conversed with many of the most influential members of Congress. I find that upon the simple question of Annexation there is little or no difference of opinion. On the details there are many opposed to the late treaty— they insist that the payment of the debt was not properly or sufficiently provided for—that the boundary was not secured as it should have been, that thier [*sic*] land titles were not sufficiently protected and that proper provision for Education was not made. They say that having conquered the country they surrender every thing and gain nothing but an equivocal protection. These points they believe can be provided for & they believe that on the part of Texas there will be no unreasonable demand.

Gen[era]l [Samuel] Houston has had other views. If he were left to himself he would put on foot an offensive war. All his arguments go to show that his mind is occupied with the conquest of Mexico and the establishment of a new Republic. He goes freely into the comparison of the two propositions, annexation and conquest. All his remarks are appeals to the passions and interests which he desires to enlist in the conquest of Mexico, & when replied to, or when he finds that he has made the desired impression he says that nothing shall tempt him from his retirement. He is enthusiastic, poetical in the description of his domestic happiness and says that notwithstanding all that has been said he is for annexation. It is easy to read all this—and I can see where it will end if the Congress of the United States delay the question beyond the *next* session. To press the question now and to fail would ["do" *interlined*] injury. If the press and our public men discuss the question properly & the Government keeps the question open, no injury will, in my opinion result from the delay until the *next* session of Congress, because they are prepared here to await the action of public opinion upon the *new* Congress.

In the mean time as the only serious impediment to annexation is to be found in the ulterior aspirations of Gen[era]l Houston, I deem it fortunate that Major Donaldson [*sic*; Andrew J. Donelson] came when he did. Armed as he was by letters from Gen[era]l [Andrew] Jackson, knowing Houston and his early history, he has used arguments and urged considerations which no one else could have done with the same effect and neutralised if he has not eradicated the purpose of Mexican conquest. Gen[era]l Houston will leave here in a few days, and has declared himself in favor of annexation, saying that Texas can do nothing but await the action of the United States.

I therefore consider the question as safe so far as Texas is concerned. She will do nothing for the next year at least that will prevent annexation.

In the mean time I am by no means sure that it will be for the interest of the United States or of Texas that the question should be closed *now*. The effort of the opposition will be to organise the north against the south—Abolition—the tariff, and native Republicanism, against South Carolina. If the new administration [of James K. Polk], keeps the Texas question as one of the measures for the new organisation of parties, it will give the administration strength, and the success of the measure will be an administration triumph which will go far to establish its power. Of this you can judge better than I. I make the suggestion, subject to your better judgment.

The people of Texas will never consent to annexation on Mr. [Thomas H.] Benton's terms, and his reelection will go far to defeat the measure, unless they can be induced to believe that the next Congress will favor annexation on the terms I have indicated.

I repeat that I do not wish my name [as Consul at Galveston] sent before the Senate, until I reach home which will be in all[?] the month of January. Yours truly, Duff Green.

P.S. Gen[era]l Houston has taken occasion to treat me with great attention, has invited me to his house and expressed a great personal respect and a wish to be on friendly terms.

ALS in ScCleA; PC in Jameson, ed., *Correspondence*, pp. 1006–1007. NOTE: An AEU by Green on the address sheet reads "Will the Consul at Galveston forward this per steamer N. York & oblige . . ."

From JAMES [EDWARD CALHOUN]

University of Virginia, Dec. 9th 1844

Dear father, I have taken this early opportunity of acknowledging the receipt of your letter handed a few days ago, containing the agre[e]able information of the good health you have all enjoyed with the exception of Mother's [Floride Colhoun Calhoun's] slight indisposition subsequent to my leaving Washington, together with the much needed advise [*sic*] respecting the regulation of my expenses, contracting good habits, and improvement of time, which have it affords me the greatest pleasure to say been conformed to. After paying the fees of the Professors with the boarding bill and many other things that a student is required to pay for in advance, out of the $200 you requested me to deposit in the hands of the Proctor [Willis H. Woodley], found there remained only a few dollars which have been expended in books and other necessaries that I have been obliged to purchase, placing me under the necessity of either applying to the Chairman of the Faculty or yourself for money, and in consequence of having to pay four or six per cent on receiving it from the former, have had recou[r]se to you. I will therefore be much obliged to you, if you would remit me as soon as convenient $150, which although being more than necessary to meet my present expenses, shall be deposited in the hands of the Proctor, from whom we are permitted to draw pocket money not exceeding $6 per month. By applying so soon for money you may infer that I have not economised but by reference to the table enclosed in this letter you will find by the addition of books &c this to be a much more expensive institution than you had supposed.

It gave me great pleasure to have you mention my improvement in writing, and could console myself with the belief that I would continue to improve, since it is an acquirement to be obtained by practice, of which my correspondence would afford me sufficient, if time was allowed me for taking pains which is so essential to one's becoming skillful.

With your letter was received the President[']s [John Tyler's] message, which I have read, with a letter from Mr. [Joseph A.] Scoville with information respecting the prices of the books I intended purchasing, and the cloak for Rob[er]t Maxwell. Tell him I am much obliged to him for the trouble he has taken in pricing them, but finding that both the books and cloak can be purchased in Charlott[e]sville as cheap if not cheaper, and seeing that I can do without them, would be unwilling to purchase at the prices in Washington.

You informed me, that Patrick [Calhoun] had arrived and intends remaining in Washington this winter, and that Johny [*sic*; John C. Calhoun, Jr.] had de[s]cended the Mississippi river on his way to brother Andrew's [Andrew Pickens Calhoun's in Ala.], that his cough was much better, and his being so pleased with his excursion; but omitted mentioning the success he met with in hunting in the West. I hope your answer or a letter from Patrick will relate this in part.

I have written to several at Pendleton, and among them Willy [William Lowndes Calhoun], but have not yet received answers. I must here conclude, my time and space being pretty much exhausted. Give my love to all and tell them to write me often, and send the papers after reading them. I would have written mother and sister [Martha Cornelia Calhoun] before this, had my time been less engaged, but having entered so late in the session, and no allowances being made for my doing so, compells me to employ most of my time in studying, and therefore hope they will ["not attribute" *interlined*] my long delay to neglect, but on the contrary, to the want of time, letting a letter to one answer for all. Your affectionate son, James.

ALS in ScCleA.

To [WILLIE P. MANGUM], President Pro Tempore of the Senate, and [JOHN W. JONES], Speaker of the House of Representatives

Department of State
Washington, Dec. 9th 1844

Sir, Agreeably to the Act of the 2d of March 1799, I have the honor to Communicate an Abstract of all the returns made to this Department, by the Collectors of Customs, pursuant to the Act of the 28th of May 1796, for the releif [*sic*] and protection of American Seamen registered in each port of entry, of the United States, during the year Commencing October 1st 1843, and ending September 30th 1844. I am, Sir, respectfully, Your obedient Servant, J.C. Calhoun.

LS (to Mangum) in DNA, RG 46 (U.S. Senate), 28A-F1; LS (to Jones) in DNA, RG 233 (U.S. House of Representatives), 28A-F1; FC in DNA, RG 59 (State Department), Reports of the Secretary of State to the President and Congress, 6:127; FC in DNA, RG 59 (State Department), Domestic Letters, 35:41 (M-40:33); variant PC with Ens in House Document No. 12, 28th Cong., 2nd Sess., pp. 1–6.

To [WILLIE P. MANGUM], President Pro Tempore of the Senate, and [JOHN W. JONES], Speaker of the House of Representatives

Department of State
Washington, Dec. 9th 1844

Sir, I have the honor to transmit, herewith, Statements Showing the number and designation of the passengers who have arrived in each Collection District of the United States, during the three first Quarters of the year 1843—and the year commencing 1st October 1843, and ending 30th September 1844, according to the returns made to the Secretary of State, pursuant to the Act of Congress of the 2d of March 1819 regulating passenger Ships and vessels.

It has been the Custom, heretofore, to render these Statements to Congress for the year beginning the 1st of January and ending the 31st of December; but the Department was unable to Complete such a Statement for the last year, in time to transmit to Congress, owing to the failure on the part of some of the Collectors to make their returns in due Season. To avoid this delay, I have thought proper to make the Statements embrace the year from the 1st of October to the 30th of September, which will give ample time to the Collectors to make Complete returns prior to the meeting of Congress. I am very respectfully Your ob[edien]t Ser[van]t, J.C. Calhoun.

LS (to Mangum) in DNA, RG 46 (U.S. Senate), 28A-F1; LS (to Jones) in DNA, RG 233 (U.S. House of Representatives), 28A-F1; FC in DNA, RG 59 (State Department), Reports of the Secretary of State to the President and Congress, 6:127; FC in DNA, RG 59 (State Department), Domestic Letters, 35:42–[43] (M-40:33); PC with En in House Document No. 13, 28th Cong., 2nd Sess., pp. 1–50.

From ALFRED SCHÜCKING

Washington, Dec. 9th [18]44
Dear Sir, If you will not consider it obtrusive, that I should venture to offer to your notice occasional extracts from the leading organ of the German population in our country, considering that on account of its idiom it is not likely to come under your observation in any other way: I beg you to view it as arising from an excusable wish not to permit to remain entirely concealed from you my continuous efforts, (hardly intermitted a week for more than two years,) to make the German population in advance of a contingency, now, I trust, not very distant, fully acquainted with one, whose exalted bearing I find them ["generally" *interlined*] so well prepared to appreciate.

Being the founder of an efficient German paper in the South (at N[ew] Orleans) imparting zeal by my strenuous efforts as principal collabor[at]er to the leading organ in the North (at New York; which being flagging some time before the election I am happy to be told by others that much of the activity of the German citizens in the late election is ascribed to my timely and stirring succour)—and being disposed, if encouraged, to assume the management of a new central organ of the Germ[an] population, in this city—if practical[,] political and personal devotion (whatever the ability may be, it suffices to know the efficiency) confer any claims, I do not yield in my claims to any man, though natural modesty and respect for you and myself may forbid my urging them with the same assurance and impetuosity. Nor would I under any circumstances, but for the stringency of familiar considerations and the evident liability to be undeservedly underrated and run over, ever render my sincerity suspected by adverting to them.

All I have to regret, therefore, as an impediment in the way of my success, is, that my very inferior official position, (conferred upon me by Mr. [John C.] Spencer, *if* with his advice as to the grade assigned in the office, certainly under the impression, that my *then* connection with the German papers furnished me additional emoluments, which I never realized to any extent) does not afford better evidence to my German-American countrymen of the approbation of one, whose endorsement would be considered as preeminently honorable by them as encouraging by me. I have the honor to be Sir, with profound respect Your obed[ien]t Serv[an]t, Alfred Schücking.

[P.S.] If the newspaper herewith [sent] should be of no further interest to you I respectfully beg its being returned to me, to be sent to Europe. A.S.

ALS in ScCleA.

From WILSON SHANNON

Legation of the U.S. of A.
Mexico, December 9th 1844
Sir, We are now in the midst of a revolution which has already prostrated the Government of Santa Anna and carried consternation into the ranks of his few remaining friends.

On the 5th Inst. the people of this city rose almost in mass and rushed to the great central square in front of the palace. Two of the Regiments pronounced against Santa Anna and the Gover[n]ment and declared for the revolution. Gen[era]l [Valentín] Canalizo the acting president, ordered the remaining troops belonging to the Government, about fifteen hundred strong, to march against the revolutionary party, and prepared to put himself at their head. They refused to obey orders and declared for the revolution, having been bought over, it is said, the night before. The military having abandoned the Government it was left powerless. The revolutionary party, headed by the military, instantly marched on the palace, took the acting president and a portion of the ministers prisoners, the others having made their escape. They are still held in confinement to undergo their trial. What will be their fate I am unable to say. The people after having taken possession of the palace and the Gover[n]ment, marched to the Santa Anna theatre, broke it open, tore down the splendid statue that had been erected to the honor of Santa

511

Anna, fastened a rope round its neck and dragged it through the streets and finally broke it into pieces. A similar statue, but made of much more costly materials had been erected in the market square; it was also tore down and removed but not destroyed. The cry of the people was "death to Santa Anna[,]," death "to the robbers," ["]live Gen[era]l [Mariano] Paredes." The city of Puebla, the second in the Republic, has also pronounced against Santa Anna and a similar scene took place there, to that which was enacted here. The whole country appears to be rising against President Santa Anna, who has yet more than four years of his presidential term to serve under the constitution. He marched some time since, at the head of about ten thousand troops, to put down Gen[era]l Paredes, who had pronounced against him in Guadalaxara a city some four hundred miles distant from Mexico. He had got about one hundred and forty miles on his march, when the transactions that I have stated took place here and in the city of Puebla. It is expected that he will immediately march on this city with his whole military force and his friends expect him in six or eight days. If his troops remain faithful to him he may take the capital and again place himself in power. The regular military force here does not exceed twenty five hundred. The revolutionary party, however, are enrolling volunteers, and bringing on reinforcements and making vigorous preparations to defend themselves. It is said Santa Anna will never yield while there is any hopes of success. The revolutionary party have organized a new Government for the time being. Mr. [José J. de] Herrera is in the exercise of the presidential functions and Mr. [Luis G.] Cuevas fills the office of Secretary of foreign relations. The city remains at this time quiet and will probably continue so until the approach of Santa Anna. At that time all expect a severe conflict—one in which each party will fight not so much for power as for life. Should the present Government continue in power the contributions, levied for the purpose of raising the four millions to carry on the war against Texas, will be repealed, as the party now in power are pledged to that measure. No one now thinks of Texas or the reconquest of that country. All other questions are absorbed in that of the revolution. Mexico instead of being able to govern Texas would seem to be entirely incapable of governing herself.

While I am writing the mail brings the news that Veracruz and the castle have declared against Santa Anna. This, if true will greatly weaken his position. I have the honor to be Yours with great respect, Wilson Shannon.

LS (No. 6) in DNA, RG 59 (State Department), Diplomatic Despatches, Mexico, vol. 12 (M-97:13), received 1/25/1845; FC in DNA, RG 84 (Foreign Posts), Mexico, Despatches; CC in DNA, RG 46 (U.S. Senate), 28A-F1.

From WILSON SHANNON, "Private"

Legation of the U.S. of A.

Mexico, Dec. 9, 1844

D[ea]r Sir, I have this day drawn a draft in favour of John Patten Esq. of St. Clairsville Ohio for the sum of $1500, in part of my salary. It will probably be presented for payment in Feb. next.

I send herewith a number of letters and have to request Mr. [Richard K.] Cralle to transmit them to their respective places of destination. Also a paper directed to B.F. Brown Esq., Huron Co[unty] Ohio.

I am waiting with some anxiety the receipt of instructions from home. I think it is exceedingly doubtful which party will be in power by the time Mr. [Ben E.] Green returns. Should the present party retain power I think they will be better disposed towards the U.S. than Santa Anna and his party. They will undoubtedly be anxious to avoid a rupture with the U.S.

I received some days since, the gratifying intel[l]igence of the election of Col. Polke [*sic*; James K. Polk] to the presidency. I have no doubt he will be desireous to retain you in your present place. I hope you will consent to remain. It is a strong position and one that your friends would prefer seeing you occupy, to any other—and it would promote their ultimate views with regard to your self. Permit me to suggest the policy of sending Gen[era]l [Lewis] Cass, Minister to England. I think it is an appointment with which he would be pleased. It would satisfy his friends and remove or at least diminish the danger of a conflict in the Democratic ranks in [18]48.

I do not desire to remain longer in Mexico than the public interest may require. In the present unsettled state of the country I could not think of bringing my family here and I am unwilling to remain any great length of time absent from them.

Be pleased to give my respects to Mr. Green. I would write to him but am uncertain whether he is yet in Washington. Yours with great respect, Wilson Shannon.

ALS in ScCleA.

From Israel D. Andrews, [U.S. Consul], St. John, New Brunswick, 12/10. "I beg leave to hand you a copy of the 'Debates of the House of Assembly of the Province of New Brunswick during the session of 1844' a copy of 'An Act Relating to the Collection of Duty on Timber and other Lumber' Exported from this Province to Great Britain and Foreign Countries—also a blank Bond to be lodged at the Provincial Treasury Department before permission is granted to load any Vessel with Lumber." ALS (No. 17) with printed Ens in DNA, RG 59 (State Department), Consular Despatches, St. John, vol. 2 (T-485:1).

From VESPASIAN ELLIS

Legation of the United States
Caracas, Dec[embe]r 10th 1844

Sir, I reached Laguayra on the 27th Ult. & Caracas on the 28th, presented my credentials to [Juan Manuel Manrique] the Minister of Foreign Affairs, on the 29th, & had an interview with President [Carlos] Soublette, by a special appointment, on the 4th of this month. In this interview, I assured the President, of the deep concern felt by the Government & people of the United States, in all that relates to the interest and prosperity of Venezuela; & was answered by him, that this friendly feeling on the part of the U.S. was reciprocated by the Government & people of this Country.

On the 8th instant, I had a longer & more interesting interview with Pres[iden]t Soublette, in which I made many enquiries, touching the late & existing Commotions, in Venezuela. He properly appreciated the motives, which led me to seek the information adverted to, & being satisfied, that the government of the U.S. are now looking with much anxiety, upon the progress of political Revolutionary movements, in this Country, he went fully, & at large into the subject. He admits, that there is cause for some alarm and apprehension, that tumults, outbreaks & riots, will prevail in different portions of the Country, at intervals, for many months—that there are many restless & ambitious spirits, who are constantly exciting & feeding the prejudices of the people, against the present administration—& that they have endeavored, & are still endeavoring, to array the black population, *as a class,* against the government. He admits, that unless these rebellious & reckless leaders, shall be signally defeated in their attempts, as often as made, *a war between the races* may be ere long produced. He entertains however, no manner of doubt, that the government will be able, promptly to suppress these rebellions, & maintain its authority. Nevertheless, he is of the opinion, that prudence requires, on the part of those nations, whose citizens are engaged in business operations here, a preparation for their protection; & especially does he regard it as ["a" *interlined*] very proper course for them, to direct their Vessels of War, to touch at Laguayra, as often as convenient. This opinion was ["given" *interlined*] in response to my own suggestions to him, upon the subject. Under these circumstances, and as a measure of prudence, I repeat the advice of my predecessor [Allen A. Hall], on this point. If our armed vessels, cruising in the West Indies, & frequenting the Atlantic Coast of South America, would occasionally show themselves at Laguayra, & if their officers would visit Caracas, it would, at least, have the effect, of warning the discontented spirits of this Country, that the United States have both the power, & the purpose, to protect the lives & property of their citizens, if endangered by internal broils & civil strife, in the Country of their temporary residence; and it is more than probable too, that it would tend to check & restrain this spirit of rebellion, which has been, in some degree encouraged, by the assurances of the leaders of the "*liberals*," that the people of the U.S. sympathise with them! Indeed it has been said, and *published*, in the papers devoted to the cause of the disorganizers, within the last few days, that the United States, had *just elected an abolitionist* for their President!! This error, I caused, through others, to be corrected, as its tendency was obviously to encourage & embolden the leaders of the "liberal" party.

President Soublette very frankly assured me, that I should be immediately advised, if any thing occurred to change his present opinions, of the ultimate ["fate" *canceled and* "result" *interlined*] of the rebellions. In this conversation, I considered the major portion of his remarks, as made with the *expectation* that they would not be ["made public" *canceled and* "published" *interlined*]. His general information & acknowledged talents, entitle his opinions to much weight, and I therefore adopt the opinion, that the danger to the free institutions of this Country, is *not* imminent. Nevertheless, there are many intelligent citizens of Caracas, who apprehend "a war of the races" here, at no very distant period. They say, that the administration is unpopular—that great injustice has been done to the officers of the Revolution, in the reduction of their pay—in depriving them of command &c &c—that the Constitution has been violated in the creation of a National Bank—that the benefits of this bank are not extended to the planting interest—(which preponderates here) that the interests & happiness of the people are not consulted; and many other like complaints are made. They say, that there must be & *will be* a revolution. Such are the opinions of a great number of intelligent men in this City.

The truth is, that there is no *general* intelligence & information amongst the people, & hence no man can judge, how they will act, in reference to questions of political excitement. The *leaders alone* possess information. Education is extremely limited. The main body of the people are *honest*, but ignorant. They are strong, but blind. The probable action of such a people, is not to be foretold. I dismiss this topic, referring you however to the several communications of my predecessor, from May to October, on the same subject, for ["*his*" *canceled*] the result of *his* observation & knowledge, of Spanish American character.

I will add however, that I do not believe the primary or even the ultimate object, of the leaders of the rebellions, is to give the political ascendancy to the *blacks*. The leaders are the rash, reckless & disappointed spirits of the *Minority party*, in the Country. Their object is political power, but they have imprudently addressed themselves to the prejudices of the *blacks*, without enquiring whether they can themselves control this element, when brought into action. The fear is, that the blacks will ascertain their own strength, and take advantage of the position they will occupy.

I have had several conversations with persons holding stations in this government, touching the tariff. The power to lay duties is vested in Congress here, as in the U.S. and the Executive can only recommend the changes he desires. It is admitted by all, that the duties upon American productions, are unjust, & by no means reciprocal. I shall address a communication to the Minister of Foreign Affairs, in a few days, showing the want of reciprocity on the subject, and urging a reduction of the onerous duties, and shall bring about such action, in regard to it, as will result, I think, in a modification of the present tariff.

The payment of the claim of the "Morris," was made known to you by my predecessor, in his despatch of October 10th, and ["*that*" *canceled*] the claim of the owners of the "Good Return" ["*had*" *altered to* "has"] been presented to the Minister of Foreign Affairs, for his consideration. It was submitted by Mr. Hall on the 15th October, & is now pending.

The flag furnished by your predecessor, at the instance of Mr. Hall, was made of *fine silk*, and is not suited to the purposes for which it was intended. If hoisted upon the staff, over the office of the le-

gation, it would not last one week. It *may* become important, in the
event of further outbreaks, to exhibit one occasionally, as is *now* done
by other legations, and I suggest, that one be sent at your earliest
convenience, which shall be made of good & strong materials, & of
a very moderate size, say 4 by 12 ft. I understand that the Messrs.
Dallett Brothers, of Philadelphia, have now three regular packets, &
will by the 1st January have *four* packets, trading to Laguayra, & that
one of them will regularly leave Philadelphia on the 1st & 15th of
each month. If you would give directions for my letters & papers to
be sent to them on the 13th & 29th of each month, it would establish
a prompt & periodical intercourse with this legation.

My communications to your department dated at Washington
Oct[obe]r 10th and at Philadelphia Oct. 26th & Nov[embe]r 6th
should be numbered 1, 2 & 3.

I have heretofore drawn in favor of Corcoran & Riggs of Washington City, for my quarter[']s salary ending on the 30th of this
month, payable when due.

No despatches of any kind, have reached me, since my arrival at
Caracas.

The word "liberals," used by me in reference to the disturbances
in this Country, denotes a *party* & has no relation to any *principle*. I
have the honor to be, with great respect, your ob[edient] Serv[an]t,
Vespasian Ellis, U.S. Charge &c.

ALS (No. 4) in DNA, RG 59 (State Department), Diplomatic Despatches,
Venezuela, vol. 2 (M-79:3), received 1/11/1845.

From Grinnell, Minturn & Co., New York [City], 12/10. Having
been requested by William B. Taylor to attest to his standing in the
New York mercantile community, Grinnell, Minturn & Co. affirm that
Taylor has been "for more than twenty years in connexion with the
Post Office in this City." Because of his integrity and efficiency Taylor
deserves a more responsible position [as U.S. Despatch Agent at New
York City]. LS in DNA, RG 59 (State Department), Applications
and Recommendations, 1837–1845, Taylor (M-687:32, frames 119–
121).

From J[AMES] C. PICKETT

Legation of the U. States
Lima, Dec[embe]r 10, 1844

Sir: I transmit herewith, a copy of a correspondence between the Peruvian Minister of Foreign Affairs [Matias Leon] and myself, relative to the Convention of the 17th of March 1841, for the adjustment of certain claims of citizens of the U. States.

In my last despatch I express the opinion that Peru ought to be coerced at once, into the payment of those claims and that not less than four hundred thousand dollars should be demanded. Or some satisfactory arrangement ought to be insisted on, at least; which might be effected I think, by blockading the Peruvian ports or by seizing Peruvian vessels. I have mentioned these measures in my 38th number—not with much approbation however, and still I would recommend them only as a last resort. A blockade of the port of Callao might produce the desired effect in a few days, or the government might hold out some time. This would depend almost entirely upon the character of the chief exercising the supreme command at the time.

What would be better perhaps than a resort either to a blockade or to reprisals, would be to embargo the islands, fifty or sixty leagues from Lima, that furnish the article called *huano* [*sic*; guano; "of" *interlined*] which I have spoken in some of my despatches. Huano when first exported to England, sold at about ninety dollars the ton: Afterwards it fell to 35 dollars and even lower. It has advanced somewhat of late however, though no very material amendment in price can be expected, so long as the article continues to be imported from Africa and sold lower, as it now is. Consequently, *huano* cannot be relied upon here, as it was three or four years ago, as a source from which to derive any very important addition to the public revenue. It was asserted in England at one time to be injurious to the soil; but this must have been a mistake. It is adapted to all soils, no doubt, and to all productions; as a manure there is nothing superior to it and nothing equal perhaps. The quantity in Peru has been estimated at from forty to ninety millions of tons, the lowest estimate being I suppose, nearest the truth. The exportation of it is now in the hands of a private company, (of foreigners) but this of course would be no obstacle to the embargo of the islands by a foreign govt.

The Minister of Foreign Affairs says (Nos. 5 & 9 of the inclosures) that the Convention will be submitted to the next Congress for its approval: But when the Congress will meet is very uncertain. The 9th of this month was fixed upon at first for the meeting; but the elections in the South having taken place under a decree of Gen. [Ramon] Castilla's government, one chamber only was elected—["the House of Representatives" *canceled*] which was intended for a constituent congress. In the ["North," *interlined*] a Senate and House of Representatives have been chosen, as the Constitution prescribes, and Gen. Castilla having submitted to the govt. at Lima, the elections in the South have to be corrected, and to correct them will require at least two months. But should a Congress be convened, I am not sure that the Convention will be submitted to it in good faith; or if it should be and should be approved, I have not the slightest hope that the instalments due will be paid. The fiscal embarrassments of the government here, ever increasing and apparently incurable, will be an obstacle to payment, and besides, the executive chiefs have generally a great aversion to paying foreign claims—some of them, because they *are* foreign, and some, because they would consider the amount paid as so much taken from their own official perquisites, for they are almost all charged with peculating, and the imputation does not in general do them much injustice, I am inclined to believe. If Gen. Castilla should reach the Presidential chair and continue to occupy it some time, he may pay the claims possibly; but I am not sanguine. He is considered to be honest about money matters, as I have said elsewhere, and as he is poor and not extravagant and has had many opportunities of plundering and has abstained, it is fair to presume that he deserves the reputation he enjoys—one enjoyed by but few of the military men in Peru. He is by no means faultless though.

In Mr. Leon's note of the 30th of Nov[embe]r (No. 9) there is some error and some tergiversation, which I have let pass, besides noticing some; thinking it better to do so, than to engage in an angry and unprofitable discussion—unprofitable, because I should have got no money for the claimants, my fellow-citizens, by it; about which, I feel much more solicitude than about getting the better of the Minister in an argument—a victory which if achieved would benefit nobody. I have the honor to be, with great respect, Your Ob[edien]t Servant, J.C. Pickett.

ALS (No. 106) with Ens in DNA, RG 59 (State Department), Diplomatic Despatches, Peru, vol. 6 (T-52:6, frames 602–631), received 3/5/1845.

From S[ARAH] C[OLES] STEVENSON

The Retreat, Dec[embe]r 10th 1844
Near Richmond

My dear Sir, May I ask the favour of you to send the enclosed letters in your next Dispatch bag to [Edward Everett] our Minister at London? as I am anxious my friends in England should receive them as soon as possible; and may I venture to say, that it would very much add to my obligation, if you would do me the kindness to *frank* my English letters, that come in your Dispatch bag. I am, with very great respect, yours truly, S.C. Stevenson.

ALS in ScCleA. NOTE: The writer was the wife of Andrew Stevenson who had been U.S. Minister to Great Britain during 1836–1841.

From Moses Taylor, New York [City], 12/10. "I have been acquainted with Mr. W[illia]m B. Taylor for the last 20 years during the most of the time he has been Connected with the Post Office department in this City. I believe him to be an Honourable high minded man & on account of his Gentlemanly deportment & Business talents as well as quickness, he is peculiarly Calculated for any situation requiring despatch." [Taylor was an applicant for U.S. Despatch Agent at New York City.] ALS in DNA, RG 59 (State Department), Applications and Recommendations, 1837–1845, Taylor (M-687:32, frames 122–123).

From JUNIUS A. WINGFIELD and GABRIEL HARRISON

Eatonton Geo[rgia,] Dec[embe]r 10th 1844

Dear Sir, Understanding that there is a vacancy in the Consulship at Tangiers, we have thought proper to lay before you the claims of our friend John D. Diomatari Esq[ui]r[e] for that post, and take great pleasure in recommending them to your favourable consideration. If we should be mistaken as to the fact of such vacancy and as it is the desire of our friend to get a Consulship at some one of the ports of the Mediterranean we would be obliged, if it should suit your pleasure to consider his among the applications for any port of that sort in that quarter.

Mr. Diomatari is a native of Greece. When quite a boy and during the last war between Turkey & his native country he was brought to our shores on board the Constitution one of our Naval vessels. He very soon became the Protegé of Mess[rs]. [James] Gadsden, Dessausure [*sic*; Henry W. DeSaussure?] and Tho[ma]s S. Grimké of Charleston. He was educated according to the wishes of his patrons in the best schools of South Carolina & Georgia; having received his preparatory education in Carolina and graduated at our own University [of Ga.]. Since leaving College about eight years ago he has been in active employment in our own & the adjacent counties; and we know his qualifications for business to be of a superior order. His profession is that of the Law. So much we have thought fit to say of his history[,] education etc.

We can add to the above that he has not a feeling which is alien to the interests & the well being of the South—the home of his adoption. And there is no man among us who is more of a Southern man in feeling. The fact that he *is* from the South we hope in connection with his qualifications will give additional weight to his application. We think that it should do so. No man knows better than yourself how unequally the patronage of the Government has been distributed between the North & the South in times past. Please refer to the Hon[ora]ble Howell Cobb [Representative from Ga.] if you can consider this application and he will confirm the foregoing statements and give you any other information which you may desire. Very Respectfully, Junius A. Wingfield, Gabriel Harrison.

LS in DNA, RG 59 (State Department), Applications and Recommendations, 1837–1845, Diomatari (M-687:9, frames 275–278).

From Silas Wood, [former Representative from N.Y.], New York [City], 12/10. Wood recommends W[illiam] B. Taylor for appointment as Despatch Agent at New York City. "I have long known Mr. Taylor as one of the most efficient and obliging Officers in our Post Office, and of irreproachable moral character." ALS in DNA, RG 59 (State Department), Applications and Recommendations, 1837–1845, Taylor (M-687:32, frames 117–118).

From CLEMENT C. BIDDLE, "Private"

Philadelphia, 11th December 1844
My dear Sir, On the 22nd of November, at the particular request of Judge [Edward] King, I felt myself bound to bear my testimony to

you in his behalf; and accordingly stated, in my letter to you, what I well knew to be here universally acknowledged, his great abilities on the bench, shown in all his decisions. My own preference, however, was for another gentleman, known also to me as an able, enlightened and upright lawyer; who, moreover, was well grounded in those principles of political economy, essential in my opinion to the proper adjudication of the highest questions under the federal compact, which involve the rights of the sovereign parties who formed it, and the eternal principles of justice, the establishment of which can alone secure its preservation and perpetuity.

We are now informed that Judge King *has* been nominated to the Senate, and most probably will be confirmed. My object is not, in any way, to interfere with the result of the nomination; but to state to you, what I have been informed, from a quarter on which I can rely, that if the nomination be *postponed* until after the *third* Tuesday in January next, when Governor [Francis R.] Shunk will be inaugurated, the vacan[c]y produced by Judge King's elevation to the Supreme Court, may be supplied by Mr. George Sharswood, a gentleman in every way well calculated to fill Judge King's place, with satisfaction to our Bar, and at the same time, a warm and able champion of "State Rights" and "Free Trade," who gave his support from the moment of his nomination, to Mr. [James K.] Polk. When Mr. [Condy] Raguet retired from the Examiner, a few months before its close, he gave the editorial department to Mr. Sharswood, knowing him to be thoroughly indoctrinated with the principles he was advocating, and well qualified to sustain them.

I have read, with great gratification, your two letters to Mr. [William R.] King and to Mr. [Wilson] Shannon, and should like to receive them in pamphlet form for preservation. The annexation, I trust will not be further postponed, the time for action is arrived. I go for the annexation of Texas to preserve and strengthen our confederation, to prevent consolidation, from the concentration and cooperation of class interests, and above all as a certain means of enlarging and establishing the most perfect freedom of trade, compatible with a tariff of revenue. No state papers, in my recollection, have produced the same sensation, as your powerfully argued and conclusive letters. With perfect respect always most faithfully yours, Clement C. Biddle.

ALS in ScCleA. NOTE: Clement Cornell Biddle (1784–1853) was engaged in banking and industrial activities in Philadelphia, at times as an associate of Condy Raguet and Richard Peters. Though of Quaker origins, his father had been a Colonel in the American Revolution, and Clement C. Biddle himself had been an officer in the War of 1812.

From W[illia]m Brent, Jr.

Buenos Ayres
Legation of the U. States
December 11th 1844

Sir, I avail myself of the opportunity afforded by the return of Hon[or-a]ble H[arvey] M. Watterson to announce to you my arrival at this place. On the 15th of the last month I presented my credentials to [Felipe Arana] the Minister of Foreign Affairs, and was properly accredited.

The most friendly expressions of good will were made by him on the part of the Argentine Confederation towards the United States, and of a desire to strengthen the cords of friendship already subsisting between them. With this I most heartily reciprocated on the part of the United States. I expressed my regret lest recent occurrences might have had a tendency to produce disagre[e]able feelings, yet that I could not but believe that these, when properly examined and explained would ultimately have the effect of cementing the friendship already subsisting between the two countries.

To this the Minister assented, expressing his great confidence in the justice of the United States. From all that passed it was obvious that the affair of Capt. [Philip F.] Voorhees, (of which you have been advised by Mr. Watterson) had not produced any change in the friendly relations or feelings that had previously subsisted. I have the honor to be Your ob[edien]t ser[van]t, Wm. Brent, Jr.

LS in DNA, RG 59 (State Department), Diplomatic Despatches, Argentina, vol. 5 (M-69:6), received 2/27/1845; FC (No. 1) in DNA, RG 84 (Foreign Posts), Argentina, Correspondence with Embassy Officials, 1820–1881.

From M[aria] D[allas] Campbell

Girard Square, Chestnut St.
[Philadelphia] Dec[embe]r 11th 1844

My excellent friend, I have offered to Mr. [John] Randolph Tucker (the 3rd son of our mutual friend Judge H[enry] St. Geo[rge] Tucker) a passport to your more particular attention, than a mere formal introduction might procure him. I know your hopes of our young Americans, to be great & ardent, & I am persuaded, if you will take a little time to converse with this young scion of a goodly tree, you will find him worthy to interest you. He is *almost* as great an enthusiast upon *your* subject personally, & politically, as your *old* friend, who presents him to your notice, & who solicits for him a more than *casual* acquaintance. I will leave his intelligence, & truthful character to develope itself, I sincerely believe he will yet be one of Virginia's distinguished sons. He is just twenty one, & is about to pursue the practice of the law in Richmond. I am sure his father[']s name will ensure him your cordial welcome, & I only beg for him a *conversation* with you, more in detail, than you have leisure to bestow on the very young. As to my former letter [of 11/20], I am disposed to think, such a position as you name, would not probably offer any temptation, to the individual for whom I am interested, to quit home & its certain comforts to an invalid. Mr. [Alexander] Campbell unites in sincere regards to you, with your unchanged & unchangeable friend, M:D: Campbell.

ALS in ScCleA.

From [EDWARD STUBBS]

Dep[artment] of State, 11 Dec. 1844
Mem[orandum]: In 1842, Congress prohibited the employment, in any of the Departments, of extra clerks, except during the Session of that body, or, when such clerks should be indispensably necessary to enable the Department to answer a call, made by either House, ["at one session," *canceled*] at the next session. Under that prohibition clerks cannot be employed, or paid, except at the time, or, for the purpose specified. The necessity for the employment of extra clerks in the Department of State, does not altogether depend upon the contingency of Congress being in session, or of calls made at one session to be answered at the next. It frequently occurs that copying, to an extent beyond the capability of the Department's regular force, is required in the course of its diplomatic affairs: How is such copying to be procured or paid for? There can be no mode of doing so, unless the prohibition be removed, or the number of regular clerks be increased.

That an increased number of regular clerks is necessary may be inferred from the following exhibit:

In the year 1818, there were 7 foreign missions and 67 consulates, making the number of both 74. The Department had then 10 Clerks at an annual compensation of $13,400.

In the year 1827, there were 16 missions and 115 consulates, together 131—and there were 13 Clerks whose comp[ensatio]n was $17,000.

In 1844, with 24 missions and 177 consulates, aggregate 201 There are 14 clerks whose compensation is $19,250.

The great increase of business in the diplomatic and Consular Bureaux, required a corresponding increase of clerks. This was had by taking them from the home bureau. One of the branches of that bureau, that of Agent for disbursements and accounts, had, in 1829 and some subsequent years two clerks. It had at a later period one regular, and one temporary clerk. It has now but one. The increase in that branch of business has been as great as in that of any other in the Department, and it is not possible for one clerk to perform its multifarious and responsible duties, in a manner that would be advantageous to the Department and creditable to himself. He therefore respectfully suggests that an application may be made to Congress, for such an addition to the regular force of the Department as may preclude the necessity, unless upon extraordinary occasions, of employing extra clerks; and for a repeal of the restriction against the employment of the latter unless when Congress is in session: He also asks to be allowed, during the present session, to have, as heretofore, the aid of an extra clerk, who may, also, occasionally assist in making copies of such papers as may be called for.

ADU in ScCleA.

From John D. Van Buren, New York [City], 12/11. Van Buren withdraws an application he made a few days previous seeking the appointment of Michael B. Van Buren to be U.S. Consul at Puerto Cabello [Venezuela]. Intervening circumstances would prevent Van Buren from traveling to that post. ALS in DNA, RG 59 (State Department), Applications and Recommendations, 1837–1845, Van Buren (M-687:33, frames 110–111).

To Mrs. Sophia [Dallas] Bache, 12/12. "My dear Madam, In reply to your note, I am happy to be able to say, that, as far as I know, there is no foundation whatever for the rumour, that it was intended to remove Mr. [George W.] Lay [as U.S. Chargé d'Affaires in

Sweden]. Indeed, your note gave me the first information, I have had, that there was such a rumour afloat." [Sophia Dallas Bache was the sister of George M. Dallas and Maria Dallas Campbell and mother of Alexander Dallas Bache, the engineer and cartographer.] ALS in DLC, George Washington Lay Papers.

From J[OHN] S. BARBOUR, "Private"

Catalpa [Culpeper County, Va.,] Dec[embe]r 12th 1844
My Dear Sir, I received a confidential letter [*not found*] from a distinguished citizen at Richmond [James A. Seddon?], who bore a very active part in the late canvass, warning me of an intrigue in progress to blight the best fruits of the late victory. He solicits my aid to defeat it, and I do not know any other means of executing his wishes than apprising you of what he writes.

He says that the plan is to place Mr. [Andrew] Stevenson in the Cabinet to the extrusion of Judge [John Y.] Mason [Secretary of the Navy] and that you will be so environed by troubles as to be powerless for useful service. Prior to the receipt of this letter I had heard directly from Washington & from another high quarter in Richmond that Mr. Stevenson would cooperate in all great measures with you. That Judge Mason wished the mission to Austria & that his continuance in the Cabinet w[oul]d be irksome & burthensome to his wishes. The vote ["in the H(ouse) of R(epresentatives)" *interlined*] on the rescision [*sic*] of the 25th rule, revealed to me more of the light of these intrigues than any other occurrence of the times. And I was carried to the belief that the intrigue was more deeply laid & widely spread than my Richmond correspondent apprehended. Mr. [James K.] Polk should be well instructed as to the existence of these intrigues, and particularly as to the precise state of publick opinion in the Southern States, that gave their votes for him. How is this to be effected? My Richmond friend supposes that my service with him in Congress & the agency I have had in his election would give weight to my opinions with him. In this I have written him that he is wholly mistaken. If any man that I know will have weight in Mr. Polk[']s deliberations, it is Judge Mason. Next to him Mr. [Littleton W.] Tazewell [former Senator from Va.]. I was on very kind terms with him *up to 1831*. During the session of the Virg[ini]a Convention Mr. P[olk] was a visitor & my relations were then very kind with him. I extended civilities to him ["which no other did &" *interlined*] for *which he was grateful.* But in the split that occurred in 1831, our intercourse ceased; & I held an ill opinion of him, which I did not conceal. In the past autumn he addressed me a respectful letter, & sent ["with it" *interlined*] the vindication, in pamphlet, of Ezekiel Polk[']s memory. At the session of 1833 when the vacancy for the Chair [that is, the Speakership] was expected, (by Stevenson[']s nomination abroad & to England,) I well remember that our friend Warren R. Davis [then a Representative from S.C.] called on me to know, if I w[oul]d vote for Polk for the Chair. I refused positively & vehemently, & this was doubtless known to him; (not through Davis, but otherwise,) for to be distinct I had an ill opinion of him from the occurrences of 1831 to 1833. And although I zealously (& with some effect,) actively sustained him in the late canvass, my course was the result of a conviction, that it was my duty to keep *out* the evil principles of his adversary, rather than a wish to bring Polk *in.* And if he now acts out the expectations which the South have indulged, of his fidelity to them, & their principles; I shall feel most happily relieved from ["many" *canceled and then interlined*] anxious apprehensions. These are my thoughts, divulged to you in the sincerity of friendship & in the tumult of much that disturbs my hopes. Virginia, Georgia, So. Carolina, & Alabama, were carried to Mr. Polk *by your friends—* certainly the three first—& those three just equal the vote of New York. He (Mr. P[olk]) has not a friend in this quarter, who does not know it to be true. And the moral power of So. Carolina & Virg[ini]a outside of their limits, gave him his success. Without them (& with those ag[ains]t him,) he could not ["have" *interlined*] brought a [*one word canceled and* "picket" *interlined*] guard to the battle. If he therefore opens his heart to the evil influence, ag[ains]t which the patriot virtues rise up in rebellion, I shall scarce ["know," *interlined*] whether most to pity his weakness, or denounce his culpability. If I knew of any step that I & others (feeling & thinking as I do,) could adopt to prevent the consummation of evil counsels, in the public ruin; I w[oul]d promptly & zealously adopt ["them"(?) *canceled*] it. I commit my thoughts in all confidence & fullest Trust to you, & await your counsels.

I send herewith one of the letters to which I allude & though marked "confidential," I know the writer w[oul]d not with[h]old it from you: and if he felt restrained *in short*[?], I know that to trust it to you, is making it as sacred, as if I committed it to the Grave. ["I know no other living man I w[oul]d so trust" *interlined.*] You can read it & return it [to] me. I wish I had some Oedipus to solve the mysteries of *another* Sphinx *than this*; & *there* is *my trouble.*

You see that I throw my thoughts to you from & with a flying pen. In great haste & all Respect Y[ou]rs Truly, J.S. Barbour.

ALS in ScCleA.

From HENRY W. CUSHMAN

Bernardston, Mass., Dec. 12 1844
Dear Sir: I have the honor to request the appointment, by your Department, of Agent, to distribute the United States Laws, at the close of the present Session of Congress. If the appointment is yet to be made, I will furnish your Department with credentials of my character and standing as a man and a politician from Gov. [Marcus] Morton & Hon. Geo[rge] Bancroft of Mass.—from the Post Master [Nathaniel Greene] & Collector [Lemuel Williams] of the Port of Boston; from Mr. Senator [Levi] Woodbury of New Hampshire; from acquaintances in South Carolina & from many other leading Democrats in New England & New York.

I trust you will pardon me, for saying, that no *taint* of *abolitionism,* will render me obnoxious to gentlemen of the slave-holding States. As a singular fact, and one that is quite uncommon in New England, I will mention, that at the late Presidential Election, *not a single abolition vote,* was given, in this, the Town of my residence!

If I cannot perform the duty of distributing the Laws in *all* the States, I should prefer the *middle, western & south-western* States.

With the hope that you will be disposed to grant me the above favour, I have the honor to be your ob[edien]t serv[an]t, Henry W. Cushman.

ALS in DNA, RG 59 (State Department), Applications and Recommendations, 1837–1845, Cushman (M-687:7, frames 342–344). NOTE: A Clerk's EU reads "Mr. Stubbs—Tell him of your standing contract."

To EDWARD EVERETT

Department of State
Washington, 12th Dec[embe]r 1844
Sir: I transmit to you, herewith, copies of documents relating to the case of the American brig "Cyrus," of New Orleans, P.C. Dumas,

Master—from which it appears that this vessel, while lying at anchor in the harbor of Cabinda [in Portuguese Africa] on the 2nd day of June last, was boarded by two officers and a boat's crew belonging to Her Britannic Majesty's brig of war "Alert," Captain [W.] Bosanquet, who searched the "Cyrus," pulled down and trampled upon the American flag, forcibly entered the cabin and broke open the trunk of her Master, and seized and carried away the ship's papers: whereupon Captain Dumas abandoned his vessel to the British Government—forthwith paid off and discharged his crew—and, on the 27th of the same month, having taken passage in the French barque "Guatimozin," sailed for Rio de Janeiro, where he duly entered his protest before the United States' Consul at that port [George William Gordon]. He subsequently proceeded on his way home to the United States and soon after his arrival at his destination appealed to his government for redress in the premises.

You will perceive, on a perusal of the enclosed evidence in the case, that the seizure and search of the "Cyrus" were attended with circumstances of a peculiarly aggravating character; and it is difficult to conceive what possible countervailing testimony can be offered in justification or palliation of the conduct of Captain Bosanquet. The statement of the whole transaction, by Captain Dumas, seems to be reasonably dispassionate, consistent, perspicuous, and conclusive; and if, on an investigation of the matter by the British Government, the facts he sets forth are found to be irrefragable—as I scarcely doubt they will be—the case is certainly one of gross outrage on the American flag and the rights of a citizen of the United States, and calls for the ready intervention of this Government. You will accordingly make a representation of the subject to Lord Aberdeen, demand prompt indemnification for the losses and injuries sustained by the owner and all others interested in the brig "Cyrus," her cargo and other property on board, and complain of the conduct of Captain Bosanquet as unwarrantable, wanton, and flagitious, and meriting the severe reprehension of Her Majesty's Government.

You will see on examining the President's Message to Congress at the commencement of the present session, that the class of claims on Great Britain for seizures and detentions of American vessels on the coast of Africa on suspicion of their being engaged in the Slave Trade, continues to be a subject of painful interest; and I trust, therefore, that you will avail yourself of every proper occasion to hasten their final adjustment and settlement.

I also send you a copy of the protest [of 4/12] of Capt. Jos: Sturdivant, of the American brig "Jos. Cowperthwait," relative to the improper conduct of Gov[erno]r H.W. Hill in detaining and searching the said brig whilst at anchor in Cape Coast Castle Roads, on the 4th of April last; and have to request that you will take such steps as you may deem expedient to obtain from Her Majesty's Government an explanation of the proceedings complained of by Mr. Sturdivant. I am, Sir, respectfully, your obed[ien]t servant, J.C. Calhoun.

LS (No. 115) with Ens in DNA, RG 84 (Foreign Posts), Great Britain, Instructions, 8:471–582, received 12/30; FC in DNA, RG 59 (State Department), Diplomatic Instructions, Great Britain, 15:235–238 (M-77:74); PEx with Ens in Senate Document No. 300, 29th Cong., 1st Sess., pp. 8–42. NOTE: Among the documents enclosed to Everett were several legal statements and accounts of the incident aboard the *Cyrus* transmitted to the State Department by George William Gordon on 9/3, extracts of Henry A. Wise's despatch of 10/14 and an enclosure, and a letter of 10/18 from Thomas Barrett to Calhoun.

From Fr[iedrich] v[on] Gerolt, [Prussian Minister to the U.S.], Washington, 12/12. Gerolt announces his arrival at Washington and presents a copy of his letter of credence from the King of Prussia appointing him Prussian Minister in place of [Friedrich Ludwig, Baron von] Roenne. He asks when he can deliver the original letter to the President. ALS (in French) in DNA, RG 59 (State Department), Notes from Foreign Legations, Prussia, vol. 1 (M-58:1).

From W[illia]m A. Gibson, Baltimore, 12/12. Having learned of a vacant Clerkship in the State Department, Gibson applies for the position. Gibson is of good character and standing in the local business community but cannot find employment "owing to the dullness of business here." He respectfully seeks the State Department position or some similar in any of the other departments. ALS in DNA, RG 59 (State Department), Applications and Recommendations, 1837–1845, Gibson (M-687:12, frames 645–646).

From Z. Collins Lee, [U.S. District Attorney at Baltimore], Washington, 12/12. Lee recommends Charles R. Leffreing for the post of U.S. Consul at Stuttgart, Würtemberg. "He is a young gentleman of education & well acquainted with our language and institutions. His family is one of the most respectable in Bavaria, & reside near Studgardt." If Calhoun seeks further recommendations of Leffreing, he can consult residents of New York City where the applicant has resided for the last two years. ALS in DNA, RG 59 (State Department), Applications and Recommendations, 1845–1853, Leffreing (M-873:52, frames 610–611).

From JOHN H. LEWIS and Others

Huntsville, Ala., Dec[embe]r 12th 1844
Sir, Aware of the deep interest you feel in the progress of the line of improvements designed to connect this region of Country with the Atlantic Seaports of Charleston, & Savannah, we send you by this day[']s mail a Report by W[illia]m Spencer Brown Esq[ui]r[e], Civil Engineer, of a survey of the line of Road between the Tennessee & Coosa Rivers.

We are endeavouring to get an appropriation by our Legislature, now in Session, out of the "Two per Cent fund" for the purpose of making this connection, & we base our claim to the money on the fact that the work comes within the specified terms of the act of Congress granting the Fund to the State of Alabama—to wit—"for the purpose of making a connection between the Tennessee River & the navigable waters of the Mobile Bay." You will perceive from the Report that the part of the line which we propose to make overcomes the only considerable barrier between the northern & Southern Parts of the State, & that an extension of the Road from a Point near the Coosa River, Southwardly over a very favourable surface will strike the most northern navigable waters of the Alabama River at Wetumpka or Selma. If our Legislature could but be inspired with the enlightened view of the magnitude & importance of this improvement which we know you to entertain, we should have no doubt about the successful issue of our application, and the consequent completion of our Road within two years, or in time to meet the Georgia Rail Road at her extreme western boundary at Rome. Individual effort would do what the fund from the State would fall short of accomplishing. We ask only one half of the 2 per cent fund, being willing to concede the other half to a similar work in the South.

If compatable with your engagements, we should be pleased to have your views on the propriety of the appropriation of a part of the "two per cent fund" relinquished to this State, to the Tennessee & Coosa Rail Road. The subject will be brought up in our Legislature some time early in the next month, & we are confident that a timely letter from you would have an extensive & salutary influence with the great body of the members. With sentiments of esteem & respect, we subscribe ourselves, Sir, Your very ob[e]d[ien]t & hum[ble] Serv[an]ts, John H. Lewis, Sam[ue]l Breck, George Cox, Corresponding Committee.

ALS with En in ScCleA. Note: The committee sent to Calhoun a printed pamphlet, *Report of Wm. Spencer Brown, (Civil Engineer,) to the Commissioners of the Tennessee and Coosa Rail Road* [n.p., 1844], which described a survey of proposed rail routes from Gunter's Landing, on the Tennessee River, to Will's Creek, on the Coosa River. The writer of the above letter signed it for all of the committee members.

From [NATHANIEL] B[EVERLEY] TUCKER

Williamsburg [Va.,] Dec. 12, 1844

My dear Sir, I beg you to accept my acknowledgments for your polite notice of my letters. It was a courtesy I had no right to expect, and which I therefore appreciate the more highly.

I am surprised to learn that there is any doubt of the authenticity of the information given to me by Mr. [Joseph M.] White. In regard to that I cannot be mistaken. The language of the Treaty of cession by France to the U.S. strongly intimates the existence of some document defining the limits of Louisiana as ceded by France to Spain, and by Spain back again to France. This, and other circumstances put Mr. W[hite] on the enquiry. His large interest in Spanish Florida grants determined him to prosecute it, at the expense of spending great part of his time in Europe. This was his chief business there. He learned that somewhere about 1760 a treaty of a secret character had been concluded between France & Spain, then governed by the two branches of the house of Bourbon, and that into that treaty an article defining the bounds of Louisiana was introduced. He applied to the Minister of foreign affairs for a copy which was refused. He then went to [Charles Maurice, Prince de] Talleyrand, then in London, to invoke his influence with the minister, and procured from him a letter expressing the opinion that the article in question, tho' in a treaty otherwise secret, might be divulged without impropriety. Thereupon a copy was furnished, from which it appeared that the Rio Bravo and the Mississippi, including the Island of New Orleans, were the agreed boundaries. Such was his account to me.

A week afterwards I repeated this conversation to [Texan leader] Branch Archer, who said he had often heard that there was such an article among the archives of Mexico, whither it had been immediately sent, for the information of the vice-regal government. The cession taking place immediately after the document was no longer of any consequence, and was not made notorious by any action upon it.

Mr. W[hite] died at St. Louis [in 1839] on a visit to a brother whose habits were not such as to cause any suspicion that his papers should have fallen into confusion. Millions of acres depended on that paper, and they whose interests were to be affected by it, may have been quite ready to secure its suppression, and Mr. W[hite]'s silence by a liberal compromise of *his* claims. The Government of the U.S. was interested to suppress it. Texas was gone from us, and was independent. Much land east of the Mississippi had been sold by the U.S. covered by Spanish grants made between 1803 & 1819. These are the lands White was claiming. Can we wonder if means were taken to silence him?

In this view of the matter the U.S. did not give up Texas gratuitously, for we got all the country east of the Mississippi that *we* call Louisiana. *We* therefore might be satisfied with the bargain. But it is of no consequence to the claim of Texas to be admitted into the union, in fulfilment of our engagement to France to that effect, whether we got any thing for the country or no. We had no authority to barter away the rights of the Texans, as they themselves immediately protested in an article, ["whi" *canceled*] an extract from which I find in the 12 No. of the Southern Review p. 486, which I have just received. That article expresses what was the universal sentiment of the far west at the time, and on that sentiment most of those who migrated to Texas acted in taking that important step. I remember being present at a meeting of the most intelligent gentlemen of St. Louis one night in the Theatre, where the matter was discussed, and the [1819 Adams-Onís?] Treaty condemned by an unanimous vote, on that ground. My memory deceives me if Col. [Thomas H.] Benton was not present.

In the Treaty of cession there is a stipulation that France shall furnish all evidences of title and boundaries in her possession. This article inserted in one of the secret treaties of the heads of the Catholic party in Europe may have been overlooked by the new men into whose hands the government had come. Can it do any harm to instruct Mr. [William R.] King [U.S. Minister to France] to enquire if there be any such article, and to demand it if there is? The disclosure might occasion some loss to the Government in the adjustment of Florida titles: but ["what" *canceled*] what are a few dollars in comparison with a great political measure, and the covenanted rights of the People of Texas?

I have just seen your letter to Mr. [Wilson] Shannon, and an abstract of his correspondence with [Manuel C.] Rejon. The aspect which this gives to the Texas question makes it of infinite importance to bring in aid of the pretensions of our government every argument and every fact which can fortify your position. I think, if you will look at the Treaty of cession, you will see in it such language as will hardly leave a doubt in your mind that before the first cession by France to Spain the boundary of Louisiana had been definitively settled and was distinctly understood between those two powers.

I am much gratified to find that the leaders of the Democratic party in this State are getting back to the ground from which they were frighted twelve years ago by the thunder of the [Force] Proclamation. I earnestly hope that no part of our Southern array will take any unconsidered step, and place themselves beyond the reach of our support. At the same time I have little hope of an extensive concert of action. I see the idea of a Southern convention at Ash[e]ville revived. You did me the honour to speak to me of that in 1833. But I have no idea that more than one or two *State Governments* can be brought to act in it. Is it not better to resort to something like the former free-trade convention, attended by all who please to go, whether as representing their neighbours or acting for themselves alone. Such a body would be [more] able than one chosen by the people, of whom a large proportion hostile to the movement would give their votes with a view to embarrass it. Such a body might discuss principles, adopt resolutions and recommendations, adjourn to meet *again—and again,* and *in due time* invite the States to send delegates. Give it this feature of perpetuity, and then, tho, at first, no bigger than a man's hand, it would soon cover the face of the heavens. A few strong but well considered and well guarded resolutions, the manifestation of a temper not less cautious than decided—the whole course of proceeding marked by that independence and discretion which characterize the conduct of men who act on their ["own" *interlined*] behalf and on their own responsibility, who have no authority to commit others, and are not bound to give to others any account of their proceedings, will bring our Northern oppressors to a stand; and the adjournment of such a body *to meet again* would startle them more than ten thousand men in arms. If ever we are driven to a Southern Confederacy, the measure must commence thus; and the North, to which the Union is as necessary as the womb to the *fetus,* will see and submit to the necessity of remitting their exactions, or losing all. They can out vote us, and always will, unless deterred by this fear.

I pray you to pardon the intrusion of these crude thoughts, and to believe me, with the highest respect Your obed[ien]t Ser[van]t, B. Tucker.

ALS in ScCleA; PEx in Jameson, ed., *Correspondence,* pp. 1008–1010.

From HENRY BALDWIN

Nashville, Dec[embe]r 13th 1844

D[ea]r Sir, Several causes prevent my return to my profession, my pecuniary embarrassments are very distressing, and I am much in want of occupation. For these reasons I take the liberty of applying to you, as a friend of [Justice Henry Baldwin] my Father's in the hope that it may be in your power to give me *some place* that will at the same time furnish me with employment, and aid me in the sustenance, and education of a large, and helpless family.

For any information you may desire as to my habits, attainments, or capacity, permit me to refer you to Judge [John] Catron [of the Supreme Court], Mr. [James] Buchanan of the Senate, or to the testimonials furnished the President in an application to him some time since.

I hope you will deem my necessities a sufficient apology for soliciting a place from you, and that if it be in your power you will gratify my wishes. You shall never have reason to complain of the ingratitude of Yours most respectfully and obediently, Henry Baldwin.

ALS in DNA, RG 59 (State Department), Applications and Recommendations, 1837–1845, Baldwin (M-687:1, frames 585–586).

From KER BOYCE

Senate Chamber [Columbia,] December 13th 1844

My dear Sir, I am desirned [*sic*] to say to you by his Excellency Governor ["o" *canceled*; William] Aiken, that he would take it very kind in you if you would from time to time to [*sic*] write him your views as to the course which this State should pursue as he feels great desire to have the best information he can obtain and he looks to you for that ["course which" *canceled*] information as he thinks you not only the able exponent of our Principles but one who he can look to as coming from a source, which always have went for the interest of the South and South Carolina. Under these circumstances I trust I will not be traspassing on your time to dedicate a few of your leasure moments to a correspondence with his Excellency who will receive it with kindness and expression of his gratitude.

You will see that Aiken received a large vote over boath [*sic*] his opponents which show[s] that our people feel great desire to weight [*sic*] and see, what the new administration will do, as we trust [James K.] Polk[']s administration will take such course as [will] give sattisfaction to the South.

I have received a letter from a distinguish[ed] Gentleman, wishing your friends to ["assist" *canceled*] insist on you to continue and not to refuse, the appointment of Secr[e]t[ar]y of State under Mr. Polk. He states that he has ["not" *canceled*] no right to say that ["you" *canceled*] Polk would offer such a[p]pointment to you but his friends wish it and none more so than himself who is a very decided friend of Polk and myself. Yours Most Sinsarrily [*sic*,] your friend, Ker Boyce.

P.S. All letters of yours will be received as confidention [*sic*] when you wish.

ALS in ScCleA.

From R[EUBEN] CHAPMAN, [Representative from Ala.]

H[ouse] of Rep[resentatives] Washington City
Dec[embe]r 13th 1844

Sir; At the request of several gentlemen of Huntsville Ala. who are members of the corresponding committee of the Tennessee and Coosa Rail Road Company, I submit for your perusal and examination the Report ["of" *interlined*] W[illia]m Spencer Brown Esq[ui]r[e] the Engineer who has lately made a survey and estimate of the route and cost of said road, with a map of the route—together with the letter [*not found*] of the Com[mittee] to me of the 6th inst.

The friends of this work having (for reasons heretofore made known) been disappointed in not having had your presence and counsel at the convention on this subject held in Huntsville last spring, are desirous of obtaining your views as to the practicability and importance of the contemplated improvement from the facts submitted now as well as from your general knowledge of the country.

I shall be gratified if you can find time to comply with their request as early as convenient. With great respect your Ob[edient] S[ervan]t, R. Chapman.

[P.S.] Private;

I will be much obliged if Mr. Calhoun can find it convenient to write the letter requested by monday next, as I shall want the Report[,] Map and letter (which Mr. C[alhoun] will please return to me) to introduce the bill for the right of way indicated. Mr. C[alhoun] will observe, that an application is made by the company to the Ala. Legislature at the present Ses[sion] for an appropriation of a portion of the 2 p[e]r c[en]t fund (relinquished by act of Congress about Feb[ruar]y 1843 to Ala. to be applied to certain improvements in the State, of which this is one) towards making this road. The Com[mittee] ask your views as to ["the propriety of" *interlined*] this appropriation, as well as to the ["work" *canceled*] advantages of the work generally. Yours, R.C.

ALS in ScCleA. Note: An AEU by Calhoun reads: "Mr. Chapman, re[l]ates to the rail Road from Tennessee to Coosa."

To [THOMAS G. CLEMSON], "Private"

Washington, 13th Dec[embe]r 1844

My dear Sir, My official buseness [*sic*], as well as my correspondence, has got so far in the rear, and I find it so difficult to bring it up, in consequence of the great increase, which is attendant on the meeting of Congress, of current business, that I am compelled to write very brief letters.

The great question of the session will be the annexation of Texas. It will be brought up without delay in both Houses & pressed with Zeal by its friends. It will, I think, pass the House almost certainly; but I fear it may be defeated in the Senate, where the whig party is very strong.

There is much Speculation, as to Mr. [James K.] Polk's Cabinet; and not a little intrigue, it is said, is going on in various quarters. I am perfectly passive and am indifferent as far as I am personally concerned and keep my decision to myself, whether I shall remain in or not, if ["it" *canceled and* "I" *interlined*] should be invited to continue. It will depend on circumstances. My friends are anxious that I should remain, but ["where" *canceled and* "whether" *interlined*] I shall or not will depend, on what will be the probable course of the administration. If there should be reasonable grounds to infer, that it will accord with my principles and views of policy, I will make the sacrafice. If not, I shall retire. The course of the Northern wing of the party has been very bad on the abo[li]tion question, which has caused much dissatisfaction among the Southern members, and will I doubt not cause much through the entire South. The excitement is already great in South Carolina. She is ready to act. If the ["Texian" *canceled*] annexation of Texas is to be defeated by the same sperit, which has induced the reception of abolition petitions, it is difficult to say, what may be the consequence.

A very angry correspondence has taken place between Our minister in Mexico [Wilson Shannon] and her Government. It will end in words. She is on the eve of anarchy & revolution and is destitute of the means of waging war. The Steamer, which takes this, will take the correspondence with Texas & Mexico, growing out of the question of annexation. It has been well received[,] especially the letter to Mr. [William R.] King [U.S. Minister to France], which has created quite a sensation.

I learn from Mr. [Charles] Serruys [Belgian Minister to the U.S.], that he has been indirectly informed, that it [is] contemplated to remove him to Denmark, because his treaty had fallen to the ground, and that he has, in consequence, become unacceptable to the United States and thereby incapable of rendering amy [*sic*] service. This impression, it seems, has grown out of the cause which it is supposed led to the removal of his predecessor Baron [Desiré] Behr.

I regret, that the impression exists, and take much pleasure in saying, that there is no foundation for it. On the contrary his conduct has been such as to make him every way acceptable to our Government, which I wish you to take some early opportunity to make known to his Government.

I have received the articles you were so kind as to get for me at Paris. They are all of a very superior quality, and are much admired; and with the exception of the Boots fit very well. They are too low in the instep, but by letting in a slip, at the point where they pinch, the difficulty will be removed, without disfiguring them materially. The part will be covered by the pantaloons.

Owing to the long passage of the Caladonia [*sic*] (the last Steamer) and the delay of the Mail two days at N. York from ["some" *interlined*] cause I did not receive the letters and dispatches by her untill yesterday. We are glad to hear, that you are all in such good health, except [John] Calhoun [Clemson] & that he is better. We were uneasy about him. We hope to hear by the next arrival of his complete restoration.

I had a letter from Andrew [Pickens Calhoun in Ala.] yesterday. John [C. Calhoun, Jr.] had arrived there. His general health is excellent, but his throat is still affected & his coughs continues.

I have not had time to turn my attention to the subject of a treaty with Belgium, but will endeavour to do so, & give my views by the next Steamer. [*The remainder of the manuscript is missing.*]

ALU (fragment) in ScCleA; PEx in Jameson, ed., *Correspondence,* pp. 633–634.

From THO[MA]S G. CLEMSON

Legation of United States, Brussels
Dec. 13th 1844

Sir, Since I wrote you last I have had an interview with Mons. Hody the Administrator of public security at this place, who informs me, that some time back he recieved [*sic*] a circular issued at Bale (Switzerland) July 20th 1844, describing a certain individual named Gerhard Koster, original[l]y from the Netherlands, & calling upon all the European authorities to aid in arresting him, he said Koster having defrauded several Banks in the United States to a large amount.

The said Gerhard Koster is now residing at Bruges in Belgium, where he appears to have taken up his residence with a view to stay an indefinite length of time.

Herewith you will recieve a note (copy) addressed to me on the subject by Mr. Hody.

There is no treaty existing between Belgium and the United States, for the delivery of fugitives from Justice. Nor is there any law by which he can be arrested in Belgium. He is accompanied by a Wife & several children & is the bearer of a passport in his true name Gerhard Koster delivered to him by the Legation of the Pays Bas at this place. Had his papers not been in order he might have been arrested on that plea. Under the circumstances of the case I can do no more than keep silent and await your instructions on the subject.

When I passed through Paris, I think our minister Mr. [William R.] King was engaged in a matter analogous, if not for the arrest of the same individual then in Switzerland. I wrote Mr. King for information of what he had done in the premises & await his reply.

539

No doubt that Koster is living in Bruges with a perfect knowledge of his security in the abscence of a treaty which could effect him. Another reason for believing so, is the fact of his passport bearing his true name, for when in Switzerland he was travelling under the assumed one of Phillips. He is doubtless on the alert & if at this time negotiations were entered into between the United States and Belgium he would escape before the ratification of the treaty. The formalities necessary to the conclusion of such a treaty, would so far as he is concerned frustrate the object in view. This however is no reason why such a treaty should not be made on the part of the two countries for which this Government is well disposed. If such treaties existed between the United States & those countries bounding Belgium his arrest could then be made in one of those countries where arrangements could be made for seizing him on his entering either of those countries, and that without a treaty between the U. States & Belgium for the Authorities here would force him to quit Belgium at the instance of the Government of the U. States expressed through their minister here. I have the honour to be most respectfully your obedient serv[an]t, Thos. G. Clemson.

ALS with En in DNA, RG 59 (State Department), Diplomatic Despatches, Belgium, vol. 3 (M-193:4), received 2/11/1845; FC (No. 6, in Clemson's hand) in DNA, RG 84 (Foreign Posts), Belgium, Despatches, vol. 4, October 21, 1844–September 27, 1848.

To John Dunham, Editor of the St. Clairsville Gazette, St. Clairsville, Ohio, 12/13. "In answer to your note of the 7th instant, I have the honor to inform you, that by the 21st section of an act of Congress, approved the 26th of August 1842, it is made the duty of the Secretary of State to cause 'the laws and resolutions of Congress, treaties and amendments of the Constitution of the United States,['] to be published in no newspapers other than those published in this City." FC in DNA, RG 59 (State Department), Domestic Letters, 35:45 (M-40:33).

From DUFF GREEN, "Private"

Washington (Texas), Dec[embe]r 13th 1844

My dear Sir, I enclose you a letter for Mrs. [Lucretia Maria Edwards] Green, which I will thank you to send to send [*sic*] to her.

By an act of the Texan Congress, merchandise imported in American vessels, pays a discriminating duty of five per cent. This has cut off the greater part of the trade with the United States.

I have made a personal interest which will I believe cause this act to be repealed, altho there is a disposition on the part of many to use every pretext to annoy the United States, by angry legislation. Some because they believe that it will promote Annexation, & others because they believe that it is the interests of Texas to give a preference to European trade, under a notion that the interests of Texas & the Southern States are opposed.

I believe that the United States should not postpone the question of annexation beyond the *next* session of Congress, & I can see many reasons why it should not take place sooner. Indeed it cannot take place sooner except by a joint resolution or act, authorising the admission of Texas as a new State, and that cannot be consummated before the *next* session. It is our interest that the Texas question shall constitute an element in the reorganisation of parties. Your friend, Duff Green.

ALS in ScCleA; PC in Boucher and Brooks, eds., *Correspondence*, p. 269.

From R[OBERT] M. T. HUNTER

[Lloyds, Va., *ca*. December 13, 1844]
My dear Sir, I was very glad to receive your letter some eight days since and much obliged to you for the document which I received this evening. Your letter I have enclosed to [James A.] Seddon with instructions to show it to [Lewis E.] Harvie of the [Va.] Legislature and a very few others who might be entirely relied upon. Seddon may be trusted with any thing. He is sagacious and faithful. I had previously written to him to ply [Thomas] Ritchie on the Texas and Tariff questions. I hope So. Ca. will keep still. Whether Ritchie intends it I do not know, but his paper [the Richmond *Enquirer*] is doing us service just now on those questions. He so designs it I suspect. But "nous verrons" as he himself so often says. The Texas question will be passed at this session I trust. Upon this subject I trust the tone of the party will be *higher* than heretofore. I am afraid that [Thomas H.] Benton will yet dodge out of the corner in which he has placed himself so as to be in a position to injure us hereafter.

Your letters to [William R.] King and [Wilson] Shannon, the former especially[,] will I think be very effective. Of course they will be attacked by all the whigs and a portion of the Democrats, but they will carry the country with them. The whigs just now seem especially anxious to get you out of the cabinet. The Northern whigs at least if I am to judge by their Jesuitical organ the [Washington] N[ational] Intelligencer. It is because they know that whilst you are there they will never be able to put off the Texas question by indirection so as to escape responsibility. That print[?] the Intelligencer ought to be unmasked. It is doing you and the South a great injury by its insidious course. I understood John Tyler Jr. to say that its bills on the Mexican ["Govt." *interlined*] were presented ["to the Ameri" *canceled*] through one of our consuls and punctually paid. Is this so? And if so why are all the presses silent on the subject?

I see the 21st rule has been repealed, Northern Democrats generally voting for it. How did the western Democrats vote on this question[?] If they voted with the South the symptoms would be decidedly favorable. The South & West combined can control the North.

Your views ["in your letter to King" *interlined*; "on" *altered to* "as"] to the interest of the continental nations on the subject of British philanthropy, ["and" *canceled*] are so just and profound that I think they must make an impression. They are gall and wormwood (I suspect) to the French King [Louis Philippe] just now, anxious as he is for the ["English" *canceled*] British support to his dynasty, but they will give the opposition the means of frightening M. [F.P.G.] Guizot from the scheme (if he entertains it) of making his partnership in the crusade against us the consideration for the British alliance which he so much covets. Yours faithfully, R.M.T. Hunter.

ALS in ScCleA. NOTE: This undated letter was postmarked at Lloyds, Va., on 12/14.

To J[OHN] K. KANE, Phil[adelphi]a

Department of State
Washington, Dec[embe]r 13th 1844

Sir, I have to acknowledge the receipt of your note of the 6th instant, with its enclosure. Circumstances beyond the controul of this Department have given to the case of Mr. [Warder] Cresson an appearance of hardship, and I much regret my inability to relieve him from the embarras[s]ments to which he may be subjected. A brief and candid statement of facts in the case will enable you to judge how far the Government is responsible for these embarras[s]ments.

Mr. Cresson asked to be appointed consul at Jerusalem in May last; and though the commercial interests of the Country did not seem to require it, yet as his object appeared laudable, his request was granted (not however, without considerable reluctance). A few weeks, afterwards information was communicated to this Department from several reliable sources, to the effect that Mr. Cresson was the victim of a species of monomania which rendered it hazardous to confer on him an official character. His excessive fanaticism was urged (and not without reason) against his appointment; and upon a reconsideration, the President considered it his duty to withhold the commission. This fact was communicated to Mr. Cresson by the Department on the 22nd of June last (some few weeks after his appointment) and before, it was supposed, he could have left the country. His present embarras[s]ment, therefore is attributable rather to his own precipitancy than to any wrong on the part of the Government. I am Sir, with high respect Your ob[edien]t servant, J.C. Calhoun.

FC in DNA, RG 59 (State Department), Domestic Letters, 35:47 (M-40:33).

To W[ILLIAM] R. KING, "Strictly confidential"

State Dept., 13th Dec[embe]r 1844
My dear Sir, I have delayed writing to you untill I should receive the letters and dispatches by the Caledonia. Owing to her long passage, and the delay in receiving, what she brought, from Boston, the letters & dispatches by her were not received untill yesterday. Among them, there was nothing from Paris.

This is the last day that communications by her on her return can be mailed, which, as I have several letters besides this to write, will compel me to be very breif [*sic*].

A copy of the correspondence of the Dept. with Texas & Mexico in reference to the question of annexation will accompany this, and among them a copy of my dispatch [of 8/12] to you. It has made, I learn, a deep impression, as far as it has been read; and I hope, it will attrack [*sic*] the attention in Europe, which the vast importance of the topicks it touches, demand[s]. They are of a character to interest every country on both Continents, in their commercial and political relations. If England ["should" *interlined*] consummate her grand scheme of commercial monopoly, disguised under the guarb [*sic*] of abolition, it would not only subject the commerce of the world to her control, but would, on all that portion of this continent lying south of Mason & Dixon line, end in a war between races of the most deadly & desolating character; to be terminated in a large portion in the ascendency of the lowest & most ["savage" *interlined*] of the races [*one word or partial word interlined and then canceled*] & a return to barbarism. England from her position, would necessarily become the patron of the coulered races ["of all hues" *interlined*], negroes, indians & mixed, ag[ai]nst the white, which unless France and the contin[ent]al powers, generally, ["but" *interlined*] especially her should become the supporter of the ["latter" *canceled and then interlined*], would give them the superiority. The intimate relations of France with Brazil & Spain would seem to make it impossible, that she should be indifferent to the fate of the former or Cuba, not to mention her old & long standing friendly relations ["to" *canceled and* "with" *interlined*] the U. States. Nor can it be supposed, that she is so deficient in segacity, as not to see, what a commanding position she might take in conjunction with them & in connection with the U. States. I throw out these suggestions to turn your attention to the great & important bearings of the present remarkable juncture in the political & commercial world. You may have occasionally opportunities of giving ["them" *canceled and* "events" *interlined*] the direction we desire.

["The measure of" *canceled*; "Measures" *and* "Measure" *interlined and then canceled*; "Resolutions for the" *interlined*] annexation ["of Texas" *interlined*] have been introduced into both Houses. I hope ["it" *canceled and* "the measure" *interlined*] may succeed; but I have my fears. Should it fail, [Thomas H.] Benton will be responsible for the result. He seems bent on doing all the ["harm" *canceled and* "mischief" *interlined*] he can, both to the country & the party. He covers & protects the whigs by his course. His conduct on the annexation question, and that of the Northern wing of the party on the reception of abolition petitions, ["&" *canceled*] and ["of" *interlined*] Mass[achuset]ts in sending an emissary to South Carolina, will be the cause of much excitement during the session. It is difficult to see in what it may all end.

I entirely agree with you, as to the importance of ["dissemanating in France" *canceled and* "disseminating" *interlined*] correct information ["in France" *interlined*] on the subject to which you refer, & you are authorised to incur an expense on that account not exceeding

$500, to be charged to the contingent fund of the Department. ["It" *canceled.*] No one can be better qualified to prepare the proper articles for the purpose than Mr. [Robert] Walsh [U.S. Consul to Paris], who you suggest.

["My" *canceled and* "The" *interlined*] time is so short that I can add no more. Yours truly, J.C. Calhoun.

Autograph draft in ScCleA; PC in Jameson, ed., *Correspondence*, pp. 631–633. NOTE: An AEU by Calhoun on the ms. reads: "Draft of a letter to Mr. King."

From J[OHN] Y. MASON, [Secretary of the Navy]

Navy Department, December 13, 1844

Sir, I have had the honor to receive, and have perused with deep regret, the papers which you did me the honor to submit to my inspection, concerning the proceedings of the Commander of the U.S. frigate Congress, in capturing the squadron of the Argentine Republic.

The regulations of this Department require that Captain [Philip F.] Voorhees's official communications be made through Commodore [Daniel] Turner, his commanding Officer, from whom I have not yet heard. I have great confidence in his judgment and discretion. His despatch, when received, will be communicated to the State Department.

Without undertaking, under existing circumstances, to express any opinion of the conduct of Captain Voorhees, I have the honor to transmit an extract from the instructions on the subject of blockades and the duties of Naval Officers in regard to such a condition of things. The extract sent is taken from the instructions to Commodore [Charles G.] Ridgely. Those to Commodore Turner were modified to suit the existing state of things. They seem to have been well digested, and, if observed, collision could hardly occur. I have the honor to be Very resp[ectfull]y Yours, J.Y. Mason.

LS with En in DNA, RG 59 (State Department), Miscellaneous Letters (M-179: 106, frames 162–164); FC in DNA, RG 45 (Naval Records), Letters Sent by the Secretary of the Navy to the President and Executive Agencies, 1821–1886, 5:70–71 (M-472:3, frame 77).

To Michael B. Van Buren, New York [City], 12/13. "I have to inform you, that agreeably to the request contained in several communications filed in this Department, the President [John Tyler] had directed a nomination of you to the Senate, for the Consulate at

Puerto Cabello [Venezuela], to be laid before him, and that, in consequence of a letter, of the 11th instant from Mr. John D. Van Buren, withdrawing the application in your favour, the nomination has been cancelled." FC in DNA, RG 59 (State Department), Domestic Letters, 35:44–45 (M-40:33).

From EDWARD EVERETT

London, 14 December 1844

Sir, With my despatch No. 219 of the 2 December I transmitted a note from Lord Aberdeen of the 20th November with accompanying documents, relative to the detention of a bearer of despatches at Liverpool, and a copy of my reply of the 2nd instant. I now forward a further communication [of 12/11] from Lord Aberdeen, from which it appears that measures have been taken by him to prevent the recurrence of similar causes of complaint.

There is, I am persuaded, no wish on the part of the heads of the government to embarrass the communications between the Department of State and our foreign legations. But so long as they are transmitted on board the Royal mail Steamers and by private passengers, difficulties like that which took place in the present instance, must be expected occasionally to recur. I am, sir, with high respect, your obedient servant, Edward Everett.

LS (No. 225) with En in DNA, RG 59 (State Department), Diplomatic Despatches, Great Britain, vol. 53 (M-30:49), received 1/27/1845; FC in DNA, RG 84 (Foreign Posts), Great Britain, Despatches, 9:95–96; FC in MHi, Edward Everett Papers, 50:439–440 (published microfilm, reel 23, frames 495–496).

From JAMES GADSDEN

Columbia, Dec[embe]r 14, 1844

My Dear Sir, I write to solicit your influence in having the duty remitted on Rail Iron particularly to those Road[s] which were commenced under the faith of the Law making Iron free & who have not yet carried out their original designs, but which have been retarded by this unexpected exaction of 25 dollars a Ton on the Iron to be used. I have written to [George] McDuffie, [Senator from S.C., Isaac E.]

Holmes [Representative from S.C.] & the Sec[re]t[ary of the] Treasury [George M. Bibb] on the subject. All the Eastern & Western States are interested, and ought to recognise a claim as more than just particularly as the former participated so largely in the benefits of the late Law from their superior Capital. Pen[n]sylvania is said to have imported under the Free duty 80,000 Tons: equivalent to a saving in the Construction of their Roads of 2 millions of Dollars. All that we ask for is some 8 or 9000 Tons to complete our enterprises.

I have made another application which I trust you will favor, in behalf of our [South Carolina Railroad] Company. It is to be permitted to import *Free of duty* the Ropes & machenery necessary for one mile of Atmospheric Rail Way which I wish to substitute on the Inclined plane at Aiken for the Rope & Locomotive there. That plane is a great obstacle to our Trade, retarding transportation & enhancing its cost. We cannot go round it but at great expense and by a large circuit.

From a correspondence with the Inventor of the Atmospheric Road, I am satisfied it can be applied advantageously to the Plane, remedying most of the difficulties at that Point. But to succeed the machenery &c must be constructed under the supervision of the Inventor & as what we import will be a model for our Machenests in the U.S. to work by, should this application succeed I do not consider our application to import free of duty unreasonable. On the contrary the public may profit from our First application of the principal [*sic*]. Do urge it through before manufacturing cupidity, in hope of a job, can rally against us.

I have read with very great interest & pleasure both of your letters to [William R.] King & [Wilson] Shannon. As models of diplomatic correspondence & on very absorbing subjects they cannot but be highly appreciated. I hope that your communication to King may bring out Lord Aberdeen from his concealment, even if it should be in the spirit of complaint. In fact that nation deserves to have their duplicity & Unhallowed designs exposed as you have done and if you succeed in *that* as well as in enlightening the world on the true character of African slavery as it exists in the U.S. you will have atchieved a monument of enduring fame & be richly entitled to the gratitude of the world, where trade is stimulated by the production of black & slave labor—Labor which is only available through slavery & which goes to the comfort of those who work. Bu [*sic*].

We have concluded to extend our Road to Camden & therefore the greater the importance of securing Rail Road Iron free of duty. Yours Truly, James Gadsden.

547

ALS in ScCleA. NOTE: As to "the Inventor of the Atmospheric Road," Samuel Clegg and Joseph Samuda held an 1840 British patent. Isambard K. Brunel, another Briton, was noted for its testing and construction.

From DUFF GREEN, "Private"

Washington (Texas), 14th De[cembe]r 1844

My dear Sir, Major Donalson [*sic*; Andrew J. Donelson] will enclose you a letter, recommending H[enry] L. Kinney of Corpus Christi as Consul for that place.

There are very strong public considerations why *he* should recieve [*sic*] the appointment in preference to any one else, and I ask it as a personal favor to myself, and I will be greatly disappointed if it is not given to him. I have not written to the President [John Tyler] on the subject because I ["not" *canceled*] do not wish to annoy him, but if a question arises, you can say that I ask it on my own account as well as because of the bearing which it will have on the questions of boundary & of annexation.

I find that the tariff constitutes the strongest argument against annexation. The current expenditures of this Govt. is about $120,000. The exports will be from ["$120"(?) *canceled*] 100,000 to 120,000 bales of cotton. This will give at 25$ each say, $2,500,000 imports, and a duty of six per cent will raise sufficient revenue to support the Govt. Many are of opinion that if England will guarantee her Independence the people will consent to pledge Texas against annexation; and I am told that Elliott [*sic*; Charles Elliot, British Minister to Texas], will be here in the next stage authorised to give assurances that Mexico will give her acknowledgement with that condition.

I will have the game blocked upon him. I am not at liberty to say more now, but give yourself no uneasiness. My answer to those who object to our tariff is that it will be reduced and that our market for the sugar of Texas will compensate for the extra duty, to say nothing of the protection, which annexation will bring, & the consequent benefits ["of" *canceled*] resulting from security and increased population. Yours truly, Duff Green.

ALS in ScCleA. NOTE: An AEU by Calhoun reads: "Gen[era]l Green recommends the appointment [of] H.L. Kinney for the Consulate of Corpus Christi."

From C[harles] G. Greene, [Editor of the Boston *Post*], Boston, 12/14. "I am personally acquainted with Mr. [William T.] Mann, and believe him to be worthy of the confidence of the government, and know the testimonials he possesses of his qualifications to be from gentlemen of the highest character." [Mann had applied for the vacant post of U.S. Consul at Puerto Cabello, Venezuela.] Greene enclosed an undated obituary clipped from an unknown newspaper, perhaps the *Post*, of Dr. Franklin Litchfield, late U.S. Consul at Puerto Cabello. The obituary was written by W.T. M[ann?]. ALS with En in DNA, RG 59 (State Department), Applications and Recommendations, 1837–1845, Mann (M-687:22, frame 107).

From Carl Ernst Ludwig Hinrichs, New York [City], 12/14. Hinrichs informs Calhoun that he has been appointed by the Duke of Saxe Coburg and Gotha to be Consul for the U.S. for that duchy. He encloses his patent dated 9/23 and requests an exequatur from the President. ALS in DNA, RG 59 (State Department), Notes from Foreign Consuls, vol. 2 (M-664:2, frames 402–403).

From [Johann Georg von Hülsemann]

Washington, 14 Dec. 1844
Mr. Hülsemann[']s compliments to the Hon. John C. Calhoun Secretary of State, and according to their conversation this morning, begs leave to transmit subjoined the project of a bill, by which, if adopted by Congress, one impediment of the navigation and commerce between the ports of Austria and the United [States] would be put an end to, And which is the more desirable, as the english, french and all other german ports—except those of Austria—have been relieved from this difficulty several years ago, and enjoy an undue advantage over Trieste and Venice.

ALU with En in DNA, RG 59 (State Department), Notes from Foreign Legations, Austria, vol. 1 (M-48:1). NOTE: Hülsemann enclosed a draft bill to fix the exchange value of Austrian florins at forty-eight cents U.S. currency.

From E[lisha] M. Huntington, [former Commissioner of the U.S. General Land Office]

Terre Haute [Ind.,] Dec[embe]r 14, 1844
Sir, Several gentlemen of our State are applicants for the Office of U.S. Marshall for this Dist[rict]. Among them are Col. A.C. Pepper and James Johnson to both of whom I have given letters vouching for

their high respectability and qualifications. A valued friend has written to me that the Hon. Jno. S. Simonson now a member of the Gen-[era]l Assembly of Indiana is also an applicant. I could not do less under any circumstances than bear testimony to Mr. Simonson[']s private & public worth. He has long been in one or the other branch of our Legislature and stands deservedly high in the State. Should the choice of the Govt. fall on him, I entertain no doubt that he will make an upright and able officer. I have the honor to be Your ob[edien]t serv[an]t, E.M. Huntington.

ALS in DNA, RG 59 (State Department), Applications and Recommendations, 1845–1853, Simonson (M-873:79, frames 430–431).

From W[illia]m T. Mann, Boston, 12/14. Mann seeks appointment to be U.S. Consul at Puerto Cabello, Venezuela, to succeed the late Dr. Franklin Litchfield. For the past eight years Mann had been associated with Litchfield in managing the Consulate and often undertook the whole business of the post. He requests that the President postpone nominating a successor until he is able to submit recommendations for himself. ALS in DNA, RG 59 (State Department), Applications and Recommendations, 1837–1845, Mann (M-687:22, frames 104–106).

From DAN[IE]L B. TALLMADGE

New York [City,] Dec[embe]r 14th 1844
D[ea]r Sir, On Wednesday last, I sent to the New York Herald a communication containing a defence of your instructions to Mr. [Wilson] Shannon at Mexico. The article was prepared in haste, under the idea that it would be published immediately[.]

Had I supposed the publication would have been delayed, I should have bestowed upon it more thought and attention.

As it is, I hope it may receive your ap[p]robation[.] I perceive the Herald promises it in the paper of tomorrow or the next day[.]

When it appears I will have the honour to enclose you a copy. With great respect yours &c, Danl. B. Tallmadge.

ALS in ScCleA.

From William A. Weaver, Department of State, 12/14. Weaver addresses to Calhoun a long memorandum entitled "Continuation of

Report on the memorials relative to the alleged errors of the 6th Census (part II)." Weaver's aim in this 256-page unpublished report is to refute specifically memorials to Congress from the American Statistical Association and others that allege errors were made in the data collection and computation of the Sixth Census. Although he addresses these questions specifically, Weaver also expands his report into a history of the Negro race and of modern black-white relations. He does this to refute the memorialists' assertions that the census misrepresents, perhaps wilfully, the true status of free blacks in the North. Weaver's overriding thesis is that New World slavery has had a civilizing influence upon the African race and has, in fact, rescued Africans from worse conditions in their native lands. To this end he compiles excerpts from travelers' accounts of Africa, some as early as 1599, that emphasize the barbarism, sexual depravity, and native cruelty of Africans. Weaver collates census and other statistical information to demonstrate that the conditions of black slaves in the South are much better than those of free blacks in the North. He expands this theme, using British government publications, to suggest that Southern slaves enjoy better social, moral, and economic conditions than white industrial laborers in Great Britain. Another aspect of Weaver's thesis, the deleterious effects of emancipation, is made through a statistical study of British and French colonies in the Caribbean region before and after the Haitian Revolution and British emancipation. He concludes that these events have both destroyed the region's economies and diminished the living conditions of former slaves. Returning to the U.S., he asserts, with copious excerpts from published and unpublished works, that the abolition movement is misguided, dangerous, and unconstitutional. At this point in his narrative, Weaver copies advertisements for slave sales from July 1776 issues of New England and Pa. newspapers, the same issues that first printed the Declaration of Independence. This is to demonstrate that modern, abolitionist interpretations of the Declaration of Independence differ significantly from the interpretations of the Revolutionary generation. He also excerpts colonial black codes and contemporary anti-miscegenation laws to emphasize that even New England abolitionists and philanthropists have racist sentiments. [Despite being entitled a "Continuation" and "part II," this report preceded and was much larger in scope and size than Weaver's report of 1/18/1845 which Calhoun transmitted to the House of Representatives. Weaver had been superintendent of the Sixth Census and had been involved in earlier controversies concerning alleged errors in the census.] ADS in DNA, RG 59 (State Department), Miscellaneous Letters (M-179:106, frames 170–297).

From W[ILLIAM] W[ILKINS, Secretary of War]

War Department, December 14, 1844
Sir, I respectfully transmit herewith, a report of the Officer in charge of the Ordnance Bureau [Col. George Bomford], relative to two horses said to have been presented to the President [John Tyler] by the Imaun [*sic*] of Muscat. It is understood that the President gave orders to have those horses sent to the Arsenal in this City, and as this Department has no direct charge of them, it is believed they should be disposed of under orders of the Department of State. W. W[ilkins].

FC in DNA, RG 107 (Secretary of War), Letters Sent Relating to Military Affairs, 1800–1861, 25:430 (M-6:25); draft in DNA, RG 156 (Records of the Office of the Chief of Ordnance), Letters Received, 1812–1894, 269.

From HENRY A. WISE

Legation of the United States
Rio de Janeiro, Dec[embe]r 14, 1844
Sir, The last Despatch from the Department, of a copy of the letter addressed to Mr. [William R.] King at Paris on the subject of our relations with Texas, was duly received; and I shall omit no proper occasion to impress its views upon the persons of this Court, and upon others within the sphere of my action and correspondence whose favorable opinions & influences it may be desirable for the U. States to have in respect to them.

I have been delaying this communication in order that I might have something definite to say concerning the leading subject of the negotiations by Brazil of any new treaties ["new treaties" *canceled*] now to be formed with any of the Great Powers. It was known that Mr. [Hamilton] Hamilton, the Minister of Great Britain, was urging a negotiation and that there were some causes which favored the success of his attempts to follow their late treaty immediately by a new one. In June last, he announced the continuance of a full power to treat, notwithstanding the, then, late failure of the special mission of

Great Britain; and at that time his overtures were postponed on the ground of the engrossing subject of the pending elections in this country. The elections having terminated, and favorably too, to the present ministry of Brazil, Mr. Hamilton again renewed his proposition to negotiate. From time to time he was put off without any satisfactory answer, or assurances, or excuses, until—to show how these things are done at this Court—it was officially announced in the public journals that Commissioners were appointed by His Imperial Majesty to *discuss* the terms of a treaty with the Minister of Great Britain. Previous to this a political pamphlet made its appearance, from a deputy of one of the northern provinces and from the neighborhood of the residence or home of [Ernesto Ferreira França] the Minister of Foreign Affairs, strongly deprecating the renewal of any treaty, and in opposition especially to any tariff regulations whatever which might enter into the terms of any treaty, if made, with Great Britain. And about the very time that the annunciation was made here of the appointment of Commissioners to discuss, the English papers arrived with the news that a new treaty had been formed with Brazil. Up to Thursday of this week nothing had been done. Then, on the 12th inst. I made a visit to the Foreign Office, where I found Gen[era]l [Tomás] Guido, the Minister of Buenos Ayres, and held a free conversation with him. He unreservedly informed me that Mr. Hamilton was indignant at the manner in which his overtures were met, and that he complained of the procrastination, and of the evident indisposition to enter upon it at all in good faith—Adding, that he (Gen[era]l G.) had expressed the decided opinion that *there would be no treaty concluded*, which he repeated to me, with the declaration, on information which he had obtained, that the Commissioners were appointed *only to satisfy Mr. Hamilton."* In a few minutes after this conversation I was admitted to the presence of Mr. França, the Secretary of State. After being very kindly received, and after requesting his attention to the claim of the [ship] John S. Bryan—that he would have the amount included in the estimates of appropriations by the coming Legislative Assembly—and after receiving the usual excuse in respect to the other claims, that they were before the Executive Council and that he himself was waiting for its decisions—and, after assuring me in the most earnest manner that Brazil *felt it to her interest* to favor the U. States as much or more than any other nation, and after offering to procure for me an interview with the Minister of the Fazenda in respect to any modification of the late tariff—the conversation with him turned upon the public announcement of the negotiations with Great Britain. This was no sooner done than the smiles of us both, involuntarily, grew into an *outright laugh*! He could not hold his countenance, I, certainly, could not mine, until he insisted to know— "Why this laugh"? I then told him I felt at liberty to *inquire whether there would be a treaty with Great Britain?* He seriously replied— "Oh! yes, *if they will come to our terms of fair and perfect equality. That we will discuss* with them. But I assure you *there is no treaty yet*, and nothing has yet been done more than what you see." He, then, rather intimated that Brazil would keep herself ["to" *canceled*] free to enlarge or diminish her tariff at will, and would not again bind herself to any given rate of imposts; and that she would not agree to terms such as she lately rejected at the proposal of the late Special mission of G[rea]t Britain. And yet, I am informed that Mr. Hamilton has no other powers or propositions than those of Mr. [Charles Augustus] Ellis. And the English ["packet" *interlined*] is now and has been for some time waiting in vain to take home to England information of some progress in the negotiation. Upon the whole I concur in the opinion of Gen[era]l Guido that there will be no treaty, at all events for the present, between Great Britain & Brazil. During this conversation, Mr. França inquired of me whether I had full powers to treat on the part of the U. States. I informed him that I had, and inquired in turn whether Brazil would consent to open negotiations at Washington—in reply to which he said they would prefer to negotiate here. I told him that the U. States would ask nothing but what was fairly equal, and to be placed on the best footing with any other nation; but we would not again enter into a *derivative* treaty—i.e. one like our former, depending upon the construction & terms of the treaty of Brazil with any other power. He said as far as duties were concerned, no treaty hereafter ought to fix their amount, and, therefore, no one treaty could be made to depend upon another in respect to that point. A stipulation to be put upon the footing "of the most favored nation," would necessarily be somewhat relative or dependent. To this I had no objection. He then asked whether it would be agreeable to the U. States for Brazil to raise the grade of her mission at Washington? I replied that I presumed it would be considered complimentary, and that it would be nothing more than was deserved by the highly respectable and very acceptable Minister resident already there [Gaspar José de Lisboa]. Here our conversation was interrupted, and I must renew it at another time. In what I have already said I have given you all the information which I can give in respect to the progress of our claims. The only answer I can get is the invariable verbal reply that they are before the Executive Council, which cannot be got to act. If all the

Corps diplomatic were not treated in the same manner I should resent this continued delay & neglect to acknowledge even the receipt of Communications; but the English, Russian, French, Buenos Ayrean and every Legation complain equally & alike; and the Pope's Nuncio, I am told, has had an outbreak with them on this & other matters in controversy with His Holiness [Gregory XVI]. I must, therefore, be patient until they all cease to be patient; or until I receive instructions from the President which will peremptorily compel them to act. Indeed these people should not be indulged in a course which would be highly offensive to Foreign Powers & their representatives any where else. Mr. França as much as admitted that Mr. [Joseph] Ray's claim was just, and yet I could get no satisfactory answer as to how or when we are to expect it to be liquidated and paid. What must I do if this silence & delay is persisted in?

The accompanying papers—No. 1 an unofficial letter addressed by me to Mr. Hamilton, at his request; No. 2 A letter from the American firm of Maxwell, Wright & Co. in Rio de Janeiro, to me; and No. 3 my reply to the same; will show the nature, connexions & extent of the African slave trade as it is, and has for some time been, unblushingly carried on by our citizens under our flag. It has grown so bold & so bad as no longer to wear a mask even to those who reside here, and who are at all acquainted with the trade between Brazil & Africa. Upon information showing more than probable grounds, I hesitated not to advise our Consul, Mr. [George William] Gordon, to cause the arrest of the Master, Mates & crew of the Brig MonteVideo, and to hold them in custody on board of the Boston sloop of war until he could examine into the case. The examination has proceeded to a great length and I have given to it my personal attention & attendance. And, I must say, it has developed a combination of persons and of means to carry on this infamous traffic, to the utter disgrace of human nature and to the dishonor of our flag and of all three nations, England, Brazil & the U. States. I have carefully abstained from mentioning names, but I earnestly submit to the Department, that the attention of Congress ought at once to be called to the amendment of our laws for the suppression of the African slave-trade; and to the crying injustice of punishing the poor ignorant officers & crews of merchant ships for high misdemeanors & felonies, when the *ship-owners* in the U. States & their *American consignees, factors & agents* abroad are left almost entirely untouched by penalties for sending the sailors on voyages notoriously for the purposes of the slave-trade. I submit too that our Consuls should be armed with more authority on this subject. The whole matter is fully treated in the accompanying papers, and I ask that they may be immediately laid before Congress. I cannot do less than justice to Mr. Gordon, our Consul, when I say that he has shown every disposition in these cases to do his whole duty. He has acted prudently & with the soundest discretion, but firmly & without shrinking from any necessary responsibility. I have advised with him at every step, and he has done nothing without my approbation, and if blame, in any respect, is attributable to him in the course which he has pursued of arresting, examining and sending home these persons, I wish it to be understood that I desire to be considered as sharing with him in all responsibility and in all censure. But I can anticipate nothing else from the President & the whole country, than commendation & approval of what he has done, and is doing, to wipe from our flag & our nation a most foul stain. The persons charged are at present on board the Brig Bainbridge, and we are waiting only for the arrival of Commodore [Daniel] Turner from the River Platte to determine how & when they shall be sent home. Any disapprobation of Mr. Gordon's course would now be regarded here, as was the removal of Mr. [George W.] Slacum from office, as nothing less than a sanction of the courses pursued by persons in Brazil to aid & abet the slave-trade. At all hazards I shall continue in the steps I have taken until peremptorily ordered to desist. There has not been the least objection to my course on the part of this Government, and the police lent Mr. Gordon its prompt aid in the arrests. With the highest personal regard & official respect, I am, Your ob[edien]t Servant, Henry A. Wise.

ALS ([No. 9]) with Ens in DNA, RG 59 (State Department), Diplomatic Despatches, Brazil, vol. 13 (M-121:15), received 1/25/1845; FC in DNA, RG 84 (Foreign Posts), Brazil, Despatches, vol. 11; CCEx in DNA, RG 233 (U.S. House of Representatives), 28A-E1; PEx with Ens in House Document No. 148, 28th Cong., 2nd Sess., pp. 54–88.

From J[ohn] S. Barbour

Catalpa [Culpeper County, Va.] Dec[embe]r 15th 1844
My Dear Sir, My son James [Barbour] will deliver you this note.

Having written you fully on [*partial word canceled*] this & other subjects recently, I have nothing to add, but the apprehension that our late victory [*one word canceled*] like that of 1829 is to be utterly fruitless of good. The tenour & drift of every Northern & New York demonstration is everything but fair or true to the South. Being the weaker part we need most support, and if our own Sentinels are to turn their arms upon us, it would be far better to ["have" *interlined*] gone over at once to the enemy; and conciliated his kindness, *as we could.* Colo[nel Thomas H.] Benton[']s step in the Senate professedly for Texas is in fact against it. If anything good comes to the public Cause, & the Southern Country, from the late election; I shall be happily relieved & agre[e]ably disappointed. Y[ou]rs Sincerely, J.S. Barbour.

ALS in ScCleA.

From A [NDREW] J. DONELSON

Washington Texas, Dec[em]b[e]r 15[t]h 1844
Sir, I have the honor to enclose you herewith, a letter [of 11/24] from Mr. [Stewart] Newell our consul at Sabine forwarding to me the complaint of Messrs. Noelle & Brown on account of certain offences charged by them against a citizen of Texas by the name of French. I send them in order that the Department may have a correct view of the character of the annoyances to which our commerce in that quarter will be subjected, as long as we are without a Treaty with Texas, or a more vigilant *police* there. Under present circumstances I have told Mr. Newell that there is no remedy for the Messrs. Noelle & Brown but in the courts of Justice. I have also informed Mr. Newell of the hope which is entertained that the Congress of Texas will amend the law ["by the repeal of the provision" *interlined*] making a discrimination of five per cent against the United States, on all goods imported in American vessels. Should this be done and the collector of Texas at the Sabine receive such instructions as will hereafter relieve our vessels from the exactions claimed in the cases of the schooners Louisiana and William Bryan, we may expect less trouble.

I also enclose you a letter from Mr. Newell, who was still at Galvezton and not at Sabine, asking for leave of absence. To this I have stated to him among other reasons declining to act on the subject, that as he was the judge of the public wants in the district of his duties, I had no doubt ["of his" *canceled*] the Department would always excuse a temporary absence from them provided the proper provisions were made ["made" *canceled*] by him against the chances of injury to the public interests under his charge.

I send with this package the vindicator and Register published at this place. They contain the inaugural addresses of the new President [Anson Jones] and Vice President [Kenneth L. Anderson], and Gen[era]l [Samuel] Houston[']s valedictory. I have the honor to be with sentiments of great respect y[ou]r ob[edien]t ser[van]t, A.J. Donelson.

P.S. Travelling with this despatch to Galvezton, where I saw Mr. Newell, and the vice Consul Col. [Elisha A.] Rhodes, and finding that no injury was likely to result from granting a short leave of absence to Mr. Newell, I have granted it to him. V[er]y respectfully &, A.J.D.

ALS (No. 6) with Ens in DNA, RG 59 (State Department), Diplomatic Despatches, Texas, vol. 2 (T-728:2, frames 421–426 and 412), received 1/2/1845.

DECEMBER 16–31, 1844

◻

"I am under a severe pressure of business," Calhoun wrote, in apology for the briefness of a letter to his son-in-law. Many matters were in course—administrative, diplomatic, and political—and were reflected in the Secretary's papers. Few of them, however, were yet near a point of resolution. The Congress had yet to complete its wrestling with Texas and many other matters. The politics of the country would lack a clear focus until the new President and Congress took office in March next and revealed something of the contours of conflict to come.

Most of Calhoun's correspondents seem to take it as a matter of course that President-elect Polk would wish to continue Calhoun as Secretary of State. Calhoun, after all, was one of the handful of occupants of the top level of American statesmanship and he and his friends had given Polk unqualified support. Calhoun was not so sure that he wanted it or that it would be offered. As to remaining in his office, Calhoun wrote a friend in Europe the day after Christmas: "I have not yet determined whether I shall or not, should Mr. Polk desire it, nor shall I, untill I shall be assured, what will be the course of his administration." And the day after that Calhoun wrote his son-in-law: "Nothing yet is known as to the intention of Mr. Polk in reference to the formation of his Cabinet. He keeps a prudent silence."

◻

From R[ICHAR]D[?] ANDREWS

Alexandria [D.C.,] Dec[embe]r 16th 1844

D[ea]r Sir, I have been a resident of this place for about twelve months—my object in coming, being the Education of my children. Possessing but little means besides my profession as a Lawyer, which my experience proves to be very unprofitable here, Several of my friends prior to my removal, being aware of my circumstances and

559

design advised me to apply to Gover[nmen]t for some office, under it. I accordingly obtained from the Hon. R[obert] M.T. Hunter, a letter of introduction to the Hon. Henry A. Wise for the purpose of obtaining his influence in my behalf. This letter I enclosed to Mr. Wise, as well as I can recollect in Jan[uar]y last, and shortly thereafter had a personal interview with him. He informed me that it would afford him pleasure to serve me and through me his friend Mr. Hunter but it would be out of his power as he was then engaged in making arrangements preparatory to his leaving the Country—that employment was difficult to obtain, unless the applicant had some influential friend at Washington who would be on the alert when ever a vacancy occur[r]ed. I afterwards addressed a letter to Mr. Wise requesting him to forward my letters including that of Mr. Hunter to Mr. [Thomas W.] Gilmer, the late Secretary of the Navy with whom I had some slight personal acquaintance for the purpose of obtaining a Clerk-ship in that Department should there be a vacancy, or when one occur[r]ed. I rec[eive]d a note from the Secreatry acknowledging the re[ceip]t of the letters referred to & which he stated had been filed with my application—and that there was no vacancy at that time. The next day I think the unfortunate disaster on board the Princeton took place. That sad event and the high state of Political excitement, till recently, ever since, caused me to make no further application, although I had some acquaintance with his successor the Hon. Judge [John Y.] Mason, to whom I was introduced in the year 1835 or '36 at the Circuit Court of Westmoreland County Virginia which court he attended, in lieu of Judge [John Tayloe] Lomax, and in which I practised regularly till I came here. I now address you this communication although personally an entire stranger, to solicit your aid and influence in obtaining for me some decent employment, which will afford a salary of about $1000 p[e]r Ann[um]. A Clerkship in any one of the Departments of Gover[nmen]t, or in the land office would be truly desirable. I am personally well acquainted with the Hon. John Taliaferro [former Representative from Va.]. With Willoughby Newton [Representative from Va.] and other members of Congress all of whom have promised me letters of recommendation when ever I require them. Should you be disposed my D[ea]r Sir to aid me in this matter these letters will be obtained and handed over to you which with that of the letter from Mr. Hunter, I hope will be fully satisfactory to you. It may be proper before I conclude to inform you how I stand in reference to the two Political parties into which our country is and has been for some time divided and this I cannot do in a better manner than by giving you an account of my acts from 1824, the first of my political acts, to the present time. In that year I voted the [Andrew] Jackson ticket—and after its defeat, opposed the administration of Mr. [John Quincy] Adams. Voted the Jackson ticket again in 1828. I was opposed to the formation of Jackson's Cabinet, censured his administration, from its commencement—and after his correspondence with you, and the subsequent dissolution of his Cabinet, I dissolved all connection with what was then called the Jackson party. His famous proclamation succeeded by the Force-Bill with his protest to the Senate, confirmed me in the opinion of the propriety of the course I had taken and I have not acted with that party, properly so called, from that day to this, nor do I think that I ever shall. In 1836 I voted what was then called the double headed ticket ([William Henry] Harrison & [Hugh L.] White)—in 1840 for Harrison—and supported [Henry] Clay after the nomination of James K. Polk by the *Locofoco* (I cannot call it democratic) Convention—not that I agreed altogether with Mr. Clay, politically, but because I have the fullest confidence in his talents and Political integrity which I have not in Polk, who voted for the Force-Bill and against the compromise[,] who was supported in the Tariff States as a Tariff man and in the Antitariff States as a free trade man[,] for these reasons and because he was called young Hickory and on account of the interference of General Jackson in his behalf I opposed him. I have said it in my public speeches and now again repeat it that had your friends stuck to you and have run you for the Presidency, regardless of the nomination of the Baltimore Convention that I would have given you freely and willingly my humble support—but under no circumstances can I ever support Polk, [Martin] Van Buren or [Thomas H.] Benton. I have called on you, my D[ea]r Sir, to assist me because I have long admired your character—and because I would scorn to ask a favor of any one who sustained Jackson's administration—especially the last four years of it. Should I be successful in obtaining an office I pledge myself not to meddle with Politics, but to devote my time and talents, such as they are exclusively to my business. If it will not be asking too much of you, I'll thank you kindly to examine the letter of Mr. Hunter to which I have refer[r]ed, now filed with my application, in the Navy department—and inform me at your earliest convenience, at what time it would best suit you to receive a call from me, as a personal interview with you would be a privilege which I should highly appreciate. I am Hon[ored] Sir, with sentiments of high regard, y[ou]r ob[e]d[ien]t servant, Rd.[?] Andrews.

ALS in ScCleA.

From LEOPOLD BIERWIRTH

Newyork [City], 16 Dec[embe]r 1844

Sir, A Statement, of which I annex a printed copy, on the subject of emigration from Germany, is travelling the rounds in the american newspapers, accompanied by editorials and communications more or less abusive of foreigners in general and Germans in particular. The Statement purports to come from an american Consul in Germany [Frederick List] and its extraordinary contents certainly deserve attention, if true; at all events they are well calculated to strengthen the growing prejudice against immigrants from Germany. The german population of this country must consider itself interested in the matter at least as much as the natives, and if the alleged discoveries of Consul List are true, the German Society of Newyork, of which I am an officer, will cheerfully, and I trust effectually, cooperate with the public authorities in preventing the evil, with which this country is said to be threatened.

But in the opinion of many the Statement itself bears evidence of inaccuracy, and it is even suspected that it never had its source in Germany, but is of native origin, and I have therefore been requested respectfully to inquire of you, whether Consul List has made a report to your Department, such as the annexed newspaper paragraph alleges, and whether the extract therefrom, as published, is correct.

In the hope that you will favor me with an answer, I subscribe myself with great esteem, Sir, Your most obed[ien]t Serv[an]t, Leopold Bierwirth.

ALS with En in DNA, RG 59 (State Department), Miscellaneous Letters (M-179:106, frames 319–321); PC with En (from the New York *Journal of Commerce*) in the Charleston, S.C., *Mercury,* January 1, 1845, p. 2; PC in the Columbus, Ohio, *Ohio State Journal,* January 9, 1845, p. 3. NOTE: Bierwirth enclosed a clipping from an unknown U.S. newspaper that reported German paupers and criminals were to be transported to the U.S. The assertion was made upon information supposedly quoted from a report to the State Department from Frederick List, U.S. Consul at Würtemberg. An AEU by Calhoun reads "Relates to Mr. List."

From James A. Black, [Representative from S.C.], 12/16. Black recommends C[harles] R. Leffreing for appointment to be U.S. Consul at Stuttgart, in Würtemberg, "his native place." ALS in DNA, RG 59 (State Department), Applications and Recommendations, 1845–1853, Leffreing (M-873:52, frames 612–613).

To JAMES ED[WARD] COLHOUN, [Abbeville District, S.C.]

Washington, 16th Dec[embe]r 1844
My dear James, Knowing the pleasure you will feel, in seeing how much [your nephew] James [Edward Calhoun] has improved, in letter writing, I enclose two letters from him, received since he entered the University [of Virginia]. He has, I think, resolved in good earnest on improving himself, and I have great hopes of his doing well.

We hear by every steamer from Mr. [Thomas G.] Clemson & Anna [Maria Calhoun Clemson]. They are in good health & sperits. Patrick [Calhoun] has returned from his western excursion, & is with us. John [C. Calhoun, Jr.] de[s]cended the Mississippi from St. Louis to N[ew] Orleans & thence proceeded to Andrew's [Andrew Pickens Calhoun's plantation in Marengo County, Ala.], where he now is, & where he will spend the winter. His general health is good, but his cough continues to affect him.

I send by the Mail, which takes this a copy of my correspondence, which accompanied the Message. The [Martin] V[an] B[uren] wing of the party will, from appear[ances] oppose the admission of Texas, which will endanger the Messure [*sic*]. They are acting badly.

We are all well, & all join their love to you. Yours affectionately, J.C. Calhoun.

ALS in ScCleA.

From ROB[ER]T R. HUNTER, "Private"

New York [City,] 16 Dec[embe]r 1844
Dear Sir, It seems although the Whig & Democratic Journals of this City cannot agree in any thing else, there exists great unanimity amongst them in their condemnation of you. Myself and another friend of yours here, have procured to be written an able reply to the attacks made upon you and Mr. [Wilson] Shannon [U.S. Minister to Mexico] by the "Morning News" and the "Evening Post" of this City; The author of the reply is one of the ablest Lawyers of the New York bar, and withal a strong friend of yours; the reply is published this morning in the "New York Herald" which paper is more extensively circulated and more generally read than any other in the Country. And I have herewith sent you the paper.

Your friends here feel much solicitude for you, and are doing all in their power to repel the attacks made upon you by [Martin] Van Buren & his friends, who are your principal assailants here. Those selfish & ignoble Spirits, well know, that your sole object is your Country's interests, honor, & prosperity; still, they oppose your measures, villify & persecute you with a malignancy that their desperate position can alone account for. I sincerely hope that you will be able notwithstanding their hostility to carry out, triumphantly, all your your [*sic*] views, and I feel confident that you will. Faithfully & Truly, I remain yours, Robt. R. Hunter.

ALS in ScCleA. NOTE: The defense of Calhoun referred to by Hunter is apparently an article entitled "The Diplomacy with Mexico," which appeared under the authorship of "T.T.T." in the New York, N.Y., *Herald*, December 16, 1844, p. 1. The author found Calhoun's diplomatic policies to be consistent with American principles and precedents.

From J.G. Klenck, Publ[ishe]r, Germ[an] Nat[ional] Gazette, Washington, 12/16. "The undersigned having become the proprietor of the German 'National Gazette' in this City begs leave to say in reply to your Circular, that the present ["regular" *interlined*] Circulation of his paper is 1500, and expected to be increased during the present session of Congress." ALS in DNA, RG 59 (State Department), Miscellaneous Letters Received Regarding Publishers of the Laws.

From T[HOMAS] M. RODNEY

Consulate of the United States of America
Matanzas [Cuba], Dec. 16th 1844

Sir, I have the honor to inform the Department that I arrived here yesterday and immediately entered upon the duties of my office.

The American prisoners have been released from prison on bail with the exception of [Thomas] Savage who has been set at liberty without security, and it is to be hoped that the excesses and cruelties perpetrated by the constituted authorities of this Island, during the late conspiracy, may never be repeated.

The effects of the recent hurricane are still visible in the country and the crop of sugar for this year will be full one third ["less" *interlined*] than last. I have the honor to be Sir, your obe[dien]t Servant, T.M. Rodney.

ALS in DNA, RG 59 (State Department), Consular Despatches, Matanzas, vol. 4 (T-339:4), received 12/27.

From W[HITEMARSH] B. SEABROOK, "(Confidential)"

Edisto Island, Dec. 16th 1844

My Dear Sir, With the result of the [S.C.] Gubernatorial election you have long since been acquainted. To the decision of the representatives of the people I bow with submission, ["I bow with submission," *canceled*] but against the means adopted to elevate the incumbent [William Aiken] I do solemnly protest. Unfounded charges, log-rolling, the untiring labours of interested individuals, inactivity on the part of my friends, and above all, money, *profusely expended*, were the agents that discomfitted me, and put another into office. The citizens of South Carolina would be astounded at the information which it is in the power of hundreds to impart in reference to this matter. By Bank accommodations to the country merchants, they were released from their present embarrassments, & for this favor conferred, they used ["their" *changed to* "the"; "most" *interlined*] zealous efforts to induce the members from their sections of the State to support Aiken. I will not however particularize. The recital would disgust you, if it do not create despair for the future welfare of So. Ca. In 24 hours after the election, the [Columbia] "South Carolinian" was in the hands of the new party, under the editorship of [Adam G.] Summer of Newberry, one of the Governor's aid[e]s. The Charleston [Southern] Patriot too has been purchased, & for the [Charleston] Mercury a bid had been made by B[artholomew R.?] Carroll. Whether he be a friend of Aiken or not I cannot inform you. Thus in subsidizing the press they hope to consummate their real object. [Robert Barnwell] Rhett & [Franklin H.] Elmore are to be trampled under foot, & [Francis W.] Pickens, the acknowledged leader of the Aiken party, is to go to the U.S. Senate. Let me in passing assure you, that So. Ca. has at last recorded on the journals of the Legislature (in her selection for Governor) her submission to Federal aggression. All hopes of a resistance to the black tariff are at an end—we must forever wear the yoke which [Ker] Boyce & his moneyed associates of Charleston have fastened on our necks. 'Tis true before I left Columbia a reaction had taken place, & very many were regretting the course they had unwittingly taken. As far as my information goes,

565

& it is extensive, but one feeling, and that of indignation, has been expressed by the people. Even the old Union men, among them Dr. [Samuel H.] Dickson, declare that the State is disgraced by putting the executive power into the hands of Aiken.

For the first week [John A.] Stuart behaved well, & bid fair to lead our party. Suddenly his old habit returned, and, so far as he was concerned, all was lost. Tho' for days I had been laboring to disabuse the minds of the members concerning my ["having" *interlined*; "being" *changed to* "been"] nominated by Rhett he one day in debate in substance declared that I was a Bluffton boy, yet it was known to him that the charge was untrue. For two days it was as much as I could do to prevent him from publicly denouncing you for having, as he said, endorsed that ["part of the" *interlined*] President[']s [John Tyler's] message in reference to the Tariff. When he made the declaration he was under the influence of strong drink. At heart I know him to be one of your strongest friends. Taking advantage of a remark made by Rhett in one of his letters to him that, if the State did not resist, he would not again serve her, he (S[tuart]) has nominated [James H.] Hammond to oppose [Samuel W.] Trotti [Representative from S.C.].

My agricultural friends, tho' for 15 years I had resisted their importunities, induced me to become a candidate for the office of Governor. When I needed their aid to accomplish the very object I & they had in view—the improvement of the agricultural condition of the State, they deserted me for the reason, among others, that my means ["were too limited" *canceled*] were inadequate to the station— & that any man who neglects his own interests for the vanity of supporting that of the State, was unfit to rule over any people. My friends now insist that I shall forthwith cease all ["my" *canceled and* "agricultural" *interlined*] labours in behalf of So. Ca. Whether I shall accede to their request will depend upon circumstances. I have suffered greatly in health & fortune, much more than any one, save the members of my family, knows to further the solid prosperity of the State, & now I feel broken hearted, not for the blow that has been inflicted upon me, but that the land of my birth has fallen from the high moral ["position" *interlined*] she has so long gloriously occupied, & is doomed to sink into the arms of the plotters of her ruin. Very truly & respectfully, W.B. Seabrook.

ALS in ScCleA; PEx in Boucher and Brooks, eds., *Correspondence*, p. 270.

From FRANCIS WHARTON

Phil[adelphia,] Dec. 16, 1844

My dear Sir, I am much obliged to you for the documents I received from you the other day. I began a review of the Texas letters in the Pennsylvania[n], to whose columns I have free access, but I found that one of my coeditors—Mr. [Henry D.] Gilpin, I believe—dissented from me in the length of concurrence to which I was disposed to go, and managed to neutralize what I said by additional comments with an opposite leaning. I fear that if public opinion settles, ["wh" *canceled and "as" interlined*] it appears to be doing, at the North, there will be great difficulty in obtaining from the Democratic Review an entrance for a review such as I am desirous to give. Even Mr. [John L.] O'Sullivan goes farther in dissenting from you than I could have supposed.

Mr. [James K.] Polk's Nashville speech has startled some of the old managers here. There are only two or three men among the leading politicians who are worthy of the confidence of the president elect. One of them is Mr. John K. Kane, who is now in Washington, & who can give you a better idea of Mr. [James] Buchanan[']s low intrigues, than almost any one else. Mr. Kane is a gentleman of very high tone, and thoroughly committed in opposition to Buchanan[']s views. You probably noticed how we brought out the Pennsylvanian in opposition to the preposterous nomination, by our electoral College, of the Secretary of State. I am y[ou]rs, Francis Wharton.

ALS in ScCleA. NOTE: John K. Kane was a Philadelphia judge.

From ISAAC E. CRARY, [former Representative from Mich.]

Marshall [Mich.,] December 17th 1844

My Dear Sir, Your letter of the 3d inst. came to hand by the mail of last evening. The Bill to foreclose the mortgage in the case of Mrs. [Placidia Mayrant] Adams [of Pendleton, S.C.] has been filed in the Court of Chancery and an order of publication obtained to bring in the Defendants. The final decree will be obtained in the month of June next. In that the time of sale will be fixed. It will probably take place as soon there after as the law will permit—but of this I will give information in time to enable Mrs. Adams to avail herself of

567

all her legal privileges. I enclose herewith a memorandum from the Auditor General's Office on the subject of the taxes. I thought it advisable to make the inquiry. On the sales since the time alluded to in the memorandum there will be two years redemption from the 1st of October last if the taxes have not already been paid.

You well say that we have achieved a great victory. To you it must give great satisfaction as almost every measure of the victors has been urged by you upon the country in days gone by and at a time too when you could hardly have expected so early a triumph. In this State we openly and boldly on all occasions, took ground against distribution, against a Bank, against a Tariff for protection— in favor of State Rights and the immediate annexation of Texas.

The fruits of the victory we may realize—but to do so will require all the firmness that Col. [James K.] Polke possesses. If he makes up his cabinet of right materials all will be well with him and with the country. I have however some misgivings growing out of his old associations. The friends of Mr. [Martin] Van Buren will labor to get the control of affairs into their own hands so far as the important appointments are concerned and with them thus distributed we shall be likely to recede as a party from the high and commanding ground we now occupy.

The friends of General [Lewis] Cass are anxious to give him a place in the Senate and it is thought he will accept if nominated, by the Legislature. The General has added to his popularity by his zeal & energy during the campaign and can probably be made Senator if he desires it.

I have to return you my thanks for the rich intellectual treat given me by the letter from your Department to our minister Mr. [William R.] King. It is a paper that will produce quite as much effect among the sovereigns at home as among the sovereigns of Europe. With great respect Yours truly, Isaac E. Crary.

ALS in ScCleA.

To Henry W. Cushman, Bernardstown, Mass., 12/17. "I have to reply to your letter of the 12th instant, that the Department has discontinued the practice of sending out Agents for distributing the laws, and that the business is confined to a forwarding House at Baltimore." FC in DNA, RG 59 (State Department), Domestic Letters, 35:50 (M-40:33).

From A[NDREW] J. DONELSON

Washington [Texas,] December 17[t]h 1844

Sir, Regarding the communication made to me on the 13th inst., by the [Acting] Secretary of State of Texas [Ebenezer Allen], as too important to entrust to the uncertain conveyances from this place at this period of the year, I have determined to send a special messenger with it, who will also bring other despatches from me of less interest.

After the receipt of the correspondence between Mr. [Wilson] Shannon & Mr. [Manuel C.] Rejon, the occasion seemed to be a proper one to call for some expression of the views of the Executive here, more definite than any presented in my previous despatches, which were rather of a private and unofficial, than public character. I accordingly addressed to the proper Department the letter of the 10th December, a copy of which is herewith enclosed, embodying some of the considerations which authorised the expectation on the part of my Government, that Texas would maintain a position consistent with that occupied by her when she entered into the Treaty. The insulting and threatening tone of Mexico towards the United States was referred to as a circumstance to strengthen this expectation, and I added such other observations on the present state of the question as seemed to be useful in obtaining the desired assurance.

The prompt reply from the acting Secretary of State, as given in the note of the 13th, is not only satisfactory as an indication of the views and feelings of the Executive on the subject, but may be relied on also as an expression of those entertained by the present congress of Texas.

Whatever may have been the revulsion of feeling caused by the long postponement of annexation, it has not changed those affections which bind the people of Texas to their kindred in the United States, and the consummation of the measure, within a reasonable period, by our Government, will be ratified here with great unanimity. It may be different, however, if their expectations and wishes are to be doomed to another disappointment. Treaties to extend their trade and intercourse with foreign powers, important changes in their Revenue system, and numerous administrative measures which will readily suggest themselves to you, as necessary, if they maintain an organization seperate from the United States, are of course suspended until this event is settled. And when we add to such urgent motives for their action that which is furnished by the fact that they have on their North and North West numerous powerful Indian tribes, and on their South & West, Mexico, ever ready to annoy them with marauding incursions, it is a matter of wonder that they await with the patience they do the deliberation the question has yet to undergo in the United States before it can come to them in a practicable form for approval.

The terms, therefore, imployed in my letter to the Secretary of State to indicate the respect and admiration due to both the Government and people of Texas, were not intended as mere diplomatic compliment. They are the result of an honest conviction that they are richly meritted. With cause enough to justify a war of aggression on Mexico, and with the confidence of success, if they begin it, they are yet quiet. With every temptation which an intelligent European diplomacy can offer to them, to persevere in a national cause independent and as a rival, of the United States, they yet repel it. They feel that their best shield in the occupation and improvement of the great resources of their Territory is in the preservation of the Republican principle and that this may be hazarded if they do not form a part of the American Union—that as a seperate nation future immigration will be chiefly supplied by the nations accustomed to the forms of monarchy and Aristocracy, and that thus the force of Republican association gradually weakening may be ultimately subverted. They see also that in the present state of the affairs of Mexico, which must ever possess a population repulsive to theirs, even if there were no war between them, new provinces from that power must be yielded to Texas considered as a seperate nation, or must become the theatre of further revolution: and that thus extension of territory outstripping the capacity to supply it with a sound population will become a disturbing element in the general peace of this continent, and pave the way for the introduction of European influence in settling the domestic as well as foreign relations of the communities which will inhabit it.

Unwilling to embark in a national career, thus surrounded with danger, and thus doubtful in its effects on the American Union, Texas tells us substantially in the letter now sent to you, that she will wait yet a reasonable period for the decision of our Government on the question of annexation. A position so elevated—so far above those prejudices which might be well allowed to spring out of the contemplation of the rich prospects held out to her by Foreign powers as a rival of the United States, and from the confidence her triumph over Mexico has been so well calculated to inspire—has been regarded by me as worthy of the highest tribute of honor and praise; and I trust in the attempt to express it, however unworthily it has been done, I have not transcended the spirit of my instructions.

Accompanying this despatch is my letter of the 6[t]h inst., enclosing copies of the correspondence between Mr. Shannon & Mr. Rejon, to the Secretary of State of Texas [Anson Jones], and his reply [of 12/7], which would have been forwarded earlier had there been an opportunity. I have the honor to be very respectfully y[ou]r ob[edien]t ser[van]t, A.J. Donelson.

[Enclosure]

A[ndrew] J. Donelson to Ebenezer Allen, Acting
Secretary of State of Texas

Legation of the United States
Washington Texas, Dec[embe]r 10 1844

Sir, The Undersigned had the honor to submit for the information of the Government of Texas, on the 6[t]h inst., copies of the correspondence between the Minister of the United States at Mexico and that Government, growing out of the veiws [*sic*] taken by the President of the United States of the renewal of the war upon Texas, and the mode of conducting ["it" *interlined*], as declared by Mexico in the orders of Gen[era]l [Adrian] Woll on the 20[t]h of June last and the decree of the Provisional President dated the 17[t]h June 1843. His object was to give this Government full information on a subject of such vital importance to the interests of Texas, and particularly to show in what manner the President of the United States [John Tyler] met the responsibility involved in the Treaty of Annexation as a measure to which Mexico had no right to object—and he is happy to acknowledge the receipt of the Hon[ora]ble Mr. Jone[s]'s note expressing the satisfaction felt by this Government at the course pursued by the President of the United States.

Nothing has been omitted within the Constitutional power of the Executive of the United States, to guard the interests of Texas from injury, resulting from the acceptance by her of the invitation which led to the Treaty of annexation. Appeals have been made to the reason of Mexico to desist from the prosecution of the war and finally the most solemn protest against her right to punish Texas for acts, for which the United States are responsible, has been presented to her, accompanied by strong indications of what may be expected from an offended people should she, in despite of these admonitions, carry out the purposes of the decree and orders referred to.

The Government of Texas has also seen that the President of the United States has avowed as frankly to other powers the considerations which led to the Treaty of Annexation. Believing that the reasons for the measure are solid, not only as they apply to Texas and the United States, but the other nations of the earth, there has been no motive or wish for their concealment. It has been treated from the beginning to the present period, as a measure called for by the common good, extending it is true the Territorial limits of the United States, but not in the spirit of unworthy ambition or aggrandizement, or as a disturbing cause in the general peace of the world, or even the special interest of Mexico herself. On the contrary the measure was adopted as one of peace, necessarily growing out of the physical features of the Territory of Texas and the character of her population, and equally important as one of security to Mexico by removing all apprehension respecting the future agitation of the question of boundary.

But it is not the intention of the Undersigned to state at large, on this occasion, the veiws taken by his Government of the question of annexation as one foreign to Texas and the United States. He adverts to them only for the purpose of introducing the observations promised in his note of the 6[t]h inst. and which relate to the question as now confined to these two countries.

If Mexico, under a mistaken sense of her duty and true policy, chooses to consider the United States as an aggressor, because of her acknowledgement of the independence of Texas, and the exercise of the right to treat with her for Territory, she cannot expect a more satisfactory answer than has been already given: and in no event, can it be supposed that she can induce the United States to abandon the measure of annexation.

But whilst the United States are thus innocently incurring a liability to the hostile action of Mexico, their Executive Government reasonably conclude, and confidently expect, that Texas herself will maintain her connection with the question of annexation so far, at least, as not to consider it lost or abandoned, on account of the late action of the Senate of the United States upon it.

The Undersigned doubts not that he has fully satisfied this Government that the measure of annexation which is still pending before the Congress of the United States has been strengthened by the recent elections in those States. Considering ["it" interlined], therefore, as now relieved from the temporary causes which were instrumental in its defeat: and considering also the confidence with which its friends may rely upon the increased strength it will gain from its intrinsic merit, the more it is examined, and the more thoroughly its bearing on the true interests of Texas and the United States, is understood—it may be safely assumed that it is destined to a speedy consummation as far as the action of the United States can accomplish it. A result so much in accordance with the early wish of Texas, and deferred by causes, which, now inoperative, have ceased to be remembered with feelings of unkindness by her citizens, cannot but be hailed with joy by all who have sympathised with their sufferings in a noble struggle for independence.

This reference to the result of the recent elections in the United States, not made without a just sense of the impropriety, as a general rule, of introducing them to the notice of Foreign Governments, has been dictated in this case by the peculiar relation of the parties to the question of annexation. Without the cooperation and sanction of the Government and people of Texas the measure cannot be consummated; and hence it is important that no mistaken veiw of the influences necessary to action, in either country should prevail. The rejection of the Treaty by the Senate of the United States was calculated to create the belief that the measure had been lost, and it was natural that this Government acting for the best interests of the Republic should be looking to those alternative measures called for by the abandonment of all hope of incorporation into the American Union. To correct this erroneous inference, the Undersigned has been authorised to allude to the failure of the Treaty as affording no evidence of the abandonment of the measure by the Government of the United States, and to the public sentiment, as developped [*sic*] by the canvass for the Presidency, as justifying the confident belief, already expressed, that if the measure is to be defeated, it will be for the want of the necessary support from Texas herself.

In this state of the question then it cannot be necessary for the undersigned to dwell upon the anxiety of his Government that Texas should maintain the position consistent with its ultimate success. If the disappointment of her wishes thus long has been productive of injury, as it doubtless has, in retarding the settlement and developement of the resources of her Territory, she is sustained by the prospect of greater ultimate good to flow from annexation. Her sacrifices in this respect, great as they are, will be soon compensated, it is trusted, not only by corresponding benefits in wealth and independence—the consequence of incorporation into the Union—but by those higher moral benefits which will result from her increasing claim on the gratitude of the millions who will hereafter review her conduct, and ["who will" *interlined*] profit by her valor and patriotism, and above all by the magnanimity, which has enabled her to rise superior to the resentment ["naturally" *interlined*] produced by the apparent insensibility of her kindred in the Motherland to her past appeals.

The magnitude of the interests at at [*sic*] stake—the sincere conviction that the correct action of the two Governments upon them at this time is all important to the success of the Republican system, and that the veiws of his Government which have been so fully and unreservedly laid before this, are wise, honorable, and just—have induced the Undersigned to make these observations. He has done so upon the assumption that Texas is still desirous of annexation and will not abandon it while there is a hope of effecting it within a reasonable period on terms of justice and honor to her citizens. He has not, therefore, felt that it was proper to notice the objections which are sometimes made to it as being a measure of exclusive self interest to the United States, because this would imply a want of respect for the judgement of the citizens of Texas who have so long and with so much unanimity sustained it.

The Undersigned looks at the question of annexation, as he believ[e]s it to be, one of mutual, equal, and vital benefit and safety to both Republics, and that Texas in perceiving its true character as such, and so much earlier, and with so much more unanimity, than has been heretofore manifested by the United States, has only availed herself of the better opportunity she has enjoyed of testing the realities which sustain the position. He knows that the United States seek no aggrandizement by the acquisition of Territory at the expense of the rights of other nations: and that the incorporation of Texas into their Union is but a restoration of what should never have been taken from it, since it is as inseperable from them in its Geography, as it is in the social and political ties of its inhabitants and their connection with the preservation of the great principle of popular sovereignty. This restoration, as far as it has advanced, has been fortunately attended by no circumstances to give color to the charge that the United States secretly promoted the colonization of Texas for the purpose of severing a province from Mexico. The gallant General who commanded at St. Jacinto, and every citizen soldier who shares with him the glory of the Revolution, will bear witness that this charge against the Government of the United States is entirely groundless. If Mexico, therefore, has lost Texas she must blame herself alone, and the free and gallant spirit which the citizens of that ["province" *canceled and* "Territory" *interlined*] brought from their Motherland. If the United States gain Texas, it will be because that same free spirit by a law of destiny naturally returns to a congenial association, to be sheltered under the flag of a common union, and to live secure while it exerts its proportional agency in extending the blessings of civil and religious liberty. The Undersigned has the honor to be with sentiments of great respect y[ou]r very ob[edien]t

Ser[van]t, A.J. Donelson, Charge d'Affaires of the United States to Texas.

[Enclosure]
Ebenezer Allen to [Andrew J. Donelson]

Department of State
Washington [Texas], Dec[em]b[e]r 13, 1844

The undersigned, Attorney General of the Republic of Texas charged, ad interim, with the direction of the Department of State, has the honor to acknowledge the receipt of the note which Mr. Donelson, Chargé d'Affaires & & & did him the honor to address to him, under date of the 10[t]h inst., communicating information as to the measures adopted by the President of the United States, to guard the interests of Texas against injuries likely to result from the renewal of the war upon Texas by Mexico, on account of the acceptance of the proposition for annexation, made by the United States, and the avowed mode of conducting that war, as detailed in the orders of Gen[era]l Woll and the previous decree of the Provisional President: also communicating the veiws and suggestions of Mr. D[onelson] on the important question of annexation, and expressing the desire and expectation of the Executive of his Government, that Texas will continue to "maintain her connection with the cause of annexation so far, at least, as not to consider it lost or abandoned, on account of the late action of the Senate of the U. States upon it."

The undersigned is directed by the President to assure Mr. Donelson, in reply that the existing relations between the United States and Texas, so far as the subject of annexation is concerned, will not be affected by any opposing or unfavorable action on the part of the executive of the latter. But in receiving this assurance Mr. Donelson cannot but perceive that the result in relation to annexation may depend upon causes, over which the President can exert little or no control. Although the popular wish and feeling of Texas have heretofore been frankly and warmly expressed by her citizens in favor of the measure, yet Mr. D[onelson] cannot have failed to perceive that the strength and ardor of that wish have been necessarily, in some degree, diminished by the delay and apparent defeat of the measure, by the rejection of the late Treaty by the Senate of the United States. Still as the measure, in the opinion of Mr. Donelson, is not lost, but destined to a speedy consummation so far as the action of the United States can effect it, the undersigned trusts that the doubts and disappointment, experienced by the people of Texas necessarily occasioned by the circumstances, alluded to, will not have ripened into a general or insurmountable opposition to the measure before the consummation so confidently anticipated by Mr. D[onelson].

The undersigned is instructed by the President to express his unqualified admiration of the elevated spirit of philanthropy, pervading the communication of Mr. Donelson and of the active friendship manifested by the President of the United States, towards this Government, in his solemn protest, and measures of opposition, against the barbarous mode in which Mexico has avowed her intention to prosecute the war upon Texas.

The Undersigned avails himself of the occasion to renew to Mr. Donelson the assurances of the distinguished consideration with which he has the honor to be His most Ob[edien]t & faithful ser-[van]t, (Signed) Ebenezer Allen.

ALS with Ens in DNA, RG 59 (State Department), Diplomatic Despatches, Texas, vol. 2 (T-728:2, frames 429–435 and 437–443), received 1/2/1845.

From A[NDREW] J. DONELSON

Washington Texas, December 17[t]h 1844
Sir, You will receive herewith a copy of a letter [of 12/13] which I have addressed to the State Department of Texas, soliciting a reconsideration of the Revenue law which makes a discrimination against our vessels of five per cent on the goods imported by them in the Texan ports.

I am advised that a bill will be introduced in the present congress to repeal that provision of the law, with a prospect of its passage.

Finding after the receipt of the letter of the 13[t]h inst. from the State Department on the subject of annexation, that there was no special work for the legation, I addressed to the [Acting] Sec[retar]y [Ebenezer Allen] the note which is enclosed stating my wish to visit New Orleans on some private business. In accordance with the interview appointed in his reply [of 12/13], which is also enclosed, I called on the President [Anson Jones] who received me very cordially and after a long conversation in relation to the two countries, I took leave of him stating my intention to be absent a few weeks unless the next mail brought despatches from my Government.

Not receiving any further despatches, I trust the Department will excuse my absence when informed that the necessity for it grows out of the hurry in which I left my private business in order to execute their instructions to me, and when the public interest cannot possibly suffer thereby. No further communications can be made to me from Washington city which I will not meet at New Orleans, and be ready to return with, if necessary, on the regular packet to Galvezton.

I felt also that at this point I could promote the objects of my mission, with more certainty than at the seat of Government of Texas, for a few weeks at least, because without a special messenger to bring me information there would be no certainty in its transmission within a reasonable period. As evidence of this fact I refer to an important communication written by me in advance of my departure from New Orleans to Gen[era]l [Samuel] Houston, some eight or ten days, which did not reach him for some ten days after my arrival at the seat of Government of Texas. I have the honor to be very Respectfully y[ou]r ob[edien]t ser[van]t, A.J. Donelson.

ALS (No. 7) with Ens in DNA, RG 59 (State Department), Diplomatic Despatches, Texas, vol. 2 (T-728:2, frames 426–429 and 435–437), received 1/2/1845.

From B.B. French, Chief Assist[ant] Clerk, Ho[use of] Rep[resentatives], 12/17. At the request of John Quincy Adams [Representative from Mass.], French calls Calhoun's attention to a House resolution of 6/14/1844 requesting "a copy of all the instructions to George W. Erving upon his appointment as minister plenipotentiary to Spain in the year 1814, and afterwards during his mission to that court, which have not heretofore been made public." The request of this resolution has not yet been answered by the State Department. (A Clerk's EU reads "Answ[ere]d verbally 18 Dec. by F[rancis] Markoe Jr.") ALS in DNA, RG 59 (State Department), Miscellaneous Letters (M-179:106, frame 322).

From BEN E. GREEN

Washington, Dec. 17th 1844
Sir, In reply to your enquiry, I am sorry to inform you that none of the three last Instalments had been paid at the time I left the city of Mexico. It is true that the Mexican Minister of Foreign Relations [Manuel C. Rejon], by note of the 2d September, informed Mr. [Wilson] Shannon that the two, which had fallen due on the 30th April and 30th July, had been satisfied. This note, a copy of which was at the time forwarded to the Department, was sent to Mr. Shannon

early on the morning after he presented his credentials, and was written, as I have reason to believe, in consequence of an impression that the Mexican Government, by having failed to pay the Instalment of the 30th April, had forfeited its right under the Convention of 1843, to pay by Instalments, and that Mr. Shannon was going out with instructions to demand payment of the whole Indemnity, under the Convention of 1839.

The fact is that various orders on the Treasury were given to the Agent appointed to receive the Instalments; but he could obtain no payment on these orders up to the day when Mr. [Ignacio] Trigueros left the Treasury Department, and the first act of his successor [Antonio de Haro y Tamariz?] was to suspend the payment of all orders.

While upon this subject I beg leave to state that our claims were used by the Mexican Govt. as a pretext for levying a forced loan. More than sufficient to pay all our claims was raised in this way; but a very small part of it has been paid to our citizens, and the rest has been applied to other purposes. At the same time it was declared in the official newspaper that our claims were unjust & that the Mexican Govt. owed our citizens nothing; but the forced loan was justified before the Mexican people on the ground that the previous administration of Bustamente [*sic*; Anastasio Bustamante] had pledged the national faith to pay those claims, and that, although they were an unjust robbery on our part, it was necessary that the national faith, pledged by Bustamente, should be maintained. I am, Sir, very respectfully Your ob[edien]t serv[an]t, Ben E. Green.

ALS in DNA, RG 59 (State Department), Diplomatic Despatches, Mexico, vol. 12 (M-97:13); CC in DNA, RG 46 (U.S. Senate), 28A-E3; CC in DNA, RG 233 (U.S. House of Representatives), 28A-E1; draft in NcU, Duff Green Papers (published microfilm, roll 5, frames 867–868); PC in House Document No. 19, 28th Cong., 2nd Sess., pp. 32–33; PC in *Congressional Globe*, 28th Cong., 2nd Sess., Appendix, p. 34; PC in the Washington, D.C., *Globe*, December 19, 1844, p. 3; PC in the Washington, D.C., *Daily National Intelligencer*, December 20, 1844, p. 2; PC in the Washington, D.C., *Daily Madisonian*, December 24, 1844, p. 2; PC in *Niles' National Register*, vol. LXVII, no. 17 (December 28, 1844), pp. 265–266; PEx in Senate Document No. 85, 29th Cong., 1st Sess., p. 15.

From W[illia]m Smith, "(Private)"

Warrenton Va., Dec[em]b[e]r 17, 1844
My Dear Sir, Since the free conversation I had with you, (in which you evinced such a regard for my wishes & interests as to place me under lasting obligations to you) it has frequently engaged my thoughts; & I am free to say I hardly know what is for the best. In this mood, confidentially, I respectfully ask your counsel. To enable you to give it understandingly, I must possess you of certain anticipated results & my wishes in connection with them.

I this evening had a conversation with Gen[era]l [J.R.] Wallace of the Va. Senate from this District, & he informs me that it is not likely we shall elect a Senator to succeed Mr. [William C.] Rives this winter, as the Democratic party will not go into the election with the slightest Danger of defeat. Assuming this to be so—that there will be no election until next winter, I think I should greatly desire to have some convenient mission to fill the interval until then, as it is the wish of many friends, in which to some extent I participate, that I should succeed Mr. Rives; & I could then with this intermediate advantage, go into the Senate, if it should be the pleasure of my State, under much more favourable & satisfactory auspices than now. What think you?

Gen[era]l Wallace also informs me that [Governor James] McDowell has no chance nor any Bentonian.

Again, the wish I have intimated, if realized, followed by my election as suggested, would have the effect, which I greatly covet, of speedily recalling me to my country. I could then hold on to my seat; but if elected now, I could not. I should, as you already know be compelled to retire, if I could into a foreign mission, with the usual party animadversions upon appointments from members of Congress; & with my return almost certainly so deferred, as to place me in the next presidential canvass, without that minute knowledge of local & general politicks, indispensable to the effective popular Speaker.

I give you these views hastily, yet frankly—be pleased, to give me yours—I doubt not, they will be such as I will cheerfully adopt.

I have read your instructions touching Mexico & Texas. They are just as I would have them. I don't well see how we can get over giving Mexico a cuff or two—she, certainly, richly deserves it. Nor, would it cost us any thing, beyond a few thousands of volunteers. England need not be feared. I should think it would be difficult to drive her into a war with us. In haste Most sincerely Y[ou]rs, Wm. Smith.

ALS in ScCleA.

From CHARLES S. YANCEY

Springfield, Greene Co[unty,] Mo.
December 17th 1844

Dear Sir, You are familiar with Politics, an[d] consequently anticipate the course of Political events. From your known worth, and unquestioned integrity, as well as your exalted talents, the people of all Parties, untram[m]elled by party and faction, are anxious for your promotion (if I may use the term) to the office of Secretary of State. Though I am confident there is a faction in the government hostile to your claims, I am still confident that public opinion sets strongly in favor of yourself or Gen[era]l [Lewis] Cass. The important Diplomatic correspondence now pending, between this and other civilized powers of the world, seems to suggest the propriety of this course, on the part of the in-coming administration. Every consideration grounded on policy and principle leads to this conclusion. I do not throw out these remarks for the purpose of eliciting your views on State secrets, for I know politicians are cautious—and more, I am to you a stranger, tho' you are not altogether unknown to me. There is much curious history connected with the re-election of Col. [Thomas H.] Benton to the Senate. I believe it is matter of pub[lic] notoriety that Benton is opposed to him, whom he pleases to term the "Disorganizer," or the "wily Southerner." I well recollect in a conversation with myself, Mr. Benton associated your name with that [of] Dan[ie]l Webster and denounced you both in bitter terms. It is unnecessary for me to say he hates you as Satan hates the Angles of light. He looks on you as the evil genius that is to thwart him in his high aspirations. His conduct clearly indicates that he claims the succession as a matter of right; but the "worthiest of blood" cannot yet be prefer[r]ed. Col. Benton is my enemy and I am his; and I am aware that in speaking thus to a stranger I am not likely to make good impressions. Be it so. I am a Democrat, and am proud of the name, but never will I chain myself to Ceasers' carr, but rather Cato like, thrust my sword in my bowels. Benton[']s policy now is not to oppose Whigs but Democrats; and he has already denounced many of us in Missouri, because we could not support his obnoxious and tyrannical course. If I am not much mistaken the cabinet is bound to be organized on the Texas question; but if unfortunately for the country, however, Benton should prevail, we shall hear one loud, long deep-toned murmur throughout the nation. The quiet acquiescence of Mr. [Martin] Van Buren in the nominations of [James K.] Polk & [George M.] Dallas is indicative not of peace, but of war. If I am correct in this, he will endeavor to organize a Party in Congress adverse to your prospects, and which how cautious soever it may be disguised will be opposed to Polk's administration, and have for its ulterior object the *fixing the succession.* The politicians of this State went for Benton from the supposed control which he had over their political existence, but they are even now ready and ripe for revolt. He is standing on a volcano, which is ready to burst and nothing but a rare accident can save him. To say nothing of principle, Polk is bound from the first law of nature, self-defence, to oppose Col. Benton, and if he does, the Col. is as dead as a stone at the bottom of a well.

A few years ago I saw you make honorable mention of a relative of mine [Charles Yancey], who as you were pleased to call him was a "wheel horse for the Democracy of Virginia." Is he still living—and where? I think in Buckingham Co[unty], but am not certain. I know but little of my relatives, having been cast off in the west in early life. I should be pleased to hear from you—I have the honor to subscribe myself your friend, Charles S. Yancey.

ALS in ScCleA. NOTE: An AEU by Calhoun reads: "Mr. Yancey, relates to Col. Benton."

To ——, 12/17. In response to a request from the Princeton [Ind.] Historical Society, Calhoun sends his autograph. ALS in InHi, Robert A. Woods–Samuel Hall Papers.

From Chester Ashley, [Senator from Ark.], 12/18. Ashley wishes to add his name to those of former Governor [William S.] Fulton, A[mbrose] H. Sevier [Senator from Ark.], and Ed[ward] Cross [Representative from Ark.] in recommendation of Solon Borland to be appointed U.S. District Attorney for Ark. "I beg leave further to add that the Hon[orab]l[e] Edward Cross who arrived in the City last evening fully concurs in the views orally communicated to you a few evenings since & unites with me in the wish to have Solon Borland Esq[ui]r[e] receive the nomination of the President for that Office."

ALS in DNA, RG 59 (State Department), Applications and Recommendations, 1837–1845, Borland (M-687:2, frames 709–710).

From J[OHN] S. BARBOUR, "Private"

Catalpa [Culpeper County, Va.,] Dec[embe]r 18th 1844
My Dear Sir, I thank you for your letter of the 16th [*not found*]. My son James [Barbour] will have reached you before this.

I am thoroughly of the opinion you advanced that Mr. [Littleton W.] Tazewell [former Senator from Va.] will have great weight with Mr. [James K.] Polk. I learn that an effort is making to urge [Andrew] Stevenson [former Speaker] to your *extrusion*. I do not believe in this. He w[oul]d gladly come in as a subordinate Secretary. I have Mr. [Thomas] Ritchie's pledge to stand to you. He is a man of honour whatever you may hear to the contrary. *And if he were not I have satisfied him that your remaining in the Cabinet is indispensable to the ascendancy of the party in this State.* Here, [Silas] Wright & [Thomas H.] Benton & [James] McDowell &c are utterly powerless. *You are strong.* The slightest intimation to the public ear that *"old Hunkerism"* is to prevail; & it is the death warrant of the Democracy. We have a recognizance (with abundant security) so far as Virginia is concerned, that your stay in the Cabinet will be demanded by all her power. Because it is indispensible to the interest of every branch of the Democracy. *We have the power to controul*; for with the exception of [William] Smith, there is not a friend of yours known to me, who desires, or expects or w[oul]d take any part of the *Spoils*. They want nothing, but a fair[,] honest & faithful administration of the Govt. on the principles upon which the late battle was fought & won. I think that the spirit which prevails in Virginia, and the interests, whose peril make up our guaranty; exist also to some extent, & like effect & tendency, in Georgia & Alabama.

This view of the subject, properly urged upon the party, is sovereign in its omnipotence. And so it will be ["with" *interlined*] Polk. They dare not touch a [*one word changed to* "hair"] of ["your" *interlined*] head. *And it is this view, which exerts a master[']s sway over them all.* Before the sun sets, I will write Ritchie again, but I have the best reason to think that with him, all is right.

Do you know Judge Bayley [*sic*; Thomas H. Bayly] of this State? I do not know him. But from all that I ["can"(?) *canceled*] know of him through others I have a very high opinion of him.

The difficulty with Mr. Tazewell is to rouse him to service. An inertion, consequent on age, with most men; & to which there is a natural proclivity with him, at all times; defies every attempt to stimulate ["it" *canceled and* "him" *interlined*] into other life. I would rather write him *direct*, than ask the interference of any Richmond friend. The incidents that carried his election for the office of Gov[erno]r a few years past, & my agency in them, created kind relations between us, that have been confirmed since then; rather than weakened.

The language we hold in this State to others of our party is; that, *first*, of patriotic obligation—& *then*, of stern & decisive defiance. "The Station in the Cabinet is due Mr. Calhoun; the public interests require ["it" *interlined*]—& *pretermit his claims if you dare.*" The last spring's election is both witness & bondsman, for our safety.

I wish that I could send you some letters I have from Richmond. And I regret, that I am without the power to do so—For they are in my hands under injunctions, that w[oul]d make me base in my own esteem were I to show them. With all Respect & Sincere Regards Y[ou]rs truly, J.S. Barbour.

[P.S.] You see my haste.

[P.S.] I have written Mr. Ritchie before sealing this to you. J.S.B.

ALS in ScCleA; PEx in Boucher and Brooks, eds., *Correspondence*, pp. 270–271.

From James M. Buchanan, Balt[imore], 12/18. Buchanan recommends C[harles] R. Leffreing for appointment to be U.S. Consul at Stuttgart, in Würtemberg. ALS in DNA, RG 59 (State Department), Applications and Recommendations, 1845–1853, Leffreing (M-873: 52, frames 614–615).

From J[ohn] Y. Mason, [Secretary of the Navy], 12/18. "I have the honor to request, that you will be pleased to furnish a copy of the Treaty, concluded at Washington, with Lord Ashburton, on the 9th August, 1842. It is wanted for the use of Commodore [Charles W.] Skinner, appointed to command the relief squadron destined to the Coast of Africa." LS in DNA, RG 59 (State Department), Miscellaneous Letters (M-179:106, frame 323); FC in DNA, RG 45 (Naval Records), Letters Sent by the Secretary of the Navy to the President and Executive Agencies, 1821–1886, 5:73–74 (M-472:3, frames 78–79).

From F[RANCIS] W. PICKENS

Senate Chamber [Columbia, S.C.]
At night, 18 Dec[embe]r '44

My dear Sir, I have written you four times and rec[eive]d no answer. I regret it as the Legislature has been from day to day excited by all sorts of letters from Washington. Amongst others Mr. [Franklin H.] Elmore informs me that Mr. [Robert Barnwell] Rhett has written that you are disponding, and have been disgusted by [James K.] Polk not writing you &c.

Now I do not know what may be the change of your views, but I have endeavoured to carry out what I supposed to be your views when I parted from you in Charleston.

[George] McDuffie has denounced my resolutions to the Speaker Mr. [William F.] Colcock but I do not know what are his substitutes. I have endeavored to do my duty and thank God that I am satisfied as far as my own judgment is concerned. I introduced resolutions on the movements in Congress as to Abolition & carried them by a unanimous vote in the senate, but such is the factious feeling of a fiew [*sic*] in the House that they even oppose them, but both sets of Resolutions will pass the House. We are about adjourning to-night. I go home in the morning. In haste but truly, F.W. Pickens.

P.S. 12 O'Clock at night—The House have just adopted my first set of Resolutions by a large majority, & then indefinitely postponed all the others. My last resolutions on Abolition were introduced to prevent ultra moves in the House that I knew would be made & they have performed their office fully. All is safe now. I dreaded foolish movements in the House. F.W.P.

ALS in ScCleA. NOTE: The resolutions mentioned by Pickens herein were introduced in the Senate on 12/16 in response to the U.S. House of Representatives having repealed the 25th rule in regard to abolition petitions. They stated that the repeal was "a flagrant outrage upon our rights, and a decided step towards the subversion of our Institution, and the dissolution of this Union"; that there was no Congressional power to legislate on slavery and such legislation would abrogate the federal compact; and that if any such legislation were passed the Governor should call a special session of the General Assembly. The resolutions were passed unanimously by the Senate. After much debate and maneuvering, they were tabled by the House of Representatives. However, the House did pass Pickens's "first set of Resolutions," those concerning the annexation of Texas which he had introduced on 11/26.

From T. Simons and ten others, Elberfeld, [Prussia], 12/18. Simons and these other merchants trading to the U.S. seek the appointment of Charles Hecker to be U.S. Consul for the Prussian Rhine Provinces. Louis Mark has been recently appointed U.S. Consul to Bavaria and the Prussian Rhine. He has transferred his office to Bavaria and appointed Charles Hecker Consular Agent for this place. Because of his absence and "public rumours touching the Person of Mr. Mark," the Elberfeld merchants seek Hecker's appointment as U.S. Consul exclusively for the Prussian Rhine Provinces. Although Hecker is not a U.S. citizen, he has performed the duties of Consular Agent since 1842 "to the entire satisfaction of the commercial community." That fact and the comparative unimportance of the U.S. trade in the region should support Hecker's claim to the post. CC in DNA, RG 59 (State Department), Applications and Recommendations, 1837–1845, Hecker (M-687:15, frames 50–53).

From SAM[UE]L R. THURSTON, *"Most Confidential"*

Brunswick Me., Dec. 18, 1844

D[ea]r Sir: I have determined to address this letter to you personally & direct. I hope for many reason[s] I will not stop to name, that you will retain your present position in Mr. [James K.] Polk[']s Cabinet. I see there is a push made to controll Mr. Polk[']s Cabinet by [Martin] V[an] B[uren] men. Mr. [John] Fairfield [Senator] from our State is led by Mr. [Thomas H.] Benton, & is talked of in this State as a candidate for a seat in Polk[']s Cabinet. I take it that Polk is unconditionally in favor of immediate annexation. But if Mr. V[an] B[uren']s friends get a majority of the Cabinet, then farewell to Texas as I believe. I am confident that Benton & his clique will do every thing in their power to displace you from the seat you now hold. I therefore hope, first, Mr. Polk will look out who he takes to his bosom, & secondly, that your friends will look out that your enemies are not put in a position to injure you if they would. But, the greatest caution should be observed, to keep on friendly terms with all, till the great object of Texas is secured. But surely[?], I have no confidence in those men for seats in Polk[']s Cabinet to secure the annexation of Texas, who were led off at the last session in opposition to that measure. *Therefore*, if Mr. Polk is in favor ["&" *interlined*] for the immediate annexation of Texas, and on the ground of your treaty, can it, *can it*, I say, be safe for him to ["take" *interlined*] men into his cabinet who, no later than the last session of Congress, were opposed to the measure, & took steps & courses, not only calculated to distract & divide the party, but to put in absolute & final jeopardy the question of annexation? I think not, & so I will hope he will govern himself accordingly, & if Texas should not be annexed during Mr. [John] Tyler[']s administration, as I hope in Heaven it may, that he will surround himself with such men as will give a hearty cooperation with him, upon a question than which to us none was ever of more importance. The Democratic party are for this measure now, and why shall designing politicians seek to delay it, in order to ag[g]randise themselves upon it. I cannot advise *you*. But believe me sincere, when I say, your friends have no other safety, nor the friends of Texas, than that which rests in the cooperation with Mr. Polk & all in favor of Texas, and of being *represented* in Mr. Polk[']s Cabinet by *a majority*. Let these things be seen to. Be wise as Leopards, yet harmless as doves. Believe me your friend & ob[edien]t Serv[an]t, Saml. R. Thurston.

P.S. I acknowledge the re[ceip]t of your document for which receive my thanks.

ALS in ScCleA.

From JOS[EPH] L. WHITE, "(Confidential)"

New York [City,] Dec. 18 1844

My Dear Sir, I am exceedingly anxious, *for reasons purely personal,* to learn whether there is any probability of war with Mexico. Of course, I would not expect you to communicate any thing, which you may have learned in your official character, but your opinion based upon unofficial information would go far to strengthen or remove any impression which I may have upon this subject. I have a deep stake in the result of the present negociations with Mexico & Texas & hence my anxiety for information, that I may shape my action accordingly.

I may, perhaps be asking too much, but in doing so I have presumed upon your character for frankness & probity, for both of which you may remember I gave you credit in the 27th Congress although differing with you upon many political questions.

Let me assure you that the reason of my enquiry is personal to myself, & your answer whatever it may be is not designed for publication nor shall it be exhibited to any one.

I ask only your *individual opinion* which I shall regard as a great favor if you do not fear to trust me with it.

I confess my inability to discover how in the present posture of affairs, a war is to be avoided. Rejohn [*sic*; Manuel C. Rejon] has with the sanction of his Government, thrown off his diplomatic character, to become the common libeller of our nation & its distinguished men. In what history of diplomacy is a paralell for this to be found, or in which tame submission to such an assault is inculcated? If this Government fails in proper retaliation, will not such failure provoke new & more audacious attacks?

Has our national honor lost its sensativeness, & is the precedent established that a *desire for gain* is the only good cause for war?

Whatever may have been the opinions of statesmen, as to the policy of fighting for the acquisition of Texas, that is not now the question. *Mexico has insulted us* & she should retract or fight. And if men could divest themselves of partizan feelings this opinion would be general, because it is just.

Excuse the liberty I have taken in asking, for the perusal of this letter, a portion of your time. Yours very Resp[ec]t[ful]ly, Jos. L. White.

ALS in ScCleA. NOTE: An AEU by Calhoun reads "Mr. White[,] Asks my opinion as to a war with Mexico." Joseph L. White was a Representative from Ind., 1841–1843.

From Ch[arles] Aug[ustu]s Davis

New York [City,] 19 Dec[embe]r 1844

D[ea]r Sir, I took the liberty some time ago to call your attention to the importance of an enterprize (in which I always took a deep interest) of securing to our Southern Country boardering [*sic*] on the Gulf of Mexico—large advantages which were sure to be derived by connecting Pensacola by a good and substantial rail road with the State of Alabama—from which branches would follow and center upon that beautiful bay and harbour—a large and growing City—a consideration of no little moment to a naval rendezvous (which must in all human probability be sustained there). The project is to run a road from Pensacola direct to Montgomery a distance of 148 miles— (a six or eight hour journey). The rail road interest now at work in Georgia and South Carolina will soon extend toward Montgomery— and ["when" *interlined*] those links are completed we have one continuous line of road from one end of the Union to the other—its last Southern link rivited [*sic*] to the harbour and public works of Pensacola. They boast in England of their "overland" rout[e] to India—but when our line of rail road is completed through *our Atlantic Southern States as far as Pensacola* & thence by Steamers to *Chagres* [New Granada]—we are brought so near the Pacific that through and by that channel one of the most interesting plans of intercourse will be secured. I need not detain you sir with any detail of the certain advantages that w[oul]d be secured to that important State Alabama and portions of States contiguous to it by securing by this artificial means an *Iron River*—navigable at all seasons and all hours—bringing that harbor & rendezvous of Pensacola into a new existence and rendering it tributary to so vast an interior now measurably separated from it.

It is capable of demonstration that this simple link in the great chain—would in a few brief years double the present representation of Alabama alone without taking a man off from any other representation—and I humbly conceive that it is the most clearly demonstrable proposition that if our Southern States were better supplied with roads their population would keep pace with our northern & western States. Much is said of the great Valley of the Mississippi—but give such a State as Alabama[,] Southern & Eastern Tennessee and western Georgia the *accessability* which roads w[oul]d give and capital and population w[oul]d go there. And Tropical productions (which have a monopoly of climate) and the peculiar labor required there will find advocates N. E. W. as well as South and "abolitionism"—that wicked and ignorant theory be signally rebuked and sent back to its original elements.

If the General Gov't which must spend vast sums at *Pensacola* would but look at the importance to *all* interests—and extend a helping hand by gifts to the road of alternate sections of land on its rout[e]—*to be given only when the road is completed*—private enterprize w[oul]d at once go to work and the result w[oul]d be that more public land w[oul]d be enter[e]d & p[ai]d for to the public Treasury (ten for one) than the land gifted—and which lands without this channel must remain valueless. A glance at the map shows the rout[e] of this road from Pensacola to Montgomery runs thro a region mid way between the Alabama & Chat[t]ahoochee rivers—and too remote for Produce to be hawled [*sic*] to either river. This road w[oul]d be as it were a new creation of resources and in no way injurious to other interests. Pensacola w[oul]d soon swell to a population that w[oul]d alone suffice to bring West Florida into a State and Alabama increase her numbers ten fold. Nature designs Pensacola for a *part* of Alabama. Trade and intercourse can['] t regard

State or territorial lines. Alabama with all her vast internal resources not yet developed is at present confined to plantations upon the banks of her precarious river navigable only at certain seasons—and with one port—*Mobile* which now can't be approach'd by vessels now in use nearer than 25 miles. Give her access to another port by an *Iron River* running 30 miles p[e]r hour either way and you will soon see a developement which your mind can readily foresee. If our Southern brethren could only be made aware of the immense amount of undeveloped resources they possess and which are capable of developement by means of these artificial appliances they w[oul]d not rest in their present condition. I am so deeply impressed with this subject[,] I have labor'd so strenuously for it—that I am glad to see a plan which I was interested in starting a few years ago and which was suspended by the unhappy prostration of all things, again revived at Pensacola. A paper [*not found*] is sent to me containing certain proceedings at Pensacola which I take the liberty to inclose to you.

If Alabama takes a right view of this matter and will add her potent voice—the enterprize will be resumed and carried to completion. But I here take the liberty to record my deep regret that when this enterprize was going on in the year 1840—(May 1840) a message was sent to Congress with sundry documents provided by Special agents of Govt. sent the year preceding to Florida of the most hostile character ag[ains]t Banks—Insurance & Trust Co[mpanies] &. &.—thus selecting the weakest part of our country and striking down there with one blow all enterprizes. If the same thing had been tried *elsewhere* at the time—equally *suspicious* statements could have been furnish'd by equally *disinterested* agents—but this did not suit the policy of the day. And a stigma has thus been left on all Southern enterprizes. I do not pretend to fathom the depth of that policy but it seem'd to me at the time as *fatal* & *suicidal*. Misfortune was call'd crime—and whatever of patriotism or glory belong'd to the measure was I believe claim'd by Mr. [Martin] Van Buren and Mr. [Thomas H.] Benton. I am led to hope that a better feeling now prevails—and the enterprize then prostrated will be allow'd to revive if not by Gov't aid at least by Gov't approval. There is not an individual in our whole northern & eastern quarter acquainted with the subject who does not regard Pensacola as among the jewels of the nation. Their only wonder is why it does not prosper. The answer is "because it has no access to the interior["]—if it had a navigable river it w[oul]d be a larger town tho' it w[oul]d not have such a harbour. What nature has denied it in one way it gives in another. It gives it a harbour of unequal'd interest—a place of rendezvous. Give it but the

Iron River I describe and it at once rises into power—*and benefit*—local and national follow on accumulating from year to year—till *"the City of the Gulf"* will be among the proudest of the nation—and the entire interior lifted up also. There will be a *mart* all the year round and what portion of our wide domain will not feel its influence? I am as certain of it as I am that I have now the honor of subscribing myself Y[ou]r ob[edien]t Ser[vant] and with all respect, Ch: Augs. Davis.

ALS in ScCleA.

From VESPASIAN ELLIS

Legation of the United States
Caracas, Dec[embe]r 19th 1844

Sir, The enclosed letter &c to Simeon Toby Esq. of Philadelphia, in answer to two letters of his therein referred to, is forwarded for your perusal & disposal. If proper to be communicated to Mr. Toby you will please forward it to him.

The Pa: Insurance Co. had a claim against Colombia on account of the Josephine, which, I understand, was arranged originally by the Convention with Colombia of March 16th 1825; but by "unintentional error" on the part of the United States a *portion* of the Claim was omitted. In 1829 Mr. [Thomas P.] Moore by Treaty obtained a further allowance for the Josephine but did not stipulate for interest from 1825 on this further allowance. See his note at the end of the Treaty. These I understand to be the plain & simple facts of the case. The grounds of the adjustment in 1829 I cannot learn. These suggestions with the remarks made in my communication to Mr. Toby & a reference to the former correspondence between this legation & your predecessors, will enable you to give me whatever further instructions if any, you may think proper to give.

I respectfully suggest that it would be very desirable, if practicable, to bring about a *final* settlement of *all* the claims of our citizens upon the former Republic of Columbia [*sic*]. These claims, whether well founded or not, are very numerous, & if settled *separately* will not be closed in thirty years, according to the present dispositions of these governments [of Venezuela, New Granada, and Ecuador]. I do not mean to say, that they are not disposed to do *Justice*, but *pro-*

crastination is a characteristic feature in South American diplomacy. The present adm[inistratio]n of Venezuela profess to be well disposed towards our claimants, but they complain *not a little* that we have been too harsh with them, in the means employed to press our claims.

I entertain no manner of doubt I shall be able to get along in a friendly and peaceable manner with them, but every thing moves slowly here in diplomatic & governmental affairs.

The Venezuelan tariff will undoubtedly be reduced as it regards American productions. I have the honor to be with great respect your obedient Serv[an]t, Vespasian Ellis.

ALS (No. 6) in DNA, RG 59 (State Department), Diplomatic Despatches, Venezuela, vol. 2 (M-79:3), received 1/11/1845.

From Robert Hanna, [former Senator from Ind.], Indianapolis, 12/19. The Indiana legislature having recently elected Courtland Cushing to a circuit judgeship, the post of U.S. District Attorney will soon be vacant. Hanna recommends Joseph W. Chapman for that office. "Mr. Chapman is now a member of the State Senate. Of his Legal attainments I say nothing, because I am unable[?] of Judging, but common fame speaks well of him in that particular." An AEU by Calhoun reads "Mr. Hanna recommends Mr. Cushing [*sic*] for the place of Dist. Attorney of Indiana." ALS in DNA, RG 59 (State Department), Applications and Recommendations, 1845–1853, Chapman (M-873:15, frames 71–72).

To Carl Ernst Ludwig Hinrichs, New York [City], 12/19. Calhoun acknowledges receipt of Hinrichs' letter of 12/14, with its enclosed commission from the Duke of Saxe Coburg and Gotha appointing him Consul for the U.S. Calhoun transmits to Hinrichs his exequatur from the President and returns herewith his commission. FC in DNA, RG 59 (State Department), Notes to Foreign Legations, German States, 6:100 (M-99:27).

From MEMUCAN HUNT

Galveston [Texas,] 19th Dec[embe]r 1844

My Dear Sir, I have the very great gratification to acknowledge the receipt of your letter of the 23rd ultimo. All your opinions & suggestions are more highly appreciated and esteemed by me than those from any other statesman in the U.S. So far as my interchanges on the great question of annexation occur in relation to our policy on the subject here, your views will be particularly recommended.

If we are annexed by a joint resolution or an act of your congress ought not there to be a provision for submit[t]ing such joint resolution or act to a vote of the people of Texas? Has our congress the right (it certainly has not authority under the constitution) to part with the sovereignty of the Texian Nation? There is no doubt of a ratification of ["a" *interlined*] joint resolution or act of your congress, annexing us, by the people of Texas. The majority would be 4, 5, 6, or 7 to one unless something unlooked for, tending to alienate ["the" *interlined*] people transpires, and it would forever silence those who are opposed to annexation, and who, in some instances, for the want of proper information on the subject, now declare it as there [*sic*] belief that a majority of the citizens of Texas are opposed to the measure.

From what I can see and from what has transpired, of late, I believe you are about to have a great commotion and revolution in parties. I should not be surprised to see the Southern & western whigs unite with the democrats who are in favor of immediate annexation and on the other hand to witness a union of the democrats, opposed to immediate annexation, with the abolitionists and the old federal party. In this event you will be the next, elected, President of the U.S. by a larger majority than Gen[era]l [William Henry] Harrison defeated Mr. [Martin] Van Buren with. I ardently hope that it may so occur.

Judge A[bner] S. Lipscombe [*sic*; Lipscomb], late of Alabama very often speaks of you—his last wife is a daughter of one of my Uncles—he recently had an heir, and had it been a Son, its name would have been Calhoun, but it is of the other sex.

Your injunctions in the close of your letter [*not found*] will be strictly regarded. I have the honor to be your devoted friend, Memucan Hunt.

ALS in ScCleA; PEx in Jameson, ed., *Correspondence*, pp. 1010–1011.

From J[ABEZ] W. HUNTINGTON, [Senator from Conn.]

Senate Chamber, Dec[embe]r 19, 1844
Sir, The nominations of the persons named in the accompanying paper, to be consuls, have been referred to the committee on Com-

merce. I will thank you to send me such papers as are on file in the Department, as relate to the character & qualifications of the nominees. With great respect, I have the honor to be, Your mo[st] obed[ient] Ser[van]t, J.W. Huntington.

ALS with En in DNA, RG 59 (State Department), Applications and Recommendations, 1845–1853, Graebe (M-873:34, frames 189–191). NOTE: Huntington enclosed a list of 15 nominees to Consular positions. They were Charles Graebe, Alexander Tod, Robert Walsh, Gabriel G. Fleurot, Robert L. McIntosh, Peter A. Brinsmade, Isaac Stone, Eneas McFaul, Jr., Franklin Lippincott, Joel W. White, Patrick J. Devine, Joseph C.C. Ellis, James J. Wright, Samuel H. Kneass, and J.B. Lacey.

From J. FR[ANCI]S HUTTON, *"Confidential"*

New York [City,] Dec: 19, 1844

Sir, The election for members of the [Democratic] general committee for the ensuing year took place yesterday, and last evening the result was announced. At two of the Wards resolutions were passed in favor of the immediate annexation [of Texas], and this would have been the case throughout the whole city if time had been allowed us. [Emanuel B. or B.S.] Hart[']s resolutions in the 5th Ward are of the right stamp and beyond doubt express fully the public mind on this subject. Every where I hear complaints made against the Morning News & Evening Post for misrepresenting the democracy of this City & State, and I think you should be advised of this state of things so that your course of proceeding with these negociations may be governed accordingly. Mr. [David C.] Broderick of the 9th Ward[,] elected to the Gen[era]l Com[mitte]e last night[,] assures me that we shall have a handsome working majority and pledges himself to have the very strongest resolutions passed in favor of the immediate Annexation without consent of any power except those contracting, and if necessary to push the matter will have a committee appointed to go to Washington for the purpose of reminding representatives of their duty. The committee have their first meeting early in January.

Our friends are not sleeping although apparently so for already the incipient steps have been taken to call a great public meeting at which either [Thomas H.] Benton[']s plans will be exposed and defeated or a complete breach be made in the party. Permit me to suggest to you the name of Gov[erno]r [Cornelius P.] Van Ness as a suitable representative of our Government to Mexico if the contingency should arrise [*sic*] of the resignation or recall of Mr. [Wilson] Shannon. This appointment would create a vancancy [*sic*] here of great importance to us, for our young men would present the name of an individual every ["way" *interlined*] satisfactory to the party, and yet true as steel to us.

If there is any probability of such contingency arrising [*sic*] may I ask sir to receive information, for one or two of our friends would seek an interview with you to explain more fully our objects. I have the honor to be Very respectfully & truly Your Ob[edien]t Serv[an]t, J. Frs. Hutton.

ALS in ScCleA.

To CHA[RLE]S J. INGERSOLL, Chairman of the Committee on Foreign Affairs, House of Representatives

Department of State
Washington, 19th Dec. 1844

Sir, I have the honor to transmit to you, for the information of the Committee on Foreign Affairs, a copy of a letter [of 11/25] from Mr. Albert Smith, Commissioner to run and mark the [northeastern] boundary between the United States and Great Britain. By it you will perceive that the Commissioners have it in contemplation to complete their duties during the ensuing season. To enable them to do so, will, agreeably to Mr. Smith's estimate, require an appropriation of seventy five thousand dollars. I have accordingly requested the Committee of Ways and means to provide for such an appropriation, and, that the whole, or, at least a moiety thereof, might be available during the residue of the current fiscal year. I have the honor to be, Sir, very respectfully, Your Ob[edien]t Servant, J.C. Calhoun.

FC in DNA, RG 59 (State Department), Accounting Records: Miscellaneous Letters Sent, 1832–1916, vol. for 10/3/1844–5/29/1845, p. 122.

To J[ames] I. McKay, Chairman of the Committee of Ways & Means, House of Representatives, 12/19. Calhoun transmits a copy of a letter [to himself, dated 11/25,] from Albert Smith, U.S. Commissioner to establish the northeastern boundary with Great Britain. According to Smith's letter, the survey can be completed during the next working season, but an appropriation of $75,000 will be necessary to accomplish that end. "I have the honor therefore to request that an appropriation of that amount may be made, and that the whole, or, at least a moiety thereof, may be available during the residue of the fiscal year ending on the 30th of June, 1845." LS with En in DNA, RG 233 (U.S. House of Representatives), 28A-D30.6; FC in DNA, RG 59 (State Department), Accounting Records: Miscellaneous Letters Sent, 1832–1916, vol. for 10/3/1844–5/29/1845, p. [123].

From ROB[ER]T M. MCLANE

Balt[imore,] Dec. 19th 1844

My Dear Sir, The enclosed letter [of 11/23] from Mr. [George Read] Riddle, the democratic candidate for Congress at the late election last month in Delaware has been upon my table for a month past nearly. I have hesitated to take any share in troubling you on this subject at this time, but not from any indisposition to serve Dr. [Edward] Worrell who is my relative, and a gentle-man entitled to the good wishes of his friends every where, as he seems from the enclosed to possess those of his fellow citizens at home. He was lately a surgeon in the army, and disbanded under the act of Congress passed two years ago reducing the staff & rank & line of the army. He has a family, and has suffered severely from being thrown upon his rescources in civil life, after years passed in military life and service. I am urged again by his friends to communicate to you at least the information furnished me on his subject by Mr. Riddle. I need not add how highly I should esteem it, if his name should receive your favor in case of a vacancy in the post he seeks.

We look to Washington just now with great anxiety on the subject of Texas & on Mexican relations. When the crisis arrives you may look with confidence to the Democracy of Baltimore for any demonstration proper to rally the country to the support of a measure so distinctly at issue and passed upon by the people in the late contest, and not now to be lost by distraction or a multiplication of "projets." Our Press here is very feeble, but such as it is, it will take up this question in proper spirit—to aid them in this I have sent for the report of the Hon. Zadoc Pratt [Representative from N.Y.] on statistics made at the close of the last session which I am informed is full of valuable matter touching the question. With great respect I have the honor to remain Your very ob[e]d[ien]t Serv[an]t, Robt. M. McLane.

ALS in ScCleA; En in DNA, RG 59 (State Department), Applications and Recommendations, 1837–1845, Worrell (M-687:35, frames 155–157). NOTE: An AEU by Calhoun reads: "Mr. McLane, ["Recommends" *canceled*] enclosing a letter recom[men]d[in]g Mr. Worrell for the ["place of" *canceled*] consulate filled by Mr. [Thomas M.] Rodney." Robert M. McLane, a son of Louis Mc-Lane, was a former officer of the U.S. Army, an attorney, and later a Represen-tative from Md. and a noted diplomat.

From TH[OMAS] B. STODDARD

Irving, Chautauqua Co[unty] N.Y.
19 Dec[embe]r 1844

Will Mr. Calhoun permit, a plain citizen to avail himself of the State Department—to procure despatch for the inclos'd? It is a private communication but of some moment to Mr. [John] Ricord—who was a Student in my [law] office. His position as [Hawaiian] King Kau-mahamas [*sic*; Kamehameha III's] Crown Lawyer will I trust relieve it from the appearance of intrusion: and Subscribe most Respectfully, Th: B. Stoddard.

[P.S.] Pardon the impertenance [*sic*]—if it be one—of expressing the regret of many Democrats—that your late Texas Correspondence had not been publish[e]d previous to Election. Mr. [James K.] Polk['s] majorities[?] would have felt most sensably [*sic*] the aid—your handling of the subject has given to our side of the Texas question.

That your giant grasp may not be relax'd under the coming Ad-ministration is the earnest wish of your ["democratic" *interlined*] readers. In the light of British policy it is in your hands capable of rousing nationality even in Mr. [James G.] Birney[']s ranks.

That the Oronoko and the Amazon in a word the torrid zone is the destined home of the Negro of the U.S. is plain perhaps—but the *interim* is pregnant with our fate. It is then in the fearless policy of Titans like yourself that we all must look for pilotage. Content with a prospect of yet seeing you at the helm—& having no office seeking to impeach my sincerity I remain Your humble Admirer, T.B.S.

ALS in ScCleA.

To President [JOHN TYLER]

Department of State
Washington, 19th Dec[embe]r 1844

To the President of the United States.

The Secretary of State has received from the President, the resolution of the Senate of the 12th instant, requesting him "to communicate to the Senate, (if not incompatible with the public interest,) copies of all the correspondence not heretofore transmitted to the Senate, which may have taken place between the Department of State and the present Minister of the United States to France [William R. King], and between that Minister and the Government of France, relating to the proposed annexation of Texas to the United States:"

And in answer thereto has the honor to transmit herewith, extracts from the instructions of this Department to Mr. King, dated April 23rd 1844, and from a despatch dated the 26th of August, 1844. These include all the instructions given to Mr. King in relation to the subject referred to in the resolution. The main object of his mission was to strengthen and confirm those friendly relations which have so long subsisted between the two countries; and, in the fulfilment of this purpose, it was left to his discretion, as he was, from his position in the government, fully acquainted with the proposed measure of annexation in all its bearings, to adopt such course as might seem to him best calculated to prevent any misunderstanding in regard to so important a subject. His correspondence with the Department in reference to it, being a narrative of informal conversations, could not, consistently with usage or propriety, be made public. The only material part of this correspondence having relation to Texas, is embraced *substantially*, in the despatch from this Department to Mr. King, dated the 12th day of August last, (already published,) and in the extracts from the despatch of August 26th 1844, herewith communicated. Respectfully submitted. J.C. Calhoun.

LS with Ens in DNA, RG 46 (U.S. Senate), 28A-E3; FC in DNA, RG 59 (State Department), Reports of the Secretary of State to the President and Congress, 6:129; PC with Ens in Senate Document No. 13, 28th Cong., 2nd Sess., pp. 1–3; PC in *Congressional Globe,* 28th Cong., 2nd Sess., p. 61; PC with Ens in the Washington, D.C., *Globe,* December 23, 1844, p. 2; PC with Ens in the Washington, D.C., *Daily National Intelligencer,* December 24, 1844, p. 2; PC with Ens in the Washington, D.C., *Daily Madisonian,* December 27, 1844, p. 2; PC with Ens in *Niles' National Register,* vol. LXVII, no. 18 (January 4, 1845), p. 281; PC with Ens in Benton, ed., *Abridgment of the Debates of Congress,* 15:169–170; PC with Ens in the London, England, *Times,* January

15, 1845, p. 5. NOTE: Tyler transmitted this report to the Senate on 12/23. The resolution to which this letter is a response can be found in DNA, RG 59 (State Department), Miscellaneous Letters (M-179:106, frames 156–157) and in *Senate Journal*, 28th Cong., 2nd Sess., pp. 29–30.

From JOHN BEARD, "Private"

Newnansville, E[ast] Florida,
Dec[embe]r 20th 1844

Dear Sir, Aware that a multiplicity of important subjects claims your attention it is with much reluctance that I encroach upon your time. And the only apology I can in truth offer is my confidence in your minute acquaintance with all that pertains to every great interest in the country, and especially *that one* so vital to the peace & prosperity of the South.

Under the belief that Iowa will ere long apply to be admitted into the confederacy as a State, many entertain the opinion that Florida should make a similar application at the same time. Hitherto I have thought that the prosperity of Florida would be promoted most by her continuing a Territory until she shall have recovered from the effects of the [Seminole] war, and shall have made greater advances in population, in wealth, and in those qualities so essential to wise self-government: and that then both her own local interests, and the policy of the whole South, would recommend the formation of *two* States out of her extensive Territory. Nevertheless if this scheme be hopeless, and the policy of the South requires that Florida should be brought in with Iowa, I would cheerfully submit to the burdens incident to such a change; but would wish that the act of admission might contain a provision for her future division, on some contingency not too improbable or remote. Feeling deeply interested in this matter both as a Floridian & a Southron I would feel gratified to have your view of it.

Is it important to Florida to be admitted now?

Would she, by postponing her admission, risk the loss of any advantages?

Would she not, by coming in as *one* State, hazard the chance of a future division?

Is it important to the slave-holding States that Florida should be admitted *now* even at the *hazard* of a future division?

This subject is one of pressing importance to Florida, and, I think, to the whole South. I confess I entertain doubts as to our proper course which may be removed by one who has looked over the whole ground.

I trust it is unnecessary to assure you, Sir, that, if you have leisure & the inclination to write to me in regard to it, no improper use will be made of what you may communicate. With sincere, and very great, respect, I am &C, John Beard.

N.B. Please, if you write, direct to St. Augustine.

ALS in ScCleA; PC in Boucher and Brooks, eds., *Correspondence*, p. 272. NOTE: John Beard, a native of N.C., was the U.S. Marshal for eastern Fla. Territory, a strong Southern rights politician, and an unsuccessful candidate for the U.S. House of Representatives in 1850.

R[ichard] K. Crallé to Leopold Bierwirth, New York [City], 12/-20. "In reply to your note of the 16th Inst. I am directed by the Secretary of State to inform you that, no communication has been received from Mr. [Frederick] List, of the character referred to at this Department." FC in DNA, RG 59 (State Department), Domestic Letters, 35:52–53 (M-40:33); PC (from the New York *Journal of Commerce* and dated 12/23) in the Charleston, S.C., *Mercury*, January 1, 1845, p. 2; PC in the Columbus, Ohio, *Ohio State Journal*, January 9, 1845, p. 3.

From LATHROP J. EDDY and Others

New York [City,] Dec[embe]r 20th 1844

Dear Sir, The Undersigned beg leave to introduce to your acquaintance & friendly regards James H. Suydam Esq[ui]r[e,] of this City. Mr. Suydam was a very efficient member of the Calhoun Central Com[mittee], and as a gentleman & politician has our most perfect confidence. With great regard we remain Your Ob[edien]t Serv[an]ts, Lathrop J. Eddy, Ed[mund] S. Derry, G[eorge] E. Baldwin, Geo[rge] Montgomery.

LS (in Eddy's hand) in ScCleA.

From DUFF GREEN

Washington Texas, 20th Dec[embe]r 1844
My dear Sir, Capt. [Charles] Elliot reached here last night. He speaks in the most open manner against annexation, and promises that if Texas will give a pledge against annexation England will obtain an acknowledgement by Mexico of the Independence of Texas. He told me that a friend of his direct from Lexington [Ky.], had said to him that he had heard Mr. [Henry] Clay say that Mr. [Silas] Wright is to be Mr. [James K.] Polk's Sec[retary of] State. This argues that the Whigs will unite with [Thomas H.] Benton in passing a resolution or bill for annexation which Texas will reject and thus defeat annexation. A friend from Galveston tells me that letters had been recieved [*sic*] there, stating that Mr. [John J.] Crittenden [Senator from Ky.] had said that the question must be sett[l]ed and that he would vote for annexation.

It will be impossible to carry the question here clogged with either of Mr. Benton's conditions, and the public mind should be informed on the plan of the new coalition. It is to drive S. Carolina into nullification that the next Presidential Election may turn on that issue. All the elements of opposition will combine against you, and among them Mr. [John] Tyler. I see that he has planted Doctor [John G.] Miller in the Post office, for which he is utterly incompetent & he will devote the whole patronage of the department to build up a Tyler party.

Nine tenths, aye 99 of every 100 here are for annexation. You need not fear one year[']s delay[;] if Benton's influence does get a bill through the Senate containing any obnoxious features amend it in the House and throw the odium of defeating it on the Senate. Yours truly, Duff Green.

ALS in ScCleA; PC in Boucher and Brooks, eds., *Correspondence*, pp. 272–273.

From J[ohn] W. Holding, Baltimore, 12/20. Holding has heard that the U.S. intends to send a diplomatic agent to Ecuador. He has in the past applied for such a post and herewith renews that application. ALS in DNA, RG 59 (State Department), Applications and Recommendations, 1837–1845, Holding (M-687:16, frames 243–244).

From W[illia]m Gibbs McNeill, "Unofficial"

Brooklyn N[ew] York, Dec[embe]r 20th 1844

Dear Sir: I have for several days designed to send you, as I now do, a copy of a *Hebrew* Dictionary with the respects thro' me of the Author "W[illiam] L. Roy Professor of Oriental Languages" &[c]a &[c]a.

I accompany it with the enclosed document [*not found*] which is so far curious that it requires an explanation of why I am "*learned*"— in the opinion of Dr. Roy; for surely, in his line at least, I am far from it unless in reminiscence of some three, or four, languages studied & somewhat understood in early boyhood—which now, I fear, amounts to little more than a "*smattering*" of either. It was not—could not have been—therefore because of my proficiency in such matters that the really learned Doctor so satiryzed [*sic*] me. It was, I suppose, because of this: It so happens that as long since as when I was stationed in Boston—in Nullification days—I foolishly used to be annoyed with the jeering of distinguished & venerable gentlemen (such as Hon: H[arrison] G[ray] Otis, Col. [Thomas H.] Perkins & others) who discovering a sensitiveness of long standing—from my very youth upward—in relation to my native section of Country & you most especially, personally & politically—seemed to delight in drawing me into discussions which I confess—as I suppose they knew—I then very imperfectly understood. The result was as you were doomed to be *hung* (as it eventuated, instead) I chose that you be *suspended* among the household Gods & accordingly y[ou]r portrait was procured (the best I ever saw of you—by [Chester] Harding—as you were when I first had the pleasure to know you when you dignified the office of Secretary of War) & it was *hung up*, where it continues, & forever will, to the notice of my children & visitors—eliciting such comment as I please & the recital of the foregoing anecdote.

In this way it was that I proved "*learned*" to a number [of guests] a few nights since in my own house & hence the humble tribute to you by Mr. Roy.

Mr. John H: Alexander of Baltimore who has the honor to have his name associated, by Dr. Roy, with yours; you may probably recollect I described to you as a "John Quincy Adams *Jun[io]r—with a heart*, besides"! *I* know, from experience, your wont was to encourage talent &[c]a—especially *in young men*: & I say Mr. Alexander has more acquirement of his age—not superficial in any thing—learned & profound in most studies, on the contrary—with the bearing & virtue which ["*distinguishes*" *altered to* "distinguish"] him & human nature:

and, therefore, my apology for this unpremeditated mention of him. Since I have mentioned & dwelt on him, Mr. Calhoun, I would most respectfully ask y[ou]r remembrance *& trial*[?] *of him.* I do not believe he will ever *ask* y[ou]r patronage—but it could never be more worthily disposed.

[*Canceled*: "Yet, it now occurs to me—and only now—he is not liked by & I believe is not particularly fond of my talented, but erratic, friend (if he will allow me to call him so) Mr. Duff Green who probably, if his name be mentioned, would so say."]

I am glad to be enabled to say that I think—from a not very circumscribed acqua[i]ntance—that you are yearly, if not—of late—daily, more & more justly appreciated (I mean, Sir, your official course) by hosts of y[ou]r fellow Citizens besides Most respectfully Y[ou]r Ob[edien]t Serv[an]t &, Wm. Gibbs McNeill.

ALS in ViU, Crallé-Campbell Papers. Note: An AEU in an unknown hand reads "Gen[era]l McNeil[l]'s Letter." A copy of William L. Roy's *A Complete Hebrew and English Critical and Pronouncing Dictionary* . . . (New York: Collins, Keese & Co., 1837) appears on a list in ScU-SC of volumes from Calhoun's library sold by his descendants in 1931 to William Todd, a Conn. book dealer. Todd's list states that the book was inscribed "To the Hon. J.C. Calhoun—with the respects of the author." A further inscription, in Calhoun's handwriting, added "and by him to James Edward Calhoun." McNeill (1800–1853) was a native of N.C., raised in N.Y., and a graduate of West Point. He had served in the Army Topographical Engineers and as a railroad engineer in the South. At the time of this letter he was Chief Engineer of the Brooklyn Dry Dock which was under construction and was considered an engineering marvel of the age.

From R[ichard] Pakenham, Washington, 12/20. In reference to his letter of 9/23 concerning claims of British woollens merchants for redress for actions against them by the N.Y. Customs House, Pakenham asks on behalf of John Taylor, Jr., that his pending case before the U.S. Supreme Court be postponed until a claim made to the President for his relief shall be decided. Enclosed is a letter of 12/20 from Taylor to Pakenham requesting assistance with the matter. LS with Ens in DNA, RG 59 (State Department), Notes from Foreign Legations, Great Britain, vol. 22 (M-50:22).

To WILSON SHANNON, [Mexico City], "not sent"

Department of State
Washington [December 20, 1844]

Sir: I herewith enclose the Message of the President [John Tyler, of 12/3/1844] to Congress, transmitting copies of your correspondence with Mr. [Manuel C.] Rejon, the Mexican Minister of Foreign Relations, which will make known to you his views in regard to it. They are such that the President would have sustained you if, on receiving the insulting communication of Mr. Rejon, you had instantly demanded your Passport. As it is I am directed by the President to say to you that your future proceedings will be determined by the circumstances by which you may ["be" *interlined*] surrounded. Your last Despatch left the country in a state of revolution which we hope may settle down in a more friendly feeling to the United States, than that which dictated the late correspondence of Mr. Rejon. Being on the spot and having a more complete survey of the whole ground, you will be best qualified to say whether, after the position you have taken, you can reopen correspondence with the Government of Mexico. It is not the desire of the Executive to suspend Diplomatic Relations with Mexico; (so long as they can be preserved with a due regard to the dignity and honor of the United States,) but the President would not desire that to be done either at the sacrifice of your personal relations to that Government, or at the expense of the national honor. If you find yourself so situated as to be precluded from resuming correspondence with that Government, under a well-grounded expectation that the correspondence will assume a tone consistent with the dignity and honor of the ["United States" *canceled*] Government of the United States, you will demand your Passport.

The President directs me also to say to you that he has read, with great satisfaction, the able and spirited arguments with which you have successfully repelled the groundless and unjust charges against the conduct of our Government, now and formerly, in reference to Texas; but, at the same time, to express his regret that you should have permitted your feelings so far to prevail as to retort the insult, great as was the provocation; and so far to follow his example as to use any language which could be construed into an appeal to the People of Mexico against their Government. In the correspondence between Governments, insulting language, if noticed at all, should be met by dignified rebuke; and as we admit no Foreign Power to make an appeal against the Government to the People, or from one portion of them to another, we should carefully avoid making any such on our part, be the provocation what it may. I have the honor to be, with high respect, Sir, Your ob[edien]t Serv[an]t, R[ichard] K. C[rallé].

Draft (in an unidentified hand) in ScCleA. NOTE: An endorsement on this document reads "Draft of a Despatch to Mr. Shannon—not sent." In the same ms. collection are found two other and incomplete drafts of this document, one of which is dated 12/20/1844. This date has been assigned to the undated final draft transcribed above. In a letter of 5/30/1845 (CC in ScCleA) to John Y. Mason, Calhoun described the discussions between himself and Tyler concerning the drafting of this unsent despatch.

From ROB[ERT] G. SHAW and Others

Boston, December [20] 1844

We the undersigned Merchants of this city & part of us engaged in the trade of Venezuela having known either personally or by representation *Mr. William T. Mann* of this city, but of late years a resident of Puerto Cabello do hereby recommend him, a suitable, worthy & responsible person for the *Consulship* of that port, now vacant by the death of the late consul Dr. Franklin Litchfield. Rob. G. Shaw, Jos[eph] V. Bacon & Son, And[re]w T. Hall & Co., Atkins & Freeman, Jno. W. Langdon & Co., Henshaw, Ward & Co., Ja[me]s H. Hicks & Co., Silas G. Whitney, Consul of Venezuela, Cushing Stetson, Harland & Aspinwall, New York December 16th 1844, P[eter] Harmony & Nephew &c, Bevan & Humphreys, Philad[elphi]a, 19th Dec. 1844, Henry H. Williams, Baltimore 20th Dec[embe]r 1844, T:W: Brune & Sons, Baltimore 20th Dec[em]ber 1844.

DS in DNA, RG 59 (State Department), Applications and Recommendations, 1837–1845, Mann (M-687:22, frame 110).

From LEVI D. SLAMM

Coleman's Hotel [Washington,] Dec. 20, 1844

Dear Sir, I beg to ask an interview of about an hour with you upon a matter, I deem, and our friends deem, of some National importance. Several of our friends, members of Congress, would be pleased to attend, and could you spare the leizure for the interview I would be obliged to be informed of the fact by note at what proper time we could call upon you. Respectfully, Levi D. Slamm.

ALS in ScCleA. NOTE: Slamm was a New York City politician.

From HENRY W. SMITH

Savannah (Ga.) Dec. 20th 1844

D[ea]r Sir! Not having the honour of an acquaintaince with you personally I must commence this note with an apology for intruding upon your time and attention, and hope you will excuse the liberty I take, when I assure you nothing but sheer necessity compells me to it. My object in addressing you is to ask your aid in securing me an appointment in one of the Navy Yards, as sail maker. I am a native of Charleston So. Ca. where I was bourn and raised and have lived for thirty years, but my business and circomstances are such I am unable any longer to support my family, a wife and five small children.

I have Just returned thus far on my way home from Mobile and New Orleans in search of employment, but without success. There is nothing to be done in this city. Under these circomstances as one of your con[s]tituents and believing from your character, you to be a humane man, and capable of sympathising ["with" *interlined*] the unfortunate, no matter how humble, I have concluded to appeal to you for aid. I am a good workman, understand my business in all its branches—and can produce the best testamonials, that I am perfectly *sober, honest* and industrious. If you can secure me a situation in any of the Navy Yards in the United States, I will immediately go to it, and promise by attention to business, and ["upriteness" *canceled and* "uprightness" *interlined*] of life [to] prove to you your kindness has not been shown to one who does not merit it.

May I ask the liberty of you to let me hear from you as soon as may be. Praying again you to excuse this liberty I Remain very Respectfully Your Ob[edien]t Ser[van]t, Henry W. Smith.

P.S. Please direct to this city to the care of the Rev[eren]d Ja[me]s E. Godfrey. Perhaps if no situation in any of the yards presents itself you may be able to get one on board some ship, Any thing, my situation is distressing.

ALS in NcU, John Young Mason Papers. NOTE: An AEI by Calhoun reads: "Submitted for the consideration of the Sec[retar]y of the Navy [Mason]."

From T[homas] L. Smith, *"Private"*

Dec[embe]r 20th[?] 1844

Dear Sir, Opinions, that form parties and make leaders, are now in active operation, as you know. Their intensity is increased from the diversities that exist and the consequences to which they lead.

From the peculiar character of the subjects that engage public attention, a crisis is approaching that must affect to some extent, those who stand prominently in the foreground of the field of controversy. Such is your position, and those who feel interested in your triumph over opposition, can but look with peculiar solicitude at the movements that are in progress, that may affect you in the great arbitrament of public opinion.

Friends, I hope may be excused for volunteering advice, when it proceeds, not only from the interest they may feel, in admiration of your high character, but, for the success of those measures and principles, upon which depend the wise and wholesome administration of our Government, and which must affect the rights and prosperity of all. Presuming upon this liberty and asking pardon for its exercise, I will venture to suggest some things, that strike me as important and not unworthy your consideration. There are certain leading gentlemen at the South, who have been long closely identified with you in the advocacy of particular great, prominent measures of public policy, and ["who" *interlined*] are supposed to derive their opinions from the superior lights of your mind. This connection, leaves them in the situation to be considered in all that they now promulgate, as the exponents of your present opinions.

With the best intentions no doubt, these gentlemen have recently expressed themselves with great boldness upon delicate and important subjects, touching the policy of the South more particularly, and which are deemed so ultra, that they find but a feeble response from abroad, and ["go to" *interlined*] alarm, rather than ["to" *interlined*] proselyte. Those who have other objects and other men around whom they are rallying, take advantage of this state of things, and are using these particular opinions of those Southern gentlemen to your prejudice, by asserting, that they are *your* opinions. Proceeding upon the hypothesis, that you are not identified with these ultra opinions in *all* their latitude, I deem it of importance, that you should in some way separate yourself from the identity, so that public opinion cannot be mislead [*sic*]; and thus take from your adversaries their weapons of assault.

Another consideration is worthy of your notice. The Presidential election through which we have just passed, involved to a great extent the discussion of the Tariff and the doctrines of free trade. The indications evolved in the progress of that struggle are too manifest not to be seen and understood—popular feeling went with the Tariff measures, and showed, that whatever may be the merits of the doctrine of free trade, as you have ably demonstrated, it is ["not" *interlined*] prepared at this time to adopt ["it" *altered to* "them"]. Let us admit that your opinions on this subject are correct, yet, if they pass the scrutiny of public opinion, with unequivocal proofs of disapprobation; is it politic to persevere in pushing these doctrines in all their latitude, against such fearful odds and marked inflexibility? Would it not be best to meet prejudices and preconceived opinions, upon the ground of compromise, where something might be gained? Whatever might be ["the" *interlined*] fruit of this compromise, it would bring you nearer to the accomplishment of your object, by making you stronger for new conquests; giving you increased power, and diminishing the antagonist force, and narrowing the space between the points of controversy.

The policy of such a measure, is to be seen in the every-day transactions of life, and is abundantly exemplified in illustrious instances in the history of our Government. It seems to be a necessary concession to that right of opinion, which under our form of Government is so stern when zealously opposed. It conquers whilst it seems to yield. Modify these two points, and you will make broader the foundation on which you stand by giving increased efficiency to the power and influence that you now have over the feelings and affections of a large portion of your countrymen.

I beg you to pardon the freedom with which I have addressed you, and appreciate the motive that has influenced me. With great respect, Your most ob[edien]t Ser[vant,] T.L. Smith.

ALS in ScCleA. NOTE: Thomas L. Smith was Register of the U.S. Treasury at this time.

Article from the [London, England,] *Morning Post,* 12/21. This untitled manuscript copy of an article, found among Calhoun's papers, asserts that the success of James K. Polk and the Democrats in the recent Presidential election has "virtually annihilated" the tariff policies of the U.S. and that forthcoming reductions in American tariff duties on cotton goods will increase pressure within England for repeal of the Corn Laws. CC in ScCleA.

From GEO[RGE] M. BIBB

Treasury Department, December 21st, 1844

Sir, I beg to refer to the Department of State, the enclosed communications addressed to this Department by [Thomas Barrett] the Collector of New Orleans, and Messrs. Stafford & Bartlett, merchants of that place, relative to the vexatious interference, on the part of the Texan authorities, with our trade on the Sabine River; and request to be informed whether, since the transmission of the despatch from the Department of State to Mr. [William S.] Murphy, chargé d'affaires at Texas, dated the 11th May last, a copy of which was communicated to this Department on the 13th May last, any alteration, affecting our navigation of the river, has been effected in the Texan revenue regulations as enjoined in the instructions of President [Samuel] Houston, dated the 22d February last, a copy of which, together with a copy of a letter from the Consul of the United States to the Collector of New Orleans, transmitting the same, is also herewith enclosed. I have the honor to be With great respect Your obed[ient] Serv[an]t, Geo. M. Bibb, Secretary of the Treasury.

LS in DNA, RG 59 (State Department), Miscellaneous Letters (M-179:106, frames 334–335); FC in DNA, RG 56 (Secretary of the Treasury), Letters to Cabinet and Bureau Officers, Series B, 1842–1847, 4:493.

From LEW[IS] CASS

Detroit, Dec. 21, 1844

Sir, I understand the office of Consul at Florence is vacant and that Mr. Joseph Mozier of Ohio is an applicant for it. I beg leave to add my testimony to the other proofs of his claims, which you will receive. I do not know Mr. Mozier personally, but my information, respecting his capacity and merits is from a source, on which I can place implicit reliance. I should be happy to learn, that his application had been successful; and I feel confident he will justify the expectations of his friends and satisfactorily execute the duties of the office. With great respect, I am, Sir, your ob[edient] Serv[an]t, Lew. Cass.

ALS in DNA, RG 59 (State Department), Applications and Recommendations, 1845–1853, Mozier (M-873:62, frames 289–290). NOTE: Cass was to begin a term as Senator from Mich. in 3/1845.

From E[dmund] S. Derry, New York [City], 12/21. "I have known Mr. James Fiora of this City who will hand you this, since boyhood and have always since I took any part in politics found him to be a most firm and unwavering democrat. His political preferences have coincided with mine and with undoubted competency and the Strictest integrity, he cannot be too warmly commended to your favorable consideration." [Fiora visited Washington seeking appointment to be U.S. Consul at Manchester.] ALS in DNA, RG 59 (State Department), Applications and Recommendations, 1845–1853, Fiora (M-873:28, frames 112–113).

To Robert McGaw, New York [City], 12/21. "I have to acknowledge the receipt of your letter [*not found*] of the 18th instant and to state in reply that the claim of the representatives of Stephen J. Lewis upon the Brazillian government shall receive all proper attention from this Department." FC in DNA, RG 59 (State Department), Domestic Letters, 35:53 (M-40:33).

From F[ranci]s [M.] Auboyneau, U.S. Consul, La Rochelle, 12/22. Auboyneau informs Calhoun that he has received his commission and his exequatur. He expresses personal thanks to Calhoun for his aid in obtaining his post. ALS in DNA, RG 59 (State Department), Consular Despatches, La Rochelle, vol. 2 (T-394:2), received 2/27/1845.

From Barclay & Livingston, and six other mercantile firms, New York [City], 12/23. The signers recommend [Crawford] Livingston for appointment to be U.S. Despatch Agent for New York City. "As head of an Express line, and as conductor of a Foreign Business Agency, Mr. Livingston gives satisfaction to the public generally." The other signers were D. & A. Kingsland & Co., J.J. Boyd, Schmidt & Balcher, Grinnell, Minturn & Co., Edw[ar]d K. Collins Co., and R[ober]t Kermit. (This letter was enclosed with Crawford Livingston's letter to Calhoun of 12/23.) LS in DNA, RG 59 (State Department), Applications and Recommendations, 1837–1845, Livingston (M-687:19, frame 526).

From W[illia]m M. Blackford

Legation of U.S.
Bogotá, Dec[embe]r 23rd 1844

Sir, I have had the honor to receive your despatches, Nos. 18, 19 & 20, together with the Ratification of the Postal Convention. Mr. [Edward] Dixon arrived at Honda, and was unable, from illness, to proceed further, & forwarded his despatches by an Indian, who delivered them to me on the 17th Inst.—sixty days from the time they left Carthagena. This extraordinary delay in their receipt has been very annoying to me, personally, & unfortunate in its bearings upon the business of the Legation as it materially impaired that moral influence, produced by his arrival, to which I alluded in my last.

The Exchange of Ratifications of the Postal Convention took place on the 20th Instant, with the usual formalities.

In my last Despatch I mentioned that I had taken up the case of the Schooner "Yankee" & expressed a hope of bringing it to a satisfactory issue. In this, I am happy to say, I was not too sanguine, as I have, this day, settled the claim. The Copies of the notes which passed between myself and the Secretary [of Foreign Affairs, Joaquin Acosta], herewith transmitted, will put you in possession of the details of the negotiation. I insisted, with some pertinacity, upon the settlement, at once, of the amount of indemnity for the Captain, whilst I expressed my willingness to refer the ascertainment of the sum, to be paid for vessel & cargo, to commissioners to be respectively appointed. I could not, however be insensible to the force of some of the objections urged by the Secretary against two Conventions in the same case; nor to the danger of Congress rejecting one, or both, if thus made by the Executive in the absence of full official information on the subject. At the same time, I could not consent to submit the amount of the personal damages to the judgment of another. It was finally agreed, in the conference of to day, as a matter of compromise, that the whole affair should be referred—but that the Granadian Commissioner should be instructed to grant the sum of Four Thousand Dollars, without interest, to Captain [Eliphalet] Robbins, as compensation for his imprisonment, wages, expenses &c. I contended, long & earnestly, for a larger sum—but the embarrassed condition of the finances was urged in mitigation of my demand. The amount, no doubt, will be quite satisfactory to Capt. Robbins, who as well as the other parties—seems to have taken no interest in the claim since it was first presented.

In naming Mr. [Joseph] Gooding as Commissioner, I was influenced, not only by my confidence in his integrity & capacity, but by the consideration of his being the Attorney in fact of the Atlantic Insurance Company of New York, which holds the assignment of the Policy on the Cargo. The Commissioners will meet about the 1st of February & the Convention which they may make will be submitted to the Congress in the first month of its session.

I have given Mr. Gooding the necessary instructions—though, of necessity, leaving much to his discretion—& have handed to him all the documents in the case, which were in this Legation. The amount which will, probably, be obtained for the vessel & cargo, will be from nine to ten thousand dollars, with interest from 1838—making, with the compensation to the captain, a total of seventeen or eighteen thousand dollars to be paid by this Government.

The effects of the Legation have been left with Mr. De Lisle, the Chargé d'Affaires of France, who has kindly appropriated two rooms of his house for their accommodation.

I send you, herewith, copies of complimentary notes which have passed between the Secretary and myself.

I intend to set out, in the morning, for Carthagena, where I hope to meet the Oregon. I greatly regret the long detention of this vessel. I have the honor to be, with high respect, Your Ob[edien]t S[ervan]t, Wm. M. Blackford.

P.S. In the hurry and confusion of my departure, I find it impossible to make out an Inventory of the effects, & a catalogue of the books, belonging to the Legation. The only additions made to the former are two book presses. A good many books, consisting chiefly of public documents, have been added to the library. No other changes would be necessary in the Inventory & catalogue of my predecessor.

ALS (No. 29) with Ens in DNA, RG 59 (State Department), Diplomatic Despatches, Colombia, vol. 10 (T-33:10, frames 293–308), received 2/14/1845; FC in DNA, RG 84 (Foreign Posts), Colombia, Despatches, vol. B4.

From [F.] BURTON CRAIGE, "(Private)"

Lincolnton (N.C.), Dec. 23rd 1844

Dear Sir, I rec[eive]d yours of the 2nd inst. and feel much gratified that you should take such an interest in my affairs, and hope that some future opportunity may occur upon which I shall be able to make a better return for it, than my present acknowledgement ["of it" *canceled*].

The situation you spoke of in your letter would not be disagreeable to me though if I could obtain one in one of the new States or territories by which I could realize as much I would prefer it, but as I know of no such situation at present, I would be very happy to receive such an appointment as I could fill with credit to myself, & usefulness to the Government and ["such an one"(?) *interlined*] as would enable me to support myself and family free from the harrasments to which I am now daily subjected.

The result of the vote upon the 21st rule in the Ho[use] of Rep-[resentatives] makes us all feel rather gloomy as to the future prospects of the South. We fear the agitation of the subject of slavery by the northern fanatics sustained as they are by some from the South, will eventuate in a dissolution of the of the [*sic*] Union.

I see [Thomas H.] Benton is again likely to oppose serious obsticles to the annexation of Texas. Can nothing be done to drive him from his course of madness and folly? Will he permit his feelings—his personal feelings to govern his conduct upon this all important measure for the South & West? Will he lend himself to the abolitionists to aid them in defeating a measure upon the success of which rests the future safety of his own constituents?

I for one begin to despair of ever seeing any legislation by the national Congress for the benefit of the slave holding part of the Confederacy, and for one I am ready to go with our old Statesright friends for any effective action that will bring the majority in Congress to their senses. I am utterly opposed idly to sit by, & daily see nothing but insult added to oppressions. I had hoped—fondly hoped that much would be gained by the late triumph of the Democratic party, but the vote upon the 21st rule has left me but little room for further hope.

As we are not disposed here to act rashly we ["look"(?) *canceled*] are looking with great anxiety to the course of those that we have heretofore regarded as the leaders of the old State-rights party. How much longer are we to wait? Until after another session of Congress? Will Congress be called together immediately after the adjournment of the present? With sentiments of the highest regard permit me to subscribe myself Your friend, Burton Craige.

ALS in ScCleA; PEx in Boucher and Brooks, eds., *Correspondence*, pp. 273–274. NOTE: Francis Burton Craige was U.S. Representative from N.C. during 1853–1861 and a member of the Confederate Provisional Congress.

From HAMILTON FISH, [Representative from N.Y.]

House of Representatives, December 23, 1844
Sir, I take the liberty to enclose a letter I have received from Willet Coles Esq. of Newyork, in relation to a claim of the owners of the Ship Hope, growing out of her capture in the Harbor of Buenos Ayres, by a British Frigate in the year 1814. Mr. Coles, in his letter expresses a desire that I should have a personal interview with the Honorable the Secretary of State, under the impression that in that mode a more full answer may be obtained. Knowing however the numerous calls upon your time, I avail myself of this mode, of requesting the information which Mr. Coles desires—but will be most happy to wait upon the Secretary, in case he should prefer that mode of communicating on this subject. With the highest esteem your very obed[ien]t Serv[an]t, Hamilton Fish.

LS with Ens in DNA, RG 76 (Records of Boundary and Claims Commissions and Arbitrations), Miscellaneous Claims Records: Buenos Aires, 1816–1849; FC in DLC, Hamilton Fish Papers, Letter Copy Book E. NOTE: One of the Ens is an LS from Secretary of State Dan[ie]l Webster to John Anthon of New York City, dated 4/19/1841, reporting no progress in settlement of the *Hope* claim.

E[dmund] W. Hubard, [Representative from Va.], to [Calhoun?], 12/23. Hubard states that Dr. W[illia]m P. Moseley seeks employment as a bearer of despatches to Texas "should the Executive design in the next few months sending out any person in that capacity. The Dr. is a Democrat, but not a [Thomas H.] Bentonian, & is a great admirer of Hon. J.C. C[alhoun]." Hubard seeks to learn if this appointment can be made and what compensation is allowed. ALS in DNA, RG 59 (State Department), Applications and Recommendations, 1837–1845, Moseley (M-687:23, frames 606–607).

To [JOHANN GEORG VON] HÜLSEMANN

Department of State
Washington, 23rd December, 1844
Sir: In reply to your note of the 14th instant, I have the honor to inform you that, upon referring its subject to the Honorable J[oseph] R. Ingersoll [Representative from Pa.], he has stated that the bill to

provide for the fixing of the value of the florin of Austria at the Custom House—which was introduced into the House of Representatives in January last, from the Committee of Ways and Means—would have been acted upon promptly, but for the absence of data to enable the House to determine with certainty that forty-eight cents is the true value of the florin. As soon as this point shall be settled, it is believed that the bill will pass. I am, Sir, with great consideration, Your obedient Servant, J.C. Calhoun.

LS in DLC, John G. Hülsemann Papers (Toner Collection); FC in DNA, RG 59 (State Department), Notes to Foreign Legations, German States, 6:100–101 (M-99:27).

From Crawford Livingston, "Foreign Agency Office," New York [City], 12/23. Livingston seeks appointment as Despatch Agent "in case any new appointment is deemed necessary to insure more prompt attention to the transmission of *Despatches* between the State Department and the American Diplomatic Agents in Foreign Countries." Livingston presently conducts a private postal agency and has recently been employed by the Post Office Department "in important matters connected with the revenue of that Department upon the route of the *Express* ["*route*" canceled] *line* with which he is connected." Livingston does not solicit any "extraneous influences" to promote his application nor to have anyone removed from office. He encloses a letter from Barclay & Livingston and six other mercantile houses dated 12/22. He also encloses an ADS by J[ohn] S. Skinner [Assistant Postmaster General], dated 12/27, affirming Livingston's qualifications. ALS with Ens in DNA, RG 59 (State Department), Applications and Recommendations, 1837–1845, Livingston (M-687: 19, frames 526–529).

To C[HARLES] H. RAYMOND, [Texas Legation]

Department of State
Washington, 23d December, 1844
Sir: I have the honor to transmit herewith a copy of a Resolution adopted by the Senate on the 6th inst. [*sic*; 12/16], calling on the President [John Tyler] for certain information in regard to the public debt and the public lands of Texas.

I invite your attention, particularly, to the two subjects of inquiry, first, whether the public debt of Texas has been increased since the signature of the treaty of annexation in April, last, and, *second* whether there have been any additional grants of the public domain since that period?   In replying to these inquiries, if you have any information in addition to that heretofore communicated by the Texan Plenipotentiaries, Messrs. [Isaac] Van Zandt and [J. Pinckney] Henderson, in reference to the other subjects referred to in the Resolution, I would also thank you to communicate the same to this Department.   I have the honor to be, with high consideration, Sir, Your obedient servant, J.C. Calhoun.

[Enclosure]

"Copy of the Resolution referred to in the above note."

In the Senate of the United States, Dec[embe]r 16, 1844 Resolved that the President be requested to inform the Senate whether the Executive Department is possessed of any definite and satisfactory information by which the present public debt of the Republic of Texas can be ascertained and if so, that he be requested to communicate it to the Senate with the aggregate amount of that debt; and also, that he be requested to inform the Senate whether any, and if any, what additions have been made to that debt since the signing of the Treaty with that Republic submitted to the Senate at its last session.

And that he be further requested to inform the Senate what amount of public lands of Texas had been granted by the Spanish, Mexican and Texan Governments, and to what extent extent [*sic*] the faith of either of said Governments had been pledged, by the issuing of scrip or other security to make grants thereof, or in any form to part with its title to or interest in the same, previous to the signing of said Treaty; what amount remained at that date ungranted and subject to no such pledge; and whether any and what grants of said domain have been made, or other evidence of title thereto, legal or equitable, issued by the Texian Government since that period.

Attest, (Signed), Asbury Dickens, Secretary.

FC in DNA, RG 59 (State Department), Notes to Foreign Legations, Texas, 6:78–79 (M-99:95); FC with En in Tx, Records of the Texas Republic Department of State, Copybooks of Letters Received from Texan and Foreign Representatives, vol. 2–1/103, pp. 35–36; CC with En in Tx, Records of the Texas Republic Department of State, U.S. Diplomatic Correspondence; DS of En in DNA, RG 59 (State Department), Miscellaneous Letters (M-179:106, frames 317–318); PC of En in *Senate Journal,* 28th Cong., 2nd Sess., p. 37. NOTE: The enclosed resolution was transcribed from the second-cited source.

From JOHN M. READ

Philadelphia, December 23, 1844

Sir, I was the attorney of The United States for this District in August 1839 when large seizures were made here of woollen goods of british manufacture for violations of our revenue laws, and was afterwards engaged, in the trial of the informations, for the United States either in that capacity or as special counsel of the government.

The first case tried, was that of The U. States vs Taylor & Blackburne. It lasted nearly eight weeks. Mr. [George M.] Dallas, Mr. [John] Cadwalader & myself appeared for The U. States. Mr. [John?] Sergeant[,] Mr. Williams and Mr. [William M.?] Meredith for the Claimants. The gross frauds practised by the parties were so clearly developed during the progress of the cause, that the Jury after a deliberation of about ten minutes returned a verdict for The United States. A motion for a new trial was unsuccessful, and on a writ of error to the Circuit Court the Judgment of the District Court was affirmed, which would have been a final one, except for the 3d section of the act of the 4th July 1840, passed after the trial of this case—under which a writ of error was taken to the Supreme Court, where it is now pending—is ready for arguments, and will be reached early this week.

In the trial of the subsequent cases, the whole scheme of fraud and villainy was laid bare, and it appeared, that these were but a few out of a long series of deliberate violations of our laws perpetrated principally by English subjects, and accompanied with perjury[,] forgery, bribery, and in some instances systematic corruption of officers of the government.

Being aware that unsuccessful applications have been made by the British Minister [Richard Pakenham] to The Attorney General [John Nelson] and [George M. Bibb] The Secretary of The Treasury for a brief suspension of the pending legal proceedings in this case and hearing that an official communication from the same source will probably be made to your department, I have felt it my duty, briefly to state the above facts. I have the honour to enclose a copy of Mr. [Henry M.] Watts' report, which contains a detailed account of all these cases. Mr. Packenham I have reason to suppose has seen it, but he has never had it officially communicated to him.

My own opinion was made up long ago, not only that the forfeitures should be strictly enforced, but that the parties concerned should deem themselves exceedingly fortunate, not to have paid in their persons, for their offences against the laws of the country. I am with great respect Y[ou]r ob[edien]t S[ervan]t, John M. Read.

ALS with En in DNA, RG 59 (State Department), Miscellaneous Letters (M-179:106, frames 339–358). NOTE: Read enclosed a copy of Senate Document No. 83, 27th Cong., 1st Sess., a compendium of information on the customs cases at Philadelphia.

To J[ohn] P. Schatzell, "app[oin]t[e]d" U.S. Consul, Matamoros, [Mexico], 12/23. Calhoun notifies Schatzell of his appointment and encloses instructions for the performance of his duties and a blank bond form to be completed and returned to the State Department. FC in DNA, RG 59 (State Department), Consular Instructions, 11: 317–318.

From James Semple, [Senator from Ill.], 12/23. "I enclose a letter [to me of 12/20] from my friend Henry H. Williams of Balt[imor]e who has been for some years engaged in the trade to Venezuela, recommending the bearer of this Mr. W[illia]m T. Mann as Consul at Puerto Cabello in the Republic of Venezuela. I know Mr. Williams to be a good Man[?], and he is interested in the appointment of a good man." [An AEU by Calhoun on the En reads "Mr. Mann applies for the Consulate at Porto Cabello."] ALS with En in DNA, RG 59 (State Department), Applications and Recommendations, 1837–1845, Mann (M-687:22, frames 108–109 and 111–112).

To GEORGE M. BIBB, Secretary of the Treasury

Department of State
Washington, 24th December, 1844
Sir: I have the honor to acknowledge the receipt of your letter of the 21st instant with the accompanying papers, relative to the exaction at the port of Sabine in Texas of tonnage duties from vessels of the United States entering the Sabine Pass; and to inform you, in reply, that no communication upon the subject has been received from that government since the 11th of May, last, the date of the instruction to Mr. [William S.] Murphy, to which you refer.

The documents which accompanied your letter are now returned. I have the honor to be, Sir, Your obedient servant, J.C. Calhoun.

LS in DNA, RG 56 (Secretary of the Treasury), Letters Received from Executive Officers, Series AB, 1844, no. 46; FC in DNA, RG 59 (State Department), Domestic Letters, 35:56 (M-40:33).

From A[NDREW] J. DONELSON

New Orleans, Dec[em]b[e]r 24, 1844

D[ea]r Sir, I reached this place last evening, and passed on my way Capt. Elliott [*sic*; Charles Elliot,] the British Chargé d'Affaires proceeding to Washington in Texas. It is said in some of the papers that he has authority to offer terms to Texas, guaranteeing her independence, and proposing to pay her for certain commercial privileges provided she will refuse incorporation into our Union. Whether this be true or not I feel no uneasiness about it, after the assurances obtained from the Govt. of Texas which will be handed to you by my Brother in law Mr. [George] Martin, who proceeds directly to Washington City with despatches from me, numbered 6, 7, & 8. Texas will make no Treaty with England until the decision of our Government on the measure of annexation is known. You may depend on this. The more I have associated with the people of Texas, the more am I satisfied that they will adhere to the hope of incorporation into our union while there is a prospect of effecting it on terms of honor and justice.

If you find that the Treaty cannot be passed, it may be well for you to know how far Texas would be willing to vary its terms.

For this purpose I have consulted with some of her most prominent citizens, and among them with [Ex-]President [Samuel] Houston. I have said to him, state to me, what are the essentials of a bill that would be ratified by Texas, securing annexation.

He answers first—full community of interests and as a Territory

second—the assumption of the national debt, or if not, Texas to keep her domain pledged to this object

third—Texas to make as many States hereafter as the United States may think proper

fourth—In running the boundary line between the U.S. and Texas, where lands fell into the U. States by misapprehension of claimants, in their locations, that they are to be reimbursed upon the same principles of equity, that citizens of the U.S. falling into Texas were reimbursed fifth—public liabilities to be redeemed *at the price at which they were issued*—(the public debt will thus fall below $10,000,000, probably will not exceed the half of this sum).

You will thus see that the 2d Article of the Treaty covers all his ground, except the suggestions in relation to the public debt, and the claimants east of the line from the 32d degree of north latitude on the Sabine, to the Red river, and I understand that there are but few of those, who have valid claims.

I am also of opinion, should you think of concession to the opposition on the subject of boundary, that you might recognize Texas as including all the Territory East of the Nuecos [*sic*] to its source, and thence north to the Red river—leaving the remainder of the territory as claimed by her to be adjusted by future negotiation with Mexico.

Or if not in this form, it might be recited that within the limits of Texas it was not intended to include any portion of territory over which she had not *extended and maintained* her jurisdiction. This would leave out Santa Fee [*sic*], or those portions of Mexican territory which are trenched upon by the act of the Texan Congress running up the Rio Grande to its source, and thence north to the line of the United States: and it would give Texas the district now represented in her Congress, between the Nuecos and the Rio Grande.

I would not fear to risk the question of annexation with the people of Texas, with this limitation upon their claim to boundary. Houston[']s suggestions are important particularly in regard to the claims cut off by the running of the boundary line. He deserves a great deal on account of the support he has given the measure of annexation, and unless you possess information in regard to those claims, which I do not, making them inadmissible, I would by no means overlook them. If they are *bona fide*, they would furnish an equitable claim against Texas, and have to be settled at any rate, and if they are not of this character, they will of course be so adjudged by the commissioners who will examine them.

I make these suggestions for your consideration and that of the President [John Tyler]. I wish the measure of annexation passed as speedily as possible. If once in the Union minor difficulties will cure themselves, and the great battle on the subject of the number of States, and the threatened restriction on slavery, can be fought without the fear of foreign influence in alienating the Territory.

Not to detain Mr. Martin, I shorten this letter and will write again by the next mail.

Mr. Martin will hand also to the Departm[en]t the bundle of

private letters addressed to the late Mr. [Tilghman A.] Howard, which were handed to me by the Consul at Galveston. He brings also some letters from Gen[era]l [Duff] Green who was at Washington [Texas] when I left, and will remain there some weeks. He is pleased with the country and says he will settle in it. In the present limited state of the trade between Texas and this country, his consulate [at Galveston] is worth but little in a pecuniary point of view. I am very truly y[ou]r ob[edien]t ser[van]t, A.J. Donelson.

ALS (Confidential) in DNA, RG 59 (State Department), Diplomatic Despatches, Texas, vol. 2 (T-728:2, frames 444–446), received 1/2/1845; retained copy in DLC, Andrew Jackson Donelson Papers.

To Hamilton Fish, Representative [from N.Y.], 12/24. Calhoun acknowledges receipt of Fish's letter of 12/23 with its enclosure concerning the claim of "Willett" [*sic*; Willet] Coles of New York against the government of Buenos Aires in the case of the ship *Hope*. William Brent, Jr., U.S. Chargé d'Affaires at Buenos Aires, has been instructed to seek an adjustment of all outstanding claims against that government. Calhoun will send special instructions to Brent "agre[e]ably to Mr. Coles['] suggestion." Fish's enclosed papers are herewith returned. FC in DNA, RG 59 (State Department), Domestic Letters, 35:55 (M-40:33).

From [Joseph] Gales [Jr.] & [William W.] Seaton, [publishers of the Washington, D.C., *Daily National Intelligencer*], 12/24. "We have the honor to state, [in] reply to your Circular of the 2d instant, accidentally overlooked until now, that the number of ["our" *interlined*] regular Subbscribers [*sic*], permanent so far as a personal engagement can be said to be permanent, has varied very little from our last reply to a similar Letter from the Department; since which the number of Subscribers has, however, rather increased than diminished." LS in DNA, RG 59 (State Department), Miscellaneous Letters Received Regarding Publishers of the Laws.

From JACOB F. HAEBULEN[?] and Others

Philadelphia, Dec. 24th 1844
Sir, The undersigned have been appointed a Committee, at a meeting of adopted Citizens of German origin, and claiming the United States as their home, have heard with regret that frequent arrivals

occur from the European Continent, of convicts and criminals. They further learn from the public papers that information has been received recently in this Country from Professor [Georg Friedrich] List [U.S. Consul at Stuttgart] stating, that this policy of the petty germanic Courts and indeed of greater governments, was again to be exerted, to the detriment of the peace and happiness of the people of the United States. We beg leave therefore to inquire whether any such information has been received, at the State Department, and desire to ascertain any Knowledge, that may have been communicated to you, on the subject, in order, that proper efforts may be taken to resist an outrage so atrocious, not only upon the character of the adopted citizen, but also upon the character of free Institutions. With high esteem & respect Y[ou]r ob[e]d[ien]t Serv[an]ts, Jacob F. Haebulen[?], Secr[e]t[ar]y, L.A. Wollenweber[?], L. Herbert, H.G. Stuebgen, G. Lembert, C. Wittig, M.D., G. Goebel.

LS in ScCleA. NOTE: A Clerk's EU reads "German Emigrants[,] to be answered by the Report to Congress."

From C[harles] J. Ingersoll, Chairman, [House] Com[mittee] on Foreign Affairs, 12/24. Ingersoll informs Calhoun that the committee has reported a bill to pay Henry Ledyard the difference between his salary as Secretary of Legation at Paris and Chargé d'Affaires there, which latter office he held ad interim. Ingersoll requests information from the State Department of the length of time Ledyard served as acting Chargé d'Affaires. ALS in DNA, RG 59 (State Department), Miscellaneous Letters (M-179:106, frames 362–363).

From WASHINGTON IRVING

Legation of the United States
Madrid, 24th December 1844

Sir, Since the date of my last I have received Despatch No. 38 containing the commission of James J. Wright as Consul at Santiago de Cuba and have applied for his Exequatur.

The flour trade to Cuba has recently been made the subject of discussion in the Madrid papers and will probably be brought before the Córtes. The inhabitants of Cuba wish that the duties on flour both from Spain and the United States should be reduced. The exporters of flour from Spain wish the reduction to be exclusively in their favor, pretending that the enormous difference which at present exists between the duty of two dollars and fifty cents per barrel on spanish and ten dollars per barrel on American flour is not sufficient to give the former an equal chance in the market. I forward three or four Madrid papers containing articles which have appeared on each side of the question. I have furnished some facts and hints for the writers in favor of American interests and shall watch the future course of the question. I transmit also this day's *Gaceta de Madrid* containing the project of a law for the suppression of the slave trade made by the Minister of State in conformity to Treaty stipulations between Spain and G[rea]t Britain and presented by him for the approbation of the Cortes. I am, Sir, respectfully your most obedient servant, Washington Irving.

LS (No. 57) in DNA, RG 59 (State Department), Diplomatic Despatches, Spain, vol. 34 (M-31:34), received 1/27/1845; FC (dated 12/23) in DNA, RG 84 (Foreign Posts), Spain, Despatches, 2:121–122; PC in Aderman et al., eds., *Complete Works of Washington Irving, Letters*, 3:853.

From WILLIAM M. McCARTY

Brookville Ind[ian]a, Dec. 24th 1844

D[ea]r Sir, I very respectfully submit my name to your consideration for the office of District att[orne]y of this State and respectfully ask that the app[ointmen]t may be delayed for a few days to enable me to furnish letters.

I was your friend for the Presidency & during my residence at Cin[cinnati] addressed an assemblage of your friends by request and was one of the committee that drafted the enclosed resolutions.

Before the Texas treaty was negotiated or the sentiments of Messrs. [Henry] Clay & [Martin] Van Buren were known—I advocated the annexation of Texas immediately after a whig meeting which had denounced the measure as "Treasonable."

In 41/2 some high Tariff resolutions were adopted at College Hall Cin[cinnat]i & myself and others of your friends challenged a discussion & moved to rescind the resolutions and after a protracted discussion of several weeks succeeded in doing it in that whig city.

Should my endorsement not be sufficient to induce your favorable action I hope that the app[ointmen]t will not be conferred upon Mr. [Joseph W.] Chapman of Laporte. It is a mere challenge to the favor—by one perhaps not entitled by the strict Law of etiquette to make such a request.

I think that I was favorably endorsed to the President some two years since for the Consulship at Rio Janeiro—but as that application was made without my express sanction by my uncle (Gen. [Enoch] McCarty) I am not aware of its extent—nor by whom. Very resp[ect]f[ull]y I have the honor to be y[ou]r friend, William M. McCarty.

ALS in DNA, RG 59 (State Department), Applications and Recommendations, 1837–1845, McCarty (M-687:21, frames 28–30). Note: The Cincinnati resolutions of 5/31/1843 are published in *Papers of John C. Calhoun*, 17:249–252.

To C[ornelius] P. Van Ness, Collector of Customs, New York [City]

Department of State
Washington, 24 Dec[embe]r 1844

Sir, By a resolution of the House of Representatives of March 23rd 1843, the Secretary of State was required to procure through the Consular and Diplomatic agents of this Government abroad, and such other means as to him may seem most suitable—

"Full and accurate information as to the wholesale and retail prices, in foreign markets, during the year commencing on the first day of September 1842, of all commodities in which duties are levied under existing laws, as well as of such as are imported free of duty."

By another resolution bearing date Jan. 24th 1844, the Secretary of State is further required in making this report—

"To state the rate of duties imposed on such articles on being imported into the United States, and where specific duties are imposed, to reduce them to ad valorem rates in the cost of such articles abroad."

In order to enable me to comply with this call of the House, I will be much obliged to you if you will, from the books of the Customs House at New York, cause a statement to be prepared, giving the rates of duties on the different articles of import, during the year commencing on the first of September 1842, reducing them all to *ad valorem* rates on the cost abroad "and exercising especial care in all instances, to give such information in Federal currency[,] weights, & measures."

As it is my intention to reply to this call of the House at as early a day as possible during the present session, your prompt attention to this communication will oblige me much. I am &c, J.C. Calhoun.

FC in DNA, RG 59 (State Department), Domestic Letters, 35:54 (M-40:33).

From THO[MA]S J. GREEN

Velasco Texas, Dec[embe]r 25th/44

Sir, The enclosed proceedings [*not found*] had two days since at Brazoria[,] our "cradle of liberty," speaks the sentiments of very nearly our whole population upon the subject of annexation; and I take the liberty of enclosing them to you under the hope that they may contain some hint useful to your negociation upon that subject. Very Respectfully your Ob[edien]t h[u]m[b]l[e] Ser[van]t, Thos. J. Green.

ALS in ScCleA.

From ABNER GREENLEAF, "Private"

Portsmouth N.H., December 25 1844

Sir: Being personally unknown to you, and living in comparative obscurity I had no reason to suppose until recently, that you had ever heard my name mentioned, although in the humble sphere of life in which I move, I have taken no small degree of American pride in advocating your nomination to the Presidency, through the medium of the N.H. Gazette, to which it has been my lot to be an unpretending contributor of editorials. But, Sir, as I have intimated, I had no reason to suppose, among the multiplicity of newspapers that must necessarily come under your daily observation, that my name in the N.H. Gazette, had ever been noticed, until recently, through letters from one of my sons, who it appears, being on a visit to Washington, had a letter of introduction to you, I learned that you had been pleased to express a favorable opinion of the course pursued by me in the Gazette. I have also, more recently learned from him, that you have very kindly taken an interest in his behalf, and repeatedly used your friendly endeavours to procure him some employment; and that it is entirely owing to your particular favor, that he has obtained the situation he now holds in the New York Custom House. For this Sir, and more particularly for the very kind manner in which your efforts to promote his interest have been proffered, you will please to accept my grateful acknowledgments. These favors, stranger as I am to you, I could not have presumed to ask at your hands, ["&" *interlined*] I sincerely hope they may have been conferred without any embarrassing impositions on his part. I am not unaware that the arduous labors of your official station, in the present peculiar state of our foreign relations, must require your unremitting application, and I would be unwilling to add to its perplexities by any unwelcome importunities from myself or any member of my family.

My position as to the Gazette is probably different from that of any other editor. I have never held any pecuniary interest in that or any other paper. I have been a pretty constant ["gratuitous" *interlined*] contributor to the Gazette since the spring of 1827, with the exception of two or three years; and up to 1833, not even one of my family had any interest in it.

Although appearing as the senior editor, I take no part in the active duties of the office, and living some two miles from town, am often unable to read a proof. My son though yet quite young, contributes a considerable portion of the editorial matter, and I hope ere long ["he" *interlined*] will be able to assume the entire management, and leave me to pursue my agricultural labors, which in the present state of my pecuniary circumstances require my undivided attention. He has had much to contend with however from an inveterate portion ["of professed democrats" *interlined*] who got up a new paper, ["which" *canceled and* "and" *interlined*] under the flag of [Martin] Van Buren have avowed their intention to run down the Gazette, and are now counting on the favor of the coming administration to sustain *it* by the government patronage, and its aiders and supporters by the government offices. But ["of" *changed to* "on"] this I will forbear to dwell.

The Presidential election, although not contested under the nominee I could have wished to support, has nevertheless terminated in a ["result" *canceled*] result as I anticipate highly auspicious to correct republican principles. Nothing, to be sure, is publicly known as to what is to be the particular *caste* of Mr. [James K.] Polk[']s cabinet, though it is a subject of much busy speculation among politicians. Whether the preponderance will be north or South of Mason & Dixon[']s line, seems the absorbing topic. Your friends here, who are free trade men, in favor of annexation and opposed to the agitation of the slavery question are very desirous, from attachment to principle, that you may continue to occupy the first place in the cabinet; in which case the country will derive more important benefits from your services, than would perhaps be possible in any other station, short of the executive chair. In such an event, we think Mr. Polk[']s administration would do much towards getting the ship of state once more on the Republican tack. Your friends every where I think anticipate this, and are led to hope for it by inferences drawn from Mr.

Polk[']s declared principles, without pretending to a knowledge of his particular designs, as to men. Whatever in this respect he *will* do, it is undoubtedly desirable should be a sealed book to the public, until his inauguration: and I am gratified to learn that Mr. Polk seems disposed to keep his own counsel. You will not however deem it obtrusive in me to say, that in the event of an invitation on the part of Mr. Polk for you to remain in the State D[e]p[artmen]t your friends here entertain an ardent hope that no considerations of a personal or private nature will induce you to decline it.

I beg your pardon Sir, for the freedom with which I have written, as well as for the unpardonable length of my letter; and ["and that you will" *interlined*] be pleased ["to accept" *interlined*] the warm assurances of my respect & high consideration. Abner Greenleaf.

ALS in ScCleA.

From Sam[uel] S. Sibley, "Floridian office," Tallahassee, 12/25. Sibley informs Calhoun that R[ichard] K. Call has been tried and convicted of one of the charges preferred against him by Sibley's brother, Charles S. Sibley, U.S. District Attorney for the Middle District of Fla. Sibley lists 14 documents that he encloses relating to the prosecution of Call and Call's attacks upon the District Attorney, all of which reveal the groundlessness of Call's charges. He encloses among these documents several affidavits attesting to the accuracy of Charles S. Sibley's claims against Call and recommending Sibley's reappointment as District Attorney. "My brother has written to Mr. [David] Levy [Yulee] to ask of you and the President that he should be renominated as his commission expires 9 Jan[uar]y 1845. I cannot believe that the President or yourself can entertain any difficulty in regard to his nomination for reappointment. His friends ask it as an act of Justice." [Sibley was renominated to be U.S. District Attorney on 1/7/1845 and his appointment confirmed by the Senate on 1/15.] ALS with Ens in DNA, RG 59 (State Department), Applications and Recommendations, 1837–1845, Sibley (M-687:30, frames 303–345).

From KER BOYCE

Charleston, December 26, 1844

Dear Sir, You will see all that was done at our Legislature, which I hope will meet your views. You will see what is called Bluffton Boys came of[f] badly in resolusions and elections. Thear is all sorts of reports hear as to your pussion [*sic*; position], that you have been badly used by [James K.] Polk[']s friends and that, Polk will not offer you Secr[e]t[ar]y [of] State and [that] you are coming home a Simon Pure Bluffton Boy and will be for action. I feel yet assured that South Carolina must not act by her self again in no event unless, States send agents hear, then that we treat them according to circumstance, even if necessary they should be hu[n]g[?] up, for I feel tymid [*sic*] of resolutions or any act which we can pass. Our only course is now to act when ever, the event comes up. I feel no doubt but Mr. Polk will offer you the place you now occupy. We will invite [him] to come this way on his way to Washington and that the Hospital[i]tyes of the City will be offered to him, and that we will give him a good reception should he visit Charleston.

I should like to know if any reduction will take place on glass and Croc[k]ery this winter or if not this winter when (if at all) such deduction will take place. I shall be glad to hear from you, on all that I have wrote either confidential or not.

["Y(ou)rs most sincerely" *canceled*.] Stewart [*sic*; John A. Stuart] of the Mercury has been reather abusive ["by" *canceled*] towards you during the Legislature, but he could do no hurt as he was drunk the whole of the session, and I think somewhat deranged. Since he has come home he has kept it up and on Knight [*sic*] before last got his head broke at the corners[?] and yesterday he got another very seveare beaten. What will become of him I do not know. He ceartainly is a lost man. Y[ou]rs most Sincerely, Ker Boyce.

P.S. I have not heard one word from your son [Andrew Pickens Calhoun] about my debt. He paid nothing last year, and I do not know what he intends to do this year. If I do not have such a payment as I desire I will have to collect it, which would give me great pain. K.B.

ALS in ScCleA.

From A[ndrew] J. Donelson, *"Private"*

New Orleans, Dec[em]b[e]r 26, 1844

My D[ea]r Sir, I have learned since my arrival here, that a package, with your frank upon it, has passed me in a new steamer, the McKim, that is making an experimental trip to Galvezton, and of whose sailing I of course knew nothing when I left Galvezton. I had taken care to wait for the regular steamer, and of course felt no apprehension of there being a despatch behind me, when I left.

Now, however, I do not feel at liberty to wait here for a despatch, but shall proceed on in the packet of the 28: to Galvezton, where I shall overtake the communication alluded to, and go on immediately to the seat of Government.

If you have any thing of much importance, growing out of the question of annexation, it had better be sent to the collector with a request to him to send a special messenger with it to me—particularly if an answer is desireable before the adjournment of Congress. Taking the fate of a letter in the mail from here to the seat of Government of Texas, a despatch from you might be two or three weeks on the way.

I discover from the papers that Mr. [Thomas H.] Benton intends to urge his plan of annexation. Anxious if possible to bring him to a point on which he may exert less force against the measure I have written to him a private letter telling him that his course is injuring his friends and his country, and that I hoped he would be willing to modify his position, so far as to leave out of view for the present, the question of slavery, & the number of States, and ["take" *interlined*] the boundary as described in my private letter to you by Mr. [George] Martin. If taken as a Territory with a general clause like that in the Treaty of 1803, incorporating Louisiana, and securing to the citizens equal immunities & rights with other citizens of the Union; and with the provisions suggested as coming from President [Samuel] Houston; I would insist on nothing more.

Let us get annexation on any terms we can, taking care not to have any thing in form or substance that would render doubtful its ratification by Texas. The battle about slavery, boundary east of the Nuesos [*sic*], and the number of States, will come up on the Constitution to be hereafter formed by the people of Texas, when there will no ["be" *interlined*; *sic*] danger of loss of the Territory from British intrigue, or other causes.

If you are not able to carry annexation by the vote of the present Congress I shall despair of the cause, not seeing a certainty of much increase of strength in the next Congress unless it can be secured by a judicious arrangement of the Cabinet. This should be a paramount object with Mr. [James K.] Polk who must of course feel himself instructed to omit nothing than [*sic*] can advance the cause of immediate annexation.

Referring to the recent elections in the United States I have said to Texas that the measure was destined to a speedy consummation, and she has said in reply that she would throw no impediment in the way. This gives us the benefit of a trial in Polk[']s administration, and is so understood by Texas, but I have endeavored to give the phraseology such a turn as to convey the idea also that I relied on the present Congress. It seemed to me that I ought to risk something to secure the measure to Mr. [John] Tyler[']s administration.

I have heard nothing from Mr. Polk and have had but one letter from Gen[era]l [Andrew] Jackson, who insists upon some action by the Congress of Texas at its present session. Before its close I hope to hear from you. On existing circumstances I should fear to ask Texas for a formal renewal of her wish to come into the Union, unless our Government were prepared to take some more energetic measure to give effect to that wish than any yet attempted. The extension of the laws over the Territory without the advice of Congress, or trusting to events to secure their sanction afterwards would be hazardous.

As I feel obliged to return without attending to my private business, in consequence of the information that a despatch from you to me has gone on to Galvezton: and have requested my family to meet me here as soon as they can, I hope you will, as soon as you think the public business will allow of my absence from Texas a few weeks, give me permission to this effect.

The Congress of Texas will adjourn about the 1st of February— then I would judge there would be nothing urgent, unless you wish me to obtain some more, or new manifestation of the feeling of the Government here on the question of annexation.

I had a great desire to see Gen[era]l Jackson this winter, and talk over the old Seminole matter and remove if possible the misconception which led to the interruption of the friendly relations once existing between yourself and him. His last letter was written with his usual firmness, and leads me to hope and trust that he may yet live a few years more. I therefore feel the less doubt of my being able to see him again, and renewing a conversation with him on this subject, the purport of which I have never communicated to you, because I thought further reflection on his part would induce him to place it on a footing equally satisfactory to yourself & him. This I wish to see and have so written to Gov[erno]r [John] Branch [of Fla. Territory], whose letter to me will be answered more fully in a few weeks. I am very truly & sincerely, A.J. Donelson.

ALS in ScCleA; variant PC in Jameson, ed., *Correspondence*, pp. 1011–1013.

From GEORGE R. GLIDDON, *"Private"*

Franklin Hotel, Philadelphia
26th Dec[embe]r 1844

Honored and dear Sir, I take the first opportunity, that my nomadic life permits, to crave your pardon, if I have been silent during the last three months; but the truth is, that I had really nothing to communicate worthy of your condescending attention; while the annexed *programmes* will explain my laborious individual avocations. I have been compelled to defer the publication of my biblico-ethnographical ["views," *interlined*] owing to the absence of *books*, until I return to Europe. "Au reste," I have satisfied *myself* that Moses (or rather the *unknown* author of Genesis,) in the three divisions of "Shem, Ham and Japheth," solely refers to the *three* grand divisions of the Caucasian family. *Negro[e]s*, Mongols, Malays, and American Indians are *entirely* omitted in the Pentateuch!

In the interim, I have read, with extreme satisfaction, the broad principles upon which, (in your powerful instructions to Mr. [William R.] *King*) the "clap-trap" of the English Anti-slavery party has been demonstrated; and as it was my fate to acquire some personal experience of the *political* humbug of the pseudo-philanthropists of *London* in 1841, I am delighted, that you have thrown a hand-grenade into their canting camp.

Your condescending kindness emboldens me to venture a suggestion, which is prompted by desire to see you victorious, and is based upon some knowledge of the *East*.

It is probable, that counter-arguments, (from the pens of [Henry, Lord] Brougham, [Sir John] Bowring, [Richard R.] Madden, "et hoc genus omne,") will appear, to cover the chicanery of those, whose interested motives you have so fearlessly denounced. Permit me to say, that the history of events along the *Mediterranean, Archipelago*, and *Black Sea*, can supply the facts the most deadly to prove, that *policy* and not philanthropy (as the *public* use the term,) induces the British Government to foster the cry of *Slavery*; and that ["the" *interlined*] indifference, with which all English Anti-slavery advocates regard *Oriental* traffic in slaves, presents a boundless field for Southern denunciations. In fact, they are entirely at your mercy, and dare not meet the light in relation to *European* carrying and traffic in *Slaves* throughout Muslim Countries; nor will all the powers of Europe alter the the [*sic*] deep-rooted doctrines of Oriental Nations.

To me it is all cant and mockery, when I see the naval forces of

England attending only to the *Atlantic* coasts of Africa in the suppression of a trade, established by Anglo-Saxons, while vessels of every Nation carry *Slaves* from Morocco to the Euxine, so long as an Ottoman subject ["is" *interlined*] their (often-simulated) proprietor—while the Baza[a]rs of Africa and Asia throng with countless Slaves of *all* Nations—and while not an effort is made to save the beautiful Circassian & Georgian *white* boys and girls from abuses, to which Southern slavery is actually a charity! The multitude of these *facts* is enormous; and I venture to drop the hint, in case any information may be opportune, to support well-founded exposures of claptrap.

So far as my poor materials may be available, you have only to command me; and I can, at any rate, indicate the *sources* for information in respect to Arab & Turkish communities. The U.S. Legations at Constantinople, the Consuls in the Levant, might be ordered to supply *statistics*, as to the Mediterranean slave-trade, by ship and caravan; before which that on the *Atlantic* sinks into insignificance. And let me add, that Mr. [William B.] *Hodgson* of Savannah is eminently qualified to supply a mass of *facts* on Oriental Slavery.

Will you pardon the intrusion of these hasty ideas? They are not dictated by presumption, but simply from my earnest desire to evince, in some Slight degree, the sincerity with which I have the honor to subscribe myself, most respectfully, Dear Sir, Y[ou]r mo[st] ob[e]d[ien]t & faithful Serv[an]t, George R. Gliddon.

P.S. I propose visiting Washington after the 15th Feb[ruar]y when I shall be proud to wait upon you with oral explanations.

ALS with Ens in ScCleA. NOTE: Enclosed were three printed announcements of lectures given at Boston and Philadelphia by Gliddon on Egyptian hieroglyphics and ancient history. Also found among Calhoun's papers, and perhaps enclosed with this letter, is a 3-pp. printed circular from Gliddon, dated 9/30/1844, containing letters from groups of Philadelphia and Boston citizens complimenting his lectures.

To C[harles] J. Ingersoll, Ch[airma]n, [House Committee on Foreign Affairs], 12/26. In reply to Ingersoll's note of 12/24, Calhoun states that [Henry] Ledyard acted in the capacity of U.S. Chargé d'Affaires at Paris from 11/12/1842, when [Lewis] Cass, U.S. Minister, left his post, until 7/1/1844, on which date [William R.] King presented his credentials as U.S. Minister. LS in DNA, RG 233 (U.S. House of Representatives), 28A-D12.2; FC in DNA, RG 59 (State Department), Domestic Letters, 35:56–57 (M-40:33); FC in DNA,

RG 59 (State Department), Reports of the Secretary of State to the President and Congress, 1790–1906, 6:129–130; PC in House Report No. 26, 28th Cong., 2nd Sess., p. 2.

From C[harles] J. Ingersoll, 12/26. [Alexander H.] Everett, former U.S. Minister to Spain, has presented a memorial to Congress requesting reimbursement of expenses he incurred at Madrid for "Office-Rent and Expences" and for "Profit in Exchange on London." Ingersoll seeks to learn if [Cornelius P.] Van Ness and [John H.] Eaton, Everett's successors to the post, had received allowances for expenses under those headings. LS in DNA, RG 59 (State Department), Miscellaneous Letters from Congressional Committees, 1801–1877.

From R[ic]h[ard] M. Johnson, [former Vice-President], *"unofficial"*

White Sulphur, Ky., Dec[em]b[e]r 26th 1844
Hon. John C. Calhoun, my old friend, I want you to appoint Doct[o]r Jessee [*sic*; Jesse] W. Griffiths as Consul to Matanzas [Cuba], in case of vacancy, or to some other place if that is not to be vacated while you remain in office. Doct[o]r Griffiths of Phi[ladelphi]a is a man of honor, of honesty, of great intelligence, temperat[e] talented & industrious. He is worth his weight in gold. It is not every day that you can get an opportunity to put such a man in office. I pledge myself to this. I write as if I was sure you would appoint him, as you are the only man with whom I have been acquainted who never refused any thing I asked when you had the power. Don[']t leave the ship at such a crisis, as surely it must depend on yourself whether you remain or not. Your friend[,] Rh. M. Johnson.

ALS in DNA, RG 59 (State Department), Applications and Recommendations, 1845–1853, Griffiths (M-873:35, frames 284–285).

From George M. Keim

Philad[elphi]a, Dec[embe]r 26, 1844
Dear Sir, With the salutations of the season, I beg leave to transmit, two of our papers, and ask your leisure moment to a perusal of them.

The Ledger although a paper "by authority", has been for some weeks disposed to be troublesome. Humble as my efforts are I have broken ground and will not rest until I have stormed its battery and spiked the cannon. Should it progress, I may want some information and would respectfully ask from you to whom at Washington I may apply. With the sincere feeling of regard I am Sir very respectfully Y[ou]r ob[e]d[ien]t Ser[van]t, George M. Keim.

ALS in ScCleA. NOTE: Keim was U.S. Marshal at Philadelphia and a former Representative from Pa.

From JAMES SEVAN, "(Private)"

Dixon[,] Lee Co[unty] Illinois
December 26, 1844

Although I am personally unknown to you, yet my advocacy of your political doctrines ever since my intel[l]igence matured judgment; standing as I do a firm friend to Mr. President [John] Tyler, who has fearlessly and triumphantly sustained the Democracy of our Country, I am constrained by a sense of duty, to advise you of the movements made in this State, through the commands of Mr. [Thomas H.] Benton aided by the co operation of Gen. [Henry] Dodge, his son [Augustus C. Dodge] of Iowa and his son in Law Col. [John] Dement, with the late speaker of the House of Representatives, Maj. [Samuel] Hackleton, and others of the Bentonian school of politics; Two Political Bentonian Missionaries Dement & Hackleton have for the last 3 months, visited every section of the State of Illinois, exhibiting various Letter[s] Confidential to the County party leaders, in which are exhibited evidence to satisfy; that the influence of Mr. [Martin] Van Buren[']s friends, are to be conjointly used with Mr. Benton to perpetuate their power, by the organization of a party, through the influence of Mr. [James K.] Polk[']s] appointees throughout the West to sunder the relations and influence of Gen. [Lewis] Cass of the north & Mr. Calhoun of the South, and they even exhibit the names of men in several States who are to perpetuate this dynasty. Surreptitious advances are made to those who have remained faithful to the President, and proscription, and denunciation to all who demur to the supremacy of Mr. Benton. The aforesaid organization in this State, is made up of disappointed party hacks, who have been hanging to the skirts of Mr. Van Buren[']s garments, anticipating the elevation, and consequent power of Mr. Van Buren to redeem the promises of

Mr. Benton. How far this influence may extend east and south, I am not fully informed, but from the confident assurances of those, who take the responsibility, as by authority, they denounce 1st all friends of the President, 2d all of those who prefer either Mr. Calhoun or Gen. Cass, to have a place in the administration of Mr. Polk—and all whose opinions, are adverse to Mr. Van B[uren's] & Benton[']s on the Texas question.

I assure you the Record of Proscription is already made out for the State of Illinois, for every Officer of the Gen[eral] Government, not a Tyler man whose relations to the Democratic party, have never been censured, but who have remained faithful to the land marks of democracy; who have expressed other preferences than for Mr. Benton['s] succession, who have refused action, to perpetuate the Van Buren dynasty but have been been [*sic*] threatened with the exercise of an irresistable combination of Mr. Van Buren['s] & Benton['s] power of political annihilation, formidable in its incipient steps, to the weak, yet honest friends to whom no counter action is visible.

You may recollect that about two years or more ago, I took the liberty of requesting from you your speeches on the Tariff, and other then[?] most important questions being agitated preparatory to the Presidential Election. Allow me to say that my confidence in your action upon the great question now agitating the Nation remains unimpa[i]red, and that you may be so far advised of the organization of influences, although minor in their character yet it followed out, through, all their ramifications, for such vile purposes, it becomes the duty of every friend to his country to resist them, and the better to effect that object in my opinion is, that a knowledge of the means should extend to the inter[e]s[t]ed[?] party and Mr. Polk has it in his power to reward the faithful and paralize the efforts for self aggrandizement on the ruins of our country. All true friends of the Democratic party are with the President in his endeavours to perpetuate the true principals which he has so faithfully advocated and by you been so ably sustained, and God grant their consummation. Faithfully and truly your friend, James Sevan, Receiver [of Public Moneys], Dixon Ill.

P.S. Should these hints interest your attention, I will give you names, and present the facts of the movement in the West in a more tangible form. J.S.

ALS in ScCleA.

To HENRY WHEATON, [Paris], "Private"

Washington, 26th Dec[embe]r 1844
My dear Sir, So great is the pressure of business on the Department, at this season of the year, that I have but little more leisure, than is bearly [*sic*] sufficient to acknowledge the receipt of your letter of the 15th Nov[embe]r, received by the last Steamer.

You needed no apology or explanation for your prolonged stay at Paris. I have no doubt, that your time was efficiently & well employed at that great centre of diplomatick relations of the civilized world. To give correct impressions there is all important, in the present state of our relations with England in reference to Texas, Mexico & this Continent generally. They are, indeed, much needed there. The policy of France is, at present, far from being deep or wise, in reference to the affairs of this Continent. It ought to be on all points antagonist to that of Great Britian [*sic*].

Should I remain where I am, you may be assured, I shall not be indifferent, as to what relates to yourself. I have not yet determined whether I shall or not, should Mr. [James K.] Polk desire it, nor shall I, untill I shall be assured, what will be the course of his administration. I was forced into my present position by the publick voice & have felt no responsibility, as to the course of the administration, beyond the questions, in reference to which I was especially called into the publick service. Such will not be my situation, should I be a member of the next administration.

The Zollverein treaty is again before the Senate. I sincerely hope it may receive the sanction of the body. As yet, there has been no manifestation of its opinion.

The fate of the great question of annexation is still uncertain. I think it will probably be consummated before the close of the session. It certainly will, if the democratick party can be brought to unite. Of that there is hazard. The portion, which was dis-appointed at Baltimore in the nomination, are still discontented, and I fear will give all the trouble they can, without losing their party connection. Yours truly, J.C. Calhoun.

ALS in NNPM, Wheaton Papers.

From C[ornelius] C. Baldwin,
"(*Confidential*)"

Balcony Falls, Rockbridge co[unty], Va.
December 27, 1844

Dear Sir: I beg leave to bring myself to your recollection by saying, that I had the honor of some correspondence with Mr. [Robert M.T.] Hunter & yourself some two or three years ago, & that I owe you my acknowledgements for copies of several of your speeches in the Senate, which I read with high gratification & great instruction. I took the liberty, about eighteen months ago, to send you, (to your residence in S.C.) a copy of a rough stump speech of mine, which I hope you received.

As your time is precious, I will come at once to the object of this note.

Upon the settlement of my father-in-law's estate, the sum of five hundred dollars has been charged upon my little farm, as my portion of his liabilities binding his real estate; &, as his creditors are pressing, there is some danger that my farm, from which, chiefly by my personal exertions, I derive a comfortable yet frugal support for my little family, will be forced into market, at a ruinous sacrifice. To ar[r]est so great a calamity to myself & family, I consider myself solemnly bound to make any personal sacrifice; & I therefore beg leave to inquire of you, most respectfully, whether you have at your disposal any employment under the government, for which I am qualified— I care not how laborious it is, or what it is—whether a clerkship, a messengership, ["a consulate," *interlined*] or what not—from which I could realize the above mentioned sum, in a twelvemonth! I neither expect nor desire you to make a vacancy for me by removing probably a better man. I have always been opposed to proscription for opinion's sake, & I *hope* the in-coming administration will be characterized by the most liberal & enlightened toleration. I wish merely to tender you my poor services, should the government need such as I can render.

I want office only for the specific purpose I have named—to clear my property of a pressing ["incumbrace" *altered to* "incumbrance"]. That object accomplished, I shall return with joy to my plough & fireside; for I would not exchange the freedom & independence of rural life—its tranquil happiness, its exemption from the labors, & responsibilities, & anxieties, & detraction of public station, for the honors & emoluments of the most exalted office upon earth. At least, I *think* I would not, but the human heart is very deceitful. If the temptation were presented, it is possible that, like the great mob of mankind, I would be weak enough to prefer splendid misery to humble happiness—But how I run on!

I make this application at this time, because it is all-important that I should know what to depend upon for the ensuing year, that I may make my arrangements accordingly. Candour, however, compels me to add that I shall not be at all disappointed at the unfavorable result of ["the" *altered to* "this"] application. I have not for a moment indulged the hope that there was any thing more than a *"remotissima potentia,"* as the law terms it, that it could be successful.

Excuse this badly-written scrawl. I write in great haste & with a wretched pen. May I hear from you at your earliest convenience? With great respect Your ob[edien]t S[er]v[a]nt, C.C. Baldwin.

ALS in ScCleA.

From Geo[rge] M. Bibb, Treasury Department, 12/27. Bibb has considered the request of [Richard Pakenham], referred through the State Department, for reparations to certain British woollen merchants for actions taken against them by officers of the N.Y. Customs House. These claims have been heard before several U.S. courts and decided against the British merchants in every case thus far. Bibb sees no reason to disagree with the court proceedings, nor can he agree to postpone the case of John Taylor, Jr., and others now pending before the Supreme Court. ALS with Ens in DNA, RG 59 (State Department), Miscellaneous Letters (M-179:106, frames 374–468 and 368–370); FC in DNA, RG 56 (Secretary of the Treasury), Letters to Cabinet and Bureau Officers, Series B, 1842–1847, 4:498–506.

To T[homas] G. Clemson, [Brussels]

Washington, 27th Dec[embe]r 1844
My dear Sir, We have been greatly distressed by the accounts, which your's [*sic*] & Anna's [Anna Maria Calhoun Clemson's] letters give of the suffering of [John] Calhoun [Clemson] from the disease with which he has been afflicted, but are much relieved ["to learn" *interlined*] that it has taken a favourable turn. We shall, however, feel much anxiety, untill we hear, that he is out of all danger, which we hope ["we" *interlined*] shall by the next Steamer. Yours & Anna's anxiety & suffering must have been intense.

I am under a severe pressure of business, and, as I have little to communicate since my last, I shall have to be brief.

Nothing has yet been done in Congress beyond the introduction of various bills & resolutions, and among others, several relating to Texas. The fate of annexation is doubtful. The whigs, from appear[an]ces, ["appear" *canceled and* "seemed" *interlined*] resolved to preserve their organization; and, I fear, will unite with little exception, ag[ai]nst the measure, while the [Martin] V[an] B[uren and Thomas H.] Benton wing of the party have evinced a strong disposition to act with them. I hope, however, publick opinion will force them to give up their opposition. Its effects are already apparent. The [Washington] Globe has changed its tone, & the attacks from that quarter on me have abated. Benton will, it is said, be certain to be instructed [by the Missouri legislature] to vote for the measure. With these indications, the the [*sic*] prospect is pretty fair, that it will pass the House of Representatives; and if it should, I hardly think, the Senate will assume the responsibility of defeating it.

Nothing ["is" *canceled*] yet is known as to the intention of Mr. [James K.] Polk in reference to the formation of his Cabinet. He keeps a prudent silence.

Cotton still continues to fall. Its average price may be said to be about 4½ c[e]nts per pound. The effects will be ruinous in the South, and will rouse the feeling of the whole section. The pressure of the Tariff begins to be *felt*, and understood, which will lead to its overthrow, either through Congress or the seperate action of the South. The feeling of resistance will be greatly increased in consequence of the course of the Northern democrats in reference to the 25th rule.

Say to Anna, that I would write to her by the present conveyance, as hard pressed as I am for time; were it not that several letters will go to her from the family by it, which will give her all the news.

I have not had time to take into consideration the subject of a treaty with Belgium, but hope I will by the time the next Steamer shall arrive.

We are all well & all join their love to you & Anna. Kiss the dear children [Calhoun and Floride Elizabeth Clemson] for their Grandfather. Your affectionate father, J.C. Calhoun.

ALS in ScCleA; PC in Jameson, ed., *Correspondence*, pp. 634–636.

From Ch[arles] Aug[ustu]s Davis

New York [City,] 27 Dec[embe]r 1844

My D[ea]r Sir, I am very much obliged to you for your kind notice of my Letter to you on the subject of Pensacola. I notice that Florida is now making application to become a State. If her good people and those of Alabama will only be induced to push for a developement of the resources they possess—West Florida alone w[oul]d soon become capable of forming a State—and the impulse given w[oul]d very soon enable middle & East Florida to form another State—whilst as I stated to you Alabama would also more than double her present representation.

I am fully pursuaded that if our Southern brethren would but advocate the system of roads and canals they would keep pace with any other quarter of the Union. Nor is there a spot in our whole Union which involves deeper interest than Pensacola. And it is a remarkable fact that I never yet met a man of any intel[l]igence who does not heart & soul advocate every measure calculated to render Pensacola a great Southern *Toulon*—which it really should be with refference to that great and important "Mediterranean" *into* which—and *through* which so vast a share of our entire Commerce passes.

So certain am I of the *productive power* of that single link of the great chain of road which would bring Pensacola in line—that *it alone*—could not only pay a fair income on its cost but pay also the interest on the entire debt of Florida. This proposition is entirely demonstrable. Such a position—with such an *interior*—and such resources if at the north would as soon as the work could be accomplish'd be provided with at least three artificial channels of intercourse. For example—we have two rail roads and one canal between this city & Phil[adelphi]a—we have one steam boat rout[e] & *five* Rail road rout[e]s hence to Boston—that is I can go by *five artificial* rout[e]s from New York to Boston.

Florida itself is too poor to do any thing. The enterprize I allude to (and which I am happy to see has your sanction and entire approbation—if it receives by that sanction the approbation of Congress—as I know it will that of the Country if you give it open advocacy) will immediately spring into being and go to completion. We shall then have our "Mississippi Valley" on this side the mountains and they will have theirs. But if we neglect this—our Southern *Atlantic States* will drop out of line. The "Great West" as it is call'd is pushing for *Capital*—the South is *quiescent*. My theory is that the "march of Empire" is but the "march of Capital." The *latter* goes first & the *owners* follow it. The true policy of our wise and patriotic Statesmen should be so to direct "the march of Capital" as to keep up a balance of power. I love my country so sincerely. I am totally divested of all & every sectional feeling. I was born in the north but losing health I was sent South to regain it. This makes me *emphatically* "a Northern man with Southern feelings"—and I feel that I have a right to claim not only my "birth right" but my "health right."

Give the South—Rail roads—and you will hear no more of "abolitionism." The "march of Capital" will soon put that *vile theory* at rest—and *climate* will (which is a monopoly of itself) settle the matter. *Ice & cotton* will take their relative place and hold their relative *influence*—& the North & South equally developed will take their position just about in a ratio that Ice holds to Cotton—the one *dispensable* the other *indispensable.* Y[ou]r ob[edien]t Ser[vant] & friend, Ch: Augs. Davis.

ALS in ScCleA.

From Tho[ma]s D. Hailes, Grand Cane, La., 12/27. Hailes renews his application for the post of U.S. Consul at Matamoros, now vacant by the death of Richard H. Belt. Hailes had applied for the post prior to Belt's appointment and had recommendations from John Slidell and P[ierre] E. Bossier, Representatives from La., and Isaac E. Holmes of S.C. According to Hailes, [Abel P.] Upshur had informed him that his application would be favorably considered when a Consular vacancy occurred. Two ALS's in DNA, RG 59 (State Department), Applications and Recommendations, 1837–1845, Hailes (M-687:14, frames 96–97).

From J[AMES] HAMILTON, [JR.], *"Private"*

Oswichee Bend, [Ala.,] Dec. 27[t]h 1844
My Dear Sir, As I leave for Texas tomorrow I have deemed it expedient to enclose you a Copy of my Letter [of 11/27] to Mr. [James K.] Polk. I hope you will think that I occupy in relation to yourself no ground inconsistent with the most delicate sense of propriety.

I prehaps [*sic*] could have said less about the reciprocity Treaty with Great Britain & my past diplomatic relations with her Govt. if at that time I had not deemed it very improbable even if Mr. Polk were to offer me the mission to St. James, ["but" *canceled and* "that

I should be able under any state of things to accept it" *interlined*] but since my arrival here & from some arrangements I was able to make in reference to my affairs on Savannah River ["I think" *interlined*] if he should tender me such an honor & you remain in the Dept. of State I shall not hesitate to ["accept it" *canceled and* "say yes" *interlined*] & stand the chance of my nomination passing the Senate. But this I ["say to you" *canceled;* "ent"(?) *interlined and then canceled;* "remark" *interlined*] in confidence as I will under no circumstance be a Candidate for the office. If he therefore responds favorably to any intimation you may make him & you hold the Port Folio ["of State" *interlined*] it will be well[,] if not I am content as the office would lose it[s] value by soliciting its bestowment.

If I am appointed I believe I can effect a reciprocity Treaty and speak without fear or shame as it becomes a Southern Man ["to speak" *interlined*] on our deeplyly [*sic*] interesting Domestic Institution. And that in spirit & tone I will be a fit organ for your sentiments on this Question and all others affecting the honor & best interests of the Country. In one word I think I can do something for the interests of the Govt. & something personally for you with John Bull. But I am content to work *there* or *here* as fate and my Stars may determine. But this matter I desire held in the most entire confidence between us & nothing said for the present on the subject. If I hear from Polk at New Orleans I will write you. On my reaching the Seat of Govt. of Texas which I expect to do by the 10[t]h Jan[uar]y you may expect a detailed view of the state of affairs in that Country. If Annexation takes place it must come thence, for I see clearly that the coalition between the [Martin] Van Buren Democrats & Whigs is quite strong enough to defeat the measure this session, & all from a base jealousy towards yourself. With this view I regret President [John] Tyler moved in the matter & did not leave the initiative to be commenced by Texas, where it must both begin & end.

I shall endeavour if Doneldson [*sic*; Andrew J. Donelson] fails with ["the" *interlined*] Congress of Texas to procure a meeting of ["the" *canceled and* "a" *interlined*] Convention of the people of Texas calling on the U. States to fulfil the obligations of the Treaty of Paris, or that they will appeal to France to ["coerce" *canceled and* "interpose for the performance of" *interlined*] its stipulations. If the South was not overrun with such a horde of base Traitors to her interests at the head of which stands that arch scoundrel [Thomas H.] Benton, we could carry by a *coup de main* this great Question. But we have the canker ["in our vitals" *interlined*] eating into our own vitals. Should you have occasion to write me direct to the care of Dick &

Hill New Orleans who will immediately forward ["my" *canceled*] your Letters to Texas. I wish my Dear Sir I was near you, to strike a blow on either floor of Congress in your vindication or support. I think I could make some of the currs [*sic*] wince & [*one word changed to* "whine"] not excepting that half spaniel & half wolf Dog the Missouri Felon. Ever with sincere esteem faithfully & respec[tfull]y Yours, J. Hamilton.

[Enclosure]

[James Hamilton, Jr., to James K. Polk,] "Private"

Rice Hope, Savannah River, Nov. 27[t]h 1844

My Dear Sir, I received in the midst of our struggle in this part of Georgia your kind favor which I should have answered before but for my unceasing occupations both agricultural and political. I now desire to tender you my sincere congratulations for being the subject of one of the most glorious triumphs that graces the History of our country. God grant that you may improve it in every particular calculated to promote your own repute and the welfare and renown of our Country.

You are aware of the relations, which I have borne to So. Carolina, on that Question, on which her people have been and are now to a certain extent deeply agitated. Since the authentic declaration of the Baltimore convention combined with your nomination I have employed every effort to soothe the irritation of public feeling in So. Carolina on the ground that we had much to hope from your election and were bound in good faith to the party with which we were acting (the Democracy of the North and West) to forbear from every expression of violence which might endanger your success. I am happy to know that my co[u]nsels ["are" *canceled and* "were" *interlined*] not without effect with my old Confederates in the struggle of 1831 and 1832. I sent you a published Letter to my former constituents of Beaufort District entirely illustrative of my of my [*sic*] course on this subject. I have to add that this cou[r]se meets with the entire concurrence of Mr. Calhoun, and indeed was the result of our joint consultation in July last in Washington. I believe with the exception of a few cases of *ultra* ["*infatuation*" *canceled and* "inflam(m)ation" *interlined*], which will exist in every party, the great body of the Old Nul[l]ifiers are quiet, under a sincere disposition to support your Standard and an equally sincere confidence that you will do all in your power to procure such a modification of the Tariff as ought to satisfy every reasonable man.

I now approach a subject of extreme delicacy. It is in relation to the individual who in your cabinet shall represent the interests of the

South. I believe taking into account the whole democracy from the Potomac to Louisiana they would in reference to numbers as well as character and intelligence prefer that Mr. Calhoun should occupy this position to any other individual. Whether he will consent to remain in his present post is a question, I can not answer. But I should think in the midst of the Negociations of the Oregon and an[n]exation Questions, as a matter of just and honourable ambition he would desire to bring these important affairs to a ["success" *canceled*] successful issue. To say nothing of the possibility at an early period of your administration, of his being instrumental under your direction by the fit employment of a suitable Plenipotentiary at the Court of St. James of forming a reciprocity Treaty with England on a new commercial basis, which by ["pecuniary" *canceled*; "reciprocal" *interlined and then canceled*; "procuring a" *interlined*] modification of her Corn laws in our favor would in effect opperate reciprocally a reduction of the duties to a strictly Revenue Standard ["on" *interlined*] our import of her staple articles of Manufacture; viz., Iron[,] Wo[o]llens and Cotton. The result of such a Negociation would be this—If the manufacturers in the Senate or those representing their interests were sufficiently powerful in that body to defeat the Treaty, the Grain Growing States of New York, Ohio, Indianna, Illinois and Michigan would cordially unite with the South in doing by Legislation, what your administration could not do under the Treaty making power. And thus set this vexed question entirely at rest by the adoption of a Tariff equivalent to the concession under the Compromise act, which in point of fact would give the manufacturers a protection of 30 percent including, freights, insurance and other charges—As much as in reason they ought to ask. I was in Europe four years in the diplomatic service of Texas—Two years as Minister Plenipotentiary to Great Britain. My ["entire" *canceled and* "inter" *interlined*] course was very intimate ["with" *canceled*] and friendly with the administration of Lord Melbourne and subsequently ["with" *interlined*] that of Sir Rob[er]t Peel. With Lord Palmerston a free trade man, and really ["more" *canceled*] the ["present" *interlined*] leader of the opposition party in the house of Commons and afterwards with Lord Aberdeen, I was as intimate as a plain Republican can be with two of the first Peers of the realm. The subject of a reciprocity Treaty was often broached between us, and I think they entertained with much favor the proposition. Their only doubt seemed to be *first* the difficulty of getting a Treaty through our own senate, in which they seem to regard the power of the Manufacturing interests a altogether [*sic*] predominant. Whilst on my part, I invariably *predicated* the impossibility of getting the landed aristocracy of England to consent to a relaxation of the Corn Laws. To this their reply was that the power of the Crown was absolute under the Treaty making power and not qualified as with us. And that it would at last resolve itself into the Question w[h]ether England recieved an equivalent for the immense boon of allowing the people of the United States to feed a part of her overgrown population. The progress which the anticorn law League (some of the members of which I am now in correspondence) bears a just proportion to the progress ["of" *canceled*] which the principles of Free Trade have made as indicated by the large majority which has signalized your election—I believe the period most propitious for attempting such a treaty arranged and defined by your instructions conjointly with those of Mr. Calhoun given to a Minister at St. James's on the part of this Country who should be an *out* and *out free trade man.*

My own experience at that court has taught me what perseverance thro' the almost inscisible [*sic*] approaches of social intercourse may accomplish in bringing about the consummation of ["measures of" *interlined*] apparently great difficulty and complication. After two years siege of Lord Melbourne's administration I carried the recognition of the Independance of Texas against the whole power of the abolitionists of Great Britain ["perhaps" *canceled*] perhaps the most potent confederation in that Kingdom excepting the Repeal association in Ireland. I had moreover to encounter the active and hostile opposition of the Liberator [Daniel O'Connell] himself. I believe with Mr. Calhoun as Secretary of State ["in your hands" *canceled*] and both of you giving an impulse to the Negociations on the other side of ["w" *canceled*] the water, the most valuable results might be accomplished. Besides from the Department of State animating and invigorating your Minister at St. James's must come the tone ["of" *canceled*] both of wisdom and moral courage ["which is" *interlined*] to disabuse the public mind of Great Britain as well as that of its Government of their ignorance ["and" *canceled*] prejudice and fanaticism on the Slave Question. I fear with all his talent and moral worth Mr. [Edward] Everett's language has not been higher in its tone than merely *apologetic* on a subject which if to be met at all must be met with unaltering firmness. I think it must be admitted that there is not in the United States a man better calculated to give a direction to these great public Questions than Mr. Calhoun and I thank God that the destinies of the country have fallen into ["the h" *canceled*] your hands—hands that are not afraid to meet them whatever aspect they may bear. I desire My dear sir that you should not misapprehend me. I do not ask you to appoint Mr. Calhoun your secretary of State, because I know that he would repudiate my authority if he supposed I was engaged in such a Mission. If the position he occupies in one of the sections of this Union (the greatest in moral power beyond all question) if his stupendous talents, great experience in public affairs, spotless private character, and incorruptible integrity are not calculated to invite him into public service in any station worthy of his distinguished ability, I am quite sure nothing I can say will have this faculty. I write this letter without his knowledge[,] privity or connivance whatsoever simply for the purpose of informing you of what I know to be the feelings of the people of the South and because I likewise know that every influence that deep cunning and sleepless malice can devise will be employed to prejudice you against him and induce you to distrust his friends. As to So. Carolina she stands forth the banner state in this great Democratic victory. You will recieve her electoral vote next Monday by an entire unanimity in both branches of the Legislature a vote which will reflect the suf[f]rages of a majority of fifty thousands in your favor. Every member of her delegation in both branches of Congress will support your administration with a confidence ever in advance of its existence. *Whilst at home we have not one whig member in either branch of our Legislature.* What State in this whole union can say as much as this but herself. Yet every corrupt and envious villain from [Thomas H.] Benton down to the lowest caitiff ["that" *canceled*] will first attempt to *denounce* and then to *proscribe* us. You see Sir altho' I have become the Citizen of another State yet I can not refrain from speaking and feeling as a South Carolinian—A cherished illusion which I shall carry to my Grave die where and how I may.

These opinions come, Dear Sir, from a man who neither *asks* nor *expects* anything at your hands beyond the privilege which he feels assured your ability and public virtue ["will" *interlined*] permit him to indulge in supporting conscientiously and ["feelingly" *canceled and* "zealously" *interlined*] your administration however limited may be the sphere of his influence.

Indeed, ["My Dear Sir," *canceled and* "what" *interlined*] have you to do but to consult the best interests of the Country and your own renown? By a self denying ordinance highly to your honour you are no candidate for a second Term. The pestilent ["rule"(?) *canceled and* "root" *interlined*] of one half the evils of our country. By this determination you are placed in a situation which enables you to divorce yourself from all *cliques* and factions either existing or to be formed—to go for the glories of an administration around which you may call the highest Genius and ["public" *canceled*] public virtue of the ["Land" *canceled*] Country.

After participating this night in the enthusiastic celebration of that victory which gives you the first office in the civilized world I shall return to my cotton fields in Alabama where I hope to find that happiness and ["ultimately that" *interlined*] independance which public station can never give. I beg you ["sir" *canceled*] to be assured my dear sir of the esteem with which I am very respectfully your obedient servant [James Hamilton, Jr.]

P.S. Should you find either leisure or inclination to write me be so kind as to direct to New Orleans to the care of Dick & Hill. As private business will take me to Texas next week, where with my friends among the most respectable and influential in that country I will be most ["happy" *canceled*] happy to aid Major Donaldson [*sic*; Andrew J. Donelson] all in my power.

ALS with En in ScCleA; recipient's copy of En (dated 11/29) in DLC, James K. Polk Papers.

From CHA[RLE]S H. RAYMOND

Legation of Texas
Washington, December 27th 1844

Sir, I have had the honor to receive your note of the 23rd Instant, inviting my attention to certain subjects of inquiry, based on a Resolution adopted by the Senate of the United States on the 16th instant, calling on the President [John Tyler] for information in regard to the public debt and the public lands of Texas, a copy of which accompanied your note.

And in reply to the first inquiry as to whether ["the" *canceled*] her public debt has been increased since the signature of the Treaty of Annexation in April last, I have the honor to state that from information and data in my possession, procured from Official and other sources, I am fully persuaded that her revenues since that period have equalled, if not exceeded her expenditures, and that such has also been the case for the last four years. I have therefore no hesitancy in saying that her public debt has not been increased since the period refer[r]ed to, except from the interest which has accrued upon a portion of it.

In answer to the second inquiry as to whether there have been any additional grants of the public domain since April last, I can only state that, if there have been any, they have not come to my knowledge. I know of but one law authorizing the Government to make grants of land, and that has been in force about four years. It authorizes the Government to issue land scrip, in redemption of its liabilities at the rate of two dollars per acre. Only a few of the holders of these liabilities have heretofore availed themselves of its provisions. If however they have done so within the last few months, the effect, as you will readily perceive, has been to decrease the public debt double the amount of the number of acres of land scrip thus issued.

I have nothing further to add to the information heretofore communicated to you by the Texian plenipotentiaries, Messrs. [Isaac] Van Zandt and [J. Pinckney] Henderson, in their note of the 15th of April, last, on the other subjects embraced in the Resolution of the Senate, but will merely state, in explanation of the report of the Commissioner of the General Land Office of Texas, which was refer[r]ed to in their note, that in his general estimate of "Lands appropriated," all the legal or equitable land claims however and whenever originated, for which the faith of that Republic stood pledged, are intended to be included. I have the honor to be with distinguished consideration Your Obedient Servant, Chas. H. Raymond.

ALS in DNA, RG 59 (State Department), Notes from Foreign Legations, Texas, vol. 1 (T-809:1); FC in Tx, Records of the Texas Republic Department of State, Letters and Dispatches Sent by the Texas Legation in Washington, 2:87; FC in Tx, Records of the Texas Republic Department of State, Copybooks of Letters Received from Texan and Foreign Representatives, vol. 2-1/103, pp. 36–37; CC in Tx, Records of the Texas Republic Department of State, U.S. Diplomatic Correspondence; CC in DNA, RG 46 (U.S. Senate), 28A-E3; PC in Senate Document No. 29, 28th Cong., 2nd Sess., pp. 2–3.

To Geo[rge] M. Bibb, Secretary of the Treasury

Department of State
Washington, 28th December, 1844
Sir: I have the honor to request that you will furnish me, from the files of your Department, with a statement of the trade between the United States and Morocco since the beginning of 1840, and if the said statement shall show a great declension in that trade, the causes of that declension, so far as they may be known to you. It is alleged

that this trade has fallen off, in the last three years, from $1,000,000 to $50,000. I am, Sir, respectfully, Your obedient Servant, J.C. Calhoun.

LS in DNA, RG 56 (Secretary of the Treasury), Letters Received from Executive Officers, Series AB, 1844, no. [48]; FC (dated 12/29) in DNA, RG 59 (State Department), Domestic Letters, 35:60 (M-40:33).

To WILLIAM BRENT, JR., [Buenos Aires]

Department of State
Washington, 28th December, 1844

Sir: The parties interested in the claim against the Buenos Ayrean government in the case of the ship Hope, have expressed a wish that you might be specially instructed upon the subject. If the length of time which has elapsed since the capture of the vessel and the consequences of the capture to the worthy individuals, her owners, be considered, the case would seem to call for your earliest and best attention. You will consequently endeavor by all proper means to bring about an acknowledgement and payment of the claim. I am, Sir, your obedient servant, J.C. Calhoun.

FC (No. 4) in DNA, RG 59 (State Department), Diplomatic Instructions, Argentina, 15:12 (M-77:10).

To WILLIAM BRENT, JR.

Department of State
Washington, 28th December, 1844

Sir: By a despatch from Mr. [Harvey M.] Watterson, dated the 11th of October, last, this Department has been informed of the capture of the Buenos Ayrean squadron, blockading the port of Monte Video, by the United States Frigate Congress, under the command of Captain [Philip F.] Voorhees, on the 29th of September, last; and that, after taking possession of the vessels, he had discharged six seamen, citizens of the United States, who had voluntarily enlisted on board of one of the ships composing the squadron. These facts, with others of minor importance, are set forth in sundry papers, transmitted with

Mr. Watterson's communication, consisting of copies of a correspondence between himself and Mr. [Felipe] Arana, the Buenos Ayrean Minister of Foreign Affairs, as well as that which took place between Commodore [Juan] Fitton, the commander of the squadron, and Captain Voorhees; together with a letter from the latter to Commodore [Daniel] Turner, giving an account of the transaction, and the statements of those on board the American Barque Rosalba.

No official report has, as yet, been received from Commodore Turner, the officer in command of the station; and until this has been communicated, it would not be proper for the government of the United States to express any decided opinion in regard to the conduct of Captain Voorhees. This report, however, is expected in a short time; as we learn from a despatch of Mr. [Henry A.] Wise, that he left Rio de Janeiro for Buenos Ayres, immediately on the receipt of the intelligence. In the mean time the President instructs you to communicate to Mr. Arana his deep regret at the transaction. Anxious to preserve the most friendly relations with the Argentine Confederacy and to maintain the strictest neutrality in respect to the belligerent parties, now unhappily engaged in war, orders were issued by our Government to the commander of our naval forces on the station, carefully to avoid any thing calculated, in the slightest degree, to impair the good understanding between the two countries: and it is therefore with deep concern that the President has heard of this unfortunate occurrence. From the facts communicated to the Department it would seem that Captain Voorhees has acted against the tenor of his orders, from some misapprehension, as it is supposed, of the circumstances of the case. This, though it may palliate, can by no means justify his conduct; and you will assure the government of Buenos Ayres, in the strongest terms that, so soon as Commodore Turner shall have made an official report of the transaction, the government of the United States will be ready to do whatever justice and the occasion may require. I have the honor to be, With high consideration, Sir, Your obedient servant, J.C. Calhoun.

LS (No. 5) in DNA, RG 84 (Foreign Posts), Argentina, Instructions, vol. 15; FC in DNA, RG 59 (State Department), Diplomatic Instructions, Argentina, 15:12–14 (M-77:10).

To the COLLECTORS OF CUSTOMS at Philadelphia and New York City

Department of State
Washington, 28 Dec[embe]r 1844
Sir: By a Resolution of the Senate of Feb[ruar]y 14th 1843, the Secretary of State is directed "to inquire into the state of our tonnage, freight, and commerce with foreign powers, and report whether it is prosperous under existing arrangements by Treaties or Laws."

In order that I may be able properly to answer this inquiry, I will be much obliged to you if you will inform me how much the cost of Ships and other vessels built in your district is increased by the existing imposts on iron, cordage, and other articles which enter into the construction of ships &c or are used in fitting out the same.

Your prompt attention to this communication is respectfully requested. I am Sir very respectfully Your ob[e]d[ien]t servant, J.C. Calhoun.

LS (to the Collector at Philadelphia) in PHi, James Hamilton Papers, Letterbook of the Collector of the Port of Philadelphia, 1844; FC (to the Collector at New York City) in DNA, RG 59 (State Department), Domestic Letters, 35:59 (M-40:33). NOTE: Cornelius P. Van Ness was Collector at New York City and Calvin Blythe at Philadelphia.

To the COLLECTORS OF CUSTOMS in Maine

Department of State
Washington, 28 Dec[embe]r 1844
Sir, By a Resolution of the Senate of Feb[ruar]y 14th 1843, the Secretary of State is directed "to inquire into the state of our tonnage, freight and commerce with foreign powers, and report whether it is prosperous under existing arrangements by Treaties or Laws."

In order that I may be able properly to answer this inquiry, I will be much obliged to you if you will inform me how much the cost of ships and other vessels, built within your district, is increased by the existing imposts on iron, cordage, and other articles which enter into the construction of ships &c, or are used in fitting out the same.

I will be further obliged to you if you will send to me a comparative statement of the cost of building and fitting out ships and other vessels in your district and in the neighbouring British Province of New Brunswick.

Your prompt attention to this communication is respectfully requested. I am Sir very respectfully your Obe[dien]t Serv[an]t, J.C. Calhoun.

LS (to the Collector at Machias) in ScU-SC, John C. Calhoun Papers; FC (to the Collector at Eastport) in DNA, RG 59 (State Department), Domestic Letters, 35:58 (M-40:33). NOTE: Judging from replies received, this letter must have been addressed to all or most of the eight Collectors in Maine.

From A [NDREW] J. DONELSON, *"Private"*

New Orleans, December 28[t]h 1844

My D[ea]r Sir, The boat is not yet off, and leaves me a moment to say to you in addition to my last private letter, that I am satisfied the whigs are becoming afraid of the responsibility of a further postponement of the measure of annexation.

A Gentleman of extensive business connections here and of much influence in Tennessee, has recently written a letter to Mr. [Ephraim H.] Foster of the Senate, in which he urges him to give up opposition to Texas, and take the measure of immediate annexation. He says Foster will not be a candidate for reelection to the Senate, but will be the candidate for his party in Tennessee to succeed Gov[erno]r [James C.] Jones, and he will be made to understand that he cannot be so used unless he now goes for Texas. My belief is that the Tennessee votes in the Senate may be counted in favor of the measure.

I mention this that you may not too readily ["yield" *interlined*] any essential feature of the bill for the purpose of securing its passage. I know not what further instruction you may send me, but if I see that a new expression on the part of the Congress of Texas can be of avail in strengthening the true friends of the measure in our congress, I shall endeavor to profit by it promptly.

I do not think it worth while to send you the newspaper accounts which are just received of the overthrow of Santa Anna. I told Gen[era]l [Duff] Green that this would be the effect of his attempt to dissolve the chambers, but Green had so poor an opinion of the public morals of the country, that he still believed Santa Anna would be sustained.

Parades [*sic*; Mariano Paredes] you are aware reproaches Santa Anna with cowardice & treachery in not pushing the war against Texas. Whatever Parades may say or threaten on that subject, my

651

impression is that the moment of his success will be the true one, for obtaining a disclaimer of the orders given to [Adrian] Woll, and if the British influence is not in the way there will now be a general assent to the cessation of hostilities preparatory to the adjustment of boundary with us, and a formal acquiescence in the measure of annexation.

But the main point is the passage of the bill with our Congress. This done, all other trouble on the subject ceases, and Mexico will soon see that whilst she has done us injustice heretofore, there is no hope in the future for her except what may be based on our friendship and protection.

I will write to you from Galvezton. Y[ou]rs truly, A.J. Donelson.

[P.S.] Gen[era]l Green spoke to me about a recommendation of Mr. [Henry L.] Kinney (now a member of the Texan Congress) as a proper appointment for the U. States Consulate at Corpus Christi. I saw him at Washington. He is a very intelligent and business[like] man and is perhaps the most proper person living at that place. Mr. [Stewart] Newell, however, has stated to me, that there were objections to him, growing out of his failure ["of" *canceled and* "in" *interlined*] the United States, and his connection with the Mexican authority as a trader.

I should consider his election to Congress as a sufficient voucher for his fidelity to Texas. Of his previous character in the U. States I know nothing, but would regard his failure in business as no objection, if his moral character stood fair. Y[ou]rs &, A.J.D.

[P.S.] I send you a slip & the last Mexican news.

ALS in ScCleA; PEx in Boucher and Brooks, eds., *Correspondence*, pp. 274–275.

From Cha[rle]s G. Ferris, New York [City], 12/28. Ferris recommends James Fiora for appointment to be U.S. Consul at Manchester, England. As a merchant, Fiora has encouraged the export of U.S. goods to Great Britain and is "acquainted with the commercial relations between the United States and Great Britain and other European powers . . . ." ALS in DNA, RG 59 (State Department), Applications and Recommendations, 1845–1853, Fiora (M-873:28, frames 114–116).

From D A V I D H A Y D E N

Surveyor[']s Office
New Orleans, Dec[em]b[er] 28th 1844

Sir, The Schooner Ventura 14 days from Vera Cruz arrived here this morning. The News is highly important. Santa Anna's power is at ["an" *interlined*] end in Mexico. He is decreed banished by both Houses of Congress—and is deserted by his army. Monsieur [Manuel C.] Rejon is in disgrace &c &c. An Extra will issue from the press here but not in time probably for the mail. I have only time to assure you of my continued Esteem & High Respect. Truly yours, David Hayden.

[P.S.] Private Letters confirm all these facts—recei[ve]d by many merchants in N[ew] O[rleans] from Mexico.

ALS in ScCleA.

To J [A B E Z] W. H U N T I N G T O N, Chairman of the Senate Committee on Commerce

Department of State
Washington, 28th Dec[embe]r 1844

Sir, I have the honor herewith to enclose certain papers in reference to the qualifications of Charles Graebe, Alexander Tod, Isaac Stone, Peter A. Brinsmade, Robert Walsh, Gabriel G. Fleurot, Eneas Mc-Faul Jr., Franklin Lippincott, and James J. Wright, named in the list transmitted with your letter of the 19th instant, and nominated to the Senate as Consuls appointed during its last recess.

In reference to the qualifications of Robert L. McIntosh, Joel W. White, Patrick J. Devine, Joseph C.C. Ellis, Samuel H. Kneass and J.B. Lacey, the other persons therein named, and in like manner nominated, there are no papers on the files of this Department.

It is understood that Mr. *McIntosh* is the son of one of the wealthiest and most respectable citizens of Norfolk in Virginia. He is well educated and accompanied, without charge to the Government, the late mission to China.

Mr. Devine came recommended by Private letters and is spoken of as a highly respectable citizen of New York.

Mr. Ellis, is the son of the present Chargé d'affaires of the U.S. to

Venezuela and a nephew of Mr. [Chesselden] Ellis [of N.Y.] of the H[ouse of] R[epresentatives].

Mr. [William] Lucas [of Va.] of the House of Representatives is believed to be acquainted with *Doctor Lacey,* who was appointed, as was also Mr. *Kneass* of Penn[sylvani]a, on verbal representations, which were regarded as satisfactory.

I will thank you, when the ["papers" *canceled*] papers shall have been examined by the Committee to cause them to be returned to this Department. I have the honor &c &c, J.C. Calhoun.

FC in DNA, RG 59 (State Department), Reports of the Secretary of State to the President and Congress, 6:130; FC in DNA, RG 59 (State Department), Domestic Letters, 35:61–62 (M-40:33).

From WILLIAM R. KING, "Private"

Paris, Dec[embe]r 28th 1844

My Dear Sir, I was much gratified by the receipt of your most friendly letter, and I congratulate you most sincerely on the success of the Democracy. I trust & hope that Mr. [James K.] Polk[']s election may prove a blessing to our Country. This however, as you Justly remark, must entirely depend on the wisdom and policy of his Administration. Should he draw around him able men, and carry out in good faith, the principles for which we have contended, all will be well, and the Democratic Party will be fixed in power, not to be shaken. There should be no wavering on the subject of the annexation of Texas. The growling of the British Lion should only stimulate to immediate action. To falter in our course from apprehension of her hostility, would disgrace us in the eyes of all Europe. The act accomplished, England will complain, perhaps threaten; and her news papers will be lavish in their abuse; but that will be all, for with all her power, she can but feel, that a war with us would be more prejudicial to her interests, than with any other nation. She will not risk the consequences. I am aware that she is exerting herself to induce France to make common cause with her on the subject of Texas, and that Mr. [F.P.G.] Guizot is much inclined to do so; but it will not succeed. It would shock the French nation, which detests all alliances with England; and the King [Louis Philippe] is to[o] wise, and too prudent, to place himself in a position, which would go far towards destroying his dynasty. It is however very desireable that we should have the means to enable us to command the service of a portion of the French press, to enlighten the public mind; and thus to counteract the misrepresentations which appear daily, in those Journals, which are notoriously in the pay of England. I hope the suggest[i]on I had the honor to make on this subject will meet with the approbation of the President [John Tyler]. Mr. [Robert] Walsh[,] our Consul [in Paris,] is an able, and efficient officer, and I trust Col. Polk will not be induced to disturb him in his position. Permit me also to ask, as a personal favor to myself, as well as an act of Justice to a long tried, and faithful public servant, that our Consul at Havre, my old Friend Beaseley [*sic*; Reuben G. Beasley], may not be displaced, to gratify any one; for I know him to be one of the best of men and a capital officer. Your letter to Gov[erno]r [Wilson] Shannon reached me nearly two weeks after those addressed to Messrs. [Washington] Irving & [Henry] Wheaton had been received— probably Sir James Graham thought proper to give it a perusal. It is written with your usual ability, and places the conduct of Mexico in the odious light in which it deserves to stand, before the civilized world. A few days past I was presented to the King [Leopold I] and Queen [Louise-Marie] of Belgium, now on a visit to this Court. They took occasion to express themselves in the kindest terms of Mr. [Thomas G.] & Mrs. [Anna Maria Calhoun] Clemson, and from all that I can learn they have succeeded in making a most favorable impression, as well on the Corps Diplomatic, as on the King. The opening of the Chambers, which took place on the 26[th] presented a bril[l]iant spectacle; and the old King read his speach [*sic*] admirably well. I enclose it to you. You will perceive nothing in it of any importance, except that he dwells with rather too much emphasis on the friendship of England, to chime in with the feelings of the French People. A majority of the Papers of Paris have attacked it ["with" *interlined*] great severity, and even in the Chamber itself ["it" *interlined*] was received in dead silence. The President[']s Message is looked for with much interest, particularly in England, as Lord Cowley said to me a few days past. I laughingly replied, I was gratified to find we were of sufficient importance to excite an interest on this side of the Atlantic. Tender my best respects to Mrs. [Floride Colhoun] Calhoun. Most faithfully your Ob[edien]t Ser-[van]t, William R. King.

ALS with En in ScCleA; PC in Jameson, ed., *Correspondence*, pp. 1013–1015. NOTE: Enclosed was a 3-pp. PC of Louis Philippe's speech on 12/26: *Discours du Roi* ([Paris:] Imprimiere Royale, 1844). A current controversy in Britain concerned Sir James Graham, the Home Secretary, and his use of an old statute to intercept mail.

To THOMAS O. LARKIN, U.S. Consul, Monterey

Department of State
Washington, Dec[embe]r 28th 1844
Sir, Your letters of the 18th August & 16th September last, *not num-bered*, the former enclosing a copy of a letter from you to the Le-gation of the U. States, at Mexico [City], relative to an order, pro-hibiting the Sale of Merchandize from on board of all Vessels engaged in the Whale fishery, arriving at the ports of the Department of Cali-fornia, six months after date, have been received.

The President [John Tyler] in his Message of the 19th Inst: to Congress, a copy of which & other Documents are enclosed, notices the unfriendly feelings manifested by Mexico towards the U. States, & makes special reference to the above order.

Since the letter to you of the 25th Oct: your Consular Bond has been received, approved, and sent to the Secretary of the Treasury [George M. Bibb] to be placed on file.

The Laws of the U. States do not authorize relief & protection to be afforded to Citizens of the U. States in Foreign Countries, who are not destitute mariners.

You will please transmit to the Department an Account, with proper Vouchers, of the expenses incurred by you, in the expedition for the relief of a Vessel, reported to be wrecked & supposed to be from Boston, of which mention is made in your letter of the 16th of September. I am, Sir, Respectfully Your obedient Servant, J.C. Cal-houn.

LS in CU, Bancroft Library, Larkin Collection; FC in DNA, RG 59 (State De-partment), Consular Instructions, 11:318–319; PC in Hammond, ed., *Larkin Papers*, 2:340.

From Sam[ue]l Lowder, Bangor, Maine, 12/28. "In the year 1832, I owned three fourths of the Schooner Topaz of this Port. Henry Rider (whose heirs I represent) was owner of the other fourth & master. In that same year the vessel was pressed into the service of the Mexican Government to carry troops; while on the pas-sage to Annahuac the troops took possession of the vessel and a large sum of money & merchandize and murdered the Captain and one or more of the crew." Previously, American commissioners judged his claim worth $13,000, but Mexican commissioners refused any com-pensation for this act of "Piracy & murder." LS in DNA, RG 59 (State Department), Miscellaneous Letters (M-179:107, frames 221–222).

From F[RANCIS] W. PICKENS

Edgewood [S.C.], 28 Dec[embe]r 1844

My dear Sir, I rec[eive]d yours [*not found*] yesterday and was glad to hear you were all well, but regret that things look so gloomy to you. I hope yet matters may take a more favourable turn.

As to your fear about a split in this State I think there is no occasion for it at all. The State never has been as united as at present since I have been acquainted with public matters. The Mercury being in the hands of a few makes a greater shew of division than really exists. There were only 21 men in the legislature all told that were bitter & opposed to the present position of the State, and they made a great shew & claimed many more but I assure you that is the amount of their strength. Take Beaufort & Col[l]eton and you will find that combining Senators & Rep[resentatives] both and there is a majority of 6 ag[ain]st the course pursued by Mr. [Robert Barnwell] Rhett. In fact I am informed that in those Dist[rict]s in the recent Congressional election a majority of the votes were actually Blank. I merely mention this to shew you that there is in fact no division except such as arises in every ["countr" *canceled*] country ag[ain]st selfishness[,] ar[r]ogance, and assumption, which must allways be the case. I think I can safely say that the State is fully informed as to her true situation & responsibilities and is determined to do what is right with unanimity at the proper time, if need be.

As to my 2d set of resolutions on Abolition &c—the reason why they were not passed was that immediately after my speech on them these 21 men called a caucus to defeat & smother them, and they selected [John] Bauskett from this [Edgefield] Dist[rict] (who was allways an uncertain man) and used him to introduce counter resolutions to produce distraction the last day & confusion, and it was on this motion they were taken from the House where the yeas & nays could operate & refer[r]ed to a Committee of the Whole House & made with all the other previous resolutions the order of the day for 10 O'Clock at night the last night of the session. I told him at the time the object of his resolutions (which were drawn by [William F.] Colcock) was to produce distraction and his motion was to smother all in the confusion of the last moments. He could not deny it, and will be held to strict account from what I hear.

If it had not been for this the last night, and they could have been brought to a vote they were obliged to pass with the exception of the 21—and strange to say the night before I introduced them (on Sunday) these very gent: were the most violent for the most violent resolutions, and I took the Senate Monday immediately after reading the journal, without consulting a single person, and they then, after I passed them by a unanimous vote immediately ["turned" *canceled*] turned moderate men.

As to a report &c. on the Gov[ernor's, James H. Hammond's,] message—I thought of it, but the great difficulty was in going into details. The Legislature of So. Ca. would not bear[?] it. There are but a very fiew [*sic*] (& none from the Low Country) who can understand or appreciate our relations to any general parties out of the State. They are no more a part of the general Democratic party than if they were out of the Union. And the consequence would have been a great division on any report that could be made. Besides it was necessary to act immediately as the Gov[ernor's] message with the Mercury were to have their run & produce all the unfavourable impressions that could be before a report could be made. And it was understood that [George] McDuffie was to be there the first day of the session to urge an immediate call of a convention. He did not go & they were disappointed and I believe now have unkind feelings towards him because he did not fulfill what was supposed to be his obligations, as he signed originally the address of Mr. Rhett to his constituents and they say agreed to stand by him in the State.

I shall write to [Franklin H.] Elmore immediately & put him right, but you must not mistake Col. Elmore. I think he is a devoted friend of yours & he told me that as your friend, and I told him then there was some mistake. These 21 gent: are now bitter towards him ["and made" *canceled*] & made the unkindest insinuations about his prospects of receiving an office from [James K.] Polk &c. Elmore acted with me *most cordially* in every thing at Columbia & did what he could to check & control others.

I hope sincerely every thing will yet work right. As far as I am concerned I am perfectly satisfied and am ag[ain]st every thing calculated to produce the slightest division in the State. We must be united—it is due to ourselves, to our liberties, & to the country; and as God is the judge of my heart there is not an emotion in it at present seperate from the honor, the rights, and the glory of So. Carolina.

I read with great pride and delight your letter to [William R.] King. It is a noble and magnificent letter, and in my opinion will produce a profound impression upon the world. The fact is that it seems to me the politics of the country are all running into our foreign relations and we now have some of the greatest questions at issue. Our rights are to be vindicated in our Diplomatic relations, & I think it a great blessing that you are where you are. The present generation do not see the power of your position, but after ages will pay tribute to what you are now doing. God grant that you may be continued there, not for yourself but for the country. As far as you are concerned personally, I sincerely believe it better for you to be at home. I know it is as far as the Presidency hereafter is concerned— but the power of your position now & for the next year is immense upon the affairs of the whole world.

I take it for granted that the moves & feelings you allude to on the Texas question & abolition are instigated with a view to drive you & your friends on the extreme Southern wing of the party exclusively, and that it is in fact a game for the succession & planned *by* [Silas] *Wright.*

I hope it will not affect you in the slightest degree, but that you will laugh at it. *Just keep quiet.* You have got the issues with you and your time is coming. If you are not President, you can be more— *you can mould the Government* for an age. Very truly, F.W. Pickens.

ALS in ScCleA; PEx in Jameson, ed., *Correspondence,* pp. 1015–1017.

From S[TEPHEN] PLEASONTON

Treasury Department
5th Auditor's Office, 28 December, 1844
Sir: In reply to the letter which you referred to me yesterday, of the Hon. C[harles] J. Ingersoll, Chairman of the Committee on Foreign Affairs, House of Representatives, of 26th instant, I have the honor to enclose herewith extracts from the Settlements made at this Office, of the accounts of Mr. [John H.] Eaton, and Mr. [Cornelius P.] Van Ness, late U.S. Ministers to the Court of Spain, shewing what was allowed to each for Office rent, and exchange on the bills drawn by them on the U.S. Bankers at London. I also enclose copies of the letters addressed to me by the then Secretary of State (Mr. [Daniel] Webster) under which the allowances were made.

It is proper for me to state that Office rent was never allowed to any of our Ministers to the Court of Spain, nor to any other Court except those of England and France, nor was any gain in exchange ever allowed to any of our foreign Ministers, previous to the incumbency of the Hon. Dan[ie]l Webster in the Department of State, nor have either of these allowances been made since; the practice being previously, in regard to exchange, to charge the respective Ministers and Chargés with the gain, and to credit them with any loss on their bills. I have the honor to be, Sir, Respectfully, Your Ob[e]d[ien]t Serv[an]t, S. Pleasonton.

LS with Ens in DNA, RG 233 (U.S. House of Representatives), 28A-D12.2; FC in DNA, RG 217 (General Accounting Office), Fifth Auditor, Letters Sent, 5:193–194; PC with Ens in House Report No. 50, 28th Cong., 2nd Sess., pp. 3–4.

To [SANTIAGO VÁSQUEZ], Minister for Foreign Affairs of the Republic of Ecuador

Department of State
Washington, 28th December, 1844
Sir: The President of the United States, animated by a desire to draw closer and to strengthen the ties of friendship which connect the two countries, has appointed Delazon Smith, Esquire, Special Agent of the United States to the Republic of Ecuador. I have now the honor of introducing him to your Excellency, and to ask for him a reception and treatment corresponding to his station and to the purposes for which he is sent. Those purposes he will in due time more particularly explain to Your Excellency. Hoping, that, through his agency they may be accomplished, I avail myself of this occasion to offer Your Excellency the assurance of my distinguished consideration. (signed) J.C. Calhoun.

CC in DNA, RG 84 (Foreign Posts), Ecuador, Instructions, vol. 1/8/1827– 12/2/1848. NOTE: An EU reads "Rec[eive]d Quito 29 July 1845."

From SHEPARD CARY, [Representative from Maine]

House of Representatives, Dec. 29th 1844
Sir, Allow me to call your attention to the stipulations of the Treaty of Washington relating to the disputed territory [fund] of New Brunswick, so called.

According to the stipulations above referred to all bonds and moneys appertaining to that fund were to be paid over to the Gov-[ernment] of the United States within six months after the ratification of the treaty, for the benifit of the States of Maine & Massachusetts. It has now been nearly two years since this stipulation should have been complied with and no disposition has been evinced on the part of the British Govt. to compell the complience of New Brunswick ["to" *erased*] with this engagement.

The parties interested in this fund feel assured that you will take m[e]asures to ["compell" *canceled and* "induce" *interlined*] an early complience ["in" *altered to* "of"] the conditions above refer[r]ed to. For a more detailed statement respecting this ["matter" *interlined*], I will refer you to my letter to you of July last upon this subject.

If you should not find the letter refer[r]ed to sufficiently explicit it will afford me pleasure to furnish you with such ad[d]itional facts in the case as you may deem usefull. Respectfully your Obedient Servant, Shepard Cary.

ALS in DNA, RG 76 (Records of Boundary and Claims Commissions and Arbitrations), Letters and Miscellaneous Documents relating to the Maine-New Brunswick Boundary Dispute, 1824–1850.

From DUFF GREEN

Wash[ingto]n, Texas, 29th De[cembe]r 1844
My dear Sir, I enclose you the Tex[as] Nat[ional] Register. You will see that the Editor is preparing the public mind here for a coalition between [Thomas H.] Benton & the whigs which will defeat Annexation this winter, but keeping open the Door of hope for the next.

[Charles] Elliot [British Chargé d'Affaires] is very active, offering Independence on a pledge against Annexation. He can do nothing. Nine tenths of the people are for Annexation, and the President [Anson Jones] assures me that he is also. He cannot if he would, defeat it, if ["yo"(?) *canceled*] Congress pass resolutions, next winter, favorable to annexation. These people however will not consent to annexation with less than the limits they claim, & will reject it if it be clogged with either of Mr. Benton's conditions. Yours truly, Duff Green.

ALS in ScCleA; PC in Jameson, ed., *Correspondence*, pp. 1017–1018.

To R[OBERT] M. T. HUNTER, [Lloyds, Va.]

Washington, 29th Dec[embe]r 1844

My dear Sir, My engagements are so onerous, that I am forced to write very few & very short letters.

In answer to your enquiry, how the Western Democrats voted on the repeal of the 21st rule, I am sorry to say, that the great body voted for it. It was, with few exceptions the votes of the two sections, slave holding & non slave holding, arrayed ag[ai]nst each other. They ["are" *canceled*] appear to me to be coming daily, ["into" *canceled*] more & more, into deadly conflict. To judge by indications, which are constantly occur[r]ing, we shall be thrown ["into" *canceled*] on our own means of defending ourselves on that vital question. It would seem, that we can look ["no longer" *interlined*] to our northern allies for support in reference to it.

The Texian question is the all important question at present. Its fate is still doubtful. The real opposition is from the [Thomas H.] Benton [Martin] V[an] Buren party, and has its centre in the Empire State, where the opposition, in the ranks of our own party ag[ai]nst the South, has ever originated. It was there the opposition of [Aaron] Burr to [Thomas] Jefferson, & of [George] Clinton to [James] Madison, originated. It was by the combined influence of N. York democrats & the nationals or whigs, that the oppressive Tariffs of 1828 & 1842 were imposed on us; & now ["that" *canceled*] by the same combination, ["the" *interlined*] annexation of Texas is opposed and is in danger of being defeated. Benton is but an instrument in its hand; and yet it is this very N. York wing of the party, which has been so ["sedulously" *canceled*] anxiously courted by Virginia for more than 15 years! It is time, that she should open her eyes to the real state of things.

Notwithstanding the strength of this combination, I am of the impression, that if the question of annexation should be properly pressed, it will pass the House this session & if it should, I can not but think the prospect is fair, that it will force its way through the Senate.

We hear nothing from Tennessee. Col. [James K.] Polk seems to be observing a prudent silence as to his course & the constitution of his cabinet. As yet, I see no unfavourable indications. Yours truly, J.C. Calhoun.

ALS in ScCleA; PC in Jameson, ed., *Correspondence*, pp. 636–637.

From WILLIAM R. KING

Paris, Dec[embe]r 29th 1844

My Dear Sir, I have the pleasure of introducing to you, John T. Wymbs Esq[ui]r[e] one of the most respectable and estimable of our Countrymen now residing in Paris. You will find Mr. Wymbs a very intelligent Gentleman; and unlike most Americans who have resided for any length of time in Europe, [he] is a firm, and unwavering Democrat in principle. I ask for him your kind attention. Your friend sincerely, William R. King.

ALS in DNA, RG 59 (State Department), Applications and Recommendations, 1845–1853, John T. Wymbs (M-873:97, frame 520).

From AYMAR & CO.

New York [City,] Dec. 30, 1844

Sir, Dr. [José M.] Camiñero, appointed by his government for the purpose, proceeds to Washington with a view to obtain the recognition of the Dominican republic by our government. The obstacles that have hitherto precluded such recognition of any part of the island of St. Domingo, do not exist in this case, the republic he represents being a republic of *white-men*, who in the late revolution have succeeded in wresting one-half of the island, the old Spanish part, from the blacks, and appear to be permanently and safely established in their independence of the negroes. They are anxious to cultivate the commercial intercourse of this country; they have already abolished the extra tonnage duties on American vessels, allowing them equal privileges with those of their own flag and have, we believe, in other instances materially reduced the duties upon American goods. Under its present population, freed from the embar[r]assment of their negro governors, a great advance may be expected in the industry and production of this part of the island and it may consequently become an important consumer of our agricultural products.

In addition to his official credentials which he will present you, we beg to add that he comes commended to us by friends in that island in whom we have every confidence as being personally a gentleman of the highest character. Begging your favorable consideration of his application We are Sir With great respect Your Obedient Servants, Aymar & Co.

ALS in ScCleA. NOTE: An AEU by Calhoun reads "Mr. Aymants [*sic*] Introducing Dr. Caminero." Aymar & Company was one of the largest mercantile firms in New York City. It specialized in commerce with the Caribbean and Latin American nations.

From ALEX[ANDE]R OSW[AL]D BRODIE

New York [City,] 30 Dec[embe]r 1844
Sir, I have the honor to hand you a d[ra]ft for acceptance drawn by W[illia]m Nelson our late Consul at Panama for the amount of $223³⁸⁄₁₀₀—which you will much oblige me by ordering ["it" *canceled*] to be paid in New York.

Mr. Nelson begs me to use my best endeavour to have him replaced in his former honorable situation as Consul—and he presumes the difficulty may not be great, as his Successor [J.A. Townsend] had not made his appearance in Panama, nor did he expect he would, and if he did would not remain for want of inducement. Mr. Nelson had delivered his Exequator back to the Gouverneur, and therefore if the President [John Tyler] thro' your recommendation of him as p[er] the highly respectable list of names attached to his request for the office, will I believe be very sufficient to enable you to do so. I hope the President will in the event of Mr. Townsend retiring from the office have the kindness to renominate him as Consul at Panama.

The Hon[ora]ble Mr. [Silas] Wright informed me the only motive for removing Mr. Nelson was that he was not a Citizen—the facts are ["these" *interlined*], he arrived in this Country at the age of 18—had taken the prelimin[ary] steps—but could not the last, as he left this ere the 5 years expired from the period of 21. Mr. Nelson considers himself an American, and thinks that ought to be considered such by his adopted Country viz. untill he has an opportunity of taking the final oath. He has never revisited his native Country and is a partner in the only American house in Panama trading with this Country, and flatters himself that he may soon be enabled to return to this Country which he considers his Country.

I hope you will pardon the liberty I have taken as a stranger to you by writing the above in favour of a most Respectable man— ["but" *changed to* "and"] certainly I cannot apply to many friends of your acquaintance to use their influence with you till I know Mr. Townsend will not retain the office. My Respected friend Judge [James] Dunlop ["of your City" *interlined*] would I am certain if I wrote to him would [*sic*] say nothing injurious to the C[h]aracter of the writer of this letter. I have the Honor to sign my name with Great Respect Your very Ob[edient] Servant, Alexr. Oswd. Brodie.

ALS in DNA, RG 59 (State Department), Applications and Recommendations, 1845–1853, Nelson (M-873:62, frames 833–835).

From S. F. CHAPMAN

Washington, 30th dec[embe]r 1844

Dear Sir: My friend, Dr. Brokenborough [*sic*; John Brockenbrough] from Virg[ini]a did me the favor on saturday morning, to hand you a note from the President of the United States [John Tyler], in relation to a vacancy in your Dept. which from his kind dispositions towards me, he was doubtless anxious, I should fill.

I need not say to you Sir, that I have not troubled myself or others to procure any letters, so usual in all applications for office, but I have rather relied upon what belongs to my character, as a southern gentleman, than upon the miserable aids, which such letters, might give to my claim.

Should it be your pleasure Sir, to confer upon me this appointment I flatter myself, that I shall not be found unworthy the office, nor of your kindness, confidence and friendship. With great respect I have the honor to be faithfully y[ou]r f[rien]d, S.F. Chapman at Gen[era]l Hunters.

ALS in ScCleA.

From FRANCIS J. GRUND

Antwerp, Dec. 30th 1844

Sir, The undersigned has the honor to inform the department that he has appointed Max Vandenbergh Esquire, Vice Consul for the port of Antwerp; hoping that this appointment will meet the approbation of the Department.

The undersigned also respectfully submits to the consideration of the Department whether it would not be well for him to visit the different manufacturing towns of Belgium, during the winter; there being, first, no vessels here during the winter, & secondly the undersigned being apprised from a most unquestionable source, that most, if not all the goods sent to the United States from Liege, Ghent and Verviers are invoiced twenty-five per cent below the actual cost. It is, namely, usual to send two invoices to the United States; one for the guidance of the Consignee, & one for the Custom House. The latter only is exhibited to the Consul for verification.

In cases where the Consul refuses to verify, a bill of sale is made out, & the goods sent to the consignee as *purchased* by the latter; because this enables him to make oath as *owner* at the Custom House. It is the undersigned's respectful opinion that the revenue of the United States is in this manner annually defrauded of at least 20 per cent of all the duties levied on foreign goods.

The undersigned, in conclusion, would yet observe that he has seen letters from the different manufacturers, in which they confess the fraud above referred to, & advise the merchants to imitate the practice. This refers especially to broad Cloths & to fire arms.

On requisition the undersigned will give the names of the parties, as also the real prices of the articles from personal inquiry at the different manufacturing towns.

The goods imported from the Prussian Province of Westphalia are, in general, treated as the Belgian goods. Were every invoice, without distinction whether the goods were purchased or consigned, required to be legalised by the U.S. Consul; & were every Consul to insist that the invoice prices are actually sworn to, as the formula states, instead of looking upon this part of the transaction as a mere form, and signing certificates without seeing the parties, this kind of fraud would, in a great measure, be prevented, & the actual collection of the duties fixed upon foreign goods would be a greater protection to the home manufacturer, than the nominal augmentation of the duty itself. All which is most respectfully submitted by Sir Your ob[edien]t humble S[ervan]t, Francis J. Grund, U.S. Consul for Antwerp.

ALS (No. 2) in DNA, RG 59 (State Department), Consular Despatches, Antwerp, vol. 3 (T-181:3), received 1/27/1845. NOTE: A Clerk's EU of 1/28/-1845 reads "Respectfully referred to the Secretary of the Treasury for his perusal with the request that it may be returned." A Treasury Department Clerk's EU reads "Read & Returned—Jan. 31, 1845."

From W[ILLIA]M SLOAN

Pendleton, Dec[e]m[ber] 30th 1844

Dear Sir, Mrs. [Margaret Hunter] Rion has on two occasions recently informed me of the mismanagement and dishonesty of Mr. Fred[e]-ricks your overseer. If the charges she makes be true, your interest must suffer very much by continueing him.

I have taken the trouble to enquire of the neighbours as to his conduct and management, none of whoom are disposed to speak out, but seem to entertain the opinion that he is not trustwort[h]y. I know nothing myself of any missmanagement [*sic*] by him, if I did I would not hesitate to make the spesiffick [*sic*] charge.

Mrs. Rion will inform you of the charges she has laid before me, and you will be the better judge ["of" *canceled*] what credit should be given to them.

Thinking it possible that you might conclude to discharge him, I have saught an intervi[e]w with Mr. Philips who has overseed the last three years for T[homas] M. Sloan, who will if you wish take charge of your farm, for $200[,] 300 lb. pork[,] 1 Bu[shel] flower & 15 Bu[shels] corn. I can reccommend him as an honest industrious man, well qualified to manage negroes. He has made better crops for my brother than aney man he has had on his place, and the only cause of his leaving is that my brother did not think the farm justi-fied the wages he required. He is at present on a small farm he has purchased in the neighbourhood.

Should you conclude it to be necessary to discharge Fred[e]ricks and wish to employ Philips, you can address T.M. Sloan on the sub-ject who will attend to it for you. I should offer my own services but shall leave in a few days for Florida and will be absent about six weeks.

You will not understand me as advising the course I have sug-gested as there is nothing coming under my own knowledge, which would justify it. The matter rests mainly upon the charges made by Mrs. Rion, & you will be the better judge what credit should be given to them.

I feel it a duty I owe to you in your absence when I eaven sup-posed your interest was suffering from bad management or dishonesty of your agent to inform you of it. Verry Respectfully Your Ob[edi-en]t Servant, Wm. Sloan.

ALS in ScCleA.

From [President] J[OHN] TYLER

[Washington] Dec. 30, 1843 [*sic*; 1844]
D[ea]r Sir, It is usual to intimate to the foreign Ministers that they
will be rec[eive]d at the President's house on the 1 January in ad-
vance of the Citizens generally. They will be received at ½ after 11
O'Clock. Will you have this communicated to them[?] Y[ou]rs
Truly, J. Tyler.

ALS in DNA, RG 59 (State Department), Miscellaneous Letters (M-179:103,
frames 343–345).

CIRCULAR [to Foreign Representatives in Washington]

Department of State
Washington, 30th December, 1844
The Secretary of State presents his compliments to Don A[ngel]
Calderon de la Barca, and has the honor to inform him, that the
President [John Tyler] will receive the Diplomatic Corps, as usual,
on the first of January, at 11½ o'clock A.M.

FC in DNA, RG 59 (State Department), Notes to Foreign Legations, Spain,
6:116 (M-99:85); FC (addressed to [Jean Corneille] Gevers) in DNA, RG 59
(State Department), Notes to Foreign Legations, Netherlands, 6:37 (M-99:75).
NOTE: Abstracts of this circular, found in DNA, RG 59 (State Department),
Notes to Foreign Legations, in various files, indicate that copies were sent to
the Ministers or Chargés d'Affaires of Great Britain, France, Belgium, Russia,
Prussia, Portugal, Austria, Sweden, and Denmark. No copies of this circular
to the representatives of Texas, Mexico, Argentina, Brazil, or Sardinia have been
found.

From FERNANDO WOOD

New York [City,] Dec[embe]r 30, 1844
D[ea]r Sir, This will introduce Hon. James H. Suydam[,] late member of the New York Legislature and present Navy Agent at this
place. Mr. S[uydam] is a gentleman of great worth and most excellent standing in this city, and in all respects entitled to your confidence and respect. He visits Washington on business with the De-

partment, and relating to his nomination before the Senate.

Any advice he may receive through your kind assistance will be appreciated by Yours very Truly &c, Fernando Wood.

ALS in ScCleA. NOTE: Suydam's appointment as Naval Agent for the Port of New York was rejected by the Senate in 1/1845.

From EDWARD EVERETT

London, 31 December, 1844

Sir, I transmit herewith a note from Lord Aberdeen of the 9th instant relative to the duties imposed upon the exportation of American Timber from New Brunswick, which formed the subject of my note to him of the 28th of June last, a copy of which accompanied my despatch Nro. 150, of that date.

Lord Aberdeen's note will, I think, be regarded by you as an insufficient reply to the arguments, by which I endeavored to show that the imposition of the Colonial export duty is inconsistent with the provisions of the third Article of the treaty of Washington.

At the same time, I am far from being clear, that it is advisable for the United States, looking to the interest of the territory whose produce is affected by the question, to contest the point farther at present.

Lord Aberdeen, you perceive, observes that the intention of the negotiators of the treaty in providing that the Produce of Maine descending the river St. John should, when within the province of New Brunswick, be dealt with as if it were the produce of the Province might perhaps have been open to discussion, but that the British Government has adopted the meaning most favorable to the United States, and has considered that this produce, when once brought within the limits of New Brunswick, was entitled to be treated in all respects upon a footing of equality with the produce of that Province; allowing it to be imported into England and into the British possessions upon the same footing and upon the payment of the same dues, as the produce of the Province itself.

As there is certainly much doubt whether under the treaty we could claim this privilege, and as it greatly outweighs the burden of the export duty, I should think it injudicious, on our part, to force the discussion which would be sure to arise, if we continue to contest the liability of American Timber to the Colonial tax.

Under the influence of this opinion, I have for the present limited

669

myself to the acknowledgment of the receipt of Lord Aberdeen's note, so that the whole subject is left open for the consideration of the President. I am, Sir, with great respect, Your obedient Servant, Edward Everett.

Transmitted with Despatch Nro. 231.
1. The Earl of Aberdeen to Mr. Everett, 9th December, 1844.
2. Mr. Everett to the Earl of Aberdeen, 31 December, 1844.

LS (No. 231) with Ens in DNA, RG 59 (State Department), Diplomatic Despatches, Great Britain, vol. 53 (M-30:49), received 1/27/1845; FC in DNA, RG 84 (Foreign Posts), Great Britain, Despatches, 9:104–107; FC in MHi, Edward Everett Papers, 51:15–18 (published microfilm, reel 23, frames 561–563); PC with Ens in House Document No. 110, 29th Cong., 1st Sess., pp. 24–27.

From WILLIAM R. KING

Legation of the United States
Paris, 31st December 1844

Sir, I have the honor to acknowledge the receipt of your Despatch No. 12, and shall, without delay, deliver to the authorized representative of the Spanish government, coupons corresponding to the amount of sixty thousand dollars.

The decisive result of the Presidential election, which was not anticipated in Europe, has given a new interest to American questions, and especially to that of Texas.

The election of the unsuccessful candidate [Henry Clay] was counted upon with certainty to extinguish annexation forever. Although I still believe that the French government will take no actively offensive steps in this matter, I cannot shut my eyes to the fact that its wishes at least, coincide with those of England, and that its influence may be lent, to a certain extent, to the support of British policy with reference to this question. The King [Louis Philippe] is, for various reasons, anxious to conciliate England. That country was the first to acknowledge the government of July, which has never been viewed with a favorable eye by the great continental monarchies. The King of the French feels that the British government is his main stay, and that with the English alliance he is able to maintain the paramount object of his policy which he deems essential to the security of his dynasty, as well as to the prosperity of France— I mean the peace of Europe. I make every allowance for the difficulties of his position, amidst hostile or unsympathizing dynasties, and threatened at every moment by the revolutionary tendencies of Europe and of France in particular. Still these apprehensions may precipitate him into dangers of another character, and in wishing to secure a powerful friend in this hemisphere, he may alienate the "natural ally" of France in America. But though too anxious, perhaps, to conciliate England, I do not suspect the King of unfriendly dispositions towards the United States. I confess I have not quite the same confidence in his minister Mr. [F.P.G.] Guizot. Though an able, and, I believe, a virtuous man, his systematic devotion to England, blinds him to other interests of hardly less importance. He is a man of the cabinet rather than of the world, and carries into public affairs the rigid theories of the speculative politician. He pursues his objects with inflexible resolution, but without a sufficient regard for the opinions, the sentiments, the prejudices if you will, of the French people. So far from seeking to win popularity, even by honorable compliances, he is suspected of taking pride in the defiance of public opinion. He has rendered the English alliance almost odious in France, by an ostentatious, if not a defying, parade, of deference to English policy. In the discussions upon the Right of Search Treaties, he was forced indeed to succumb, but without the grace of good will. He unhesitatingly declared that the English alliance was more important, politically and morally, than any modification of the Treaties. Fortunately public opinion, even among the supporters of the Administration, is ["so" *canceled and* "unchangeably" *interlined*] hostile to these obnoxious Treaties.

It is thought that one of the objects of the late Royal visit to England, when the King was accompanied by his Minister, was to obtain the modification of ["those" *interlined*] Treaties ["and the abrogation of the last Convention," *interlined*] which must remain a dead letter for every purpose, but that of keeping alive national antipathies. The British government might have conceded the point, had it not been deterred by apprehension of offending the fanatics, who from their numbers and influence however diminished, must yet be treated with a certain consideration.

Upon the whole, I apprehend nothing from European influence upon American questions, if we have the firmness to despise and resist the brutum fulmen of mere diplomatic remonstrance. Public sentiment in France ["reta" *canceled*] restrains the British tendencies of the Minister, and even renders ["the" *canceled and* "his" *interlined*] tenure of power, precarious by reason of these obvious dispositions. The cold reception of the Royal speech at the opening of the Session of the Chamber of Deputies, was mainly caused by this feeling, and was a significant indication for the King and his Ministry. The éclat of the African victories was tarnished in French estimation by the eagerness to tranquillize British susceptibilities, as evinced by the conclusion of a treaty with the Emperor of Morocco [Abd-ar-Rahman] without the exaction of substantial guarantees, and the evacuation of Mogadore even before the ratification of the Convention. As to France, then, the fears of her government, if not the wisdom of her rulers, will deter her from multiplying the difficulties of her foreign relations which have proved to her already a source of so much embarrassment.

From England, there is not, in reality, more to apprehend. Her debt, her financial difficulties with a property tax in time of peace, her East India embarrassments, her Canadian troubles, the scarcely slumbering volcano of Ireland, are all salutary checks upon her hostile disposition. She will be but too happy, if she can thwart the policy of the United States by the cheap weapons of diplomatic remonstrance or newspaper menace. I trust, then, as I have remarked in a former communication, that the course of our government will be determined by duty and patriotism alone, and that it will not permit itself to be influenced, in the slightest degree, by the empty demonstrations which timid politicians dread, or artful ones affect to apprehend.

I confess I fear more from Texas herself, than from European hostility. It is to be apprehended that two rejections of proffered annexation have given some effect to foreign intrigue, if they have not somewhat cooled the disposition of her people for union with the United States. The hostility to annexation of the new Administration [of Anson Jones] in Texas, is hardly concealed, and it may not be amiss to state that the late Chargé d'Affaires of that republic here [Ashbel Smith], who will probably be the new Secretary of State, frankly avowed to myself as well as to others, his opposition to the measure. Nothing will be left undone by England, and perhaps by France, to foster this adverse feeling, and this, doubtless, ["is" *interlined*] the direction which their hostility will take, it is to be feared not without effect. But it is superfluous to press considerations which have, without doubt, suggested themselves to your mind, with sufficient clearness and force. I will add a word before closing upon a topic which I think requires attention. Passports are granted to American citizens coming abroad by various authorities besides the Department of State, and especially by the Mayors of the great cities. Without enquiring into the right or propriety of this custom, it becomes unquestionably an abuse when they are given to persons not citizens. Such passports have been presented at the Legation by aliens, and what is not a little curious, in two instances, at least, they were given by the Mayor of New York [James Harper], who was elected by the, so-called, Native American party. In all such cases I have refused to acknowledge them, or to permit the customary visa to be attached, since protection and privileges are thereby claimed of European governments, for the subjects of foreign powers. Should the parties become involved in difficulties, how could the American minister interfere in their behalf, with propriety or effect? Would it not be advisable to publish a notice that passports given to any but American citizens, will not be recognized by the representatives of the American government abroad? I suggest this, because no simpler or more effectual method occurs to me of putting an end to an abuse which certainly deserves to be corrected. I am very respectfully your obedient servant, William R. King.

LS (No. 9) in DNA, RG 59 (State Department), Diplomatic Despatches, France, vol. 30 (M-34:33), received 1/27/1845.

From RICHMOND LORING

Aux Cayes, 31st December 1844
Sir! I have the honor to forward herewith the returns, (No. 4) of this Agency for the last six months. I think it my duty to apprise you of the following occurance. There was a dispute between some Haytians and a Seaman on board the American Brig Corvo. The former were the aggressors, and it was of so serious a character, that I made a representation thereof to the Delegates of the Government in this City, who sent the offenders to be tried before the Civil tribunal, where two of the most violent were condemned to a fine of sixteen dollars each, and one month's imprisonment. This in the end was merely a form, for the judgment has never been executed.

This circumstance has tended to increase the Insolence towards foreigners, of that portion of the population who are workmen on the wharves; and in several instances, lives have been endangered. The English and French are readily protected by the authorities, which I attribute to the occasional visits of their vessels of war. Some demonstration of a power to protect is absolutely necessary to enforce attention to my complaints.

By a recent arrival, I have every reason to beleive that my consular bond; forwarded to the United States for the signatures of my security, has been miscarried, and in all probability lost, this obliges me to trouble the Department for another blank bond, so that I may be able to execute the required obligation. I am, Sir, With great respect Your most ob[edien]t Serv[an]t, Richmond Loring.

LS (No. 5) with Ens in DNA, RG 59 (State Department), Consular Despatches, Aux Cayes, vol. 2 (T-330:2), received 2/28/1845.

To President [JOHN TYLER]

Department of State
Washington, 31st December, 1844
To the President of the United States.

The Secretary of State, to whom was referred the Resolution of the Senate of the 16th inst: requesting the President to "inform the Senate whether the Executive Department is possessed of any definite information by which the present public debt of the Republic of Texas can be ascertained; and if so, to communicate it to the Senate with the aggregate amount of that debt; and also that he be requested to inform the Senate whether any, and if any, what additions have been made to that debt since the signing of the Treaty with that Republic submitted to the Senate at its last session.

"And that he be further requested to inform the Senate what amount of public lands of Texas had been granted by the Spanish, Mexican and Texan Governments, and to what extent the faith of either of said governments had been pledged, by the issuing of scrip or other security, to make grants thereof, or in any form to part with its title to, or interest in the same, previous to the signing of said Treaty; what amount remained at that date ungranted and subject to no such pledge; whether and what grants of said domain have been made, or other evidence of title thereto, legal or equitable, issued by the Texan Government, since that period;"

Has the honor to state, in reply, that this Department is in possession of no information additional to that contained in the note of Messrs. [Isaac] Van Zandt and [J. Pinckney] Henderson of the 15th of April, last, which has any relation to the subjects of inquiry proposed in the said Resolution, so far as they relate to the amount of the public debt of Texas and the grants of land made previous to the signature of the Treaty. The note of Messrs. Van Zandt and Henderson was communicated to the Senate with other documents accompanying the Treaty of Annexation, and was published by its order. It is therefore only necessary to refer to it.

With a view to ascertain whether the public debt of Texas has been increased since the signature of the Treaty in April, last; and whether there had been any additional grants of the public domain made by the Texan Government since that period, a letter [of 12/23] has been addressed by this Department to Mr. [Charles H.] Raymond, Acting Chargé d'Affaires of the Republic of Texas, a copy of whose reply [of 12/27] is herewith communicated. Respectfully submitted, J.C. Calhoun.

LS with En in DNA, RG 46 (U.S. Senate), 28A-E3; FC in DNA, RG 59 (State Department), Reports of the Secretary of State to the President and Congress, 6:119–120; PC with En in Senate Document No. 29, 28th Cong., 2nd Sess., pp. 1–3. NOTE: This report was transmitted by Tyler to the Senate on 1/2/1845.

To President [JOHN TYLER]

Department of State
31st December 1844

To the President of the United States.

The Secretary of State to whom has been referred the Resolution of the Senate of the 19th instant requesting the President "to inform the Senate whether the Executive Department is informed of the various Treaty stipulations now subsisting between the Republic of Texas, and other independent Powers; and that he be requested to communicate such stipulations if in the Possession of the Department to the Senate," has the honor to transmit herewith copies of two Treaties, the one of commerce and navigation between the Republic of Texas and Great Britain, concluded at London on the 13th of November 1840, the other of Amity, Navigation and Commerce between the said Republic and France concluded at Paris on the 25th of September 1839, which embrace all the information on the files of this Department, in relation to the subjects mentioned in the said Resolution. Respectfully submitted, J.C. Calhoun.

LS in DNA, RG 46 (U.S. Senate), 28A-E3; FC in DNA, RG 59 (State Department), Reports of the Secretary of State to the President and Congress, 6:120; PC with Ens in Senate Document No. 30, 28th Cong., 2nd Sess., pp. 1–11. NOTE: Tyler transmitted this to the Senate on 1/2/1845. The resolution to which the above is a response can be found in DNA, RG 59 (State Department), Miscellaneous Letters (M-179:106, frame 325) and in *Senate Journal*, 28th Cong., 2nd Sess., p. 43.

To the U. S. SENATE and HOUSE OF REPRESENTATIVES

Department of State
December 31st 1844

The Secretary of State has the honor to lay before Congress, in compliance with the Act of August 16th 1842 an account of such changes and modifications in the commercial systems of other nations, by treaties, duties on imports and exports & other regulations, as have come to the knowledge of the Department since the date of the last annual report. J.C. Calhoun.

LS (to the Senate) in DNA, RG 46 (U.S. Senate), 28A-F1; LS (to the House) in DNA, RG 233 (U.S. House of Representatives), 28A-F1; PC with En in Senate Document No. 135, 28th Cong., 2nd Sess., pp. 1–259; PC with En in House Document No. 45, 28th Cong., 2nd Sess., pp. 1–255.

From H[ENRY] WHEATON, "Private"

["Berlin" *canceled and* "Paris" *interlined*], 31 Dec. 1844

My dear Sir, Referring you to my former letters in respect to my future employment in the diplomatic service, I beg leave to state that although I deem a communication of my wishes & views in that respect amply sufficient as ["already" *interlined*] made through you, being the proper official channel, further reflection has induced me to address the President [John Tyler] directly on that subject, a course which I trust will meet with your approbation. I take the liberty of subjoining a Copy of my Letter to him, & as I have already troubled you perhaps too much with my concerns, will only add that I am extremely anxious to have my future destination ascertained, if possible, during the present Administration. I am, my dear Sir, ever truly your obliged friend, H. Wheaton.

P.S. The enclosed was written intended to be forwarded from Berlin but I have been unfortunately detained here by a hurt in my foot beyond the period I had intended.

[Enclosure]

H. Wheaton to President [John] Tyler, "Private," "Copy"

["Berlin" *canceled and* "Paris" *interlined*] 31 Dec. 1844

My dear Sir, Having succeeded in accomplishing the principal objects of my mission to this [Prussian] Court, & my conduct in the late negotiation with the *Zollverein* having received your approbation

& that of a large portion of our constituents the American people, I hope the suggestion that my public services may be considered as affording a well grounded claim to the only sort of promotion our diplomatic establishment admits of, in the shape of a *transfer*, will not be considered as indelicate or presumptuous on my part.

It being understood that Mr. Jennifer [*sic*; Daniel Jenifer] has asked for his recall from Vienna, I beg leave to suggest for your consideration that an opportunity is now afforded of transferring me to that Court, which if availed of, will leave a vacancy at Berlin to be filled as the Executive may think proper. Our relations with the Austrian empire are already very important, opening a new field to be explored, which will become still more interesting, should the project be realized of a commercial league, similar to the Prussian *Zollverein*, to be established between that Empire & the Italian States. An opportunity would thus be afforded of rendering available for the public service whatever experience I may have acquired in this line by long practice; my knowledge of the French, German, & Italian languages; & whatever zeal, industry, & perseverance I may be supposed to possess. Should you think fit to nominate me to the Senate for this post, I flatter myself that no opposition would be encountered in that body. I should be very much obliged by this proof of your confidence; & should the new mission be succes[s]ful, it would reflect additional lustre on the close of an Administration already distinguished by the important results of its political & commercial negotiations. I have the honour to be, Sir (Signed), H. Wheaton.

ALS with En in ScCleA. Note: An AEU by Calhoun reads "Mr. Wheaton, Desires to be transferred to ["Berli" *canceled*] Vienna."

From ALB[ERT] S. WHITE, [Senator from Ind.]

Senate Chamber, Washington, Dec. 31, 1844
Sir: The enclosed letter [to me, dated 12/25, from Rufus Haymond] was probably not written with an expectation that it would be submitted to you, but as I have declined recommending any person for the office therein named, and as I believe the District Attorneyship appertains to the State Department, I have taken the liberty of forwarding Doctor Haymond's letter to you as the most appropriate method of making known the candidacy of his friend [William M. McCarty], requesting you to overlook its bluntness which I am cer-

tain is well meant. The writer & his nominee are both of the first respectability.

It may be proper to add in this connection that it has been made known to me that E. Dumont Esq. of Lawrenceburgh and William Hendricks Esq. of Madison (both respectable) are also Candidates for the same appointment. I have the honor to be very resp[ectful]ly Y[ou]r ob[edient] ser[van]t, Alb. S. White.

ALS with En in DNA, RG 59 (State Department), Applications and Recommendations, 1837–1845, McCarty (M-687:21, frames 31–33). NOTE: In the En, Haymond described McCarty as "a Calhoun locofoco of the first water— and as much entitled to the office as any one of that party and as well qualified to discharge its duties." According to Haymond, if Calhoun learns this, he will support McCarty's claim "in preference to those of the Van Buren democratic School."

CH[ARLES] H. WINDER to R[ichard] K. Crallé

Department of State
Washington, 31st Dec. 1844

Sir, In relation to the Resolution of the House of Representatives of the 14th of June last, calling for copies of all instructions to Geo[rge] W. Erving Esq[ui]re from 1814, and afterwards, whilst he represented the U.S. at the Court of Spain, and which had not already been made public—I have the honor to report—That I applied to the appropriate Bureau for the Record of Such instructions, and that after strict Search none Such could be found. A book in which they were Supposed to be, was handed to me, labelled, on the back in printing—"Foreign Letters Vol. VII" and in manuscript—"1800–11— principally to Consuls 1816—Hiatus from 1811 to 1816." No instructions of the Character called for in the Resolution are to be found in that Book. It is impossible, at this day, to account for the Hiatus.

Failing to discover them in the proper Bureau, I naturally supposed no traces of them could be found in the Department, I therefore returned the Resolution to the Hon. the Secretary stating this fact. Afterwards, papers, copies of which I have already placed in your hands, were found among the old, neglected papers of the Department. If their [*sic*] be any merit in their discovery, it is due to Mr. [William A.] Weaver.

There is no other evidence of their official Authority than is presented by the papers themselves. I have on this account copied, the endorsement of each literally.

I return the three files placed in my hands for examination. There is nothing in them bearing on the Resolution. I am resp[ectfull]y Your ob[edien]t Ser[van]t, Ch. H. Winder.

ALS in DNA, RG 59 (State Department), Miscellaneous Letters (M-179:106, frames 477–478).

Thomas Hedycock, "Master Royal Navy of Great Britain," and Sam[ue]l Lee, "Merchant," London, to Daniel Webster, "Treasury Secretary of the United States of America," [1844?]. They recommend a plan of levying a low duty on every package of goods imported or exported, for the purpose of "raising finances from a very low Taxaxtion." They assert that E[dward] Everett, U.S. Minister to Great Britain, in a letter of 6/4/1844, agreed with their proposed plan. They claim that this plan is in the process of becoming law in Great Britain and think it would be beneficial to the U.S. as well. [It is unknown why this document is found among Calhoun's papers, but a Clerk's EU seems to indicate that it was received in the State Department on 7/5/(1844?).] LS in ScCleA.

From "POLYBIUS"

[1844?]

The Union. The effeminate South. The South unable to stand alone without the North—

The value of the Union is so obvious that I shall not at present enter into any elaborate argument to establish it. Few men set a higher value on the Union than I do; and I have not spared the expression of that opinion under circumstances that made it personally perilous.

But we must ever recollect that it is for the aggregate amount of blessings which it brings, that rational men value the Union. Such men do not act without a reason for action. If by oppressive enactments, producing more injury than benefit to the whole country, the federal Legislature depart from the object of the Constitution which is "to promote the General welfare" the purposes of the institution of the General Government are transcended and abrogated, and the worth of the Union, if such measures be long persisted in, ceases. A mere arbitrary union it will be admitted, can no more be binding than mere arbitrary decisions of a judge in ordinary cases. If the judge, therefore, adopting the course supposed, were to be arraigned before an adequate tribunal, he would be justly liable to condemnation. Under those circumstances impeached for his misdemeanors and high crimes, his commission would be rescinded and he would be consigned to that judicial death which justice inflicts. And the habitual exercise of the powers of the constitution to the ends of injustice by the federal Govt., would upon the same principles, but with greater force, from the immensely greater magnitude of the interests affected, bring on the death of the Government. It requires a hand delicately exact and scrupulously careful, to adjust the burdens of this Govt. so that it may move in the orbit of the Constitution, and not to oppress a part of the union by unequal taxation.

Moreover this Government is a *compact with specific and limited powers*. A breach of this compact by one party to it as much infringes its validity as a breach of it by the other party to it. And when this breach is long continued & material to the ends of its institution, the party against whom it operates is released from the obligation; and is entitled to a division of whatever portion of the assets have accumulated as a common fund—a division upon principles of equity—and a peaceable quit claim from the party who has broken it.

The conclusion is that the Union is of immense value when maintained in practical harmony with the purposes for which it was formed, but if converted into a engine of oppression it is a machinery that cannot last.

At the North they have multiplied institutions, schools, and newspapers, considerably more proportionally to population & resources, than at the South. These are means of knowledge & improvement excellent in themselves, but susceptible of abuse, as all human institutions are. Such institutions are adapted to give a concentrated action to public opinion whether for good or evil. Any idea to which they choose to give the ascendancy, will obtain a more complete dominion, at least one more active & effervescent, than in a community less abundantly supplied with them. Hence there are several opinions propagated at the North and North East, which have gained a vast diffusion, and received general credence; nay, may be considered as established maxims, such as the great Superiority of the North and East in religion, morals, intellect, and as articles of the same creed of humility and christian fellowship, the effeminicacy of the South and its inability to stand alone without the kind propping and ready aid of its strong and charitable brothers at the North & East.

But there is a multitude of persons at the South who feel disposed to enter a demurrer to these assertions, and while they grant much to the North & East, they appeal to the past in refutation of these pretensions, in their full extent. The long continued acquiescence of the South in a system of measures ruinous to its own interests, is decisively indicative of its attachment to the Union; but it ought to be to the North and East a matter of prudent calculation, whether it will not expire under the constant load of direct & indirect taxation which a high tariff ensures. *Moderation* should be volunteered by them while the opportunity exists. *In the exercise of moderation & mutual concession, the Union was formed;* where there is so great a *contrariety* of *interests,* it is only by the watchful and enlightened application of these invaluable principles that it can be *preserved.*

The effeminate South, unable to stand alone! But it did stand alone when it had but little more than half of its present strength. It stood alone when ["Mr. Adams's letter to Levitt (*sic;* Levett) Harris" *interpolated*] "the gigantic power of England, ready to crush us at a blow" filled the sturdy Mr. [John Quincy] Adams, "the parliamentary general," with dismay [at the time of the War of 1812]. Who ["crushed the Creeks," *canceled*] subdued the Cherokees? who crushed the Creeks? who drove the far famed troops of Wellington back to old ocean's stormy billows? The effeminate South, unable to stand alone! They are now essentially the same men they were in the revolution, and in the last war, excepting that they are more pacific in their general views. But their courage is not abated, nor their skill diminished; and their ["reso" *canceled*] warlike resources, from the concentration and increase of population, ["and" *canceled*] and the invention and practical ["at" *canceled*] use in their section, of railways & steamboats, are fourfold augmented beyond what they were in 1813–14: That is to say, the population of the South is now equal in the event of war—to accomplish as much ["defensively" *interlined and then canceled*] with the same exertion, as sixteen millions of people ["on the same territory" *interlined*] could have done at the former period, ["on the same" *erased*.] [Signed,] Polybius.

LS in ScCleA. Note: The only evidence to date this letter, which lacks dateline and postmark, is its address to Calhoun as Secretary of State.

From S. N. WASHBURN

[1844?]

D[ea]r Sir, We will take all the cotton factorys of this country together and call it one factory—likewise those of England & call it one. Now destroy one factory, then the demand will be less for the raw material, & consequently prices low, consequently the Cotton grower will have to submit & the remaining cotton factory would be a monopolizer, and make tremendous profits—and the citizens around the dilapidated factory would have to pay a double freight, double expenses, & at len[g]th themselves would be double[d] up into a cocked hat.

Now I want to ["know" *interlined*] which factory you support, or which factory you want to destroy, the English or the American one. If you want to put down the English one (which is impossible) I do indeed admire your desires & wishes—& think it would be an excellent plan, for then the American manufactories would flourish, but oh! the South would be in a bad dish. If you want to put down the American (which might be possible) then indeed, the English one would flourish, and oh! the South would be in a worse dish.

Well, I say, let the English take care of theirs, and let us take care of ours—keep the two mills agoing—and grind a double quantity, consequently a greater demand for cotton to supply the mills—& where the demand is kept up, the price will be kept up. Yours &c, S.N. Washburn.

ALS in ScCleA. NOTE: This letter was addressed to Calhoun as Secretary of State, which provides the only clue to its approximate date. Another letter from Washburn to Calhoun, undated and undatable, is found among the Calhoun Papers at ScCleA. In the latter document, which is labelled "Private" and carries a Washington postmark of 8/14, Washburn describes himself as "a Baptist by trade" and delivers a long homily in the hope that "God may make me the means of bringing *effectually* to your mind those things which belong to our eternal peace & welfare."

SYMBOLS

▯

The following symbols have been used in this volume as abbreviations for the forms in which documents of John C. Calhoun have been found and for the repositories in which they are preserved. (Full citations to printed sources of documents can be found in the Bibliography.)

Abs	—abstract (a summary)
ADS	—autograph document, signed
ADU	—autograph document, unsigned
AEI	—autograph endorsement, initialed
AES	—autograph endorsement, signed
AEU	—autograph endorsement, unsigned
ALS	—autograph letter, signed
ALU	—autograph letter, unsigned
CC	—clerk's copy (a secondary ms. copy)
CCEx	—clerk's copy of an extract
CU	—University of California-Berkeley
DLC	—Library of Congress, Washington
DNA	—National Archives, Washington
DS	—document, signed
DU	—document, unsigned
En	—enclosure
Ens	—enclosures
ES	—endorsement, signed
EU	—endorsement, unsigned
FC	—file copy (usually a letterbook copy retained by the sender)
InHi	—Indiana Historical Society, Indianapolis
LS	—letter, signed
LU	—letter, unsigned
M-	—(followed by a number) published microcopy of the National Archives
MHi	—Massachusetts Historical Society, Boston
NcU	—Southern Historical Collection, University of North Carolina at Chapel Hill
NNPM	—Pierpont Morgan Library, New York City
PC	—printed copy
PDS	—printed document, signed
PEx	—printed extract
PHi	—Historical Society of Pennsylvania, Philadelphia
RG	—Record Group in the National Archives
ScCleA	—Clemson University, Clemson, S.C.
ScU-SC	—South Caroliniana Library, University of South Carolina, Columbia

ScSpW	—Wofford College, Spartanburg, S.C.
T-	—(followed by number) published microfilm of the National Archives
Tx	—Texas State Library, Austin
ViHi	—Virginia Historical Society, Richmond
ViU	—University of Virginia, Charlottesville
ViW	—College of William and Mary, Williamsburg, Va.

BIBLIOGRAPHY

▯

This Bibliography is limited to sources of and previous printings of documents published in this volume.

Aderman, Ralph M., and others, eds., *Letters [of Washington Irving]*. 4 vols. Boston: Twayne, 1978–1982. (Vols. 23–26 of *The Complete Works of Washington Irving*.)

Alexandria, D.C. and Va., *Gazette*, 1808–.

American Farmer, The. Baltimore, 1819–1897?.

Anderson, S.C., *Gazette*, 1843–1855.

Benton, Thomas H., ed., *Abridgment of the Debates of Congress*. 16 vols. New York: D. Appleton & Co., 1854–1861.

Boucher, Chauncey S., and Robert P. Brooks, eds., *Correspondence Addressed to John C. Calhoun, 1837–1849*, in *American Historical Association Annual Report* for 1929 (Washington: U.S. Government Printing Office, 1930).

Bourne, Kenneth, ed., *British Documents on Foreign Affairs. Reports and Papers from the Foreign Office Confidential Print*. Part One, Series C: *North America, 1838–1914* (4 vols. Frederick, Md.: University Publications of America, 1986).

British and Foreign State Papers (170 vols. London: HMSO, 1812–1968), vols. 33 and 34.

Carolina Planter. Columbia, S.C., 1844–1845.

Charleston, S.C., *Mercury*, 1822–1868.

Christian Citizen. Worcester, Mass., 1844–1851?.

Collector, The. New York, 1887–.

Columbus, Ohio, *Ohio State Journal*, 1811–1904.

Congressional Globe . . . 1833–1873 . . . . 46 vols. Washington: Blair & Rives and others, 1834–1873.

Crallé, Richard K., ed., *The Works of John C. Calhoun*. 6 vols. Columbia, S.C.: printed by A.S. Johnston, 1851, and New York: D. Appleton & Co., 1853–1857.

Davids, Jules, ed., *American Diplomatic and Public Papers: The United States and China*, Series I [1842–1860], 2 vols. Wilmington, Del.: Scholarly Resources, Inc., 1973.

Garrison, George P., ed., *Diplomatic Correspondence of the Republic of Texas*, in the *American Historical Association Annual Report* for 1907, vol. II, and for 1908, vol. II. Washington: U.S. Government Printing Office, 1908–1911.

Greenville, S.C., *Mountaineer*, 1829–1901.

Hammond, George P., ed., *The Larkin Papers. Personal, Business, and Official Correspondence of Thomas Oliver Larkin, Merchant and United States Consul in California*. 11 vols. Berkeley: University of California Press, 1951–1968.

[Hammond, Jabez D.] "Hamden," *Letter to the Hon. John C. Calhoun, on the Annexation of Texas.* Cooperstown [N.Y.]: printed by H. & E. Phinney, 1844.

Hellman, George S., *Washington Irving, Esquire, Ambassador at Large from the New World to the Old.* London: Jonathan Cape, 1925.

Holmes, Alester G., and George R. Sherrill, *Thomas Green Clemson: His Life and Work.* Richmond: Garrett & Massie, 1937.

Jameson, J. Franklin, ed., *Correspondence of John C. Calhoun,* in the *American Historical Association Annual Report* for 1899 (2 vols. Washington: U.S. Government Printing Office, 1900), vol. II.

Liberator, The. Boston, 1831–1865.

London, England, *Times,* 1785–.

Manning, William R., ed., *Diplomatic Correspondence of the United States: Canadian Relations, 1784–1860.* 4 vols. Washington: Carnegie Endowment for International Peace, 1940–1945.

Manning, William R., ed., *Diplomatic Correspondence of the United States: Inter-American Affairs, 1831–1860.* 12 vols. Washington: Carnegie Endowment for International Peace, 1932–1939.

Niles' Register. Baltimore, 1811–1849.

Pendleton, S.C., *Messenger,* 1807–?.

Southern Cultivator. Atlanta, 1843–1935.

Thruston, G.P., ed., "Autograph Collections and Historic Manuscripts," in *Sewanee Review,* vol. X, no. 1 (January, 1902).

Tyler, Lyon G., *The Letters and Times of the Tylers.* 3 vols. Richmond: Whittet & Shepperson, 1884–1896.

U.S. House of Representatives, *House Documents,* 28th and 29th Congresses.

U.S. House of Representatives, *House Reports,* 28th and 29th Congresses.

U.S. Senate, *Senate Documents,* 28th and 29th Congresses.

U.S. Senate, *Senate Journal,* 28th Congress.

Washington, D.C., *Constitution,* 1844–1845.

Washington, D.C., *Daily National Intelligencer,* 1800–1870.

Washington, D.C., *Madisonian,* 1837–1845.

Washington, D.C., *The Globe,* 1830–1845.

INDEX

II

"A.A.A." (pseudonym): from, 227.
Abd-ar-Rahman (Emperor of Morocco): mentioned, 672.
Aberdeen, Lord: mentioned, 30, 72, 74, 87, 95–96, 207–208, 211–213, 292, 339–340, 345–346, 351–354, 398, 529, 546–547, 643, 669–670; to, 208.
Aberdeen, Scotland: 55.
Abingdon, Va.: 401.
Abolition: xi–xiii, 7, 15, 30–31, 34, 43, 51–52, 61–62, 64, 71–75, 87, 92, 95–96, 98, 102, 107, 113, 137–139, 157, 180–182, 187, 190–192, 201–202, 207–214, 219–220, 236–238, 250, 252–253, 255–257, 261–264, 270–271, 282–287, 290–291, 318, 336, 339–341, 345–346, 351–355, 363, 365, 368, 374–377, 381, 398, 417–419, 432, 435–439, 450–451, 456–458, 463, 471, 486–487, 490, 492, 506, 514–516, 526, 528–530, 538, 542, 544, 547, 550–552, 555, 564, 568, 570–571, 584, 588, 592, 596–599, 612, 619, 622, 625, 628, 630–631, 638, 640–641, 644, 657–659, 662, 679–681.
Acapulco, Mexico: 248.
Acosta, Joaquin: mentioned, 94, 193–195, 198, 391–392, 610–611.
A'Court, Sir William: mentioned, 386.
Adams, John: mentioned, 437, 463.
Adams, John P.: mentioned, 344; to, 345.
Adams, John Quincy: mentioned, 261, 263, 326, 418, 422, 425, 432–433, 435, 437, 462–463, 561, 577, 601, 681.

Adams, Placidia Mayrant: mentioned, 567–568.
Adams-Onís Treaty: 149, 254–255, 271–272, 285, 326, 432, 533.
Admiralty law: 38, 116.
Africa: 16, 71–75, 87, 95–96, 159, 204–206, 209, 311, 347–348, 371, 376–377, 443–444, 453–455, 476–477, 491, 494–498, 518, 528–530, 551, 555–556, 583, 630–631, 647–648, 671–672.
"Agricola" (pseudonym): mentioned, 185.
Agriculture: in Calhoun family, ix, 3, 42–43, 66, 90, 102, 104–105, 119, 193, 229–230, 667; mentioned, 53, 199, 202, 518, 625, 636; Southern, 13–15, 21, 30–31, 49, 56–57, 95, 103–104, 198–199, 292, 312–313, 318, 356, 363–364, 435, 449, 534, 541, 566, 587–590, 638–640, 643, 682.
Aiken, S.C.: 502, 547.
Aiken, William: mentioned, 126, 535–536, 565–566, 584.
Alabama: xii, 3, 14, 29, 43, 102, 181, 229, 290, 364, 449, 460, 487–488, 508, 527, 531–532, 536–537, 539, 563, 582, 587–590, 592, 639–640, 646.
Albers, John H.: mentioned, 68, 314.
Alexander, John H.: mentioned, 601–602.
Alexandria, D.C.: 559–561.
Alexandria, D.C., *Gazette & Virginia Advertiser*: document in, 127.
Algiers: 180.
Allen, Ebenezer: from, 575; mentioned, 569, 576; to, 571.

Arkansas: 45–46, 482–483, 581.
Army, U.S. *See* Calhoun, Patrick (son); War Department, U.S.
Art: 54, 131, 337, 601.
Arthur, Sir George: mentioned, 292.
Artigas, José Gervasio: mentioned, 115.
Ashburton, Lord: mentioned, 96, 583.
Asheville, N.C.: 534.
Ashley, Chester: from, 581.
Astor, John Jacob: mentioned, 407.
Athens, Ga.: 230–231, 322.
Athens, Greece: 56.
Atkins & Freeman: from, 604.
Atmospheric Railway: 547–548.
Attakapas, La.: 177.
Attorney General, U.S.: 9, 221, 227, 616.
Auboyneau, Francis M.: from, 609.
Augsburg, Bavaria: 241.
Augusta, Ga.: 101, 452.
Aumale, Duke: mentioned, 404.
Aurora, N.Y.: 388.
Austin, Moses: mentioned, 151.
Austin, Tex.: 64.
Australia: 32, 84–85.
Austria: 39, 192, 235, 237, 240–241, 309–310, 387, 397, 499, 526, 549, 613–614, 668, 677.
Aux Cayes, Haiti: 673–674.
Aymar & Co.: from, 663; mentioned, 324.

Bache, Alexander Dallas: mentioned, 526.
Bache, Sophia Dallas: to, 525.
Backman, Louis: mentioned, 108.
Bacon, Joseph V., & Son: from, 604.
Bahamas: 339–341, 351–354.
Bahia, Brazil: 73, 204–205.
Bailey, Henry: from, 217.
Bainbridge, U.S.S.: 99–100, 281, 477, 496–497, 556.
Baker, John M.: mentioned, 77.
Baker, Robert: mentioned, 348.
Baker, Simmons: mentioned, 13.
Balderana, Capt. ——: mentioned, 170.

Baldwin, Cornelius C.: from, 636.
Baldwin, George E.: from, 599.
Baldwin, Henry: mentioned, 326, 535.
Baldwin, Henry (Jr.): from, 535.
Baldwin, John: from, 206.
Balestier, Joseph: from, 86.
Baltimore, Md.: 34–36, 60, 159, 177, 180, 221, 226–227, 238, 280, 342, 348, 370–371, 386, 405, 504, 530, 568, 583, 595, 600–601, 617.
Bamberg, Bavaria: 68.
Bancroft, George: mentioned, 528.
Bangor, Maine: 656.
Bankhead, Charles: mentioned, 50, 157, 234, 393–394.
Bank of the State of South Carolina: 436, 565.
Bank of the United States: 437, 568.
Banks and bankers: 51, 58, 199, 229, 237, 308, 338, 356, 369, 388, 436–437, 452, 515, 522, 539, 565, 568, 589, 659.
Baptist Church: 682.
Barbour, Calhoun: mentioned, 401.
Barbour, James: mentioned, 400, 556, 582.
Barbour, John S.: from, 338, 400, 526, 556, 582.
Barclay & Livingston: from, 609; mentioned, 614.
Baring Brothers & Co.: mentioned, 77, 289, 659.
Barney, Vincent G.: mentioned, 299.
Barnwell, Robert W.: mentioned, 126.
Barrett, Thomas: from, 98; mentioned, 65, 98, 242–243, 530, 608.
Barrow, Alexander: mentioned, 440.
Bartlett & Wilford: to, 465.
Basadre, Ignacio: mentioned, 415–416.
Basil (slave): mentioned, 105.
Basto, J. Antonio de Souza: mentioned, 496.
Bate, R.B.: from, 45.
Bauskett, John: mentioned, 657.
Bavaria: 25, 68–69, 93, 103, 241, 530, 585.
Bayly, Thomas H.: mentioned, 582.
Bayou Goula, La.: 49, 198, 292.

Fairburne, John: mentioned, 227, 347, 444, 460.
Fairfield, John: mentioned, 585.
Fannin, James W.: mentioned, 148.
Farias, Gomez: mentioned, 440.
Farrington, Thomas: mentioned, 17–19.
Fay, Theodore S.: from, 24, 27, 102, 109, 330, 430, 459.
Federalist party: 33, 97, 182, 226, 295, 365–366, 437, 477, 592.
Ferdinand I (Emperor of Austria): mentioned, 39, 240, 499.
Ferdinand II (of the Two Sicilies): mentioned, 401, 403–404, 413.
Ferris, Charles G.: from, 652.
Field, Richard H.: mentioned, 400.
Figaniere e Morão, J.C. de: mentioned, 390, 455, 491; to, 390.
Fillmore, Millard: mentioned, 307–308.
Fine, John: mentioned, 445–446.
Finland: 385.
Fiora, James: mentioned, 323, 370, 377–378, 389, 609, 652.
Fish, Hamilton: from, 613; to, 620.
Fisher, George: mentioned, 44–45.
Fisher, John W.: from, 129; mentioned, 490.
Fisheries: 54–55, 131, 175, 220, 275–276, 289.
Fisk, Theophilus: mentioned, 102, 130–131.
Fitton, Juan: mentioned, 649.
Flagg, Azariah C.: mentioned, 446.
Fleurot, Gabriel G.: mentioned, 112, 593, 653.
Florence: 608.
Florida Territory: 13–16, 48, 56, 114, 125, 160, 162–163, 187, 230, 286, 291–292, 296–297, 351–353, 420, 489, 532–533, 587–590, 598–599, 626, 629, 639–640, 667.
Flour: 82, 287, 621, 622.
Floyd, John G.: from, 215.
Forbes, Paul S.: mentioned, 409.
Forbes, Robert B.: mentioned, 409.
Force bill: 287.
Forney, Walter: mentioned, 369–370.
Forsyth, John: mentioned, 117.

Fort Gibson, Indian Territory: 483.
Fort Hill: ix, 3, 42–43, 66, 90, 119, 192–193, 228–229, 667. *See also frontispiece.*
Fort Jesup, La.: 112.
Fort Leavenworth: 228.
Fort Smith, Ark.: 482–483.
Fort Towson, Indian Territory: 482.
Fort Washita, Indian Territory: 482.
Foster, Ephraim H.: mentioned, 651.
Foster, Winslow: mentioned, 11.
Fox, Henry S.: mentioned, 346.
França, Ernesto F.: mentioned, 71, 73, 76–77, 201–202, 206, 287–288, 553–555.
France: xii–xiii, 8, 12, 47, 53, 55–56, 63–64, 85–86, 106, 111–112, 131, 185, 236, 302–304, 353, 384, 396–402, 406–407, 414, 424, 465–468, 487, 499–500, 538–539, 549, 609, 621, 631, 639, 659, 663, 668; in Caribbean and Central America, 61–62, 92, 112, 129–130, 194, 196, 220, 544, 551, 611, 673; in relation to Texas and Mexico, 20–21, 37, 63–64, 91, 102, 224, 233, 241, 254, 285, 302–303, 317–318, 349–350, 361, 373, 396–398, 439, 470, 472, 532–534, 538, 542–545, 570–571, 597, 635, 641, 654–655, 670–673, 675; in South America, 201–202, 276–277, 289, 529, 555; Minister of to U.S. (*see* Pageot, Alphonse); U.S. Minister to (*see* King, William R.). *See also individual French cities and colonies.*
Francisco, Count Trapani: mentioned, 499.
Francois-Eugene, Duc d'Harcourt: mentioned, 401.
Frederick, Archduke of Austria: mentioned, 499.
Fredericks, ——: mentioned, 667.
Fredericksburg, Va.: 400.
Frederick William IV: mentioned, 25, 530.
Freeman, William H.: mentioned, 59–60; to, 217.
Free trade: 20–22, 30, 39–40, 45, 53–54, 91, 103–104, 114, 174–175,

Missionaries: x, 488–489, 492–493, 542–543.
Mississippi: 129, 282.
Missouri: 91, 105, 118, 283–286, 533, 580–581, 638. *See also* St. Louis, Mo.
Missouri, U.S.S.: 409.
Missouri Compromise: 107, 282–287, 438, 492.
Mobile, Ala.: 158, 449, 531–532, 589, 605.
Mobley, John: mentioned, 104–105, 229.
Moffat, Samuel: mentioned, 7, 49, 50, 155–156, 564.
Monasterio, José M. Ortiz: mentioned, 17–18.
Monroe, James: mentioned, 326, 432–433.
Monroe Doctrine: 202–204.
Monterey, Cal.: 123, 248, 656.
Montevideo. *See* Uruguay.
Montezuma (Mexican warship): 4–6, 9, 27–29, 35, 81, 88–89, 144.
Montgomery, Ala.: 587–588.
Montgomery, George: from, 599.
Moore, Samuel: mentioned, 60, 386.
Moore, Mrs. Samuel: mentioned, 60.
Moore, Thomas P.: mentioned, 590.
Morling, Solomon: mentioned, 28, 88.
Mormons: 237.
Moro, Cayetano: mentioned, 24.
Morocco: 631, 647–648, 672.
Morrill, John A.: from, 333; mentioned, 405, 464.
Morris (brig): 58–59, 173–175, 193–194, 198, 390–391, 516.
Morse, ——: mentioned, 342.
Morton, Marcus: mentioned, 528.
Moseley, William P.: mentioned, 613.
Mosquera, Manuel M.: mentioned, 24.
Mosquera, Tomás C.: mentioned, 196–197.
Mower, James B.: from, 349.
Mozier, Joseph: mentioned, 608.
Mulattoes: 137–139, 159, 544.
Mules: 138.
Munich: 68.
Murat, Joachim: mentioned, 402.
Murphy, Henry C.: from, 304.

Murphy, Lucy Maria: mentioned, 243.
Murphy, William S.: mentioned, 11, 157, 243, 474, 608, 617.
Murray, Hugh: mentioned, 376.
Murray County, Ga.: 231.
Muscat: 552.

Namesakes: of John C. Calhoun, 367, 401, 486, 592.
Naples. *See* Two Sicilies.
Narvaez, Joaquin Baldomero: mentioned, 499–500.
Nash, Alanson: mentioned, 88.
Nashville, Tenn.: 101, 364, 433, 535, 567.
Natchez, Miss.: 129.
National Archives, U.S.: Calhoun documents in described, x; documents in (more than 280 included herein).
National Bank: 437, 568.
Native American party. *See* American party.
Nativism: 190–192, 228, 230, 236–237, 315, 325, 336, 355, 365, 506, 562, 599, 620–621, 673.
Navarro, José Antonio: mentioned, 44.
Navigation: 13–15, 54, 93, 103, 602. *See also* Seamen, American; Steamboats.
Navy Department, U.S.: 8, 13–15, 45, 48, 52, 70–71, 77–78, 90, 93, 99–100, 103, 110, 130, 132, 139–140, 163, 200, 203, 205, 225, 275–278, 280, 282, 289, 292–293, 297, 305–306, 327–328, 348, 391, 405, 409, 477, 496–497, 515, 518, 521, 523, 545, 555–556, 583, 587–590, 611, 648–649, 673. *See also* Applications and recommendations: for Navy Department; Appointments and removals: in Navy Department.
Negroes, free: 109–111, 158–160, 486–487, 490, 514–516, 550–552, 596, 663, 673–674. *See also* Haiti; Jamaica.
Nelson, John: mentioned, 9, 64, 221, 227, 402, 616.